The WORLD'S BEST WINES

2009-2010

First published 2009 by Elliott and Thompson Limited
27 John Street, London WC1N 2BX
www.eandtbooks.com

ISBN 978-1-9040-2780-5

With thanks to:
James Collins, Mike Florence, Matthew Johnson, Charles Metcalfe,
Ray O'Connor, Andrew Reed, Lee Sharkey, Lottie West and
everyone associated with the International Wine Challenge

9 8 7 6 5 4 3 2 1

A CIP catalogue record for this book is available
from the British Library.

Printed in China by 1010 Printing

The
WORLD'S
BEST WINES
2009-2010

MORE THAN 3,500 AWARD WINNING
WINES AND WHERE TO BUY THEM

E&T

VIRTUALLY
TAINT FREE
JUST ISN'T
GOOD ENOUGH

Others claim to have reduced TCA. We have eliminated it. Each DIAM cork is certified to contain releasable TCA below detectable levels; < 0.5 ng.

This means your winemakers can concentrate on what they do best, safe in the knowledge that every time a bottle of their wine is opened, it tastes the way it should.

Find out more at **www.oeneo.co.uk** or contact us at: **info@oeneo.co.uk**

Contents

Foreword

Imagine having to judge over 9,000 wines in a five-day week. That's an average of more than 1,800 wines a day. It helps if you have 20 teams of excellent tasters, and if you've been running the competition for over 25 years.

Each year teaches you a little more, shows just a few more ways to improve the system, nets ideas offered to make the process simpler and more effective. But there's more to the International Wine Challenge (IWC) than that first week. That's just an elimination round. It separates the potential medallists from the rest. In the second week, we retaste those potential medal wines, more slowly, and award the medals.

At every stage of the process, there is a safety net – the five Co-Chairmen. I, and my colleagues Tim Atkin MW, Sam Harrop MW, Derek Smedley MW and our overseas guest Co-Chairman Joshua Greene, retaste every wine that has been knocked out in the first round, and every wine tasted in the second. Why? Because the producers and retailers who enter their wines deserve every chance. In the first week, we are the safety net. In the second, we are the levellers. We retaste the wines coming through from all the teams of tasters. If there are tables marking higher or lower than others, we can adjust the marks, so the standard of medals is exactly the same throughout the results. And every time we want to change something,

we have to seek approval from another Co-Chair.

By the time it wins a medal, every wine has been tasted at least three times, sometimes as many as six. It goes without saying that everything is tasted blind. The bottles are covered by plastic bags, and none of the judges or the Co-Chairmen has the faintest idea who made each wine.

And what results they have been this year! Entries from 41 different countries, over 300 judges from 19 different countries, 188 Trophies, 304 Gold medals, 1304 Silvers, 2154 Bronzes and 2625 Commended wines. Top-scoring nations for Gold medals are France, then Australia, then Portugal. England has had its best ever year, winning 23 medals. Japan wins 12 Trophies and 18 Gold medals for its Sakes.

So, dive in and find out who were the winners of the 2009 IWC. They have won their accolades in the world's most scrupulously judged wine competition.

Huge thanks to the producers who submitted their wines, the tasters, and our fantastic admin team who coordinated the event, especially to Mike Florence, who moves on after masterminding the IWC for nine years.

We at the IWC hope you enjoy the results of our two weeks of hard work. Because that's what it's all about, in the end, selecting the world's best wines, so you can enjoy drinking them.

Charles Metcalfe

In the hot seats

The experts at the front line of the International Wine Challenge

The IWC has four resident co-chairmen and one guest chairman, who oversee the judging panels and assist the judges with any tough decisions.

Tim Atkin MW

Tim Atkin MW is one of Britain's leading wine writers and an internationally recognised expert. He is the wine correspondent of The Observer and wine editor at large of OLN. He also writes for many other publications and appears on the BBC1's Saturday Kitchen.

Atkin has won more than 20 awards for his journalism, including the Glenfiddich Wine Writer Award and the Lanson Wine Writer of the Year Award.

Sam Harrop MW

Sam Harrop MW started his career as a trainee winemaker at Villa Maria Wines in his native New Zealand. He spent seven years with Marks & Spencer before beginning his own consultancy.

Joshua Greene

Editor and Publisher of Wine & Spirits magazine since 1986, Joshua Greene has travelled extensively through the wine regions of Bordeaux, Burgundy, Portugal, Italy, Spain, Australia and Chile, as well as all the major regions of the United States.

Charles Metcalfe

Charles Metcalfe co-founded Wine International with Robert Joseph in 1983. They started the International Wine Challenge in 1984 and built it into the world's largest wine competition.

As well as writing books on Spanish and Portuguese wines, and on matching wine with food, Metcalfe has been a television drinks presenter for 17 years.

His latest book is *The Wine & Food Lover's Guide To Portugal* (Inn House Publishing) written with his wife, Kathryn McWhirter.

Derek Smedley MW

Derek Smedley MW joined the wine trade in the great vintage of 1961, working for John Harvey & Sons in Bristol. From there he moved to Gilbeys (IDV), where he worked in buying and sales.

In 1985, he started Smedley Vintners, as well as developing a consultancy string to his bow, helping the likes of Tuscan wine house Antinori. He sold Smedley Vintners in 1999 so he could concentrate full-time on his growing consultancy work.

He joined as co-chairman of the IWC in 2002.

Rites of passage

Just how does the IWC work? Ray O'Connor follows the path of a bottle through the rigorous test of the Challenge

It's not easy being a bottle of wine. As if being at the mercy of local weather conditions wasn't enough, the grapes have to go through a selection of winemaking techniques to make them stand out from the crowd.

Next, the juice is trained and modelled into a style of drink that will stand up and represent its region proudly on the podium of international wines.

Finally, once it's deemed ready to do the locals proud, it's bottled and sent to London to pass the ultimate test – to get past the International Wine Challenge judges.

Five weeks before the main event, delivery trucks loaded with palettes of wine start to roll into London's Barbican Centre.

Sorted by grape variety, the bottles stretch the length of the 200ft floor like a vinous game of dominos. Four samples of each bottle are sent to allow for faulty wine and qualification to the next round and the trophy round, should it make it that far.

This is the last chance the bottles have to show off their labels and individual curves. All identity is concealed as each is bagged and given a unique code to identify it all the way through the competition. Armed with clipboards and trollies, the staff work their way through the hall, collecting the wines according to their number, creating flights of similar styles.

This enables the judges to focus on a single grape from a particular region and vintage in order to assess its relative merits.

Round 1: qualifying heats

With the contenders lined up on tables, the time has come for the judges - five to a table – to sniff, taste and spit their way through each flight, making notes about each

again, to ensure integrity, wines are sent to co-chairs for reassessment, but scores are rarely altered – testifying to the high standard of judging.

By the end of play each day, hordes of three-quarters-full bottles are waiting to be disposed of. In line with the competition's Planet Earth Awards, the IWC holds sustainability in high regard. Instead of filling London's drains with fermented grape juice, the leftover wine is poured into huge containers to be taken away and used for cooking. The glass bottles and cardboard boxes are collected by the council for recycling. Even the corks are reused in pinboards and decorative coffee tables.

bottle. As this is round one, it's a straightforward matter for the group to decide whether the wine should stay in the competition or be given its marching orders.

A negative result sees the wine sent to the co-chairmen, who grant it a second chance at qualifying for round two by retasting it. This ensures nothing slips through the net and every single bottle is given the fairest chance possible. In this first week a selection of the world's wine experts put around 2,000 wines a day through their paces.

Round 2: medal table
In the second round, wines are scored out of 100 to determine the medal status: 95-100 = gold, 90-94.9 = silver, 85-89.9 = bronze and 80-84.9 = commended. It's in this second week that the competition really comes alive.

With fewer wines as a result of the first round eliminations, more time is spent on each bottle. Judges debate the qualities of each wine and conclude a final score, led by the tables' panel chair. Once

Trophies and Champions
In the last leg, wines deemed to be of trophy status are selected from the handful of gold-medal winners, to determine the leaders of their class.

As impressive as this lot are, the five co-chairmen still have the task of choosing the overall champions in the following categories: red, white, sparkling, sweet, fortified and sake. These wines make up the most celebrated selection in the competition.

As you flick through the results on the following pages, spare a thought for the bottles that passed this most rigorous of examinations – they've been through a lot.

Matchmaking

	Snacks	Salads	Fish	Poultry	Pork	Game
Light & flora Think: German Riesling	●	●	●		●	
Light & spicy Think: Soave, Pinot Grigio	●	●	●	●	●	
Light & fruity (orchard fruits) Think: Chablis	●	●	●	●	●	
Big & fruity Think: NZ Sauvignon Blanc		●	●	●	●	
Big & buttery Think: Australian Chardonnay				●	●	●
Rosé Think: Spanish Garnacha Rosado	●		●		●	●
Aromatic red Think: Loire Cabernet Franc		●		●	●	
Gamey red Think: Burgundy Pinot Noir			●	●		●
Smoky red Think: South African Pinotage						●
Spicy red Think: Rhône Syrah					●	

Wine is designed for food. But which wines go with which dishes? Our handy chart reveals some tasty choices

Beef	Lamb	Light curry	Spicy curry	Creamy pasta	Tomato pasta	Cheese
		🍷	🍷			🍷
		🍷				
						🍷
				🍷		🍷
				🍷		🍷
					🍷	
🍷	🍷			🍷	🍷	🍷
🍷	🍷					🍷
🍷	🍷					🍷
🍷						🍷

White Winemaker
Neil McGuigan, Australian Vintage

With a father, grandfather and older brother in the Australian wine industry, Neil McGuigan could hardly have considered any other career. Now he is in charge of the winemaking at his family's company, McGuigan Wines.

McGuigan trained as a winemaker in South Australia, before joining his entrepreneurial brother Brian at Wyndham Estate in the Hunter Valley, where they founded McGuigan Brothers. After a while, Neil moved on to Briar Ridge Wines in the Hunter Valley, and then to Rothbury Estate as General Manager and Chief Winemaker.

In 2004, Neil rejoined his brother Brian as General Manager of Production and Wine Supply at McGuigan Simeon Wines, which has since been renamed Australian Vintage. Neil has always been recognised as a particularly gifted winemaker, whether crafting small quantities of handmade wines at Briar Ridge, or overseeing the quality of millions of litres at McGuigan Wines. He oversees the winemaking at the company's two wineries, in the Barossa and Hunter Valleys.

16 wines entered (1 Trophy, 1 gold, 4 silver, 8 bronze)

Red Winemaker
J.P. Trollet, Caves Saint Pierre

Jean-Philippe Trollet comes from Pau, and worked his first vintage in the Blaye region of Bordeaux. He soon caught the wine bug and studied oenology at Bordeaux University, doing stints at smart estates, such as Châteaux La Garde, Rayne-Vigneau and Smith Haut-Lafitte. A job in the Languedoc region with Foncalieu, the giant union of co-ops, enabled him to work vintages in Chile with Santa Rita, as well as in France for three years.

In 2003, he was taken on by the Skalli Group, owners of Caves Saint-Pierre, and one of the most forward-looking wine groups in southern France. Now he is Chief Winemaker, responsible for liaison with growers as well as winemaking. "The Skalli system of working with growers is fundamental." Trollet says. "I work with 30 grape-growers, helping them get the best results out of their vineyards. We discuss pruning, training, leaf-plucking, everything." He loves working with Syrah on the granite soils of St-Joseph, and with old Grenache in the southern Rhône.

11 wines entered (1 Trophy, 1 gold, 1 silver, 4 bronze, 1 commended, 3 out)

Sweet Winemaker
Luis Kracher, Weingut Kracher

Luis Kracher made the sweet wines that swept the board in the 2009 IWC, just like 2008, when he also won Sweet Winemaker of the Year. But we don't have many more of his wines to delight us. Luis died of cancer in December 2007, at the tragically early age of 48.

Kracher's region of Neusiedlersee, a vast inland lake to the south-east of Vienna in Austria, is a region where the autumn mists and warm days make it perfect for the formation of 'noble rot', one of the most important elements in the cultivation of grapes for great sweet wines. He was one of the foremost evangelists for Austrian wines.

He made sweet wines in two styles. 'Zwischen den Seen' ('between the lakes') were fermented and aged in stainless steel vats (or very occasionally large oak ones), and usually made from Welschriesling, Scheurebe or Muskat Ottonel. 'Nouvelle Vague' ('new wave') wines were fermented and aged in oak barrels (occasionally big oak vats), from Chardonnay, Traminer, Zweigelt or blends.

They are fabulous wines, and Luis Kracher is deeply missed by wine lovers all over the world.

14 wines entered (3 gold, 8 silver, 3 bronze)

Sparkling Winemaker
Regis Camus, P.&C. Heidsieck

Following in the steps of his very illustrious predecessor, Daniel Thibault, Régis Camus has begun to make a habit of winning the Sparkling Winemaker of the Year award. Régis is a no-nonsense kind of guy, who learned a great deal from his mentor Daniel (before Daniel died in 2002). He is not a native of the Champagne region, but comes originally from Thiérache (50 kilometres to the north of Reims), better known for Maroilles, one of the smelliest cheeses in France.

The cheeses of his youth have obviously not harmed Régis's sense of smell or taste, however, and he studied winemaking at Reims University, in the heart of the Champagne region. He has continued Daniel's success with the champagnes of Charles Heidsieck, and has raised the Piper Heidsieck champagnes to new levels of quality. At the same time, Régis keeps the character of the non-vintage wines very different: 'Charles is a wine for fine dining; complex and powerful,' he says. 'Piper has to have freshness and vivacity. Not simple, but good as an aperitif.'

12 wines entered (2 Trophy, 3 gold, 2 silver, 4 bronze)

Fortified Winemaker
Juan Fuentes, Emilio Lustau

'Making truly fine sherry is a long-term business.' So says Manolo Arcila, who has worked for Emilio Lustau for 37 years. As MD he oversees production, as well as all the other aspects of the company. 'You need the right basic wines, the right bodegas, good cellar-masters, and time.'

Back in the early 1980s, Rafael Balao (then head of Lustau) and Manolo started selling small amounts of high-quality sherry from sherry devotees known as almacenistas. These private individuals sell mature sherries to large companies to improve their blends. The almacenista sherries established Emilio Lustau as a producer to watch.

In 1990, Luis Caballero bought Emilio Lustau and subsequently bought a bodega in Puerto de Santa María.

'The skill of the cellar-master in guiding the maturation and selection of the wines is very important', Manolo continued. 'We have three, one each in Jerez and Puerto, and Juan Fuentes, our head cellar-master. But the most important thing is time. On average, our finos are five years old, and the rest between 10 and 20 years.'

---

19 wines entered (3 Trophy, 2 gold, 4 silver, 5 bronze, 4 commended, 1 out)

Lifetime Achievement Award
Peter Lehmann

Peter Lehmann (known widely as PL) is one of the pillars of the Australian wine industry, and the man who has done more than anyone to preserve the vine-growing heritage of the Barossa Valley.

PL started working life in a winery, and rose to the position of running Saltram, a medium-sized Barossa winery. One year in the late 1970s, when times were very hard, the owners of Saltram told PL not to buy any grapes from Barossa growers. So, rather than let his suppliers down, PL started a new company and bought the grapes himself, on credit. His independent venture prospered. It could be argued that his actions have saved that some of the Barossa's oldest and most precious vineyards, together with the livelihoods of the grape growers who own them.

Peter Lehmann Wines has gone on to be listed on the Australian Stock Exchange, and is now owned by the Hess Group. The company is run by Doug Lehmann, PL's son. Phil Lehmann, PL's grandson, is one of the younger winemakers. PL should be proud of his achievements.

Len Evans Trophy
Gonzalez Byass

The Len Evans Trophy rewards consistently excellent results in the IWC over a period of five years. During the last five years, González Byass have won three Trophies, eight Golds, 11 Silvers and four Commendeds. This year bag included three Trophies, the Palo Cortado and Pedro Ximénez Sherry Trophies, and the top Sherry Trophy itself (for the Apóstoles Palo Cortado VORS).

González Byass has always been family-owned, since its founding in 1885. Their Tio Pepe bodega in Jerez is a temple to sherry, filled with majestic butts of sherry, maturing quietly until the time comes for them to release their contents to an admiring audience. From their iconic dry fino, Tio Pepe, to their great range of VORS sherries (Very Old Rare Sherry – at least 30 years old), Matusalem, Apóstoles, Del Duque and Noé, González Byass is a worthy winner of the Len Evans Trophy.

43 wines have been entered over 5 years with 2 trophies, 8 gold, 11 silver, 11 bronze and 7 commended

Personality of the Year Award
Oz Clarke & James May

You may know them as solo performers, Oz as a wine expert and former actor, James as a car journalist and music lover. But the world has now been seduced by their new double-take on drink, particularly wine. Oz and James's Big Wine Adventure, Parts One & Two, have been seen on TV screens all over the world, not just in the UK.

Oz and James have done more to make wine 'cool' with a new generation of drinkers than anyone since UB40 sang Red, Red Wine.

Their road trips took TV viewers through wine regions in France, then California.

More recently they travelled throughout the British Isles, in Oz and James Drink to Britain, with a more comprehensive view of the drinks and drinking spots of our fair and pleasant land. Beer, cider, whisky and gin had their moments of glory, but Oz and James included English wine as well.

They have proved that drinking – then sleeping it off in a tent, caravan or Winnebago – before you drive is an entertaining way to see a wine country. They have also passed on much useful information in a light-hearted and entertaining way along the road.

Trophy Winners
White

The Champion White Wine

International Chardonnay Trophy, French White Trophy, White Burgundy Trophy, Meursault Trophy Meursault Clos De La Baronne 2007, Château Labouré Roi, Burgundy, France

Beautiful, fresh floral nose, quite perfumed, with apple, and a restrained, nutty flavour. It has very fine depth on the palate, with real freshness - really quite stylish.

Australian Chardonnay Trophy, South Australian White Trophy, Adelaide Hills White Trophy
Mcguigan Shortlist Chardonnay 2007, Australian Vintage Ltd, South Australia

Australian White Trophy, International Semillon Trophy, Australian Semillon Trophy, Hunter Valley Semillon Trophy
Marks & Spencer Hunter Valley Semillon 2005, Tyrrells, New South Wales
£18.00 M&S

Austrian White Trophy
Grauburgunder Hasel 2007, Winery Allram, Kamptal
£14.80

Barossa Valley Semillon Trophy
Peter Lehmann Wines, Margaret Semillon 2004, Australia
£13.30 VDV, LAI,

Barossa Valley White Trophy, Barossa Valley Riesling Trophy
Wolf Blass Gold Label Riesling 2005, South Australia

Bordeaux White Trophy
Château Brown 2007, Yvon-Mau, France

Cape Agulhas Trophy
Lomond Snowbush 2007, Cape Agulhas, South Africa

Chablis Trophy
Domaine De La Grande Chaume Chablis 1er Cru Vau De Vey 2007, Romain Bouchard, France
JAS, RAR, TPE

Chilean White Trophy, Chilean Sauvignon Blanc Trophy
Cono Sur 20 Barrels Limited Edition Sauvignon Blanc 2008, Casablanca Valley, Chile

Eden Valley Trophy, Eden Valley Riesling Trophy
Pewsey Vale Eden Valley Riesling 2008, South Australia
£10.40 FLA

Eden Valley Viognier Trophy
Yalumba Eden Valley Viognier 2008, South Australia
£10.80 FLA, NFW, VDV, WAIT

English Trophy
Camel Valley, 2007 Camel Valley Bacchus 2007, South West England
£11.00 WAIT, CVV, WBR

French Cabernet
Sauvignon Trophy
Famille Skalli Cabernet Sauvignon
2007, Vin De Pays d'Oc, France
£6.00

Greek White Trophy
Ovilos White 2008, Ktima Biblia
Chora S.A., Greece

International Alvarinho Trophy,
Portuguese White Trophy
Muros Antigos Alvarinho 2008,
Anselmo Mendes Vinhos Lda
(Wines & Winemakers By
Saven), Vinho Verde, Portugal

International Cabernet Franc
Trophy, Loire Valley Red Trophy
French Connection Classics
Samur Champigny 2008,
Alliance Loire, France

International Chenin Blanc
Trophy, Stellen-bosch White
Trophy
Kleine Zalze Vineyard
Selection Chenin Blanc 2008,
Stellenbosch, South Africa
£8.00

International Riesling Trophy,
Rheingau Trophy
Winkeler Jesuitengarten
Riesling 1. Gewächs 2007,
Weingut Prinz Von Hessen,
Rheingau, Germany

International Viognier Trophy,
Languedoc-Roussillon White
Trophy
Laurent Miquel Vérité Viognier
2007, France
£14.00

Italian White Trophy,
Pecorino Trophy
Unico Pecorino Terre Di Chieti
IGT 2008, Tenuta Ulisse,
Abruzzo, Italy

Loire Valley White Trophy,
Sancerre Trophy
Sancerre 2008, Domaine
Naudet, France
ABY

Lombardia Trophy
Cabanon Riesling O.p. DOC
2007, Fattoria Cabanon Of Elena
Mercandelli, Lombardia, Italy

Moscophilero Trophy
Orinos Helios-Mountain Sun
White 2008, Semeli Winery,
Peloponnese, Greece
£6.00

Mosel Off-Dry Trophy,
Mosel Trophy
Riesling Kabinett Mosel 2004,
S.A.Prum, Mosel, Germany
£12.20

Great Value Champion White

Australian Riesling Trophy, Clare Valley White Trophy, Great Value White between £5 And £10
Tim Adams Riesling 2008, South Australia
Clean, green, and complex. Lime and tropical
fruit, with a dry, apple core, and notes of
oatmeal. Lots of fresh acidity. Palate has nice
pleasing roundness, with quite a long finish.
£8.60 TESC, AWC

Great Value
White Between
£10 And £15
Louis Latour
Pouilly-Vinzelles
En Paradis 2006,
£10.00 MWW

New Zealand Chardonnay
Trophy
Ata Rangi, Craighall
Chardonnay 2007, Wairarapa
£23.20 NZH, LIB

New Zealand White Trophy,
International Sauvignon
Blanc Trophy, New Zealand
Sauvignon Blanc Trophy
Clifford Bay Awatere Valley
Sauvignon Blanc 2008,
Vavasour Wines Limited,
Marlborough
£9.00 B&J

Pouilly Fumé Trophy
Pouilly-Fumé 2008, Domaine
De Bel Air, France
£13.00 LIB

Puligny Montrachet Trophy
Marks & Spencer Puligny
Montrachet Ier Cru Les
Chalumeaux 2007, Domaine

Jean Pascal Et Fils, France
£35.00 M&S

South African White Trophy,
South African Sauvignon Blanc
Trophy, Western Cape Trophy
Groot Constantia Sauvignon
Blanc 2008, Western Cape,
South Africa
£10.00 HOH

Spanish White Trophy
Maior De Mendoza 2007,
Galicia

Retsina Trophy
The Pine 2008, Kechris Winery,
Macedonia, Greece

Western Australian
White Trophy
Evans & Tate The Reserve
Chardonnay 2005, Australia
HWL

 Trophy Winners
Red

The Champion Red Wine

**International Cabernet Sauvignon Trophy, South
African Red Trophy, Stellenbosch Red Trophy
Guardian Peak, Lapa Cabernet, Sauvignon 2007,
Stellenbosch, South Africa**
Flashy black fruit, cassis, and plum. Firm, dense, and
extracted, with some dryness too. Elegant, big, powerful,
and youthful, with good length.
£16.50 SAO, DBY, L&C

Adelaide Hills Red Trophy
Shaw & Smith Shiraz 2007,
South Australia
£18.90 HEN, LIB

Aglianico Trophy
Gudarrà Aglianico Del Vulture DOC
2005, Bisceglia, Basilicata, Italy
£14.50

Great Value Champion Red

International Malbec Trophy, Argentinean Red Trophy, Mendoza Red Trophy, Mendoza, Malbec Trophy, Great Value Red Between £5 and £10
Pascual Toso Malbec 2008, Mendoza
Ripe, sweet cherry yoghurt on the nose, with meaty and wood-smoke notes. Complex coffee, raspberry, and liquorice on the palate. Fruity, spicy finish, which is very long.
£8.00 SWS

Great Value Red Under £5
Misterio Malbec 2008, Bodega Finca Flichman, Mendoza
£5.00

Alentejo Trophy
Herdade Das Barras 2005, Soc. Agro-pecuaria Do Oeste Alentejano, Lda., Alentejo, Portugal

Australian Red Trophy, South Australian Red Trophy, Barossa Valley Red Trophy
Yalumba The Signature Barossa Cabernet Sauvignon Shiraz 2005, South Australia
£24.50 FLA, VDV

Australian Cabernet Sauvignon Trophy, Western Australian Red Trophy
Clairault Estate Cabernet Sauvignon 2005, Western Australia
£18.00 M&S

Australian Shiraz Trophy, Barossa Valley Shiraz Trophy
Pirathon By Kalleske Shiraz 2007, South Australia

Austrian Red Trophy, Kamptal Trophy, Zweigelt Trophy
Zweigelt Granit 2007, Weingut Kurt Angerer, Kamptal
NYW

Catalonia Trophy
Grupo Codorníu Scala Dei Cartoixa 2006, Catalonia, Spain
£25.00 CPB, HRW, RWW

Central Otago Pinot Noir Trophy
Hinton Estate Vineyard Barrel Selection 2007, Central Otago, New Zealand

Chianti Trophy
Tenuta Di Capraia Chianti Classico Riserva Docg 2005, Rocca Di Castagnoli, Tuscany, Italy
£21.30 EUW, EVW

Chilean Cabernet Sauvignon Trophy
Doña Bernarda 2006, Viña Luis Felipe Edwards, Colchagua Valley, Chile

Chilean Red Trophy, Chilean Syrah Trophy, San Antonio Valley Trophy
Matetic EQ Syrah 2007, San Antonio Valley
£18.00 GNS, MWW, WSO

Clare Valley Red Trophy
O'leary Walker Claire Clare Reserve Shiraz 2004, South Australia
£37.50 WAIT

Colchagua Valley Malbec Trophy
Viu Manent Malbec Single Vineyard El Olivar 2007, Colchagua Valley, Chile

Great Value Champion Rosé

Great Value Rosé Between £5 and £10
Côtes Du Rhône Parallele 45 Rose 2008, Paul Jaboulet Aine
Clean, pure, fresh strawberry fruit. A well-balanced wine with
fresh, lively acidity, carrying the flavours to a long finish.
£9.00 LIB, V&C, WIA

Colchagua Valley Trophy
Novas Carmenère / Cabernet
2007, Viñedos Emiliana,
Colchagua Valley, Chile
£7.80

Dão Trophy
Quinta Da Garrida 2006,
Alianca, Dão
£8.70

**Edmund Penning-
Rowsell Trophy**
Château Caronne Ste
Gemme 2004, Sce Vignobles
Nony Borie, France
£13.00 MWW

Elqui Valley Trophy
Falernia Syrah Reserva
2007, Viña Falernia S.A.,
Elquí Valley
£11.00 FFT, FNW, GWW, HOF,
HVN

**French Red Trophy,
International Pinot Noir
Trophy, Red Burgundy Trophy**
Clos De Vougeot Grand Cru
2006, Domaine De La Vougeraie

**Great Value Red
Between £10 And £15
Caves Saint Pierre-
Préférence Gigondas 2007,
Les Vins Skalli**
£14.00 TESC

Hawke's Bay Syrah Trophy
Mission Estate Winery Reserve
Syrah 2007, Hawke's Bay, New
Zealand

International Carmenere Trophy
Falernia Carmenère Reserva
2006, Viña Falernia S.A., Elqui
Valley, Chile
£11.00 CAM, DEF, GWW,
HVN, NYW, TAN

International Merlot Trophy
Galatrona 2006, Fattoria Petrolo,
Tuscany, Italy
£80.00 LIB

**International Nebbiolo Trophy,
Piedmont Trophy**
Barbaresco 2005, Beni Di Batasiolo,
Piedmont, Italy
£23.00 MON

International Tempranillo Trophy
Campillo Gran Reserva 1995, Rioja
£23.50 EVW

**Italian Red Trophy, Veneto
Trophy, Amarone Trophy**
Campolongo Di Torbe 2004, Masi
Agricola, Veneto, Italy

Languedoc-Roussillon Red Trophy
La Garrigue 2007, Scea Château
Camplazens, France
£9.20

Lujan de Cuyo Trophy
Andean Vineyards, Waxed Bat
2008, Mendoza
£8.00 LAI

Maule Valley Trophy
Chilcas Single Vineyard Cabernet
Franc 2006, Via Wines, Maule
Valley, Chile
£9.00 BWL

New Zealand Red Trophy,
International Syrah Trophy,
New Zealand Syrah Trophy,
Auckland Syrah Trophy
Kennedy Point Waiheke Syrah
2007, Auckland, New Zealand

New Zealand Pinot Noir Trophy,
Marlborough Pinot Noir Trophy
Pioneer Block 15 Strip Block
Pinot Noir 2007, Saint Clair,
Marlborough, New Zealand
£16.10 NZH, HOH

Puglia Trophy
Selvarossa Salice Salentino
Rosso DOC Riserva 2005,
Cantine Due Palme Soc. Coop.
Agricola, Puglia, Italy

Spanish Red Trophy, Rioja Trophy
Inspiracion Valdemar Edicion
Limitada 2004, Rioja, Spain

St Laurent Trophy
St Laurent Classic 2007,
Heinrich Hartl, Thermenregion
£ 14.50 MWD, CEE

Terras do Sado Trophy
Palácio Da Bacalhôa 2005,
Bacalhôa Vinhos De Portugal,
Terras Do Sado, Portugal
£17.00

Tuscan Red Trophy, Brunello di
Montalcino Trophy
Brunello Di Montalcino Riserva
DOCG 2003, Loacker Corte
Pavone, Tuscany, Italy
£61.00 GWW

Ripasso Trophy
Ripasso Valpolicella 2007,
Cortegiara, Veneto, Italy
£9.00 TESC, LIB

Victorian Red Trophy
Plunkett Fowles Ladies Who
Shoot Their Lunch Shiraz 2006,
Victoria Red

Wairarapa Pinot Noir Trophy
Gladstone Pinot Noir 2007,
Wairarapa, New Zealand
£13.80 CAM, FFT, GWW,
NYW

Trophy Winners
Fortified

Amontillado Sherry Trophy
Sainsburys Taste The Difference
Amontillado NV, Emilio Lustau
S.a. Jerez-xérès-sherry
£6.50 SAIN

Boal Madeira Trophy
Blandy's Colheita Bual 1993,
Madeira Wine Company, Madeira

Fino Sherry Trophy
Waitrose Solera Jerezana Fino
Sherry NV, Emilio Lustau Sa,
Jerez-xérès-sherry, Spain
£8.00 WAIT

Fortified Muscat Trophy
Angelas Blend Rare Muscat NV,
Buller Wines, Victoria, Australia

LBV Port Trophy
Warre's Lbv 2000, Symington
Family Estates, Douro, Portugal

Malmsey Madeira Trophy
Marks & Spencer Malmsey
Madeira 2001, Henriques &
Henriques, Madeira
£17.00 M&S

Champion Fortified

Madeira Trophy, Verdelho Madeira Trophy
**Verdelho Old Reserve 10 Year Old NV, Vinhos
Barbeito Madeira Lda, Madeira, Portugal**
Lovely rich fruit, with a powerful and concentrated
palate of walnut and sultana. Clean and bright, with
elegance and a long finish. A gorgeous Madeira.
£25.00 REY

Great Value
Fortified
Between £10
and £15
Krohn LBV
2004, Wiese &
Krohn, Douro
£12.60 GGR
HFW WWN

Great Value
Champion Fortified

Manzanilla Sherry Trophy, Great Value
**Fortified Wine Between £5 And £10
Marks & Spencer Manzanilla Sherry NV,
Williams & Humbert, Jerez-xérès-sherry**
Pale gold straw in colour. Nose of lifted salt and
bacon rind. Clean and mineral with carnation
blossom and hints of lime and a very elegant finish.
£6.00 M&S

Moscatel Sherry Trophy
Lustau Solera Reserva Moscatel
Emilin NV, Jerez-xérès-sherry
£14.00

Pedro Ximénez Sherry Trophy
Nectar Pedro Ximénez
NV, González Byass
Jerez-xérès-sherry, Spain

Port Trophy, Vintage Port Trophy
Quinta Seara D'ordens Vintage
2005, Douro, Portugal

Sherry Trophy, Palo Cortado
Sherry Trophy
Apostoles Palo Cortado Vors NV,
González Byass, Jerez-xérès-sherry
£15.00 WAIT

Tawny Port Trophy
Porto Ferreira 20 Years Old Tawny
NV, Sogrape Vinhos S.A., Douro

Vermouth Trophy
Quady Winery Vya Sweet
Vermouth 2010, California, USA
£15.00 HOH

Trophy Winners
Sweet

Austrian Chardonnay
Botrytis Trophy
Chardonnay TBA
2005, Hans Tschida,
Burgenland

Austrian Sweet Trophy,
Austrian Botrytis Trophy,
Austrian Samling Botrytis
Trophy, Burgenland Trophy
Sämling TBA 2005, Hans
Tschida, Burgenland

James Rogers Trophy

Eiswein Welschriesling Höchleit´n 2007, Weingut Felberjörgl, Südsteiermark

Decadently rich honey aroma, leading to an equally rich apricot palate that is, by turns, sweet and apple-like. A chewy sweetness on the finish, which is very long and luscious.

Champion Sweet

International Botrytis Trophy, German Sweet Trophy, German Botrytis Trophy, Franken Trophy, Alois Kracher Trophy Escherndorfer Lump Riesling Trockenbeer-enauslese 2007, Weingut Horst Sauer, Franken

Very sweet and honeyed, with a hint of spice. Marked by considerable freshness on the palate, with plenty of fruit, and great length and complexity.
J&B

Canadian Icewine Trophy
Jackson-Triggs Niagara
Estate, Proprietors' Reserve
Vidal Icewine 2007, Niagara
Peninsula, Canada

German Late Harvest Trophy,
Mosel Late Harvest Trophy
Kanzemer Altenberg
Trockenbeerenauslese 2007,
Bischöfliche Weingüter, Mosel

Greek Vinsanto Trophy
Sigalas Vinsanto Santorini
2003, Greece
£17.60 VKB

International Gewürztraminer
Trophy, Pfalz Trophy
Gewürztraminer Spätlese 2007,
Weingut Heinz Pfaffmann,
Pfalz, Germany

International Icewine Trophy,
Austrian Eiswein Trophy
Eiswein Welschriesling
Höchleit´n 2007, Weingut
Felberjörgl, Südsteiermark

International Late Harvest
Trophy, South African Late
Harvest Trophy
Nederburg Winemasters
Reserve Noble Late Harvest
2008, Paarl, South Africa

Great Value Champion Sweet

Great Value Sweet Between £10 And £15
Marks & Spencer Scheurebe 2005, Weingut Darting, Pfalz
Pale gold straw colour. Pink grapefruit, ripe honey, and stone fruit on the nose, with lifted apricot notes. Great balance and length, with a terrific finish. £15.00 M&S

Italian Sweet Trophy, Vin
Santo Trophy, Italian Vin
Santo Trophy
Tegrino Vinsanto 2004,
Leonardo, Tuscany , Italy
£21.70 HEN, LIB

Loire Valley Sweet Trophy
Bonnezeaux Les Melleresses
2007, Château La Varière

Tokaji Trophy
Dobogo' Tokaji Aszu' 6 Puttonyos
2004, Dobogo', Tokaji, Hungary

 Trophy Winners
Sake

Champion Sake

Koshu Trophy
Kinmon Akita Shuzo Co Ltd, Yamabuki 1995
With elegant notes of apricot and dried flowers on
the nose and palate, this has a beautiful bright gold
colour, and a nice hint of sweetness on the finish.

Daiginjo Mie Regional Trophy
Shimizu Jozo Co, Zaku Daiginjo
2008

Ginjo, Daiginjo Trophy
Nemoto Shuzo Co Ltd, Daiginjo
Kujinoyama 2008

**Honjozo Okayama
Regional Trophyv**
Kamikokoro Shuzo Co Ltd,
Kamikokoro Hihou Honjozo 2008

Honjozo Trophy
Shindo Sake Brewery Co Ltd,
Ura Gasanryu 'koka' 2008

**Junmai Daiginjo Kyoto
Regional Trophy**
Sasaki Shuzo Co Ltd, Jurakudai
Junmai Daiginjo-shu 2008

**Junmai Daiginjo Miyagi
Regional Trophy**
Uchigasaki Shuzouten Ltd,
Junmai Daiginjo Hoyo 2008

**Junmai Daiginjo Yamagata
Regional Trophy**
Takenotsuyu Sake Brewery
Co Ltd, Takenotsuyu Junmai
Daiginjo Hakurosuishu 2008
£65.00 TZK

**Junmai Ginjo, Junmai
Daiginjo Trophy**
Kodama Brewing Co Ltd, Taiheizan
Junmai Daiginjo Tenko 2008

Junmai Trophy
Yoshida Sake Brewery Co Ltd,
Yamahaishikomi Junmai-shu
Tedorigawa 2008

Koshu Miyagi Regional Trophy
Saura Co Ltd, Yamadanishiki
Junmai Daiginjo Koshu
Urakasumi 2005

Koshu Nara Regional Trophy
Choryo Shuzo Co Ltd, Tsukihi
Kasanete 1992

Trophy Winners
Sparkling

Asti Trophy, Great Value
Sparkling under £5
Canti Asti DOCG NV, Fratelli
Martini Secondo Luigi Spa,
Piedmont, France
£5.00 MRN

Great Value Sparkling
Between £5 and £10
Bluff Hill Brut NV, France
£9.00 M&S

Great Value Sparkling
Between £10 And £15
Prosecco Valdobbiadene Brut
Villa Sandi NV, Villa Sandi
Veneto, Italy
£12.60 PLA

Mature Vintage
Champagne Trophy
Charles Heidsieck Blanc Des
Millénaires 1983, France
£245.00 BB&R

Non Vintage
Champagne Trophy
Taittinger Prelude Grands
Crus NV, France
£39.20 FLA, HMA

Rose Champagne Trophy
Rosé De Castellane NV

The Champion Sparkling Wine
Daniel Thibault Trophy

**Young Vintage Champagne Trophy
Charles Heidsieck Blanc Des
Millénaires 1995**

Elegant Chardonnay character, with lime custard notes on a leesy,
lively, fresh palate, which shows lovely Chardonnay flavour. Long,
fresh citrus flavour, and an elegant finish.
£93.00 WUO

Great Value Champion Sparkling

**Great Value Sparkling Between £15 And £20
Sainsbury's Blanc De Noirs Champagne NV, Société Coopérative
De Producteurs Des Grands Terroirs De La Champagne**

Lifted soft red fruits aromas. Attractive, with good integrated fizz. Full
of flavour, with notes of golden apple, and a full mouthfeel, with nice
creamy texture.
£16.00 SAIN

Planet Earth Awards

Organic Trophy

Clos De Vougeot Grand Cru 2006, Domaine De La Vougeraie

Dark, heady aromas of berry fruit, mingled with cocoa and light oak spice. The palate is similar, but with rich mulberry and bramble fruit flavours, and brisk tannins.

Biodynamic Trophy

Brunello Di Montalcino Riserva DOCG 2003, Loacker Corte Pavone, Tuscany

Magnificent nose of ripe black cherry and plum. On the palate it has an attractive, slightly bitter note, with hints of tobacco, and evident new French oak. Lots of potential and really great length.
£61.00 GWW

Sustainable Trophy

Guardian Peak, Lapa Cabernet, Sauvignon 2007, Stellenbosch, South Africa

Flashy black fruit, cassis, and plum. Firm, dense, and extracted, with some dryness too. Elegant, big, powerful, and youthful, with good length.
£16.50 SAO, DBY, L&C

Get the most out of your guide

This guide lists award-winning wines from the 2009 International Wine Challenge. To make individual wines easy to find, they are organised first by country of origin, then according to the type of medal they won: Gold Medal winners first, then Silver and then Bronze. Within these groupings each entry is sorted alphabetically by producer name for New World wines, and by wine name for Old World wines.

Individual entries are colourfully designed to offer information at a glance ...

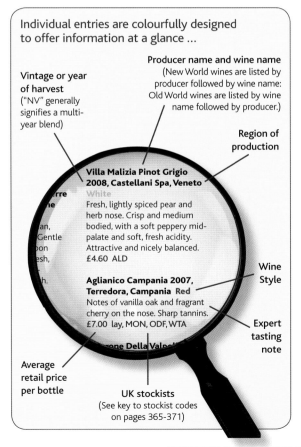

Vintage or year of harvest
("NV" generally signifies a multi-year blend)

Producer name and wine name
(New World wines are listed by producer followed by wine name: Old World wines are listed by wine name followed by producer.)

Region of production

Villa Malizia Pinot Grigio 2008, Castellani Spa, Veneto
White
Fresh, lightly spiced pear and herb nose. Crisp and medium bodied, with a soft peppery mid-palate and soft, fresh acidity. Attractive and nicely balanced.
£4.60 ALD

Aglianico Campania 2007, Terredora, Campania Red
Notes of vanilla oak and fragrant cherry on the nose. Sharp tannins.
£7.00 lay, MON, ODF, WTA

Wine Style

Expert tasting note

Average retail price per bottle

UK stockists
(See key to stockist codes on pages 365-371)

Argentina

Home to the highest cultivated vineyard in the world, the average altitude for grape growing in Argentina is over 900 metres above sea level. This freshness, along with state-of-the-art technology in the winery, is enabling winemakers to produce wines with immense elegance and unparalleled promise. This is reflected in this year's results, showing a steady improvement year-on-year. With all ten Gold medal wines coming from red and black grapes, Argentina has mastered the art of tannins, most notably in the black and brooding Malbec. Once again the altitude plays a vital role in preserving the fragrant aromas found in the national white grape Torrontés and the abundance of Chardonnay widely planted.

2009 IWC PERFORMANCE

Trophies	5
Gold	10
Silver	43
Bronze	63
Great Value Awards	2

GOLD

 **LUJAN DE CUYO TROPHY**

Andean Vineyards, Waxed Bat 2008, Mendoza Red
Terrific nose of violets and blackberries, showing lovely oak complexity. Huge youthful palate of ripe fruit, with real depth and a fresh finish.
£8.00 LAI

Chakana Reserve Malbec 2007, Mendoza Red
A beautifully deep ruby colour. Intense, ripe fruit aromas of blackberries, blueberries, and morello cherries. Lovely floral overtones. Well-integrated acidity and tannins, culminating in an excellent length.

Fabre Montmayou Patagonia Barrel Selection Malbec 2007, Domaine Vistalba S.A., Rio Negro Red
Sweet red berry nose, with a purée-like aroma. Lovely sweet fruity wine, with smooth tannins and lovely acidity. Everything is in balance, with intense sweet fruit and good length.
£9.00 VGN

Felino Malbec 2007, Viña Cobos S.A., Mendoza Red
Lots of jammy dark fruit on the nose, leading to a ripe, dark chocolatey palate. Ripe, black, juicy fruit, with ripe tannins and intense flavour. Great balance and structure. A very modern style of wine.
£9.40 AAW

Jean Bousquet Malbec 2007, Mendoza Red
Fruity nose of nicely lifted black fruit. Very nice expression of flavour, with good depth. A classy wine which will improve with time.
£7.50

Jean Bousquet Malbec Reserva 2007, Mendoza Red
An intense nose with loads of power. Very structured, dark, ripe fruit on the palate. Long length of flavour. A brooding wine that can age. Exceptional stuff.
£9.90 VRT

Magdalena Toso 2006, Bodegas Y Viñedos Pascual Toso S.A., Mendoza Red
Beautifully vibrant, juicy blackberry fruit. Sweet, savoury, and lovely spicy and smoky notes. Good structure and freshness. Nice tannins and a long finish.
£60.00 SWS

 **INTERNATIONAL MALBEC TROPHY, ARGENTINEAN RED TROPHY, MENDOZA RED TROPHY, MENDOZA MALBEC TROPHY**

GREAT VALUE CHAMPION RED, GREAT VALUE RED BETWEEN £5 AND £10

Pascual Toso Malbec 2008, Mendoza Red
Ripe, sweet cherry yoghurt on the nose, with meaty and wood-smoke notes. Complex coffee, raspberry, and liquorice on the palate. Fruity, spicy finish, which is very long.
£8.00 SWS

Santa Julia Reserva Tempranillo, Familia Zuccardi, 2008, Mendoza Red
Bright, ruby red colour. Clean nose, with a soft attack of fresh fruit and toast. Good weight on the palate, well-balanced, with a vanilla oak finish.

Trivento Reserve Malbec 2007, Mendoza Red

Very good varietal expression. Rich and ripe, concentrated and extracted. Spicy, juicy fruit, with good balance and a velvety smooth texture. Not for wimps, but a very good modern wine nonetheless!
£11.00 FLA CYT

SILVER

Alamos Seleccion Chardonnay 2008, Bodegas Esmeralda - Wines Of Catena, Mendoza White

Big, rich nose with a warm citrussy palate. This charming wine has really good body and creamy texture. Well-balanced, with good length.
BWL

Asda Argentinian Torrontes 2008, Trivento Bodegas Y Viñedos S.A., Mendoza White

Star-bright, pale lemon yellow in colour. The nose shows youthful elderflower fruit. Lovely apricot tones on the palate, with good fruit intensity.
£4.30 ASDA

Doña Paula Estate Sauvignon Blanc 2008, Mendoza White

Masses of juicy fruit on the nose, with aromas of asparagus coming through. Huge acidity, some length, and a satisfyingly dry finish.

Finca El Origen Torrontes Reserve 2008, Bodegas Y Viñedos La Esperanza S.A., Mendoza White

Lifted floral notes on the nose, with hints of rose petal and white pepper. Rounded mouthfeel. Well-made, with good length.

Las Moras Black Label Viognier 2006, San Juan White

Clean, classic apricot, with some spicy honey. Balanced acidity and a creamy edge, with depth and good length.
£10.00

Alta Vista Atemporal Blend 2007, Mendoza Red

Fresh, fruity, almost floral nose, of raspberry, leather, tobacco, indian spice, and cherry. Sweet and sour flavours, light tannins, long length, and a slightly spicy finish.

Alta Vista Grande Reserve Terroir Selection 2006, Mendoza Red

Purple in colour. Quite subtle, with dark cherry and vanilla leaf character. Palate is full, rich, and deep. Round, with nice spice and peppery length.

Andean Vineyards Malbec 2007, Mendoza Red

Initially oaky, but fruit comes through. Lush, plummy, and spicy, with ripe mulberry and chocolatey fruit. Well-made, with a long finish.
£6.00 LAI

Black River Reserve Malbec 2007, Humberto Canale Winery, Patagonia Red
Deep plum red in colour, with a nose of perfumed berry fruit and cinnamon. Palate of cassis and blackberry fruit, with firm tannins and fruit acidity.
£10.00

Bodega Del Fin Del Mundo Gran Reserva 2006, Neuquen Red
Sweet tobacco notes, with elegant fruit and liquorice flavours. Full-bodied, with jammy chocolate and coffee notes coming through on the finish.

Bodega Del Fin Del Mundo Reserva Malbec 2007, Neuquen Red
Dark berry fruit and smoked meat on the nose. A jammy, juicy palate with nicely integrated acidity, and a linear texture.

Caro 2006, Les Domaines Barons De Rothschild (Lafite) Distribution, Mendoza Red
Lovely deep red in colour. Nice coffee and leather notes, with a rich, spicy taste. Very juicy, with a meaty, chocolate finish.
£25.00 AVB, BWL, LAI

Chakana Malbec 2008, Mendoza Red
Excellent lifted fruit. Great varietal character. Crunchy black fruit with a touch of perfume. Rich, full-bodied, and smooth.

Colomé Estate Malbec 2007, Salta Red
Elegant lifted nose, soft and fruity, with black cherry notes, good construction, and showing some real complexity.
£13.40 WTSCOE, NYW, ODD, SWG

Dedicado 2006, Bodega Finca Flichman, Mendoza Red
Deep dark cherry colour, with intense spice notes, full body, rich tannins, and a good finish.
£17.00

Doña Paula Estate Malbec 2008, Mendoza Red
Lifted toasty new oak. Ripe, plummy fruit flavours, with caramel on the finish. Richly textured, with fresh acidity and supple tannins.

Estilo Pampas Malbec 2007, Trivento Bodegas Y Viñedos S.A., Mendoza Red
Rich cassis fruit aromas. Fresh lifted fruit palate. Smooth tannins, with a light violet and creamy note. Good length.
£6.00 MVN

Fabre Montmayou Reserva Malbec 2007, Domaine Vistalba S.A., Mendoza Red
Very ripe and juicy on the nose, very deep, dark, brooding notes. Lovely aged fruit, delicious palate, and well-integrated oak – beautiful!
£8.70 LAI, DKS, VGN

Finca El Origen Cabernet Sauvignon Reserve 2007, Bodegas Y Viñedos La Esperanza S.A.,Mendoza Red
Intense colour. Pronounced Cabernet nose, with a palate of juicy black fruit. Crisp acidity and good length.

Finca El Portillo Malbec 2008, Bodegas Salentein, Mendoza Red
Big chunky vanilla, blackberry, and smoky aromas. Juicy sour cherry palate with floral notes. Good freshness and chunky tannins.
£7.00 D&D

Graffigna Centenario Shiraz 2006, San Juan Red
A smoky, blackberry nose with black pepper notes. Full, dry, and intense palate of ripe fruit, black pepper, with smooth tannins, some chocolatey oak, and a clean, bright finish.

Gran Pampas Malbec 2006, Trivento Bodegas Y Viñedos S.A., Mendoza Red
Juicy black fruit, with slightly chunky tannins. A bit dry, but with very nice length. Needs time to evolve.
CYT

La Consulta Malbec 2007, Finca La Celia, San Carlos Red
Spicy, ripe fruit, with lovely chocolate and water biscuits on the nose. Earthy palate, with very grippy tannins and a nice long finish.

La Mascota Malbec 2007, Bodegas Santa Ana, Mendoza Red
Intense, deep and brooding, with masses of dark fruit. Full and fruit-driven, with tight tannins, balanced acidity, and a slightly hot finish.

Las Moras Black Label Cabernet Cabernet 2006, San Juan Red
Black fruits, oak, and vanilla, with good varietal character. Firm structure, with dark fruit on the palate. Ripe tannins and balanced acidity.
£10.00

Las Moras Black Label Shiraz 2006, San Juan Red
Clean nose of perfumed spice and blackberry fruit. Concentrated mulberry palate, with silky tannins and a pure finish.
£10.00 CWS

La Puerta Reserva Bonarda 2007, La Rioja Red
Very attractive nose, with lots of fruit and toasty juiciness. Well-balanced, with good length and intensity.
£7.00

> **GREAT VALUE RED UNDER £5**

Misterio Malbec 2008, Bodega Finca Flichman, Mendoza Red
Big nose of creamy ripe plum fruit. Fresh black fruit with toffee and nice weight. Good and chewy.
£5.00

Nieto Senetiner Reserva Malbec 2007, Mendoza Red
Deep cherry red in colour. Meaty tones and red berries on the nose. Intense palate. Good balance and excellent concentration.
£7.80 CHH, WES

Pascual Toso Alta Reserva Malbec 2007, Mendoza Red
Deep colour, with a spicy, slightly woody nose, and notes of fresh ripe black plums, damsons, chocolate, and eucalyptus. Smooth attack, with a juicy morello cherry palate, good balance, and a long vibrant finish.
£23.00 SWS

Pascual Toso Alta Reserva Syrah 2007, Mendoza Red
Rich, complex palate of black cherries, spice, and toast. Full and powerful, yet silky and elegant.
£23.00 SWS

Pascual Toso Cabernet Sauvignon Reserva 2007, Mendoza Red
Very rich, ripe nose. Sexy wine with great structure, harmonious acidity, and sweet length.
£12.50 SWS

Pascual Toso Finca Pedregal Single Vineyard 2005, Mendoza Red
Big, super-ripe, Porty nose, with some lifted fruit and dark chocolate notes. Palate has sweet blue and black fruit. Big and linear, with lovely fruit and chocolatey persistence.
£35.00 SWS

Pampas Del Sur Reserve Malbec 2007, Trivento Bodegas Y Viñedos S.A., Mendoza Red
Attractive nose of black cherry fruit, almond, crushed black pepper, and spice. Lovely balance on the palate. Fine tannin and soft black fruit.
CYT

Salentein Numina Gran Corte 2005, Mendoza Red
Lovely savoury black fruit aromas, with oaky juicy fruits. Well-defined fruit character on the palate. Chewy tannins and well-balanced acidity. Excellent length.
£15.00

Santa Ana Malbec Reserve 2007, Mendoza Red
Fruit compote on the nose. Deep crimson plum and raspberry palate. Firm, crunchy tannins, finishing on a bitter cherry note.
£10.30 EDC

Terrazas de los Andes Afincado Malbec 2006, Mendoza Red
Aristocratic. Tastes expensive and low yielding. Jammy and fruity, with dark chocolate and high tannins. A wine with attitude.
£30.00

Trivento Golden Reserve Malbec 2006, Mendoza Red
Inviting perfumed nose of jammy bramble fruit. Some hints of cloves and spice. Spicy fruit palate, balanced with brisk tannins.
£8.00 FLA

Umbral De Los Tiempos 2006, Bodega Cruz De Piedra S.A., Mendoza Red
Intense blackcurrant notes. Very oaky, with an inky eucalyptus aroma, and silky tannins. A well-balanced, elegant wine with length. Bordeaux-like.

Viñalba Reserva Cabernet Sauvignon 2007, Domaine Vistalba, Mendoza Red
Lovely intense nose with hints of chocolate. Very serious, well-made wine - long and elegant.
£10.00 BUC

Vineyard Selection Reserva Altos Las Hormigos Malbec 2007, Mendoza Red
Deep black-red colour, with blackberries and plenty of ripe strawberries and cinnamon on the palate. Very chewy tannins, and very long finish, with a clean minty note.
£17.50 LIB

Zuccardi Q Tempranillo 2006, Familia Zuccardi, Mendoza Red
Fresh, spearmint nose with coffee and oak notes. Succulent attack, good acidity, and vibrant fruit, with engaging complexity on the finish.
£12.60 HEN

Santa Julia Syrah Rosé 2009, Familia Zuccardi, Mendoza Rosé
Rich red fruit aromas. Vibrant, soft red fruits give a bold, rich, concentrated palate. Good finish and length.
£6.00 SMF

Alto Pampas Del Sur Viognier 2008, Trivento Bodegas Y Viñedos S.A., Mendoza White
Tropical, apricot richness, with hints of sweetness, and some good fruit. An easy drinking style.
£6.00 MVN

Argento Chardonnay 2008, Mendoza White
Oaky aromas, but with good, ripe tropical fruit as well. Acidity is crisp, and balances the oakiness. Decent fruit and length.
£6.00 WES, TESC, WAIT, BWL, MWW

Colomé Torrontes 2008, Salta White
Pungent floral aromas on the nose, which carry through to the palate. Grippy, refreshing acidity.
£8.00 COE, EVW, SWG

Finca El Portillo Sauvignon Blanc 2008, Bodegas Salentein, Mendoza White
Pale yellow green in colour, with sweet peach and banana notes.
£7.00 D&D

Finca Sophenia Reserve Chardonnay 2008, Mendoza White
Pure and bright, with citrus aromas and zippy acidity. Good length.
£11.00 EOR, RWA

Grupo Codorníu Septima Chardonnay 2008, Mendoza White
An attractive nose of almond and coconut. Nice definition, well-balanced, with good acidity, and a touch of spice on the long finish.
£7.00

Pascual Toso Chardonnay 2008, Mendoza White
Oak, vanilla, and citrus on the nose, with a palate of citrus and sherbet. Crisp acidity and a fruit-driven, zesty finish.
£8.00 SWS

Santa Ana Viognier Reserve 2008, Mendoza White
Clean apricot and apple nose, with some nice weight on the palate and an elegant finish.
£7.00

Sophenia Synthesis Sauvignon Blanc 2008, Mendoza White
Grapefruit nose. The palate has good weight, with plenty of acidity and minerality.
£11.00 EOR, RWA

Terrazas de los Andes Reserva Torrontes 2007, Mendoza White
Star-bright, pale lemon green hue. Lifted floral nose. Light body and a grapey finish.
£12.00

The Co-operative Fairtrade Argentine Torrontés Chardonnay 2008, La Riojana Co-op., La Rioja White
Pale lemon colour. Lovely citrus fruit on the nose, leading to a clean, balanced palate.
£4.50 CWS

Trivento Colección Fincas Sauvignon Blanc 2008, Mendoza White
Nice, fruity, clean nose. Firm and polished, with good texture and balance.
£16.50 LAI, CYT

Alamos Seleccion Malbec 2008, Bodegas Esmeralda - Wines Of Catena, Mendoza Red
Baked fruit aromas on the nose. Intense fruit on the palate. Dry finish.

Discover your inner tango.

Wines of Argentina

www.winesofargentina.org

Argento Reserva Malbec 2008, Mendoza Red
Aromas of rich red plums, with dried figgy fruits, and spicy tannins.
£6.60 WES, BWL,

Bodega Del Fin Del Mundo Reserva Cabernet Sauvignon 2006, Neuquen Red
Elegant cassis and cinnamon nose. Silky, multi-layered palate, well-balanced, with a long, spicy, dry finish.

Bodega Del Fin Del Mundo Special Blend 2006, Neuquen Red
Plum, cherry, and chocolatey nose. Very fruity, rich, juicy, and complex. Sweet, long finish.

Bramare Lujan De Cuyo Malbec 2006, Viña Cobos, Mendoza Red
Excellent high notes of violet and plum, with a rich, round, smooth, and fruity palate. Long and balanced, with heaps of finesse on the finish.
£18.30 AAW

Canale Black River Reserve 2007, Patagonia Red
Deep in colour, with characteristics of currant, blackberry, and pepper. Chewy tannins are evident on the palate, which has fabulous length.
£10.00

Canale Estate Reserve Merlot 2007, Patagonia Red
Rich, powerful nose, with complex currant flavours, and a clean, juicy, well-balanced.
£10.00 M&S

Coleccion Malbec 2008, Michel Torino, Cafayate Red
Good solid black fruit. Lovely sweetness on the palate with a burgeoning richness, and plenty of spice. A good, simple style.
£7.50 BNK, HOH

Coleccion Pinot Noir 2008, Michel Torino, Cafayate Red
Red berry nose, with clear cherry and raspberry flavours. Full, ripe, and warming.
£7.00 HOH

Colomé, Amalaya 2007, Salta Red
Clean, lifted, elegant sweet raspberry fruit. Soft, juicy palate. Clean, with good complexity.
£8.00 SWG

Colomé Direct Wines Ascension 2007, Salta Red
Broad, bramble fruit nose, with some cranberry fruit on the palate. Medium length.
£10.00 LAI

Colomé Tannat 2008, Salta Red
Ripe, dark, rustic fruit, with a spicy, leafy edge. Palate of blackberry, red fruit, plum, and cherry, with soft tannins.
£10.00 M&S

Ecológica Fairtrade Organic Shiraz Malbec 2008, La Riojana Co-op.,La Rioja Red
Deep plum red, with chocolate and cherries on the nose, and juicy berry fruit on the palate. Intense, long finish.
£5.00

Finca El Origen Malbec Gran Reserve 2007, Bodegas Y Viñedos La Esperanza S.A., Mendoza Red
Blackcurrant and roasted coffee bean notes. Dense, chewy tannins, with a nice long finish.

Finca Sophenia Reserve Malbec 2008, Mendoza Red
Nice wine, with tight juicy fruit,

and a lean backbone. A wine for keeping.
£11.00 EOR, RWA, SAO

Gestos Malbec 2008, Bodega Finca Flichman, Mendoza Red
Violet, spice, and spirity nose. Lots of raisiny fruit on the palate, leading to a fresh, dry finish.
£7.00

Gran Lurton Corte Friulano 2008, François Lurton, Mendoza Red
Fresh, spicy, and clean. Spicy, bready, and dry,with a pithy edge, and some hints of citrus peel. Good balance of acid and fruit.

La Celia Reserva Malbec 2006, San Carlos Red
Jammy, leathery nose, with blueberry fruit and a touch of spice. Summer fruit on the finish.

La Celia Reserve Cabernet Franc 2006, San Carlos Red
Very pure nose of plum and herbs. Medium body, creamy fruit tannins, and chocolatey oak.

La Chamiza Polo Amateur Malbec 2008, Mendoza Red
Earthy nose. Soft plummy fruit, with light spice and pepper. Medium spicy finish.
£6.00

La Chamiza Polo Profesional Shiraz 2007, Mendoza Red
Clean, fresh fruit, with a jammy edge. Nice, elegant style, with good acitdity and balance.
£8.00

Las Moras Black Label Bonarda 2006, San Juan Red
Medium-powered, juicy, aromatic fruit nose. Nice refreshing structure, and a savoury finish.
£10.00 FTD

Las Moras Black Label Malbec 2006, San Juan Red
Minty nose leads to a great fruity, plummy, cassis palate. Good tannins.
£10.00

Las Moras Reserve Cabernet Sauvignon, Shiraz 2007, San Juan Red
Soft, ripe fruit, with chewy tannins, and a long, crisp, dry finish.
£6.50 CWS, HAX

Las Moras Reserve Malbec 2007, San Juan Red
Intense vibrant ruby in colour. Broad bramble nose, with spicy wood-chip characteristics. Soft tannic structure, which leads to a medium-bodied wine. Excellent complexity and superb long finish.
£6.50 BOF, QTK

Las Moras Reserve Tannat 2007, San Juan Red
Very dark in colour, with sweet, stewed black fruit, and lifted floral nuances. The palate has lean aromas of nuts and autumn fruits.
£6.50 MWW

La Puerta Reserva Malbec 2006, La Rioja Red
Deep plum red in colour. Lively, juicy nose, with delicious fruit on the palate, good acidity, and floral fruit .

Malbec Caligiore 2008, Mendoza Red
Good savoury meaty aromas. Ripe, fruity spice on the palate, with grippy tannins.
£7.00 VER

Marks & Spencer Altos Del Condo Malbec 2008, Trapiche, Mendoza Red
Rich, perfumed, and toasty on the nose. Highly-flavoured, with

vibrant grapefruit character.
Well-balanced.
£7.00 M&S

Marks & Spencer Dominio Del Plato 2006, Susanna Balbo, Mendoza Red
A lovely juicy wine, full of rich, brambly flavours, leading to a lingering finish.
£9.00 M&S

Paisaje De Barrancas 2006, Bodega Finca Flichman, Mendoza Red
Concentrated fruit on a full, round palate, with a very pleasant mouthfeel, and good balance.
£11.00 SGL

Pascual Toso Cabernet Sauvignon 2008, Mendoza Red
Floral, oaky, violet nose. Sweet concentrated black fruit, which balances the strong oak presence.
£8.00 SWS

Pascual Toso Malbec Reserva 2007, Mendoza Red
Cold cream and smoked fruit aromas. Velvety fruit palate, balanced by gentle tannins.
£12.50 SWS

Piedra Negra 2006, François Lurton, Mendoza Red
Meaty nose with stewed plum aromas. Big fruit attack, and supporting tannins on the palate.

Punto Final Malbec 2007, Bodega Renacer, Mendoza Red
Very good varietal expression. Intense black fruits - rich and spicy.
£8.00 LIB

Sainsbury's Argentinian Malbec 2007, Kaiken S.A., Mendoza Red
Ripe berry nose, with fresh, juicy raspberry and morello cherry on the palate. Smooth attack, good crispness, and long finish.
£6.00 SAIN

Salentein Primus Malbec 2004, Mendoza Red
Bready, earthy, gamey, red fruit on the nose. Raspberry palate, with fresh chewy tannins. Meaty finish, and a moderate length.
£28.00 CAV

Salentein Primus Pinot Noir 2005, Mendoza Red
Earthy and creamy notes, with hints of woodland undergrowth and fruit sweetness. Lovely wine, with an uncomplicated finish.
£28.00

Salentein Reserve Malbec 2007, Mendoza Red
Nice mix of peppery spice, dark fruit, and savoury notes on the nose. The palate is dense and dark.
£10.00 CAV

Santa Julia Reserva Cabernet Sauvignon 2008, Familia Zuccardi, Mendoza Red
Blackcurrant juice, intense and concentrated, with fruit tannins, and some vanilla notes in the background.

Santa Julia Reserva Malbec 2008, Familia Zuccardi, Mendoza Red
Cooked prunes on the nose. Intense fruit, with a nice tannic grip on the palate.

Sophenia Synthesis The Blend 2007, Mendoza Red
A whiff of stables, with herbaceous notes. Showing great concentration and real class. Balanced fruit and acidity, with high tannins, and a fine finish.
£26.50 DVY, EOR, HAR

Sur De Los Andes Malbec 2007, Mendoza Red

Crushed red and black fruit aromas, with a hint of spice. Balanced, medium to full-bodied palate.

Terrazas de los Andes Reserva Malbec 2007, Mendoza Red

Restrained nose. Dense, dark fruit with a savoury note. Rustic charm, and evident oak.
£11.50 FLA

Tiasta 2007, Bodega Cruz De Piedra S.A.,Mendoza Red

Jammy ripe strawberries on the nose. Fresh, juicy fruit, nice purity and good balance.

Vinalta Malbec 2008, Domaine Vistalba, Mendoza Red

Fresh, fruity nose, with hints of violets. Lovely palate of berry fruits. Very long length.
£5.20 M&S, BUC

Viñalba Reserva Malbec 2007, Domaine Vistalba, Mendoza Red

Creamy blackcurrant aromas, with a lifted floral note. Big and powerful, with smooth tannins. A very good wine.
£10.00 BUC

Vistalba Corte B 2005, Carlos Pulenta Wines, Mendoza Red

A beautiful nose of morello cherry and violet. Palate of juicy fruit, supported by well-integrated acidity. Supple tannins, delightfully spicy oak, and long length.
£13.00 FNW, GWW, SEL

Zuccardi Q Cabernet Sauvignon 2006, Mendoza Red

Deep colour, with a vanilla nose and good concentration. Earthy, dusty flavours, leading to a dry finish.
£11.80 HEN, WAIT

Zuccardi Q Malbec 2007, Mendoza Red

Restrained aromas, with a savoury note. Juicy, fruity palate, with creamy oak and good depth.
£12.60 HEN

Zuccardi Serie A Bonarda 2008, Mendoza Red

Structured, with black cherry aromas and a clean, fruity palate. Not complex, but a little floral.

Australia

Total production
9.62m hectolitres

Total vineyard
173,794ha

Top 10 grapes
1 Chardonnay
2 Shiraz
3 Cabernet
   Sauvignon
4 Merlot
5 Semillon
6 Colombard
7 Muscat Gordo
   Blanco
8 Sauvignon Blanc
9 Riesling
10 Pinot Noir

Top regions
Riverland, Murray
Darling Victoria,
Riverina, Murray
Darling NSW,
Barossa, McLaren
Vale, Langhorne
Creek, Swan Valley
Victoria, Padthaway,
Limestone Coast,
Margaret River,
Clare Valley, Hunter
Valley, Coonawarra

Producers
2,299

When European settlers landed in Australia in the nineteenth century, many brought vine cuttings from their homelands. Few could have imagined the sensation these plantings were destined to become. As the largest exporter of wine to the UK, Australia is slowly moving its image away from being a one-trick pony of juicy, jammy reds. They aim to convey regional expression in their wines; what the French call terroir. Amongst their successes, Hunter Valley Semillon proved it can still go the distance, with a Gold for a white wine from 1998, while 'Ladies who Shoot Their Lunch', a possible homage to its pioneers, struck Gold with a moderately cool climate Shiraz from Victoria.

2009 IWC PERFORMANCE	
Trophies	27
Gold	43
Silver	206
Bronze	338
Great Value Awards	2

7th Continent Hunter Valley Semillon 2006, Cheviot Bridge, New South Wales White
Waxy minerally lemon curd. Lovely palate, with a backbone of citrus and mineral acidity. Just starting to get into its stride.
£9.00 WRC

Bethany Wines Semillon Barossa 2007, South Australia White
Toasty citrus and lemon peel character, with mineral and smoky aromas. Intense fruit, with delicate flavours. Slightly woody and savoury, with bright, rich fruit on the palate.
£10.00

WESTERN AUSTRALIAN WHITE TROPHY

Evans & Tate The Reserve Chardonnay 2005, Western Australia White
Clean, punchy, and really nicely aged mix of pear, musk, nutty maturity, and toast. Flinty, zesty, and fresh on the palate. Really superb complexity and elegance. A great wine!
HWL

Mcguigan Earth's Portrait Riesling 2004, Australian Vintage Ltd, South Australia White
Medium lime-yellow in colour, with a limey nose, and spicy salty attack. Complex lime flavours, with depth and fine acidity coming up from the back. Exceptional length.

AUSTRALIAN CHARDONNAY TROPHY, SOUTH AUSTRALIAN WHITE TROPHY, ADELAIDE HILLS WHITE TROPHY

Mcguigan Shortlist Chardonnay 2007, Australian Vintage Ltd, South Australia White
Fresh, clean, complex nose, with a nutty character, and citrus aromas. Showing minerality, oiliness, and astringence.

AUSTRALIAN WHITE TROPHY, INTERNATIONAL SEMILLON TROPHY, AUSTRALIAN SEMILLON TROPHY, HUNTER VALLEY SEMILLON TROPHY

Marks & Spencer Hunter Valley Semillon 2005, Tyrrells, New South Wales White
Distinctive elderflower notes on nose, with high acidity on palate, and fruit coming through at the end. A lovely, light, spritzy wine.
£18.00 M&S

Palandri Vita Novus Riesling 2007, 3 Oceans Wine Company, Western Australia White
Thick oily nose. Mineral, steely character, with lovely weight of fruit, and abundant tropical mango and papaya. Good vibrancy and length. Very stylish.
£9.00 3OW, EHL, WIE

Peter Lehmann Wines Margaret Semillon 2003, South Australia White
Very delicate aromas of flowers, with toasty citrus notes. Elegant bright lemon flavours, with soft

toasty character. Clean, fresh
acidity, leading to a long finish.
£13.30 VDV

 **BAROSSA VALLEY
SEMILLON TROPHY**

**Peter Lehmann Wines,
Margaret Semillon 2004,
South Australia** White
Restrained nose of
broad coconut, with flowers and
delicate notes of toast, straw,
and lemon. Well-balanced fresh
acidity, with broad structure,
and good length.
£13.30 VDV, LAI,

**EDEN VALLEY
TROPHY, EDEN VALLEY
RIESLING TROPHY**

**Pewsey Vale Eden Valley
Riesling 2008, South Australia**
White
Clean fruit - lime citrus, with
some floral honeysuckle on
the nose. Zingy citrus fruit on
the palate, a good deal of crisp
acidity, and a lovely zesty finish.
£10.40 FLA

**Tahbilk Marsanne 2007,
Victoria** White
Smoky, buttery nose with some
deep peach notes, a toasty
caramel-honey nose with
pronounced oak, and a clean,
simple palate.
£9.50 FLA, WSO, SAIN, MWW

**AUSTRALIAN
RIESLING TROPHY,
CLARE VALLEY
WHITE TROPHY**

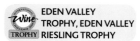 **GREAT VALUE CHAMPION
WHITE, GREAT VALUE WHITE
BETWEEN £5 AND £10**

**Tim Adams Riesling 2008,
South Australia** White
Clean, green, and complex.
Lime and tropical fruit, with a
dry, apple core, and notes of
oatmeal. Lots of fresh acidity.
Palate has nice pleasing
roundness, with quite a long
finish.
£8.60 TESC, AWC

**Tim Adams Semillon 2008,
South Australia** White
Honeyed, citrus, floral, and
waxy aromas. Mandarin and
ginger character on the palate.
Mineral acidity, which is
structured for ageing. Full, with
tremendous depth. Very long,
lingering flavour.
£9.60 TOSAWC

**Tomich Hill Riesling 2008,
South Australia** White
Lime and citrus nose. Hints of
kerosene on the palate. Young,
fresh acidity. Beautiful floral
Riesling - complex and tasty.
Needs time to bring out the
delicateness, but it has a good
future ahead of it.

**Tyrrell's Winemakers
Selection Vat 1 Hunter
Valley Semillon 1998,
New South Wales** White
Lime and mandarin, with
leesy creamy notes, and masses
of buttery croissant. This has a
fresh, lively palate, with smoky,
toasty elements, exceptional
balance and length. Wow.
£20.00 WAIT

Vasse Felix Semillon/ Sauvignon Blanc 2007, Western Australia White
Lemon-fresh, with notes of melon, balanced by white porcelain notes. The freshness on the palate is emphasised by citrus notes and minerality. Rich mouthfeel, with vigour on the back palate.
£10.90 BNK, FLA, VDV, WAIT, WRC

BAROSSA VALLEY WHITE TROPHY, BAROSSA VALLEY RIESLING TROPHY

Wolf Blass Gold Label Riesling 2005, South Australia White
Pronounced kerosene on the nose. Great lift. Very good varietal character. Delicate palate of fresh apple, lime, and kiwi. Good persistence. Excellent wine.

EDEN VALLEY VIOGNIER TROPHY

Yalumba Eden Valley Viognier 2008, South Australia White
Very fresh, clean white peach and Viognier character, with alluring aromas. Some very soft, fresh citrus fruit flavours, and a finish that is clean, pure, and slightly oily.
£10.80 FLA, NFW, VDV, WAIT

Baldivis Estate Shiraz 2007, 3 Oceans Wine Company, Western Australia Red
Very dark, thick, blackberry fruit with just a glimpse of violet and floral character, with notes of sandalwood oak. Rich, concentrated fruit palate.
£7.00 3OW, EHL

AUSTRALIAN CABERNET SAUVIGNON TROPHY, WESTERN AUSTRALIAN RED TROPHY

Clairault Estate Cabernet Sauvignon 2005, Western Australia Red
Very typical Margaret River nose – ripe, maturing aromas of black fruit, and a palate of pencil shavings and bell pepper. Very good structure, with ripe tannins, and spice. The finish has liquorice notes, and is elegant and satisfying.
£18.00 M&S

Dead Ringer Cabernet Sauvignon 2007, Wirra Wirra Vineyards, South Australia Red
A very rich, dark red colour, this wine has sweet red and black fruit, with a cassis nose, and lovely, well-balanced, crisp acidity. There is spicy oak, mint, and eucalyptus on the finish.
£25.00 WAIT

Dorrien Margaret River Cabernet Sauvignon Merlot 2007, Cellarmasters, Western Australia Red
Very complex fruit, with a really lovely elegance. Perfumed. Palate of smooth brambles, with soft tannins, and a rich, deep, and exceedingly long finish.

Eldredge Vineyards Sangiovese 2005, South Australia Red
Very minty, rich, creamy, and raisined. A nice even mineral note, with firm, rich tannins. Very powerful and ripe, but really well-made. A lovely wine.
£10.00 AWC

Evans & Tate Margaret River Shiraz 2005, Western Australia Red
A clean, quite savoury nose, with silky, spicy fruit. This is juicy and well-structured, with nice acidity, good length, and an attractive refreshing style.
HWL

Fox Creek Reserve Shiraz 2006, South Australia Red
Blueberry and cream bouquet, with an ultra-ripe plummy palate, balancing acidity, supple tannins, and a complex, spicy finish, with notes of black olive.

Heathfield Ridge Cabernet Sauvignon 2005, Tidswell Wines, South Australia Red
Really good length, with an elegant bouquet of cassis and creamy oak. On the palate there is a very nice balance of fruit acidity and silky tannins, plus plenty of floral and cedar nuances.

Houghton The Bandit Shiraz Tempranillo 2007, Western Australia Red
Sweet ripe fruit, supported by coffee and toffee oak. Buttery and minty, with broad, ripe tannins, and integrated oak.
£10.00

Jim Barry Mcrae Wood Shiraz 2005, South Australia Red
Very deep purple-black colour. Succulent blackcurrant nose. Rich and concentrated, with spicy fresh cassis, and well-integrated oak. Tannins are velvety and supple, but supportive. Rich-textured, with a long fresh finish.
£21.30 CHH, EDC, FLA, NFW, VDV, WAIT

Kilikanoon The Duke Grenache 2006, South Australia Red
Lovely, restrained, perfumed

nose of sweet blackcurrants. Rich fruit on a very voluptuous palate, showing balance, finesse, and elegance, with a delightfully long finish.

 **CLARE VALLEY RED TROPHY**

O'leary Walker Claire Clare Reserve Shiraz 2004, South Australia Red
Intense red-orange colour, hot fruit, and very fresh, intense leather. Good structure and grip, on a fresh, fruity palate. Delicious.
£37.50 WAIT

Palandri Vita Novus Shiraz 2007, 3 Oceans Wine Company, Western Australia Red
Cedary and rich, with lots of clove spice, and creamy raspberries. Quite tight and focused, culminating in a lovely curranty finish, with power and length.
£11.00 3OW, BOF, EHL, OWC, RWW, SAD, WIE, WIW

Penfolds Bin 28 Shiraz 2006, South Australia Red
Fresh red fruit with a firm vanilla note, elegant, with a balsamic, peppery note. Rounded, with gentle tannins, with some smoky depth, leading to a dry finish.

Peter Lehmann Wines Mentor 2004, South Australia Red
The nose shows a deep Ribena character, with peppery spice leading to a dense, rich, smoky character. Full, rounded cherry notes on a very ripe palate. Great typicity.
£18.60 VDV, SWG

 AUSTRALIAN
SHIRAZ TROPHY,
BAROSSA VALLEY
SHIRAZ TROPHY

Pirathon By Kalleske Shiraz 2007, South Australia Red

Exotic yet elegant blueberry fruit, with cocoa, spice, and freshness on the nose. Sweet fruit, very creamy oak, and silky texture. Clean, fine, and long.

 VICTORIAN RED
TROPHY

Plunkett Fowles Ladies Who Shoot Their Lunch Shiraz 2006, Victoria Red

Cool climate nose of smoky, ripe eucalyptus, and aromatic berry fruit, with some menthol, mint, and pepper. Juicy palate, with crunchy fruit, and lovely minty freshness, supported by solid spice.

Primo Estate Joseph Angel Gully Shiraz 2007, South Australia Red

Lovely complex nose of black fruit, basil, and tobacco. Dense, chewy, rich, and fruit-driven palate. Good structure, with sweet tannins and a long finish.
£20.00 AWC

Shaw & Smith Shiraz 2007, South Australia Red

A very taut nose, with soft, juicy plum and damson flavours, soft creamy tannins, and a fresh, rich, brambly finish.
£18.90 HEN, LIB

Shotfire Shiraz 2007, Thorn-Clarke Wines, South Australia Red

A nose of intense black cherry, with lots of berries and fresh plum. Black fruit, leather, and tobacco on a highly extracted palate. Nice texture and jammy fruit, with chocolate, elegant aromas, and good tannins.
£11.50 VDV

Wolf Blass Platinum Label 2006, South Australia Red

Intense sweet cassis and blackberry aromas, with lots of very spicy oak. Young and concentrated, with ripe but fresh fruit, and a huge amount of tasty oak.

Yalumba The Octavius Barossa Shiraz 2005, South Australia Red

Aromatic blackberry aromas. Really velvety chocolate and raisin fruit, with fresh acidity. Supple, silky texture; stylish and fragrant, with a sustaining finish.
£43.70 FLA, NFW, VDV, WAIT

 AUSTRALIAN RED
TROPHY, SOUTH
AUSTRALIAN RED
TROPHY, BAROSSA VALLEY
RED TROPHY

Yalumba The Signature Barossa Cabernet Sauvignon Shiraz 2005, South Australia Red

Attractive warming black fruit and spice. Pleasing palate of fine cherry and blackberry. Balanced and fresh, with an enduring finish. Good overall harmony. Mature. An excellent wine.
£24.50 FLA, VDV

FORTIFIED MUSCAT TROPHY

Angelas Blend Rare Muscat NV, Buller Wines, Victoria Fortified
Chocolate brown in colour. Lifted white chocolate and molasses on the nose, with notes of coffee and ripe fruit. Vibrant, deep, and sophisticated. Fine balance and great intensity.

De Bortoli Wines Old Boys NV, New South Wales Port
Very old, rich, and complex. Good acidity, fresh and round, with huge concentration of raisin, honey. and toffee. Great length and structure.
£16.70 BNK, FHM, NFW

SILVER

Asda Extra Special Riesling 2008, Knappstein Wines, South Australia White
Lemon sorbet nose with good clarity. The palate is really sharp and crisp, with lime and lemon fruit, excellent acidity, and an extraordinary finish.
£8.00 ASDA

Australian Reserve Riesling Gewurtztraminer 2008, Angove Family Winemakers, South Australia White
Light yellow in colour, with complex lemon-lime and petrol aromas, which follow through to the palate, which results in an excellent, crisp, fruity, long finish.
£6.00 D&D

Bylines Hunter Valley Chardonnay 2008, Songlines Estates, New South Wales White
Quite Burgundian nose, with notes of vanilla and toasted walnuts. A well-balanced palate

of green fruit, nuts, and subtle spice.
£17.50 JAS, MWW, PVC

Cape Mentelle Sauvignon Blanc Semillon 2008, Western Australia White
Fragrant elderflower, asparagus,and lemongrass nose. Fresh and appetising with intense, fresh primary fruit, good acidity, and a clean finish.
£12.30 BNK, FHM, FLA, WSO, WAIT

Clairault Semillon Sauvignon Blanc 2008, Western Australia White
The nose has gooseberry crispness, backed by sweet melon. Good depth of fruit on the palate, with a fleshy feel at the back.
WAV

D'arenberg, The Money Spider 2008, South Australia White
Pale yellow in colour with green tones. Warm mouthfeel with a juicy, oily texture, showing terroir and hints of spice.
£11.00 WAIT

De Bortoli Wines Yarra Valley Estate Grown Chardonnay 2007, Victoria White
Smoky, cigar nose with flinty struck match notes, elegantly balanced with pure peach and citrus fruit. Rich yet fresh.

Dorrien Estate Black Wattle Chardonnay 2007, South Australia White
Melon and white chocolate on the nose, with a bold, persistent and intense palate. Finish is fine and long. Very good quality.

Dorrien Bin 1a Chardonnay 2006 White
Spicy clove and peach nose, with a lovely palate of rich peach and

tangerine flavours, and a ripe finish.

Eden Springs High Eden Riesling 2008, South Australia White
Delicate, floral, steely nose. Fresh, limey, citrus fruit palate with some minerality. Slightly spritzy, youthful character. Long, balanced finish.

Evans & Tate Margaret River Classic White 2008, Western Australia White
The nose has white peach and fresh tropical aromas, which follow through to a fragrant, fresh, fruity palate, showing some sweetness.
HWL

Eileen Hardy Chardonnay 2006, Hardy Wine Company, South Australia White
Nose is herbal and oaky, but very fresh, with excellent fruit. Intensely flavoured, with brisk acidity and great length. Top class!

Eileen Hardy Chardonnay 2007, Hardy Wine Company, South Australia White
A nose full of elegant, toasted oak aromas, flavoured with creamy hazelnuts, almond, and balanced fruit on the palate. Slightly vegetal finish.
£20.00 NYW

Hardys VR Chardonnay 2008, South Eastern Australia White
Creamy lemon meringue pie aromas on the nose. Balanced fruit on the palate. The oak integration is very good, and the finish is nice and clean.
£5.40 TESC, WAIT

Haselgrove Vincent's Breeze Chardonnay 2007, South Australia White
Mineral, yeasty-leesy nose,

with a smoky veneer overlaying stone fruit. Moderate acidity, an attractive wine, with delicate style, finesse, and elegance.

Highland Heritage Estate, Wellwood Estate Riesling 2006, New South Wales White
An attractive Mosel-like nose. Floral, with nice weight and good acidity. Notes of lime leaf and green apple, with honeyed tones on the finish. Good balance.

Howard Park Chardonnay 2007, Western Australia White
Light yellow in colour. Nose of fine oak with plenty of citrus aromas, citrussy tropical fruit, and long, firm, fine acidity. Great balance.

Jim Barry The Lodge Hill Riesling 2008, South Australia White
Floral and citrus aromas. Lime zest on the palate, with some chalky texture. Well-balanced, with fresh acidity and lingering finish.
£10.70 CHH, FLA, NFW

Katnook Estate Chardonnay 2006, South Australia White
A very well-made wine which is nice and rich on the nose, with lots of lemony and grapefruit freshness on the palate, and a good finish.
BWL

Katnook Founder's Block Chardonnay 2006, South Australia White
Lovely lemony, oaky nose. Lovely balance on the palate, with lots of fruit and viscosity. Good acidity with attractive flavours.
BWL

Kilikanoon Barrel Fermented Semillon 2008, South Australia White
Peachy apple aroma, with white

flower perfume. Sherbet apple
and peachy pineapple on palate.
Mineral, crisp acidity. Good
length, and exceptionally well-
balanced.

Kilikanoon Morts Block
Riesling 2008, South Australia
White

Clean and crisp, with a touch
of peaches and almonds, soft
and round with a hint of juicy
sweetness. Good acidity and a
gentle long finish.

Knappstein Handpicked
Riesling 2008, South Australia
White

A touch of waxy minerality, with
smoky notes on the nose. Some
very sweet fruits, with enduring
tangy acidity, and a fresh,
vibrant, long finish.
MWW, ODD

Kooky Village Reserve
Riesling 2008, South Australia
White

Elegant nose, with floral and
citrus aromas. Well-balanced,
with great fruit intensity. Long
finish. Typically Eden Valley.

Leasingham Bin 7 Riesling
2008, South Australia White

Lively lemon sorbet character.
Full of sunshine, with canteloupe
melon and lots of fresh fruit
acidity. Very pleasing on the
palate.
£12.00 MCT

Leasingham Magnus Riesling
2008, South Australia White

Lots of grip, with very fresh
sherbet lemon, apple, and pear.
Quite zingy, with a lemon zest
punch, and good length.
£8.50 SAIN, WRC

Logan 2008, New South
Wales White

Massively aromatic nose of
spring vegetables, with herbal
notes. Lively palate, with lots
of fruit and acidity. Great
balance, good finish, deliciously
viscous.

Mcguigan Bin 9000 2004,
Australian Vintage Ltd, New
South Wales White

Lemon-cream nose, with viscous
rich depth on a honeyed palate.
Lovely balanced acidity, and a
fresh, clean finish.

Mcguigan Earth's Portrait
Riesling 2005, Australian
Vintage Ltd, South Australia
White

Lively fresh wine. Good intensity
on the nose, with a touch of
petrol and elderflower. Stone
fruit palate. Lovely slippery
acidity, and a long finish.

Mcguigan Personal
Reserve 2007, Australian
Vintage Ltd, New South
Wales White

Heady aromas of blossom, citrus,
and green spice. Refreshing
citrussy palate with layers of fat,
crunchy tropical fruit.

Mcguigan Regions
Chardonnay 2007, Australian
Vintage Ltd, New South
Wales White

Long, complex, nutty, and
toasty nose, with beautiful fruit
expression. The palate is richly
fruited, with good complexity
and length.

Marks & Spencer Brothers
& Sisters Viognier 2008,
Fox Gordon, South Australia
White

Apple blossom and white
peach aromas, quite fleshy
in the mouth. Rounded and
opulent, with a slight fresh, leafy
character.
£11.00 M&S

Marks & Spencer Knappstein Ackland Riesling 2007, Lion Nathan, South Australia White

Good intensity on the nose with notes of petrol, green apple, and cut grass. Quite full-on palate, with a very fine fruit character and long finish.

£10.00 M&S

Mesh Eden Valley Riesling 2008, South Australia White

Serious nose of aromatic lime, with hints of kerosene. Stony, mineral aroma. Lime juice flavours, and zingy fruit on the palate. Long finish and good balance.

£14.00 FLA, VDV

One Chain Vineyards "the Opportunist" 2008, Alliance Wine Australia, South Australia White

Bright gooseberry flavours, with a warm finish. A well-structured wine, with attractive acidity and good weight.

£5.00 AAW

Penfolds Reserve Bin 07a Chardonnay 2007, South Australia White

Concentrated, toasty, and attractively nutty nose, with ripe melon and crisp lemon on a zesty palate. Integrated oak, with a dry, mineral finish.

Pepper Tree Venus Block Chardonnay 2008, New South Wales White

Really appealing fruity nose, showing good complexity, and leading to a soft, sweet, long, and fruity palate. Very good quality.

Peter Lehmann Wines Eden Valley Riesling 2008, South Australia White

Nice nose, with real aromatic

purity, and notes of petrol, lime, and appley varietal character. Elegant, with good acidity and balance.

£10.00 VDV, COE, NYW

Pewsey Vale The Contours Eden Valley Riesling 2003, South Australia White

Quite restrained, petrol-like nose, with sweet ripeness balancing the bright acid. Shifts to a long, elegant finish.

£12.60

Pikes "Traditionale" Riesling 2008, South Australia White

Herbal nuances, with clean lime and lemon-grapefruit aromas. A touch phenolic, full and quite complex, with richness and a long finish.

£11.10 FLA, VDV, LEA

Primo Estate La Biondina 2008, South Australia White

Pale in colour, with nice, clean Colombard aromas giving some broadness, which is lifted by the Sauvignon Blanc component. Good depth and weight, with nice acidity.

£10.00 FLA, AWC,

Red Hill Estate Chardonnay 2007, Victoria White

Lovely nose full of buttered biscuits. The palate is flavoured with zippy, citrus fruits, and the finish is mellow and creamy.

Rosily Vineyard Semillon Sauvignon Blanc 2008, Western Australia White

Slight coffee notes, with fresh lemon and nettles on the nose. Dry, full, and herbal on palate. Fresh, with good length.

Seville Estate Chardonnay 2006, Victoria White

Pineapple nose, leading into a fresh, fruity palate, with more layers of fruit and vanilla. Clean and complex, with depth.

Shelmerdine Chardonnay 2007, Victoria White
Crunchy biscuit aromas, with lovely lees character, layered on apple fruit flavours. Super freshness; a terrific wine, with potential to age for 4-5 years.

Stella Bella Chardonnay 2007, Western Australia White
Fresh, fruity, and open, with a lively, crisp, and citrussy palate. Fragrant and slightly sweet, with a balanced finish.
£12.60 HEN, AAW

Stella Bella Suckfizzle Sauvignon Blanc Semillon 2006, Western Australia White
Herbal, minty, and asparagus perfume. Interesting and concentrated, slightly buttery, with a long, crisp finish.
£19.30 HEN, AAW

Tahbilk Marsanne 2008, Victoria White
Light, clean, and fresh. Limey and bright, with a racy edge. There are fresh fruit notes, with good intensity and freshness, leading to perfect, balanced finish.
£10.00 FLA, MWW, THS

Tim Adams Riesling 2007, South Australia White
Racy, lively lime flavour, with fresh, bright acidity, good depth, and a very nice long length. A classic!
£8.60 TESC, AWC

Vasse Felix Heytesbury Chardonnay 2007, Western Australia White
Clean, fresh, mineral nose, leading to a smoky palate of guava, peach, pineapple, and hazelnut, with a long, elegant finish.
£19.80 FLA, VDV

Voyager Estate Chardonnay 2006, Western Australia White
Gentle, ripe, creamy nose, with citrus notes. Fruity palate of pineapple, guava, pear, and cashew.. Good length; clean and youthful.
£14.30

Whispering Hill Riesling 2008, Capel Vale Wines, Western Australia White
Aromatic, stone fruit, and orange blossom notes, with gorgeous minerality. This is a lively, long, and complex wine, with real freshness.

Wolf Blass Gold Label Adelaide Hills Chardonnay 2007, South Australia White
A distinct nose of lemon mousse, and an oak-laced, creamy lemon palate. The finish is zesty, fruity, and firm. An elegant wine.

Wolf Blass Presidents Selection Chardonnay 2008, South Eastern Australia White
Attractive lifted, pronounced nose, with lovely meaty fruits. Extremely well-balanced, with gentle complexity.
£11.00 WAIT

Wolf Blass Yellow Label Riesling 2006, South Eastern Australia White
Mild straw in colour, with some honey, and creamy concentrated aromas. Hints of petrol and development on the palate. A very nice wine.

Wyndham Estate Show Reserve Chardonnay 2005, South Eastern Australia White
Bright mandarin and pineapple fruit, framed by smoky oak,

and supported by crisp acidity. There is a touch of minerality and a creamy texture. Showing excellent balance and maturity showing.
£10.00

Yalumba The Virgilius Eden Valley Viognier 2008, South Australia White
Bright colours and apricot fruit. Good depth of juicy fruit flavour, with a long, elegant finish.
£22.50 FLA, VDV, WAIT

2006 Trevor Jones Wild Witch Shiraz 2006, Kellermeister Holdings Pty Ltd, South Australia Red
Cassis on the nose. Smooth mouthfeel, with a palate of ripe fruit, and a hint of bitter chocolate. Very spicy on the finish.

Allanmere Shiraz 2005, New South Wales Red
Fresh, spicy berry fruit, with good acidity, gentle oak, and a nice finish. This is a gentle crowd-pleaser.

Amon-ra 2007, Glaetzer Wines, South Australia Red
Some chocolate notes, with a fruity, juicy taste. The wine offers good fullness on the palate, with soft, smooth tannins, good acidity, and a sweet finish.
£42.90 NFW, WSO, CVS, FFT, GWW, LAY, SWG

Arrowfield Estate Show Reserve Shiraz 2006, New South Wales Red
Good; ripe, firm, juicy, and open. This has a balanced eucalyptus edge, leading to cassis notes on the finish.

Averys Pioneer Range Yarra Shiraz 2005, The Cheviot Bridge Wine Co., Victoria Red
Tertiary notes of leather and

cigar on the nose, underpinned with sweet red berry and cassis. Well-balanced palate, showing attractive evolution.
£9.00 AVB

Barossa Valley Estate E&E Black Pepper Shiraz 2004, South Australia Red
Lifted minty black fruit aromas, with a gentle palate that shows good typicity, smooth tannins, and a long lasting finish.
£50.00 HAR

Berton Reserve Coonawarra Cabernet Sauvignon 2007, South Australia Red
Violet hue. Good ripe, fruity nose. Inviting style, with a palate of rich, supple fruit. Generous flavour and lovely balance, with well-integrated oak."
£9.20 NFW, HOH

Bethany Gr9 Reserve Shiraz Barossa 2004, South Australia Red
A slight note of attractive struck match. Really good, rich ripe fruit, with smooth tannins and complex flavours.
£35.00

Camelback Block Two Shiraz 2006, Victoria Red
Perfumed, spicy, and meaty. Bright, juicy palate, with good fruit and oak. Acidity is nicely balanced, and the wine is rich in texture.

Cape Mentelle Cabernet Merlot 2007, Western Australia Red
Spicy, rich and herbaceous, with a blueberry palate, culminating in a long, red plum finish, supported by drying, well-structured tannins.
£14.20 FHM, FLA, WAIT

Chapel Hill McLaren Vale Cabernet Sauvignon 2007, South Australia Red
Deep ruby in colour, with excellent intensity on the nose, rich berries, spice, and fruit tannin, with good intensity and length.
£12.00

Chapel Hill The Vicar 2007, South Australia Red
Lovely dark chocolatey nose. Good balance of oak and concentrated fruit on a big, rich , savoury wine.
£23.00

Chateau Reynella Shiraz 2006, South Australia Red
Rather peppery, herbal, smoky oak nose. Chewy and savoury. A well-made wine.
£11.00 WAIT

Church Block 2007, Wirra Wirra Vineyards, South Australia Red
Concentrated black fruit, spice, and vanilla on the nose, following through to a smooth, well-balanced palate, with good length.
£10.00 WAIT

Clairault Cabernet Sauvignon 2005, Western Australia Red
Green bell pepper, tobacco leaf, and black fruit on the nose, with cooked fruit on the palate. Slightly minty, underpinned by fine tannins. Elegant finish, with complexity and good balance.
£10.00 M&S

Crackerjack Shiraz Viognier 2006, Wingara Wine Group, South Eastern Australia Red
Herbal and creamy aromas, showing red fruit and some pleasant black pepper notes. A nod to Rhône-style syrah.
BWL

D'arenberg The Cadenzia 2006, South Australia Red
Good intense fruit character of dark cherry and blackcurrant. Good ripe, jammy fruit with chocolate, and vanilla oak notes running through to a lingering finish, with chocolate tones.

D'arenberg The Dead Arm 2006, South Australia Red
Good intense black fruit, with plum, and deep-spiced fruit, some vegetable notes, and chunky tannins.
£25.70 NFW, WSO, WAIT

D'arenberg, The Galvo Garage 2006, South Australia Red
Ripe, juicy blackcurrant and blackberry nose, with sweet spice, liquorice, and cedary notes. Good tannic, berried fruit, with a hint of mintiness Attractive balance.
£12.00 WAIT

D'arenberg The Ironstone Pressings 2006, South Australia Red
Cherry fruit, with a slight hint of mint, and spicy tones on the nose. Good ripe fruit, with a touch of heat on the finish. Well-balanced with ripe tannins.
£25.00 WAIT

De Bortoli Wines Gulf Station Pinot Noir 2008, Victoria Red
Light in colour, with a vibrant, sweet cherry fruit palate, and hints of leather and tobacco. Viscous velvety mouthfeel, with great balance and fruit.

Domaine Terlato & Chapoutier Shiraz/viognier 2007, Victoria Red
Subtle red berry fruit on the nose. Fresh palate of elegant berries, and a pleasant finish.
£12.00 HAR, HWE, NYW

Dorrien Bin 1 Cabernet Sauvignon 2006, South Australia Red
Inky, almost black in colour, with a subdued nose. Crisp, dry blackcurrant and leaf palate. Good freshness and firm tannins.

Dorrien Grower's Shiraz 2006, South Australia Red
Complex wine with a nose of mint, chocolate, and blackcurrant. Oak integration is good, with fresh acidity and a long, elegant finish.

Eden Springs High Eden Shiraz 2006, South Australia Red
Rich raspberry fruit on the nose, leading to a concentrated palate of spiced berries, with a creamy texture, and good acidic balance.

Eldredge Vineyards Blue Chip Shiraz 2006, South Australia Red
Very ripe on the nose, with blackberry, and a touch of tinned prune. Lovely succulent palate, very harmonious, sensuous, and pure. Slips gently down the throat.
£12.00 AWC

Fonty's Pool Pinot Noir 2008, Western Australia Red
Elegant berry aromas, with hints of coffee. A juicy structure, with soft sweet tannins, and a long creamy finish.
£10.00

Four Sisters Shiraz 2006, Victoria Red
Quite rich on the nose, with hints of peppery spice and oak. Juicy, vibrant palate, with plush blackcurrant fruit. High-toned, with subtle creamy oak.
£8.00 FFT, IRV,

Fox Creek Short Row Shiraz 2007, South Australia Red
Blackberry and spice on a fruity nose. A rich, ripe, mouth-filling wine, with a hint of toffee and dry tannins.

Geoff Merrill Reserve Cabernet Sauvignon 2002, South Australia Red
Lush fruit, with sour cherry, notes of meat, violet, and blackberry. Big tannins, with a cigar note on the finish.
£14.00 BAW, EOR, HDS, HRW

Geoff Merrill Reserve Shiraz 2004, South Australia Red
Deep red in colour. A balanced, harmonious palate of lovely ripe fruit and chocolate, with a long, persistent finish.
£20.00 EOR, HDS, HRW

Glaetzer Bishop 2007, South Australia Red
Lovely rich, full fruit nose. Nice explosion of blackcurrant and cherry fruit, with good complexity and structure, and a long finish.
£20.00 CAM, CVS, GWW, HVN, LAY, SWG

Gralyn Estate Cabernet Sauvignon 2005, Western Australia Red
Herbal aromas on the nose. Clean, with fresh juicy fruits, good balance and structure, and an elegant finish.

Grant Burge Cameron Vale Cabernet Sauvignon 2006, South Australia Red
Elegant, with juicy, ripe red fruit. Fine and fresh, with good purity. Hints of eucalyptus and pine. Medium body and tannins, with richness, and a good finish.
£11.20 NFW, HMA

Grant Burge Hillcot Merlot 2007, South Australia Red

Good concentration of plummy flavours. Nice supporting acidity. Fresh, crisp, and enduring.
£11.20 FLA, NFW, HMA

Grant Burge Miamba Shiraz 2006, South Australia Red

Herbaceous mint, good fruit, and gentle tannins. A wine that is well-balanced, with finesse and elegance.
£11.70 FHM, NFW, HMA

Grant Burge Filsell Shiraz 2006, South Australia Red

A mixture of marzipan and white chocolate, with huge blackcurrant and black cherry flavours, and wonderful balance of tannins.
£16.90 FLA, NFW, WSO, HMA

Grant Burge Meshach 2004, South Australia Red

Complex aromas of red berries, mint, cream, and spice. Developing well, and showing smooth tannins, and fresh acidity, along with multi-layered flavours.
£48.30 FHM, NFW, HMA

Green Point Heathcote Shiraz 2006, Victoria Red

Green sappy edge to the nose, with some warmer spicy notes. The palate is vibrant, forward, and a bit meaty.
£14.00 FLA

Green Point Reserve Shiraz 2006, Victoria Red

Very rich, sweet, spicy nose with an apricot lift. Lively, vibrant palate, with notes of peppery spice
£17.00

Hardys Heritage Reserve Bin Cabernet Sauvignon 2007, South & Western Australia Red

Notes of black olive, cherry, creamy vanilla, and black fruit. A very Mediterranean take on Cabernet.

Hardys Oomoo Grenache Shiraz Mouvèdre 2006, South Australia Red

Dark ruby in colour, with a tawny rim. An elegant nose of raspberry fruit, with smoky aromas. Good concentration of fruit on the palate, with an elegant finish.
£10.00 TESC, MCT

Heggies Vineyard Eden Valley Chardonnay 2007, South Australia Red

Toasty white peach on the nose, with a slight leesy character. Oily palate with notes of lees, peach, and light oak. Balanced acidity.
£11.00 CHH, NFW

Pillar Box Red 2007, Henry's Drive Vignerons, South Australia Red

Inviting aromas of light fruit. Rich palate with good fruit flavours. Promising.

The Trial of John Montford 2007, Henry's Drive Vignerons, South Australia Red

Meaty eucalyptus and blackcurrant on the nose, with a very good, structured palate, and great balance.

Houghton Cabernet Sauvignon 2008, Western Australia Red

Densely aromatic, funky, and fleshy; a very supple palate. Touch of savoury fruit, with quite a dry linear finish.

Houghton Jack Mann Cabernet Sauvignon 2004, Western Australia Red

Bright ruby in colour, with a clean, cedary nose. Sweet, attractive fruit, and lots of tannins. Nice wood, good length, and fresh acidity.

Irvine Wines Grand Merlot 2005, South Australia Red
Black fruit, honey, and elderflower on the nose. Structured tannins are still very young. Black cherry note on the finish.
£48.30 VDV, PLA

Jacob's Creek Cabernet Sauvignon 2006, South Eastern Australia Red
Opulent nose of macerated black cherries, liquorice, and cedar. Full-bodied, with peppery black fruit. Showing pleasant savoury maturity, yet still fresh.
£6.90 TESC, WAIT

Jacob's Creek St Hugo Cabernet Sauvignon 2005, South Australia Red
Minty chocolate nose, firmly supported black fruit, with good depth of flavour, lots of chocolate, coffee, and cedar notes. Good length.
£25.00

John Duval Eligo 2006, South Australia Red
Fragant, floral, blackberry fruit. Big and powerful, with nice structure, this is a well-balanced, voluptuous, and appealing wine.
£39.00 LIB

K1 By Geoff Hardy Shiraz 2007, South Australia Red
Eucalyptus nose, with sweet ripe fruit, and a creamy, juicy palate. Supple tannins, with bramble fruit and spice prevailing on the palate. Long, savoury finish.
£16.00 VDV

K1 By Geoff Hardy Shiraz Viognier 2006, South Australia Red
Intense aromas of ripe, red berry

fruits, with a sweet summer pudding character on the palate, and hints of tropical fruit and chocolate. A pleasantly elegant wine.

Kilikanoon 'killerman's Run' Cabernet Sauvignon 2007, South Australia Red
Dark ruby in colour, with big nose of berries and cherries, and an elegant spicy character Chocolate-cocoa palate; powerful and drinkable, with a soft finish.

Kilikanoon 'Killerman's Run' Shiraz Grenache 2007, South Australia Red
Forward style, with a soft cherry nose, leading to a juicy, ripe cherry and plum palate. Balanced and medium bodied, with a long finish.

Kilikanoon 'm' Shiraz 2006, South Australia Red
Intensely dark black in colour, with attractive ripe blackberry and menthol aromas, and a black fruit palate, developing notes of jam, milk chocolate, and mocha.

Kilikanoon Oracle Shiraz 2006, South Australia Red
Slightly mushroomy on the nose, with a touch of white pepper. Very well-balanced, pure, black, peppery fruit, and long, puckering tannins.

Kilikanoon Prodigal Grenache 2006, South Australia Red
Big, bold, and fudge-like, with meaty aromas. Lots of lip-smacking juicy fruit quality, with a very nice, sweet finish.

Kilikanoon 'r' Shiraz 2006, South Australia Red
Cedar, plums, and prunes, with fresh black fruit, white pepper,

and juicy, creamy oak and spice. Good savoury length.

Kilikanoon Testament Shiraz 2006, South Australia Red
Intense Syrah aromas, with a buttery character. Long palate, with well rounded tannins and lots of fruit.

Kilikanoon The Medley 2006, South Australia Red
Ripe fruits with hints of eucalyptus, which carry through from the nose to the palate. Good concentration and balance, with a strong tannic structure that carries the wine's length.

Knappstein Cabernet Merlot 2006, South Australia Red
Dark red in colour, with good chewy fruit. Nicely aromatic, with spicy tarry fruit. The palate is berryish and plummy, with nice structure and length.
£10.00 FLA

Knappstein Shiraz 2006, South Australia Red
Restrained nose, withsubtle black fruit, lifted floral notes, redcurrant, and mocha. Notes of sweet red berry, bitter chocolate, spice, and cherry. Well-crafted and integrated oak and tannin. Soft and silky, with a subtle, long finish.
MWW

Kooky Village Reserve Shiraz 2005, South Australia Red
Coffee and dark chocolate, with preserved cherry notes on the nose, and a complex, sweet blend of big tannins and fruit.

Leasingham Classic Clare Cabernet Sauvignon 2006, South Australia Red
Fresh, elegant fruit with floral notes on the nose. Clean palate with fine-grained tannins.

Longview Devil's Elbow 2007, South Australia Red
Pure inky appearance in the glass, packed with berries and rosemary on the palate, with firm tannins, and pleasant length of flavour.

"The Malleea" By Majella 2005, South Australia Red
Raisined prune, mocha, mint, and cream predominate. Lots of flavour, with fine tannic structure. An impressive wine.
£28.10 FLA, NFW, VDV, AAW, HAR, ODD

Mcguigan Shortlist Cabernet Sauvignon 2006, Australian Vintage Ltd, South Australia Red
Aromas of blackberries, cedar wood, mint, and cassis. Good upfront fruit, with chocolate and coffee on finish. Balanced wine, with good length.

Mcguigan Shortlist Cabernet Sauvignon 2007, Australian Vintage Ltd, South Australia Red
Very rich in berries and eucalyptus. Round and smooth on the palate, with rich, minty notes.

Mcguigan Shortlist Shiraz 2006, Australian Vintage Ltd, South Australia Red
Intense spice, mint, and nuts. With lovely fruit elegance, this is balanced, long, and in wonderful harmony. Above all, it shows great freshness.

Mcguigan Shortlist Shiraz 2007, Australian Vintage Ltd, South Australia Red
Intense blackberries, black cherries, spice, smoke, and meat on the nose. Dark chocolate, spice, ripe morello cherries, ripe raspberry, and mint flavours

come through on a jammy palate.

Mcpherson Family Shiraz 2008, Victoria Red
Nose of young, jammy raspberry fruit, with a clean palate of cherries. Nice balance, with good acidity, and a pure finish.
LAI

McWilliam's Icons Maurice O'Shea Shiraz 2006, South Eastern Australia Red
Attractive floral, violet, and blackberry aromas. With flavours of mocha, and grainy tannins, this promises to be a good food wine.
£30.00

Mitchelton Crescent 2006, Victoria Red
Ruby in colour, with an unusual, liquorice spice nose. Well-balanced, with round tannins and a peppery finish, on a very harmonious and elegant wine.

Mitolo Jester Shiraz 2007, South Australia Red
Restrained red fruits on the nose. Nice sweet spice and good varietal character. Structure and acidity are well-balanced, and the finish is long and soft.
£11.90 HEN, VDV, LIB

Mitolo Savitar Shiraz 2006, South Australia Red
Soft, ripe, concentrated nose, with red and black plum aromas. Pure fruit on the palate, with good, balanced acidity.
£30.00 VDV, LIB

Nepenthe Tryst Cabernet Sauvignon Tempranillo Zinfandel 2006, South Australia Red
Ripe, rich mulled blackcurrant and spice nose, and a palate of ripe,

dense black fruit. Nicely balanced, with a long, fresh finish.

O'Leary Walker Clare Valley McLaren Vale Shiraz 2006, South Australia Red
Intense fresh fruit, with a full body, and good tannins. The finish is warm, silky, and round.

Palandri The Estates Cabernet Sauvignon 2007, 3 Oceans Wine Company, Western Australia Red
Big, fleshy, earthy tannins. Serious, chunky, structured style. Polished berry and cassis flavours. Good length.
£9.00 3OW, EHL, WIE

Palandri The Estates Merlot 2007, 3 Oceans Wine Company, Western Australia Red
Plum and blackcurrant, with creamy oak. Lively acidity, with textured tannins, and a eucalyptus note on the finish.
£9.00 3OW

Palandri The Estates Shiraz 2005, 3 Oceans Wine Company, Western Australia Red
Cool berry fruit and a savoury mid-palate. Velvety structure, with medium body, plenty of acid ity and good length. Nicely mature.
£8.90

Paul Conti Pinot Noir 2007, Western Australia Red
The nose shows an attractive savoury, almost biscuity note. Clean fruit and good definition, with lots of character and great balance.

Paxton EJ Shiraz 2006, South Australia Red
A meaty, evolved Rhône-style

nose, with bacon and herbaceous notes on the palate, with a full, long finish.
£32.00 SWS

Penfolds Bin 389 Cabernet Sauvignon Shiraz 2006, South Australia Red
Notes of smoky spiced oak, with layers of ripe berry. Full palate, with soft, structured tannins and silky length.

Penfolds Bin 707 Cabernet Sauvignon 2006, South Australia Red
Intense, concentrated, slightly cooked fruit character on the nose. The palate is intense, dark, and strapping, with perfumed fruit, and a long finish.
£52.50 VDV, WAIT

Penfolds Magill Estate Shiraz 2006, South Australia Red
Dark ruby in colour. Clean, with smoky violet and dark fruit on the nose. Nicely wooded, with spice and fair acidity, but still fruity.
£36.50 VDV, WAIT

Penfolds Rwt Barossa Valley Shiraz 2006, South Australia Red
Sweet, syrupy raspberry aromas. Typical Barossa Shiraz, with good acidity and freshness. Firm but well-handled tannins. Well-made and freshly drinkable.
£45.00 WAIT

Penfolds St Henri Shiraz 2005, South Australia Red
Ripe, plummy black fruit and slightly dusty oak. Concentrated spicy black fruit on the palate. Smooth oak texture, balanced with good length. Nicely evolved.
£28.70 VDV, WAIT

Penley Estate Chertsey 2006, South Australia Red
Minty aromatic character, with

a core of ripe fruit. Plush, firm tannins, with a thread of acidity adding structure.
£20.00 MOR

Penley Estate Hyland Shiraz 2007, South Australia Red
Bright ruby red in colour, with a classic nose of menthol, vanilla, and berry fruit. Rich, viscous palate, with notes of coffee, and good length.
£10.00 MOR

Penley Estate Special Select Shiraz 2006, South Australia Red
Nose of red and black fruit, with attractive layers of vanilla oak. Moderate tannins and fresh acidity, which lead to a good finish.
£20.00 MOR

Penny's Hill Mclaren Vale Shiraz 2007, Galvanized Wine Group, South Australia Red
Clean, red and black fruit notes, with a spice-laden palate, some feminine softness, forward fruit, and a long, intense finish.
£13.00 HOH

Pertaringa Undercover Shiraz 2007, South Australia Red
Lovely, rich and fruity, with blackberry, spice, and menthol. Good fruit definition and oak flavours.
£12.00 VDV, SWS

Petaluma Adelaide Hills Shiraz 2006, South Australia Red
Elegantly oaky and spicy, with a stylish fruity nose. A plummy, juicy palate of blackberry and complex fruit, with good length.
MWW

Peter Lehmann Wines Eight Songs Shiraz 2004, South Australia Red
Black fruit and creaminess on

the nose, showing good typicity and pleasant mouthfeel. Firm tannin and balanced acidity.
£24.60 VDV, CMR, SWG

Peter Lehmann Wines Stonewell Shiraz 2003, South Australia Red

Showing some maturity and spicy richness. Big, juicy tannins, good acidity and structure.
£30.00 NFW, VDV, WAIT

Plan B! Shiraz 2007, Western Australia Red

Deep plum in colour, with a subtle olive and cherry nose. Soft attack and velvety structure, with good acidity, elegant, ripe tannins, and a long finish.
£10.00 3OW

Plunkett Fowles The Rule Reserve Shiraz 2006, Victoria Red

Plum pie, vanilla, and nutmeg aromas. Chunky, firm tannins on a peppery mid-palate.

Primo Estate Joseph "Moda" 2007, South Australia Red

Very sweet, spicy, oaky nose, with hints of ginger and tar. The palate is intense and rich, with notes of oak and ripe fruit.
£18.00 FLA, AWC

Punt Road 2006, Victoria Red

Elegant, ripe, dark, peppery fruit on the nose. Palate of rich spice and berries, with medium length, and a creamy finish.
£11.00

Richard Hamilton Hut Block, Cabernet Sauvignon 2006, South Australia Red

Youthful cassis and creamy vanilla nose. Balanced, supple palate, with complex coffee and mocha notes. Easy, elegant style, with a long finish.

Rifle & Hunt Cabernet Sauvignon 2007, Pertaringa, South Australia Red

Lovely blackcurrant fruit on the nose. A hint of mint, and a fresh, dark palate, with great intensity.
£16.60 VDV, SWS

Rosemount Estate Show Reserve Traditional 2004, South Australia Red

Good development and integration, with notes of subtle leather, spice, and earthiness. The palate has plenty of black fruit, and a good acidic structure, built for ageing.

Rosemount Show Reserve Balmoral Syrah 2004, South Australia Red

Clean, rounded plummy fruit and pepper, with soft, ripe tannins, good concentration, and a balanced finish.

Serafino Sharktooth Shiraz 2007, South Australia Red

Cardamom, sesame seeds, and mace, with good length and a pleasant finish.

Shingleback D Block McLaren Vale Shiraz 2006, South Australia Red

Densely structured, with dark fruit flavours. Sweet, but well defined. Firm and focused, with a savoury edge.

Shingleback The Gate Shiraz 2006, South Australia Red

Blackberry jam, with pronounced toasty oak aromas. Very ripe, with moderate acidity and supple tannins, and a long, savoury finish.

Songlines Estates Leylines McLaren Vale Shiraz 2007, South Australia Red

Very pure and fresh, showing mint and spice on the nose. An

elegant and subtle wine, with lovely balance.
£12.00 JAS, MWW, PVC

St Hallett Blackwell Shiraz 2006, South Australia Red

Deep, youthful, intense, and savoury aromas, with notes of black treacle. Fine fruit, with lovely freshness and mintiness. Long, intense, and flavoursome.
£15.50 NFW, SAIN

Tahbilk Shiraz 2004, Victoria Red

Lovely opulent nose, with a refined, complex, and svelte palate of berry fruit, with gamey notes. Long and toothsome.
£10.00 BOF, CAM, OWC, ROD, TAN, WIE

Shotfire Quartage 2006, Thorn-Clarke Wines, South Australia Red

Intense raspberry palate with plenty of fruit. Good integration of oak. A wine with fragrance and length.
£11.50 VDV

Terra Barossa Cabernet Sauvignon 2007, Thorn-Clarke Wines, South Australia Red

Spice and pepper on the nose, with a palate of luscious balanced fruit. Rich in body, well-made, and powerful. A nourishing wine!
£9.00 VDV

Tim Adams Cabernet 2005, South Australia Red

Mature, with sweet blackcurrant fruit on the nose, and notes of juicy black fruit. Pleasant tannins. Enjoy soon.
£10.00 AWC

Tim Adams Reserve Tempranillo 2006, South Australia Red

Pronounced minty, herbal nose, with notes of fresh herbs, toffee, and dry, plummy fruit. There is an overlay of attractive, integrated oak, and a long, chewy finish.
£20.00 AWC

Tim Adams The Aberfeldy 2006, South Australia Red

Deep colour, penetrating black fruit, menthol, and dark chocolate. Concentrated ripe black fruit, and spicy, mocha oak flavours. Ripe tannins.
£26.00 TESC, AWC

Vasse Felix Cabernet Sauvignon 2007, Western Australia Red

Youthful with cassis, cedar, and eucalyptus aromas. Palate of concentrated black fruit and cherry, with firm tannins, and balanced acidity and alcohol. Good flavour and length.
£14.70 BNK, FLA, VDV

Voyager Estate Girt By Sea Cabernet Merlot 2007, Western Australia Red

Dense, firm, and intense. Bordeaux-like, with an elegant texture, and serious, ripe tannins designed for longer ageing – this deserves to be kept for some time.
£10.40

Voyager Estate Shiraz 2007, Western Australia Red

Deep ruby in colour, with a nose of black fruit, leading to juicy fruit on the palate, with some smokiness and good length.
£12.40

Wakefield Eighty Acres Shiraz Viognier 2006, South Australia Red

Minty eucalyptus notes on the nose. Dense blackberries, with mulled spice and raisins, on a generous palate. Big structure, and long hot finish.
£9.50 SWS

Wakefield Shiraz 2007, South Australia Red
Plummy, brambly nose, with a hint of eucalyptus and chocolate. Clean, ripe, red stone fruit palate, and a long concentrated finish.
£9.50 SWS

Wakefield St Andrews Shiraz 2003, South Australia Red
Eucalyptus nose, with spice, blackberries, and plum. Fresh, with good structure, and a long, warm finish of berries and spice.
£30.00 SWS

Whispering Hill Shiraz 2007, Capel Vale Wines, Western Australia Red
Deep plum and ripe menthol cherry nose. Soft attack of fresh brambly fruit and velvety structure, bolstered by firm tannins.

Willunga Creek Black Duck Merlot 2006, South Australia Red
Sweet, slightly jammy strawberry-fruit nose. The palate shows ripe, sweet fruit. Rich and balanced.
THO

Willunga Creek Black Duck Shiraz 2006, South Australia Red
Lots of eucalyptus and smoky fruit on the nose. Ripe, concentrated, pleasant berry fruit, with lovely, spicy complexity.
THO

WILLUNGA CREEK WINES

Wine INTERNATIONAL WINE CHALLENGE 2008
SILVER

P.O. Box 773
Willunga,
South Australia 5172
Tel: +61 88 556 2244
www.willungacreekwines.com.au

Wirra Wirra Vineyards Rsw Shiraz 2007, South Australia Red
Dense and creamy, with black fruit and oak nose. Big and rich, with morello cherry liqueur and creamy oak. Long and delicious.

Wolf Blass Black Label 2005, South Australia Red
Attractive roasted aromas and sweet black fruit. Excellent intensity on the palate. Full of fruit, with balanced oak and good freshness.

Wyndham Estate Black Cluster Shiraz 2005, New South Wales Red
Quite closed on the nose, but launches into a palate of ripe summer fruit. Sweet, succulent tannins, with good acidity. A class act.
£35.00

Wynns Coonawarra Cabernet Sauvignon 2005, South Australia Red
Dark and brooding, with a rich, spicy, ripe fruit character. Lovely balanced, minty herbaceousness, with a spicy, chocolatey finish. Long and powerful.

Next Of Kin Shiraz 2007, Xanadu Wines, Western Australia Red
Sweet bramble and black fruit nose, with floral aromas. Some pepper on the palate, with cherry and raspberry fruit, with good acidity leading to a well-balanced finish.
£8.00

Yaldara Farms Shiraz 2007, Australian Vintage Ltd, South Australia Red
Very sweet black fruit, with exotic spice and liquorice on the nose. Spice, blackberries, and some smoky chocolate on the

palate, a full-bodied wine with layers of flavour.

Yalumba Barossa Patchwork Shiraz 2007, South Australia Red

Creamy redcurrant, with earthy aromas and smokiness on the nose. A medium-bodied palate, with good fruitiness, attractive tannins, and good length.
£10.50 FLA, NFW

Yalumba The Menzies Coonawarra Cabernet Sauvignon 2006, South Australia Red

Fresh black and red fruit, underlayered with some mint and spice. Complex flavours of cooked fruits and coffee.
£30.00 FLA

Turkey Flat Rosé 2008, South Australia Rosé

Fresh wild strawberry and pleasant citrus notes. Savoury and pithy, with good structure on the palate. A fresh, fruity finish.
£9.90 EDC, HTG, NYW, SEL

Brown Brothers Wines Prosecco 2008, Victoria Sparkling

Notes of honeysuckle and grapefruit on the nose. Almonds and lime on the palate, with a long finish.

E&e Black Pepper Sparkling Shiraz 2004, Barossa Valley Estates, South Australia Sparkling Red

A cauldron of fruit; dark and brooding, with excellent fruit sweetness, and enough acidity to balance. Tasty; perhaps the only wine to be able to withstand a fried breakfast!

Mount Horrocks Cordon Cut Riesling 2008, South Australia Sweet

Lovely rich golden colour. Spicy

fruit character on the nose and palate, with some whiffs of petroleum. Clean, simple, and sweet.
£17.10 VDV, LIB

Peter Lehmann Wines Wigan Eden Valley Riesling 2004, South Australia Sweet

Lime-yellow in colour, with sherbet and lime pastille on the nose. Clean attack, nice balance, with a long lime finish. Clean and fresh.
£13.30 VDV, ABW, COE, CWA, WAD, WSO

Beverford Gold Botrytis Semillon 2006, Buller Wines, Victoria Botrytis

Rich and waxy nose, but with good freshness. Intense, tangy fruit with spice and brioche notes. Good acidity, concentration, and length.

McGuigan Botrytis Semillon 2005, Australian Vintage Ltd, New South Wales Botrytis

Deep yellow in colour, with a marmalade and honey nose, fresh lively acidity, and notes of lemon and wax on the palate. Excellent length and complexity.

Primo Estate, Primo Estate Joseph La Magia 2008, South Australia Botrytis

Perfumed floral, mineral, orange blossom nose, with hints of toffee and marmalade. Rich, sweet, honey-cream palate, with lovely balancing acidity, excellent concentration. Long and delicate.
£11.50 FLA, AWC

Black Noble NV, De Bortoli Wines Pty Ltd, New South Wales Fortified

Amber in colour, with a good, complex nose of orange peel,

DISCOVER... THE GREAT DIVERSITY OF **AUSTRALIA'S** WINES AND **REGIONS!**

crème brulée, and figs. Very good balance, with a long, complex, silky finish.
£15.70 FHM, VDV

Buller Fine Old Muscat NV, Victoria Fortified
Deep fruit, with intense apricots on the nose. Complex, lasting, and balanced. Good length. Well-made.

Campbells Rutherglen Muscat NV, Victoria Fortified
Attractive amber-orange colour. Very intense nose of ripe raisins, with toffee and caramel notes. Strong and harmonious, with a wonderful finish.
£9.50 CPW, RDS, WON

Stanton & Killeen Classic Rutherglen Muscat NV, Victoria Fortified
Deep amber in colour. Lifted raisins and hints of chocolate, with fresh oranges and rose petals on the nose. Elegant and harmonious palate.
£14.20 WAIT, ARL, CSS

Stanton & Killeen Rutherglen Muscat NV, Victoria Fortified
Deep amber in colour. Lifted tea leaf and raisins, with fresh fruitcake, and layers of dried fruit on the nose. Very complex finish.
£9.10 VDV, EVW, WIL, WSO

Grant Burge 20 Year Old Tawny NV, South Australia Port
Coffee, mocha, and white chocolate on the nose. Peppery intensity, with plenty of power, and a pungent finish.
£32.00 HMA

Pirramimma Digby Mclaren Vale Old Tawny NV, Geoff Johnston Wines Pty Ltd, South Australia Port
Creamy caramel nose, which

is full and raisined, with a concentrated, intensely sweet palate of oaky caramel, culminating in a nutty finish.

Seppeltsfield Para 21 Year Old 1987, South Australia Port
Liquid honey and caramel character. Very luscious crème brulée palate, showing volatility and age, with a complex exhilarating finish.
£29.60

Yaldara 15 Year Old Tawny Port NV, Australian Vintage Ltd, South Australia Port
Black treacle and caramel nose. Intense black treacle and white pepper palate. A pungent, classic 15 year-old tawny, with a long finish.

BRONZE

Athena's Vineyard Chardonnay 2007, Bellvale Wine, Victoria White
Intense nose with ripe fruit, fresh herbaceous palate, and clean finish.

Baldivis Estate Semillon Sauvignon Blanc Chardonnay 2008, 3 Oceans Wine Company, Western Australia White
Russet apple on the nose and palate, with well-intergrated flavour, and a rich, crisp finish
£7.00 3OW, EHL

Barwick Estates Semillon Sauvignon Blanc 2008, Western Australia White
Grassy and fresh nose. Fresh, bright gooseberry fruit, with some pineapple, on a clean, straightforward palate.

Berton Reserve Eden Valley Chardonnay 2007, South Australia White
Lovely citrus tones on the nose.

Fresh clean apricot fruit on the palate, with a dry intense finish.
£9.20 NFW, HOH

Bethany Riesling Eden Valley 2008, South Australia White
Aromatic nose of lime, lemon, and blossom. Citrus and lime palate. Powerful flavours. Tangy.
£9.00

Brown Brothers Wines Dry Muscat 2008, South Eastern Australia White
Very attractive grapey nose, with clear varietal character, in a very commercial style.
£6.00 TESC

Brown Brothers Wines Pinot Grigio 2008, Victoria White
Clean and bright, with a fresh pineapple note. Mineral and crisp, dry and pleasant, with a balanced finish, in an easy-drinking style.
£7.00 WAIT

Brown Brothers Wines Viognier 2008, Victoria White
Lovely typical Viognier nose. Bright, fresh, and pleasant.

Cape Mentelle Chardonnay 2008, Western Australia White
Tropical fruit nose, with a ripe fruit palate. Rich, full-bodied, and concentrated.
£15.80 BNK, FHM, FLA

Clairault Sauvignon Blanc 2008, Western Australia White
Intense flavour, with asparagus and passion fruit notes. Good, balanced, medium-weight body, with a persistent finish.
£10.00 M&S, WAV

Clare Valley Riesling 2008, Angove Family Winemakers, South Australia White
Zesty lime nose. Crisp, soft citrus

palate, with a long, limey finish.
£10.00 D&D

Climbing Chardonnay 2008, Cumulus Wines Pty Ltd, New South Wales White
Creamy tropical nose. Good oak support. Elegant fruit and good balance.
£10.00

Climbing Sauvignon Blanc 2008, Cumulus Wines Pty Ltd, New South Wales White
Showing elegance and varietal character, with a very light body, and some complex flavours of myrrh.

Currency Creek Chardonnay 2008, Ballast Stone, South Australia White
Smoky, creamy nose, with flinty strikes, and a fresh, elegant palate.
ABY

D'arenberg The Dry Dam 2008, South Australia White
Lovely, forward elderflower, and light kerosene aromas and flavours. A touch of leesy cheesiness, and fresh, racy acidity, with a balancing note of sweetness.
£8.00

D'arenberg The Hermit Crab 2008, South Australia White
Blowsy nose, with apricots and candied pears. Extremely fruity palate, with powerful length.
£8.80 WES, WSO, WAIT

Deen De Bortoli Verdelho 2007, New South Wales White
Subdued tropicality, with a mineral wax nuance. Surprising intensity and fruitiness, with clean acidity and potential.

Evans & Tate Margaret River Chardonnay 2007, Western Australia White
Light toasty oak. Elegant palate

of peaches and pears, supported by crisp acidity. Balanced, with a nice spicy finish.
£11.00 TESC, HWL

Ferngrove Cossack Riesling 2008, Western Australia White
Orange and lemon fruit, with green apple and sweetness on the nose. Fresh, balanced lemon juice palate.
£15.50 VDV

Forester Estate Chardonnay 2007, Western Australia White
Lemon, lime, and mango flavours with honeyed tones. Good structure, with a nice floral finish.

Grant Burge Zerk Semillon / Viognier 2007, South Australia White
Floral nose, with crispy notes and real finesse. Moderate depth of citrus flavours.
£9.70 FLA, NFW, HMA

Hardys Heritage Reserve Bin Chardonnay 2007, South & Western Australia White
Attractive creamy aromas, with a toasty note. Appetising, with lovely fruit and freshness. Good balance and acidity.

Hardys Heritage Reserve Bin Riesling 2008, South & Western Australia White
Lime and orange flowers on a perfumed nose. Mandarin, orange, and apricot flavours, framed by lively acidity. Textured wine, with chalky finish.

Hardys Oomoo Chardonnay 2007, South Australia White
Complex, nutty, oaky nose, with lovely expressive citrus character, and very pleasant finish.
£10.00

Heggies Vineyard Reserve Eden Valley Chardonnay 2007, South Australia White
Pungent, fruity nose. Rich, ripe fruit on the palate, with good length.
£15.10

Houghton Stripe Sauvignon Blanc Semillon 2008, Western Australia White
Classy herbaceous nose, and a palate that is elegant and grassy, with good acidity, and a clean melon finish.
£7.00

Houghton The Bandit Chardonnay Viognier 2008, Western Australia White
Elegantly balanced wine, with pretty peachy fruit and understated smoke. Medium acidity and creamy texture. Plenty of interest.
£10.00

Houghton The Bandit Sauvignon Blanc Pinot Gris 2008, Western Australia White
Lovely fresh nose, with lots of tropical fruit. Floral, fresh finish, and good balance.
£10.00

Howard Park Riesling 2008, Western Australia White
Light yellow in colour, with clean, fresh juice on the nose, opening into intense tropical notes and attractive fruitiness.

Jacob's Creek Chardonnay 2008, South Eastern Australia White
Pale tropical fruit character, with a good body, balanced fruit, and gentle acidity. Long, creamy finish.
£6.90 TESC, WAIT

Jacob's Creek Pinot Grigio 2008, South Eastern Australia White
Clear, pale colour, with a delicate,

but moderately pronounced smoky oatmeal nose, and ripe fruit on a clean, bright palate.
£6.90 TESC

Jacob's Creek Steingarten Riesling 2007, South Australia
White
Notes of white flower and cooking apple. Nice clean fruit, with apple and gooseberry predominating. Lively and vivacious.
£13.30 TESC

K1 By Geoff Hardy Silver Label Semillon Viognier 2008, South Australia White
Rich, fresh apricot fruit on the nose. Ripe white fruit on the palate, and a fresh, clean finish.

Kangarilla Road Chardonnay 2008, South Australia White
Fresh and appealing tropical fruit on the nose. Fruity, elegant palate, with balanced acidity.
£10.00 MWW

Kilikanoon Morts Reserve Riesling 2008, South Australia
White
Punchy nose of tropical pineapple, with citrus and apple core notes. Lovely acidic lift.

2008 Kirrihill Single Vineyard Series Riesling 2008, South Australia White
Fruity wine with aromas of lemon zest and lime, with a long fruity finish.

Kooky Village Riesling 2008, South Australia White
Zesty lime and ripe apple on the nose. Some varietal fruit character, with notes of citrus apple. Clean, crisp finish.

Limestone Coast Chardonnay 2008, Angove Family Winemakers, South Australia White
Intriguing lime meringue pie

notes, heavy texture and weight; a big Chardonnay.
£9.00 D&D

Mcguigan Bin 9000 1999, Australian Vintage Ltd, New South Wales White
Orange blossom and buttered toast character, with a complex nose and palate. Supple texture, and a creamy finish.

Mcguigan Bin 9000 2003, Australian Vintage Ltd, New South Wales White
Lemongrass and lime leaves, with notes of honey and custard. Textured and mineral, with a fresh, citrus acidity and a lovely chalky finish.

Mcguigan Bin 9000 2007, Australian Vintage Ltd, New South Wales White
Lime in colour, notes of bay leaves and hay, with some elegance. Cotton wool fruit.

Mcguigan Discover Sauvignon Blanc 2008, Australian Vintage Ltd, South Australia White
Nice intensity of aromas, with appley and lemony notes, and a sweet zingy lemon palate.

Mcguigan Earth's Portrait Riesling 2003, Australian Vintage Ltd, South Australia White
Citrus and mineral notes. Lovely fruit intensity. Medium length, with good mouthfeel.

Mcguigan Genus 4 Riesling 2007, Australian Vintage Ltd, South Australia White
Characteristic exotic fruit nose. Well-opened, with good balance, and a lovely finish.

Mcguigan Genus 4 Riesling 2008, Australian Vintage Ltd, South Australia White
Great pungency of tertiary aromas

and primary fruit. Very youthful with great potential.

Mcguigan Shortlist Chardonnay 2008, Australian Vintage Ltd, South Australia White
Pale lemon in colour. Melon and lemon on the nose, with a slight oakiness. Lovely high acidity. Very pleasant and extremely quaffable.

McHenry Hohnen Margaret River Semillon Sauvignon Blanc 2008, Western Australia White
Crisp gooseberry, with fleshy tropical fruits on the palate. Fresh, approachable style.
£9.90 CHH, FLA, WSO, FAW, GWI, NDJ, WWS

Marks & Spencer Tallarook Marsanne 2006, Victoria White
Elegant structure, with fresh, fragrant fruit. Long, nutty, savoury finish.
£10.00 M&S

Nepenthe Sauvignon Blanc 2008, South Australia White
Beautiful nose, with green citrus and gooseberries. Sweetness on the palate, leading to a clean lime finish.
£8.60 TESC, WAIT

Nine Vines Viognier 2008, Angove Family Winemakers, South Australia White
Some burnt match and steely overtones. Cool and fresh, well-balanced, with a light finish.
£7.00 D&D

Nugan Estate Frascas Lane Vineyard King Valley Chardonnay 2008, Victoria White
Rich fruit and toasty palate, with

crisp acidity, and a fresh, long finish.

O'Leary Walker Adelaide Hills Sauvignon Blanc 2008, South Australia White
Clean, fresh, ripe and elegant aromas, with grassy notes. Light citrus acidity.

O'Leary Walker Polish Hill River Riesling 2008, South Australia White
Star-bright pale lemon hue. Good intensity on the nose, with fruit and hints of petrol. Good length.
£9.00 WAIT

O'Leary Walker Watervale Riesling 2008, South Australia White
Full, long, and complex. Quintessential Clare Valley Riesling. Light body and dry finish.

One Chain Vineyards "The Googly" Chardonnay 2008, Alliance Wine Australia, White
Fresh, light, and fruity, with an attractive lemony edge. Slightly warm finish.
£5.80 HEN, AAW

Oxford Landing Viognier 2008, South Australia White
Aromatic white peach and apricot with violet notes. Creamy and spicy, with good acidity.
£5.00 NFW

Palandri The Estates Sauvignon Blanc 2008, 3 Oceans Wine Company, Western Australia White
Fresh, herbaceous nose, notes of exotic melon and grapefruits, with notes of green bell pepper, and hints of tropical fruit. The palate is

braced by good acidity, and nuance of spice.
£8.90

Palandri Vita Novus Chardonnay 2005, 3 Oceans Wine Company, Western Australia White
Seductive oak edges, with peachy tropical fruit. Fleshy and tasty.
£11.00 3OW, BOF, EHL, OWC, RWW, SAD, WIE, WIW

Paxton Chardonnay 2007, South Australia White
Sweet vanilla notes with an elegant peach and mango fruit palate.
£15.50 SWS

Penfolds Bin 311 Tumbarumba 2006, New South Wales White
Judicious use of oak, allowing the fruit to shine. Medium body.

Penfolds Bin 51 Eden Valley Riesling 2007, South Australia White
Steely, fresh lemon nose. Lovely acidity, and good mineral character. Finish is clean and crisp.

Penfolds Bin 51 Riesling 2007, South Australia White
Lighter on the nose, then developing oily richness. Zesty acidity, and rich youthful fruit, culminating in an elegant, long finish.

Penfolds Yattarna 2006, South Australia White
Fresh, oaky, tropical, and sweet. Juicy and toasty, with white stone fruit flavours.

Peos Four Aces Chardonnay 2008, Western Australia White
Oak-tinged tropical nose.

Bright acidity supporting tropical fruit flavours. A well-balanced wine.

Petaluma Chardonnay 2006, South Australia White
Ripe mango and pineapple, with gentle oak and fresh bread. Moderate acidity, with cinnamon and all-spice on the finish.
£16.00 BNK, SAIN, TESC, WAIT, ODD

Petaluma Hanlin Hill Riesling 2008, South Australia White
Nice, bright, clean, fresh and elegant - balanced and persistent.
£11.00 BNK, WAIT, ODD

Peter Lehmann Wines Wigan Eden Valley Riesling 2003, South Australia White
Very powerful kerosene nose, with a toffee edge. Real elegance in the long finish.
£13.30 VDV, LAI

Pewsey Vale Prima Riesling 2008, South Australia White
Floral, leesy, citric aromas. Palate shows some residual sugar, with a little spice. Soft but fresh, with good balancing acidity.
£10.70

Pike & Joyce Chardonnay 2007, South Australia White
Restrained and evolving nose. Some toasty buttery oak, and a full mouthfeel on the finish.
LEA

Prospector's Riesling Viognier Clare Valley 2008, Pikes Vintners Pty Ltd, South Australia White
Extremely tropical, ripe, soft honeydew melon and peach aromas. Palate is slightly nutty with ripe peach, and decent length.
£9.00 LAI

Plantagenet Riesling 2008, Western Australia White
Soft, light but elegant fruit, leading to palate of lovely acidity and stone fruit, with a spicy, crisp, fresh finish.
£10.40 VDV, LIB

Plunkett Fowles Stone Dwellers Riesling 2008, Victoria White
Breezy, fresh nose with an ozone-like quality. Hint of possible botrytis. Crisp and balanced.

Punt Road 2008, Victoria White
Lovely peach and apricot aromas, with a floral fragrance. A long, attractive wine.
£11.00

Punt Road Wines 2007, Victoria White
Lovely tropical aromas. Palate of citrus, with balanced oak, and elegant creamy ripe fruit. Medium intensity and length.
£11.00

Ravenswood Lane Chardonnay 2007, South Australia White
Pale in colour. Nose shows Chardonnay fruit, not overpowered by oak. Palate holds good varietal character and underlying oak. Nice balance of acidity.
WRC

Rockbare Tinderbox Chardonnay 2008, South Australia White
Banana, bubblegum, and appley notes on the nose. Good balance of fruit and acidity, with a long grapefruity finish.
£10.00 M&S

Rosemount Show Reserve Hunter Valley Chardonnay

2006, New South Wales White
Oak spice aromas, showing crispness on the palate, with rich peach flavours and vanilla tones.
£12.00 WAIT

Seven Scenes Viognier 2007, Sirromet Wines, Granite Belt White
Orange and honey on a lengthy, floral nose. Fairly rich on the palate, with good depth and weight.

Shaw & Smith M3 Chardonnay 2008, South Australia White
Gentle smoky aromas. Lively acidity with citrus fruit. Lemon confection finish.
£19.10 HEN, WAIT, LIB

Shaw & Smith Sauvignon Blanc 2008, South Australia White
Light floral and mineral notes, with soft vanilla aromas. Pleasant, ripe gooseberry notes on the palate.
£12.30 CHH, HEN, VDV, WAIT, LIB

Skuttlebutt Sauvignon Semillon 2008, Western Australia White
Tropical fruit and melon, with good freshness on the palate. Good balanced acidity.
£9.10 HEN, AAW

Speckled House Riesling 2007, Setanta Wines, South Australia White
Fresh citrussy nose, with nice lift and decent freshness on the palate. Crisp green fruit, with kiwi and pineapple notes.
£14.00 NOV

Spring Seed Wines 'Four O'Clock' Chardonnay 2008, South Australia White
Lychees, pineapple, and

grapefruit on the nose. Lovely sweet fruit on the palate, with well balanced acidity.

St Hallett Poachers Blend 2008, South Australia White
Delicate aromas of fresh citrus. Good depth, well-balanced, with some pleasant citrus flavours on the finish.
£7.70 BNK, NFW, TESC, WAIT, CWS

Stella Bella Viognier 2007, Western Australia White
Perfumed orange and subtle flowers on the nose. Moderately soft on the palate, with a touch of honey, good texture and length.
£10.20 AAW

Terra Barossa Riesling 2008, Thorn-Clarke Wines, South Australia White
Lime and lemon aromas, with petrol notes coming through. Off-dry, with crisp acidity, and a refreshing finish.
£10.00

Tesco Australian Reserve Riesling Gwertztraminer 2008, Angove's Pty Ltd, South Australia White
Very light yellow in colour, with a floral, spicy lychee nose. Good balance of fruit, with a creamy attack, and crisp acidity providing freshness.
£4.90 TESC

Tesco Finest* Denman Vineyard Reserve Semillon 2006, Australian Vintage Ltd, New South Wales White
A calm wine, makes its way deliberately across the palate. Well-achieved; a unique style.
£7.10 TESC

The Black Chook Vmr 2008, South Australia White
Nice peachy notes, with

creaminess, and good acid balance. An attractive blend.
£10.00 GZB

Tomich Hill Sauvignon Blanc 2008, South Australia White
Green herbaceous notes. Pear flavours on the palate, with good crisp acidity.

Trentham Estate, Albariño 2008, South Eastern Australia White
Crisp nose, with clean lime notes. Bright, racy palate with brioche complexity and soft fruitiness. Well-balanced, with a good mouthfeel.
£9.00 GGR, VDV

Voyager Estate Chardonnay 2007, Western Australia White
Vibrant, restrained fruit on a creamy, elegant palate. Fresh finish and good weight.
£14.30

Voyager Estate Sauvignon Blanc Semillon 2008, Western Australia White
Touches of green pepper and coffee on the nose. Good intensity of zesty, herbal fruit, which is well sustained through the palate.
£9.50

Wakefield Jaraman Sauvignon Blanc 2008, South Australia White
Bright clean fruit on the nose, with touches of honey and gooseberry. High acidity and good intensity of flavour.
£16.00 SWS

Wakefield Riesling 2008, South Australia White
A touch of minerality, with subtle lemon and limes, sour apple, and lemon on the palate. Clean zippy acidity; well-made

and well-pitched.
£9.60 EDC, SWS

Wakefield St Andrews Riesling 2005, South Australia White
Fresh petrolly nose. Apple, grapefruit, mango, and guava. Fine definition and fresh balance.
£17.50 SWS

Wirra Wirra Vineyards Lost Watch Riesling 2008, South Australia White
Clean, with dry, intense, tangy acidity, fresh complexity, and a rich finish.

Wolf Blass Gold Label Riesling 2008, South Eastern Australia White
Bright lemon-lime aromas, with mineral notes. Dry, with lovely citrus acidity, and a creamy mid-palate. Good length.

Wolf Blass Red Label Semillon Sauvignon Blanc 2008, South Eastern Australia White
Fresh lemon and honey nose, with some herbaceous tones. Medium-weight with grapefruit notes on the palate.

Woodside Valley Estate Le Bas Chardonnay 2007, Western Australia White
Mango, tangerine, and pineapple on the nose. Good definition with a fresh, lively mid-palate.

Wyndham Estate Bin 222 Chardonnay 2007, South Eastern Australia White
Fresh lime and stone fruit aromas, with a creamy soft mouthfeel.
£7.00

Yalumba Y Series Viognier 2008, South Australia White
A shy nose, with hints of white fruit and flowers, on a gentle palate.
£7.50 FLA, NFW, TESC, WAIT

Yering Station Chardonnay 2006, Victoria White
Beautiful creamy, spicy nose, leading to a gentle mandarin and pineapple palate. Very nice acidity and well-integrated oak.
£11.00

Allanmere Cabernet Sauvignon 2004, New South Wales Red
Mature, attractive, currant fruit. Some warmth, with a strong cassis note, and good sweet fruit. Rich and minty.

Amphora Wine Group Rigoletto 2006, South Australia Red
Lovely wine; well-balanced, with smoky leather on full palate. Good, balancing acidity: enjoy it beside an open fire!

Angove Family Winemakers Brightlands Cabernet Merlot 2007 South Australia Red
Subtle, spicy, ripe, fat nose, with hints of violet, tar and cedar. Well-textured and balanced.
£9.00 D&D

Angove Family Winemakers Coonawarra Cabernet Sauvignon 2007, South Australia Red
Fresh and youthful, with minty fig aromas. Fine-grained tannins add elegance to this promising wine.
£13.00 D&D

Angove Family Winemakers Limestone Coast Cabernet Sauvignon 2006, South Australia Red
Minty, herbal, and liquorice notes on the nose. Ripe red fruit on the palate. Nice texture and finish.
£9.50 D&D

dried black fruits, and light floral notes on the nose. Bold, chocolatey palate, with fresh acidity.

Ceravolo Sangiovese 2007, South Australia Red
Restrained red berry, and light herbal aromas. Fresh acidity and lifted palate. Refreshing.

Ceravolo Shiraz 2006, South Australia Red
Good deep colour, with a full mouthfeel, jammy black fruit, sweet chocolate, and fresh acidity holding the fruit on the finish.

Chapel Hill Bush Vine Grenache 2007, South Australia Red
Ripe, crunchy black fruit. Smooth, well-defined palate, with juicy fruit and crisp acidity.
£12.00

Chapel Hill, McLaren Vale Shiraz 2007, South Australia Red
Red and black berry fruit, with spice on a fresh palate of raspberry, plum and spice.
£12.00

Chateau Tanunda Three Graces 2006, South Australia Red
Juicy, young, tangy, blackcurrant and blackberry. Good weight and length.

Coriole, Mary Kathleen 2006, South Australia Red
Floral and mulberry nose. Palate is full of juice, with fruity tannins.
£19.60 DBY, VDV

Coriole Redstone Shiraz 2006, South Australia Red
Black fruit and meat on the nose, with a deep, rich palate of spicy oak, balancing acidity, and chewy tannins. A coconut-tinged finish, which is meaty, with salty nuances.
£11.00 GGR, VDV, HVN

Coriole, The Soloist, Shiraz 2006, South Australia Red
Rounded, full, and chocolatey, with slightly edgy tannins and acidity, though it maintains good balance.
£18.30 GGR, THC, VDV

Climbing Cabernet Sauvignon 2007, Cumulus Wines Pty Ltd, New South Wales Red
Deep red in colour. Tight, leathery nose. Complex, balanced palate, with good structure.
£10.00

D'arenberg The Coppermine Road 2006, South Australia Red
Nose of black fruit and raspberry juice. Concentrated fruit on the palate, with crunchy tannins.
£13.00 WAIT

D'arenberg The Feathered Dinosaur Cabernet Sauvignon 2004, South Australia Red
Vibrant aromas with spicy oak. A little bretty and slightly earthy, but elegant.
£19.00 TESC

D'arenberg The Footbolt 2006, South Australia Red
Blueberries and toasty oak aromas, with jammy fruit on the palate; a very serious wine.
£9.80 WES, WSO, WAIT

D'arenberg The High Trellis 2006, South Australia Red
Deep, black fruit nose. The palate is broad and sweet, showing some evolution.
£10.30 FLA, WES

D'arenberg The Twenty-eight Road 2006, South Australia
Red
Black fruit and meat on the nose, with a sweet rich palate of spicy oak, with bracing acidity, cherry tannins, and a coconut finish.

Dead Letter Office 2007, Henry's Drive Vignerons, South Australia Red
Earthy, leathery notes on the nose, with mulberry fruit showing on the palate. Rich, with hints of chocolate and spice.

Deen De Bortoli Petite Sirah 2007, New South Wales Red
Blueberry nose with concentrated black fruit palate and mouth-coating tannin.

De Bortoli Wines Windy Peak Pinot Noir 2008, Victoria Red
Light bodied, with soft cherry fruit, and fresh acidity. Decent length.

Eden Springs High Eden Cabernet Sauvignon 2006, South Australia Red
Savoury black fruit on the nose. Black fruit carries through to the palate, which also shows notes of leather, balanced tannins, and good length.

Elderton Barossa Shiraz 2006, South Australia Red
Red and black berry fruit on an attractive nose, with notes of vanilla oak and rich coffee. Palate of intense spice and bramble fruit, with notes of white pepper, and integrated, silky tannins.

Elderton Command Single Vineyard Shiraz 2006, South Australia Red
Minty nose, leading to a powerful and grippy fruit palate, with vanilla edges, and a very long finish.

Elderton Ode To Lorraine Cabernet Sauvigon, Shiraz, Merlot 2006, South Australia Red
Surprisingly light fruit. Good acidity and tannins. Well-balanced, and beginning to mellow.

Evans & Tate Margaret River Classic Red 2007, Western Australia Red
Ruby red in colour with a restrained herbal nose, and a spicy bramble palate.
HWL

Evans & Tate The Reserve Cabernet Sauvignon 2005, Western Australia Red
Minty, blackcurrant nose, with ripe but fresh fruit, with a trace of bitterness.
HWL

Evans & Tate The Reserve Shiraz 2007, Western Australia Red
Bright, dark ruby in colour. Clean, with quite a perfumed violet note, attractive balance, and some chocolatey notes.
HWL

Fonty's Pool Cabernet Merlot 2007, Western Australia Red
Light purple in colour. Rich, with good fruit, and very juicy.
£8.20

Fox Creek Jsm Shiraz Cabernet Sauvignon Cabernet Franc 2007, South Australia Red
Smooth ripe plum and spice on the palate. Well-balanced, with good complexity and length.

Gemtree Vineyards Uncut Shiraz 2006, South Australia Red
Concentrated, ripe, deep raspberry fruit on the nose, with rich, ripe eucalyptus notes, and chunky tannins.
£14.40 VDV, CAM

K1 By Geoff Hardy Merlot 2006, South Australia Red
Sweet, forward, black fruit nose, with hints of mint and spice. The palate is fresh, with nice plummy fruit.

Geoff Merrill 2005, South Australia Red
Lovely length. A nice wine; heavy-weight, and almost sweet.
£8.00 EOR, HDS, HRW

George Wyndham Shiraz 2005, South Australia Red
Clean menthol aromas. Spicy, herbal palate, with notes of blackcurrant and a hint of smoke.
£10.00

Anaperenna 2007, Glaetzer Wines, South Australia Red
Peppery nose, with firm tannins on the palate. Well-developed, with good oak integration, and a long finish.
£32.10 NFW, WSO, CAM, CVS, GWW, SWG

Grant Burge Shadrach 2006, South Australia Red
Firm tannin and fresh black fruit, with a long, crisp blackcurranty finish.
£25.00 NFW, HMA

Grant Burge The Holy Trinity 2004, South Australia Red
Very savoury, developing fruit, with a tangy raspberry character. Well-integrated structure and good length.
£18.50 FHM, NFW, HMA

Eileen Hardy Shiraz 2004, Hardy Wine Company, South Australia Red
Concentrated, ripe plummy fruit, with good balance and a long finish.

Eileen Hardy Shiraz 2005, Hardy Wine Company, South Australia Red
Full and ripe, with smooth, woody black fruit. Elegant and powerful, with a salty note, offering good complexity.
£40.00 HAR

Hardys VR Merlot 2008, South Eastern Australia Red
Oaky nose, showing some complexity, with notes of youthful redcurrant fruit, with vanilla spice and pepper. Soft, well-integrated tannins.
£5.30 TESC

Hardys Oomoo Shiraz 2007, South Australia Red
Coffee, mocha, and smoke aromas. Polished, velvety tannins, and a hint of eucalyptus on a smooth, minty, berry palate.
£10.00 THS

Hardy Wine Company, Thomas Hardy Cabernet Sauvignon 2004, South & Western Australia Red
Elegant and fresh, with attractive cassis and accents of cedar. Vibrant fruit on the palate, framed by velvety tannins, and lively acidity, with meaty flavours, and a very long finish.
£40.00

Haselgrove Hrs Reserve Shiraz 2007, South Australia Red
Dark vanilla and spice, with black fruit, concentrated blackberry, and ripe, minty fruit.

Haselgrove Vincent's Breeze Cabernet Sauvignon 2006, South Australia Red
Ruby red in colour. Creamy and liquorice notes on the nose. Juicy dark fruit on the palate, finishing on a ripe fruity note..
£10.00 WRC

Haselgrove Vincent's Breeze Shiraz 2007, South Australia Red
Raspberry, blackberry, plum, and juicy fruit on a rounded, sweet, fruity palate.

Heartland Shiraz 2006, South Australia Red
Smoky rich fruit on the nose. Palate of cinnamon and minty fruit, showing good length.
£9.20 WSO, FNW, GWW, JAS, OZW, SWG

Heathfield Ridge Shiraz 2005, Tidswell Wines, South Australia Red
Menthol on the nose, with a fresh peppery palate, chunky tannins, and a long, powerful finish.

Henry's Drive 2007, South Australia Red
Good colour. Fruity nose with some earthy and gamey notes.

Houghton Stripe Cabernet Shiraz Merlot 2007, Western Australia Red
Cedar and spice on the nose. Leafy green palate, with a subtle fruity finish.
£7.00

Howard Park Leston Cabernet Sauvignon 2007, Western Australia Red
Raspberry and blackberry fruit, with a nuance of eucalyptus, and subtle oak. Lively fruit palate, nicely balanced, with moderate length and a spicy finish.

Howard Park Leston Shiraz 2007, Western Australia Red
Jammy fruit nose. Rich black fruit on the palate, with some liquorice and leather, leading to a spicy, oaky finish.

Howard Park Scotsdale Cabernet Sauvignon 2007, Western Australia Red
Deep ruby in colour, with notes of ripe forest fruits and violet, leading to a dry, menthol finish.

Howard Park Madbay Shiraz 2007, Western Australia Red
Smoky, creamy, dark fruit nose. Dry, with lots of cool fruit on a firm palate.
£9.10 TESC

Howard Park Scotsdale Shiraz 2007, Western Australia Red
Ripe, sweet nose. Cherry flavours on the palate, with medium weight, and a dry, concentrated finish.

Irvine Wines Premium Grand Merlot 2005, South Australia Red
Deep ruby in colour, with concentrated blackberry and spicy savoury mint character. Concentrated blackberry character, with good acidity and light tannins.
£39.00 VDV, PLA

Jacob's Creek Reserve Shiraz 2006, South Australia Red
Light spicy fruit on the nose. A soft-textured wine, with a

medium body, and smooth finish.
£7.50 TESC, WAIT

Jim Barry The Lodge Hill Shiraz 2007, South Australia Red
Raspberry aromas on a complex nose, with a palate of sweet, concentrated fruit, and a long finish.
£10.30 EDC, FLA, NFW

John Duval Entity 2007, South Australia Red
Ripe cherries, coffee, and leather aromas, with a juicy, fruity, velvety palate, which is elegant and delicate.
£21.20 VDV, LIB

John Duval Plexus 2007, South Australia Red
Interesting aromas, and surprisingly fragrant. Looks and smells pretty mature, with a pleasing fruit flavour, and a fresh finish.
£19.20 VDV, LIB

Kalleske Greenock Shiraz 2007, South Australia Red
Spicy raspberry on the nose, with classy oak, sweet raspberries, and fresh black pepper on the palate.

Kangarilla Road Shiraz 2006, South Australia Red
Warm, dense, spicy nose, and an attractive, warm, spicy palate.
£10.00 MWW

Katnook Estate Cabernet Sauvignon 2005, South Australia Red
Very ripe aromas of cassis and mint. Fresh and jammy, with nice balance, and a sweet, ripe fruit character.
BWL

Katnook Estate Odyssey Cabernet Sauvignon 2004, South Australia Red
Good cherry and spice aromas, with round fruit, cool mint, and an elegant finish.
£25.00 WAIT, BWL

Katnook Estate Prodigy Shiraz 2005, South Australia Red
Blackberry fruit and hints of vanilla, with powerful, but well-integrated oak.
£30.00 WAIT, BWL

Katnook Estate Shiraz 2006, South Australia Red
Ripe red berry nose, with hints of vanilla and cocoa. Fresh palate, with raspberry acidity.
BWL

Katnook Founder's Block Shiraz 2006, South Australia Red
Soft, spicy fruit with herbal undertones. Understated and stylish, with a rounded mouthfeel and excellent length.
BWL

Trevor Jones Dry Grown Shiraz 2006, Kellermeister Holdings Pty Ltd, South Australia Red
Menthol and spice on the nose. Well-balanced, with good length.

Kilikanoon Covenant Shiraz 2006, South Australia Red
A clean, fresh bouquet of ripe blackberries. Oaky, with good fruit concentration, and a fruity finish.

Kilikanoon 'killerman's Run' Shiraz 2007, South Australia Red
Complex, with red fruit, and a spicy nose, with a hint of liquorice. Palate is juicy, moreish, and well-structured.

Kilikanoon Killermans Run Shiraz 2005, South Australia Red
Savoury fruit notes, with subtle oak, a gentle fruit palate, and a balanced finish.
WRC

Kingston Estate Cabernet Sauvignon 2008, South Australia Red
Good concentration of fresh but ripe cassis flavours, and fine tannins. Well-balanced, with nice weight. A pleasant wine.

Kirrihill Clare Valley Shiraz 2008, South Australia Red
Liquorice and jam nose, very rich yet youthful, with concentrated dark fruit character, and a crisp finish.

Krondorf Symmetry Barossa Valley Cabernet Sauvignon 2006, Dorrien Estate, South Australia Red
Powerful dark fruit on the nose, and a refreshing palate, showing good concentration.

Krondorf Symmetry Barossa Valley Shiraz 2007, Dorrien Estate, South Australia Red
Ripe black plum fruit and spice on the nose, with a big, concentrated palate of sweet spicy fruit.

Leconfield Cabernet Sauvignon 2006, South Australia Red
Cedar, cassis, black fruit and savoury notes combine with spice and fresh mint. Good fruit, with oaky spiciness and firm tannins.
£17.00 NFW, FTH

Richard Hamilton Centurion Shiraz 2007, Leconfield Wines Pty Ltd, South Australia Red
Pronounced floral and fruit notes.

Toasty oak, polished, with fine tannins, and lifted by attractive freshness.

Lindemans Bin45 Cabernet Sauvignon 2008, South Eastern Australia Red
Clean cassis nose, with a touch of leafiness, and light menthol. Good fruit weight, which follows through to lengthy finish.

Longview, Yakka 2007, South Australia Red
Violet hue, with a spicy elegant nose, and jammy, fresh blackberry fruit, on a woody and creamy palate.

Mcguigan Handmade Shiraz 2006, Australian Vintage Ltd, South Australia Red
Hearty, with a hint of mushroom and chocolate on a complete palate.

Majella Wines Pty Ltd, "The Musician" 2007, South Australia Red
Bright berry fruit, with minty notes. Good weight and crunchy style.
£9.90 FLA, NFW, VDV, AAW, JCC, NYW

Majella Cabernet Sauvignon 2006, South Australia Red
Minty and berry character on the nose. Nice medium weight, with lovely texture.
£15.80 FLA, NFW, VDV, AAW, BHL, ODD, SCA

Majella Shiraz 2006, South Australia Red
A delicate, perfumed nose with hints of eucalyptus. Lovely ripe fruit on the palate, and a smooth, minty finish.
£15.90 FLA, NFW, VDV, AAW, HSW, ODD

McWilliam's Hanwood Estate Shiraz 2007, South Eastern Australia Red
Fresh, bright, intense fruit. Quite dark, with a full, tannic body, and a chocolatey finish.
£7.40 TESC, WAIT, SMF

McWilliam's Icons "1877" Shiraz Cabernet Merlot 2004, South Eastern Australia Red
Leafy nose. Complex palate, with hints of cedar and spice. Grippy finish. £20.00

Marks & Spencer Ebenezer Blackwell Shiraz 2007, Lion Nathan, South Australia Red
Fresh, minty chocolatey nose, with well-defined fruit. Broad, spicy, and oaky, with a medium length finish.
£10.00 M&S

Mitolo G.A.M. Shiraz 2006, South Australia Red
Deep red in colour, with young, chewy fruit, liquorice notes.Good concentration, with balanced tannins.
£22.10 HEN, VDV, LIB

Mitolo Reiver Shiraz 2007, South Australia Red
Nice structured fruit, firm tannins, and a complex structure. Classic varietal character, with real length.
£21.50 HEN, VDV

Moppity Vineyards Reserve Shiraz 2006, New South Wales Red
Interesting nose of green peppers and eucalyptus. The fruit is integrated with soft tannins, and structured acidity.
£24.00 WLY

Moppity Vineyards Reserve Shiraz 2006, New South Wales Red
Chocolatey, cherry menthol nose. Slightly stewed fruit on a balanced palate.
£24.00 WLY

Mount Langi Ghiran, Billi Billi Shiraz 2006, Victoria Red
Dense black and bramble fruit with a mineral, liquorice character. Lush ripe palate with creamy oak.
£8.00

Mount Langi Ghiran, Cliff Edge Shiraz 2005, Victoria Red
Pronouced menthol nose, with a refreshing palate of herbal black fruit, and a long spicy finish.
£12.00

Mr. Riggs The Gaffer Shiraz 2007, South Australia Red
Sweet, nutty, warm, and relatively restrained. Ripe fruit, with fresh acidity. Well-balanced and pleasing, with a fresh spicy finish.
£12.00 GZB

Nardone Baker The Wara Manta Reserve Shiraz 2006, South Australia Red
Ripe berry fruit and spice, with a hint of black pepper. Soft, long fruity finish.

Neagles Rock One Black Dog Reserve Cabernet Shiraz 2006, South Australia Red
Chocolate and nuttiness on the nose. Rich and complex palate of coffee and cherry. Very smooth, with an elegant finish.

Nepenthe Good Doctor Pinot Noir 2005, South Australia Red
Ripe, balsamic character; a very Australian nose. Soft red fruit and dry, earthy tannins.

Nugan Estate Manuka Grove Durif 2007, South Eastern Australia Red
Intense, rich palate, with good

complexity and structured tannins.

Nugan Estate McLaren Parish Shiraz 2007, South Australia Red
Blackberry, plum, and spicy oak, with a rich, ripe fruit palate, displaying concentrated flavours and a hint of spice, with good length and balance.

O'Leary Walker Clare Valley Cabernet Sauvignon 2006, South Australia Red
Warm, ripe, macerated fruit character. Jammy and ripe on the palate. Firm tannins.
£10.00 WAIT

Favourite Son Cabernet Merlot 2005, Parker Coonawarra Estate, South Australia Red
Minty blackberry aromas, with notes of milk chocolate. Evident grippy tannin, with a smooth lifted finish.

Mariginiup Shiraz 2007, Paul Conti, Western Australia Red
Meaty Rhône-style wine, with a slightly buttery edge. Full and ripe on the palate.

Palandri The Estates Cabernet Sauvignon 2005, 3 Oceans Wine Company, Western Australia Red
Nose of cherry and eucalyptus. Soft mouthfeel, with notes of ripe cassis and grippy tannins.
£9.00 3OW, EHL, WIE

Palandri The Estates Cabernet Sauvignon Merlot 2007, 3 Oceans Wine Company, Western Australia Red
Leggy with deep colour. Good grape definition here – the softness of Merlot stands out. Good style and purity of fruit.

Long cassis finish.
£8.90

Palandri The Estates Shiraz 2007, 3 Oceans Wine Company, Western Australia Red
Ripe dark fruits, with a toasty, brambly edge on the nose. Medium intensity, with a nice fruit attack.
£8.90

Palandri Vita Novus Cabernet Sauvignon 2005, 3 Oceans Wine Company, Western Australia Red
Deep, intense nose of plum, menthol, eucalyptus, and cherry. Soft palate, with good varietal character.
£11.00 3OW, BOF, EHL, OWC, RWW, SAD, WIE, WIW

Paxton Jones Block Shiraz 2005, South Australia Red
Big, rich fruit aromas on the nose, with a peppery palate, and an attractive balance of chocolate and plum.
£18.00 SWS

Penfolds Bin128 Coonawarra Shiraz 2006, South Australia Red
Nose of smoky cherry, with notes of black fruit and oak on the palate.

Penfolds Koonunga Hill Shiraz Cabernet Sauvignon 2007, South Eastern Australia Red
Bright, cherry red colour. Complex chocolate and leather flavours, with rich tannins, full body, and fresh acidity.
£8.00 WAIT

Penfolds Thomas Hyland Shiraz 2006, South Eastern Australia Red
Mint and mulberry fruit aromas.

Lots of chocolatey oak and black olive notes on the palate of this big chunky wine.

Penley Estate Condor Shiraz Cabernet 2007, South Australia Red
Rich ruby in colour, with deep red fruit and some spice. Warm, powerful, and well-balanced.
£10.00 MOR

Penley Estate Reserve Cabernet Sauvignon 2006, South Australia Red
Rich aromas of blackberry, cedar, and vanilla oak, on a concentrated ripe black fruit palate, with some hints of coffee cake.
£20.00 MOR

Pertaringa Over The Top Shiraz 2007, South Australia Red
Elegant, almost gamey nose. Juicy, with ripe red fruits, creamy oak, and ripe tannins.
£17.50 SWS

Pertaringa Two Gentlemens Grenache 2007, South Australia Red
Peppery nose, with soft, sweet raspberry and bramble palate, underpinned by soft, ripe tannins.
£12.00 SWS

Pertaringa Understudy Cabernet Petit Verdot 2007, South Australia Red
Delicate perfumed nose, with a hint of violet. Rich fruitcake palate, with good balance and length.
£11.00 EDC, VDV, SWS

Petaluma Coonawarra Cabernet Merlot 2005, South Australia Red
Leathery tobacco and black fruit aromas. Powerful tannic palate, with some nice savoury notes,

and good length.
£23.00 BNK, ODD

Peter Lehmann Futures Shiraz 2006, South Australia Red
Minty eucalyptus and blackcurrant nose, with good complexity and balanced structure.
£13.20 NFW, VDV, BTH, OST

Peter Lehmann Wines Barossa Cabernet Sauvignon 2006, South Australia Red
Clean and straightforward. Slightly vegetal nose. Fresh black fruit on the palate, with a long, crisp blackcurranty finish, and nice balance.
£9.00 CAM, CMR, NYW, ODD

Peter Lehmann Wines Clancy's Red 2005, South Australia Red
Classic, well-balanced wine, which is sweet, with fresh tannins and fruit, finishing on a spicy notes.
£7.60 TESC, WAIT, BTH, ODD, OST

Peter Lehmann Wines Semillon 2006, South Australia Red
Soft, honeyed nose, with silky notes of asparagus and citrus, and a limey palate. A well-made wine.
£6.50 TESC, ODD

Pipers Brook Estate Pinot Noir 2007, Tasmania Red
A nose of pure, concentrated red fruit, and some floral notes. This profile is matched on a palate, which is very focused, with quite pronounced oaky tannins.
£16.20 PBA

Plantagenet Cabernet Sauvignon 2007, Western Australia Red
Big, fruity, young wine. There is lots of oak, but it does not

dominate. Fleshy berry character, tinged with spearmint.
£15.00 VDV, LIB

Primo Estate Il Briccone 2006, South Australia Red
Rich black fruit, cherry, and ferrous notes on the nose, with a solid ripe fruit palate, and sleek flavour.
£11.50 FLA, AWC

Primo Estate Il Briccone 2007, South Australia Red
Attractive coffee notes, with juicy, meaty tannins, and a long, pleasant finish.
£10.00 AWC

Primo Estate Shale Stone Shiraz 2005, South Australia Red
Big, rich fruit on the nose, with a peppery palate, and an attractive balance of chocolate and plum.
£15.00 AWC

Johnny Q Shiraz 2008, Quarisa Wines, New South Wales Red
A vibrant peppery red, this is juicy and spicy, with a dry, medium-bodied character.

Johnny Q Shiraz Viognier 2008, Quarisa Wines, South Eastern Australia Red
Lovely, rich plummy red colour. Bags of fruit, and pleasing tannins on the finish.

Ravenswood Lane Shiraz 2007, South Australia Red
Warm red berry and spice nose, with fresh, soft, supple juicy fruit. A simple and well-made wine.
WRC

Ringbolt Margaret River Cabernet Sauvignon 2007, Western Australia Red
Intense cassis fruit and toasty oak on the nose. Bold flavours are accented by eucalpytus and spice. Nicely integrated structure, with good concentration and weight.
£9.20 FLA, TESC

Rock Bare Tinder Box Shiraz 2007, South Australia Red
Raspberry red fruits and fresh floral notes on the nose. Minty eucalyptus on a palate of amazing complexity, with high acidity and a clean finish.
£10.00 M&S

Rockbare Shiraz 2006, South Australia Red
Deep black-garnet in colour, with a vanilla nose, and some development on a smoky, dark palate.
£11.00 CHH

Rosemount Diamond Label Cabernet Sauvignon 2006, South Eastern Australia Red
Dark, vegetal nose, with lots of concentrated fruit; dry but with clean, smooth tannins and good structure.

Rosemount Diamond Label Sangiovese 2006 Red
Intense, rich flavours, with piercing acidity. A lovely food wine.

Rosemount Show Reserve Coonawarra Cabernet Sauvignon 2005, South Australia Red
Minty cassis overlaying a warm ripe fruit character. Firm tannin, which drives up the palate. Good depth of black fruit and length.

Rosemount Show Reserve McLaren Vale GSM 2004, South Australia Red
An elegant nose of plums, black fruit, and spice. Raspberry notes

combine with excellent spicy fruit on the palate.

Samuels Gorge Shiraz 2006, South Australia Red
Deep plum in colour, with a soft, sweet attack of wood and vanilla. Warm, creamy, elegant style, with low tannin and a long finish.
£20.00 VDV

Schild Estate Ben Schild Reserve Shiraz 2006, South Australia Red
Aromatic violet notes, with textured tannins, and lively acidity framing morello cherry flavours.
H&H

Schild Estate Old Bush Vine GSM 2008, South Australia Red
Redcurrant nose, which carries through to a fresh palate, with zippy fruit, and a long finish.
H&H

Shaw Vineyard Estate Winemakers Selection Cabernet Sauvignon 2008, Canberra Red
Minty green, leafy nose, which is light and clean on palate, with medium length, supported by fruit.

Shaw Vineyard Estate, Winemakers Selection Merlot 2008, Canberra Red
Minty, bright, and aromatic nose. Pure, well-balanced, and fresh on the palate, with lovely bright, berry fruit.

Shelmerdine Shiraz 2006, Victoria Red
Gamey nose, leading to a juicy palate with redcurrant and pepper nuances. Good acidity.

Shingleback Cellar Door McLaren Vale Shiraz 2007, South Australia Red
Nose of light pepper and

pleasant berry fruit. Soft tannins, with a hint of coffee on the finish.
£8.00

Shingleback D Block Mclaren Vale Cabernet Sauvignon 2006, South Australia Red
Approachable, sweet, fruited nose, with herbs, liquorice, and mulberry notes. Well-balanced but firm palate.

Shingleback McLaren Vale Cabernet Sauvignon 2006, South Australia Red
Restrained but promising herbal nose. Well-balanced, with firm, grippy tannins. Subtle black fruit, and good finish.

Shingleback Mclaren Vale Shiraz 2006, South Australia Red
Aromatic, with a floral and spiced accent, leading to an earthy, leathery palate, with soft, plummy fruit.

Shottesbrooke Eliza Reserve Shiraz 2007, South Australia Red
Fragrant, deep, savoury fruit. Well-articulated, balanced, and elegant.

Marks & Spencer Barossa Shiraz 2007, St Hallet, South Australia Red
Raspberry, chocolate, and spice on the nose. Full, dry, and spicy, with a solid, sound, and chocolatey character.
£8.00 M&S

St Hallett Gamekeepers Reserve 2007, South Australia Red
Some attractive fruit and liquorice on the nose, as on the palate, which is medium-bodied,

with medium level tannins, and good length.
£7.80 BNK, NFW, SAIN, TESC, WAIT, CWS

Stella Bella Sangiovese 2007, Western Australia Red
Dominated by red cherry, berry, and black fruit on both the nose and palate. Dry and tannic with fresh acidity.
£13.50 AAW

Tatachilla Foundation Shiraz 2004, South Australia Red
Minty, fruity nose. Very ripe and rounded on the palate, with good structure.
MWW

Terra Barossa Shiraz 2007, Thorn-Clarke Wines, South Australia Red
Spicy oak and dark fruit aromas. Chocolatey sweet, with a dry finish.
£9.00 VDV

Tesco Finest* Howcroft Estate Cabernet Sauvignon Merlot 2006, Australian Vintage Ltd, South Australia Red
Cherry and prune notes, showing some maturity and edge. Good acidity.
£7.10 TESC

Thomson Estate Antiquarian Shiraz 2006, Byrne & Smith Wines, South Australia Red
Lovely ripe blackberries, spice, and chocolate. Savoury character, with a long, fruity finish and good tannins.

Tim Adams Shiraz 2006, South Australia Red
Sweet, fruity cassis character, with juicy fresh fruit on the finish.
£10.50 TESC, AWC

Tintara Blewitt Springs Shiraz 2005, South Australia Red
Lively and dense, with a strawberry-fresh jammy nose, fresh acidity, and big tannins.

Tyrrell's Rufus Stone Heathcote Shiraz 2006, Victoria Red
Gamey, with black pepper on the nose. Juicy palate, with high acidity and bramble fruit, backed up with spicy oak.
£12.30 VDV

Victory Point Cabernet Sauvignon 2006, Western Australia Red
Pure, relaxed, and lively, with lovely, juicy, tangy blackcurrant. Showing nice evolution; a good wine.

Voyager Estate Cabernet Sauvignon Merlot 2005, Western Australia Red
Slightly closed nose, with blackcurrant and herbal notes. Initial ripe fruit on the palate, with building pepper, and good, balancing acidity.
£19.10

Waitrose Reserve Shiraz, St Hallett 2007, South Australia Red
Spicy on the nose, and very fruity on the palate, with black cherry aromas, soft, smoky tannins, and chocolate on the finish of this elegant wine.
£9.00 WAIT

Wakefield Cabernet Sauvignon 2007, South Australia Red
Dark ruby-red in colour, with attractive berry and blackcurrant fruit, some spice, and lots of tannins. Showing signs of more life ahead!
£9.50 SWS

Wakefield Jaraman Cabernet Sauvignon 2006, South Australia Red
Vibrant, herbaceous, eucalyptus character. Juicy, herbal, and liquorice on the palate. Medium-weight and earthy.
£16.00 SWS

Wakefield Merlot 2007, South Australia Red
Pleasant oaky nose, with cherries and violets. Sweet tannins, with a long rich finish. Will keep and improve.
£9.50 SWS

Wakefield Pinot Noir 2008, South Australia Red
Aromas of fresh, yet elegant strawberry fruit, which is also evident on the palate. Good balance between fruit and acidity, and a long finish.
£9.60 EDC, SWS

Wakefield St Andrews Cabernet Sauvignon 2005, South Australia Red
Ripe and fragrant nose. Very juicy and succulent palate, with red fruits, and firm tannins on the finish.
£30.00 SWS

Hedonist Shiraz 2006, Walter Clappis Wine Co, South Australia Red
Lovely Northern Rhône-esque spice and leather nose. Elegant fruit, white pepper, and silky tannins. A creamy mineral and soft spice finish.
£10.00 WAIT

Yaldara Farms Shiraz 2004, Australian Vintage Ltd, South Australia Red
Savoury leathery fruit on the nose, with a lush balance of fruit on the palate. Showing some complexity, with a warm finish.

Yarra Valley 2008, William Downie, Victoria Red
Leather, tobacco, and liquorice flavours predominate. Medium tannins lend structure, giving the wine a smooth, supple finish.
£37.00

Willowbridge Dragonfly Cabernet Merlot 2007, Western Australia Red
Fresh, herbaceous, green pepper flavours, with plums to round out the finish.
WRC

Willows Vineyard Cabernet Sauvignon 2006, South Australia Red
Pure, herbal, and floral, with sweet chocolatey notes Well balanced; a lovely wine with real finesse.
£17.00 VDV

Willunga 100 Cabernet Shiraz 2006, South Australia Red
Intense nose of blackberry, redcurrant, spicy black pepper, and vanilla oak. On the palate, there is rich red and black fruit, with supple tannins and good length.
£8.00 LIB

Willunga Creek Black Duck Shiraz 2005, South Australia Red
Lifted black fruit, with spice, elegance, and smooth pepper notes.
THO

Catapult Shiraz Viognier 2007, Wirra Wirra Vineyards, South Australia Red
Vanilla fudge nose, with a rich, ripe, silky texture, and balanced acidity.

Woodhenge Shiraz 2007, Wirra Wirra Vineyards, South Australia Red
Attractive oaky nose, with rich

fruit aromas. Juicy, creamy style; full and savoury.

Wolf Blass Grey Label Cabernet Sauvignon 2004, South Eastern Australia Red
Complex, peppery, intense, and ready to drink. Good tannins and medium structure.

Wolf Blass Presidents Selection Shiraz 2006, South Eastern Australia Red
Fruit-forward, with blackberry and cream aromas. Velvety texture and intense flavours, in a big hedonistic style.

Bissy Merlot 2006, Woodside Valley Estate, Western Australia Red
Lovely leafy nose, with herbal tones. The palate shows attractive bright leafy fruit.

Bonnefoy Shiraz 2006, Woodside Valley Estate, Western Australia Red
Oaky aromatic nose, with a touch of coffee. Good balance, with notes of spicy mocha and grilled meat.

Woody Nook Cabernet Sauvignon 2004, Western Australia Red
Fresh, clear notes of green pepper and green peas, with an intense cassis character on the palate, and a good balance of acidity. Good length.
£16.80 JAV, WNW

Wynns Coonawarra Cabernet Shiraz Merlot 2006, South Australia Red
Heady black fruit and cream aromas. Smooth and silky, with a nice note of pepper on the mid-palate.

Wynns Coonawarra Shiraz 2007, South Australia Red

Black fruit, with hints of tobacco and spice. Good concentration and structure. Pleasant finish.

Wynns John Riddoch 2003, South Australia Red
Cool, minty, red berry on the nose, l;eading to rich fruit and chocolate on the palate, and a long dry finish.
£35.00 VDV

Xanadu Cabernet Sauvignon 2007, Western Australia Red
Bright, ruby in colour, with a clean cedary nose. Savoury, with herbal fruit and dark, spicy notes. A big wine.
£11.00

Yalumba Barossa Bush Vine Grenache 2008, South Australia Red
Textbook Grenache, with a very attractive, well-made, raspberry and strawberry character, showing red fruits, white pepper, and spice. This is nicely vibrant on the palate, with good length.
£10.30 FLA, NFW, VDV

Yalumba Barossa Shiraz & Viognier 2006, South Australia Red
A real mixture of herbaceous notes with cloves and cinnamon, approachable pure blueberry fruit, and a balanced body.
£13.10 CHH, FLA, NFW, VDV

Yering Frog Pinot Noir 2008, Victoria Red
A very expressive nose of plum jam and red fruit. Smooth on the palate, with soft supple finish.
£8.00

Yering Station Pinot Noir 2008, Victoria Red
Light intensity, with subtle fruit and mild spice. Soft and easy-drinking.
£11.00

Yering Station Shiraz Viognier 2006, Victoria Red
There is a fresh, minty, herby edge to the slightly meaty, berry fruit nose. Nice fresh, bright fruit on an attractive palate.
£11.00

Zonte's Footstep Cabernet Sauvignon 2007, South Australia Red
Dark, meaty nose. Rich and full-flavoured. Slightly dry tannins.

Zonte's Footstep, Shiraz Rows 8-18 2008, South Australia Red
Violet-red in colour. Young, jammy, and rich, with powerful fruit.

Beverford Moscato Rosso 2008, Buller Wines, Victoria Rosé
Perfumed Muscat-style nose. Layered fruit flavours and good acidity. Sweet but not cloying.

Eldredge Vineyards Sangiovese Rosé 2008, South Australia Rosé
Pretty, bright pinky-red colour. Rhubarb cherry perfume, and spicy notes. Quince and rhubarb flavours. Balanced, with a lingering finish.
£9.00 AWC

Rococo NV, De Bortoli Wines Pty Ltd, Victoria Sparkling
Good clean colour, with a lemon nose. Elegant, with some custard notes, a soft attack and crisp finish.

Green Point Brut NV, Victoria Sparkling
Clean leesy nose, soft attack, and a light-medium palate. Good depth on the finish. Clean and well-made.
£14.00 FLA

Green Point Vintage Brut 2005, Victoria Sparkling
Creamy, rich and nutty nose. Good Chardonnay-based sparkling wine with a rich, creamy finish.
£15.80 FLA, MWW

House of Arras Chardonnay Pinot Noir 2002, Tasmania Sparkling
Brioche notes, turning to caramel on the palate. Fine mousse, and ready to drink now.
£7.00

Jansz Tasmania Premium Non Vintage Cuveé NV, Tasmania Sparkling
Lemon zest nose. Crunchy finesse ,with a soft tangy finish and great balance.
£11.20 FLA, VDV

Jansz Tasmania Premium Vintage Cuveé 2004, Tasmania Sparkling
Bright and clear, with toasty toffee aromas carrying through to the palate. Clean, light, and medium-sweet.
£16.40 FLA, VDV

Green Point Vintage Brut Rosé 2005, Victoria Sparkling Rosé
Very good fine and delicate mousse. Persistent bead, with a fresh pink look, pure fruit, and a long, clean finish.
MWW

Griffith Park Sparking Rose NV, South Eastern Australia Sparkling Rosé
Good fizz, with small bubbles, a delicate coral colour, and a clean, fresh nose, with some appley summer berry fruit.
£6.40 ASDA, TESC, MRN

Jacob's Creek Sparkling Rosé NV, South Eastern Australia
Sparkling Rosé
Pale pink in colour, this is decent fizz, with a bright nose and clean palate. Balanced acidity, with some fruit to soften.
£9.00 TESC, WAIT

Jansz Tasmania Premium Non Vintage Rosé NV, Tasmania
Sparkling Rosé
Delicate colour, with a lean, mineral and floral nose. Champagne-like juicy sour fruit.
£11.20 FLA, VDV

Brown Brothers Wines Dolcetto & Syrah 2008, Victoria Sweet
A nice mixture of spicy red and black berry fruit on the nose, and similarly on the palate. Very sweet, but lifted by some balancing acidity.

Brown Brothers Wines Orange Muscat & Flora 2008, Victoria
Sweet
Sweet and citrussy. Pleasant palate with good acidity, much more citrus than the typically floral Muscat character. Good and crisp.
£6.50 TESC

Noble One 2006, De Bortoli Wines Pty Ltd, New South Wales Botrytis
Nose of toast and apricots. Marmalade, jam,and sweet apricots on the palate, leading to a nice finish with good acidity.
£14.70 FHM, FLA, NFW, VDV

Yalumba Hand Picked Botrytis Viognier 2008, South Australia Botrytis
Fresh, bright, spicy nose. Waxiness and honey, on a fresh palate. Sweet, with reasonable acidity.
£14.70 FLA, NFW

Show Liqueur Muscat NV, De Bortoli Wines Pty Ltd, New South Wales
Fortified
Brown in colour. Intense nose, with some cedar aromas. Good balance and elegant finish.
£13.00 FHM

Seppeltsfield Cellar No. 9 Muscat NV, Victoria Fortified
Dark amber in colour, with a light caramel nose. Mouthfilling. Good finish, with very sweet flavours.
£12.00 FLA

Seppeltsfield Grand Muscat NV, Victoria Fortified
Dark amber in colour. Attractive nose, with some exotic wood aromas. Very long finish and good acidity.
£16.00 FLA

Buller Fine Old Tawny NV, Victoria Fortified
Toffee brittle and hazelnut nose, showing poise, lovely balance, sweet fruit, and a spicy finish.

Seppeltsfield Para Grand NV, South Australia Fortified
Pale amber in colour, with a delicate honeyed nose, and a sweet palate of marmalade, cloves, and peppercorn.
£15.90

Austria

If only the best will do, if quality is the influential factor in your choice of wine, then you need look no further than Austria. This is a country that focuses its passion and creativity on delivering individual excellence rather than brands. Vineyards prosper in the east of the country, surrounding the bountiful culture in Vienna, and extend southwards to line the borders with Hungary and Slovenia. Many grape varieties grown here are found nowhere else in the world, and all are exceptional partners for food. The number of Austrian wines judged this year shows the greatest average tally of medals in the competition, a success rate augmented by an almost twofold increase in the number of Golds awarded, compared with last year.

2009 IWC PERFORMANCE

Trophies	12
Gold	17
Silver	34
Bronze	46

Bricha 2006, Weingut Robert Grill, Thermenregion White
Bright green in colour, with hints of straw. Loads of lemony oak, but this is well supported by fruit on a rich and creamy mid-palate with lovely texture.

 AUSTRIAN WHITE TROPHY

Grauburgunder Hasel 2007, Winery Allram, Kamptal White
Greeny-gold in colour, with some mineral and spice intensity on the nose. Ginger and pepper dominate the palate, with good weight, wood and minerality.
£14.80

ST LAURENT TROPHY

St Laurent Classic 2007, Heinrich Hartl, Thermenregion Red
Clean, floral nose. Lovely palate of wild strawberry, raspberry, and pomegranate fruit, with a silky edge. Good balance and length. Very good, traditional example of its kind.
£14.50 MWD, CEE

Wachtberg 2007, Weingut Frank, Niederösterreich Red
Nose of rich forest fruit and toast. Spicy palate with black pepper, and excellent oak integration. Dry and well-balanced, with silky tannins. Beautifully made and sophisticated, showing great finesse.

 **AUSTRIAN RED TROPHY, KAMPTAL TROPHY, ZWEIGELT TROPHY**

Zweigelt Granit 2007, Weingut Kurt Angerer, Kamptal Red
Nose of pepper and liqueur cherries. Rich silky fruit. A touch of oak, with finesse and structure. Very well-balanced, with good concentration.
NYW

 **INTERNATIONAL ICEWINE TROPHY, AUSTRIAN EISWEIN TROPHY**

Eiswein Welschriesling Höchleit´n 2007, Weingut Felberjörgl, Südsteiermark Sweet
Decadently rich honey aroma, leading to an equally rich apricot palate that is, by turns, sweet and apple-like. A chewy sweetness on the finish, which is very long and luscious.

Florian's Essenz Nr. 1 Strohwein 2006, Weingut Felberjörgl, Südsteiermark Sweet
Complex nose of lemon, honey, and white flowers. Jammy, lemony flavours on the palate, leading to a piercing acidity, with a delicious finish.

 **AUSTRIAN CHARDONNAY BOTRYTIS TROPHY**

Chardonnay TBA 2005, Hans Tschida, Burgenland Botrytis
Pale straw in colour. Nose of honeyed almond, with rich apricot and peach on the palate. Good length, with a hint of minerality. A glorious wine.

Fink Chardonnay TBA 2006, Fink Hermann, Burgenland
Botrytis

Clean golden yellow colour. Ripe and jammy, with lovely balance. Tangy, with a pure, fresh, clean style. Notes of fennel, tangy honey, and apricot, with a long finish.

Fink Welschriesling TBA 2007, Fink Hermann, Burgenland
Botrytis

Pretty, gentle wine, with long legs. Lychee and mango on the nose, with a hint of toffee. Well-balanced, with ripe fruit.

Merry Widows Sämling Dessert Wine Trockenbeerenauslese 2006, Bernd Heiling (of Fam. Heiling), Burgenland Botrytis

A pretty wine, with pear fruits and hints of almond. A delicate mix of fragrances and tastes, which come together to produce a wine of elegant distinction, with evolving flavours.
£18.95, MWD, CEE

Rotgipfler 2005, Harald Zierer, Thermenregion
Botrytis

Burnished amber in colour. Digestive biscuit aromas, with a rich, honeyed palate of intense sultana, fruitcake, and roast nuts. Good acidity, and a long glorious finish. Dessert in a glass!

Wine TROPHY AUSTRIAN SWEET TROPHY, AUSTRIAN BOTRYTIS TROPHY, AUSTRIAN SAMLING BOTRYTIS TROPHY, BURGENLAND TROPHY

Sämling TBA 2005, Hans Tschida, Burgenland
Botrytis

Lime peel, tangerine, dried apricot, apple, and honey notes. Spicy and intensely sweet, with fresh acidity. A well-structured wine, with a complex, long, and persistent finish.

Sämling TBA 2006, Hans Tschida, Burgenland Botrytis

Stunning nose of crystaline grapefruit and tropical fruit. Fabulous acidity. Tingles with a great length. A wonderful wine.

Trockenbeerenauslese No.3 Zwischen Den Seen 2006, Weinlaubenhof Kracher, Burgenland Botrytis

Nose of pear and lychee, with a rose petal colour. Light, smooth palate, with heavy sweetness balanced by good acidity. Excellent!
£35.00 NYW

Trockenbeerenauslese No.7 Zwischen Den Seen 2006, Weinlaubenhof Kracher, Burgenland Botrytis

An incredibly beautiful nose. A very high class Welschriesling. Refreshing, clean acidity, and flavour characteristics of dates, figs, peaches, and dried apricots. Never-ending length.
£34.00 NYW

Trockenbeerenauslese No.8 Nouvelle Vague 2006, Weinlaubenhof Kracher, Burgenland Botrytis

Golden in colour. Clear, clean, honeyed nose, with botrytis character. A very sweet wine, with fresh honey, marmalade, and elegant fruit on the palate. Well-balanced, with a long, sweet finish.
£35.00 NYW

SILVER

Fred Loimer Riesling Seeberg 2007, Fred Loimer, Niederösterreich White

Pale straw colour. Guava and

cantaloupe on the nose. Clean fresh green apple and split pea on the palate, with a flinty steely acid finish.
£32.00 LIB

Grüner Veltliner Lauschenkreuz Kremstal Dac Reserve 2007, Wolfgang Zeileis, Kremstal White
Lifted perfumed nose, with a pungent fruit palate, showing hints of tropical fruit. Balanced and long.

Grüner Veltliner 'Nussberg' 2008, Weingut Wieninger, Vienna White
A classy wine with smoky complexity. Good weight and finish.
£14.00 NYW

Grüner Veltliner Schiefer 2008, Meinhard Forstreiter, Niederösterreich White
Elegant spicy nose. Dry palate of fruit, with a hint of smoke. Some petrol character is apparent. Finish is nutty and spicy.

Grüner Veltliner Wachau 2008, Niederösterreich White
Herbal white pepper and floral aromas. White peach palate. Good breadth of flavour, in a spicy, but soft and fruity style. Very good length.
£8.00 WAIT

Huber Riesling Traisental 2008, Weingut Markus Huber, Traisental White
Clean, pure, and varietally distinct, with a steely limey character, showing good minerality. Palate is rich and complex, with floral and lime notes.

Johannesbergen Grüner Veltliner 2008, Weingut

Frank, Niederösterreich White
Lovely nose of intense peach and honey. Fresh, savoury note on the palate. A really elegant, well-made wine.

Jurtschitsch Grüner Veltliner Dechant Alte Reben 2007, Jurtschitsch, Kamptal White
Very bright, ripe, and tropical, with peach fruit on the nose. Full-flavoured creamy peach and pineapple on the palate. Very fresh acidity and long finish.
£20.00 CSS, P&S, UNC

Merry Widows Muskat Ottonel Refreshing 2007, Bernd Heiling (of Fam. Heiling) White
Elegant floral nose. Clean and fruity, with zingy light fruit. Nicely judged and balanced, with good texture.
£9.50 MWD, CEE

Peter Schweiger Grüner Veltliner Kamptal 2008, Kamptal White
Oily, honeyed nose, with notes of asparagus. Juicy palate, with crisp acidity and a very long finish.

Riesling Heiligenstein 2007, Weingut Birgit Eichinger, Niederösterreich White
Bright, clean, and attractive, with some lemon, pears, and ripe peach on the nose. Not high in acidity, but with good weight.

Sauvignon Blanc "Alte Reben" 2008, Weingut Josef Sailer, Burgenland White
Clean firm fruit. Soft and easy, with a lovely depth of herbaceous notes and quince. Well-made, with lovely acidity and length.

TASTE **CULTURE**

AUSTRIAN WINE

Nowhere on earth are great wines
more refreshing or refreshing wines
more distinctively delicious.
www.austrianwine.com

Walter Skoff Morillon Classique 2008, Südsteiermark White
Very ripe nose of white flowers, peach, and apple blossom. Good freshness and perfect balance.

Walter Skoff Royal Sauvignon Blanc 2007, Südsteiermark White
Pale straw colour, with a light spritz. A herbaceous Sauvignon nose, with notes of grapefruit and guava. Good length, and well-balanced.

Illmitz Zweigelt 2006, Weinlaubenhof Kracher, Burgenland Red
Vibrant morello cherry and toasty oak. Lively acidity, finely built, with soft, structured tannins.
£11.00 BUT, HVN, NYW, SEL, WWN

Pinot Noir Classic - Heinrich Hartl 2007, Thermenregion Red
Restrained plum nose, with hints of earthiness. Typical Pinot Noir fruit character on the palate, underpinned with creamy oak.
£14.50 MWD, CEE

Lyss Doux Cuvée 1999, Karl Kadlec, Burgenland Sweet
Orangey, floral nose, with touches of caramel. Ripe, juicy style, with firm acidity and an elegant, floral, honeyed finish. Good length.

Muskat Ottonel Schilfwein 2006, Hans Tschida, Burgenland Sweet
Clean and grapey, with a hint of herbs on the nose. Very sweet. Good finish, with hints of orange blossom.

Schwarz 'Schwarz' 2006, Johann Schwarz, Burgenland Sweet
Strawberry nose, with some chocolatey notes. Rich, complex palate, with smoky tones and plum flavours. Good volume, fresh acidity, and a coffee note on the finish.
£39.00 NYW

Beerenauslese Cuvée 2006, Weinlaubenhof Kracher, Burgenland Botrytis
Pale straw colour. Honeyed almond on the nose, with apricot richness on the palate. Well-integrated acidity, and hints of peach kernel and apricot. Long finish.
NYW

Fink Chardonnay TBA 2007, Fink Hermann, Burgenland Botrytis
Intense honey, melon, and spice on the nose. Dense citrus fruit on the palate, with good, balancing acidity. Long finish.

Lenz Moser Prestige Trockenbeerenauslese 2006, Weinkellerei Lenz Moser Ag, Burgenland Botrytis
Hints of lemon on the nose. Intense sweetness, with notes of honey and beeswax.
FTH

Lyss Doux Muskat Ottonel Tba 1999, Karl Kadlec, Burgenland Botrytis
Intense gold in colour. Aromatic, sweet, spicy nose, leading to a rich palate, with herbal notes and a long finish.

Ruster Ausbruch Essenz 2006, Weingut Feiler-Artinger, Burgenland Botrytis
Clean, bright gold colour. Big, heavy toffee apple notes, very creamy and round, with balanced acidity, and a sweet finish.

Ruster Ausbruch Essenz Chardonnay 2006, Weingut Feiler-Artinger, Burgenland Botrytis
Varietal Chardonnay character. Honeyed, with some apricot and nuttiness. Good balance of acidity, raisin, and dried fruit on the finish.

Schloss Halbturn Grand Vin TBA 2006, Schloss Halbturn, Burgenland Botrytis
Deep lemon-gold in colour. Lovely aromatic acacia honey and peach on the nose. Beautifully luscious and creamy, with orange peel notes, and well-balanced acidity. Sweet and tantalising.
COE

Trockenbeerenauslese 2007, Höpler, Burgenland Botrytis
Botrytised flavours, and fruity aromas. Rich tropical fruit notes and acidity help balance this glorious wine.

Trockenbeerenauslese No.1 Nouvelle Vague 2006, Weinlaubenhof Kracher, Burgenland Botrytis
Orange-red colour. Clear, clean, fresh nose, this is a sweet, rich, honeyed wine. Notes of marmalade and high acidity, but well-balanced, with an elegant, medium-to-long finish.
£28.00 NYW

Trockenbeerenauslese No.10 Nouvelle Vague 2006, Weinlaubenhof Kracher, Burgenland Botrytis
Delicate roasted almonds and spices combine with peach compote and tropical fruit. Super luscious fruit.
£36.00 NYW

Trockenbeerenauslese No.12 Zwischen Den Seen 2006, Weinlaubenhof Kracher, Burgenland Botrytis
Lemon-gold colour, with honeyed concentration and complexity on the nose. Lovely acidity balances the sweetness , and the finish is long.
£40.00 NYW

Trockenbeerenauslese No.2 Zwischen Den Seen 2006, Weinlaubenhof Kracher, Burgenland Botrytis
Very rich apricot, lemon, and honey on the nose. Palate is very sweet and delicious, with a delicate finish..
£28.00 NYW

Trockenbeerenauslese No.5 Zwischen Den Seen 2006, Weinlaubenhof Kracher, Burgenland Botrytis
Vibrant, golden yellow colour, with notes of lemon, candy, and honeysuckle, and lovely acidity balancing the sweetness. 100% pure and clean.
£31.00 NYW

Trockenbeerenauslese No.6 Grande Cuvée Nouvelle Vague 2006, Weinlaubenhof Kracher, Burgenland Botrytis
Mid-straw to gold in colour. Honeyed nose, with fruit salad on the palate. Waxy, rich pineapple notes. Fresh acidity and complexity.
£34.00 NYW

Trockenbeerenauslese No.9 Zwischen Den Seen 2006, Weinlaubenhof Kracher, Burgenland Botrytis
Spankingly good Welschriesling,

with golden botrytis. Rich, ripe, and elegant. One for the long haul. Full, minerally finish,
£35.00 NYW

BRONZE

Chardonnay 2006, Harald Zierer, Thermenregion White
Creamy fruit notes, with intense honeyed nose. Good acidity and balance on the palate.

Chardonnay Steinbach 2008, Meinhardt Hube, Styria White
Bright floral aromas, with a hint of lees. Clean palate, with crisp acidity.
£10.70 HPW

Gelber Muskateller Steinbach 2008, Meinhardt Hube, Styria White
Pale in colour, with a light Muscat blush. Good acidity, with a fresh, dry mid-palate.
£10.50 HPW

Grüner Veltliner Alte Reben Oberfeld Kremstal Dac Reserve NV, Petra Unger, Kremstal White
Steely nose, with fresh cut fennel, and a subtle spicy fruit palate. Easy style.
£9.80

Grüner Veltliner Berg Vogelsang 2008, Willi Bründlmayer White
Lovely freshness and a peppery character. Good fruit and nice balance.
£13.60 WAIT, RWD

Grüner Veltliner Federspiel Terrassen 2008, Domäne Wachau, Niederösterreich White
Lemon-yellow colour. Concentrated aromatic nose of tropical fruits and pineapple.

Grüner Veltliner Federspiel Weingärten Weissenkirchen 2008, Domäne Wachau, Niederösterreich White
Lemon, pear, and honey on the nose. Lovely fresh, peachy palate. Good concentration of flavour, with balanced acidity.

Grüner Veltliner 'Gebling' 2008, Weingut Sepp Moser, Kremstal White
Nutty, with notes of pepper on the nose. Lovely wine, with good persistence and lift. No harshness. Long, refreshing finish.
£12.80

Grüner Veltliner Kremser Kogl 2008, Meinhard Forstreiter, Niederösterreich White
Pungent, unusually bold style of Grüner Veltliner. Nice acidity and good balance.

Grüner Veltliner Langenlois Terrassen 2007, Fred Loimer, Niederösterreich White
A restrained mineral nose, with a youthful mineral palate. Very fresh acidity, and a long green apple finish.
£16.00 LIB

Grüner Veltliner Loibner Reserve 2007, Weingut Johann Donabaum, Wachau White
Lovely floral nose, with hints of richness. Sweetness on the palate, with a pleasant and lengthy finish.
£21.00 NOV

Grüner Veltliner Prestige 2008, Ing. W. Baumgartner, Niederösterreich White
Lemony fruit aromas, with an elegant entry on the palate, pleasant structure, and complexity.

Grüner Veltliner Smaragd Achleiten 2008, Domäne Wachau, Niederösterreich
White
Classic Grüner Veltliner style. Nose of lifted white pepper, leading to a refreshing palate with lemony intensity.
£16.00 WAIT

Grüner Veltliner Smaragd Pichlpoint 2008, Domäne Wachau, Niederösterreich
White
Fresh, floral nose. Lemon and honey on the palate. Very balanced, with a long attractive finish.

Huber Grüner Veltliner Obere Steigen 2008, Weingut Markus Huber, Traisental White
Bright, lively aromas with clean minerality on the palate. Very balanced, with good length.

Huber Grüner Veltliner Alte Setzen 2008, Weingut Markus Huber, Traisental
White
Lively grapefruit aromas, with light, clean acidity. Soft palate and light weight. Elegant and fresh.

Huber - Riesling Engelreich 2008, Weingut Markus Huber
White
Floral nose, with hints of petal on the palate. Lovely citrus flavours, with a good acidic backbone.

Jurtschitsch Grüner Veltliner Käferberg 2007, Jurtschitsch, Kamptal White
Restrained tropical fruit nose, with mineral undertones. Fresh, clean, zingy notes, with some added acidity.
EVW

Jurtschitsch Riesling Zöbinger Heiligenstein 2007, Jurtschitsch, Kamptal White
Clean, with citrus and melon intensity, zingy acidity, and mineral undertones. Concentrated limey finish.
£17.50 EVW

Laurenz and Sophie Singing Grüner Veltliner 2008, Laurenz V., Lower Austria
White
Spicy, floral, and smooth, with a very clean, milky finish.
£9.00 BWL, FAW

Laurenz V. Friendly Grüner Veltliner 2008, Laurenz V., Lower Austria White
Mineral, aromatic, perfumed nose. Very pretty, stylish, and balanced. Showing some complexity and good length.
£10.00 BWL, FAW

Lenz Moser Prestige Pinot Gris 2008, Weinkellerei Lenz Moser Ag, Burgenland White
Elegant nose of apple musk and white flowers; rich, full, and bright, with a lingering finish.
FTH

Linea Gewürztraminer 2007, Wein Von Ploder - Rosenberg, Südsteiermark White
Very restrained. Rose water character, with considerable residual sweetness on the palate, balanced by energetic acidity.

Merry Widows Sämling 88 During Dinner 2007, Bernd Heiling (of Fam. Heiling)
White
Very good example of Sämling. Rich and intense, with a sweet finish.
£10.40 MWD, CEE

Peter Schweiger Riesling Kamptal Terrassen 2008, Kamptal White
Appley, almost creamy nose. Gentle, rounded palate.

Pinot & Co. 2008, Weingut Frank, Niederösterreich White
Clean and rich, with good varietal character. Fresh pineapple on the palate, with good acid grip.

Rabl Grüner Veltliner Kaferberg 2007, Weingut Rabl, Kamptal White
Asparagus nose, with a rich, ripe, and fruit-laden palate. Nice length.
£16.60 HOH

Riesling Ametzberg 2008, Weingut Kurt Angerer, Kamptal White
Clean, delicate nose. Crisp acidity, and good concentration of fruit, with notes of minerality.
NYW

Riesling Smaragd Achleiten 2008, Domäne Wachau White
Attractive fruity, citrussy nose. Palate is crisp, limey, and floral. Good balance and length.

Rotes Haus Am Nussberg Reserve 2008, Vwg Vienna 19, Wien White
Bright and lively, with apricot and herb aromas. Crisp, pure palate of peach and apricot. Long finish.

Sauvignon Blanc 2008, Branigg, Styria White
A clean green floral nose, with spritzy, spicy green fruits, kiwi and celery on the palate. Mouthwatering acidity and moderate length.
£12.20 HPW

Walter Skoff Sauvignon Blanc Classique 2008, Südsteiermark White
Tropical fresh fruit salad on the nose, with greengage and ripe kiwi fruit on the palate. Lovely fruity finish and soft acidity.

Weinviertel Dac 2008, Weingut Frank, Weinviertel White
Clean light colour, with a fruity palate. Good body and acidity.

Blauer Portugieser 2007, Ing. W. Baumgartner, Niederösterreich Red
Bright black cherry character, with a mineral edge and great purity. Well-balanced, gentle red wine with texture and a long, silky finish.

Blauer Zweigelt 2008, Ing.w. Baumgartner, Niederösterreich Red
Bright and youthful, with a vibrant redcurrant character. Fresh, juicy blackcurrant palate. Spicy, supple, delicate, and appealing, with fine tannins. Bright and fresh.

Lorenz 2007, Ing. W. Baumgartner, Niederösterreich Red
Vibrant redcurrant fruit. Bright and youthful, with grippy tannin and lots of acidity, but well-balanced.

Prädium 2007, Erich Scheiblhofer, Burgenland Red
Youthful, with a nose of smoke, toast, and pepper. Excellent example of a cool-climate wine.

Ried Hallebühl 2000, Weingut Umathum, Burgenland Red
Juicy fruit with lively, balanced

acidity, and corduroy tannins, plenty of oak, and a spicy finish.

Shiraz 2007, Erich Scheiblhofer, Burgenland Red
Black fruits on the nose. Palate shows oak and minty flavours, with pleasant crispness, and a long finish.

Lenz Moser Selection Zweigelt Rose 2008, Niederösterreich Rosé
Mineral quince aroma, with firm acidity, and some herbal notes on the palate. Elegant and balanced.

Sparkling Brut 2007, Schlumberger Wein-Und Sektkellerei Gmbh, Weinviertel Sparkling
Lovely fresh, sea-breezy nose. Palate of ripe fruit, with well-balanced acidity.

Lyss Doux Chardonnay TBA 1999, Karl Kadlec, Burgenland Botrytis
Amber in colour, with luscious apricot, baked pineapple, and orange zest on the nose. A powerful wine that explodes on the palate, with a finish of toasted almonds.

Lyss Doux Scheurebe TBA 1995, Karl Kadlec, Burgenland Botrytis
Deep amber in colour, with dry apricot and honey on the nose. Oxidative, elegant, and complex.

Trockenbeerenauslese No.11 Zwischen Den Seen 2006, Weinlaubenhof Kracher, Burgenland
Honey and peach candy, with lovely acidity to balance out the sweetness.
£38.00 NYW

Trockenbeerenauslese No.4 Nouvelle Vague 2006, Weinlaubenhof Kracher, Burgenland Botrytis
Pale gold colour. Nose of dark honey and peachy fruit, with tropical fruit on the palate.
£29.00 NYW

Trockenbeerenauslese Non Vintage NV, Weinlaubenhof Kracher, Burgenland Botrytis
A lovely nose; very pretty and delicate, with hints of lychees, mango, and honey. Noteable acidity, and a lovely mid-palate, with a medium length finish.
£12.00 HVN, NYW, SEL

Chile

To its advantage, Chile depicts isolation like nowhere else. Stretching 4,500 kilometres from north to south, it is surrounded by ocean, desert, mountains and Antarctica. Vineyards here have been specifically selected for the regional attributes of the surrounding environments. Beyond the local hero Carmenère, Chile continues to hit the spot with just about every international grape, and is generally regarded as a strong contender for the best-value wine on the planet. An increase in Gold, Silver and Bronze medals has made this year's triumph in the International Wine Challenge the most successful yet for some of the 350 producers throughout the country. Look out for a strong presence of Cabernet Sauvignon blends taking top prizes.

2009 IWC PERFORMANCE	
Trophies	11
Gold	21
Silver	90
Bronze	161

Veramonte Sauvignon Blanc Reserva 2008, Alto De Casablanca S.A., Casablanca Valley White

Lime and asparagus nose, with aromas of fruit salad. Silky entry on a full, well-balanced, mineral and floral palate. Good passion fruit character on a long finish.
£8.00 MCT, THS

CHILEAN WHITE TROPHY, CHILEAN SAUVIGNON BLANC TROPHY

Cono Sur 20 Barrels Limited Edition Sauvignon Blanc 2008, Casablanca Valley White

Very aromatic, pronounced nettle nose, with grapefruit, grass and green pea notes. Ripe gooseberry flavours, followed by crisp, enduring lemon and lime. Very well-balanced acidity and good weight. Very refreshing.

Errazuriz Single Vineyard Sauvignon Blanc 2008, Casablanca Valley White

Fresh, vibrant fruit aromas, with nutty notes and hints of green asparagus. Attractive balance and fresh palate, with intense fruit and herbal flavours. Well-balanced, with good acidity.
£9.00 HMA

Antu Ninquen Cabernet/ Carmenère 2007, Colchagua Valley Red

Inky colour, with vinous aromas, and notes of coffee, oriental spice, and damson. Explosion of silky tannins on the palate, with well-integrated oak, satisfying texture, and a long finish.
£10.00

Casa La Joya Cabernet Sauvignon Gran Reserve 2007, Viña Bisquertt, Rapel Valley Red

Clean, pure, elegant nose of blackberry and cassis fruit. Rich, complex, and harmonious flavours on the palate, with sensitive use of oak, smooth tannins, and lovely length.

MAULE VALLEY TROPHY

Chilcas Single Vineyard Cabernet Franc 2006, Via Wines, Maule Valley Red

Ripe, rounded, red fruit aromas. Polished, concentrated palate, with amazing flavours. Full of complexity, with firm but fine tannins, and real length and power.
£9.00 BWL

Coyam 2006, Viñedos Emiliana, Colchagua Valley Red

Attractive nose of spice, with a note of gravelly minerality. Lovely rich, dark fruit on the palate. A classy wine, with true intensity.
£14.80

CHILEAN CABERNET SAUVIGNON TROPHY

Doña Bernarda 2006, Viña Luis Felipe Edwards, Colchagua Valley Red

Ripe, with rich blackberry and well-integrated oak, and notes of mint and plum on the nose, as well as cocoa and chocolate nuances. Great balance of alcohol and tannin, with a soft, generous, impressively long finish.

Doña Dominga Gran Reserva Cabernet Sauvignon 2007, Viña Casa Silva S.A., Colchagua Valley Red

Nose of pure cassis, leading to

an elegant blackcurrant palate, balanced by good acidity and supple tannins, with well-integrated, spicy oak. Will age well.

 **INTERNATIONAL CARMENERE TROPHY**

Falernia Carmenère Reserva 2006, Viña Falernia S.A., Elqui Valley Red
Opaque wine, with a nose of damson, coconut, and curry. Smooth entry, leading to an explosion of flavour on the palate. Plummy, juicy fruit on the mid-palate, with a beautiful, long finish.
£11.00 CAM, DEF, GWW, HVN, NYW, TAN

 **ELQUI VALLEY TROPHY**

Falernia Syrah Reserva 2007, Viña Falernia S.A., Elquí Valley Red
Violet intensity, with rich, good, vigorous fruit on the nose, and a hint of leafiness. Juicy fruit on the palate, and a pleasing, long finish.
£11.00 FFT, FNW, GWW, HOF, HVN

G7 Reserva Carmenère 2008, Viña Carta Vieja S.A., Maule Valley Red
Classic Carmenère nose of leafiness and green spice. The palate shows some savoury, meaty complexity, along with great finesse and elegance . Sweet ripe fruit holds sway. Really well put-together.

La Porfia Grand Reserve Cabernet Franc 2007, Viña Y Bodega Botalcura S.A., Curicó Valley Red
Red colour, with excellent red

fruit notes, and flavours of soft fruit and green peppers, combining with leafy tobacco. Amazing texture, and incredible intensity on the palate.
£11.70

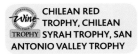 **CHILEAN RED TROPHY, CHILEAN SYRAH TROPHY, SAN ANTONIO VALLEY TROPHY**

Matetic EQ Syrah 2007, San Antonio Valley Red
Intense, dark, meaty, and minerally, with an almost pencil-lead character. Lovely spicy white pepper character, with notes of graphite, black pepper, and dark cherry. Very long, with good varietal definition.
£18.00 GNS, MWW, WSO

 **COLCHAGUA VALLEY TROPHY**

Novas Carmenère / Cabernet 2007, Viñedos Emiliana, Colchagua Valley Red
Brooding nose, with complex, ripe black fruit, vibrant bramble and cedar, with vanilla and herbaceous notes. Sweet, juicy, and powerful, with youthful, grippy tannins and gentle oak.
£7.80

Novas Winemaker's Selection Syrah / Mourvèdre 2006, Viñedos Emiliana, Colchagua Valley Red
Deeply coloured wine, with a nose of spiced vanilla, blackberry, and plum. Concentrated berries follow through on the palate, underpinned by mouthwatering acidity and good tannic grip.
£11.80

Tarapaca Gran Reserva Etiqueta Negra Cabernet Sauvignon 2007, Maipo Valley Red

Ripe blackcurrant fruit, which is well-balanced with herbaceousness. There are also notes of olive, meat, and some oak. Well-integrated tannins, and a persistent finish.
£10.00 LAI

Terra Andina Reserva Carmenère 2007 Red

Deep nose of ripe berry fruit, with lovely raspberry and chocolate, and a touch of green pepper. Balanced acidity, with soft tannins, and a long, juicy, attractive finish.

Veranda Cabernet Carmenère 2007, Viñedos Y Bodegas Corpora S.A., Central Valley Red

Notes of black and green peppercorn, with brambly fruit, and lots of toasty spice. Elegant texture and rich body, with very impressive Carmenère ripeness. A great wine, with a very long life ahead.
£18.00

 COLCHAGUA VALLEY MALBEC TROPHY

Viu Manent Malbec Single Vineyard El Olivar 2007, Colchagua Valley Red

Violets and black truffles on the nose, with hints of rich, brambly and forest fruit flavours, and a spicy finish. Deeply opulent; a beautifully well-made wine.

Marks & Spencer Secano Estate Pinot Noir Rosé 2008, Viña Leyda, Leyda Valley Rosé

Restrained perfumed nose, with attractive soft fruit aromas. Clean and fresh on the palate, showing good weight, with excellent balance and acidity, and a summer-fresh finish.
£7.50 M&S

SILVER

Amelia Chardonnay 2007, Viña Concha Y Toro S.A, Casablanca Valley White

Wonderful balance of cloves, baked apples, and raisins. Elegant oak on the palate, with good spice and coconut notes. Lovely finish.

Cono Sur Vision Riesling 2008, Bío Bío Valley White

Pale yellow in colour, with attractive aromas of intense lime and pink grapefruit. Complex, with refreshing acidity.

Errazuriz Tapihue Block Sauvignon Blanc 2008, Casablanca Valley White

Green fruit and melon on the nose, leading to a smooth palate, with balanced sweetness and acidity. Good concentration, with a vibrant finish.
£8.00 TESC, HMA

Leyda Single Vineyard Sauvignon Blanc Garuma 2008, Leyda Valley White

Highly aromatic, with a herby, grassy, gooseberry nose. Exuberant, forward palate, with real intensity, and stewed apple fruit flavours.
£9.00

Matetic EQ Coastal Sauvignon Blanc 2008, San Antonio Valley White

Bright lemon-green in colour, with zingy, fresh goosebery fruit on the nose. The palate shows fresh, clean acidity, with a creamy finish.
£9.00 GNS, MWW, SSU

Maycas Del Limarí Reserva Especial Sauvignon Blanc 2008, Limarí Valley White
Pale colour. Elegant, fresh and fruity, displaying notes of grassy greengage, with some ripe fruit and minerality. Good weight and concentration on the palate; well-balanced and crisp.

Reserva Castillo De Molina Sauvignon Blanc Elquí 2008, Viña San Pedro, Elquí Valley White
Exuberant nose, with intense lemon, gooseberry, asparagus, and green bean aromas. Crisp palate, with good acidity, and real balance.
MWW

Santa Camila, Valle Andino Reserva Especial Chardonnay 2008, Casablanca Valley White
Deep lemon-green colour. Restrained and mineral, with ripe, peachy fruit. The style is essentially subtle, with fresh acidity.

Mhv San Andrés Vino Blanco NV, Les Grands Chais De France White
Lovely floral apricot freshness, with a stylish, racy palate, with notes of tropical fruit adding interest.

Trio Chardonnay 2008, Viña Concha Y Toro S.A, Casablanca Valley White
Fresh nose, with savoury, well-knitted oak, and a concentrated, clean, polished finish, showing good acidity, minerality, and length.
£7.30 FLA

Viña Mar Reserva Sauvignon Blanc 2008, Casablanca Valley White
Intense aromas of sweet fruit and lemon zest. The palate shows a floral character, with nice acidity, and a fresh finish.
£7.00 C&B

Anakena, Anakena Ona Syrah 2007, Rapel Valley Red
Inky colour, with opulent aromas of ripe fruit and chocolate. Full-bodied, with plenty of ripe fruit, and a firm finish.
£10.00 SWS

Apaltagua Envero Gran Reserva 2007, Colchagua Valley Red
Notes of violet, thyme, oregano, nutmeg, and marmalade on the nose. The palate has a wild, savoury character, with a medium body, and good length and balance.
£7.00

Aresti Family Collection 2006, Curicó Valley Red
Sweet toasty oak, with notes of menthol, olive and black fruit on the nose. Ripe black fruit and eucalyptus notes come through on the palate. Elegant, with good length and a fine finish.

Aresti Late Harvest Gewürztraminer 2007, Curicó Valley Botrytis
Very floral nose, with notes of sweet fruit and spice. Nicely balanced sugar on silky palate, with light acidity.

Agustinos Pinot Noir Gran Reserva 2007, Bío Bío Valley Red
This wine has good, typical Pinot Noir colour, with a pronounced nose, and a palate of good fruit, with fresh acidity and a nice finish.
£10.00

The natural choice
Chile – a great place to make wine

The long, thin country running down the west coast of South America - blessed with perfect conditions for winemaking.

Wine Regions

- Elqui Valley
- Limarí Valley
- Choapa Valley
- Aconcagua Valley
- Casablanca Valley
- San Antonio Valley
- Maipo Valley
- Cachapoal Valley } Rapel Valley
- Colchagua Valley }
- Curicó Valley
- Maule Valley
- Itata Valley
- Bío Bío Valley
- Malleco Valley

WINES OF CHILE

If you want further information about Chile's wines, please contact Wines of Chile UK: info@winesofchile.org.uk
Tel: 01344 872229 www.winesofchile.org

Chile
All Ways Surprising

Caliterra Estate Grown Merlot 2008, Colchagua Valley Red

Blue-toned, youthful colour. The nose is sweet, heady, and clean, with notes of blackcurrant cream and spice. Quite chewy, with a good weight of ripe fruit, balanced by good structure and length.
£7.00 HMA, MWW

Caliterra Reserva Merlot Estate Grown 2008, Colchagua Valley Red

Deep colour, with interesting leafy notes on the palate. Smoky black fruit character, with some cream and spice. Firm muscular style; this is a serious wine, with some juicy acidity, balanced by rich, ripe black fruit.
£7.00 HMA

Caliterra Tributo Edición Limitada Carmenère / Malbec 2006, Colchagua Valley Red

Leafy nose, with notes of blackcurrants and loganberry, combining with vanilla oak. Masculine tannins wrap around the bright red fruits, supported by balanced acidity.
£13.00 HMA

Caliterra Tributo Shiraz 2007, Colchagua Valley Red

Raspberry and loganberry nose, with earthiness, and layers of vanilla oak. Balanced and stylish, with good grip and length.
£9.00 HMA

Canepa Finísimo Cabernet Sauvignon 2007, Colchagua Valley Red

Spicy plum and prune on the nose, with a concentrated palate of attractive black fruit and cinnamon, leading to a long clean finish.

Carmenère Reserva Privada Ochotierras 2008, Limarí Valley Red

Ripe black cherry nose. Full-on and complete. Soft in the mouth, with an elegant, complex mid-palate of black cherry, leading to a sweet finish.

Carmen Winemaker's Reserve Red 2005 Red

Deep ruby colour. Typical Chilean style. The attack is simple, soft, and clean, leading into a medium-light body, with a slightly dry finish.

Carta Vieja, Tierra Merlot 2008, Colchagua Valley Red

Purple edged hue. Lean and supple, with good juicy fruit. A positive style, showing harmonious oak, fine Carmenère varietal character, and a mid-length finish.
£5.80

Casablanca Nimbus Merlot 2007, Casablanca Valley Red

Deep in colour, with rich, dense fruit, and restrained herbal cedar oak. Soft palate, with integrated tannins, showing good balance, complexity, and a long finish – an elegant wine.

Casa Rivas Gran Reserva Carmenère 2007, Maipo Valley Red

Vibrant nose of dark fruits and cinnamon spice, leading to a blackcurrant palate, which shows fine structure and balanced acidity, hinting at good ageing potential.
£9.00 ADN

Casa Silva Los Lingues Gran Reserva Carmenère 2007, Colchagua Valley Red

Slightly lifted, bubblegum character on the nose, with a sweet, ripe attack, and a bitter chocolate finish.

Casa Silva Reserva Carmenère 2008, Colchagua Valley Red
Terrific berry fruit and creamy oak on the nose. A well-made wine, with good balance and fine tannins.

Casa Lapostolle, Cuvée Alexandre Cabernet Sauvignon 2006, Colchagua Valley Red
Wonderful, full, balanced nose, with a hint of acacia and orange blossom, combined with a blend of mint, red fruit, and integrated oak. Lovely long finish. New World meets Old World.
£12.00 BWC, EVW, TVY, WNN

Casa Lapostolle, Cuvée Alexandre Syrah 2006, Cachapoal Valley Red
Serious restrained nose of plum, blackcurrant, and mulberry fruit, with good tannic grip. Long, balanced finish. Very good.
£20.00 BWC, MWW, SEL

Cono Sur 20 Barrels Limited Edition Merlot 2007, Colchagua Valley Red
Nose of cedar and cassis, with integrated oak. Ripe fruit, good fresh acidity, and ripe tannins on the palate. There is some alcohol heat, with fresh acidity, and leafy notes.

Cono Sur 20 Barrels Limited Edition Pinot Noir 2007, Casablanca Valley Red
An intense nose of red fruit, with a lovely palate of crushed redcurrant, raspberry, and plum. Slightly earthy mouthfeel, with a fresh alluring finish.

Cono Sur Reserva Merlot 2007, Colchagua Valley Red
Elegant fruit on the nose, with soft, round, elegant fruit on the palate, leading to a clean, long finish. A fine wine.

De Martino 347 Vineyards Cabernet Sauvignon 2007 Red
Rich, juicy menthol and cassis on the nose, with a slight green, leafy edge. Nice underlying hints of leather and spice. Nice tannins and long finish; an elegant wine. VGN

Errazuriz Kai 2006, Aconcagua Valley Red
Floral and peppery, with intense black fruit aromas. Smooth palate of ripe black cherries, with well-integrated oak.
£30.00 HMA

Errazuriz Max Reserva Cabernet Sauvignon 2007, Aconcagua Valley Red
Gentle, soft, and subtle, with a caramel and oak edge, and pure currant on the palate. Fine grip, with bracing acidity. Elegant and long lasting.
£11.00 HMA

Errazuriz Max Reserva Merlot 2007, Aconcagua Valley Red
Ripe black fruits, with vanilla oak on the palate. Fresh, moderately assertive tannins, with good flavour concentration. Balanced, with great length of spice and black fruit.
£11.00 HMA

Falernia Carmenère Syrah Reserva 2006, Elquí Valley Red
Deep and brooding, showing a typical Syrah leathery character, with a sweet edge. Ripe, fresh, sweet fruit, with good acidity to drive it through.
£8.30 CAM, FNW, GWW, TAN

Gran Reserva Korta 2007, Maule Valley Red
Sweet vanilla oak on a backdrop of black spice and berry fruit.

Very well-made and powerful; a bit of a bruiser. Intense, concentrated, and very long.

Henríquez Hermanos Ltda, Aromo Barrel Selection 2007, Maule Valley Red

Sweetly creamy fruit on the nose, leading to a clean, elegant palate of soft fruit, with a very pleasant mouthfeel. A very well-made wine.

Indomita Zardoz 2007, Maipo Valley Red

Elegant, complex nose, with oak, violets, spice, and blackcurrant. High acidity, with a good backbone of fruit, and a tannic finish.

James Maxwell, Barrica Petit Verdot 2007, Rapel Valley Red

Plummy fruit on the nose, leading to peppery chocolate and mineral notes on the palate. Lovely, fine, long finish, with balanced tannins.

Korta Barrel Selection Cabernet Sauvignon 2007, Maule Valley Red

Pure blackcurrant andblueberry nose. Palate of rich, dense black fruit, with creamy mocha oak, showing pure, refined balance. Restrained and extremely elegant. Delicious.

Korta Barrel Selection Carmenère 2007, Maule Valley Red

Intense, rich bramble, spice, and oak on the nose. Sweet coffee oak comes to the fore on the palate. Very spicy, with plenty of black fruit.

Lagar De Bezana Winery, Limited Edition Syrah 2007, Cachapoal Valley Red

Rich, inviting fruity nose, with

floral and oaky tones, and lovely plummy fruit with a good savoury character. Stylish wine, with a long, spicy finish.

Les Domaines Barons De Rothschild (Lafite), Los Vascos Grande Réserve 2007, Curicó Valley Red

Rich body, with chewy plums wrapped in peppery flavours, culminating in a creamy, lingering finish of pepper and plummy fruit. Extremely well-balanced and integrated.
£15.00 L&W

Lot 21 Pinot Noir 2007, Leyda Valley Red

Really classy aromas of violet and black fruit. Lovely sweet fruit flavours, with balanced acidity.
£17.00

Mayu Syrah Reserva 2007, Elquí Valley Red

Deep damson red in colour, with a meaty, savoury nose. Rich fruitcake, and hints of spice on the palate, leading to a long finish. A wine with good appeal.
£9.50 CAM, DEF, GWW, HVN, NYW, TAN

Maycas Del Limarí Reserva Especial Syrah 2006, Limarí Valley Red

Concentrated black fruit, with notes of chocolate and spice.Well-structured, with good length.

Millaman Limited Reserve Barrel-Aged Malbec 2005, Curicó Valley Red

Big sweet violets on the nose, and a palate of dark chocolate and dark fruit, with velvety tannins, and a smoky finish.

Millaman Limited Reserve Zinfandel 2007, Maipo Valley Red

Perfumed ripe fruit and

strawberry jam nose, with a rich palate of ripe fruit, and powerful, well-balanced tannins.

Misiones De Rengo Reserva Cabernet Sauvignon/Syrah 2007, Rapel Valley **Red**
Cigar and tobacco leaf notes, with buttery undertones. Full and ripe, with rich black fruit and oak spice balanced over a fine tannic scaffold.
£7.00 EHL

Montgras Reserva Cabernet/ Syrah 2008, Colchagua Valley Red
Powerful nose of milk chocolate oak over notes of cassis. Soft, broad base of tannins, with a crisp crunch of black fruit and spice.
£8.00 WAIT

Montgras Reserva Merlot 2008, Colchagua Valley **Red**
Really good, plummy fruit, with satisfyingly ripe tannins, and integrated oak. Good balance and concentration.
£7.80 ASDA, EDC

Morandé Edición Limitada Cabernet Franc 2007, Maipo Valley **Red**
Balanced nose of herbs and flowers. Creamy texture, with supple tannin and good freshness.
LAY

Morandé Reserva Carmenère 2006, Maipo Valley **Red**
Purple in colour, with a nose of young berries, and an intense, sweet palate, showing good potential for ageing.
LAY

Orzada Syrah 2006, Odfjell Vineyards, Maipo Valley **Red**
Ripe, sweet, and chocolatey, with notes of vanilla and cassis,

showing some leafy freshness and a smoky oak nose. Big and chunky, with ripe black fruit and dark chocolate, freshened by eucalyptus nuances.
£10.30 AAW

Palo Alto Reserva Cabernet Sauvignon Syrah 2008, Maipo Valley **Red**
Lovely nose; very balanced and fresh - typically Chilean in style. Palate of cassis and creamy fruit, with hints of smoke.

Pérez Cruz Carmenère Reserva Limited Edition 2007, Maipo Valley **Red**
Subtle nose of plums, with a hint of spice. Refreshing acidity and balanced tannins. Plums, liquorice, cedar, and tar predominate on the palate.
£11.00 MWW

Santa Alicia Carmenère Gran Reserva De Los Andes 2005, Maipo Valley **Red**
Ruby in colour, notes of blackberry, spice, and tomato leaf, showing characteristic Carmenère tannin. Good potential for ageing.
MYL

Santa Alicia Merlot Gran Reserva De Los Andes 2005, Maipo Valley **Red**
Deep brick red in colour. Hot spice, with hints of tobacco and chocolate, and good mature fruit. A gutsy wine with layers of fruit.
MYL

Santa Rita Floresta Apalta Cabernet Sauvignon 2005 Red
Nice smoky nose, leading to a smooth palate showing balanced fruit, menthol, and cinnamon. High acidity, with balanced tannins.

Santa Rita Medalla Real Cabernet Sauvignon 2006 Red
Very clean nose. Thick, full body, with ripe tannins and a very long finish.

Santa Rita Medalla Real Carmenère 2007 Red
Spicy smoke and tobacco aromas, and a palate of chocolate and ripe fruit, with grippy tannins, and a long finish.

Santa Rita Reserva Carmenère 2007 Red
Sweet, dark fruit character, with black cherry and spice, and a tinge of greenness, with elegant, grippy tannins on the finish.

Tabalí Encantado Reserva Syrah 2007, Limarí Valley Red
Cherry and spice and all things nice! Ripe, floral, aromatic fruit, with hints of coffee. Good depth and length.
£10.00 WAIT

Tamaya Syrah Reserve 2007, Coquimbo Red
Dense, opaque purple-red in colour. Nose of plum, leather, and spice, and a savoury palate with notes of liquorice, and velvety tannins.

Terranoble Gran Reserva Cabernet Sauvignon 2006, Colchagua Valley Red
Hints of ripasso on the nose. Integrated through the mid-palate, with hints of cherry and black chocolate, finishing on a note of dried apricots. Balanced acidity.
£8.00 PIM

Terranoble Reserva Pinot Noir 2008, Casablanca Valley Red
Savoury, peppery nose, with some perfumed raspberry character. Red berry and oak on the palate, with high acidity, nice balance, and a clean,medium-length finish.
£9.00 PIM

Terrunyo Carmenère 2006, Rapel Valley Red
Summer fruit and herbs on the nose, opening up nicely on the palate, with sweet, luscious and minty flavours.
£12.00 FLA

Terrunyo Syrah 2006, Central Valley Red
Good fruit, with a nose of aromatic bay leaf, black pepper, and sun-baked raspberries. Clean, focused, and harmonious.
£12.00 FLA

Trio Merlot 2007, Viña Concha Y Toro S.A., Central Valley Red
Ruby in colour. Medium-bodied, with lifted perfume, and flavours of plums, peppers, and violets. Soft tannins, and a plummy, spicy character, which follows through to the finish..
£7.30 FLA

Valdivieso Merlot Reserva 2007, Central Valley Red
Deep purple core, with a nose of spicy bramble and loganberry. Nice, soft tannins, with bramble and blackcurrant fruit, and a spicy smoky finish.

Valdivieso Single Vineyard Malbec 2007, Central Valley Red
Nice oaky character, with red berry fruit, and notes of coffee, chocolate and mint on the palate. Juicy ripe tannins, with a chocolatey finish.

Valdivieso Single Vineyard Merlot 2007, Central Valley Red
Deep ruby in colour. Soft attack,

with a palate of attractive fruit, with tannins on the finish. Rich and concentrated, yet elegant.

Valle Andino Gran Reserva Cabernet Sauvignon 2006, Colchagua Valley Red
Deep colour, with a fruity nose of pepper and blackberry. Easy palate, with a smooth, fruity finish, showing incredible intensity of flavour.

Valle Andino Gran Reserva Carmenère 2007, Maule Valley Red
Deep ruby in colour, with a nose of intense cedar and pencil lead, with restrained, elegant black cherry. Soft attack, with balanced fruit and oak, and a clean, medium-length finish.

Veranda Pinot Noir Oda 2007, Viñedos Y Bodegas Corpora S.A., Bío Bío Valley Red
This wine has a lovely ruby colour, with a typical Pinot Noir nose of bramble fruit, which continues onto the palate, leading to a finish of nice length.

Veranda Syrah 2007, Viñedos Y Bodegas Corpora S.A., Central Valley Red
Vibrant nose of bright red fruit, and a very well-balanced, fresh, silky palate, showing lots of bright fruit, with a mild tannic bite on the finish.
£18.00

Viña Los Boldos, Momentos De Chile Merlot 2007, Maipo Valley Red
Deep cherry colour, with mature fruit on the nose, and berries on the palate. Soft, integrated tannins come through on the finish, which is long, and very stylish.

Viña Los Boldos, Sensaciones Reserva Cabernet Sauvignon 2007, Maipo Valley Red
Restrained red berries, with ripe fruit and spice. Nicely balanced, ripe, soft tannins, with a smooth texture and warming finish.

Viña Luis Felipe Edwards, Cabernet Sauvignon Family Selection Gran Reserva 2007, Colchagua Valley Red
Nose of blackcurrants with just a touch of mint. Black fruit and brambles on the palate, with toasty oak and a lingering finish.

Viña Luis Felipe Edwards Carmenere Family Selection Gran Reserva 2007, Colchagua Valley Red
Leafy, smoky nose. Cooling fruit with a herbal edge on the palate. Good depth and length, with balanced alcohol.

Viña Maipo Limited Edition Syrah 2006, Maipo Valley Red
Old style Syrah nose; a touch of brett, with creamy cassis jam. Soft, with lovely length, and really delicious character.

Viña Ochotierras, Syrah Reserva Ochotierras 2008, Limarí Valley Red
Delicate spice, with some white peppery Syrah character, and chocolatey notes on the nose. Medium-weight palate of black fruit, with vanilla and fresh pepper.

Viña San Pedro, 1865 Single Vineyard Carmenère 2007, Maule Valley Red
Leafy cedar and spice on the nose, with a woody, oaky edge. Good fine grip on the full, rich palate.

Viña San Pedro, 1865 Single Vineyard Syrah 2007, Cachapoal Valley Red
Violet hue, with a good,

satisfying, fruity nose. Lovely, plummy fruit on the palate, with good acidity and fantastic length. Stylish wine.
RVL

Viu Manent Cabernet Sauvignon Single Vineyard 2007, Colchagua Valley Red
Soft, round palate of cassis, with good acidity, fleshy fruit, and spicy herbs, leading to a long finish.

BRONZE

Agustinos, Chardonnay Reserva 2008, Bío Bío Valley White
The nose is fresh, with toasty oak and sweet fruit. Fresh, zesty palate, with nutty oak and pineapple fruit.
£7.50 HOH

Agustinos Chardonnay Reserva 2008, Viñedos Y Bodegas Corpora S.A., Bío Bío Valley White
Pale straw-green hue, with well-balanced oak character on a slightly oily, silky palate, which leads to a long, crisp, lemon-fruity finish.
£7.00

Agustinos, Gewurztraminer Reserva 2007 White
Lean and lemony. Quite high in acidity, with medium-sweetness. Grapefruity, with minerality, and elderflower fragrance.
£7.50 HOH

Amaral Chardonnay 2007, Leyda Valley White
The nose is yeasty, with greengage and wet stone minerality. Stewed herb palate, with bright acidity, and a touch of honeyed sweetness.
£9.00

Apaltagua Chardonnay Reserva 2008, Casablanca Valley White
Ripe nose showing floral notes, and a touch of clean honey, with a little bit of confection. Sweet palate, with fresh acidity on the finish.

Asda Extra Special Sauvignon Blanc 2008, Viña Errazuriz, Casablanca Valley White
Orange and tropical fruit on the nose. Fresh, creamy palate with sweet fruit, and medium intensity on finish.

Caliterra Tributo Sauvignon Blanc 2008, Casablanca Valley White
Pale straw colour, with intense aromas of citrus zest and grapefruit. Soft, sweet attack, and a touch of asparagus. Restrained and balanced.
£9.00 HMA

Casa Silva Gran Reserva Lolol Viognier 2008, Colchagua Valley White
Pale straw appearance, with light peach and apple fruit flavours, on a wine which is straightforward, but well-made.

Casillero Del Diablo Pinot Grigio 2008, Viña Concha Y Toro S.A, Casablanca Valley White
Pale, clean, and fresh. Notes of fragrant pear, with balanced almonds. A great example of this variety.

Casillero Del Diablo Sauvignon Blanc Casablanca 2008, Viña Concha Y Toro S.A, Casablanca Valley White
Restrained nose of fresh, pure citrus. Good balance of acidity and fruit.
£6.70 FLA, TESC

Cono Sur 20 Barrels Limited Edition Chardonnay 2007, Casablanca Valley White
Lovely, strident citrus and vanilla nose, showing a terrific balance of warm fruit and marzipan, with an intense finish.

Cono Sur Reserva Chardonnay 2008, Casablanca Valley White
Creamy, lemony aromas. A touch of sweetness, with big flavours of ripe peach, balanced by crisp acidity. Attractive.

Cono Sur Reserva Riesling 2008, Bío Bío Valley White
Pale yellow in colour, with a restrained citrus nose. Refreshing in the mouth, with good balance.
£8.10 TESC

Cono Sur Reserva Sauvignon Blanc 2008, Casablanca Valley White
Creamy, ripe fruit nose. Gentle, ripe gooseberry, rhubarb, and lemon flavours, with a long, fruity finish.

Cono Sur Reserva Viognier 2008, Colchagua Valley White
Well-balanced, soft, and light, with gentle apple and peach fruit, plenty of acidity, and a crisp finish.
£8.10 TESC

Cono Sur Vision Chardonnay 2008, Casablanca Valley White
Fresh, clean, lightly nutty nose, with a bright, sweet fruit palate, ending on a slightly sweet note.

Cono Sur Vision Sauvignon Blanc 2008, Casablanca Valley White
Gentle fresh green fruit nose, with soft, ripe greengage and citrus. Long, fruity finish.

Cono Sur Vision Viognier 2008, Colchagua Valley White
Clean, citrus fruit flavours on a fresh, well-balanced palate.

De Martino Legado Chardonnay 2007 White
Decent nose with oak, tropical fruit, melon, and apple. The palate is quite rich, with full, good fruit, and a medium finish.
BWC

Doña Dominga Reserva Sauvignon Blanc Viognier 2008, Viña Casa Silva S.A., Colchagua Valley White
The nose is full of pink grapefruit and zest. The palate is just dry, and zesty, with notes of spice, and good length.

Errazuriz Max Reserva Chardonnay 2007, Casablanca Valley White
Broad tropical aromas, with a gentle mouthfeel, and good acidity. Clean finish.
£9.50 HMA

Gracia Sauvignon Blanc Luminoso Reserva 2008, Viñedos Y Bodegas Corpora S.A., Bío Bío Valley White
Delicate, attractive green plum aromas. A tea-like character, with some refreshing green fruit, combined with notes of honeydew melon.
£6.50

Gran Tarapaca Viognier 2008, Maipo Valley White
Crisp, clean, and pale and straw-like in appearance. Floral aromas, with a gentle citrus note, and crisp acidity carrying a long finish.
£8.00 LAI

Leyda Single Vineyard Chardonnay Falaris Hill 2008, Leyda Valley White
Creamy peach and apricot, in a lovely gentle relaxed style. Finish is fresh and tangy, with a hint of vanilla.
£9.00

Leyda Single Vineyard Riesling Neblina 2008, Leyda Valley White
Light yellow in colour, with mineral aromas, and a tinge of oiliness on the palate. Fresh, round, and elegant, with ripe tropical fruit and a medium-length finish.
£9.00

Leyda Single Vineyard Sauvignon Gris Kadun 2008, Leyda Valley White
Lively, lifted aromas and flavours. A plump, rich, unoaked style.
£9.00

Lidl Chilean Pedro Jiménez 2008, Coquimbo White
Nose of delicate tropical fruit, with a perfume of fragrant spice. Nice acidity and balance.
£4.00 LDL

Marks & Spencer PX - Elquí 2008, Viña Falernia, Elquí Valley White
Floral perfume on the nose, with pungent tropical fruit and peach on the palate.
£5.00 M&S

Matetic EQ Chardonnay 2007, San Antonio Valley White
Smoky oak combines with ripe apple fruit notes. Lively acidity, and a leesy texture, with excellent balance.
£13.00 GNS

Maycas Del Limarí Reserva Chardonnay 2007, Limarí Valley White
Attractive green apple fruit, with

La Porfia Sauvignon Blanc 2008, Viña Y Bodega Botalcura S.A., Casablanca Valley White
Gooseberries, lychees, and tropical fruit on the nose. Smooth palate, with silky texture and balanced acidity.

Leyda Lot 5 Chardonnay 2007, Leyda Valley White
Dry and clean, with elegant fruity flavours. Good balance of acidity, fruit, and oak. Elegant finish.
£14.00

Leyda Secano Sauvignon Blanc 2008, Leyda Valley White
Soft nose, with hints of pear and apple. Elegant, clean palate, with soft acidity and apple freshness, and a decent length finish.
£7.00

Leyda Secano Sauvignon Gris 2008, Leyda Valley White
Flinty, mineral, dry, and quite rich. Plump, plush palate, with rhubarb tones. A well-balanced, friendly wine.
£7.00

tropical nuances, with toasty oak, fresh acidity, and lovely length.

Maycas Del Limarí Reserva Especial Chardonnay 2007, Limarí Valley White
Lovely apple fruit and creamy oak on the nose. Vibrant melon and passion fruit palate, with hints of spice, and a leesy texture.

Novas Winemaker's Selection Chardonnay / Viognier / Marsanne 2007, Viñedos Emiliana, Casablanca Valley White
Powerful exotic, tropical fruit aromas, with a toasty oak overlay. Rich fruit palate, with crisp acidity and a creamy finish.
£9.80

Santa Alicia Reserva Chardonnay Espíritu De Los Andes 2008, Maipo Valley White
Tropical fruit with banana and orange on the nose. Medium body.
MYL

Santa Carolina Reserva De Familia Chardonnay 2007, James Maxwell, Casablanca Valley White
Smoky yellow plum nose, leading to a leesy palate with lemon acidity, and a spicy finish.

Santa Rita Floresta Sauvignon Blanc 2008 White
A fragrant and tropical fruit-laden nose leads onto a crisp palate, with a long finish.

Santa Rita Medalla Real Sauvignon Blanc 2008 White
Aromas are strong, floral, fruity, and fresh, with clean green fruit and good, refreshing acidity on the palate.

Somerfield Cabalito Reserve Chardonnay 2008, Emiliana Vineyards, Casablanca Valley White
Nutty pineapple and sweet lemon nose, with a full, ripe, fruity palate, leading to a clean finish.
£5.00 SMF

Tabalí Encantado Reserva Chardonnay 2007, Limarí Valley White
Rich, balanced, and subtly toasty, with a nice clean, nutty finish.
£9.00 WAIT

Tabalí Reserva Sauvignon Blanc 2008, Limarí Valley White
Dusty, with ripe lemon and a juicy attack. Clean acidity, and a long finish, showing good potential.
£8.00 PBA

Tamaya Chardonnay Reserve 2007, Coquimbo White
Banana and apricot aromas, leading to a very fruity, smooth, rounded palate, with a long finish.

Terrunyo Sauvignon Blanc 2008, Viña Concha Y Toro S.A., Casablanca Valley White
Green fruit and herbaceous notes on the nose, leading to a crisp, fresh, clean, and fruity palate.
£11.00 FLA

Tesco Finest* Los Nogales Sauvignon Blanc 2008, Montes S.A., Leyda Valley White
Assertive grassy, green pepper nose, leading to a rounded palate, which shows attractive fruit.
£7.60 TESC

Tarapaca Terroir La Isla 2008, Leyda Valley White
Aromatic, herby nose, with nice minerality on the palate. Quite

juicy, with fresh apple character and good length.
£7.00 LAI

Valdivieso Sauvignon Blanc Reserva 2008, Central Valley
White

Bright citrus nose, leading to a zingy lemon-cream mid-palate, showing good balance, and a soft, creamy finish.

Viña Casas Del Bosque Sauvignon Blanc Gran Reserva 2008, Casablanca Valley White

Lime and passion fruit on the nose, with some grass and inerality. The palate is crisp, with grapefruit acidity carrying a long finish.
£9.00

Viña Casas Del Bosque Sauvignon Blanc Reserva 2008, Casablanca Valley White

Soft and ripe, with light lemon fruit, and very good acidity. Showing refreshing notes, with good elegance and balance.
£7.00

Viña San Esteban, In Situ Winemaker's Selection Chardonnay 2008, Aconcagua Valley White

Fresh, waxy, melony, nutty nose, leading to a big, ripe, hot palate, which shows slight sweetness, yet is still fresh.
£8.00 DFW, OWC

Viña Undurraga, T.H. Sauvignon Blanc Lo Abarca 2008, San Antonio Valley
White

Very refreshing and spritzy, with citrus and grapefruit on a crisp, well-balanced palate.

Yali National Reserve Chardonnay 2008, Viña Ventisquero White

Lively, fruity nose with lemony

freshness. The palate is rounded, fruity, and a bit nutty.
PLB

Agustinos Carmenère Reserva 2007, Rapel Valley Red

Chewy nose of light vanilla, leading to a peppery palate, with chunky tannins, and a chocolatey finish.
£8.50 HOH

Aluvion - Gran Reserva 2006, Lagar De Bezana Winery, Cachapoal Valley Red

Clean, pronounced nose with notes of violet and youthful fruit. Spicy and well-balanced, with a good finish.

Anakena Ona Pinot Noir 2008, Casablanca Valley Red

Light coloured, with slightly lifted bright fruit. Soft, approachable tannins.
£10.00 SWS

Antu Ninquen Syrah 2007, Colchagua Valley Red

Notes of black fruit and spice, with a savoury character. High tannins balance with ripe flavours.
£10.00 HAR

Annuela Merlot By Caliterra 2008, Colchagua Valley Red

Fresh fruit, with a slightly oily character. Aromas of chocolate, coffee, figs, red berry, and raspberry, which follow through onto a palate which is fresh fresh, spicy, peppery, mineral, fruity, and dry.
£7.00 HMA

Apaltagua Carmenère Reserva 2007, Colchagua Valley Red

Very fruity aromas, characteristic of the varietal. Chewy and juicy, with ripe, clean tannins.
£5.00

Aresti Reserva Malbec 2006, Curicó Valley Red
Great fresh nose of red fruits and well-balanced oak. Soft tannins.

Aromo Reserva Privada Cabernet Sauvignon 2007, Henríquez Hermanos Ltda, Maule Valley Red
Bright, charming cherry and black fruit on the nose. Elegant palate, with tasty fruit tannins.

Agustinos Cabernet Sauvignon Gran Reserva 2007, Viñedos Y Bodegas Corpora S.A., Aconcagua Valley Red
Nose of green pepper and coffee beans, with a touch of eucalyptus. The palate shows a nice mix of sweet fruit and green pepper, with good tannins and a long finish.
£10.00

Agustinos Malbec Gran Reserva 2007, Viñedos Y Bodegas Corpora S.A., Bío Bío Valley Red
Intense dark raspberry nose, with notes of spice and vanilla. Smooth tannins and good balance.
£10.00

Agustinos Syrah Gran Reserva 2007, Viñedos Y Bodegas Corpora S.A., Aconcagua Valley Red
Balsamic notes at the start, with a nice bouquet of juicy fruits. Refreshing and very long.
£11.00

Caliterra Tributo Carmenère 2007, Colchagua Valley Red
Blackcurrant nose. Notes of bitter chocolate on the palate, with softish tannins. Juicy, with good depth of flavour.
£9.00 HMA

Canepa Magnificum Cabernet Sauvignon 2006, Maipo Valley Red
Deep in colour. With a nose of ripe sweet cassis and chocolatey oak, and a full palate of dense ripe fruit, with lots of oak and tannin.

Cantaluna Cabernet Sauvignon Reserva 2006, Colchagua Valley Red
Medium ruby in colour. Powerful minty aromas, with some nutmeg on the palate. Generous cherry and blueberry fruit. Easy-drinking with a long finish.
£8.50 PAT

Carmen Winemaker's Reserve Syrah 2006 Red
Attractive perfumed nose of ripe intense fruits. Rich, chewy structure, with fresh, balanced acidity.

Carmen Nativa Cabernet Sauvignon 2006 Red
Lovely, ripe cassis nose. Palate shows freshness and very good balance, with smooth oak, and nice ripe tannins.

Casa Lapostolle Cuvée Alexandre Merlot 2006, Colchagua Valley Red
Dark as night, with notes of liquorice, spice, and slightly burnt fruit. Good acidity; will develop nicely.
£15.00 BWC, DBY, HVN, MWW

Casa Silva Lolol Gran Reserva Shiraz 2007, Colchagua Valley Red
Lifted red and black fruit flavours, with some hints of white pepper, and oaky nuances.
JKN

Casa Silva Quinta Generación Tinto 2007, Colchagua Valley Red
Blackcurrant pastille nose, with

a palate of simple blackcurrant fruit and slight toastiness, with hallmark acidity.

Casillero Del Diablo Reserva Privada Cabernet Sauvignon Syrah 2006, Viña Concha Y Toro S.A., Maipo Valley Red
Deep in colour, with an oaky nose, and dark blackcurrant fruit. Simple but enjoyable.

Chocalán Reserva Cabernet Franc 2006, Maipo Valley Red
A little oak and hints of ripe blueberry, with chocolatey notes, and a cedary finish.
£13.00

Cono Sur, Marks & Spencer Soleado Merlot 2008, Central Valley Red
Lush damsons and plums, with dry savoury tannins, crisp acidity, and good length.
£4.30 M&S

Cono Sur 20 Barrels Limited Edition Cabernet Sauvignon 2007, Maipo Valley Red
Attractive blackcurranty fruit, with some cherry and plum notes.

Cono Sur Ocio Pinot Noir 2007, Casablanca Valley Red
Attractive balanced red berry fruit on the nose. Good lively fresh fruit palate, with lavish tannins.

Cono Sur Orgánico Cabernet Sauvignon - Carmenère 2008, Colchagua Valley Red
The nose has vibrant berry fruit, and some floral and herbal notes. The palate has vanilla, plums, fresh acidity, and medium length.
£7.10 TESC

Cono Sur Reserva Cabernet Sauvignon 2007, Maipo Valley Red
Ripe cassis fruit on the nose,

with almond, cassis, prune and plum on the palate. Nice use of oak.

Cono Sur Vision Carmenère 2007, Rapel Valley Red
Carmenère nose, showing black fruit and a touch of brett. Balanced and long; good quality, with a creamy texture.

Cono Sur Vision Syrah 2007, Colchagua Valley Red
Youthful nose of concentrated juicy fruit, with good complexity. Good balance of acidity and tannin, with a powerful finish.

Co-op Premium Pinot Noir 2008, Viña Santa Helena, Casablanca Valley Red
Perfumed lilies on the nose, and a palate of sweet, ripe fruit, with soft tannins, leading to a peppery finish.
£8.00 CWS

Cousino Macul Antiguas Reservas Cabernet Sauvignon 2006, Maipo Valley Red
Ripe, dark fruit on the nose. Dry, blackberry characteristics on the palate. Good acidity, structure, and length.
£8.60 WAIT, BEN, CAM, CAS, CPW, TAN, TAU

De Martino Legado Carmenère 2007 Red
Deep purple in colour, with a mild, jammy character. Showing black fruit on the palate, with a supple finish.
£10.70 FLA

De Martino Legado Syrah 2007 Red
Slightly reduced nose, giving a Camp Coffee character, with a palate of ripe blackcurrant and chocolate, and a smooth mouthfeel.
ODD, ODF

Doña Dominga Gran Reserva Carmenere 2007, Viña Casa Silva S.A., Colchagua Valley Red
Fresh, fruity aromas on a herbal background. Light and smoky, with cherry fruit character.

Doña Dominga Gran Reserva Merlot 2007, Viña Casa Silva S.A., Colchagua Valley Red
Deep cherry colour, with soft mature fruit on the nose, and a palate of apple, blackberry, and spice. Long finish.

Doña Dominga Reserva Cabernet Sauvignon 2008, Viña Casa Silva S.A., Colchagua Valley Red
Leafy currant nose, with a fresh blackcurrant and blackberry palate. Good, fresh structure, and a chocolatey finish.

Doña Dominga Reserva Carmenère 2008, Viña Casa Silva S.A., Colchagua Valley Red
Spicy, with sweet red fruit on the nose. Good balance. Well-made.

Doña Dominga Single Vineyard Carmenère 2008, Viña Casa Silva S.A., Colchagua Valley Red
Restrained fruit aromas, with a savoury, powdery palate of plummy red fruit.

Encierra 2006, Colchagua Valley Red
Well-defined black fruit and vanilla oak on the nose. Broad palate, with plenty of pepper and spice. Syrah-driven fruit with an accent of green olive.
£10.50

Espíritu De Chile Gran Reserva Carmenère 2006, Curicó Valley Red
Medium ruby in colour, with

restrained damson aromas. Austere mid-palate, with juicy red fruit on a fresh finish.

Errazuriz Max Reserva Shiraz 2007, Aconcagua Valley Red
Attractive lifted floral nose, with white pepper spice. Quite jammy fruit on the palate. Very drinkable.
£11.00 HMA

Errazuriz Single Vineyard Carmenère 2007, Aconcagua Valley Red
Deep in colour, with black fruit aromas. The palate shows chocolate and tobacco notes, with high tannins, lovely fruitiness, and good potential.
£14.00 HMA

Errazuriz The Blend 2006, Aconcagua Valley Red
Deep in colour, with ripe fruit carried through from the nose to the palate. High tannins, with chocolate and coffee aromas.
£16.00 HMA

Estampa Gold Syrah 2007, Colchagua Valley Red
Attractive colour. Nose of blackberry, with floral aromas and chocolate. Pleasant tannic structure.

Gracia Cabernet Sauvignon Pasajero Reserva Lo Mejor 2007, Viñedos Y Bodegas Corpora S.A., Maipo Valley Red
Dense, dark blackcurrant fruit nose, with a hint of rubber. The palate shows sweet, dense blackcurrants on the finish.
£10.00

Gracia Syrah Grenache Viognier Travesía Reserva Superior 2007, Viñedos Y Bodegas Corpora S.A., Central Valley Red
There is evident Viognier

peachiness on the nose, with a hint of fruit salad. Full-bodied and peppery, with a slight vegetal character, and plenty ripe fruit.
£9.50

Indomita Duette Cabernet Sauvignon-Carmenère 2007, Maipo Valley Red
A well-made wine, with lovely soft raspberry and cherry fruit.

In Situ Gran Reserva Carmenere 2008, Aconcagua Valley Red
Herbal, floral nose, with hints of spice. Good structure and earthy finish.
£10.00 DFW, OWC

In Situ Reserva Cabernet-Syrah 2007, Aconcagua Valley Red
Quite sweet fruit, leading to a dry tannic palate, with a definite juicy edge.
£6.00 DFW, OWC

La Capitana Shiraz 2008, Viña La Rosa, Rapel Valley Red
Minty blackberry aromas, with a smooth palate of juicy fruit and hints of liquorice. Herbal notes come through on the finish.

Las Niñas Cabernet Sauvignon 2007, Colchagua Valley Red
Aromas of cassis and vanilla plum. Silky palate, with plenty of ripe fruit, and a restrained finish.

Leyda Single Vineyard Pinot Noir Las Brisas 2008, Leyda Valley Red
Youthful primary fruit nose, leading to a palate of raspberries and loganberries, with generous fruit, and silky texture.
£10.00

Manso De Velasco 2006, Miguel Torres Chile, Curicó Valley Red
Deep purple in colour. Well-structured, with ripe fruit. Great ageing potential.

Maquis Lien 2006, Colchagua Valley Red
Spicy red berries and bramble fruit on the palate, with a firm tannic structure, well-integrated acidity, and balanced fruit.

Marks & Spencer Secano Estate Pinot Noir 2008, Viña Leyda, Leyda Valley Red
Attractive, fragrant, and subtle. Ripe and full bodied, with creamy oak.
£7.50 M&S

Marqués De Casa Concha Cabernet Sauvignon 2007, Viña Concha Y Toro S.A., Maipo Valley Red
Rich, dense wine, with dark fruit notes. Herby intensity, with well-integrated tannins, and a lingering finish.
£9.30 FLA

Marqués De Casa Concha Syrah 2007, Viña Concha Y Toro S.A., Rapel Valley Red
Inky in colour, with opulent cassis, blueberry, and vanilla on the nose. Good structure and acidity.
£9.30 FLA

Matetic Corralillo Syrah 2007, San Antonio Valley Red
Incredibly dense nose of blackcurrant and meat. Deeply coloured, with pronounced acidity on a dense, chewy palate.
£12.00 GNS, MWW, ODD

Matetic Corralillo Winemaker's Blend 2006, San Antonio Valley Red
Deep in colour, and ripe in style.

Vibrant, brambly fruit.
£12.00 GNS, MWW, ODD

**Matetic EQ Pinot Noir 2007,
San Antonio Valley Red**
Nose of red fruit, with a toasty
character. Spiced complexity on
a silky, balanced finish.
£18.00 GNS, MWW, WSO

**Maycas Del Limarí Reserva
Especial Cabernet Sauvignon
2006, Limarí Valley Red**
Deep in colour, with cassis,
menthol, eucalyptus, and coffee
on the nose. Slightly bitter on
the finish.

**Maycas Del Limarí Reserva
Syrah 2007, Limarí Valley Red**
Rich, concentrated nose of red
fruit, with a well-balanced palate,
showing nice, soft tannins.
£8.60 TESC

**Miguel Torres Chile Cordillera
2006, Curicó Valley Red**
Nice red fruit on the nose.
Good structure, with quite
chunky tannins, and an earthy
finish.

**Morandé Reserva Cabernet
Sauvignon 2007, Maipo Valley
Red**
Nice fruitiness on the nose, with
red fruit, cherries, plums, and
pepper. The palate is fresh and
mineral, with pointed acidity. An
easy-drinking wine.
LAY

**Odfjell Vineyards Armador
Carmenere 2007, Central
Valley Red**
Mulberry, plum and damson
aromas, with a touch of spice on
the palate, and dark fruit flavours
on the finish.
£6.90 AAW

**Orzada Carignan 2005,
Odfjell Vineyards, Maule**

Valley Red
Lovely, complex nose of ripe red
berry, with jamminess and spicy
notes. Rich palate, with a silky
tannic finish.
£10.30 AAW

**Ossa Sixth Generation 2004,
Viña La Rosa, Rapel Valley
Red**
Ripe black fruit, with hints of
coffee and cedar. Dense and
tannic, with a very ripe palate.

**Pérez Cruz Cabernet
Sauvignon Reserva 2008,
Maipo Valley Red**
Medium ruby colour, with notes of
spicy plums and blackberries. Good
acidity, with youthful tannins.
£8.20 NOV

**Pérez Cruz Cot Limited
Edition Reserva 2007, Maipo
Valley Red**
Minty eucalyptus character, with
a nice fruity structure, and long
sweet finish.
£11.40 NOV

**Porta Cabernet Sauvignon
Orgánico Boldo 2006,
Viñedos Y Bodegas Corpora
S.A., Aconcagua Valley Red**
Engaging nose, with flinty
eucalyptus and black fruit on the
palate. Clean, soft tannins.
£9.50

**Porta Pinot Noir Gran Reserva
2007, Viñedos Y Bodegas
Corpora S.A., Bío Bío Valley Red**
Varietally typical ruby red in colour,
with a pleasant, quite extracted
nose. On the palate, there is
warm fruit, with a slightly bitter
edge. The finish is strong and dry.
£10.00

**Primus 2006, Alto De
Casablanca S.A., Colchagua
Valley Red**
Fresh crushed red and black

berries, with a floral accent and gentle oak. Juicy palate, showing great freshness, with silky texture and a lifted finish. Luscious.
£13.00 MCT

Santa Mónica Reserva Merlot 2003, Rapel Valley Red
Chocolatey, showing light richness, with black fruit and mulberries. An easy-drinking style with good maturity.
£20.00 HWG

Santa Carolina Reserva De Familia Cabernet Sauvignon 2007, James Maxwell, Maipo Valley Red
A rich, full-bodied wine, with well-integrated tannins, and a long, rich finish. A little tannic, but will soften with time.

Somerfield Cabalito Cabernet Sauvignon 2008, Emiliana Vineyards, Rapel Valley Red
A green and leafy wine, with slightly drying tannins.
£4.00 SMF

Sutil Reserve Cabernet Sauvignon 2007, Rapel Valley Red
Ripe, red and black berries, with a floral lift, building acidity, and gentle tannins, leading to a crisp, fragrant finish.
£7.50 CTL

Sutil Reserve Merlot 2007, Rapel Valley Red
Velvety, berry fruit nose. Very elegant and seductive.
£7.50 CTL, HBC

Syrah Reserva Privada Ochotierras 2008, Limarí Valley Red
Lively raspberry red in colour. Nose of white pepper and blackcurrant. On the palate, there is sweet fruit with mocha and oak.

Tabalí Reserva Especial Pinot Noir 2008, Limarí Valley Red
Very perfumed, fresh, almost minty nose. Dry, fruity flavours with fine tannins, and a lingering finish.
£12.00 PBA

Tabalí Reserva Especial Syrah 2007, Limarí Valley Red
Deep in colour, with black fruit on the nose, and vanilla, ripe fruit, and oak on the palate. Good tannins, notes of tobacco and chocolate, with a long finish.
£13.00 PBA

Tabalí Reserva Especial Tinto 2007, Limarí Valley Red
Peppery blackberry fruit, with a complex structure.
£13.00 PBA

Tabalí, Tabalí Reserva Syrah 2007, Limarí Valley Red
Black colour, with oaky liquorice, dark chocolate, and ripe black fruit on the palate. Good character, with a dark chocolate and coffee kick.
£10.00 PBA

Tarapacá Gran Reserva Syrah 2007, Maipo Valley Red
Ripe black and blue fruit, with spicy oak, slight minerality, and a dusty finish.
£13.00 LAI

Terramater S.A. Limited Reserve 2006, Maipo Valley Red
Bright, expressive wine, with a good berry character, and some spicy tannins.
£7.00

Tierra Antica Merlot 2008 Red
Very juicy and quite bold, if a touch leafy. High acidity and full body.
£6.00 HOH

Trio Cabernet Sauvignon 2007, Viña Concha Y Toro S.A., Maipo Valley Red
Big, creamy, minty nose. Lots of cedar notes overlaying black fruit.
£7.30 FLA

Valdivieso Cabernet Sauvignon Single Vineyard 2007, Central Valley Red
Medium intensity, with coffee and cherries on the nose. Sweet ripeness on the palate, with some depth.

Valdivieso Carmenère Reserva 2007, Central Valley Red
Light, smoky fruit on the nose. Powerful palate, with appealing fruit.

Valdivieso Eclat 2006 Red
Red fruit and a leafy overtone on the nose. Juicy, textured tannins, with lively acidity.

Valle Andino Reserva Especial Pinot Noir 2008, Santa Camila, Casablanca Valley Red
Attractively perfumed nose of lily flowers and raspberry. Good fresh acidity, with nice length.

Viña La Rosa, La Capitana Merlot 2008, Rapel Valley Red
Dark purple in colour. Jammy black cherry flavours, with good texture, and ripe tannins. Rich in aromas, with notes of chocolate and tobacco on a long finish.

Viña Los Boldos Grand Reserve Merlot 2007, Rapel Valley Red
Bright deep ruby colour, with notes of eucalyptus, mint, and blackcurrant fruit. Fresh and soft.

Viña Los Boldos Sensaciones Reserva Syrah 2007, Rapel Valley Red
Vinous minty blackberry aroma. Smooth attack, with an elegant, multi-layered palate, and a vibrant, never-ending finish.

Viña Luis Felipe Edwards Merlot Reserva 2008, Colchagua Valley Red
Spice and chocolatey fruit, with oak coming through on the palate. Medium-length finish.

Viña Luis Felipe Edwards Shiraz Family Selection Gran Reserva 2007, Colchagua Valley Red
Nose of new vanilla oak, with a juicy, dark berry palate.

Viña Luis Felipe Edwards Shiraz Reserva 2008, Colchagua Valley Red
Spicy red and black fruit, with firm tannins and good length.

Viña Mar Reserva Pinot Noir 2008, Casablanca Valley Red
Light oak combines with with sumptuous fruit on the nose. Attractive, gentle flavours of raspberry and plum, with a hint of spice.
£7.00 C&B

Viña Montgras De Gras Reserva Cabernet Sauvignon 2008, Colchagua Valley Red
Nose of confectionery and some mintiness, with well-integrated oak, good structure and length.
£7.00

Viña Montgras De Gras Reserva Merlot 2008, Colchagua Valley Red
Simple, straightforward wine, with big, dark, plummy fruit and tannins.
£7.00

Viña San Pedro 1865 Single Vineyard Cabernet Sauvignon 2007, Maipo Valley Red

Attractive sun-kissed blackcurrant fruit on a lingering palate, with supportive structure, and a vibrant finish. A well-made wine.

Viña Santa Helena, Selección Del Directorio Pinot Noir 2008, Casablanca Valley Red

Strawberry and plum aromas, with juicy fruit on the palate and good length.
£9.00 TESC

Viña Ventisquero Pangea 2006 Red

Restrained, meaty dark fruit, with hints of chocolate and hazelnut. Rich, concentrated palate of savoury black fruit, tobacco leaf, and plum. Firm tannins, with good length.
PLB

Vistamar Sepia Cabernet Sauvignon 2008, Central Valley Red

Intense spicy notes at the start, with a nice, full body, and rich tannins.

Viu Manent Malbec Single Vineyard San Carlos 2007, Colchagua Valley Red

Rich, complex nose, with some oaky notes. The palate is very juicy and meaty, with a nice long, sweet finish.

Yali Three Lagoons Carmenère, Viña Ventisquero, 2007 Red

White pepper on the nose, leading to a soft, juicy palate with ripe tannins. Quite enjoyable.
PLB

Ycaro Merlot 2008, Viñedos Emiliana, Rapel Valley Red

Rather dusty red fruit, with savoury tannins, good length, and some real persistence.
£6.00 VGN

Casillero Del Diablo Shiraz Rose 2008, Viña Concha Y Toro S.A., Central Valley Rosé

Boiled sweet aromas, with good squishy fruits on the palate, leading to a lengthy finish of wild strawberries.
£7.00 TESC

Leyda Single Vineyard Pinot Noir Rosé Loica 2008, Leyda Valley Rosé

Salmon hue, with some lifted fruit on a dry palate, showing good acidity, which carries through to a nice finish.
£9.20

San Medin Rosé 2008, Miguel Torres Chile, Curicó Valley Rosé

Vivid, luminous red in colour. Vibrant, juicy, dry, and long.

France: Bordeaux

Bordeaux has established itself as the world's most illustrious wine regions, with wine nuts around the world bowing to its historical virtues. The high-end châteaux have been charging through the teeth for their 2005 wines, as a result of an ideal vintage, but you don't have to be a City roller to appreciate what Bordeaux has to offer. There are some bargains to be found at the more reasonable end of the price spectrum, which you'll find here. Don't let the reds take all the credit for quality in this neck of the woods either. The whites are versatile and fresh, with the majority made to drink young. A blend of Sauvignon Blanc and Sémillon, with some local varieties also added, warranted a Gold medal from our judges.

KEY FACTS

Total production
4.79 Mhl in 2008

Total vineyard
119,000ha

Top 10 grapes
1 Merlot
2 Cabernet Sauvignon
3 Cabernet Franc
4 Semillon
5 Sauvignon Blanc
6 Malbec
7 Muscadelle
8 Petit Verdot
9 Ugni Blanc
10 Colombard

Top 10 production per appellation
1 Bordeaux
2 Premieres Cotes de Blaye
3 Bordeaux Blanc
4 Medoc
5 Bordeaux Superieur
6 Haut Medoc
7 Saint Emilion Grand Cru
8 Red Graves
9 Saint Emilion
10 Entre deux Mers

Producers
9044 winegrowers in 2008, 43 wine co-operatives

2009 IWC PERFORMANCE

Trophies	2
Gold	2
Silver	31
Bronze	54

BORDEAUX WHITE TROPHY

Château Brown 2007, Yvon-Mau White
Buttered toast with marmalade on the nose. Nice aromatics and spice, with ripe sweet citrus fruit on the palate. Good acidity and length. Very classy.

 EDMUND PENNING-ROWSELL TROPHY

Château Caronne Ste Gemme 2004, Sce Vignobles Nony Borie Red
Nicely restrained, but complex, with jammy and dark fruit notes, and nice aromas of cedarwood and leather. Tannins are firm but smooth. Excellent quality.
£ 13.00 MWW

Château Bauduc Bordeaux Blanc Sec 2008, Château Bauduc White
Fruity and fresh aromas, with good acidity, and a full, quite weighty mouthfeel. Some ripe, stewed apple fruit notes, with good complexity, structure and length.
£ 9.00

Château Ducla Experience 2007, Yvon-Mau White
Restrained beeswax, honey, and dried herb aromas. Clotted cream rises from the palate, which also shows oak, and a smooth, elegant array of flavours. A stylish wine.

Château La Hargue 2008, Ducourt White
Very lovely fragrance, with lots of punchy tropical fruit and exotic jasmine and floral notes. Juicy lemon and grapefruit character.

Château Marjosse 2008, Earl Pierre Lurton White
A touch of green gooseberry on the nose, with floral hints. Palate has good fruit, with a bit of intensity driving through to a mouthwatering finish.

Dourthe Grands Terroirs Bordeaux 2008, Dourthe White
Punchy on the nose, with green fruit, and a little nettle lift over tropical fruit. Good attack, with building intensity.
£ 5.50

Ducourt Sauvignon Gris - Réserve De Famille 2008, Ducourt White
Extremely pale in colour, with good gooseberry aromas. Crisp and fresh; a lovely Sauvignon Gris style with good varietal expression.

Les Trois Hectares 2007, Château Bauduc White
Deep lemony colour. Aromas of honeyed lemon and toffee. Fresh acidity and good lemon fruit on the palate. Plenty of complexity, and a long, rich finish.
£ 11.00

Sauvignon Blanc 2007, Château La Levrette White
Complex, lemony nose with oak, caramel, and waxy tones. Lovely depth of fruit, with good length.

Averys Fine Médoc 2005, Diva Red
Big, ripe, and explosive on the nose. Clean, and showing signs of maturity. Dry, tight tannins, with rich, complex, spicy fruit,

and lovely blackcurrant and chocolate notes, culminating in a sweet berry finish.
£ 10.00 AVB

Château Brown 2005, Yvon-Mau Red
Elegant and rounded, with a lot of intensity. Fully integrated oak. Earthy, with some gravelly notes, and good red fruit intensity.

Château Cambon La Pelouse 2006, Marie Red
Spicy and woody, with plum and sweet fruit on the nose. Soft, open palate, with expressive fruit and good, chewy tannins.
£ 15.00 A&B, CAM, DNL, EVW, FWL, HHC, MGM

Château Clauzet 2004, Baron Velge S.A. Red
Bright ruby colour. Cassis and black fruit on the nose, with hints of coffee and tobacco. Tannins are dry but fine-grained.

Château De Come 2004, Baron Velge S.A. Red
Vibrant, elegant nose, with vegetal and fruit notes, and showing some development. Good fruit, well-structured, with some grippy tannins.

Château De Roquebrune 2006, Famille Guinjard Red
Good colour, with lovely fruity aroma. Ripe, yet soft Merlot fruit is accented on the palate. Gentle acidity and balanced fruit.
£ 12.00

Château Deryem Valentin Margaux Cru Bourgois 2006, Château Deryem Valentin Red
Fresh scented violets and black fruit. Very fresh and balanced, with good purity and length. Potential for up to 5 years' ageing.
£ 24.40 HEN, DLATKW, WRC

Château Garraud 2007, Vignobles Léon Nony Red
Youthful colour, with plummy aromas. Palate of black cherry fruit, with mouthwatering tannins, and a nice, medium length plummy finish.

Château Haut Condissas 2005, Domaine Rollan De By Red
Gorgeous colour, with a nose of cedar, plum, and red fruit. Rich, silky palate. Bright, silky texture.

Château Laroque 2001, Laroque Red
Mid-raspberry red in colour. Sweet fruit and complex spice on the nose. Rich, sweet, developed fruit and cedar on the palate. Good length.
£ 24.50 WAIT

Château Pey La Tour 2008, Dourthe Red
Light purple in colour, with clean primary fruit aromas. Fresh and plummy, with soft tannins, and some attractive sunshine character from the Merlot.
£ 6.80 TESC

Château Serilhan 2007, Scea Marcelis Red
Good deep crimson colour, with a dark core. Fine tannins, and excellent fruit characteristics including cassis, soft plum, tobacco box and chocolate. Good use of oak, with structured acidity, and a long, elegant, perfumed length.
£ 18.00 HAR

Château Tourteau 2005, Sc Du Château Tourteau-Chollet Red
Oriental spice character on the nose. There is ripe fruit on the palate, complemented by firm tannin. A good food wine, which has potential for ageing.

Château Tourteau-Chollet 2006, Sc Du Château Tourteau-Chollet Red
Soft plum and minerality on the nose, with a palate of gentle ripe plum fruit, complemented by velvety tannins, and an undercurrent of stony minerality.

Lamotte Robin 2006, Cheval Quancard S.A. Red
Ruby-garnet colour, with medium depth redcurrant and woody aromas. Plummy palate, with spicy oak and chewy tannins, and a hint of smoke on the finish.

L'Enclos Gallen 2005, Château Meyre S.A. Red
Lovely colour, showing sweet fruit and cassis on a highly-flavoured palate .Toasty and evolved. Very integrated, very long, very Bordeaux.
£ 25.00

Lvcvllvs Cuvée D'exception 2004, Scea Château Hostens-picant Red
Red fruit aromas, with a youthful colour. Loads of red fruit and lively tannins. Dense, with a graphite and loganberry finish.
£ 30.00

Marks & Spencer Château Saÿe 2006, Saÿe Red
Complex nose of red and black fruits, with tasty notes of oak. The palate is full, with good fruit intensity, and well-integrated oak. A very well-made wine.
£ 9.00 M&S

Marks & Spencer Margaux 2005, Lucien Lurton & Fils Red
Elegant, perfumed, ripe blackcurrant nose, with liquorice, cedar, and slightly savoury notes. Well-structured, with integrated

acidity and tannin, and well-defined fruit.
£ 15.00 M&S

R De Ramage 2006, Sci Château Ramage La Batisse Red
Delicious classic aromas of plum, cassis, and pepper. Balanced palate, with savoury tannins and medium length.

Vieux Château Les Jouans 2007, Calvet Red
Deep, dark, enclosed fruit. Tight, spicy oak, tobacco, and leafy notes. Smoky dark fruit, encouraging chocolate oak through the palate.

Tesco Finest* Sauternes 2005, Yvon Mau Botrytis
Apricot, orange peel, and marmalade nose, with a palate of candied marmalade, orange, lemon, and oak. Firm acidity, and attractive long finish. A real food wine.
£ 12.00 TESC

Waitrose Sauternes, Château Suduiraut 2005 Botrytis
Orange zest and marmalade nose,

with a luscious honey, apricot, white peach and lime palate. Balanced acidity, with a citrussy sensation, and good length.
£ 10.00 WAIT

BRONZE

Chapelle De Tutiac Bordeaux Sauvignon Blanc 2008, S.a.s. Vignerons De Tutiac White
Some asparagus notes, with sweet, fruity character, and good acidity.
£ 10.00 GYW

Château Haut Grelot 2008, Joel Bonneau White
Very light in colour, with floral undertones on the nose, this is fresh, crisp, and dry, with notes of gooseberry.

Châteaux Selection Bordeaux White Benoit Valerie Calvet 2008, Benoit Valerie Calvet Sas White
Ripe, gooseberry and grassy nose, with a pleasant, ripe gooseberry palate: a nice simple wine.
£ 4.60 ALD

Cheval Quancard Reserve Blanc 2007, Cheval Quancard S.A. White
Spicy apricot and peach aromas. Lifted mid-palate, with a note of dried herbs and white flowers, and some woody spice.

French Connection Classics Bordeaux Blanc 2008, Cheval Quancard White
Subdued mineral nose, but intensity develops on the palate, and the finish is good.

Premius 2008, Yvon Mau White
A little bit of pear drop, with sherbetty-lemon fruit on the nose. Palate shows lemon and lime intensity, with a nice bite.

Prestige De Calvet 2008, Calvet White
Smoky nose, with apple acidity, and quite a rich palate, with a nutty character, and good length.

Averys Pioneer Range Montagne Saint Emilion 2007, Olivier Cazenave Red
Dark chocolate and tobacco on the nose. Good structure, with red fruit and high tannins. Good potential.
£ 13.00 AVB

Blaye Sélection 3 D Wines 2006, Château Monconseil Gazin Red
Delicate nose of fennel and blackberry. Gentle structure, with well-integrated new oak tannins. Soft and silky mouthfeel.
£ 13.80 3DW

Cellar Estates Saint Emilion 2007, Les Grands Chais De France Group Red
Quite fragrant, with a little notes of lifted cherry and kirsch. Juicy, with a bit of crunch.

Château Bellisle Mondotte 2004, Heritiers Escure Red
Farmyard aromas, with notes of cedar and spice. Rich, ripe and complex. Full, lingering finish.
£ 23.50

Château Braude Fellonneau Haut - Médoc 2006, Château Mongravey Red
Prototypical nose, demonstrating excellent wine-making, with truly wonderful balance, a dense mouth-filling body, and great length.
£ 19.50 3DW

Château D'Arche 2006, Château D'Arche Red
Oak and blackcurrant on the nose. Dry rich fruit palate, with a long, rich finish. Will improve with age.

Château De Braude Haut - Médoc 2006, Château Mongravey Red
Attractive, ripe flavours of red and black berry fruit.
£ 14.70 3DW

Château Du Cartillon 2005, Crus Et Domaines De France Red
Blackcurrant aromas, with dark berries and woody spiciness. Stewed fruit on the palate.

Château Fonchereau "Le Grand" 2006, Sca Château Fonchereau Red
Nose of light, soft, red fruit. Hints of spice on the palate, with good balance and length.

Château Fonreaud 2006, Jean Chanfreau Red
Fragrant, spicy nose of plum and currants. Palate has cherry characteristics, with dry tannins, and a long finish.

Château Guadet St.Emilion Grand Cru Classe 2005, Château Guadet Red
Very dark, creamy, cherry fruit. Youthful, with big dry tannins. Good potential and balance.
£ 35.00 WRC

Château Haut-Vigneau 2007, Erric Perrin Red
Elegant nose of black cherries, tobacco, and a hint of oak. Palate of black fruit, with high tannins.

Château La Fleur Peyrabon 2006, Bernard Patrick Red
Textbook Pauillac - scented fragrant black fruits, with a bright cassis character. Youthful, with chewy tannins.
£ 25.00

Château Larrivet Haut Brion 2004, Château Larrivet Haut Brion Red
Mature fruit, Autumnal, with coffee, and sweet earthy tones. Elegant, with a good finish.
£ 23.50 WAIT, MWW

Château Meyre 2005, Château Meyre S.a.s Red
Clean, mature cassis and light fennel on the nose. Dry, with good tannic grip, gentle acidity, clean upfront fruit, with a cocoa finish.
£ 10.00

Château Montlabert 2007, Castel Freres Red
Redcurrants and violet on the nose. The palate is compact and savoury, with a touch of oak.

Château Pey La Tour Réserve Du Château 2006, Dourthe Red
Perfumed notes on the nose, with good tannin and fruit balance, and medium weight. Lovely fruit, with a long finish.
£ 10.00 BTH, WSO

Château Pey La Tour Réserve Du Château 2007, Dourthe Red
Bright primary fruit, with lots of cherry juice. Drying tannin, with a charming cherry lift on finish.
£ 10.00 BTH, WSO

Château Peyrabon 2006, Bernard Patrick Red
Restrained black fruit nose, with hints of violet. Firm, spicy tannins, and medium length.
£ 12.00

Château Preuillac 2005, Yvon-Mau Red
Big, open nose of cherry and berry fruit. Smooth and velvety, with some freshness on the finish. Good length.

**Château Rousseau De Sipian
2005** Red
Gentle cassis nose. The palate
is swollen with mature fruit.
Medium-to-full bodied.
£ 15.00 AWW, FHW, MBS

**Château Segonzac Reserve
Oak Age 2007** Red
Floral aromas, with some
complexity. Youthful colour, with
good black and red berry fruit.
Long finish. Will age well.
£ 9.00 WAIT

**Château Tourteau-chollet
2005** Red
Soft currants are complemented
by herbal notes on the nose. Palate
of ripe plum and currant, with
ample spice and some earthiness.

**Château Treytins Montagne
Saint Emilion 2007, Vignobles
Léon Nony** Red
Fine fruit on the nose, and even
better on the palate - good
length and tannins.

**Château Trimoulet Cuvée
Émilius 2006, Yvon-Mau** Red
Fruity and rich, still very tannic.
Bright and lively, with more fruit
available on the palate.

**Clos Des Quinze 2006,
Château Bauduc** Red
Plummy, gamey, warm, jammy,
and ripe. Complex flavours of
fruit and boot polish, with a
boiled sweet and cherry finish.
£ 10.00

**Diane De Belgrave 2006,
Dourthe** Red
Very ripe berries, plums, and fruit
compote on the nose. Soft, spicy
tannins, with medium length.
£ 11.00

**Dourthe Grands Terroirs
Bordeaux Rouge 2007** Red
Fruity, with some freshness on

the nose. Elegant style, with fair
length.
£ 6.00

**Dourthe La Grande Cuvée
Médoc 2006**
Red
Clean, herbal nose, with light
smoke and sweet cassis aromas.
Dry, intense acidity, with ripe
tannins. Good concentration and
structure.
£ 9.00

**Dourthe La Grande Cuvée
Saint Emilion 2006** Red
Mid-cherry red in colour. Notes
of tamarind, fruit, and leafiness
on the nose. Quite rich, with
supple fruit on the palate.
Medium length.
£ 11.00

Dourthe N.1 Rouge 2007 Red
Spicy nose showing blackcurrants
and cedar. Juicy, fresh palate with
soft tannins.

**Dourthe Terroirs D'exception
Croix Des Menuts 2006** Red
Excellent integration of oak and
fruit on the nose, with notes
of wine gums. Persistent in the
mouth, with grippy tannins. This
wine has plenty of time left to
age.
£ 10.00 BTH

**Dourthe Terroirs D'exception
Terrasse De La Jalle 2006**
Red
Brooding, tight nose, with hints
of redcurrants. Dry, tight tannins,
well-balanced with acidity.
Showing mature fruit and good
quality.
£ 9.00

Il Est Q 2008, Univitis Red
Fragrant Merlot character frames
the nose. Light, bright, juicy to
drink. Soft tannins, and a nice
finish.

La Croix Lugagnac 2006, Cordier Mestrezat Grands Crus Red
Sophisticated oak, with a firm, edgy palate. Will soften and age well.

Les Abeilles Saint Emilion Grand Cru 2006, J.n Boidron Red
Lifted plum cake nose. Light and soft, with chewy raisins, and good length.
WRC

Marks & Spencer Bordeaux Merlot 2007, Sichel Red
Nose of cassis, with an attractive, fruity palate, leading to a long, sweet finish with hints of cherry.
£ 6.00 M&S

Marquis De Mascaret Bordeaux Merlot 2007, S.a.s. Vignerons De Tutiac Red
Nice lifted bouquet, which grows in the glass. Firm tannins, and touch of cigar box and chestnut.
£ 8.00 GYW

Seigneurs D'Aiguilhe 2006, Comtes De Neipperg Red
Linear black fruit nose, with floral glimpses. A nice dry, savoury palate.
£ 9.50 WAIT

Taillefer 2004, Yvon-Mau Red
Soft, vegetal nose. Meaty, earthy character, with integrated oak. Rustic style.
£ 19.00 TESC

Taste The Difference Saint Emilion 2007, CVBG Red
Scented oaky nose, with sweet curranty fruit, good freshness and acidity, with fine tannins.
£ 9.00 SAIN

Château De Sours Rose 2008 Rosé
Good depth, with a palate of juicy red fruit, backed up by refreshing acidity.
£ 8.00 BCR, GHC, MWW, PVC

Grand Theatre Rosé 2008, Univitis Rosé
Nice strawberry colour and aromas. Well-balanced and fresh, with good acidity.

La Rosée De Ramage 2008, Sci Château Ramage La Batisse Rosé
Bright pink in colour. Youthful, with vibrant cherry fruit and a herby tang.

La Tulipe 2008, Univitis Rosé
Salmon pink in colour, with fresh raspberry aromas, good weight and mouthfeel, and a reasonably firm finish.

Richemont Du Château De Sours Rose 2008 Rosé
Juicy fruit and lifted berry flavours. Very pleasant.
£ 7.50

Château Haut-Coustet 2007, Philippe Mercadier Botrytis
Deep old gold colour, with a rich, old oak nose. Relatively light body, and quite simple, but sweet and toasty, with fruit peel character. Very attractive.

France: Burgundy

The style of wines produced from Pinot Noir and Chardonnay in Burgundy are revered by winemakers all over the world. The respect for the French vignerons who work the land lies in their selfless commitment and hours of hand-pruning that produce such world-class wines. The locals, on the other hand, would claim none of the glory, insisting it's the terroir; a reflection on the local environment. Without blowing the budget, you'll find suppleness in the red Savigny-Les-Beaune, and an elegant nuttiness in the whites Montagny and Rully. Five times smaller than its eminent counterpart, Bordeaux, this region continues to deliver top quality wines from a compact space, claiming an impressive eleven Golds from France's total of forty-nine.

2009 IWC PERFORMANCE

Trophies	9
Gold	11
Silver	61
Bronze	96
Great Value Awards	1

Chablis - Grains Dorés 2006, Domaine Garnier Et Fils White
Bright yellow appearance and clean nose, with notes of ripe melon, dry honey, and artichoke, with a mineral, smoky, minty character. Ripe attack, with mineral fruity flavour and medium length.

Chablis Premier Cru Les Vaillons, Vieilles Vignes Domaine Laroche 2006 White
Lovely lemon colour in the glass. Charming, floral nose, with butter, biscuit, and honey tones. Really freshing on the palate, with a very long, nicely juicy finish.
£ 21.80

Chablis Premier Cru Vaucoupin 2007, J.Moreau & Fils White
Fresh note of citrus and creaminess on the unevolved nose. Crisp acidity on the palate, which is lifted and lingering in style. Very dry, and good with food. Will certainly keep. Top class.
FTH, MCT

Côte De Nuits Villages Blanc 2007, Domaine Désertaux Ferrand White
Lots of butter, citrus fruit, and toasty oak on the nose. Big citrus concentration on the palate, with attractive lime flavours. An inviting fruity taste, with good length and lovely balance.
£ 12.70 3DW

 CHABLIS TROPHY

Domaine De La Grande Chaume Chablis 1er Cru Vau De Vey 2007, Romain Bouchard White
Toasty, mealy, butterscotch nose. Taut minerals and acidity balance with layers of tart apple, and some spice. Crisp, clean lemon and cream notes. Balanced acidity, and a persistent mineral finish.
JAS, RAR, TPE

GREAT VALUE WHITE BETWEEN £10 AND £15

Louis Latour Pouilly-Vinzelles En Paradis 2006 White
The nose is creamy, quite melony, and rich. Soft tropical and passion fruit, with notes of grapefruit. Apple fruit pulses through. Well-structured and balanced.
£ 10.00 MWW

 PULIGNY MONTRACHET TROPHY

Marks & Spencer Puligny Montrachet Ier Cru Les Chalumeaux 2007, Domaine Jean Pascal Et Fils White
Youthful nose with toasty oak to the fore, alongside minerality, citrus and white floral notes. A fragrant, rounded, honeyed palate with lingering weight. Elegant finish with balance, integrity, and considerable potential.
£ 35.00 M&S

THE CHAMPION WHITE WINE, INTERNATIONAL CHARDONNAY TROPHY, FRENCH WHITE TROPHY, WHITE BURGUNDY TROPHY, MEURSAULT TROPHY

Meursault Clos De La Baronne 2007, Château Labouré Roi White
Beautiful, fresh floral nose, quite perfumed, with apple, and a restrained, nutty flavour. It has very fine depth on the palate, with real freshness - really quite stylish.

Vougeot 1er Cru "Le Clos Blanc De Vougeot" Monopole 2006, Domaine De La Vougeraie White

Delicate bouquet of melon and apple, with gentle oak. Wonderfully concentrated, layered, minerally wine. Lovely integration and superb length.

FRENCH RED TROPHY, INTERNATIONAL PINOT NOIR TROPHY, RED BURGUNDY TROPHY

Clos De Vougeot Grand Cru 2006, Domaine De La Vougeraie Red

Dark, heady aromas of berry fruit, mingled with cocoa and light oak spice. The palate is similar, but with rich mulberry and bramble fruit flavours, and brisk tannins.

Grands Echezeaux Grand Cru Domaine Du Clos Frantin 2007, Albert Bichot Red

Pale, elegant, and ethereal. Spicy perfumed nose. Bright, fresh palate, with good weight and silky tannins leading to a long, dry finish.

SILVER

Beaune Clos Des Mouches 1er Cru 2007, Domaine Chanson White

Nicely made wine with good, bright citrussy fruit. Clean nutty palate, with zippy acidity and an attractive, long-lasting finish.
£ 40.00 MZC

Bourgogne Hautes Cotes De Nuits 2007, Jean-Claude Boisset White

A vegetal, but clean, creamy, and appley nose, filled out with hazelnut. Very complex, and a little sweet, but full-flavoured. Good finish.
£ 14.50 LIB

Bourgogne Hautes-Côtes De Nuits Blanc "Dames Huguettes" Domaine Guy Et Yvan Dufouleur 2007 White

A wine with a lovely, light, mineral acidity. Apple and citrus nose, with light oak, leading to a well-balanced, lemony finish.
£ 15.00

Blason De Bourgogne Chablis 2007, Union Des Viticulteurs De Chablis White

This has a lovely bright, restrained, delicate nose, which is slightly lemony, with notes of honey, herbs, green apples, and cream. A lovely elegant Chardonnay.

Chablis 1er Cru - Mont De Milieu 2007, Garnier Et Fils White

Mid-yellow appearance, with a slightly vegetal nose. Soft attack, with notes of mint and artichoke. The palate is broad and clean, with some mineral notes; a zesty, elegant Chardonnay.

Chablis 1er Cru Montmains - Domaine De Vauroux 2007, Olivier Tricon White

Pale gold in colour. Elegant nose, with some minerality, and aromas of Golden Delicious apples. Good, clean palate, with acidity and some freshness to match the ripe fruit. A classic Chablis.

Chablis 1er Cru Vaulorent 2006, La Chablisienne White

Biscuit and straw aromas. Intense flavours of biscuit and toast on the palate. Balanced acidity, and a really long finish.

Chablis 2007, Union Des Viticulteurs De Chablis
White
A very fresh wine, with exceptionally good acidity. Very ripe, but showing good Chablis character, with a nutty, lightly oxidative nose.

Chablis Domaine Sainte Claire 2007, Jean-Marc Brocard White
Bright, clean, fresh lemon peel aromas, with a good toasty, complex nose. The palate has nice weight and a really attractive structure. Very good.
£ 13.50

Chablis Extra Special 2007, Domaine De La Levée White
Apple and stone fruit on the nose. Showing some development. The palate shows some concentration of flavour on the palate, with racy acidity, and a hint of spice on the finish. Youthful and firm, with good potential.
£ 9.00 ASDA

Chablis Grand Cru Bougros 2007, Jean-Marc Brocard
White
Rounded, buttery nose with lemon, pear, and tropical aromas and notes of minerality. Very fresh and attractive, with a good lemony finish.
£ 33.00

Chablis Grand Cru Château Grenouilles 2006, La Chablisienne White
Buttery nose with smoky, flinty aromas. Smooth nutty palate of kiwis and pineapples, with a medium body, and a rich, zesty finish.

Chablis Grand Cru Les Clos Domaine Laroche 2006
White
Fresh creamy and flinty nose.

> **DID YOU KNOW?**
> The average age of a French oak tree harvested for use in wine barrels is 170 years.

Buttery, with sweet apples on the palate. Intense lemony flavours, followed by a rounded, balanced finish
£ 57.30

Chablis La Sereine 2007, La Chablisienne White
Pale lemon hue, with good mineral Chardonnay fruit on the nose, and a really good, rich stylish, fruity palate, with good minerality.

Chablis Mineral Jean-Marc Brocard 2006 White
Showing elegant finesse on the nose, with creamy lemon notes. Rounded and smooth, with fruit and oak flavours on the palate. Creamy, nutty finish.
£ 16.00 TESC

Chablis Premier Cru Fourchaume 2007, Domaine Vrignaud White
Elegant fruit on the nose. Crisp juicy palate, with lovely minerality, and a touch of creaminess on the lingering finish. A classic.

Chablis Premier Cru Fourchaume 2007, J.Moreau & Fils White
Restrained and complex, with layered apple, and lactic butterscotch. Full, textured, taut palate with excellent balance of fruit and acidity. Persistent mineral finish.
FTH, MCT

Chablis Premier Cru Les Vaudeveys Domaine Laroche 2006 White
Nice straw-yellow colour. Aromas of citrus fruit and oak, with full body, and really nice, fresh acidity.
£ 20.50

Chablis Premier Cru Montmains 2007, Jean-Marc Brocard White
Bright yellow in colour, with a big nose of fragrant lemon, honey, and cut grass. Hints of sweet almonds and citrus jam on the palate. Crisp acidity.
£ 18.50

Chablis Premier Cru Vau De Vey 2007, Jean-Marc Brocard White
Stone fruit and cherry oak aromas. Good acidity, with a palate of apple pie, and a touch of spice on the finish.

Chassagne-Montrachet Blanc 2007, Vaucher Père Et Fils White
Creamy, nutty aromas, with notes of banana and biscuit. Very lean at present, with high acidity, but creamy richness underneath. Just needs 5 years or so.

Château Genot-Boulanger Mercurey Les Bacs 2006, Chateau Genot-boulanger White
Bright pale yellow colour, with a nose which is rich, ripe, and oaky, but still fresh. Toasty, creamy oak, and a slightly oily texture. Classic Burgundy.
£ 16.00 DLA, WRC

Domaine Vessigaud Vielles Vignes 2007 White
Pale colour, with stone fruit and lemon aromas. Yellow stone fruit and floral notes on the palate, with lovely acidity and finish, and subtle, well-integrated, subtle oak.
£ 18.00 CHH, DLA, WRC

Joseph Drouhin Puligny-Montrachet Folatieres 1er Cru 2007 White
Soft stone fruit character. Tightly structured, yet round, with a soft, smooth palate showing good fruit. An open, inviting wine.
£ 45.00 WAIT

Louis Jadot Bourgogne Chardonnay 2007 White
Pleasingly complex, mineral, herby nose. The palate is complex and nutty, with dried lemony fruit. Well-made, with appealing concentration and depth.
£ 11.00 TESC, HMA

Mâcon-Villages Clos De Pize 2007, Vignerons De Terres Secretes White
Juicy, citrus, orange, and almond notes. The palate shows focused citrus and apple, with tight acidity carrying a longish finish.
£ 10.00 THS

Mâcon-Péronne 2007, Jaffelin White
A little honeyed, showing nice tropical fruit, with pineapple, and some apple fruit behind. Full palate of dry melon and apple fruit, pithy, with a great long finish.

Marks & Spencer Mâcon Uchizy 2006, Raphaël Sallet White
A touch vegetal, quite rich, creamy, and full. Lots of tangy, fruity brightness, with a hint of pineapple and exotic fruit. Long finish.
£ 9.00 M&S

Meursault 1er Cru Boucles Chères 2007, Château Labouré Roi White
Very good, verging on excellent.

Rich, ripe, and really mouth-filling, with a finish that is fruity, creamy, long, and nutty.

Meursault 1er Cru Poruzot 2007, Château Labouré Roi
White
The nose is perfumed, enticing, and gently oaky. Typically complex, with loads of minerality, and a clean, lifted palate. Lovely bite. Long, crisp finish.

Meursault 2007, Ropiteau Frères White
Classic white Burgundy nose, with balanced creamy oak, ripe fruit, and flavours of crisp lemon on a juicy mid-palate. Long and lovely.
£ 28.00 WAV

Montagny Premier Cru Les Resses 2007, Domaine Michel - Andreotti White
Open, ripe, nutty, and slightly earthy nose, with crisp citrus aromas. Rounded, lightly nutty palate, with fresh fruit, good balance, and a nice fresh finish.
£ 10.40 3DW

Petit Chablis 2008, Château De Maligny White
Nice, concentrated fruit. Really quite expressive. Pure fruit character, with great mouthfeel and balance. Long, harmonious finish.
ABY

Petit Chablis Goulley 2007, Goulley Père et Fils White
Mineral, yeasty, leesy aromas, with underlying green apple fruit. Elegant wine, beautifully defined, with racy acidity and a creamy texture.
£ 12.00 HOH

Pouilly-Fuissé Les Ancolies 2007, Loron Et Fils White
Toasted nose, with lots of tropical fruit flavours on the palate. Extremely well-balanced, with a gorgeous, long finish.
£ 12.10

Pouilly-Fuissé Vieilles Vignes 2007, Maison Auvigue White
Green fruit and fine oak aromas. Buttery and fat, with medium body and good balance. Fresh, long, and pleasant.
£ 22.50 NYW, WBW

Rully St Jacques 2007, Maison Albert Sounit White
Gentle nose with correct, clean, smooth finish. Intense mid-palate. Very drinkable; a very good job well-done.
£ 20.00 SWG

Simonnet-Febvre Chablis 2007, Maison Simonnet-Febvre White
Lemon-lime nose, showing delicate lightness of touch, and some really appealing, clean, dry fruit. With a steely, young Chablis limestone character, this wine has a good future ahead of it.
£ 11.80 CHH, FLA, BAB, GWI, HFB

Beaune 1er Cru Les Bressandes Domaine Du Château Gris 2006, Lupe-Cholet Red
A nose of raspberry and strawberry, with is matched on the palate. This is a full, smoky wine, with good minerality.
CRI, DAY

Bourgogne Hautes-Côtes De Nuits Le Prieuré 2006, Cave Des Hautes-Côtes Red
Nicely aromatic, with cherry fruit, stony mineral aromas, and some oak. The palate shows some oak, but with clear, well-delineated fruit with a touch of spice.

Bourgogne Hautes-Côtes De Nuits Rouge "Dames Huguettes" Domaine Guy Et Yvan Dufouleur 2006, Domaine Guy Et Yvan Dufouleur Red
Pure, with notes of raspberry, rose petal, and savoury spice. Sweet fruit on the palate, with silky texture, well-integrated oak, and a fine backbone.
£ 15.00

Brouilly 2007, Château De Pierreux Red
Mid-ruby to cherry red colour. Clean, earthy tinge of redcurrant fruit on the nose. Well-balanced fruit on the palate, with a clean finish and good length.

Clos De Vougeot Grand Cru Domaine Du Clos Frantin 2007, Albert Bichot Red
A fragrant nose, showing plums and almonds with some vegetal notes in the background. On the palate there is fine sweet fruit, with good length and overall balance.

Domaine L.Muzard & Fils Santenay "Champs Claude" Vv 2006, Domaine L.Muzard & Fils Red
Firm cherry and mineral aromas. Showing firm acidity on the palate, with stylish ripe fruit, and good rusticity. This has good length, and will benefit from a further 3-5 years ageing.
£ 23.00 DLA, WRC

Gevrey-Chambertin "Vieilles Vignes" 2006, Domaine Heresztyn Red
Complex oak and red fruit ripeness, with lovely floral length.
£ 26.00

Louis Jadot Pommard 2006 Red
A lovely perfumed plum fruit nose. Fresh and silky smooth, with fine tannins, and a lovely concentration of ripe summer fruit flavours, leading to a smoky finish.
£ 25.00 HMA

Marks & Spencer Moulin-À-Vent 2007, Domaine Du Petit Chêne Red
Good colour, with gentle banana flavours and a sweet cherry finish. The palate has generous fruit, and attractively soft tannins.
£ 10.00 M&S

Moulin-À-Vent Des Hospices De Romaneche Thorins 2007, Collin Bourisset Red
Structured, cherry and raspberry scented wine, with lovely, fresh acidity, and a touch of tannin. Very good ageing potential.

Nuits-Saint-Georges 2007, Domaine Michel Gros Red
Dark berried fruit, with a savoury hint of wood polish on the nose. Chunky palate and good acidity.

Nuits-Saint-Georges Mhv Hlf 2005, Fgvs Boisset Red
Fragrant summer fruit pudding nose with good intensity. Firm, grainy tannins, and balanced acidity with a loganberry finish.
£ 27.50 MHV

Nuits-Saint-Georges 1er Cru Clos De Thorey Monopole 2006, Antonin Rodet Red
Strawberry fragrance, and ripe red fruit aromas. A balanced, attractive, and elegant wine, with medium concentration and balance.
£ 50.00

Nuits-Saint-Georges 1er Cru Les Poullettes Domaine Guy Et Yvan Dufouleur 2006 Red
Lovely spicy nose, with ripe

balanced fruit, good acidity, and a medium length finish.
£ 40.00

Patriarche Chambolle - Musigny 2007 Red
Well-supported black fruit, with a silky texture, nice balance, and some length. Nicely perfumed and elegant.
£ 36.00 PAT

Savigny-Les-Beaune Les Picotins Domaine Du Château Gris 2006, Lupe-Cholet Red
Pale ruby appearance, with delicate peony aromas. Tight-knit palate, with vibrant fruit, leading to a juicy finish.
CRI, DAY

Savigny-Les-Beaune 1er Cru "Les Marconnets" 2007, Domaine De La Vougeraie Red
This wine has a lightish ruby-violet colour, and shows cloves, pepper, and pure raspberries on the nose. It is balanced by youthful, gently herbal cherry flavours, with a spicy finish of plums, backed by moderate tannins.

Volnay Premier Cru 2007, Domaine Poulleau Michel Red
Lovely nose of ripe black cherry, framboise, and violets, with a touch of gameyness adding depth. There are young spicy cherry and tea flavours, surrounded by fine but solid tannins, and some sweetness.

Vosne-Romanée 1er Cru Clos Des Réas Monopole 2007, Domaine Michel Gros Red
Fragrant, floral, rose-scented, and savoury on the nose. On the palate, there is a good depth of cherry fruit.

Vosne-Romanée 1er Cru Les Malconsorts Domaine Du Clos Frantin 2007, Albert Bichot Red
Classic nose of wild strawberries. Tight but ripe fruit tannins. Good potential for ageing, with a long, satisfying aftertaste.

Vosne-Romanée 2005, Vaucher Père Et Fils Red
Deep crimson in colour, with a light, perfumed nose of cherry fruit. Good concentration and balanced oak. Fresh, with a long finish.

Vougeot 1er Cru "Les Cras" 2006, Domaine De La Vougeraie Red
A nose of dark, earthy fruit, and a full, velvety palate, with balanced fruit and an earthy character. Deep fruit on the mid-palate, backed by light tannin. Long finish.

Simonnet-Febvre Crémant De Bourgogne Vintage 2005 Sparkling
Honeyed ripe apple nose. Soft, creamy palate, with appley notes. Rich mousse and long finish.
£ 18.00 LOL

BRONZE

Beaune Du Château Blanc 2006, Bouchard Père & Fils White
Good smoky complexity on the nose. Clean citrus fruit, and a soft finish.
£ 25.00 WAIT

Bourgogne Chardonnay 2007, Ropiteau Freres White
The nose is lemony, herby, light, minerally, and nutty. Spicy palate, with a balanced finish.
£ 9.00 WAV

Bourgogne Chardonnay Beaucharme 2008, Louis Max
White
Creamy, with ripe oak, and good fruit beneath. Fresh palate and clean finish.

Chablis - Domaine De Vauroux 2007, Olivier Tricon
White
Creamy, delicate lemon, with a hint of honey on the nose. Smooth, creamy entry. Medium weight, with good, fresh honey and acidity on the palate.

Chablis "Les Pierres Blanches" André Tremblay 2008, Pascal Bouchard White
Peach, melon, and stone fruit notes. Green fruit on the palate. Good acidity.
£ 11.50 TESC, WAIT

Blason De Bourgogne Chablis 2008, Union Des Viticulteurs De Chablis White
Attractive tropical fruit on the nose, with creamy apple, peach, and melon notes. Refreshing acidity, balanced by apple and citrus fruit.

Chablis 1er Cru Fourchaumes 2008, Lamblin Et Fils White
Classic light lemon-rind aromas, with notes of elderflower. Delightful balance and relaxed elegance, with nice structure and finish.
£ 15.40 WES

Chablis 1er Cru La Singulière 2007, La Chablisienne White
Textbook nose of citrus and cotton wool, with notes of creaminess. Dry, fresh, harmonious palate.

Chablis 1er Cru Mont De Milieu 2008, Lamblin Et Fils
White
Citrus aromas, with medium-intensity fruit, and some lees character. The palate is fresh and broad, with crisp but balanced acidity and green apple notes.
£ 14.50 WES

Chablis 1er Cru Montée De Tonnerre - Domaine De Vauroux 2007, Olivier Tricon
White
Mineral with some iodine notes. Complex and classic nose, with notes of greengage and some creaminess. Lovely mouthfeel.

Chablis 1er Cru Montmains 2006, Goulley Père et Fils
White
Simple pear and peach fruit, with tropical notes. Medium weight palate, which is good and complex.
£ 19.50 HOH

Chablis 1er Cru Vaillons Domaine Louis Moreau 2006
White
Fragrant lemony biscuit aromas, with hints of white flowers. Good quality.
£ 15.70 ICL, WWN

Chablis 1er Cru Vaillons Gvjcb 2007, Fgvs Boisset
White
Pale in colour, with nice clean aromas. The palate is creamy, with slight bitterness and grassy notes.
£ 18.80 MHV

Chablis 2006, Union Des Viticulteurs De Chablis
White
Ripe, waxy, woody style, with ripe green apples, and light citrus on the nose. Good texture and acidity.
£ 8.00 SPR

Chablis 2007, Domaine Séguinot Bordet White
Ripe tropical fruit on the nose.

Soft, clean palate, with a nice mouthfeel.
3DW

Chablis AOC Domaine Louis Moreau 2007 White
Creamy, honeyed nose. Sharp green apple fruit; fresh, with very good acidity.
£ 9.30 CMR, WIW

Chablis Domaine William Fèvre 2007 White
Rocky, fruity, stone fruit, grapefruit, and a touch of oak. Good balance and length, with a buttery finish.

Chablis Grand Cru Bougros - Domaine De Vauroux 2006, Olivier Tricon White
Elegant, nutty, citrus nose, with a soft cream and apple character. Fresh finish of lemon and cream.

Chablis Grand Cru Clos Des Hospices Dans Les Clos Domaine Louis Moreau 2006 White
Intense nose of pear, mushroom, and lime. Flinty, buttery, and toasty notes on the palate.

Chablis Grand Cru Les Blanchots Domaine Laroche 2005 White
Yellow crystal colour. Intense toasted and flinty nose. Good complexity on the palate, showing balanced acidity on the finish.
£ 42.50

Chablis Grand Cru Valmur 2007, J.Moreau & Fils White
Clean, oaky, complex nose, with a palate of lively oak and fruit, with honey notes and a lemony finish.
FTH, MCT

Chablis Grand Cru Vaudésirs 2006, J.Moreau & Fils White
White stone fruit on the nose. Well-made, with harmonious

fruit, and a minerally finish.
FTH, MCT

Chablis La Pierrelée 2007, La Chablisienne White
Ripe tropical fruit on the nose. Good balance and nice mouthfeel.

Chablis Laroche 2008 White
Ripe apple, and notes of citrus blossom. Refreshing acidity is balanced with fruit. Good length, and a spicy finish.
£ 13.00

Chablis Premier Cru Fourchaume 2007, Château De Maligny White
Great lifted lanolin notes. Floral, lean, and mineral. Good length with lees complexity.
ABY

Chablis Premier Cru Fourchaume 2007, Domaine Séguinot Bordet White
Lemon in colour with green tinges, and Granny Smith apple aromas. Crisp acidity, with fresh apples on the palate; and a zingy finish.
£ 16.30 3DW

Chablis Premier Cru Fourchaume 2007, Jean-Marc Brocard White
The nose shows fruit and oak flavours, with some distinction and elegance.
£ 19.30

Chablis Premier Cru Montmains 2007, J.Moreau & Fils White
Clear, pale lemon in colour. Clean, with some minerality and lemon flavours on the palate. Showing apple and spice, with some chalkiness, and a crisp acid finish. Polished.
FTH, MCT

Chablis Premier Cru Selection 2007, Domaines Brocard
White
Nice Chardonnay character, with green apple and crisp acidity. The style is fresh and fruity, rather than mineral-driven. Creamy and simple, but elegant.
£ 13.00 SAIN

Chablis Premier Cru Vaulorent 2007, Jean-Marc Brocard White
Medium intensity, with a fine backbone. Textbook salty notes. Delicate and mineral, with lovely structure.

Chablis Saint Martin Domaine Laroche 2007 White
Fresh and a little sweet, with good acidity and freshness on the palate.
£ 14.50

Chablis Sainte-Céline Taste The Difference 2007, Famille Brocard White
Green apples on the nose and palate, with citric minerality. Fresh, long, and harmonious.
JBF

Chablis Vieilles Vignes 2007, Domaine Séguinot Bordet
White
Bright, fresh nose of apple, peach, and melon. Fresh acidity and good balance.
£ 13.40 3DW

Chablis, Paul Deloux 2007, Matthew Clark White
Minerally fruit on the nose, with a palate which opens up to reveal nice citrus concentration, with a clean finish.
£ 13.10

Chassagne-Montrachet Blanc 2007, Domaine Lamy Pillot
White
Light, fresh, citrus-blossom

scents, with a little lees and honey, in a clean, light style.
ABY

Chassagne-Montrachet 1er Cru "Morgeot Vignes Blanches" 2007, Château De La Maltroye White
Subtle exotic spice and minerals. Quite rich, with integrated, toasty oak and immediate appeal.
£ 45.00

Domaine J&G Lafouge Auxey-Duresses "Les Hautés" 2007, Domaine J&G Lafouge White
Appetising lemon and hazelnut, with some oak on nose. Clean, focused lemony fruit and hazelnut, with textured acidity, good length, and minerality.
£ 23.00 DLA, WRC

Fixin Jean-Claude Boisset 2007 White
Heavy oak influence, with nice fresh melon fruit. Youthful, but complex, with great length.
£ 25.00 LIB

French Connection Classics Bourgogne Chardonnay 2008, Collin Bourisset White
Minerality on the nose, which gives way to lots of ripe white peach and citrus notes. Good balance.

Limited Release Bourgogne Blanc Remoissenet 2007
White
Earthy nose with notes of musty hay and citrus fruit. Well-balanced palate, with a long, rich finish.
£ 14.00 AVB

Louis Jadot Meursault 2007
White
Fresh, fruity, floral nose. Clean, crisp, fresh, light, and refreshing.
£ 25.00 SAIN, WAIT, HMA

Mâcon-Villages Mhv Hlf 2008, Fgvs Thorin White
Crisp, light, and clean, showing elegant tropical fruit. Notes of melon and guava, with slate character, good acidity, softness, and complexity.
£ 7.90 BNK, MHV

Marsannay Blanc Champ Perdrix 2005 White
Pale lemon in colour. Lovely rich, soft-textured palate. Hints of white peachy flavours, with traces of vanilla, and nutty leesy nuances. Full of complexity, with a structured finish.
£ 19.00 PAT

Meursault Premier Cru Poruzots 2007, Pierre André White
Soft, neutral, fruity, and balanced, with good acidity and a long, crisp finish.
RBC

Montagny 1er Cru Les Coeres 2006, Vignerons De Buxy White
Fresh and creamy, with a nose of fresh apple and lemon fruit. Rounded creamy texture, with crisp, well-defined fruit on the palate, and good acidity. Well-made.

Morrisons The Best Chablis 2007, Louis Moreau White
Lemon green hue, with a bright wheatsheaf, yeasty nose. Light bodied, and supple Chardonnay character, with good length.
£ 9.00 MRN

Nuits-Saint-Georges Les Terrasses Domaine Du Chateau Gris 2007, Lupe-Cholet White
Lemon-green hue, with good, aromatic, ripe fruit. Medium length, and showing promise.
£ 35.00 WAIT

Oak Aged Burgundy 2007, Cave Des Vignerons De Buxy White
Taut, mineral nose, with fresh, light palate, showing subtle nuttiness, and lively acidity.

Pernand-Vergelesses Les Caradeux 1er Cru 2007, Domaine Chanson White
Nose of softly defined oak and minerality, with restrained fruit, and a balanced, gentle leesy character.
£ 29.00 MZC

Petit Chablis 2007, Bertrand Capdevigne White
Intense lemon in colour, with restrained, grassy minerality, strong acidity, and good length.

Petit Chablis Pas Si Petit 2008, La Chablisienne White
Pale straw colour, with a restrained nose. Medium complexity, with fresh, clean acidity on the finish. Well-made.

Puligny Montrachet 1er Cru Champ Gain 2007, Jean-Claude Boisset White
Restrained nose, with a fresh, mineral palate, showing subtle lees notes. Smooth and clean, with good weight.
£ 58.00 LIB

Rully 1er Cru Clos Du Chaigne 2007, Louis Picamelot White
Stone fruit, butterscotch, and light, toasty oak, with freshness and notes of green apple.

Rully 1er Cru La Bressande Château De Rully Monopole 2007, Antonin Rodet White
Lemon curd and grapefruit on the nose and palate. Lively and fresh, with really lovely expression. Well-made.
£ 25.00

Rully 2007, Pierre André
White
Nicely supported orchard fruit flavours, with integrated oak and a nice minerally finish.
RBC

Rully 2007, Ropiteau Freres
White
Stone fruit, toasty butterscotch, and light, fresh acidity. Nice buttery length.
£ 11.50 WAV

Saint Véran 2007, Cave De Prisse White
Good concentration of pineapple and citrus character. There is attractive ripeness on palate, which is balanced with refreshing acidity.
£ 11.00 THS

Simonnet-Febvre Chablis Preuses Grand Cru 2006, Maison Simonnet-Febvre
White
Fresh, flinty nose, with intense aromas of pear and toasted bread. Very smooth, oily structure and complex taste.
£ 40.00 FAW, FNC, HFB

Tesco Finest* Chablis 1er Cru 2007, Unions Des Viticulteurs De Chablis White
White stone fruit character, with notes of apple, creamy lees, and mineral acidity. Zesty and clean.
£ 8.00 TESC

Vire Clesse Cuvée À L'ancienne 2005, Boutinot
White
Almond aromas, with a buttery palate, showing ripe fruit, and full creaminess.
£ 11.10 WES

White Burgundy Cuvée Philippe Bourgogne 2005, Boutinot White
Waxy, creamy palate, with stone fruit flavours. A good wine; elegant and harmonious.
£ 11.40 WES

Avery's Fine Red Burgundy 2006, Sarl Nicolas Potel Red
A vegetal nose, showing some age and development, with good structure, and a clean finish.
£ 11.00 AVB

Beaujolais-Villages Château De La Pierre 2008, Loron Et Fils Red
Bubblegum and banana nose, with supple cherry fruit on the palate, and a medium finish.
£ 8.00 CHH

Beaujolais-Villages 2008, Domaine De Saint-Ennemond Red
Freshly crushed strawberries and raspberries, with lively acidity and spice on the finish. A gluggable wine.
AVB

Beaune Du Château 2006, Bouchard Père & Fils Red
Pure fruit aromas, with plenty of fragrance. Maturing quickly overall, this is a fresh and flavoursome wine.

Beaune Grèves Premier Cru 2006, Domaine Du Château De Meursault Red
Lightly perfumed with red berries, matched on the palate with new oak undertones and fresh tannins.
£ 27.50 PAT

Beaune Premier Cru Les Avaux 2007, Domaine Lucien Jacob Red
This wine is attractive to the eye, with a pure red fruit character. Crisp, light, elegant, and harmonious.
£ 19.20 3DW

Bourgogne Grand Ordinaire Rouge 2008, Labouré Roi Red
Intense rich strawberry notes. Soft and pleasant on the palate, with carbonic maceration character.

Chambolle-Musigny 2007, Domaine Michel Gros Red
Rich, ripe, and spicy nose, showing delicate fruitcake on the palate.

Chambolle-Musigny Dufouleur Père Et Fils 2006 Red
Nutty, sweet cherry nose, and stone fruit character on the palate.
£ 30.00

Chassagne-Montrachet 2007, Domaine Lamy Pillot Red
A nose of lovely ripe red berries with a touch of oak, which follow through to the palate. A little on the lean side, but very fresh and persistent.
ABY

Château De La Terriere Brouilly 2008, Scea Des Deux Châteaux Red
Bright cherry fruit on the nose, with nice, rounded, balanced fruit on the palate.

Château De Meursault Bourgogne Pinot Noir 2005 Red
Pale red in colour, with a brown-tinged edge. Hints of spice on the nose, with meaty, tobacco notes on the palate.
£ 15.00 PAT

Fixin 2007, Domaine Mongeard-Mugneret Red
A lovely rich berry fruit nose, leading to an attractive base of strawberry and cassis on the palate. Long finish.
£ 30.00 LIB

Fleurie Calvet 2008, Pasquier Des Vignes Red
Lovely ruby purple colour. Full, fresh aromas. Good summer berry and cherry notes, with touch of banana. Firm, spicy finish with persistent length.

Fleurie Hospices De Belleville 2008 Red
Pure nose, with real depth of fruit, packed full of maraschino cherries. Fresh, clean finish.
£ 13.50 LIB

Gevrey-Chambertin En Songe 2007, Domaine Lucien Jacob Red
This wine is crisp and fresh, with fruit giving way to some fragile notes, with plenty of chocolate on the palate, which finishes on a long, smooth, and dry note.
£ 19.20 3DW

Gevrey-Chambertin Le Creot 2007, Jean-Claude Boisset Red
This wine starts very nicely, and is well-balanced, with slight bitterness on the finish.
£ 35.00 LIB

Gevrey-Chambertin "Les Evocelles" 2007, Domaine De La Vougeraie Red
This wine has a lovely colour, and a nose of soft black cherry fruit, with a soft body, and nicely textured fruit.

Henry Fessy Château Des Ressiers Regnie 2008, Henry Fessy Red
Floral violet nose, smooth, with a good uncomplicated finish and decent balance.
£ 11.50 FLA, LOL

Joseph Drouhin Rully Rouge 2006 Red
Smooth palate, with good grip, a sweet red fruit character and very nice oak. The finish is tannic but will soften.
£ 13.00 WAIT

Louis Jadot Beaujolais Villages Combe Aux Jacques 2008 Red
Very fresh strawberry fruit on the nose. Attractive juicy palate, supported by lively acidity. Easy-drinking.
£ 9.00 WAIT, HMA

Louis Jadot Lantignie 2008 Red
Jammy bubblegum nose, with palate of dark cherry and intense strawberry, with good tannins.
£ 9.00 HMA

Mazis-Chambertin Grand Cru 2007, Albert Bichot Red
Earthy nose, with rich, deep flavours on the palate. Persistent and elegant, displaying great finesse.

Mercurey 1er Cru Les Vasees 2007, Louis Max Red
A subtle nose, with elegant, floral fruit aromas. Crisp tannins, balanced acidity, and a moderately intense finish.

Monthélie 1er Cru "Le Meix Bataille" Cuvee Signature 2007, Bouchard Aine & Fils Red
A very elegant nose, with soft attack on a savoury palate. Nicely balanced, with a good finish.

Nuits-Saint-Georges Aux Lavières 2007, Jean-Claude Boisset Red
Bright floral aromas, with strawberry and leather notes. Soft, silky tannins, and a long finish.
£ 40.00 LIB

Nuits-Saint-Georges 2007, Labouré Roi Red
Pale crimson in colour, with a stewed stone fruit nose. Fruity light body, with savoury flavours.

Patriarche Gevrey-Chambertin 2007 Red
Very light red hue, with a funky rhubarb and strawberry nose, and a soft, textured palate.
£ 30.00 PAT

Pommard Premier Cru Clos De La Commaraine 2007, Pierre André Red
Perfumed plum and black fruit aromas. Creamy and spicy, with fresh acidity and some fine-grained tannins evident.
RBC

Savigny-Les-Beaune 1er Cru Les Peuillets Cuvée Signature 2007, Bouchard Aine & Fils Red
This wine has a ripe, full nose of gamey, black cherry fruit. An intense spicy, floral, fruity palate supported by oak, with a medium body and finish.

Vosne-Romanée 1er Cru Aux Brûlées 2007, Domaine Michel Gros Red
Earthy, mushroomy nose. Great richness of flavour, which is intense and persistent.

Marsannay Rosé 2007, Domaine Du Château De Marsannay Rosé
Ripe strawberry fruit with hints of herbs on the nose. Good balanced acidity and length.
£ 13.50 PAT

Cremant De Bourgogne NV, Cave De Lugny Sparkling
Very clean with nice acidity. Fresh green apples predominate on the palate, with hints of lime zest.
£ 10.00

Fête De Famille 2002, Domaine De La Vougeraie Sparkling Red
Attractive, bright red apple fruit, with yeasty aromas. Full-flavoured, with a broad palate and vibrant mouthfeel.

Crémant De Bourgogne Rosé NV, Domaine Brelière Sparkling Rosé
Pleasant, with a touch of cherry, showing good weight and balance, with some oaky fruit.
£ 11.80 3DW

France:
Champagne

Imagine a world without Champagne. While sparkling wine hits the spot for a refreshing aperitif and social occasions, there are times where only the world's finest will do. It's the blending expertise of these Gallic alchemists that gives each bottle its own house style. Grown on chalky French soils, a combination of one white grape (Chardonnay), and the white juice of two red grapes (Pinot Noir and Pinot Meunier) are brought together in perfect proportions, to give unique French flavours to a style imitated worldwide. This year saw success through gold tinted flutes for a UK supermarket's own-label Champagne; a sensible purchase considering the quality of grape-growers sourced to make this wine.

KEY FACTS

Total production
2.9 m hectolitres, 3.96 million bottles (2007)

Total vineyard
35,280ha of which 32,706ha is productive: 23,722ha in the Marne Department; 6,681ha in the Aube and Haute-Marne; 2,303ha in the Aisne and Seine-et-Marne

Top varieties
● Pinot Noir
● Pinot Meunier
● Chardonnay

Producers
15,000 wine-growers including 4,733 who produce their own Champagne (Récoltants Expéditeurs), 65 co-operatives and 284 negocians

2009 IWC PERFORMANCE

Trophies	5
Gold	17
Silver	74
Bronze	78
Great Value Awards	2

Champagne Jacquart Allegra Millésime 2002 Sparkling
Creamy, moussy, toasty, integrated palate, with toasty ripe fruit, heaps of brioche, and old, bruised apple nuances. Incredible layered complexity, with excellent balance, and real length.

 **MATURE VINTAGE CHAMPAGNE TROPHY**

Charles Heidsieck Blanc Des Millénaires 1983 Sparkling
Well-evolved, good fruity nose, with notes of honey and hazelnut. Deliciously tart fruit,, multi-layered, with a very good length of toasty, citrus intensity.
£ 245.00 BB&R

 **DANIEL THIBAULT TROPHY (CHAMPION SPARKLING), YOUNG VINTAGE CHAMPAGNE TROPHY**

Charles Heidsieck Blanc Des Millénaires 1995 Sparkling
Elegant Chardonnay character, with lime custard notes on a leesy, lively, fresh palate, which shows lovely Chardonnay flavour. Long, fresh citrus flavour, and an elegant finish.
£93.00 WUO

Charles Heidsieck Brut Millésimé 1982 Sparkling
Lovely mature wine, with aromas of toast and old mahogany. The fizz is beginning to fade, but it still has wonderful toasty, woody persistence, with fresh acidity and good length.

Charles Heidsieck Brut Millésimé 2000 Sparkling
Delicious, crisp, complex

aromas of minerality, brioche, and nuts. Great balance, with notes of complex apple, nuts, and honey, with a gentle, creamy mousse.
£50.00 BB&R, HAR, VHS

Charles Heidsieck Champagne Charlie 1985 Sparkling
An even stream of small bubbles, with a lovely, toasty, bready, yeasty nose. Good weight of ripe fruit and acidity, with a long fresh palate.

Grand Vintage Collection 1990, Moët & Chandon Sparkling
Pale yellow in colour. Very fresh on the nose, with hints of toast and lime marmalade. Intense citrus palate, with a lovely creamy mousse, and great length, leading to a lovely fresh finish.

Henriot Vintage 1998 Sparkling
Pale yellow in colour, with a good mousse. Fresh citrus nose, showing elegant maturity. Lovely balanced fruit palate, with pineapple, melon, and lemon notes. Complex flavours and good length.
£35.00 BUT, CAM, SEL, WHR

Le Brun De Neuville Lady De N Chardonnay NV Sparkling
Well-developed, with aromas of toast, wheat, and minerals, with lemon fruit on the nose. The palate is dry, toasty, and biscuity, showing minerality, good acidity, and great length.
£32.00 WAW

Noble Cuvée De Lanson Blanc De Blancs 1998 Sparkling
Delicious, toasty, complex nose, with a palate which displays complex, savoury notes over brightly intense Chardonnay

fruit. Very harmonious and delicate.
£88.00 BEL, BWL, HAR

Pommery Louise 1998
Sparkling
Very intense, mineral, and flinty, showing richness and depth. Very complex, with hints of tropical fruit joining the toasty chocolatey flavours, backed up by lovely acidity.
£94.00 HAR, J&B

Taittinger Comtes De Champagne Blanc De Blancs 1999 Sparkling
Fine, youthful, and restrained, with a complex mineral and toasty citrus nose. Lovely palate of fresh, creamy fruit, with a delicate, very long finish.
£117.50 WAIT, HMA

 **NON VINTAGE CHAMPAGNE TROPHY**

Taittinger Prelude Grands Crus NV Sparkling
Strong full character. A very vivacious mousse, with a complex biscuit and bread palate, showing hints of lemon and nuttiness, and leading to a full, long finish.
£39.20 FLA, HMA

Waitrose Brut NV Champagne NV Sparkling
Yeasty brioche on the nose, with apricot tones. Toasty and fruity, yet poised, with fine mousse. Gentle acidity, with pleasant flavours of marmalade and brioche.
£19.00 WAIT

Rosé Brut NV, Champagne Duval-Leroy Sparkling Rosé
Vibrant spiced plum and raspberry nose. Lovely balance of acidity, with fine bubbles, a touch of honey, and elegant

notes of cherries and cream; an extremely attractive wine.

 **ROSE CHAMPAGNE TROPHY**

Rosé De Castellane NV
Sparkling Rosé
Attractive pale salmon pink in colour. Creamy mineral and toasty aromas with notes of red apple. A savoury note on the palate combines with red apple skin. Lovely, finely-integrated mousse.

Veuve Clicquot La Grande Dame Rose 1998
Sparkling Rosé
Supple, very Pinot Noir heavy, with rich strawberry notes. Showing lovely development, and a good toasty character. A sexy, alluring wine with excellent length and balance.
£150.00 EDC, MWW

SILVER

Asda Extra Special Vintage Champagne 2002, Fabien Henry Sparkling
Straw colour, with medium-sized bubbles. Grapey, marzipan aromas, with a palate of creamy almonds. Good acidity and body. Zesty and elegant.
£20.00 ASDA

Besserat De Bellefon Cuvée Des Moines Brut NV
Sparkling
Fresh, with good purity of fruit, and steely elegance on the palate, leading to a long, fresh finish. Brisk, lively flavours and good complexity.
£30.00

Blanc De Blancs Brut 1er Cru 2004, Champagne Mandois
Sparkling
Deep straw colour, with biscuity

aromas. Well-balanced vibrant palate, leading to a long, creamy finish.

Blanc De Blancs Brut NV, Champagne Napoléon
Buttery brioche on the nose, with a yeasty and autolytic character. Medium intensity, with flavours that follow through on palate. Medium length and good acidity. Drinking well now.

Brut De Castellane NV
Very fresh, clean citrus nose. Lovely mousse, with zesty lemon fruit, fresh acidity, and good staying power.

Brut Elite NV, Champagne Binet   Sparkling
Deep golden colour. The nose shows hints of yeast and toast. Full palate, almost vintage in style.

Brut Imperial NV, Moët & Chandon   Sparkling
Showing some maturity, with bold, tangy fruit. Hints of brioche and hazelnut, with a creamy mouthfeel, and good acidic balance.
£27.00 BNK, CHH, FLA, TESC, WAIT

Canard-Duchêne Cuvée Leonie NV, Canard Duchêne
Creamy aromas, with soft biscuit tones. Good yeast influence and nice strawberry fruit, with a good, long, almondy finish.
£20.00 EDC

Champagne Chanoine Brut Grande Réserve NV   Sparkling
Subtle yeasty nose, with lovely apple and pear palate, and exuberant notes of strawberry. Refined, with good length.
CRI

Champagne Forget Brimont Brut Premier Cru NV
Fresh, creamy, sweet fruit nose, with light toast. Full, ripe appley fruit, with a touch of brioche on a crisp palate. Good mousse, with balanced acidity.
£18.00 GWI, J&B, JNW, PEA, ROD

Champagne G.H.Mumm Cordon Rouge Millésime 1999, Didier Mariotti
Nutty and rich aromas, with fruity edges. Texture is deep and satisfying texture, without excessive weight. Good minerally length.
£33.00 SAIN, MWW

Champagne G.H.Mumm Cordon Rouge NV, Didier Mariotti   Sparkling
Clean, floral nose, and a fresh lemony taste, with light, elegant bitterness. Nice bead. Truly drinkable.
£26.40 SAIN, TESC, WAIT, ODD, THS

Champagne Jacquart Katarina NV   Sparkling
Bready nose, with some development and subtle floral notes. Fresh palate of citrus zest and stone fruit, leading to good length.

Champagne Lenoble Brut Intense NV   Sparkling
Pale yellow in colour. Good, yeasty, fruity nose, with a hint of minerality. Positive rounded palate, with yeasty complexity on the finish, and a pleasant length.
£20.00 CMI, EOR, RWA

Champagne Lenoble Brut Nature NV   Sparkling
Pale yellow in appearence. Clean

and minerally, with delicate fruit, and an elegant yet simple finish. £20.00 CMI, EOR, RWA

Champagne Michel Lenique Grand Cru Blanc De Blancs 2004 Sparkling

Nose of bread and chalky minerality, with a fine, delicate mousse, and ripe fruity character, with savoury undertones.
£29.40 3DW

Champagne Perrier-Jouët Grand Brut Millésime 1998, Hervé Deschamps Sparkling

Clear pale yellow appearance, with a good mousse of small bubbles. Fresh, clean nose of lemon and lime. Clean and refreshing, with a satisfying, light richness.
£37.00 HAR, HVN, MWW, SEL

Champagne Ritz Brut NV, Alliance Champagne Sparkling

Elegant, complex nose, showing a yeasty autolytic character. Rich-textured, with clean, fresh acidity. Crisp appley fruit on the palate, with hints of minerality.
£25.00 HAR

Champagne Roger Legros - Extra-brut NV Sparkling

Biscuity nose, and quite a rich palate, with fresh acidity and a fine mousse. Good acidity, with a long, citrus finish.
£14.80

Chanoine Vintage Champagne 2002 Sparkling

Straw-coloured wine, with brioche flavours, and notes of biscuit, green apple, and lees. Well-balanced, persistent acidity, and a crisp, refreshing finish.
£40.10 TESC

Charles Ellner Carte Blanche NV, Jean-Pierre Ellner Sparkling

Creamy, yeasty nose, with some

toasted bread aromas. Very smooth and elegant. Slightly flinty, with a lasting finish.
£26.00 M&S

Cuvée 225 Vintage 2003, Centre Vinicole-Champagne Nicolas Feuillatte Sparkling

Blossom and lemon on the nose, with elegant hints of cream and minerality.

Cuvée Des Sires Grand Cru 2004, Roger Brun Sparkling

Clean and intense, with fine, yeasty hints. Medium body, with excellent acidity and mousse.
£35.50 LIB

Cuvée Lady Millésime - Brut 2000, Champagne Paul Goerg Sparkling

A touch of caramel biscuit on the nose, leading into an elegant palate of tropical fruit. Very firm acidity, and a long, crisp finish.

Cuvée Perle D'Ayala 2000 Sparkling

The nose shows nice leesy character. Very fine, with a persistent mousse, and crunchy acidity. Showing good, elegant autolytic character, and a nice lemon soufflé finish.
£50.00 M&S

D De Devaux L'Ultra NV Sparkling

Young, yeasty nose, with hints of soft red fruit. There are lots of perfumed, dry floral notes, with young, fresh intensity. Creamy texture and length, with balanced finesse. This has potential.
£40.00 LIB

De Saint Gall Brut Blanc De Blancs 2004, Union Champagne Sparkling

Fine mousse, with opulent

aromas. Minerality and developing complexity on palate, leading to a long citrus finish.
£24.00 M&S

Design Paris NV, Champagne Duval-Leroy Sparkling
Fine bubbles. Toasty, with peach and butterscotch aromas. Plenty of ripe apple and citrus notes on mid-palate, with almonds and white peach to finish.
HAR, MCT, WUO,

Devaux Blanc De Noirs NV
Sparkling
Intriguing collection of flavours. Hints of nutmeg and clove spice on a soft fruit palate, with fine mousse and decent length.
£28.50 LIB

Devaux Grande Réserve NV
Sparkling
Attractive creamy nose, with undertones of soft red fruit. Starting to show subtle age-related development, with good persistence.
£27.00 LIB

Femme De Champagne 1996, Champagne Duval-Leroy
Sparkling
Pale yellow in colour. Clean, fresh, and elegant, with a leesy character. Full-flavoured, with an intense mousse.
HAR, MCT, WUO,

Fleur De L'Europe Brut NV, Champagne Fleury Sparkling
Pale colour and delicate mousse. Yeasty apple flavours, with a steely mid-palate. High acidity, with a long, elderflower finish.

Grande Reserve NV Champagne Prin Pere & Fils NV, Sparkling
Pale golden yellow in colour. Bready and biscuity, with an

attractive mousse, and a big, rich, yeasty nose and finish.

Heidsieck Gold Top 2002, Vranken Pommery Monopole
Sparkling
Delicate, elegant nose. Creamy mouthfeel, leading to a dry mid-palate, with fine acidity. Cool and long.
£33.00 MWW

J.Charpentier Champagne Cuvée Pierre Henri Brut NV
Sparkling
Showing a lot of finesse for Pinot Meunier, with delicate notes of strawberry, underlined by a bready character and creamy texture.
£32.00 CPE

Janisson Et Fils Premier Cru NV Sparkling
Attractive and soft, with nice fruit on the nose. Quite mineral in the mouth; long, tasty, crisp, and balanced; an elegant style.
£22.80 ASDA

Lanson Gold Label Brut Vintage 1998 Sparkling
Medium gold colour, with an intense nose of brioche and yeast, with some toasty notes. Rich and full palate, which is powerful and toasty, with great length.
£37.00 BEL, BWL, HAR, MWW

Lelac Brut NV, Sarl Lallement Dubois Sparkling
Seductive Champagne, with a lush creamy nose and good definition. The palate shows poise and elegant acidity, leading to a chalky finish.

Marks & Spencer Oudinot Brut NV, Château Malakoff
Sparkling
Lively, mineral, and pure news, with fresh, focused appley fruit.

wineRACK

Wine Rack are proud to offer you a discerning range of still wines, sparkling wines and Champagne from all corners of the globe.

We make choosing the perfect wine easier, with recommendations, helpful suggestions and something special whatever the occasion.

Wine Rack Manager's Promise*

Buy with confidence and experiment because if you're not completely happy with your bottle of wine or Champagne, you can bring it back and we'll replace it with another bottle of equal value free of charge. That's our promise to you. Just ask in store for details.

So why not visit us and experience

Over 300 wines and Champagnes

Terms and conditions apply, ask in store for details.

www.winerack.co.uk

The palate is clean, fine, dry, and focused, with fine texture and good length. Well-balanced, with real potential to age.
£20.00 M&S

Marquis De La Fayette Champagne Brut NV, S.A. Champagne Pierrel Et Associés Sparkling
Tight, steely apple mousse, and a complex nose and palate. Clean, elegant style, with balanced pear and apple fruit, leading to a lovely long finish.
£22.50 CPE

Millésime Brut 2002, Champagne Paul Goerg
Sparkling
Bright apple and citrus aromas, with notes of bready honey. Fresh acidity, with an underlying apple and autolytic character. Creamy lees note, with a fresh, balanced finish.
£29.00 LAI

Noble Cuvée De Lanson Brut 1998 Sparkling
Elegant, with citrus aromas and baked apple on the nose. Subtle autolytic character, with zesty acidity, and good concentration.
£77.00 BWL

Nostalgie 1999, Champagne Beaumont Des Crayeres
Sparkling
Rounded, creamy nose, with a nice toasty character. Crisp and dry, with good richness, a honeyed mid-palate, and a long, quite powerful finish.

Orpale Grand Cru 1998, Union Champagne Sparkling
Rich, leesy nose with lots of autolytic character. Clean, light Chardonnay fruit, with rounded elegance, and a great, long finish.
£50.00 M&S

Philipponnat Réserve Millésimée 2002, Champagne Philipponnat Sparkling
Nice golden colour. Very bright and youthful. Hints of brioche and crunchy apple, with some greenness. Rich, mouth-filling mousse, and sparkling acidity.

Pierrel Champagne Cuvée 'Traditions' Brut NV, S.A. Champagne Pierrel Et Associés Sparkling
Firm positive flavours, with baked apple and brioche character. Round and supple, with a fine mousse and a clean finish.
£21.60 CPE

Piper-Heidsieck Brut NV, Champagnes P. & C. Heidsieck Sparkling
Rich, yeasty, and fresh. Full, ripe, and toasty, with lively orange and red berry fruit on the palate. Good texture, with a delicate finish.
£24.20 ASDA, TESC, CWS, HOF, HVN, MCT, SBS

Piper-Heidsieck Rare Millésimé 1999, Champagnes P. & C. Heidsieck Sparkling
Complex brioche aromas, with obvious oak, and rich tertiary flavours. Keen mid-palate, with a fresh, creamy finish.
£102.00 BB&R, VHS

Pommery Grand Cru 1998
Sparkling
Pale lemon colour, with a good mousse. Citrussy nose, leading to a palate which is full of well-balanced fruit and acidity, with a dry pineapple and lime character. Good length, on a very attractive wine.
£40.00 J&B

Radcliffes De Brissar Vintage 2002, Chanoine Sparkling
Golden straw colour, with a

nutty, honeyed nose. Weighty mouthfeel, with a good toasty character and crisp high acidity.

Reserve 1er Cru Brut NV, Edouard Brun Sparkling
Opulent aromas of ripe yellow plums. Fresh, and well-balanced with a long, peachy, lemon zest finish.
£30.00 LIB

> **GREAT VALUE CHAMPION SPARKLING, GREAT VALUE SPARKLING BETWEEN £15 AND £20**

Sainsbury's Blanc De Noirs Champagne NV, Société Coopérative De Producteurs Des Grands Terroirs De La Champagne Sparkling
Lifted soft red fruits aromas. Attractive, with good integrated fizz. Full of flavour, with notes of golden apple, and a full mouthfeel, with nice creamy texture.
£16.00 SAIN

Somerfield Prince William Champagne NV, Union Champagne Sparkling
Bright, fresh and citrussy, with a hint of yeasty complexity. Rich, creamy palate of soft brioche, with notes of minerality.
£17.00 SMF

Tesco Finest* Premier Cru NV, Union Champagne Sparkling
Gentle, creamy, and vigorous, with a really good core of flavour; there is a crisp, bready character, with some yeasty richness.
£19.00 TESC

Tesco Finest* Vintage Champagne 2004, Union Champagne Sparkling
Fine nose of brioche and apple. Well-balanced palate with zingy,

fresh apple acidity, and showing some richness.
£20.00 TESC

Veuve Clicquot La Grande Dame 1998 Sparkling
Mature honeyed notes of cream and ginger. Relatively dry, biscuity, and mature - it's delicious now.
MWW

Vinothèque 1996, Champagne J. Dumangin Fils Sparkling
Pale gold in colour, this is soft, dry, and elegant. Lots of acidity and finesse, with a long finish.
YAP

Vintage Brut Reserve 2002, Veuve Clicquot Ponsardin Sparkling
Medium gold in colour, with broad solid bubbles. The nose shows developmental toasty, savoury notes and a rich, yeasty brioche character. The body is tight and taught, falling away slightly on the mid-palate. Long and soft.
£45.20 CHH, TESC, WAIT

Vintage Cave Privée 1980, Veuve Clicquot Ponsardin Sparkling
Good complexity and a great nose, which is clean and biscuity. Crisp palate, with hints of mushroom and brioche, leading to a fine finish.

Vintage Cave Privée 1990, Veuve Clicquot Ponsardin Sparkling
Fine mousse, with a textured nose of fresh apple, with hints of mushroom. The palate is equally fresh, dry, and crisp, with an elegant, lasting finish.

Vintage Rich Reserve 2002, Veuve Clicquot Ponsardin Sparkling
Good autolytic notes, with a

clean, fine spritz. Rich structure, with balanced acidity.

Waitrose Blanc De Noirs Brut Champagne NV Sparkling
Understated, toasty, and yeasty, with some richness and a fresh finish. Delicate complexity, with nice balance.
£18.00 WAIT

Waitrose Special Reserve Vintage Brut Champagne 2002 Sparkling
Full, fine, creamy mousse. Rich palate of soft strawberries, with ample fruit and weight, balanced with high acidity.
£27.00 WAIT

Alexandre Bonnet Extra Rosé NV Sparkling Rosé
Lovely delicate nose with a yeasty biscuit character. Floral notes with hints of citrus, leading to a dry finish. Complete, and showing good finesse.

Besserat De Bellefon Cuvée Des Moines Brut Rosé NV
Sparkling Rosé
Very fine mousse. Pale pink in colour, with orange blossom tints, and a strong autolytic character on the nose. Very elegant, with delicate fruit on the palate, and fresh acidity.
£34.00

Champagne Forget Brimont Rose Premier Cru NV
Sparkling Rosé
Lifted pear and red apple fruit. Palate is fresh, but smooth and rounded. Fine bubbles and elegant texture; an attractive style.
£19.50 GWI, J&B, JNW, PEA, ROD

Champagne G.H.Mumm Rosé NV, Didier Mariotti
Sparkling Rosé
Aged and complex, with toasty

notes of biscuit and yeast on the nose. Soft, rounded palate, showing good concentration and autolytic character.
£34.30 SAIN, WAIT, ODD

Champagne Le Brun De Neuville - Cuvée Rosé Brut NV Sparkling Rosé
Vivid orange-pink colour, with firm black fruit aromas. Fresh attack on the palate with good fruitiness - very attractive. Balanced with a touch of minerality.

Grand Vintage Brut 2003, Moët & Chandon
Sparkling Rosé
Intense, with lovely flavour development and maturity. Thick toast and earthiness on the nose, which come through to the palate.
£40.00 WAIT

Marks & Spencer Oudinot Rosé NV, Château Malakoff
Sparkling Rosé
Appealingly light and fragrant, with floral aromas, and red berry fruit. Lifted and light; a fresh style, with nice elegance.
£23.00 M&S

Rosé Brut NV, Edouard Brun
Sparkling Rosé
Good delicate nose, and a palate of juicy red fruit, underlayed with a fine-beaded, persistent mousse. Balanced and harmonious, with a lingering finish.
£33.00 LIB

Taittinger Brut Prestige Rosé NV Sparkling Rosé
Gentle strawberry notes, quite vinous, in a restrained way. Good, fresh fruit and flavour, with surprising length and grip.
£40.50 FLA, WAIT, HMA

Taittinger Comtes Des Champagne Rosé 2004
Sparkling Rosé
Clean, fresh, and vibrant nose. Good mouthfeel, with clean, citrus fruit, a creamy body, and lovely balance and finish.
£210.00 HMA

Tesco Rosé Champagne NV, Champagne Chanoine
Sparkling Rosé
Salmon pink in colour. Restrained, leafy, raspberry nose. Delicate, fruity, and refreshing, with good small, frothy bubbles, and a light autolytic note.
£18.00 TESC

BRONZE

Authentis Cumières 2003, Champagne Duval-Leroy
Sparkling
Toasty, spicy nose. Notes of rich, fresh, cream, sherry, and nuttiness. An exciting wine, with a long and irresistible finish.
HVB, MCT, WUO

Besserat De Bellefon Cuvée Des Moines Brut Millésime 2002 Sparkling
Pale green golden colour, with a subtle, persistent mousse, and flavours of ripe apples, yeast and toastiness. Lively mid-palate, with good balance.
£36.00

Bredon Brut NV, Piper & Charles Hiedsieck Sparkling
Lovely bready nose, with fresh fruit and some yeastiness, which carries through to the finish.
£19.00 WAIT

Brut Tradition NV, Champagne H.Blin & Cie
Sparkling
Attractive colour, with flavours of yeast and bread, showing good freshness. Well-balanced and long.
£20.00 ACG, CLC, HTW, ODD, ODF, PTD

Brut Vintage 2003, Champagne H.Blin & Cie
Sparkling
Citrus fruit on the nose. Abundant large bubbles, with raspberry and citrus fruit on the palate.
ADN, DMR, EHB, HTW, ODD

Champagne Blanc De Blancs Brut NV, Vollereaux
Sparkling
Light, fresh citrus nose. Lightly sweet, with pear character on a crisp, racy palate.

Champagne Brut Tradition NV, Serge Matthieu Sparkling
Very clean, iconic Champagne. Light and elegant, with an excellent finish and good length.
£28.00 LIB

Champagne Deutz Brut Classic NV Sparkling
Fresh, with bready lees character, brisk acidity, and moderate length.
£30.00 FLA, BCC, BWC

Champagne G.H.Mumm De Cramant NV, Didier Mariotti
Sparkling
The nose is open and round,

with creamy richness. Full, round palate, with biscuity flavours, and a dash of hazelnut. Nice weight and richness, with good length and acidity.
£45.70 WAIT, HAR

Champagne G.H.Mumm Grand Cru NV, Didier Mariotti Sparkling
Intense nose of yeast and butter. Creamy entry, with fine bubbles and fresh acidity.
£36.70 WAIT, HAR, HOF

Champagne Georges Gardet Brut Special NV Sparkling
Notes of yeast and toast, with fresh acidity, and a peppery finish.
ALE, CNL, GHC, GHL, HOT, OSB, THC

Champagne Georges Gardet Cuvée Saint Flavy (Brut Tradition) NV Sparkling
Interesting nose, showing balanced fruit, with some yeasty notes. Nice smooth palate, with good, persistent finish.

Champagne Grand Cru 2004, Philizot & Fils Sparkling
Pale straw colour. Clean, elegant nose of honey, with some green apple. Smooth mousse and good acidity.
£32.70 3DW

Champagne Gremillet Brut Grande Reserve NV Sparkling
Interesting nose of raisins and biscuits. Fresh, light, lemony, and fruity. Persistent fine bubbles.
£21.50 FLA, WES

Champagne Jacquart Blanc De Blancs Millésime 2004 Sparkling
Fine mousse and attractive nose of honeyed apple and toasted nuts. Light, youthful palate.

Champagne Jacquart Brut De Nominée NV Sparkling
Pale straw in colour. Aromas of tropical fruits, with lifted guava, paw-paw, and mango. Long, clean finish.
£45.00 HAR

Champagne Jacquart Brut Millésime 2002 Sparkling
Frothy, medium-intensity bubbles. Nutty, with creamy strawberries and zingy acidity. Good mouthfeel and a yeasty finish.
£35.00 MWW

Champagne Jacquart Brut Oenothèque Grand Millésime 2000 Sparkling
Clean style. Quite austere, steely, and very dry, with plenty of concentration, and a long, fruit-focused finish.
£45.00 HAR

Champagne Jacquart Extra Brut NV Sparkling
Clean and minerally, with a floral hint on the nose. Finish is crisp and rounded, yet fresh, with good length.
£27.80 ASDA, TESC, MWW

Champagne Mailly Grand Cru Les Echansons 1999 Sparkling
Good, rounded, creamy fruit, with good minerality. The finish is quite long and clean.
£65.00 BB&R

Champagne Michel Lenique Brut 2004 Sparkling
Pale lemon hue. Good mousse, with some full, ripe fruit, and lovely length.
£24.90 3DW

Champagne Michel Lenique Réserve Blanc De Blancs NV Sparkling
Yeasty nose, underpinned by

apple and flowers. Fairly full fruit palate, good acidity and a biscuit crumb texture.
£18.30 3DW

Champagne Perrier-Jouët Grand Brut NV, Hervé Deschamps Sparkling
Floral nose, with a hint of yeastiness. The palate shows stone fruit, leading to a long finish.
£30.00 HAR, HOF, MWW, ODD, SEL

Champagne Pierre Bertrand Brut 1er Cru NV, Champagne Pierre Bertrand Sparkling
Fresh, floral, lightly biscuity, and chalky on the nose. Crisp, perfumed red berry fruit, with some biscuity notes.
£24.00 CAM

Champagne Raoul Collet Blanc De Blancs NV Sparkling
Very clean and light, with notes of white flowers. Pleasant and creamy, with excellent balance.
FUL

Champagne Ritz Brut Millésime 2000, Alliance Champagne Sparkling
Nice elegant bouquet, with a fresh, fine mousse, and notes of grilled nuts on the palate.
£35.00 HAR

Champagne Tsarine Cuvée Premium Brut NV, Chanoine Frères Sparkling
Fine, honeyed notes of maturity, with a fresh, vibrant, biscuity palate. Clean, with a good mousse, well-intergrated fizz, and nice balance.

Charles Heidsieck Brut Réserve NV Sparkling
Fresh apple aromas, which carry through to a fresh palate, with a crisp, appealing finish.
£29.00 WAIT

Charles Lafitte Vintage 2001, Vranken Pommery Monopole Sparkling
Bright yellowy-green colour, with a nose of peachy toasted brioche, and rounded ripe fruit. The palate is smooth and quite elegant.
£36.00 J&B

Clos Des Bouveries 2003, Champagne Duval-Leroy Sparkling
Ripe, Mediterranean-style nose. Soft, warm bread texture, with a delicious palate of light fruit, and well-balanced acidity.
HVB, MCT, WUO

Comte De Brismand Champagne Brut Réserve NV, Lidl Sparkling
Apple and brioche aromas, with a touch of smoked cheese. Creamy mousse, with notes of vanilla.
£14.00 LDL

Cuvée Speciale Vintage 2000, Centre Vinicole-Champagne Nicolas Feuillatte Sparkling
Clean, with medium intensity. Toasty and balanced, with soft acidity and a fine, juicy finish.

D De Devaux La Cuvée NV, Champagne Devaux Sparkling
The nose shows development, with nutty, floral notes underpinned by fresh fruit.
£35.00 LIB

De Saint Gall Blanc De Blancs 1er Cru NV, Union Champagne Sparkling
Youthful nose, with chalky, minerally notes overlaying sweet lemon and apple fruit aromas. Good depth of well-defined fruit, with good acidity. Plenty of potential.
£23.00 M&S

De Saint Gall Brut Tradition 1er Cru NV, Union Champagne Sparkling
Delicate aromas of white flowers and spice, with some yeasty, toasty complexity, fresh good citrus fruit, and a creamy mousse.
£20.00 M&S

Demi-Sec NV, Champagne Duval-Leroy Sparkling
Sweet, fragrant nose, with notes of citrus. Sweet ripe fruit, and a gentle mousse.
BTH

Fleur De Champagne Brut 1er Cru NV, Champagne Duval-Leroy Sparkling
Full, weighty nose, with good bready character. Medium-bodied, with balanced acidity.
£27.00 WAIT, HVB

Fleur Noire 2003, Champagne Beaumont Des Crayeres Sparkling
Fresh and clean on the nose, with aromas of blossom, and ripe apple. Refreshing, quite creamy, and well-balanced.

François Dubois Brut NV, Champagne Nicolas Dubois Sparkling
Aged savoury nose, with a delicate mousse. Crisp, balanced acidity and good length.
£29.00 TESC

François Dubois Cuvée Divine NV, Champagne Nicolas Dubois Sparkling
Baked apple on the nose. Thre palate shows hints of strawberry and apple, with nice acidity and a fresh finish.
£17.00 TESC

Grande Sendrée 2002, Champagne Drappier Sparkling
Elegant ripe nose, with an

excellent balance of acidity and sugar, and a fresh finish.
ABY

Heidsieck Blue Top NV, Vranken Pommery Monopole Sparkling
Discreet nose. Flavoursome and easy-drinking, with good grip.
£22.70 SAIN, TESC, MRN

Heidsieck Red Top NV, Vranken Pommery Monopole Sparkling
A subtle nose, hinting at minerality and almond. Well-defined, with good acidity and balance.
£24.00 ASDA

Henriot Blanc Souverain NV Sparkling
Clean, light, and delicate, with a nose of fresh white flowers. Delicate, fresh, and pure, with a fine mousse. A young, lighter style, with good acidity.
£31.00 CAM, HAR, L&W, SEL

Henriot Brut Souverain NV Sparkling
Palate of intense fruit, with good balance and a crisp, citrus finish.
£29.00 CAM, PAR, SEL, WHR

Janisson Et Fils Blanc De Noirs Grand Cru NV Sparkling
Toasty ripe fruit on the nose, with good weight, and a rich finish.

Le Brun De Neuville Blanc De Blancs NV Sparkling
Nicely developed, with biscuity, toasty, macaroon notes. Round, silky palate, with fresh sweet fruit, and a delicate finish. Upfront and full-flavoured.
£22.00 WAW

Marks & Spencer Vintage Oudinot 2002, Chateau Malakoff Sparkling
Medium bubbles, with currant

bun flavours, overlayed by yeasty notes. Crisp acidity and a refreshing, citric finish.
£24.00 M&S

Millésime Brut 1995, Champagne Napoléon
Sparkling

Powerful nose, with hints of cheese tart. Spicy character, with some hints of baked apple; deep-flavoured and savoury.

Millésime De Castellane 2002
Sparkling

Straw coloured, with a persistant mousse, and an intense, yeasty sensation on the palate. Good overall balance, and a moderate finish.

Philipponnat Cuvée 1522 Gran Cru 2002, Champagne Philipponnat Sparkling
Clean, elegant nose with biscuity notes. Good acidity and balance. Well-structured.

Philipponnat Royale Réserve NV, Champagne Philipponnat
Sparkling

Rich, toasty Champagne, with good autolytic character, and an elegant, creamy mousse.

Pierre Darcys Brut NV, Champagne Paul Laurent
Sparkling

Very fine, elegant Champagne. Pinot Meunier character adds complexity. Showing hints of maturity, but there is still ample freshness.
£24.00 ASDA

Piper-Heidsieck Cuvée Sublime NV Sparkling
Green apple freshness, with lovely, creamy honeyed sweetness, and lively balancing acidity.
£29.00 CWS

Pol Roger Brut Reserve NV
Sparkling

Warm brioche notes. Clean, crisp and appley, with medium length.
£34.10 CHH, WAIT, BB&R, BEC, BEN, TAN, TAU

Radcliffes De Brissar Brut NV, Chanoine Sparkling
Gentle, fresh apple nose, leading to a crisp, slightly nutty palate. Fine bubbles and lingering finish.
£17.00 WRC

Sainsbury's Taste The Difference Premier Cru 2003, Champagne Duval-Leroy
Sparkling

Taught nose. Showing good acidity, bearing in mind the vintage, with nice honeyed fruit, and very tasty length.
£20.00 SAIN

Taittinger Brut Vintage 2003
Sparkling

Rich, full, and creamy brioche aromas, with hints of fresh citrus. Full, young, and yeasty, rich in fruit, with good acidity. Still very young.
£44.90 FLA, HMA

Taittinger Les Folies De La Marquetterie NV Sparkling
Citrus aromas, with hints of yeastiness on a clean, fresh palate.
£48.00 HMA

Tesco Blanc De Noirs Champagne NV, Champagne Chanoine Sparkling
Complex yeasty nose, with mineral notes, and hints of biscuit. Intense steely palate of citrus and flint.
£15.80 TESC

Vintage 1999, Champagne Duval-Leroy Sparkling
Freshly developed, with tertiary aromas and freshness. Rich, nutty

flavours, and a long, textured, creamy finish.

Waitrose Blanc De Blancs Nv Brut Champagne NV Sparkling
Buttery, creamy, and lightly floral. The palate shows creamy flavours and texture, with a fruity length. Well-balanced, with a long finish.
£22.00 WAIT

Alexandre Bonnet Rosé NV Sparkling Rosé
Lifted berry nose, with a light autolytic character. Lovely understated mousse, and creamy texture.
£25.00 WAIT

Asda Rosé Champagne NV, Jacquart Sparkling Rosé
Biscuity nose, with soft fruit on a mid-weight palate. Fine bubbles and crisp acidity.
£19.00 ASDA

Brut Rosé NV, Champagne H.Blin & Cie Sparkling Rosé
Deep colour, with fresh berry aromas. Fresh finish and good structure.
£28.00 DMR, HTW, LAI, PTD

Champagne Aspasie Brut Rosé NV, Ariston Sparkling Rosé
Salmon pink in colour, with fine bubbles, and pronounced strawberry and red apple aromas. Fresh style, with crisp acidity.

Champagne Jacquart Brut Rosé Grand Millésime 2004 Sparkling Rosé
Attractive pale salmon colour. Yeasty, bready nose, with red fruit and good balancing acidity.

Champagne Jacquart Brut Rosé Mosaïque NV Sparkling Rosé
Young and fresh, with a fruity mid-palate. Good aperitif style.
£35.00 MWW

Champagne Perrier-Jouët Blason Rosé NV, Hervé Deschamps Sparkling Rosé
Pale pink in colour, with a soft floral nose, leading to a delicate body, with hints of biscuit.
£39.50 HAR, HVN, MWW, SEL, VHS

Champagne Tsarine Rosé Brut NV, Chanoine Frères Sparkling Rosé
Forward orchard fruit aromas combine with earthy breadiness. Full and fleshy, with good fruit.
£35.00 WAIT

Charles Heidsieck Rosé Millésimé 1999 Sparkling Rosé
Clean, fresh, and appealing. Beautiful colour, with silky fruit on the palate. Delicate, yet pleasing.
£75.00 HAR

Charles Heidsieck Rosé Réserve NV Sparkling Rosé
Very pale salmon in colour. Red apple aromas, with good acidity, and a mouth-filling mousse.
£40.00 BB&R, VHS

Fleur De Rosé 2003, Champagne Beaumont Des Crayeres Sparkling Rosé
Deep pink colour, with a lasting mousse. Good balance of fruit and yeast on the nose, with notes of red fruit and biscuit.

Fleury Brut Rosé De Saignée NV, Champagne Fleury Sparkling Rosé
Nose of fresh rhubarb and

raspberry, following through to the palate, which also displays fresh yeastiness.

Heidsieck Rose Top NV, Vranken Pommery Monopole
Sparkling **Rosé**
Floral nose, with a touch of yeastiness. Light, refreshing palate, with good length and elegance.
£27.00 TESC, MRN

Henriot Rosé NV Sparkling Rosé
Gentle and creamy, with notes of strawberry. Fine, creamy, and soft, with lovely balance. Not too dry; this is flavoursome and easy-drinking.
£32.00 SEL

Lanson Rosé Label Brut Rosé NV Sparkling **Rosé**
Clean, delicate fruit nose. Restrained, balanced, and well-structured.
£32.40 ASDA, SAIN, TESC, BWL, MWW

Louis Dubrince Brut Rosé NV
Sparkling **Rosé**
Deep cherry red in colour, with attractive red and black fruit aromas. Full-flavoured, with a touch of residual sweetness, and notes of cream and spice.
MRN

France:
Languedoc-Roussillon

The world's largest wine-making region, Languedoc-Roussillon produces wines that exhibit the greatest qualities of stone, vine, and sun. The region has witnessed an increasing number of organic and biodynamic producers making wine that reflect the area's finest traits. Offering some of France's – and indeed the world's – best value wines, the consistent Mediterranean climate rarely fails to deliver. The area comprises almost 30,000 winemakers, amongst them French film star Gérard Depardieu, who has been making wine here since the early 1980s. With an aim to making the wines more comprehensible, an umbrella title of Sud de France has been introduced, representing wines from Nimes in the East, to as far as the Spanish border town of Banyuls in the West.

2009 IWC PERFORMANCE

Trophies	4
Gold	5
Silver	27
Bronze	53

 INTERNATIONAL VIOGNIER TROPHY, LANGUEDOC-ROUSSILLON WHITE TROPHY

Laurent Miquel Vérité Viognier 2007 White
Lush, ripe apricot fruit, with balanced acidity. This has a nicely concentrated, aromatic style; an elegant, soft, dry wine, with super-long, ripe fruit on the finish.
£14.00

Domaine Fontsèque 2007, Gérard Bertrand Red
Wild blueberry and redcurrant;, with gorgeously layered blackberries, smokiness, orange peel, and rosemary. Wonderful mouthfeel, and a long and luxurious finish.

 FRENCH CABERNET SAUVIGNON TROPHY

Famille Skalli -Cabernet Sauvignon 2007, Vin De Pays d'Oc Red
This wine displays exquisite use of subtle, and no doubt expensive, oak. Notes of dark currants and leather. Extremely suave and stylish palate.
£6.00

 LANGUEDOC-ROUSSILLON RED TROPHY

La Garrigue 2007, Scea Château Camplazens Red
Traditional style, with a touch of brett. Rich tutti-frutti nose, with red berries, meatiness, and well-integrated oak. Long, complex, and balanced, with a spicy finish.
£9.20

L'absolu De Château Rouquette Sur Mer 2007, Jacques Boscary Red
Aromas of black olive, with bold, meaty sausage, and mild herbs. Fruity, sweet, and creamy, with elegant, soft tannins. A delicious example.
£59.00

Trois Terres 2007, Graeme Angus Red
This is a very exciting example of Grenache from the Hârault, with lots of raspberry, white pepper, and spice flavours. Elegant structure, with fine floral tannins.

4 Clochers 2007, Sieur D'arques White
Lovely nutty, savoury fruit on the nose. Stylish, long, complete, and pure on the palate. Juicy, satisfying finish. Very good.
£7.00 TESC

Abbotts Zephyr 2007, Abbotts Brothers Sas White
Bright sweet fruit on the nose, with a palate showing spicy new wood and citrus and generous barrel treatment. Creamy tropical fruit quality, and gorgeous length.
£14.50

Domaine De La Baume - Chardonnay - Les Vignes De Madame 2008 White
Star-bright lemon hue. Lightly toasted, with zingy citrus notes. Well-integrated oak and lovely balance, leading to good length.
£8.00

Domaine De La Baume - Sauvignon Blanc - Les Mariés 2008 White
Pungent nose of smokiness and grass. Nice nutty dried herb

character, with passionfruit and good balancing acidity, leading to a dry finish.
£8.00

Domaine Ventenac 2008, Sarl Vignobles A. Maurel White
Plum and herbal notes, with hints of straw. Tangy green fruit on the palate, with a honeyed mouthfeel. Full and concentrated, with good length and minerality.
£7.00 WAIT

Les Jamelles Viognier 2008, Badet Clément & Co White
Bright lemony fruit, with delicate apricot tones, nice intense floral perfume, good balanced acidity, and great length.
£5.50 ASDA, CWS

Réserve Saint Martin Chardonnay 2008, Coop Val D'Orbieu White
Pale gold in colour. The nose is unoaked, with notes of fresh citrus, leading to a creamy lemon palate. Mouthfilling, with good length and acidity

Tête De Cuvée De La Jasse 2008, Sarl Blb Vignobles / La Jasse White
Fruit is green, yet ripe, with tea-like hints, and notes of citrus and pineapple on the nose. Lengthy finish and very nice lemony tang, with zip of acidity.
£9.00 L&W, WHR

3 Naissances 2005, Domaine De Familongue Scea Quinquarlet Red
Slightly reduced, spicy, dark nose, with an open palate, which is meaty and spicy, and culminates in a long, dark fruit finish.

Asda Extra Special Shiraz 2008, Domaines Paul Mas Red
Fresh and fruity. Delicate floral palate, with a rounded finish.
£6.00 SWS, ASDA

Château De Lastours "Réserve" 2005, Sca Famille P. & J. Allard Red
Attractive, open, and floral, with garrigue character. Chunky, pleasantly rustic black fruit, with a good balance of moderate acidity and medium-firm tannin.

Château De Pennautier "Terroir D'altitude" 2006, Vignobles Lorgeril Red
Medium-depth ruby colour. Flavours of plum, currant, and black pepper come through on the palate, with soft tannins, toasty oak, and a lingering finish.
£10.00 DNL

Château L'Hospitalet Réserve 2007, Gérard Bertrand Red
Attractive pepper spice note. Hint of greenness, with spicy oak, good complexity, and a firm finish.

Château Rouquette Sur Mer Cuvée "Henry Lapierre" 2007, Jacques Boscary Red
Hints of meatiness, with a stylish, oily texture. Firm but well-integrated tannins. Very attractive black olive flavours.

Château Triniac 2007, Cazes Sas - A Part Of Jean Jean Group Red
Long, profound, and complex. A great wine, with a lovely, rich, peppery finish.

Fitou Château De Segure 2007, Mont Tauch Red
Pungent, fruity, smoky nose, with rich, ripe fruitcake tones.

Flavoursome, pure, and well-integrated tannins. Clean and long.

Fitou Domaine Saint Roch 2007, Mont Tauch Red
Lifted perfumed, with fine bright aromas. Juicy, flavoursome, chewy, and highly refreshing. An excellent wine – crying out for food.

La Difference Carignan 2008, Vindivin Red
Elegant, with nice fruit intensity, tart flavours of burnt fruit, with hints of plum. Good tannins lead to a dry finish.
£5.10 ASDA, TESC, CWS

Le Vent Du Nord 2007, Domaine De Sainte Rose Red
Nose of open, frank fruit and vanilla oak. The palate is quite tightly-wound, with a fresh finish and good length. Delicious!
MWW

Les Fiefs D'Aupenac 2007, Cave De Roquebrun Red
Lovely ripe fruit and earthy spice on the nose, with a clean, enduring, blackberry fruit-driven palate.
£8.00

Mas Gabinèle Cuvée Rarissime 2006, Thierry Rodriguez Red
Intense black fruit on the nose, with notes of pepper. Modern style, with bitter tannins, good structure, and excellent length.

Pic Saint Loup: Mas Bruguière L'Arbouse 2007, Xavier Bruguière Red
Slightly reduced roasted nose, with sweet fruit. The palate shows rich fruit, with some meaty notes.

Premium 2007, Scea Chateau Camplazens Red
Medium-bodied, with very floral herby aromas. Very ripe, sweet fruit, with mineral notes.
£15.00

Roche Mazet Cabernet Sauvignon 2008, Castel Frères Red
Elegant fruitiness on the nose, with vanilla aromas. Smooth, fruity, floral, and rounded, with soft tannins and chocolate on the palate.

St Chinian Roches Noires 2006, Caves De Roquebrun Red
The palate shows grippy tannins, with hints of liquorice and bramble jelly. Gentle spice and dark raspberries on the finish.
£8.00 TESC

Arnaud De Villeneuve Ambré Hors D'Age 1982, Les Vignobles Du Rivesaltais Fortified
Orange-amber colour. Nose of lifted butterscotch and vanilla, with marmalade, orange peel, and hints of honey and cantaloupe on the palate.
£11.30 WAIT

Cornet & Cie Banyuls Rimage 2007, Abbe Rous Fortified
Bright cherry-red colour, with notes of lifted cloves and plums on the nose. Fresh blackberry and jelly bean on the palate, with attractive powdery tannins.
£15.00 MJW

BRONZE

Aigle Noir Chardonnay 2008, Gérard Bertrand White
Gentle, pleasing, nutty aromas. Fresh, balanced, appetising, young, and fresh.

Aigle Royal 2007, Gérard Bertrand White
Rich, creamy, pleasantly toasty, and flavoursome, with well-integrated oak, and some minerality.

Ancien Comté Cuvée De La Comtesse 2008, Mont Tauch White
This is a fun wine, with a fresh melon nose, good acidity, and an attractive glycerol texture.

Asda Extra Special Chardonnay 2008, Domaines Paul Mas White
Zippy, tangy apple and lemon, with creamy notes. Young fruity taste on the palate, with nice sourness on the finish.
£6.00 SWS, ASDA

Asda Extra Special Viognier 2008, Domaines Paul Mas White
Clean, aromatic nose, with fresh peach and stone fruit, and a long, fresh finish.
£6.00 SWS, ASDA

Asda French Oc Marsanne 2008, Les Vignobles Foncalieu White
Notes of pear and light stone fruit, with a pleasant mouthfeel, good length, and an oily finish.
£3.20 ASDA, BWL

Cigalus Blanc 2007, Gérard Bertrand White
Notes of peach and apricot; lemony rich, with a tropical fruit finish.

Famille Castel Chardonnay 2008, Castel Frères White
Pale lemon colour, with a creamy unoaked nose showing lemon notes, which follow through to the palate. Good length.

Famille Skalli - Chardonnay 2007, Vin De Pays d'Oc White
Well constructed, with spicy wood conditioning. Clean and refreshing.
£6.00

La Difference Viognier Muscat 2008, Vindivin White
Positive perfume, with well-structured, exotic fruit, this is refreshing, with a simple, dry finish.
£5.00 ASDA, TESC

La Forge Estate Chardonnay 2008, Les Domaines Paul Mas White
Ripe, well-developed fruit on the nose. Zingy citrus character, with good length on the palate.
£8.00 SWS, THS

Laurent Miquel Viognier Nord-Sud 2007, Laurent Miquel White
Soft, floral apricot fruit, and a light, crisp finish.
£8.00 TESC, MWW

Paul Mas Estate Single Vineyard Marsanne 2008 White
Notes of vanilla, green apple, and custard, with a creamy palate of sour apple and hints of cream, leading to a fresh lemony finish.
£7.80 TESC, MWW

Robert Skalli Viognier 2008, Skalli, Vin De Pays d'Oc White
Concentrated fruit, with pear and apricot, on a floral, fruity nose. On the palate, there is plenty of pineapple fruit. Stylish, with good length.
£8.00

Unicorn Chardonnay 2007, Abbotts Brothers Sas White
Light, clean, fruity nose, with

The short cut
to the great wines
from Languedoc-Roussillon

Sud de France

Maison de la Région Languedoc-Roussillon - London
Tel. + 44 (0) 207 079 33 44 / Fax. + 44 (0) 207 079 33 45
contactuk@suddefrance-export.com / www.maisondelaregionlanguedocroussillon.com

la Région
Languedoc
Roussillon

notes of orange blossom, and a crisp, fresh, lemony palate.
£5.30

Vignes De St Pierre Sauvignon Blanc 2008, Domaine Paul Mas White
Creamy, with typical Sauvignon Blanc character. Fresh, lively acidity, and a pleasant mouthfeel.

Wild Pig Viognier 2008, Vin De Pays d'Oc White
A fresh, peachy nose, following onto a sweet fruit palate, with a soft, ripe character. Mid-palate is quite fat, with a good finish.
£6.30 GYW

3 Naissances 2006, Domaine De Familongue Scea Quinquarlet Red
A nose of violet and raspberry, with sweet broad fruit and vanilla oak, layered over interesting chewy tannins.

Abbotts Cumulo Nimbus 2006 Red
Nice ripe fruit, with good concentration and rich tannins. Complex, with a peppery finish.
£14.50

Asda Corbières 2006, Les Vignobles Foncalieu Red
Very intense aromas of violet Lifted, ripe dark fruit, with gentle spice, and easy tannins on a soft finish.
£3.20 ASDA, BWL

Asda Extra Special Merlot 2008, Domaines Paul Mas Red
Purple in colour, with a nose of fresh red berries. Good concentration of fruit, with balanced tannin and acidity.
£6.00 SWS, ASDA

Asda Vin de Pays d'Oc Syrah 2007, Les Vignobles Foncalieu Red
Attractive red ripe fruit. Just fresh enough, but very clean, modern, and appealing.
£3.20 ASDA, BWL

Averys French Country Red 'Syrah - Grenache' Vin de Pays d'Oc 2008, Xavier Roger Red
Cherries on the nose. The palate shows dry tannins, with a rich, sweet chocolate finish.
£6.00 AVB

Black Beret Grenache Syrah 2005, Union Des Producteurs Du Haut Minervois Red
Earthy developing nose, with notes of red cherry and currants, On the palate there is white pepper, with ripe tannins and harmonious acidity.

Cazal Viel Cuvée Des Fées 2007, Laurent Miquel Red
Bright nose of red cherries. Soft juicy palate, backed up by vibrant acidity.
£9.00 MWW

Château De Lascaux Classique 2007 Red
Very perfumed nose. An elegant wine, with complex layers of vibrant fruit and vanilla, with silky tannins.
£10.00 BB&R, LEA

Château De Lascaux Pic Saint Loup 2007 Red
Blackberry nose, with a palate of soft bramble fruit, underpinned by good chewy tannins.
£9.50 BB&R, LEA

Château De Sérame Réserve Du Château Mourvèdre Grenache Carignan 2007, Dourthe Red
Aromas of dark fruit and garrigue,

with savoury notes. Ripe dark fruit combines with chocolate on the palate. Good length.
£10.00

Chevalier De Puydeval 2008, Jeff Carrel Red
Red and chunky, with a youthful pepper note and with vanilla undertones. Palate of rich red cherry and pepper, with a violet perfume.

Church Mouse Grenache Shiraz 2008, Riviera Wine Company Red
Sweet ripe berry fruit on the nose, with spicy warmth and a rich, sweet, spicy palate. Made in a modern style.
£6.00 GYW

Cigalus 2007, Gérard Bertrand Red
Intense, super-ripe nose, with cassis and plum character, and vanilla oak. Classy.

Collection Daniel Bessiere AOC Corbières 2008, Bessiere Red
Vibrant colour, with a nose of sweet red fruit and white pepper. Jammy raspberry on the palate, with ripe cherries and well-integrated oak.

Cuvée Des Hospices Catalans 2007, Cazes Red
Bright, ripe red berry fruit. Excellent drying tannins and superb acidity, with lovely structure and balance.
CBK

Domaine De L'Aigle Pinot Noir 2007, Gérard Bertrand Red
Notes of cherry liqueur combine with toasty, smoky oak. A smooth rounded palate, with good glycerol texture, and a savoury finish.

Domaine Des Garennes 2007, Gérard Bertrand Red
Jammy big fruit, both on the nose and the palate, with a full body, big tannins, and a herbal finish.

Domaine Montlobre La Chapelle 2007, Sarl Blb Vignobles/Colonie De Montlobre Red
Ripe black fruity nose, with quite a lot of oak. Sweet fruit on the palate.
£10.00 BB&R

Domus Maximus 2006, Venes Red
Bright polished note, showing fine black fruit, attractive perfume and juicy fruit, with balanced acidity and tannin.
£35.00

Famille Castel Cabernet Sauvignon 2008, Castel Frères Red
Good medium intensity colour. Wonderful complexity and good fruitiness, with soft leather and green pepper notes. Solid mouthfeel, not too tannic; very pretty.

Famille Castel Merlot 2008, Castel Frères Red
Restrained red fruit nose, with soft supple tannins and a sweet fruit palate.

Fitou Réserve Du Château De Segure 2007, Mont Tauch Red
Refreshing style, with fresh red berries, and a fleshy, juicy texture. An uncomplicated style, but well-made.

Fitou Villa De Pazuls 2006, Mont Tauch Red
Interesting freshness, with some new oak. Notes of blackberry and attractive spicy fruit, with lovely freshness of flavour.

Grand Canal 2007, Cave De Roquebrun Red
Earthy, leathery nose, leading to a delicious palate of blackberry and ripe fruit.

Grand Terroir Tautavel 2006, Gérard Bertrand Red
Dense, baked, spicy, and earthy aromas. Lots of fruit and bold oak influence. Very long.

La Difference Grenache Noir 2008, Vindivin Red
Very full-flavoured and jammy. Black cherry fruit, with lots of flavoursome fruit and pronounced alcohol. A typical, appealing, supple Grenache from a sunny climate.
£5.50 MRN

La Forge Estate Cabernet Sauvignon 2008, Les Domaines Paul Mas Red
The nose is inky and pure, with a smooth, silky, balanced palate. Ripe and very, very stylish.
£7.70 SWS, ASDA

La Forge Estate Merlot 2008, Les Domaines Paul Mas Red
Rich and complex, with jammy fruit and smooth sweetness on the palate.
£8.20 SWS, THS

La Masquerade Shiraz Vin de Pays D'oc 2006, Boutinot Red
Juicy fruit on the nose, with a smooth palate showing well-balanced oak. Long and persistent.
£6.60

Largesse Shiraz 2008, Les Producteurs Reunis Af 34360 Cebazan Red
Big, rich, smoky, peppery nose, with structured red berry fruit and smooth tannins.
£6.00 AAW

Le Mas 2007, Domaine De Nizas, Vin De Pays d'Oc Red
Interesting tarry redcurrant aromas. Fresh, clean palate, with nice length.
£8.00 GWW

Les Douze Fitou 2007, Mont Tauch Red
Summer pudding overtones on the nose. Fresh fruit salad, with lovely acidity and good tannins on the palate.
£7.00 MWW

Les Quatre Fitou 2007, Mont Tauch Red
Restrained liquorice aromas, with notes of oak. Palate of ripe fruit, with grainy tannins. Well-structured, with good, refreshing flavour.
£8.00 WAIT

L'Ostal Cazes - Estibals 2006, Jean-Michel Cazes Red
Nose of vinous plummy spice. Smooth, multi-layered palate, with plenty of ripe fruit, and a long, lingering finish.

L'Ostal Cazes 2006, Jean-Michel Cazes Red
Well-made wine, with compact fruit, and good depth and complexity, leading to a long, savoury finish.

Marks & Spencer Cuvée Extrême 2006, Vignerons Catalans, South France Red
Chocolate, mocha, and violets on the nose, with blackberry fruit and lacy tannins.
£9.00 M&S

Marks & Spencer St Chinian Bardou 2005, Laurent Miquel South France Red
The palate delivers black pepper, red fruit, and chocolate, with ripe tannins.
£16.00 M&S

Mont Tauch Varietals Marselan 2008 Red

Youthful, sweet fruit, with a good mouthfeel, and some elegance on the finish. Clean, fresh, and attractive.

Paul Mas La Forge Malbec 2008, Les Domaines Paul Mas Red

Intense raspberry and blueberry on the nose. Ripe, juicy palate, with good structure and length.

Riviera Merlot 2008, Vin De Pays d'Oc Red

Clean nose, with a palate of juicy fruit. Nicely balanced.
GYW

Robert Skalli Garrigue 2006, Les Vins Skalli Red

Nose of black fruits, with a palate of leather, savoury notes, dark fruit, and cocoa, with supple tannins and fresh acidity.
£10.00

Robert Skalli Syrah 2007, Vin De Pays d'Oc Red

With silky black fruit aromas, this is really quite serious and savoury. Evident firm, smooth tannins, and good intensity of flavour.
£8.00

Ropiteau L'Emage 2008, Vin De Pays d'Oc Red

Nose of ripe red fruit, with hints of fresh leaf. Clean, vibrant palate.
£6.00

Cazal Viel Vielles Vignes 2008, Laurent Miquel Rosé

Pale salmon pink in colour. Herbal, with mild red berry fruit. Attractive garrigue notes, and good French character.
£7.50 MWW

Château De Caraguilhes 2008, Pierre Gabison Rosé

Bright cherry red in colour. Attractive strawberry fruit aromas, with good ripe summer berry flavours, and a touch of cream.
£7.00 WAIT

Esprit Des Peyrals 2008, Les Vins Skalli Rosé

Cherry red in colour, with light vanilla and plum aromas. Very fresh palate, with good fruit concentration.
£8.00

The Real Rosé Company Cinsault Syrah 2007, Laurent Miquel Rosé

Pretty strawberry pink colour. Nice bright summer berries. Ripe fruit and good acidity.
£6.00 TESC, CWS

1531 Blanquette De Limoux NV, Sieur D'arques Sparkling

Lovely fruity nose, with smoky notes. Crisp, clean fruit on the palate, with good acidity and a long finish.
£10.00 TESC

Rivesaltes Ambre NV, Jean-Marc Lafage Sweet

Dark amber colour, with an elegant, subtle nose. Notes of caramel and marmalade on the palate.
£13.00 BWL

France: Regional

France has an unrivalled wealth of diversity of style amongst its wine regions, home to the majority of the greatest known grapes in the world.

Alsace
The strict vineyard area control ensures quality wines, even at entry level prices. Laced with intense aromatics and flavours, the wines are often recommended to best accompany Asian food.

Loire
An abundance of choice is on offer here when selecting a wine style, from light reds to sparkling wines and of course world class 'stickies' with varying degrees of sweetness.

Rhône
There are two sides to this coin, but either one is a winner. Syrah dominates the wines in the north, sometimes with a dash of white for aromatics. Down south, as many as thirteen different grapes are permitted in the wines of Chateauneuf du Pape. In general, it's the spiciness and fruit character of Grenache, Syrah and Mouvedre that give Rhône wines their global appeal.

South West
When you tire of the same old branded wines, take a walk on the cultured side of life with grapes from this area. The thinking man's wine, South West France is as honest a drop as you'll ever get from a bottle. Prepare to be converted.

2009 IWC PERFORMANCE

Trophies	11
Gold	14
Silver	65
Bronze	184
Great Value Awards	3

LOIRE VALLEY

GOLD

 POUILLY FUMÉ TROPHY

Pouilly-Fumé 2008, Domaine De Bel Air
White
Good intensity on the nose, with dried fruit, walnuts, chalk, and candied fruits. Attractive palate, with very good weight and balance. Vibrant citrus fruit, with a spicy finish.
£13.00 LIB

 LOIRE VALLEY WHITE TROPHY, SANCERRE TROPHY

Sancerre 2008, Domaine Naudet White
Classy mineral white flowers on the nose. Crisp, refreshing lemon fruit, with good richness and depth. Long green apple finish. Classic Sancerre.
ABY

 INTERNATIONAL CABERNET FRANC TROPHY, LOIRE VALLEY RED TROPHY

French Connection Classics Samur Champigny 2008, Alliance Loire Red
Red and black berry fruit, with fragrant leafiness on the nose. Some coconut and spicy oak on the palate, with bananas and redcurrants. Acidity carries the wine to a fresh, warm finish.

 **LOIRE VALLEY SWEET TROPHY**

Bonnezeaux Les Melleresses 2007, Château La Varière
Botrytis
Light lemon-gold in colour. Delightful honeyed botrytis nose. Luscious sweetness and superb acidity. A glass of liquid gold - delicious.

SILVER

Cellar Estates Sancerre 2008, Les Grands Chais De France Group White
Zingy, fresh gooseberry aromas, with crisp, mineral acidity. Good body, with lots of fruit and grassy flavours. Oily texture, with a lingering finish.

Château De Fesles 2006, Sauvion White
Bright and clean, with wet wood and honeyed, waxy notes. Plenty of good, fresh acidity, with a nice finish.

Cuvée Domaine 2008, Domaine Du Tremblay
White
Creamy flavours, with sweet notes of papaya, pineapple, and other tropical fruits. The palate is dry and slightly metallic, with fruit flavours on the finish and strong acidity.
£12.00 LIB

Marks & Spencer Vouvray Domaine Pouvraie 2008, Ackerman Laurance White
Fruity, smoky nose, with hints of green apple. Zesty sweet apple palate. Honeyed, with lively, crisp acidity and some sweetness, ending on a clean finish.
£7.00 M&S

Muscadet de Sèvre Et Maine Sur Lie Domaines Des Hautes Noelles 2008, Lacheteau
White
A truly lovely Muscadet. Astoundingly balanced for this variety. Unctuous citrus blossom notes on a terrific food wine - a good match for roast chicken.
£7.00 MWW, ALD

Philippe Portier 2008, White
Lychees, melon, green apple, and grapefruit on the nose. Slightly salty palate, with citrus, gooseberry and green apple flavours. Good length.
£10.50

Sancerre 'Cuvée Antique', Domaine Claude Riffault 2007, Domaine Claude Riffault White
Very mineral, with restrained white flower notes. Crisp, fresh citrus fruits, with riper stone fruit too. Balanced, with a good, rich finish.
MWW

Tesco Finest* Pouilly-Fumé 2007, Fournier Pere Et Fils
White
Delightful fresh fruity nose of asparagus, with smoky and mineral aromas. Fresh spicy lemon on the palate. Well-balanced, with good acidity.
£11.00 TESC

Château De Targé Quintessence 2006, Edouard Pisani-Ferry Red
Ripe black berry fruits and oak. A full, rich style, with high extract and ripeness. Good flavour, with lots of appeal.

Crémant De Loire Brut NV, Langlois-Château
Sparkling
Delicate restrained fruit, with citrus aromas and hints of aniseed. Good mouthfeel, with some biscuity notes on the palate. Light fizz and good acidity. Well-balanced and refreshing.
£10.30 WES, FAW, LAI, MWW, ODD

BRONZE

Anjou Cuvée 1895 2008, Domaine De Salvert White
Crisp apple and pear aromas which follow through to the palate. Crisp acidity, and youthful character.
£7.40 3DW

Château Du Coing De Saint Fiacre 2008, Véronique Günther-Chéreau, Vin de Pays du Val De Loire White
Clear and bright. Lime character on the nose, with notes of young fresh pears. Lively acidity on the palate, with good follow-through of lime and pears. Easy-drinking.

Château De Targé Les Fresnettes 2007, Edouard Pisani-Ferry White
The nose has some honey, plus toasty oak, and ripe apple and lime fruit. Intense oak toastiness dominates the finish.

Château Soucherie Savennières Clos Des Perrières 2007 White
Fresh delicate nose of perfumed apples. Appley mineral palate, with a hint of apricot. Bone dry, with a pure long finish.

Cuvée Vieilles Vignes 2008, Domaine Du Tremblay White
Restrained nose of melon, citrus,and vegetables. Fresh palate, with good, balanced fruit, and grippy acidity.
£16.00 LIB

Domaine Gauither Jasnieres 2008 White
Nose of fragrant jasmine, green apple, and apricot. Floral palate, with intense spiced green fruit.
£9.00 DLA, MWW

Grande Garde 2005, Boullault Frères White
Pale gold colour. Pears and honey on the nose, with notes of white flowers and summer straw. Complex character, with terrific balance - utterly intriguing.

Haute Culture Château Du Cleray 2007, Sauvion White
Vanilla, Golden Delicious apples, and pear on the nose. Good acidity. Pleasant drinking.
£17.00 BWC

Joël Delaunay Domaine Sauvignon Blanc 2008 White
Ripe lemon and hints of grass. Dry, restrained, and very pleasant, with linear acidity and a good, fresh finish.
£8.00 ALE, MWW, SGL

Le Rochoy 2007, Domaine Laporte White
Bright, with grapefruit and limes on the palate. Crisp fruit, very balanced, with elegant citrus and lime fruit flavours.
ARL, EOR, PAT, RWM

Marks & Spencer Touraine Sauvignon 2008, Jacky Marteau White
Grassy, nutty notes on the nose. The palate shows zesty acidity and good flavour concentration, with some nice savoury flavours.
£6.50 M&S

Marks & Spencer Vin de Pays du Val de Loire Sauvignon 2008, Lacheteau White
Aromatic, with asparagus and grass on the nose. Citrus notes, supported by high acidity on a nicely rounded palate.
£5.00 M&S

Muscadet de Sèvre Et Maine Sur Lie Tesco 2007, Les Grands Chais De France Group White
Pale straw colour. Fresh, lively, and highly aromatic notes. Modernist nose of green fruit, lime, and pears. Pleasant drinking.

Pascal & Nicholas Reverdy Sancerre 'Terre De Maimbray' 2008, Gaec Reverdy White
Lovely grassy, gooseberry aromas. Crisp and well-balanced, with floral notes and a lime-fresh finish.
£15.00 AVB

Pouilly-Fumé 2008, Lacheteau White
Pale straw in colour, with a delicate bouquet of tropical fruit and marmalade. Rich and balanced, with a great finish.

Pouilly-Fumé Sainsbury Taste The Difference 2008, Figeat White
Fresh nose of lovely apple and chalkiness, with a honey-scented palate of ripe, zesty orange and lemon peel.
£11.00 SAIN

Quincy, Jean-Charles Borgnat 2007, Domaine De La Commanderie White
Green mango, gooseberry, and mineral aromas, with hints of truffle and ripe acidity.
£8.00 MWW

Reuilly 2008, Domaine Henri Beurdin White
Intense aromas of gooseberry and grass, with some mineral notes. Fresh, light palate, with

green notes and high acidity.
£10.00 MWW, SDC, SGL, UPT

Sancerre Blanc Les Collinettes 2008, Joseph Mellot Sas White
Clean, vibrant mineral fruit. Zesty and quite acidic, with a blackcurrant leaf finish.

Sancerre Chavignol, Paul Thomas 2008 White
Green tropical aromas. Good acidity and light body, with some minerality coming through on the palate. Lifted, lingering finish.
£12.00 MWW

Sancerre 'Cuvée Edmonde', Alphonse Mellot 2007 White
Soft fruit and oaky spice, with a rounded palate. Clean and well-made.
£25.00 MWW

Sancerre Les Espailles, Domaine Sautereau 2008 White
Elegant, green, herbal aromas. Good gooseberry fruit, and some sherbet minerality, with a good finish.
£13.40 RIC, TBO, UPT

Sancerre Selection "Latuiliere" 2008, Cave Des Vins De Sancerre White
Dried hay aromas. Minerality and elegance on a palate, which shows crisp acidity, with a good, rounded finish.
£11.00 ALD

Sancerre Taste The Difference 2008, Florian Mollet White
Fresh, grassy aromas. Rounded palate, showing hints of asparagus, and an oily texture, with minerality on the finish.
£12.00 SAIN

Sauvignon Vin De Pays Du Val De Loire 2008, Ackerman

Rémy Pannier, Vins Du Val De Loire White
Summertime in a bottle. Delightful, fragrant, sweet, edgy gooseberry character. Unpretentious, fresh, and clean.
£5.00

Vouvray 2008, Ackerman Rémy Pannier White
Nose of flinty mnerality, with green apple following though to the palate, which also displays hints of herbal apricot.
£7.00

Anjou Villages Brissac Cuvée J. Beaujeau 2008, Château La Varière Red
Intense ripe berry fruit, with ripe tannins, and good balance and length.

good raspberry fruit aromas. The palate shows soft ripe tannins, and good balance and length.

Domaine Du Roncée, Clos Des Marronniers 2007, Baudry-dutour Red

Earthy, soft, ripe tannins, with good black fruit intensity and oaky complexity. The palate is fresh and moderate, with a soft, round attack.

Saumur-Champigny 2008, Domaine De La Cune Red

Nose of redcurrant, leafiness, violet, and oak. Dry, firm tannins, with persistent red fruit.
£9.00 3DW

Saumur-Champigny Les 3 Jean 2007, Domaine De La Cune Red

Perfume of violet, oak, plums, and red fruit. Light body, with redcurrants on the palate.
£11.30 3DW

La Grille - The Classic Loire 2008, Union Des Vignerons De Saint-Pourçain Rosé

Pale salmon pink colour, with a palate that is crisp and lively, delicate yet tangy, leading to a tangy strawberry finish.

Les Deux Clochers 2008, Union Des Vignerons De Saint-Pourçain Rosé

Charming and fresh. Appealing and dry, yet fruity, with a pleasantly dry finish.

Sancerre Rose La Demoiselle 2008, Joseph Mellot Sas Rosé

Floral on the nose, with hints of fresh strawberries. Refreshing, crisp acidity.

Bouvet Saumur Brut Blanc Gd Excell. Mx NV, Bouvet Ladubay Sparkling

Fresh clean nose. Excellent fruit

Anjou Villages Brissac Vieilles Vignes 2007, Château La Varière Red

Dark red in colour, with a fresh palate of dark berries and earthiness, with grassy and toasty notes. Fair complexity, clean tannins, and a medium length, fresh finish.

Charles Joguet Les Petites Roches 2006 Red

Intense red colour, with a nose of fruity cassis, and leafy reduced notes. The palate displays red fruit, with firm, dry, tight tannins, and good acidity.
£10.00 WAIT

Domaine Du Roncée 2008, Baudry-Dutour Red

Pale to medium red in colour. A lifted nose, full of fruit, with attack on the palate, with good flavour and well-integrated fizz.

Bouvet Saumur Brut Blanc Saphir Mx 2006, Bouvet Ladubay Sparkling
Apple and pear aromas, with hints of minerality. Showing some complexity on an attractive, crisp palate. Clean and consistent.

Bouvet Saumur Brut Blanc Trésor 2006, Bouvet Ladubay
Sparkling
Attractive herby fruit on the nose. Pure, clean fruit palate, with crisp acidity and notes of pear.

Marks & Spencer Château Moncontour Vouvray 2006
Sparkling
Fresh appealing aromas. Typical pale gold Chenin Blanc colour. Small bubbles, and nice fruity palate.
£10.00 M&S

Réserve Du Château Grandin NV Sparkling
Nice yeasty aromas. Rich, yeasty, biscuity flavours on the palate, with hints of almond, and some light, delicate fizz.

Saumur Mousseux 1811 Brut NV, Ackerman Rémy Pannier
Sparkling
Lifted notes of strawberry with good sweetness of fruit. Very fresh and clean, with a long finish.
£9.00

Crémant Rosé 2007, Domaine Pibaleau
Sparkling Rosé
Light strawberry notes, with a citrus edge. High acidity and good length.
£9.20 3DW

RHÔNE VALLEY

GOLD

Chêne Bleu Aliot 2006 White
Honeyed beeswax nose, with ripe stone fruit character. Delicious ripe soft peach and honeysuckle fruit, with light oak. Persistent, rounded flavours; an attractive style.
£32.00

GREAT VALUE RED BETWEEN £10 AND £15

Caves Saint Pierre-Préférence Gigondas 2007, Les Vins Skalli Red
Sweet, peppery, black fruit nose, with a very ripe, dense blackcurrant palate, which is earthy, stony, and very fruity. This is balanced with some complexity, and excellent structure.
£14.00 TESC

 **CÔTES DU RHÔNE TROPHY**

Caves Saint Pierre- Préférence Signargues 2007, Les Vins Skalli Red
Good fruit intensity, with soft tannins and balanced acidity. Good depth of fruit. Racy and elegant, with good length.
£10.00

Crozes-Hermitage Domaine Des Grands Chemins 2006, Delas Frères Red
Big savoury Syrah scent, with a touch of violet. Very classic, true Syrah character on the palate, with good structure. Concentrated and controlled.
£18.00 BWC

Cuvée Les Pierres Châteauneuf-du-Pape 2007,

Cellier Des Princes Red
Nose of raspberry and fruity
sweetness, with a nice
suggestion of coffee. Delightful
mid-palate sweetness. Tangy,
with good length.
THS

HERMITAGE TROPHY

**Hermitage Marquise De La
Tourette Rouge 2006, Delas
Frères Red**
Open, spicy meaty nose, which is
aromatic and fresh. The palate is
juicy, complex, and focused, with
some meaty, spicy character, and
lovely density.
£38.50 BWC, FWL

**RHÔNE VALLEY
TROPHY,
CHÂTEAUNEUF-
DU-PAPE TROPHY**

**Marks & Spencer Châteauneuf
Du Pape Domaine Des
Sénéchaux 2006 Red**
Young intense aromas, which
are sweet and rich on the nose,
with lots of white pepper and
fresh fruit coming through on the
palate. A smoky, rather rustic style.
£23.00 M&S

**Saint Joseph Cave De Tain
2007 Red**
Huge aromatic structure, with
nice vanilla aromas and good
black fruit. Delightful freshness
and gentle tannin, with chocolate,
and toasty oak on the finish.

SILVER

**Les Terres Salees Christophe
Barbier Vin de Pays des Côtes
De Perignan 2007, Christophe
Barbier** White
Pale lemon hue in the glass, good

lemon and lime fruit on the nose
and palate. Really good length.
Very attractive.
£13.00 AVB

**Cairanne Réserve Des
Hospitaliers 2006, Boutinot
Red**
Spice and slightly savoury notes
over aromas of red fruit. Ripe
red fruit on the palate, with firm
structure and good balance.
£8.00 WAIT

**Caves Saint Pierre- Préférence
Stjo 2007, Les Vins Skalli Red**
Soft fruit on a background of
game and leather. Closed yet
well-structured.
£14.00

**Caves Saint Pierre-
Préférence Vacqueyras 2008,
Les Vins Skalli Red**
Dark and earthy, with a slightly
herbaceous nose. Big, well-
structured palate, with a dry,
elegant, soft spice finish.
£12.00

**Cellier Des Princes
Châteauneuf-du-Pape 2007
Red**
Crunchy raspberries and
sweetness on the palate, with
a hint of an animal, earthy
character. Rich style, with a long,
tangy finish.

**Château Beauchene
Châteauneuf-du-Pape Grande
Réserve 2006, Château
Beauchene Red**
Toasty, perfumed, ripe plum
nose. Beautifully developed,
with juicy ripe fruit and real
complexity. Well-structured,
with some tannic grip.
C&B

Chêne Bleu Abelard 2006 Red
Lifted, high-toned aromas of
abundant red fruit, with deep,

and heavily dark bramble notes.
£36.50

Chêne Bleu Heloise 2006,
Red
Firm dark fruit aromas. Really
big and chunky, with firm tannin,
lots of power, and a meaty, oaky
structure.
£42.00

Côte-Rôtie Seigneur De
Maugiron 2007, Delas Frères
Red
Spicy bold dark fruit on the
nose, with a nuance of pepper
and vanilla. Grippy structure and
silky oak.
£39.50 BWC

Côtes Du Rhône Domaine De
St Roman 2008, Fgvs Boisset
Red
Bright, vibrant nose of wild
strawberries and red liquorice,
with a palate that is crisp, and
full of spice flavours.
£6.80 BNK, MHV

Côtes Du Rhône Parallele
45 Red 2007, Paul Jaboulet
Aine Red
Bright red and black fruit, with
intense concentration. Jammy
blackcurrant palate, with a
good finish.
£8.00 LIB

Côtes-du-Rhône, Belleruche
2007, M. Chapoutier Red
Deep garnet colour. Earthy nose,
with notes of cherry and currant.
Velvety palate, with nice balance.
Elegant, good, and interesting.
£8.00 WES, BTH, MWW, WIM

Domaine Bastide d'Eole 2008,
Vignerons de Caractère Red
Plummy blackberry nose, with a
hint of pepper. Soft plum, cassis,
and blackberry on the palate.
Juicy and rounded, with plenty of
tannins.

Domaine de la Curnière 2008,
Vignerons de Caractère Red
Unmistakably meaty, with spicy
oak and redcurrants. Lots of spicy
black fruits and pepper on the
palate, with balancing acidity,
vanilla oak, and integrated
tannins.

Domaine de la Maurelle 2008,
Vignerons de Caractère Red
Soft red and black fruit. Peppery,
with crushed plums on a fresh,
ripe palate, with good balance
between tannin and fruit.

Domaine Des Escaravailles
Les Antimagnes Côtes-du-
Rhône Rouge 2007 Red
Light ruby in colour. Vanilla
and oak nose, with some violet
aromas. Concentrated fruit on
palate, with great length.
£10.00 CAM

Domaine Des Sénéchaux
2006, Jean-Michel Cazes Red
Full of beef tomatoes, cherries,
and plummy fruit on the nose.
A rich, chocolate-sweet palate,
with chewy baked rhubarb, and a
long finish.

Domaine Guy Jullian 2007
Red
Baked cherry pie on the nose.
Crisp acidity, and a rounded
palate of concentrated black
fruit.

Joncier Lirac Rouge 2007 Red
Vibrant red fruit, with a nuance
of garrigue, and lovely acidity.
Floral body, with white pepper
spice, and good length.
£9.00 WAIT

La Chasse Du Pape Grande
Réserve Côtes-du-Rhône
Villages Plan De Dieu 2007,
Gabriel Meffre Red
Spices and black fruit on the
nose. Ripe fruity tannins, with

good structure and depth.
leading to a long, fruity finish.
£8.00 GYW

Lavau Vacqueyras 2008 Red
Peppery, floral Rhône nose,
with notes of blackberry and
strawberry. Fresh acidity, and a
spicy, peppery palate, with firm
structure; a good food wine.

Les Figuières 2008, Vignerons de Caractère Red
Perfumed nose of black cherries,
raspberries, and violets. Peppery
palate, with a good balance of
fruit and acidity.

M&S Crozes Hermitage 2007, Cave De Tain Red
Attractive savoury aromas of
freshly ground black pepper,
backed up by dense black berry
fruit.
£9.00 M&S

M&S Hermitage 2006, Cave De Tain Red
Elegant and cedary, with notes
of nutmeg and cinnamon.
Well-structured acidity, and
well-integrated tannins. Long,
lingering finish, developing
complexity and finesse.
£24.00 M&S

Maison Bouachon - Les Rabassières 2007, Les Vins Skalli Red
Lovely raspberry fruit on the
nose. Sweet red berries on the
palate, with pepper, orange peel,
and some lavender. Soft attack
of black pepper, with well-
integrated oak.
£8.00

Maison Bouachon - Prince De Montvert 2006, Les Vins Skalli Red
Youthful and perfumed, with
violet, pepper, and red and black
berry fruit. The juicy fruit is

framed by lovely acidity and silky
tannins.
£30.00

Maison Bouachon - Roc De Monges 2006, Les Vins Skalli Red
Black fruit, sweet spice, cedar,
and pepper on the palate. Silky
tannins and balanced acidity.
Restrained and elegant.
£30.00

Maison Bouachon Dédication 2005, Les Vins Skalli Red
Peppery spice nose, with a juicy,
zesty, sweet palate, and a long
finish. Balanced, harmonious, and
soft, in an attractive, commercial
style.
£35.00

Marquis De Valclair 2007, Ogier Red
Ripe green pepper and berry
fruit on the nose, with dense
black fruit, and a smoky peppery
note on the concentrated palate.
Lowish acidity and high alcohol,
but in balance.
£12.00 ASDA

Ortas Rasteau Côtes Du Rhône Villages Tradition 2007, Cave De Rasteau Red
Lovely Rhône typicity, with an
aromatic violet nose. Sweet red
fruit and ripe tannins, leading to
a long finish.
£12.00

Palais Des Anciens Gigondas 2007, Boisset Red
Very sweet, spicy, black pepper
nose, with dark bramble fruit
and good oak. This is real Syrah;
a big chunky ripper, with a long,
balanced finish.

Robert Skalli Côtes Du Rhône Villages 2007, Les Vins Skalli Red
Scented, spicy nose of juicy

currants and cherry. Fleshy fruit, with good lift and balance. Good potential for ageing.
£9.00

Seigneur de Fontimple 2008, Vignerons de Caractère Red
Light purple in colour. Creamy, herbaceous, and peppery on the nose. Very peppery palate, with red berries and evident tannins.

Tesco Finest* Châteauneuf-Du-Pape 2007, Les Vins Skalli Red
Hints of orange peel and warm spice on the nose. Notes of garrigue, with a full structure. Good ageing potential.
£14.00 TESC

Tesco Finest* Gigondas 2006, Sica Vignerons De Beaumes De Venise Red
Showing some sweet, nutty development on the nose, but also some sweet herbal flavours. Dry fiinish, on a slightly chewy palate, which is savoury and concentrated.
£12.00 TESC

GREAT VALUE CHAMPION ROSÉ, GREAT VALUE ROSÉ BETWEEN £5 AND £10

Côtes Du Rhône Parallele 45 Rose 2008, Paul Jaboulet Aine Rosé
Clean, pure, fresh strawberry fruit. A well-balanced wine with fresh, lively acidity, carrying the flavours to a long finish.
£9.00 LIB, V&C, WIA

La Chapelle Rosé 2008, Enclave Des Papes Rosé
Very pale in colour. Attractive red fruit, showing richness and elegance, with fresh, balancing acidity. Good purity and length.

J Vidal-Fleury Condrieu 2006
White
Sweet, rich aromas of barley sugar and banana, which carry through to the palate. Rich and wholesome, with high alcohol and sweetness.
£30.00 LOL

7 Collines Côtes Du Rhône Villages Rouge 2008, Wineway Red
Intense strawberry and red fruit on the nose. Fruity and balanced on the palate, with dry tannins, full body, and fresh acidity.
£7.00 PAT

Asda Côtes Du Rhône Villages 2007, Les Vins Skalli Red
Black fruit and spice, with a floral accent on the nose. Firm and dry, but juicy.
£4.10 ASDA, THI

Averys Fine Côtes Du Rhône Rouge 2007, Domaine Fond Crozes Red
Youthful nose of jammy fruit which jumps out of the glass. Blackberries and raspberries on the palate, with good balance, making for an easy drinking wine.
£7.00 AVB

Cave De Monterail 2008, Benoit Valerie Calvet Sas Red
Faint berry nose, with notes of ripe cherries, well-balanced with oak. Well-structured fruit palate.
£13.00 ALD

Caves Saint Pierre-Préférence 2008, Les Vins Skalli Red
Aromatic berries and cherries on the nose, with a palate of rich, ripe black cherries, nicely balanced with oak, leading to a long fruity finish.
£17.00

Caves Saint Pierre-Préférence Côtes Du Rhône Rouge 2008, Les Vins Skalli Red

Intense sweet red berries on the nose. Lovely and simple; a well-made wine with great presence.
£9.00

Caves Saint Pierre-Préférence Rouge 2008, Les Vins Skalli Red

Subtle candied red fruit, with an earthy rugged nose, and a delicately smooth finish on the palate.
£7.00

Caves Saint Pierre-Préférence Signargues 2008, Les Vins Skalli Red

Intense cherry and red berry aromas. Juicy, rich palate with hints of coffe on the finish. Full-bodied.
£10.00

cdr 2007, Sarl Image Du Sud Red

Bold, fruity and savoury, this has some weight, with a really good, fine, refreshing finish.

Cellar Estates Châteauneuf-du-Pape 2007, Cellier Des Princes Red

Crunchy redcurrant and raspberry fruit. Vibrant flavours lead to a big, lemony finish.
BES

Château Beauchene Châteauneuf-du-Pape Vignoble De La Serriere 2006, Château Beauchene Red

Elegant and spicy, with a ripe, robust bramble nose, and ripe fruits on the palate, balanced by refreshing acidity.
HTW, PVC

Château des Hautes Ribes 2008, Vignerons de Caractère Red

Fresh, soft palate, with mineral notes and black cherries.

Château Les Quatre Filles Rochegude Côtes-du-Rhône Villages Rouge 2007 Red

Black fruit character. Lovely fruit intensity, with balanced acidity and tannins.
£10.00 AVB

Châteauneuf-du-Pape 2006, La Fagotière Red

Ripe plums and brambles, with hints of violet, leading to a palate of liquorice and cedar, with refreshing acidity.
£18.50 3DW

Côtes Du Rhône 2007, Domaine Des Pasquiers Red

Complex fruit flavours of raspberry and blackberry. Gentle on the palate, this is a well-balanced wine, with a dry finish.

Côtes Du Rhône Villages Calvet 2008, Pasquier Des Vignes Red

Nice cherries on the nose, with hints of red berries. Rich tannic taste, with a sweet finish.

Côtes Du Rhône Villages Plan De Dieu 2007, Domaine Des Pasquiers Red

Sweet blackberries on the nose, with fine, spicy, bramble fruit. Rich and flavoursome on the palate, it has a spicy, almost Zinfandel-like quality, making it highly expressive for a Côtes du Rhône.

Côtes-du-Rhône, Croix Des Grives 2007, M. Chapoutier Red

Elegant nose, with strong berry notes. Well-integrated fruit and

acidity, with a smoky finish.
£10.00 LAI

Crozes Hermitage 2006, Cave De Tain Red
Gentle and attractively perfumed, with big ripe flavours, in a juicy, creamy, modern style.
£11.40 WES

Crozes Hermitage '3 Lys' 2006, Cave De Tain Red
Intense nose of briars and blackberries, with a very nice lift. Good balance, fine concentration, and a harmonious finish.
£8.00

Crozes Hermitage 'Hauts Du Fief' 2006, Cave De Tain Red
Leathery, woody nose, with black fruit flavours, and a peppery dark fruit finish. Good balance.
£13.00

Crozes Hermitage Les Jalets Red 2006, Paul Jaboulet Aîné Red
Black cherry and damson jam, with leafy and liquorice notes. On the palate there are flavours of cherry, blackcurrant, and toasty oak, with black pepper to finish. Good weight and subtle balance.
£12.00 LIB

Cuvée Des Toques 2007, Balma Venitia Vignerons De Beaumes De Venise & Producteur De Vacqueyras Red
Lifted floral spice aromas, with some black fruit. Sweet fruit palate; upfront, with a dry finish.
VLW

Domaine De Carobelle Grenache Syrah Mourvèdre 2008, Vignerons De Caractère Red
Cassis and dark chocolate on the nose. Dark cherries on the palate, with oaky tannins leading to a sweet finish.

Domaine du Grand Prieur 2008, Vignerons de Caractère Red
Nose of dark fruit, with forest aromas. Long finish.

Famille Skalli - Côtes-du-Rhône Villages 2007 Red
Well-made and elegant, with fresh violet aromas, and nicely balanced tannins.
£9.00

Heritages 2007, Ogier Red
Floral aromas, with cherry, raspberry, and slightly spicy white pepper. On the palate, it is meaty, with strawberries, red fruit, and well-balanced oak.

Hermitage 2006, Cave De Tain Red
Fresh, bright palate, with an attractive red fruit character, and good acidity.
£29.00 WES

J Vidal-Fleury Châteauneuf-du-Pape 2006 Red
Seductive dark cherry nose gives way to a palate of sweet red fruit, slight syrupy, with notes of chocolate, dry tannins, and a long sweet finish
£30.00 LOL

J. Vidal-Fleury Cairanne Côtes-du-Rhône Villages 2007 Red
Fantastic nose of ripe cherries and plums. Spiciness and red fruit on the palate, with some complexity on the finish.
£11.00 LOL

La Chapelle Notre Dame D'Aubune 2007, Balma Venitia Vignerons De

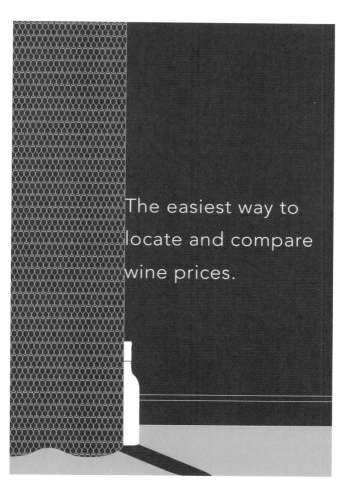

The easiest way to locate and compare wine prices.

Search for your wine– You have over 3 million choices.
Locate your nearest wine merchant – We have over 9000 merchants worldwide.
Pay the best price – We do the comparison for you.
Promote yourself – We offer you 600,000 visitors per month.
List your wines – It costs you nothing.

wine-searcher.com

Information. Location. And price.

Beaumes De Venise Red
Intriguing floral and spice notes, giving way to a firm, dry, medium weight palate of red fruit, with nice balance.
£5.00 MWW

La Chasse Du Pape Reserve Côtes-du-Rhône 2008, Gabriel Meffre Red
Intense cherry fruit on the nose, with rich strawberry flavours, and dry tannins.
£6.20 ASDA, SAIN, TESC, GYW, CWS

La Promesse 2007, Ogier Red
Notes of orange peel and red berries, with some almonds. This is a very soft, juicy wine, with some pepper on the palate, and good length.

Lavau Gigondas 2008 Red
Young, spicy, peppery raspberry nose, with smoky and focused fruit, offering a fresh, balanced palate.

Les Paillanches 2007, Ogier Red
Spicy, meaty aromas of pepper and red fruit, in a bold jammy style.

Les Perdrigolles Crozes-Hermitage 2006, Cave De Tain Red
Ripe, fleshy cranberry and pepper nose. Good lift and vigour, with nice definition on finish.

Lirac La Fermade: Domaine Maby 2007 Red
Smoky, meaty aromas, followed by bold black fruit and white pepper spice, balanced by good freshness, and quality tannins, with a firm, balanced finish.

Marks & Spencer Gigondas 2006, Perrin Red
Slightly gamey, bretty, animal

nose, with sweet, ripe fruit, some tannin, and good balance.
£17.00 M&S

Marquis de Fonséguille 2008, Vignerons de Caractère Red
Animal and vegetable notes, with red berries, and spicy, herbaceous aromas. Light bodied, with red berry flavours on the palate.

Orca Vi 2007, Marrenon Red
Summer fruits on a pepper spiced nose. The palate shows fruit and chocolate, with notes of black olive. Good texture, and brooding nuances.

Palais Des Anciens Vacqueyras 2007, Boisset Red
Light fruit on the nose. Firm structure; juicy and angular.

Perrin Réserve 2007 Red
Freshly perfumed, with good spicy fruit. Dry and mouth-watering; an excellent example of its type.
BCR, GHC, JNW, MWW, WIA

Premiere The Rhône, Côtes Du Rhône Villages 2007, Boutinot Red
Positive, vibrant red and black fruit. Perfect balance, with good length on a high-toned finish.
£8.00

Rasteau Côtes Du Rhône Villages Domaine De Pisan 2006, Cave De Rasteau Red
Good intensity on the nose, with mulberry and honeyed fruit. Good ripeness, and full body. A superb, vibrant example of the style.
£20.00

Roche Bastide (Organic) 2007, Clvd Red
Light tawny rim, with a youthful nose, and spicy, ripe Grenache

fruit on the palate. This is well-integrated, with a very pleasant finish.

Saint Joseph Sainte Epine Rouge 2007, Delas Frères Red
Intensely peppery. An attractive wine, with notes of black fruit, quince, and cherry. Creamy, with good freshness, and balanced oak.

Saint-Joseph 2005, E.Guigal Red
Juicy blackberry fruit, with eucalyptus and spice on both the nose and palate. Grippy tannins.

Taste The Difference Côtes Du Rhône Villages 2007, M. Chapoutier Red
Ripe blackberries on the nose. Good balanced tannins, with redcurrant flavours on the finish.
£6.00 SAIN

Tesco Finest Hermitage 2005, Cave De Tain Red
Fresh and herby, with bright red berry fruit. Good acidity and structure. Quite elegant.
£20.00 TESC

Waitrose Côtes Du Rhône Villages 2008, Gabriel Meffre Red
Ruby-violet colour, with intense cherry and red berry aromas. Good volume, with ripe tannins, and an elegant finish.
£6.00 WAIT, GYW

Waitrose Le Chemin Des Mulets 2006, Perrin & Fils Red
Savoury nose, with hints of pepper, raspberry, and violet. Fresh fruit, and great intensity
£20.00 WAIT

Caves Saint Pierre-Préférence Rosé 2008, Les Vins Skalli Rosé
Pale in colour. Full, rich nose, with

a hint of sweetness on the palate.
£7.00

La Chasse Du Pape Costières De Nîmes Rosé 2008, Gabriel Meffre Rosé
Lovely fragrant raspberry and strawberry fruit on a fresh palate, with a pleasant finish.
£5.50 GYW

La Chasse Du Pape Blanc De Blancs Chardonnay NV, Gabriel Meffre Sparkling
Gently yeasty, with bright apple fruit, and lovely freshness. A good, honest, bready wine, with nice balance.
£10.00 GYW, MRN, THS

La Gourgeonne 2007, Balma Venitia Vignerons De Beaumes De Venise Fortified
Brilliant green-tinged colour. Intense floral aromas, with good balance, and a pleasant finish.
BWC

REGIONAL FRANCE

GOLD

 FRENCH SWEET TROPHY

Riesling Herrenreben Sélection De Grains Nobles - Cuvée Aurélie 2005, Schoenheitz, Alsace Botrytis
Beautifuly delineated, with lime marmalade and floral notes. Unctuous honey character. Refreshing palate, with lemon acidity, minerality, and a very long length.

SILVER

Domaine Du Tariquet Sauvignon 2008, South West White
Pale ,brightly vivid colour. Zippy

flavours of green papaya and gooseberry. Fresh, elegant, approachable, and long. Try with salmon or Asian food.
FRD

Gewürztraminer Grand Cru Vorbourg 2007, Domaine Gruss, Alsace White
Medium colour, with a clean, soft nose. Slightly phenolic character. Soft, clean flavours. Well-balanced, with reasonable length.
£15.20 3DW

Gewürztraminer Vieilles Vignes 2007, Cave De Turckheim, Alsace White
Opulent aromas of fresh rose petals. The palate displays ginger, spice, and glacé cherries. Rounded spice balances the low acidity. Luscious and long, with quite a zesty fruit finish.
£9.70 WES

Kiwi Cuvée Sauvignon Blanc 2008, Les Grands Chais De France Group White
Defined nose of minerality, gooseberries, citrus, and grass. Slightly creamy palate, with delicate, elegant fruit, leading to a clean finish.
£5.50 BNK

Les Palombieres Colombard Ugni-Blanc 2008, Rigal - A Part Of Jean Jean Group, South West White
Crisp herbaceous nose. Clean, firm fruit, and a citrus finish, with good balance and length.

Les Vignes Retrouvées St-Mont 2007, Producteurs Plaimont, South West White
Sappy, attractive, mineral white blend, with a hint of tropical fruit, and tangy fresh acidity.
£9.00

Riesling Grand Vin Kuehn 2007, Alsace White
Pale lemon and honeyed grapefruit nose. Soft and approachable, with medium weight, great ripe acidity, and a soft, pleasing finish.

Riesling Herrenreben 2006, Schoenheitz, Alsace White
Big, lovely, rich, ripe limey style. Charming off-dry palate, with classic mineral, lime, and citrus peel character. Good balance and body. Delicious.

Riesling Silberbeng 2007, Domaine Pfister, Alsace White
Pale and fresh, with a good attack. Complex, pithy, mineral lemon and lime. A good honest, grippy style, with nice weight and finish.
£15.50 LIB

Riesling Terroir 2007, Zinck Paul, Alsace White
Big, toasty mineral and sulphur attack, with plenty of richness on a rounded, complex palate. Strong, long-lasting finish.

Saint Mont 2008, Vignoble De Gascogne, South West White
Crisp white peach nose. Zesty mineral palate, with a long finish.
£7.00 M&S

Alain Grignon Cabernet Franc 2008, Les Producteurs Reunis Af 34360 Cebazan, Vin De Pays d'Oc Red
Aromas of bright redcurrant, leafiness, and wood come through to the palate, with hints of raspberry. Fruity finish, with a touch of smokiness.
£7.00 MWW

Clos Poggiale 2006, Les Vins Skalli, Corsica Red
Ripe fruit, with a hint of raisin,

vanilla, and liquorice. Structured tannins and interesting balance.
£13.00

Domaine Richeaume, Cuvée Columelle 2007, Provence Red
Big mulberry, chocolate, and wild herb aromas. Rich, ripe, and fruity. Quite floral, with good complexity.
£19.00 VER

Famille Skalli - Côtes De Provence 2008, Provence Rosé
Good restrained, gentle palate weight, with rounded earthy and red summer fruit flavours on the finish.
£9.00

Château De Fesles 2005, Sauvion Sweet
The nose shows nice honey, with light marmalade. There is clear honeysuckle fruit on the palate, with balanced zesty fruit, good acidity, and a long finish.

Cuvée Thibault: Domaine Bellegarde 2006, Pascal Labasse, South West Sweet
Powerful herbs, spice, and vanilla on the nose, followed by a fruity palate of spicy straw, with honeyed green notes, red leaves, and pear. Long finish.
£17.00 YAP

Dernières Grives 2007, Domaine Du Tariquet South West Sweet
Nice rustic nose of peach and apricot nose, with good weight of pineapple and candied citrus on the palate. Zingy acidity, with a buttery citrus twist.
FRD

Alsace One 2008, Pierre Sparr Alsace White
Delicate citrus fruits, oatmeal,

and hints of floral Muscat character. Good acidity.

Asda Extra Special Gewürztraminer Tradition 2007, Cave De Turckheim Alsace White
Pleasant aromas and flavours of soft exotic spice and flowers. Round and smooth.
£7.00 ASDA

Chignin Bergeron Prestige De Rocailles 2007, Savoie White
Light gold colour, with elegant fruit, full body, and good balance. Clean, with almost tropical fruit. Simple and full.
£13.00 SGL

Gewürztraminer Grand Cru Eichberg 2007, Zinck Paul, Alsace White
Medium yellow in colour. Peachy Gewürztraminer character on the nose. Soft, light attack. A clean, elegant, well-balanced wine, with good acidity.
£12.00

Gewürztraminer Grand Vin Kuehn 2008, Alsace White
This wine has understated aromas. Medium-sweet, with moderate balancing acidity. Overall, an attractive, forward style.

Gewürztraminer Vieilles Vignes 2007, Domaine Gruss, Alsace White
Clean yellow colour. Nose of Turkish delight and rose petal. The palate contains notes of orange peel, with some spicy rose petals, and a smoky finish.
£13.10 3DW

Grand Héron Gascogne 2008, Vignoble De Gascogne, South West White
Aromatic stone fruit character. Delicate balance on a peachy

palate, with lemon acidity, and a medium-length finish.
£5.00 MWW

Largesse Sauvignon 2008, Les Producteurs Reunis Af34360 Cebazan, South West White
Elegant fruitiness on the nose. Fruit palate, with medium body, good acidity, and a long finish.
£6.00 AAW

Pinot Blanc Terroir 2007, Zinck Paul, Alsace White
Creamy and rich, on a background of nutty oak, with notes of dry apple fruit, and good grapefruity acidity.

Reserve Gewürztraminer 2008, Pierre Sparr, Alsace White
Delicate nose, with spicy floral notes and pink fruit. Lovely balanced acidity, on a smooth, subtly weighted palate, with a fragrant finish.

Riesling Cuvée Des Prélats 2007, Domaine Gruss, Alsace White
Honeyed floral nose. Lime fruit, balanced with oiliness on the palate. Good finish and length.
£11.30 3DW

Riesling Grand Cru Brand 2006, Vignobles François Baur, Alsace White
Rich but dry, with floral, lavender, and elderflower palate. The wine finishes clean, with some citrus and toast.
£14.10 3DW

Sauvignon Blanc 2007, Domaine Gourdon, South West White
Muted lilac notes on the nose. Firm backbone, with a good combination of fruit and

structure. Stylish and focused.
£6.50 QFW

Selection Riesling 2008, Pierre Sparr, Alsace White
Lovely limey style, with balanced juicy fruit. Clean and pleasant, with floral mineral notes on the finish.

Cellar Estates Vin De Table Fruity NV, Les Grands Chais De France Group Red
Rich red berry fruit, with hints of spice. Fresh palate, with good weight, and soft tannins

Château D'Aydie 2006, Vignobles Laplace, South West Red
Ripe, savoury, rustic fruit, and dark raspberries on the palate. Good structure, with a hint of liquorice on the finish.
£12.50 WAIT, WSO

Château Montdoyen Cuvée Tout Simplement 2005, Jean Paul Hembise, South West Red
Slightly leathery fruit on the nose, with medicinal, savoury red fruit on the palate.

Classic 2007, Château Bouissel, South West Red
Soft red berry fruit, with a hint of liquorice. Good structure and acidity.
£9.00 WSO

Cuvée Patricia 2005, Domaine Des Deux Ruisseaux Red
A serious wine, with solid varietal character, dry cherries, and firm tannin.

Fat Bastard Shiraz 2008 Red
Good nose of red fruits and spice nose. Soft, supple, and fruity. Attractive and easy drinking.
CBK

Fortant Merlot 2008, Les Vins Skalli, Vin De Pays d'Oc Red
Clean plummy nose, with a palate of sweet spiced plum fruit. A very sound, easy-drinking, everyday wine.
£6.00

Fortant Syrah 2008, Les Vins Skalli, Vin De Pays d'Oc Red
Blackcurrant jam, with a lovely peppery note on a simple, appealing mid-palate.
£6.00

Reserve Anglais 2007, Pierre Roque & Richard Speirs Red
Bright ruby in colour, showing peppery notes, with some spice. Simple palate. Well-made.

Clos Poggiale 2008, Les Vins Skalli, Corsica Rosé
Peardrop nose, with a nose of confected fruit and sweetness. Red fruit on the palate, with good length.
£13.00

Mhv Sparkling Chardonnay NV, Cfgv Sparkling
Light-bodied, with fresh acidity, and touches of fresh bread and brioche. Creamy mousse; a delicious drink.

Germany

We can only assume that Germans will be laughing in their lederhosen this year. Not only did they pick up the Champion Sweet Trophy, but they were also duly awarded international trophies for Riesling and Gewürtztraminer, the beloved grapes of the nation. The German proficiency in capturing the lip-smacking freshness of these varieties, while also making them capable of ageing, is a talent sought after by winemakers in cool climates around the world. Once you've deciphered the wine label, you'll find extremely attractive prices for superb quality wines. The low percentage of alcohol in most whites works a treat when enjoying a glass or two over lunch, while the latest hero, Spätburgunder (Pinot Noir) has also opened cellar doors for German red wine.

2009 IWC PERFORMANCE	
Trophies	14
Gold	16
Silver	50
Bronze	46
Great Value Awards	2

GOLD

2007 Winkel Jesuitengarten Riesling Erstes Gewächs, Weingut Fritz Allendorf, Rheingau White

Intense bright gold in colour, with notes of honey and creaminess on the nose. Lovely balance of sweetness and cleansing lemony acidity on the palate. Really well-made, with good length.

Hochheimer Hölle Riesling Kabinett 2007, Domdechant Werner'sches Weingut, Rheingau White

Promising petrol aroma, backed up with a highly complex nose of lychees, grapefruit, and subtle spice. On the palate, it is sweet, with notes of bitter marmalade, and a gorgeous, long crisp, complex finish.
£19.00

Hochheimer Kirchenstück Riesling Spätlese Trocken 2007, Domdechant Werner'sches Weingut, Rheingau White

Floral honey notes on the nose. Palate of green apple, citrus, and sherbet acidity, with stone fruit and rich apple flavours on the palate. A delicious wine!
£25.00

Johannisberger Klaus Kabinett Trocken 2007, Weingut Prinz Von Hessen, Rheingau White

Nose of jasmine, layered over lime fruit. Fresh, vibrant acidity, with noticeable CO2. Tropical flavours come through on the palate, combined with white flower and lime. Good balance.

 MOSEL OFF-DRY TROPHY, MOSEL TROPHY

Riesling Kabinett Mosel 2004, S.A.Prum, Mosel White

Lovely expression of developed, minerally fruit. An elegant wine, with lovely length - and nicely balanced fruit and acidity. Tremendous quality and character. Delicious!
£12.20

Schloss Johannisberg Riesling Spätlese Green Seal 2007, Rheingau White

Clean and very fresh, with elegant lime and peach flavours. Balanced acidity and sugar, with great intensity of flavour. This wine really builds on the palate. Effortless, and compelling; a keeper.
£28.00 HOH

 INTERNATIONAL RIESLING TROPHY, RHEINGAU TROPHY

Winkeler Jesuitengarten Riesling 1. Gewächs 2007, Weingut Prinz Von Hessen, Rheingau White

Nose of honey and barley sugar, with notes of spice and richness coming through on the mid-palate. Interesting, clean, fresh, and pure, with great intensity. Excellent example of this style.

Dr Loosen Riesling Eiswein 2007, Mosel Sweet

Delicious floral expression; a fresh and very youthful Riesling. Pretty and lime-fresh, with lovely balance, and a very honeyed finish. Elegant, pure, and long.
£49.50 BDX

Gewürztraminer Spätlese 2007, Weingut Heinz Pfaffmann, Pfalz Sweet
Bright, spicy aroma, with tropical flavours leaping out of the glass. Rounded, elegant, and balanced, with wonderful ginger and spice on the palate, an almost creamy texture, and great flavour and lift. Terrific.

Kanzemer Altenberg Trockenbeerenauslese 2007, Bischöfliche Weingüter, Mosel Sweet
Intense and concentrated sweet fruit on the nose, with hints of flower blossom, honey, and mango. Lovely balance of sugar with high acidity. Long, clean, fresh finish.

Marks & Spencer Scheurebe 2005, Weingut Darting, Pfalz Sweet
Pale gold straw colour. Pink grapefruit, ripe honey, and stone fruit on the nose, with lifted apricot notes. Great balance and length, with a terrific finish.
£15.00 M&S

Thomas Schmitt Private Collection Auslese 2007, Schmitt Söhne Gmbh, Mosel Sweet
Great iconic nose of orange

blossom, with masses of other flowers including jasmine. Notes of mint, and distinctive spices add real interest to the wine, which has excellent length, and smooth balance.
£8.90

Burg-layer Schlosberg Riesling Beerenauslese 1999, Weingut Michael Schaefer, Nahe Botrytis
Lovely rich honey and lemons, with some oiliness on the nose. Well-balanced palate, with length that goes on and on.

Escherndorfer Lump Riesling Trockenbeerenauslese 2007, Weingut Horst Sauer, Franken Botrytis
Very sweet and honeyed, with a hint of spice. Marked by considerable freshness on the palate, with plenty of fruit, and great length and complexity. J&B

Escherndorfer Lump Silvaner Beerenauslese 2007, Winzergenosssenschaft Escherndorf Eg, Franken Botrytis
Attractive nose of ginger spice, with fresh acidity. Medium-weight palate, with flavours of botrytis, honey, and spice. Fresh acidity, with a zesty, clean finish.

Riesling Trockenbeerenauslese 2007, Weingut Langenwalter, Pfalz Botrytis
Medium gold in colour, with amber tints. Nose of apricot and

sweet marmalade, followed by a fresh, very appealing palate, with honeyed notes of rich fruit and gingerbread.

SILVER

Divino Grauer Burgunder Trocken 2007, Divino Nordheim Eg, Franken White
Mid-yellow colour, with a rich, full, ripe tropical and spicy nose. The palate is clean and fresh, with plenty of power and weight.

Divino Weisser Burgunder Trocken 2007, Divino Nordheim Eg, Franken White
Ripe and full-flavoured, with a character that is floral, apricoty, and slightly mineral. There is well-defined stone fruit and good acidity.

Escherndorfer Lump Silvaner Spätlese Trocken 2007, Winzergemeinschaft Franken Eg (gwf), Franken White
Pale golden-green hue, with an aromatic, nose of very fresh peach. High-toned, with full body and balanced fruit acidity. Good quality.

Franconia Rieslaner Spätlese Trocken Nordheimer Vögelein 2007, Divino Nordheim Eg, Franken White
Richly textured palate, with ripe stone fruit and some minerality, with good weight and balance.

Hochheimer Hölle Riesling Trocken 2005, Franz Künstler, Rheingau White
Pale yellow in colour. Honey-toned nose, with aromatic jasmine notes. Lots of ripe fruit on the palate, combining with honey and white flower flavours.

Iphöfer Julius-echter-berg Silvaner Spätlese Trocken 2007, Staatlicher Hofkeller Würzburg, Franken White
Pale gold in colour, with classic stoney and gravelly aromas. The palate shows lovely open peachy stone fruit, with good balance, nice fruit, and a complex finish.

Hocheimer Stein Riesling Kabinett Halbtrocken 2007, Domdechant Werner'sches Weingut, Rheingau White
Good concentration of spicy, peach-tinged fruit. Lovely mineral notes, which extend right to the finish.
£19.00

Hochheimer Hölle Erstes Gewächs Riesling Trocken 2007, Franz Künstler, Rheingau White
Deep straw in colour, with a lovely honeyed floral nose. Loads of complexity on the palate, with notes of white peach, and a touch of minerality.

Hochheimer Hölle Riesling Trocken 2007, Franz Künstler, Rheingau White
Opulent aromas of mineral white peach, flowers, and apples. Elegant and light, with a spicy finish. A superb aperitif.
£13.50 WAIT

Hochheimer Kirchenstück Riesling Trocken 2007, Franz Künstler, Rheingau White
Lovely nose of honey and lemons, leading to a really good, long, rich palate. Creamy and balanced; a wonderful, well-made wine.

Johannisberger Klaus Riesling 1.gewächs 2007, Weingut Prinz Von Hessen, Rheingau White
Delicately balanced nose of

honey and lemon fruit, with floral and barley sugar notes. Lively, vibrant acidity balances the palate.

Lorcher Schlossberg 2007, Weingut Friedrich Altenkirch Gmbh & Co. Kg, Rheingau
White
Moderately intense aromas of pure, clean fruit, with baked apple notes. Well-balanced, with tangy acidity and an interesting finish.

Marks & Spencer Ernst Loosen Erdener Treppchen Riesling Kabinett 2007, Mosel
White
Fine, pure baked apple, with elegant, mineral Riesling aromas, and wonderful briskness and lift. Exhilaratingly fresh and invigorating.
£12.00 M&S

Piesporter Goldtröpfchen Riesling Spätlese 2007, Nik Weis, Weingut St. Urbans-hof, Mosel White
Clean, ripe, tense, and grippy. A beautiful wine, made in a lovely fine-boned and honeyed style. Very good.
WBN

Randersackerer Marsberg Riesling >s< Spätlese Trocken 2007, Weingut Günther Bardorf, Franken White
Citrus zesty nose, with lovely clean Riesling character. Good depth and mouthfeel, with mineral length, and good intensity. This is good stuff!

Randersackerer Pfülben Riesling Spätlese Trocken 2007, Weingut Reiss, Franken
White
Vibrant nose of citrus peel, which is reflected on the palate. Off-dry, with good acidity, and a lively lemon-lime finish.

RK Riesling Mosel, Reichsgraf von Kesselstatt 2007, Mosel
White
Nicely honeyed, well-balanced, floral, and fruity, with steely minerality, and good acidic balance. Potential to develop for up to two years.
£10.30

Schloss Johannisberg Riesling Silberlack 2007, Schloss Johannisberg, Rheingau
White
Floral, musk, and peach aromas on the nose. On the palate, fresh acidity combines with concentrated stone fruit, apple, and apricot flavours. Full, rich style, with good balance and length.
£44.00 HOH

Trabener Kräuterhaus Riesling Spätlese 2007, Foundation Estate "Gütervewaltung Stiftungsweingut" White
This wine is big and tense with a fine, juicy aromatic nose, and a similarly tangy, flavoursome palate. A lovely open, balanced style, yet still keeps one on the edge.
£8.00

Würzburger Innere Leiste Riesling Spätlese Trocken 2007, Staatlicher Hofkeller Würzburg, Franken White
Clean mineral nose, with fresh crisp acidity on the palate, and flavours of juicy pear, green apple, and a touch of white pepper. Well-balanced, with good length.

Winzersekt Kerner Frankensekt B.a. Brut 2006, Winzergemeinschaft Franken Eg (gwf), Franken
Sparkling
Floral aromas with hints of honey. Apricot palate, with good balance.

> **DID YOU KNOW?**
> Wine has so many organic chemical compounds it is considered more complex than blood serum.

The palate shows bread and honey, with hints of minerality, papaya, and mango. Good acidity and balance.

Dhron Hofberger Auslese 2007, Bischöfliche Weingüter, Mosel Sweet
Pleasant light lime colour. Some clementines on the nose, with gentle honey aromas. Fresh tropical fruit on the palate, accompanying balanced acidity.

Dhron Hofberger Beerenauslese 2007, Bischöfliche Weingüter, Mosel Sweet
Creamy, delicate fresh fruit and concentrated honey flavours. Fresh and balanced, with a great, long finish.

Dr Loosen Ürziger Würzgarten Riesling Kabinett 2008, Mosel Sweet
Floral nose, with a bunch of violet, tropical fruit, and orange blossom flavours, plus some stony minerality. Really good length.
£13.30 WAIT, RKL, SHJ

Escherndorfer Lump Riesling Auslese 2007, Winzergenosssenschaft Escherndorf Eg, Franken Sweet
Honey and apricot aromas on the nose, with a palate of sweet apples, papaya, and molasses, leading to an attractive, fruity finish.

Franconia Rieslaner Auslese Nordheimer Vögelein 2006, Divino Nordheim, Franken Sweet
Earthy and fruity on the nose.

Graacher Domprobst Spätlese 2007, Bischöfliche Weingüter, Mosel Sweet
Floral, apple, and citrus notes, with botrytis, honey, and luscious concentration of flavour, topped off by some acidic zest, with balanced sweetness and texture.

Hattenheim Nussbrunnen Riesling Auslese 2007, Balthasar Ress, Rheingau Sweet
Lemon-coloured, with a fresh bouquet of green apple, honeyed apricot, and toasty nuttiness. Hints of botrytis, even acidity, and a long finish.
£40.00 BWC

Kendermanns Eiswein 2007, Reh Kendermann Gmbh Weinkellerei, Rheinhessen Sweet
A touch honeyed, with lovely apple blossom. Fresh and easy, with good acidity and a velvety finish. Extremely elegant, honeyed finish.

Laubenheimer Vogelsang Riesling Spätlese 2006, Weingut Michael Schafer, Nahe Sweet
This wine is pleasant, and showing great typicity on the nose, with big, concentrated fruit on the palate. Balanced and fresh.
£11.60 PON

Leitz Rüdesheimer Magdalenenkreuz Riesling Spätlese 2008, Rheingau Sweet
Grippy and tense, yet well-

balanced and open. A lovely mixture of sweet and sour, with an almost minty edge to the finish.
£13.50 ADN, BRI, WON

Leitz Rüdesheimer Rosengarten Riesling Kabinett 2008, Rheingau
Sweet
Watery white colour. The palate is spritzy, with citrus and sherbet. Very clean, with lovely acidity, and great potential to develop further.
£9.00 WAIT

Riesling Eiswein 2007, Collegium Wirtemberg, Baden
Sweet
Bright lifted apricot nose, with lemon sherbet aromas. The palate shows rich apricot and fresh lively acidity, and is lemony all the way through. Good length.

Scharzhofberger Spätlese 2007, Bischöfliche Weingüter, Mosel Sweet
Fruity nose of sweet apples, pears, and peaches. Elegant and fantastically balanced, with a lovely freshness.

Ürziger Würzgarten Spätlese 2007, Bischöfliche Weingüter, Mosel Sweet
Fresh, clean, bright nose of orange blossom and white fruits. Juicy limes and honey on the palate, with a long zesty finish.

Wittlicher Portnersberg Riesling Trockenbeerenauslese 2005, Weingut Losen-bockstanz, Thomas Losen, Mosel Sweet
Intensely sweet and multi-layered, with notes of honeyed

Escherndorfer Lump Silvaner Trockenbeerenauslese 2007, Weingut Horst Sauer, Franken
Botrytis

Thick, ultra-sweet, and complex, with a rich, concentrated palate of honey and ripe apple, with hints of tropical fruit.

Franconia Silvaner Beerenauslese Nordheimer Vögelein 2007, Divino Nordheim Eg, Franken Botrytis

Deep gold in colour, with a rich honeyed nose. Clear, clean botrytised notes. Sweet, with medium acidity, and a sugary syrup character. Well-made wine with good, pleasant fruit and a medium-to-long finish. This will keep a long time.

Iphoefer Julius-echter-berg Riesling Trockenbeerenauslese 2005, Ernst Popp, Franken
Botrytis

A brilliant wine! Pale gold in colour, with fabulous, zesty lemon curd aromas. Sweet, but not overly so, beautifully balanced by great acidity. Positively mouth-watering!

Iphoefer Julius-echter-berg Silvaner Trockenbeerenauslese 2007, Ernst Popp, Franken
Botrytis

Deep gold in colour, with an elegant, concentrated nose. Weighty palate, with a succulent mouthfeel, good acidity, and a very long finish.

Iphoefer Kronsberg Silvaner Beerenauslese 2007, Ernst Popp, Franken Botrytis

Medium gold in colour, with an attractive nose of sweet lemon and lime. Super-sweet ripe fruit on the palate, leading to a juicy finish.

apricot, raisins, spice, and orange peel. Very good acidity, and excellent finish.

2007 Rüdesheimer Berg Roseneck Riesling Trockenbeerenauslese 2007, Weingut Fritz Allendorf, Rheingau Botrytis

Deep gold in colour. Unctuous, and honeyed, with great sweetness, balanced by good acidity. Showing intensity and balance, which will age well, and deepen in complexity.

Escherndorfer Lump Riesling Beerenauslese 2007, Weingut Horst Sauer, Franken Botrytis

Nice balance and extremely fresh and attractive, with notes of honey and lemon.
J&B

Randersackerer Pfulben Rieslaner Beerenauslese Edelsuss 2006, Burgerspital Zum Hl. Geist - Weingut, Franken Botrytis
Opulent fruit, with apricot and musk. Luscious palate of grapefruit and orange blossom, with an element of minerality.

Sommeracher Katzenkopf Silvaner Trockenbeerenauslese 2007, Winzer Sommerach - Der Winzerkeller, Franken Botrytis
Golden hue, with an aromatic nose of mango and peach. Voluptuous, rich, and concentrated, with vibrant acidity. Good length and complexity, with superb balance.

Würzburger Pfaffenberg Silvaner Beerenauslese 2007, Weingut Reiss, Franken Botrytis
Light amber in colour, with a nose of honey, peach, and grapefruit marmalade. Luscious sweetness, with a lemon and honey character. Good acidity and length.

Würzburger Stein Weißburgunder Beerenauslese 2007, Staatlicher Hofkeller Würzburg, Franken Botrytis
Deep, dark, toasty aromas, with lots of vanilla, dark muscavado sugar notes, and deep caramel fruit. Massively sweet, but moderated by good acidity.

Wurzburger Abtsleite Rieslaner Beerenauslese Edelsuss 2006, Burgerspital Zum Hl. Geist - Weingut, Franken Botrytis
Honey, quince, and sweet apricot, with notes of marmalade, lemon, and honeycomb. Luscious; a fine wine, with well balanced acidity.

Wurzburger Stein-harfe Rieslaner Trockenbeerenauslese Edelsuss 1994, Burgerspital Zum Hl. Geist - Weingut, Franken Botrytis
Tawny in colour. The nose is quite evolved, with sweet notes of marmalade, and hints of nuts and dried fruit. Good length with lively acidity.

BRONZE

Avelsbacher Altenberg Spätlese Feinherb 2007, Bischöfliche Weingüter, Mosel White
Pale lemon-yellow colour. White blossom and orchard aromas. Good concentration on a tight, elegant citrus palate, with mineral undertones. Medium body and length.

Domdechaney Hochheim Riesling Erstes Gewächs 2007, Rheingau White
Delicate aromas of floral honey, with vibrant citrus and pineapple notes on the palate and finish. Complex and elegant.
£30.00

Domdechant Werner Hochheimer Riesling Classic 2007, Rheingau White
Aromatic orange blossoms, lychee, and tropical fruit on the nose, leading to a palate of spicy tropical fruit, with balanced acidity and good length. Very drinkable.
£19.00

Ehrenkircher Weißburgunder Spätlese Trocken -sl- 2007, Weinkeller Ehrenkirchen Eg, Baden White
Fresh nose, with notes of cream and honey. Apple and a touch of quince on the palate. Fresh supporting acidity.

Escherndorfer Lump Riesling Spätlese Trocken 2007, Winzergenossenschaft Escherndorf Eg, Franken White
Lovely lime and honey character, with intense citrus flower notes. Complex length, showing finesse.

Escherndorfer Lump Riesling Trocken Grosses Gewächs 2007, Weingut Horst Sauer, Franken White
Lovely ripe fruit nose, with sweet ripe apple and pear aromas. Good complexity, and great length. J&B

Escherndorfer Lump Silvaner Trocken Grosses Gewächs 2007, Weingut Horst Sauer, Franken White
Delicately scented and honeyed. Relatively dry, with considerable texture and grip. Fat style, saved by a fresh finish.

Franconia Müller-Thurgau Spätlese Trocken Nordheimer Vögelein 2007, Divino Nordheim Eg, Franken White
Hints of botrytis and clean, light citrus, on a spicy medium-weight palate.

Franconia Riesling Spätlese Trocken Nordheimer Vögelein 2007, Divino Nordheim Eg, Franken White
Citrus nose, with notes of dry stones. Palate shows good weight, forward fruit, and limey acidity, culminating in a dry finish.

Franconia Silvaner Spätlese Trocken Nordheimer Vögelein 2007, Divino Nordheim Eg, Franken White
Deep in colour, with fresh lime and tropical fruit, with a full body and long finish.

Hochheimer Domdechaney Riesling Spätlese 2007, Rheingau White
Vinous, as well as fragrant and youthful. Good balance and grip, with lots of structure.
£25.00

Iphoefer Julius-echter-berg Silvaner Spätlese Trocken 2007, Ernst Popp, Franken White
Very strong, toned fruit on the nose, with a palate of citrus, apricot, and melon. Rounded acidity, and a sweet aftertaste.

Kendermanns Dry Riesling Roter Hang 2007, Rheinhessen White
Spicy and herby character, and a stone fruit palate, with firm mineral acidity balancing the subtle sweetness.

Kirchenstück Hocheim Riesling Erstes Gewächs 2007, Domdechant Werner'sches Weingut, Rheingau White
Spicy aromas of white pepper, with crisp apple, and concentrated honey flavours, leading to a mouthwatering finish.
£30.00

Leiwener Laurentiuslay Riesling Spätlese Feinherb, 1. Lage 2007, Nik Weis, Weingut St. Urbans-hof, Mosel White
Complex nose, with evident development, progressing towards a petrolly quality. The palate shows earth and minerality.
£21.00 WBN

Lorcher Krone 2007, Weingut Friedrich Altenkirch Gmbh & Co. Kg, Rheingau White
Developed aromas. Notes

of green apple fruit, with
good flavour concentration,
and a lovely, clean, long, and
flavoursome finish. Will improve
with time.

Naked Grape Riesling 2008, Villa Wolf, Pfalz White
Fresh, spicy nose, with a
lively prickle on the palate.
High acidity and good
freshness.
£7.70 WAIT, BCR, FFT

Oberbergener Bassgeige Grauburgunder 2007, Weingut Franz Keller Schwarzer Adler, Baden White
Pale yellow in colour, with
an elegant floral nose of apple
and almond. Soft full body,
with fresh chalky notes and
good length.
£14.00 WBN

Pechstein Forst Grosses Gewächs 2007, Reichsrat Von Buhl, Pfalz White
Very elegant notes of honey and
white flower. Good intensity,
clean, and finely balanced, with
good length.

Prinz Von Hessen Dachsfilet Riesling Trocken 2007, Rheingau White
Light yellow in colour, with
oily pineapple, peach, and
citrus on the nose. Light
acidity, and elegant notes of
lemon, spice, and pepper on
the long finish.

Rüdesheim Berg Roseneck Riesling Erstes Gewächs 2007, Weingut Fritz Allendorf, Rheingau White
Fresh and clean, with
honeysuckle and lime juice
flavours, and a lemony
character on the finish.

S.a.prüm 2007, Weinhaus R. Prüm, Mosel White
Tangy and crisp, with juicy fruit
and good intensity, leading to a
grapefruity finish.

Seinsheimer Hohenbühl Traminer Spätlese Lieblich 2007, Winzergemeinschaft Franken Eg (gwf), Franken White
Lovely aromatic nose of white
peach and apricot. Palate of
spicy pineapple and dried mango,
with medium body, and good
length.

Sehnsucht Silvaner Trocken 2007, Weingut Horst Sauer, Franken White
Toasted honey, on a ripe citrus
nose, with a palate that has good
weight and acidity.

Thomas Schmitt Private Collection Spätlese 2007, Schmitt Söhne Gmbh, Mosel White
Scented nose of passion fruit,
lime, and marmalade, with
citrussy notes and minerality on
the palate.
£6.30

Weißburgunder Spätlese Trocken 2007, Weingut Horst Sauer, Franken White
Tropical fruit, which is sufficiently
ripe. Short and tangy, with a
simple Pinot Blanc character.

Winkeler Hasensprung Favorit Riesling Trocken 2007, Weingut Prinz Von Hessen, Rheingau White
Vibrant fruit, with concentrated
aromas, and good acidity and
balance. Limey drying finish, with
firm minerality.

Würzburger Stein Weißburgunder Spätlese

Trocken 2007, Staatlicher Hofkeller Würzburg, Franken White

Cream and apricot on the nose, with hints of minerality. Ripe creamy palate, with good concentration of fruit, and balanced acidity.

Allendorf Quercus Pinot Noir Trocken 2006, Weingut Fritz Allendorf, Rheingau Red

An elegant, fine nose, leading to a good, balanced palate showing medium-sweet fruit, balanced by good minerality. Very long finish with some spicy notes.

Cuvée Wirtemberg 2006, Baden Red

Deep-coloured, with warm, chewy, robust tannins. Nice texture and structure.

Oberbergener Bassgeige Spätburgunder Rotwein Auslese "franz Anton" 2007, Weingut Franz Keller Schwarzer Adler, Baden Red

Fairly pale, bright garnet colour, with a nose of pure wet cherry fruit, edged with spice. Clean and nicely textured, with pure vibrant fruit, and a long finish.
£28.00 WBN

Spätburgunder Selection A 2007, Weingut Franz Keller Schwarzer Adler, Baden Red

Sweet red fruit and violets, with a palate of dry, rounded bitter fruit and dry tannin.
£45.00 WBN

Burg-layer Schlosberg Riesling Auslese 2005, Weingut Michael Schaefer, Nahe Sweet

Pale lemon in colour, with floral, petrol and lemon notes. There is rich, fresh green apple on the palate, with good acidity, lovely complexity, and a long finish.

Leitz Rüdesheimer Berg Roseneck Riesling Spätlese 2008, Rheingau Sweet

Fragrant; like sugared candy. Juicy and tangy on the palate.
£22.00 BB&R, BRI, TAN

Leitz Rüdesheimer Berg Roseneck Riesling Spätlese "Old Vine" 2008, Rheingau Sweet

Youthful and tangy, with candied sugar fruit, backed up with a little sulphur. Ripe, plush, and elegant.
£18.00 M&S

Lorcher Kapellenberg Auslese 2007, Weingut Friedrich Altenkirch Gmbh & Co. Kg, Rheingau Sweet

Pale straw in colour, with a perfumed nose. Sugared water sensation, with hits of grapefruits, decent acidity, and medium length.

Ockfener Bockstein Riesling Auslese 2007, Nik Weis, Weingut St. Urbans-hof, Mosel Sweet

Subtle, attractive nose of honey, orange peel, and lemon. Rounded, ripe fruity palate with long finish.
WBN

Piesporter Goldtröpfchen Riesling Auslese 2007, Nik Weis, Weingut St. Urbans-hof, Mosel Sweet

Clear, floral notes, with gardenia, butterscotch, and pineapple. Good acidity and balanced sweetness on the finish.
WBN

Randersackerer Teufelskeller Spätburgunder Eiswein Blanc

De Noirs 2005, Weingut Günther Bardorf, Franken
Sweet
Ripe, heady, tropical and exotic. Nice flavours, with honeyed apple and lemon fruit on a soft finish.

Riesling Auslese 2007, Collegium Wirtemberg, Baden
Sweet
Fragrant white honeysuckle flowers, with a lovely palate of papaya and orange flower.

Rüdesheim Berg Rottland Riesling Spätlese 2007, Balthasar Ress, Rheingau
Sweet
Delicate nose, with a palate of lush, concentrated, complex fruit flavours, and good balance.
£27.00 BWC

Ungeheuer Forst Riesling Auslese 2007, Reichsrat Von Buhl, Pfalz Sweet
Pale yellow in colour, with elderflower on the nose, and sugared candied lemon on the palate. Good acidity, with a well-balanced, floral end-palate.

Ürziger Würzgarten Kabinett 2007, Bischöfliche Weingüter, Mosel Sweet
Very pale lemon colour, with a restrained nose of lemon and smoky nuances. There are hints of glycerol, with balanced acidity, and medium length.

Ürziger Würzgarten Riesling Auslese 2007, Weingut Losen-bockstanz, Thomas Losen, Mosel Sweet
Intense honeyed lemon nose. Fruity palate with a long appley finish.

Handthaler Stollberg Silvaner Trockenbeerenauslese 2007, Staatlicher Hofkeller Würzburg, Franken Botrytis
Peachy nose with lots of honey, which is reflected on the palate, which also shows melon flavours. Very rich, with balanced acidity.

Würzburger Stein Riesling Trockenbeerenauslese 2006, Staatlicher Hofkeller Würzburg, Franken Botrytis
A mouthful of intense citrus, passion fruit, and apples. Flavours are honeyed, rich, and concentrated, with a long, lasting finish.

Italy

With an assortment of eighty grape varieties submitted from Italy this year, there was never a dull moment for our judges. While not all the wines tasted were perfect, there was an improvement in overall quality on results seen in previous years. Look out for the curiously delicious white styles of Pecorino and Nosiola, or discover the power of Aglianco and Negramaro; red wines with dark ripe fruits. The Veneto, Piedmont, and Tuscany were regions that excelled this year, with a large haul of Gold medals between them, giving the Mezzogiorno something to look up to. On the whole, these are wines to enjoy with meals full of lively conversation and great food.

KEY FACTS

Total production
60m hectolitres

Total vineyard
860,000ha

Top 10 regions
1 Sicily
2 Veneto
3 Tuscany
4 Emilia-Romagna
5 Piedmont
6 Latium
7 Sardinia
8 Campania
9 Lombardy
10 Calabria

Top 10 grapes
1 Sangiovese
2 Catarratto
3 Trebbiano Toscano
4 Barbera
5 Merlot
6 Negroamaro
7 Montepulciano
8 Trebbiano Romagnolo
9 Primitivo
10 Malvasia

2009 IWC PERFORMANCE

Trophies	19
Gold	28
Silver	132
Bronze	246
Great Value Awards	2

LOMBARDIA TROPHY

Cabanon Riesling O.p. DOC 2007, Fattoria Cabanon Of Elena Mercandelli, Lombardia White

Yum! Steely, minerally, crisp, and lemony. Showing Alpine freshness, this is a dry Italian white that actually tastes of something! Great balance and very good length.

Simboli Nosiola Trentino DOC 2008, La Vis Sca, Trentino White

Very fresh and vibrant, with leafy grassy notes and hints of blossom. Ripe citrus style, with a very long finish and nutty complexity. Well-balanced, crisp, and zesty - excellent.
£7.00 HWL

 **ITALIAN WHITE TROPHY, PECORINO TROPHY**

Unico Pecorino Terre Di Chieti IGT 2008, Tenuta Ulisse, Abruzzo White

A rich, mineral, multi-dimensional wine, with a gunflint and smoke quality following a persistent, vibrant palate. Excellent.

Amarone Classico 2005, Allegrini, Veneto Red

Dark in colour, with an intense nose of perfumed violets. Rich and mouth-filling, with great complexity, showing flavours of berry, coffee, and liquorice on the palate, culminating in a lingering finish.
£48.50 CHH, WAIT, LIB

Amarone Classico Domini Veneti 2006, Cantina Valpolicella Negrar, Veneto Red

Sweet, pure cherry fruit nose. Lush and attractive. Fruity and well-balanced, with a lovely, sweet palate and a deliciously smooth finish. Superbly well-made wine.
£20.00

 **INTERNATIONAL NEBBIOLO TROPHY, PIEDMONT TROPHY**

Barbaresco 2005, Beni Di Batasiolo, Piedmont Red

Brick red in colour. Complex dried fruit on the nose, with hints of straw. Cherries, leather, and tobacco on the nose. Well-balanced, with drying tannins and a good finish. A very good quality wine.
£23.00 MON

Barbaresco Bordino 2005, Tenuta Carretta, Piedmont Red

Fresh, bright red fruit, with blueberries, spice, and tar on the nose. High levels of well-structured drying tannins, with good concentration and complexity. Mouthcoating tannins and good acidity indicate longevity for this very high quality wine. A wine to keep.
£23.50 AFI

Barolo Enrico V I DOCG 2005, Cordero Di Montezemolo, Piedmont Red

Earthy and spicy, with notes of violet, cedar, and sour cherry coming through on the nose. Mouthwatering acidity, and fine, integrated tannins underpinning fruit and spice. Good length.
£68.50 EUW, EVW

Barolo Monfalletto DOCG 2005, Cordero Di Montezemolo, Piedmont Red

Beautifully crafted wine, with a clean nose of cherry, dark fruit, and cedar, with notes of vanilla spice. High acidity and firm, well-integrated tannins on a concentrated fruit palate.
£23.00 EUW, EVW

Bottega Vinai Lagrein Dunkel Trentino DOC 2006, Cavit, Trentino Red

Ripe juicy red berries on the nose. Slightly green, but intense and attractive fruit, with lots of pleasing tannin and bitterness. Made in a modern, commercial style, with lots of well-judged oak. Excellent.
£7.00 PBA

 TUSCAN RED TROPHY, BRUNELLO DI MONTALCINO TROPHY

Brunello Di Montalcino Riserva DOCG 2003, Loacker Corte Pavone, Tuscany Red

Magnificent nose of ripe black cherry and plum. On the palate it has an attractive, slightly bitter note, with hints of tobacco, and evident new French oak. Lots of potential and really great length.
£61.00 GWW

 ITALIAN RED TROPHY, VENETO TROPHY, AMARONE TROPHY

Campolongo Di Torbe 2004, Masi Agricola, Veneto Red

Lifted floral, sour cherry, and herbal aromas. Evident chalky tannin, with fresh acidity and rich raisin flavours. Rich silky structure, with nice grip. Deliciously long and balanced, with a truly great finish.

Capitel San Rocco Valpolicella 2006, F.lli Tedeschi, Veneto Red

Aromatic, spicy, earthy nose, with notes of red fruit, cherries and figs. Lovely palate, with open, sweet, spicy fruit and a real savoury intensity.
£9.00 HOH

 INTERNATIONAL MERLOT TROPHY

Galatrona 2006, Fattoria Petrolo, Tuscany Red

Very deep colour, showing intense, dark well-ripened fruit, spice, and smoke, with touch of menthol on the nose. Lots of chocolatey oak on the appetisingly fresh palate. Tannins are prominent but ripe, with rich fruit; this wine has great potential.
£80.00 LIB

 AGLIANICO TROPHY

Gudarrà Aglianico Del Vulture DOC 2005, Bisceglia, Basilicata Red

Dark, rich, and spicy with notes of tobacco and chocolate. A herby, earthy nose leads to a palate of attractive dark cherry and plum fruit, with a spicy finish. Extremely high quality wine with great character.
£14.50

Il Pino Di Biserno 2006, Tenuta Campo Di Sasso, Tuscany Red

Nose of vibrant black fruit, with leafy, spicy, peppery notes, and vanilla oak. On the palate it shows bright red and black fruit, bramble, and blackcurrants. Silky integrated tannins, with balanced acidity.
£42.50 B&J, COL, HSW, P&S, POG, SOH, SOM, WIL

RIPASSO TROPHY

Ripasso Valpolicella 2007, Cortegiara, Veneto Red

Lovely ripe cherry fruit, with a touch of raisin on the nose. Clean, dense, chewy and fruity, with an elegant attack, notes of spiced chocolate, and a fruity finish. Superb!
£9.00 TESC, LIB

Ripasso Valpolicella DOC Rocca Alata 2007, Cantina Di Soave, Veneto Red

Lovely floral, dark cherry nose, with hints of chocolate. Ripe juicy attack, with good concentration, great depth, and excellent length. A delicious wine.
£24.70 TESC, AIL, VSO

Riserva Di Costasera 2004, Masi Agricola, Veneto Red

Intense concentrated black fruit. Rich cherry fruit palate, with notes of wood and big tannins. Great depth of flavour and length. Excellent quality; a really characterful wine.

Sasso Al Leccio Toscana IGT 2005, Piccini, Tuscany Red

Open fruit and spice on the nose, with notes of primary fruit and aged chocolate. Red fruit with lovely oak underpinning complex plum and damson notes on the palate. Wonderfully soft tannins.

 PUGLIA TROPHY

Selvarossa Salice Salentino Rosso DOC Riserva 2005, Cantine Due Palme Soc. Coop. Agricola, Puglia Red

Rich, deep, brooding nose of plum and bramble. The palate is oaky, but this is seamlessly stitched

through the fruit. Dense and rich, with a sweet fruit finish. Perfect balance.

Sondraia IGT Toscana 2006, Poggio Al Tesoro, Tuscany Red

Cream, plum, and cedarwood aromas. Fresh and very modern, with firm, fine-grained tannins, and a long smooth finish. Wonderful mouthfeel. A big, powerful wine.
£22.00 LIB

CHIANTI TROPHY

Tenuta Di Capraia Chianti Classico Riserva Docg 2005, Rocca Di Castagnoli, Tuscany Red

Medium ruby in colour, with bright intensity. Soft and subtle, portraying flavour characteristics of cassis, wild raspberries, baked cherries, and spice. A lovely intense palate reflecting the characteristics on the nose. A very complex wine, with excellent acidity and an extremely long length.
£21.30 EUW, EVW

W IGT Toscana 2006, Poggio Al Tesoro, Tuscany Red

Opaque, with restrained liquorice and plummy tobacco aromas. Explosion of liquorice, mocha, and raspberry compote, supported by silky tannins on the palate. A classy wine with a never-ending finish.
£43.00 LIB

ASTI TROPHY

GREAT VALUE SPARKLING UNDER £5

Canti Asti DOCG NV, Fratelli Martini Secondo Luigi Spa, Piedmont
Sparkling
Elegant, tropical, muscat-like aromas. Medium-soft texture, with a sensation of sweetness and balanced acidity.
£5.00 MRN

GREAT VALUE SPARKLING BETWEEN £10 AND £15

Prosecco Valdobbiadene Brut Villa Sandi NV, Villa Sandi Veneto Sparkling
Pure, clean, elegant and youthful, with a nose which is rich, fruity, and a touch floral. Rich, creamy palate with clean fruit and good length.
£12.60 PLA

 **ITALIAN SWEET TROPHY, VIN SANTO TROPHY, ITALIAN VIN SANTO TROPHY**

Tegrino Vinsanto 2004, Leonardo, Tuscany Sweet
Burnished amber in colour. Oxidative sultana and Dundee cake aromas, with a palate of lovely, attractive toasted nut and sultana, and hints of orange peel. A lovely, well-made wine.
£21.70 HEN, LIB

Arele Vino Santo Trentino DOC 1997, Cavit, Trentino, Botrytis
Very deep gold in colour. The nose is complex, honeyed, and oxidative, with figgy, apricot

fruit. There is a crystallised fruit character and a note of caramel. Complex and contemplative.
£22.00 PBA

SILVER

Amorino Pecorino Colline Pescaresi 2008, Podere Castorani, Abruzzo White
A well-focused wine whose savoury finish and honeyed quality make for a complex food wine.
£10.00 HOH

Contesa Pecorino Colline Pescaresi 2008, Contesa, Abruzzo White
Open and fruity on the nose, with some subtle, herby, waxy notes. The palate is fresh and fruity, with nice minerality.
£12.50

Costeggiola Classico DOC 2008, Guerrieri Rizzardi, Veneto White
Bright yellow-green in colour, with clean, tropical aromas. The palate shows nice acidity and crisp, clean lemon-scented fruit. Very attractive modern wine, with a long finish.
£9.00 F&M

Fiano Di Avellino Terre Di Dora 2008, Terredora, Campania White
Good balanced fruit and minerality on the nose, with a palate of sweet watermelon and grapefruit. Acidity is very high, but crisp, with great depth. Good balance and a lively medium-length, finish.
£13.00 LAY, MON, ODF

Fontana Candida Frascati Superiore Vigneto Santa Teresa 2007, GIV, Latium White
Straw appearance, with waxy fruit and nutty flavours on the

nose. Good expression on the palate, with quite complex fruit and good length.
£7.50

Franz Haas Pinot Bianco 2007, Alto Adige White
Vibrant nose of citrus, following through on a palate which shows some stone fruit character, with crisp acidity and a long finish. This is a food wine: broad and tender.
£11.30 HEN, LIB

Gavi Luciana 2008, Araldica Piedmont White
Good structure, fresh acidity, and a bit herbaceous, with a hint of minerality.
£7.50 FLA, WAIT

Greco Di Tufo Loggia Della Serra 2008, Terredora, Campania White
Clean and creamy, with a soft tropical nose. Rich, pure palate with balanced citrus and an oily character. Full, waxy, and nutty, with a mineral edge, and a balanced, long citrus finish.
£11.00 LAY, MON, ODD, ODF

Le Vele Verdicchio Dei Castelli Di Jesi Classico 2008, Terre Cortesi Moncaro, Marche White
Very good, fragrant nose, with concentrated flavours and subtle savoury hints on a lively citrus palate, which shows balanced acidity.
£8.80 EUW, EVW

Lugana Riserva Sergio Zenato DOC 2006, Veneto White
Pale yellow in colour. Hints of stone fruit on a nose, which is ripe and rich, without being showy. The palate is ripe, rich, wheaty, fresh, and herbal. A full, dry wine, with good length.
£27.00 EUW, EVW

Mandrarossa Fiano 2008, Settesoli, Sicily White
Bright green-gold in colour, with a honeyed nose of soft orange peel and honeysuckle. The palate is round, full, and soft, with lots of minerality and ripe fruit. Good length.
£7.40 FLA, WSO

Manna Cru 2007, Franz Haas, Alto Adige White
Intense yellow colour, with floral aromas, and some mineral, tropical fruit notes. The palate shows a nice balanced of sweetness and acidity.
£18.40 HEN, LIB

Marks & Spencer Pecorino 2007, Rocco Pasetti - Az. Agr. Contesa, Abruzzo White
Pale yellow colour, with fresh, oaky, vanilla, creamy, and glycerine aromas. The palate is dry, fresh, and complex, with intense, nutty almond notes.
£10.00 M&S

Pinot Grigio Collio 2007, Pighin, Friuli Venezia-giulia White
Fragrant and floral, with a lively, sappy nose. Creamy peach and mineral palate. Good concentration, balance, and length; powerful yet elegant.
£14.00 MON

Pinot Grigio Trentino DOC 2008, Concilio S.p.a., Trentino White
Lovely nose of ripe fruit. Fine, balanced palate, with good length. Fresh, long, and mineral. Very good.

San Sisto Verdicchio Dei Castelli Di Jesi Superiore Riserva 2005, Fazi Battaglia, Marché White
Medium lime-yellow colour. Developed luscious character

on the nose. Soft attack, with notable acidity, good weight, and a clean, medium-length finish.
£14.70

Südtirol Pinot Bianco Alto Adige 2008, Kellerei Kaltern Caldaro, South Tyrol White
Light, spicy, floral aromas, with a good, broad palate of pear and red apple fruit. Balanced acidity and reasonable length.
£4.70

Terra Di Vulcano Falanghina IGT Beneventano 2008, Bisceglia, Campania White
Slight muted nuttiness on the nose, with vegetal artichoke tones. Soft light attack, with sweet, juicy, primary fruit characteristics.
£8.50

Tesco Finest* Fiano 2008, Cantine Settesoli, Sicily White
Bright yellow in colour, with a clean, attractive, floral nose. Soft and attractive, with fresh floral and peachy notes, with a touch of oak and very good length – a lovely wine.
£6.00 TESC

Toledana Gavi Di Gavi DOCG 2008, La Toledana S.s. - Distribuito Da Domini Villae Lanata, Piedmont White
Deep, rich notes of honeysuckle on the nose. Fresh, vibrant palate, with terrific lime and pear flavours, and lovely, fresh intensity.
£10.00

Torricella 2007, Barone Ricasoli, Tuscany White
Smoky, toasty nose with notes of lemon notes. The palate is leesy and Burgundian, with well-crafted fruit, and a satisfying, stylish finish.
£14.20 EDC

Unico Trebbiano D'abruzzo Doc 2008, Tenuta Ulisse, Abruzzo White
Bright, young bubblegum character. Moderate depth of minerality, with apple fruit, pleasant supporting acidity, and a bit of length. Clean, fresh, and tasty.

Vermouth Di Torino Bianco NV, Ravini, Piedmont White
Very fresh and pure, with aniseed aromas. Lovely fruit and great purity; this is incredibly refreshing - a mouthwatering and uplifting wine.

Vernaccia Di S. Gimignano DOCG "ab Vinea Doni" 2007, Azienda Agricola Casale Di Falchini R., Tuscany White
Star-bright, pale straw appearance, with light acacia floral notes on the nose. Good, clean fruity palate, with a long finish.
ADN, BB&R, COE, PLA, RAE, RWD, SOM

Vesevo Sannio Falanghina DOC 2008, Campania White
Attractive bright floral and tropical nose. Light attack and weight. Bright, fresh, and crisp, with tropical fruit sweetness.
LIB

Vignetti Fantinel Pinot Grigio Grave del Friuli "Borgo Tesis" 2007, Friuli Venezia-Giulia White
Fresh, although somewhat evolved. Attractive aromas of apricot and spice, which follow through to the palate. Nice freshness and purity, with decent length, and a clean finish.
£7.70

Amarone Classico Della Valpolicella 2005, Bixio Emilio, Veneto Red
Damson red in colour, with a nose of cloves and damson fruit.

Supple palate, with vibrant fruit, mocha, and chocolate.

Amarone Classico DOC Cantina Di Negrar 2006, Cantina Valpolicella Negrar, Veneto Red
Attractive sweet berry fruit on the nose, with hints of coffee. Beautifully smooth dark cherry fruit, with a plummy tang - delicious.
£17.00 WAIT

Amarone Della Valpolicella - Cadis 2006, Cantina Di Soave, Veneto Red
Sweet berries and pepper on the nose. Excellent balance of tannins, with chewy fruit and hints of chocolate. There is lots of interest here.
£60.00 CTL, VSO

Amarone della Valpolicella Classico 2005, F.lli. Tedeschi, Veneto Red
Ruby red in colour, with fruity characteristics of cherries, spice, and a hint of soft redcurrants. Well-integrated oakiness, with a long, fruity, complex finish.
£25.00 BNK, HOH

Amarone Della Valpolicella Classico DOC 2005, Zenato, Veneto Red
Gentle scented herbs and tar. Dry, attractive flavours, with a long finish. Effortless style, with a long, fresh finish.
£44.00 EUW, EVW

Amarone Della Valpolicella Classico DOC "Vigneti Di Osan" 2001, Az.agr. Corteforte, Veneto Red
Nose of almond and morello cherry. Smooth, well-balanced palate of tobacco and oriental spices. Elegant and complex, with a lengthy finish.
£70.00

Amarone Della Valpolicella Classico Riserva Sergio Zenato DOC 2004, Zenato, Veneto Red
Soft plum fruit aromas, with nose of intense raisin fruit and wild herb flowers. Lovely smooth texture, with great complexity.
£83.60 EUW, EVW

Amarone Della Valpolicella Terre Di Verona 2006, Cantina Sociale Della Valpantena Sca, Veneto Red
Lifted aromatics of dark cherry fruits. Rich dense palate, with notes of caramelised plum and walnut. Good length.

Amarone Della Valpolicella Torre Del Falasco 2005, Cantina Sociale Della Valpantena Sca, Veneto Red
Moderate depth of dark fruit, with nicely balanced acidity, and some firm, grippy tannins. A lot of length.
£31.00 FLA

Asda Extra Special Valpolicella Ripaso 2007, Cantina Sociale Di Soave, Veneto Red
Some black fruits on the nose, with spicy aromas. Plenty of black fruit and earthy flavour, with good acidity and backbone.
£6.20 ASDA

Barbaresco Bricco Asili Bernardot 2005, Ceretto, Piedmont Red
Medium red in colour. Showing signs of development, with good intensity of red fruit and leather, with cherries and a hint of bitterness. Tight tannins and crisp finish.
£41.00 BWL

Barbera D'asti Superiore La Luna E I Falo' 2006, Terre Da Vino, Piedmont Red
Soft earthy notes on the nose.

Dense mid-palate, with chewy tannins, high acidity, and long-lasting notes of bramble and acidity.
£16.00 EHB, EVW, VIN

Barolo Bricco Delle Viole 2004, Gd Vajra, Piedmont Red

Elegant nose of vanilla, leather, and spice, wrapped around chocolatey black cherries. Rich and full bodied, with excellent integration of fruit and tannin. Classic Barolo style.
£50.00 LIB

Barolo Bricco Gattera Docg 2005, Cordero Di Montezemolo, Piedmont Red

Dark fruit, with hints of chocolate. Red and black fruit combine with vanilla spice, on a backdrop of crisp acidity. Developed, with tertiary notes coming through.
£56.70 WAIT, EUW, EVW

Barolo Bricco Rocche Brunate 2004, Ceretto, Piedmont Red

Quite evolved, showing dried fruit, with cherry and medicinal undertones on the nose. Firm, ripe, dry tannins on the palate, leading to a good finish.
£47.00 BWL, MWW

Barolo Essenze 2004, Terre Da Vino, Piedmont Red

Fragrant nose of black cherries and oak, showing complex hints of violet. Rich and full-bodied, demonstrating good maturity, culminating in a long, rich finish.
£28.00 EUW, HAR, VIN

Barolo La Corda Della Briccolina 2004, Beni Di Batasiolo, Piedmont Red

Fragrant, mature nose of oak, mulberries, chocolate, truffles, and plums. A well-made wine, with a rich palate expertly

balancing acidity, fruit, and tannins.
£43.00 MON

Bottega Vinai Teroldego Rotaliano DOC 2007, Cavit, Trentino Red

Deep, dark red-garnet core. Nice herbaceous nose with blackcurrant and red cherry aromas. The palate is harmonious, elegant, rich, and full-bodied, with flavours of black fruit, violet, and bitter plum, with well-balanced tannins and some minerality.
£7.00 PBA

Brolio 2007, Barone Ricasoli, Tuscany Red

Ripe berry fruit on the nose. light-bodied, sleek, and dry on the palate, with complex floral notes and plum flavours. Good, red fruit finish.
£14.10 FLA, EDC

Caldora Montepulciano D'abruzzo DOC 2008, Caldora Vini, Abruzzo Red

Deep, dense colour, with a nose of blackberry and spicy cherry. Good concentration of flavour, with well balanced tannin and acidity.
ATM, THI

Cantina Di Merlara Valpolicella Ripasso DOC 2006, Casa Vinicola Sartori Spa, Veneto Red

Mid-ruby colour, with some leather and red cherry on the nose. Medium-weight palate, with clean, soft tannins and fruit. Nice balance and some complexity.

Capitel Monte Olmi Amarone della 2005, F.lli. Tedeschi, Veneto Red

Tannic, dark, attractive cherry flavours. Nice balanced acidity,

with and some length and a really attractive edge on the finish.
£50.00 HOH

Castero Brunello Di Montalcino 2004, Schenk Italia, Tuscany Red
A rich nose of fleshy black cherry, leading to mulberry and bright red cherry on the palate. Great depth of flavour, and lovely length.

Cerro Del Masso 2007, Poggiotondo, Tuscany Red
Attractive vegetal nose with oak, mulberry, liquorice, and violet tones. Blackcurrant, vanilla, spice, and chocolate on the palate, with good acidity and complexity. A rich full-bodied wine.
£9.10 HEN, LIB

Chianti Classico Berardenga 2007, Felsina, Tuscany Red
Pale garnet in colour, with a delicate nose bolstered by meaty red fruit. Firm tannins and fresh acidity, with underlying savoury tones.
£18.00 LIB

Chianti Classico Riserva 2005, Castello Della Paneretta, Tuscany Red
Bright raspberry red in colour, with medium intensity. Lovely fruit sensations of cassis and black cherries, with hints of dark chocolate. Soft drying tannins. A beautiful mid-palate and decent length.
VIN

Chianti Classico Riserva DOCG 2005, Fattoria Di Valiano, Tuscany Red
Savoury cherry flavours, with hints of chocolate. Tight tannic structure, with good depth of flavour and nice length.

Chianti DOCG Botter 2007, Casa Vinicola Botter Carlo & C. S.p.a., Tuscany Red
Mature, oaky nose, with blackcurrant, violet, and chocolate notes. Good ripe palate of blackcurrant and spicy oak, with ripe tannins.

Chianti Riserva 2006, Leonardo, Tuscany Red
Restrained dark leathery aromas. Dry chalky tannin and damson fruit on the palate, leading to a long herbal finish. A good food wine.
£12.00 HEN, LIB

Colle Dei Venti Montepulciano D'abruzzo DOC 2006, Caldora Vin, Abruzzo Red
Showing very ripe, creamy black fruit, and good intensity. Full-bodied and well-balanced, with a very pleasant, long, and elegant finish.
ATM, THI

Cresasso IGT 2005, Zenato, Veneto Red
Very pleasant, extremely fruity nose. On the palate, there is a measure of attractive, old wood character, which adds complexity.
£41.60 EUW, EVW

Dama 2007, Azienda Marramiero, Abruzzo Red
Showing some development on the nose, with hints of leather, along with spiced fruit and defined grapefruit. Very pleasant, with plenty of refreshing fruit and perfume, and mouthfilling tannins. Very good length.

Feudi Di San Marzano Negroamaro Puglia IGT. 2008, Feudi Di San Marzano, Puglia Red
Vivid vermilion hue. Nose of dried leaves, leading to a clean,

savoury palate, with flavours of dried cranberry and prune. Very good quality.
ATM, TAN

Fondo Filara Etna Rosso Doc 2006, Cantine Nicosia S.r.l., Sicily Red
Interesting spice on the nose, with attractive tones of red fruit. Soft, rounded, and smooth, with a slightly jammy taste on the finish.

Forca Di Lupo Rosso IGT Terre Di Chieti 2006, Cantine Spinelli, Abruzzo Red
Lovely fragrant aromas of plums, tea, and tobacco. The palate is spicy, meaty, and intense, but not heavy. Fine, sweet fruit, with a fresh, curranty, minty finish. Excellent!

Ginepreta 2006, Valentino Cirulli, Umbria Red
Very good fruit. Well-balanced and complex, crammed full of dark berry fruits. Very chunky, big, and bold.

Gran Sasso Montepulciano D'abruzzo DOCG 2006, Farnese Vini, Abruzzo Red
Restrained nose of almond and cherry, leading to a smooth palate of red fruit and mint, with well-balanced acidity. Well-made.
LIB

Il Ruffiano 2005, Azienda Agricola Buglioni, Veneto Red
Complex nose of fruit, figs, cherries, and eucalyptus. The palate is very nice and fresh, with a long finish.
£13.80 CAM, GWW

Itynera Primitivo IGT Salento 2007, Mgm Mondo Del Vino, Puglia Red
Complex nose, with a surprisingly velvety outcome. Big fruit flavours

come through on a seriously dense palate. There is fruit from start to finish. Very good.
CBG

La Court Barbera d'Asti Superiore "Nizza" 2006, Michele Chiarlo, Piedmont Red
Deep rich colour. Perfumed nose of damson, liquorice, and floral notes. Classy, with concentrated ripe fruit and balanced tannins.
£36.00 HOH

La Grola IGT Veronese 2006, Allegrini, Veneto Red
Spice and cherry, with wood notes. Clean black fruit flavour on the palate.
£16.10 HEN, LIB

Lacrima Del Pozzo Buono 2007, Vicari Vico, Marche Red
Aromatic dark fruit and floral aromas, with and a hint of Muscat character. Opaque, plummy aroma, with a firm chocolatey finish. A good food wine.

and leathery aromatics over black cherry fruit. Intense black cherry fruit entry, with lots of weight and supple tannins. Long finish. £19.00

Memento 2006, Giuseppe E Riccardo Olivi, Tuscany Red
Red berry and soft ripe fruit on the nose, with some lovely sweet and concentrated berry fruits on the palate. Soft tannins, and a good finish.

Merlot Affinato In Barrique 2004, Moletto, Veneto Red
The nose is rich, ripe, sweet, developed, and spicy. Well-developed palate showing spicy sweetness, with a touch of velvety cocoa texture. Supple tannins and good balance.

Monferrato Rosso Luce Monaca 2004, Araldica, Piedmont Red
Vivacious, fruity aromas of pepper and black fruit. Good weight on the palate, with well-integrated new oak.
£13.20

Morellino Di Scansano Lohsa 2007, Poliziano, Tuscany Red
A wine of distinction, with lovely perfume and a hint of tar and light spice. Pleasant and warm, with depth on the mid-palate, and notes of stewed fruit. Ready to drink.

Morrisons The Best Chianti Riserva DOCG 2005, Uggiano, Tuscany Red
Intense floral aromas combine with notes of raisins and herbs. Showing nice development, with fine chalky tannins, fresh acidity, and complex notes of tobacco.
£7.20 MRN

Nero D'Avola 2007, Fondo Antico, Sicily Red
Light red fruit on a velvety

Lacrima Di Morro D'alba 2008, Monte Schiavo, Marché Red
Inky and opulent, with plummy aromas. This is a very well-balanced wine, with lots of ripe fruit on the mid-palate, and a vibrant finish.

Lacrima Di Morro D'alba Superiore DOC 2007, Marconi Vini Srl, Marché Red
Packed full of juicy berry fruits, and elevated with herbal tones. There are big ripe tannins and notes of blackberries, blueberries, and wild herbs, with a fleshy, austere backbone.

Le Buche 2006, Giuseppe E Riccardo Olivi, Tuscany Red
Red fruits on the nose, leading to a palate of cherry fruit, with dense, chewy, very ripe tannins. Very well-balanced. Will certainly improve with age.

Lo Zoccolaio Barolo DOCG 2004, Cascina Lo Zoccolaio - Distribuito Da Domini Villae Lanata Srl, Piedmont Red
Full red-brick colour. Spicy tar

nose. Full, ripe red fruit on the palate, balanced with tannin and acidity.

Nerone Conero Riserva 2005, Terre Cortesi Moncaro, Marche Red

Nicely developed oak, with spiced fruit and chocolate on the nose. A fruity palate with good freshness. Chunky, chewy, and chocolate-sweet.
£39.90 EUW, EVW

Opi Montepulciano D'abruzzo DOCG Colline Teramane "Riserva" 2005, Farnese Vini, Abruzzo Red

Nose of dark plum and ripe bramble fruit, with lots of coconuty oak. Intense palate of vibrant dark plum and cinnamon, balanced by refreshing acidity.
£9.00 LAI

Palazzo Della Torre IGT Veronese 2006, Allegrini, Veneto Red

Cherry wood notes on the nose, with attractively soft tannins, dense flavours, and a smooth concentrated length.
£13.70 HEN, LIB

Piemonte DOC Barbera-Rivasole 2008, Cantine Del Castello Di Santa Vittoria Srl - Part Of Fotanafredda, Piedmont Red

Youthful, dry, primary fruit. Tight, paintbox nose, with floral notes. Rounded tannins on a very dry palate, balanced by juicy cherry tones. Good to enjoy now.

Poggio De' Paoli 2007, Tenuta Lenzini, Tuscany Red

Clean, pure fruit, with intense toastiness, and spicy blackcurrant aromas and flavours. The oak is balanced and well-integrated.

Refosco Dal Peduncolo Rosso Superiore 2006, Valpanera, Friuli Venezia-Giulia Red

Liquorice and coffee nose, leading to a juicy palate, with good acidity, lots of fruit, and lovely balance. A wine with future.

Regolo Rosso Veronese 2005, Casa Vinicola Sartori Spa, Veneto Red

Good fruit on the nose and palate. Very attractive black cherry and savoury oak flavours. Excellent length.
WAV

Ripa Delle Mandorle 2007, John Matta, Tenuta Vicchiomaggio Srl., Tuscany Red

Rich, bright red fruit and spice character on the nose and palate. Round and complex, with a very attractive, fresh sweetness. Very good.

Rosso Di Toscana 2006, Fossacolle, Tuscany Red

Violet hue, promising lovely fruit on the nose. Lovely rich fruit on the palate, with good spice and depth, and a fresh lengthy finish.
£18.00 LIB

Sangiovese di Romagna Riserva 2006, Umberto Cesari, Emilia-Romagna Red

Dense, ripe spicy fruit on the nose, which has seductive violet overtones. Berries dominate the palate, ending on a lovely spicy note.
£14.00 HOH

Scialo 2006, Viticultori Associati Canicatti, Sicily Red

Deep blackcurrant appearance. Attack of fruit and spices, with approachable ripe fruit and high tannins. A well-made wine with great balance.
£13.00 EVW, VIN

Scirus IGT Toscana Rosso 2006, Fattoria Le Sorgenti, Tuscany Red
A very perfumed, almost Margaux-like nose, showing fragrant Petit Verdot character, and elegant tannins. A very feminine style, with intensity on the back palate. High quality.

Sessantanni Primitivo Di Manduria DOC 2006, Feudi Di San Marzano, Puglia Red
Dense brooding style, with an ultra-ripe palate of vibrant black fruit, underpinned by soft tannins and moderate acidity. Savoury notes on the finish.
ATM, TAN

Sud Primitivo-Merlot IGT Tarantino 2008, Feudi Di San Marzano S.r.l., Puglia Red
Nose of vanilla and tobacco, leading to an opulent, smooth palate, developing red berries and spice, with a hint of bitter almond on the finish.
ATM, TAN

Syrah 2007, Tenuta Lenzini, Tuscany Red
Subtle nose of leather, mulberry, and cherry fruit, with silky chocolate tannins on the palate. Elegant and fresh, with nice complexity.

Syrah Sicilia Itynera 2006, Mgm Mondo Del Vino S.r.l., Sicily Red
Nose of gorgeous berry fruit and black pepper, with a very dense palate of blackberry fruit. Quite solid, with ripe tannins.

Tolos Montepulciano D'abruzzo DOC 2005, Cantine Spinelli, Abruzzo Red
Red fruit compote and cinnamon notes on the nose. Vibrant palate of liquorice and damson, leading to a long, juicy finish.

Tommasi Amarone Della Valpolicella Classico DOC 2005, Tommasi Viticoltori, Veneto Red
Lovely, elegant nose, showing good definition. A cohesive palate, which is straight and pure, with dark fruit nicely balanced with acidity, and a long finish.
£30.00 WAIT

Toscana IGT Tenuta Di Burchino 2004, Castellani Spa, Tuscany Red
Medium raspberry red in colour. Earthy tobacco and liquorice nose, with hints of almond. Well-constructed palate, with beautifully soft velvety tannins, lovely concentration of fruit, and good length.

Trentino Superiore DOC Marzemino Dei Ziresi 2007, Vivallis S.c.a., Trentino Red
Peppery, plummy nose. These aromas are carried onto a juicy palate, showing earthiness, fresh black fruit, and a bouncy structure.

Trionfo Amarone Della Valpolicella 2005, Vinea S.r.l., Veneto Red
Big style, showing firm grip and dark cherry flavours. Pleasant long length and lovely balance. Very attractive.

Vaio Armaron 2004, Serego Alighieri, Veneto Red
Very bright red cherry aromas. The palate shows bitter herbs, fine tannins, and fresh acidity, with lovely balance and attractive aromatics.

Valpolicella Classico DOC Superiore 2006, Terre Di Leone Srl, Veneto Red
Cherry red in colour. Vanilla and oak on the nose, with redcurrant

and cherry fruit coming through on the palate. Long, mature finish on a pleasant, well-balanced wine.

Valpolicella Classico Superiore Ripasso 'la Casetta' 2005, Cantina Valpolicella Negrar S.c.a, Veneto Red
Medium intensity of colour, with a nice, tight structure and juicy fruit. Long, dry, clean finish.
£15.00 MWW

Valpolicella Ripasso Superiore 2007, Alpha Zeta, Veneto Red
Ripe cherry fruit, with hints of spice. Good fruit and chocolate attack on the palate, with lovely raisined flavours. Good structure, showing finesse.
£10.60 HEN, LIB

Valpolicella Superiore Ripasso Bosan 2006, Gerardo Cesari Spa, Veneto Red
Deep ruby-garnet colour. Ripe black fruit profile on the nose, with smoky spice and complexity. This follows through to a palate, which displays ripe fruit with an edge. Full-bodied, with soft tannins and good length.
£19.50

Varramista 2004, Tuscany Red
Very classy Syrah, showing raspberry fruit with gamey aromas on the nose. Ripe and round, with a soft silky texture and gentle tannins.

Via Collina Dolcetto Di Diano D'alba 2008, Cantina Terre Del Barolo, Piedmont Red
Complex, aromatic nose, with a fresh yet firm structure. Elegant and stylish, with a juicy palate, and a lovely scented finish.
£7.20 WAIT, GYW

Vigna Di Fontalle Chianti Classico Riserva DOCG 2005, Machiavelli, Tuscany Red
Deep ruby hue, with intense flavours of cherry pie and spice, combined with undertones of cassis fruit and smoky spice. Rather attractive flavour profile, with balanced acidity and tannins. Very complex, with a great long length.
£13.00

Villa Borghetti Amarone Della Valpolicella 2005, Pasqua Vigneti E Cantine, Veneto Red
Garnet in colour. Rather restrained, and showing some complexity, with meaty toastiness, and hints of smoke and cloves. Juicy mid palate, with a long finish. Well-made.
£24.00 CBK, CTL, THI

Villa Cafaggio Cortaccio IGT 2004, Tuscany Red
Oaky blackcurrant, plum, and blackberry on the nose. Full-bodied, with an attractive sweet finish.
£25.00 HWL

Villa Donoratico DOC 2006, Tenuta Argentiera, Tuscany Red
Warming savoury plum and black fruit aromas. Tannins are firm but silky, with a supple, lush texture.
£23.20 EUW, EVW

Villa Martis Langhe Rosso 2005, Marchesi Di Gresy, Piedmont Red
Pale colour indicating maturity. Nice distinct aromas of cherry fruit. Pleasantly textured palate, with Nebbiolo character showing through. Nice, soft, ripe tannins.
£16.50

Villa Rizzardi Amarone Della Valpolicella 2004, Guerrieri Rizzardi, Veneto Red
Restrained but developed, with sour cherry and wild herb aromas on a complex and elegant nose. Harmonious and balanced, with a long, savoury finish.
£28.00 DVY

Virtuoso Primitivo IGT Puglia 2006, Casa Girelli Spa Puglia Red
Rich crimson in colour, showing hints of maturity. Beautifully integrated palate, with a full body and a long lingering finish.
£10.00 HWL

Zanna Montepulciano D'abruzzo Colline Teramane 2005, Illuminati Abruzzo Red
Deep colour, with opulent blackberry and mocha aromas. Well-integrated palate of ripe vanilla and spiced plum, with damson on the finish.
£20.00 MON

Chiaretto DOC Classico 2008, Guerrieri Rizzardi, Veneto Rosé
Sweet ripe fruit nose, with pink grapefruit aromas and redcurrant on the palate. Lingering, with lots of acid and good balance.
£8.00 F&M

Ario' Prosecco Di Conegliano DOC Extra Dry 2007, L'antica Quercia, Veneto Sparkling
Intense nose, which is clean, pure, and fresh. Zesty, mouthwatering acidity and pure varietal character. Citrus and apple notes, with a balanced, lingering finish.

Berlucchi Cuvée Imperiale Brut NV, Guido Berlucchi & C. S.p.a., Lombardia Sparkling
Complex nose, with notes of butter and light almonds on the palate. Good balance between acidity and sugar, and a persistent bead.
£25.00

Deltetto Extra Brut Vsq 2005, Piedmont Sparkling
Clean nose of relaxed ripe fruit, with a fat palate of marmalade and bready sourdough. A good, well-balanced food wine.
£12.80 LIB

Eliseo Bisol Cuvèe Del Fondatore Talento Metodo Classico 2001, Bisol Desiderio & Figli Sparkling
Tight, fresh nose, with subtle, toasty, aged notes. A light and easy palate. An effortless wine, which is complex, with a savoury-sweet finish, and real length.

La Gioiosa Prosecco Valdobbiadene Doc NV, Veneto Sparkling
Very pale colour. Light, primary fruit nose of pear drops, with a soft attack, and good, clean fruit. Fresh pear drops on a medium length palate, with a crisp finish, and a balanced, fine mousse.
£8.10 TESC

Prosecco Di Valdobbiadene DOC - Maschio Dei Cavalieri NV, Cantine Maschio, Veneto Sparkling
Pears and cream, with hints of candy and caramel on the nose. Intense, but smooth and elegant.
WAV

Prosecco Di Valdobbiadene Millesimato Doc 2008, Cantina Produttori Di Valdobbiadene Sac, Veneto Sparkling
Fine bubbles. Good varietal character, with fine floral aromas. Clean, full, fresh palate, with herbaceous notes on the finish.

Prosecco Monte Santo Agricoltura Biologica IGT NV, Soyo Foods, Veneto Sparkling
Rich and creamy; more vinous than a typical Prosecco. Notes of sunflower, with a good body, and a crisp, clean finish.

Tenuta S.anna - Prosecco Millesimato 2007, Genagricola Spa, Veneto Sparkling
Pungent nose, with pleasant notes of vanilla fruit. Crisp acidity, with a touch of vanilla following through on the palate. Good length.

Rosé Bisol Talento Metodo Classico 2001, Bisol Desiderio & Figli Sparkling Rosé
Pretty pale pink salmon colour. Light, delicate red fruit and cream notes on the nose, with a lively palate showing some delicate red fruit. Good length and finish.

Alto Adige Bianco Comtess DOC 2006, San Michele Appiano, Alto Adige Sweet
Mid-yellow colour. Nose of floral spice, rose petal, and dried white flowers. Broad attack, with rich apricot flavour, leading to a clean, long finish.
£30.40 EUW, EVW

Ben Rye 2007, Donna Fugata, Sicily Sweet
Vibrant old gold colour. Rich, with notes of apricot jam, and great acidity and length. Kick back and enjoy with a bread and butter pudding!.
£28.00 LIB

liatico Aleatico Di Puglia 2007, Feudi Di San Marzano, Puglia Sweet
Intense nose of black cherry, with gingerbread, damson jam, and a super-sweet, fruity palate, leading to a Port-like finish.
ATM, TAN

Marks & Spencer Vin Santo 1990, Grati Fattorie Di Galiga E Vetrice, Tuscany Sweet
Amber colour. Very developed nose of walnut and raisin. Good acidity on a palate which is smooth, nutty, spicy, and slightly spirity, with good length.
£15.00 M&S

Vin Santo Chianti Rufina Prunatelli 1990, Azienda Agricola Prunatelli, Tuscany Sweet
Attractive brown colour, with a citric, cedarwood nose. Very well-balanced palate, with good length.
£22.20

Vinsanto Di Carmignano 2003, Capezzana, Tuscany Sweet
Nut brown in colour, with amber tints. Volatile, heady oxidative aromas, with prunes and quite a lot of smoky sweetness on the palate. Creamy and luscious.
£30.00 LIB

Tordiruta Verdicchio Dei Castelli Di Jesi Passito 2005, Terre Cortesi Moncaro Marché, Botrytis
Deep golden colour, with peach and exotic fruit on the nose. Powerful rich palate, with oily fruit, sweet, stylish, creaminess, and good length.
£37.20 EUW, EVW

BRONZE

Altare 2006, Azienda Marramiero, Abruzzo White
Hints of old-style white Rioja, with a note of sherry, apple crumble complexity, spice, nutmeg, and honeyed citrus.

Alto Adige Pinot Grigio DOC 2008, San Michele Appiano, Alto Adige White
Fine, fruity nose, with good

ripeness. Good fruity palate, with a long finish.
£12.00 WAIT, EUW, EVW

Amarone 2006, Alpha Zeta, Veneto White
Complex flavours of plum, vanilla, and caramel. Very smooth palate, with balanced acidity and fruit, notes of cinnamon, and a long, round length of floral and prune notes.
£24.50 HEN, LIB

Bianco Del Cavaliere 2008, Cantina Todini Srl, Umbria White
Attractive nose of ripe, exotic fruit and lemon, with fresh yeastiness and high acidity. Well-balanced.

Bigi Orvieto Classico Secco Vigneto Torricella 2007, GIV, Umbria White
Lactic, creamy, grapey fruit, with a ripe, soft nose. Full grapey style, with good oak and fresh acidity.
£7.30

Canaletto Müller-Thurgau Trentino DOC 2008, Casa Girelli Spa, Trentino White
Clean, hot flavours,and good intensity of exotic fruit, with notes of banana on the nose. High in alcohol, with good intensity on the palate.
£6.00

Casale Vecchio Passerina Colli Aprutini IGT 2008, Farnese Vini White
Intense peach nose, and a very aromatic palate, with notes of peach and a touch of orange.Rich depth, with freshness on the finish.
LAI

Casale Vecchio Pecorino Terre Di Chieti Igt 2008, Farnese Vini, Abruzzo White
Light green in colour, with a

nose comprising candy, lemon, glycerine, pineapple, peas, and a touch of volatile acidity. The palate is lemony and fresh, with persistent peach notes.
LAI

Cellar Estates Frascati Doc 2008, Fratelli Martini Secondo Luigi Spa, Lazio White
Fragrant orange blossom and apricot on the nose and palate. Delicate. Good.
£4.50 BES

Cellar Estates Lambrusco Emilia Bianco 4% NV, Fratelli Martini Secondo Luigi Spa, Emilia-Romagna White
Elderflower notes on the nose, with hints of apple and lemon. Fruity and simple, with good appeal.
£3.00 BES

Colle Dei Venti Pecorino IGT Terre Di Chieti 2008, Caldora Vini, Abruzzo White
Pale lemon in colour, with a fresh citrus nose. Dry, with very strong lime notes. Well-made, with good balance. Ready to drink now, but best with food.
THI

Controguerra Bianco Ciafre' 2006, Illuminati, Abruzzo White
Quite deep in colour, with a very oaky nose, and well-structured palate. There is a honeyed edge, with great complexity and freshness. A special wine.
£12.00 MON

Controguerra Bianco Daniele 2006, Illuminati, Abruzzo White
Deep straw in colour, with notes of spicy oak on the nose,. The palate is broad in style, with toasty honey flavours.
£16.00 MON

Cubia 2007, Cusumano
Sicily White
Fresh, clean almond blossom, with notes of pear and lemon. Crisp character, with good length.
£20.40 EUW, EVW

Custoza DOC Val Dei Molini 2008, Cantina Di Custoza, Veneto White
Fresh, herbal, understated nose, leading to a delicate, clean herbal palate of apple and spiced apricot, with balanced acidity, and medium length.
£9.20 EUW, EVW

Dicembra Müller-Thurgau Trentino DOC 2008, Valle Di Cembra Cantina Di Montagna, Trentino White
Strong floral notes, with a touch of tropical fruit. Peach fruit palate. Clean, with medium intensity.
£8.00 HWL

Ekeos Verdicchio Dei Castelli Di Jesi Classico Superiore 2008, Fazi Battaglia, Marche White
Creamy, herbal aromas, with fresh vibrant acidity and balanced citrussy finish.

Falanghina 2008, Feudi Di San Gregorio, Campania White
Mid-yellow in colour, with nutty notes on the nose. Broad, ripe palate, which is soft and attractive.
£14.50

Falanghina Campania 2008, Terredora, Campania White
Some floral notes on the nose, over a touch of oak. Good balance, with some bright sherbet.
£9.00 DIW, LAY, MON, ODF

Farnese Trebbiano D'abruzzo Doc 2008, Abruzzo White
Water-white in colour, with a fresh, sappy, leafy nose. On the palate, there is some weight and concentration, with good acidity.
LAI

Fossili Gavi del Comune di Gavi 2008, San Silvestro, Piedmont White
Creamy length on the nose. Light and delicate, with notes of lime and lemon. Good intensity on a gently structured palate.
£10.00 HOH

Frascati DOC Superiore Spar 2008, Cantina Cerquetta, Lazio White
Sappy, white floral fruit expression, with light, sharp fruit on the palate.

Friulano DOC Collio Marco Scolaris 2008, Scolaris Vini, Friuli Venezia-Giulia White
Attractive peach and spicy nose, leading to a delicate spicy palate, with moderate acidity, nutty fruit, and a concentrated finish.

Gavi del Comune di Gavi 2008, Michele Chiarlo, Piedmont White
Nose of floral honey, blossom, and minerality. Fresh acidity, complex, with good length.
£17.00 HOH

Gavi Del Comune Di Gavi Granee 2008, Beni Di Batasiolo, Piedmont White
Light floral and citrus aromas on the nose. Palate shows fresh acidity, with notes of blossom, honey, and orange, leading to a medium length finish.
£12.00 MON

Gavi Del Comune Di Gavi Masseria Dei Carmelitani 2008, Terre Da Vino Piedmont White
Nice mineral nose and palate,

with pleasant pear and apple flavours.
£15.00 EHB, EVW, VIN

Gavi Di Gavi Nuovo Quadro 2008, La Battisitina, Piedmont White
Big, broad, leesy nose. The palate is creamy with decent concentration. Classic style.
£10.90 CHH, FLA

Greco Di Tufo Terre Degli Angeli 2008, Terredora, Campania White
Rich and peachy; a good, honest, ripe, and friendly style. A little simple, but tangy.
£11.00 DIW, LAY, MON, ODD, ODF

Grillo Sauvignon Blanc Sicilia IGT 2008, Barone Montalto S.p.a., Sicily White
Light herbs and citrus, with overtones of nutmeg. Full dry palate of lemon and herbs, and a slightly oily texture, with good acidity and balance. An interesting wine.

Il Nostro Grecanico 2008, Oenoforos Ab, Sicily White
Lovely, smoky, and aromatic. Quite good and typical, well-balanced, with medium length.
£3.90

Inycon Chardonnay Pinot Grigio 2008, Settesoli, Sicily White
Ripe, creamy, and appley, with lively balance, and a pleasant, persistent finish.
£5.00

Inycon Growers Fiano 2008, Settesoli, Sicily White
Pale yellow in colour, with a light, lifted pear drop nose. Soft, well made, and approachable.
£5.60 WAIT, BTH

Inycon Unoaked Chardonnay 2008, Settesoli, Sicily White
Ripe fruit on the nose, reflected nicely on the palate. Good length - a fine wine.

Kue 2008, Brugnano Srl, Sicily White
Pronounced nose of lovely ripe white peach fruit, with good fruit and acidity on the palate, and good length.

La Segreta Bianco 2008, Planeta, Sicily White
Oaky and creamy, quite ripe a nd rich, with a pronounced n ose of minerals and green fruit. Pleasant wine, with a good finish.
£10.50 COO, HAR, LBS, P&R

Langhe Arneis Blangé 2008, Ceretto, Piedmont White
Floral and honeyed, with a hint of spice on the nose. Almonds and nutty sweetness come through on the palate, with some bitterness, and a delicate length.
£15.00 EUW

Macrina Verdicchio dei Castelli di Jesi 2008, Gioacchino Garofoli, Marché White
Clean, ripe, and creamy, with medium concentration, and a dry citrussy, nutty, solid edge to the long finish.
£9.00 HOH

Manifesto Inzolia Chardonnay 2008, Oenoforos Ab, Sicily White
Delicate fruit on the nose, with a palate of clean, fresh pear and melon fruit. Crisp and fresh, with a creamy finish, a well-made wine.
£5.20

Marks & Spencer Chardonnay Piedmont 2008, Araldica, Piedmont White
Restrained nose of mineral

herbs, with a floral note from Cortese. Smoky, with mouth watering acidity. A refreshing and attractive wine.
£5.00 M&S

Marks & Spencer Quadro Sei Gavi 2008, Araldica, Piedmont White
Nice floral nose, with good perfume. Fruity and well-balanced, with a long silky finish.
£7.00 M&S

Maso Toresella Chardonnay Trentino DOC Superiore 2007, Cavit, Trentino White
Delicate nose, opening up with big fruits on the palate. Good length.
£12.00 PBA

Masseria Torre Rossa Verdeca Puglia IGT 2008, Terre Di Sava S.r.l. Puglia White
Pear drop notes, with some complexity, showing tropical fruit, fresh acidity, and an elegant mineral finish.
HOH

Ofithe Offida Pecorino 2008, Terre Cortesi Moncaro Marché White
Pure, slightly smoky fruit dominates, with herbs and nuts to the fore.

Olivar IGT Bianco 2007, Cesconi, Trentino White
Obvious oak. A serious, robust flavoured style. Balanced, with good concentration, long finish, and good structure.
£21.50 LIB

Pecorino 2008, Azienda Marramiero, White
Earthy, pungent style, well-balanced fruit and acidity, notes of lime, lemon, and pineapple, with good length.

Pinot Grigio 2008, Bidoli - Margherita & Arrigo Srl, Friuli Venezia-Giulia White
Perfumed, slightly earthy, mineral nose, with notes of pear drops. Crisp, steely palate, with green apple acidity. Quite simple style, but showing some concentration and reasonable length.
£8.00 M&S

Pinot Grigio "i Feudi Di Romans" 2008, Azienda Agricola Lorenzon, Friuli Venezia-Giulia White
Fresh pear and apple nose, with good Pinot Grigio character. Pure, clean, simple pear and fruit flavours. Clean and dry, with a peardrop finish.
£11.00 LIB

Previata Frascati DOC Superiore 2008, San Marco, Latium White
Charming, light, slightly yeasty nose, with refreshing light lemon fruit. Bright and fresh, with a medium finish.

Quota 311 2008, Casa Vinicola S. Piersanti & C, Marche White
Peachy, tropical nose. Aromatic, with balanced acidity and freshness. Good length and complexity.
£6.50 ARL, EXC, VNS

Roero Arneis San Michele 2008, Deletto, Piedmont White
Floral and slightly honeyed on the nose, with a Viognier-like character, and notes of marzipan and peach. Attracive palate.
£13.00 LIB

Sauvignon Trentino DOC 2008, Concilio S.p.a., Trentino White
Daffodil notes on the nose, with a floral fruit palate, fresh acidity,

Selezione Lugana "Fabio Contato" 2007, Azienda Agricola Provenza, Lombardia White
Herbal, lemony citrus peel aromas, with a touch of oaky spice, tight structure, and good balance and texture.
£40.00 CTL, VSO

Soave Classico DOC - Duca Del Frassino 2008, Cantina Di Soave, Veneto White
Very pale, with a slightly reductive nose, showing clean, crisp citrus fruit aromas, with good acidity and length.
£15.00 PLB

Soave Classico DOC Rocca Sveva 2008, Cantina Di Soave, Veneto White
Pale yellow in colour, with lovely minerality and good balance.
£20.00 CTL, VSO

Soave Fiorellino Fattori 2008, Fattori Srl, Veneto White
Pronounced nose, with good fruit and acidity, delicate pear flavours and a medium finish.
£6.00 AVB

Staforte Soave Classico 2007, Azienda Agricola Pra, Veneto White
Medium-deep lemon in colour, with a bright, clean nose, with some wood character and good intensity.
£17.70

Sud Verdeca Puglia IGT. 2008, Feudi Di San Marzano, Puglia White
Fresh, grapey, and waxy, with a hint of Muscat character, good mouthfeel, and a pleasant finish.
ATM, TAN

Südtirol Pinot Grigio Alto Adige 2008, Kellerei Kaltern Caldaro, Alto Adige / South Tirol White
Some ripe fruit on the nose, with a lovely fruity palate. Well-balanced, with good length.
£5.20

Terre Di Ginestra Catarratto 2008, Calatrasi Mediterranean Domains, Sicily White
Rich, ripe and fat; a very good Catarratto, with fresh, juicy, tropical fruit, and plenty of acidity.
£9.80

Trentino DOC Chardonnay 2008, Vivallis S.c.a., Trentino White
Smoky, grassy, mineral, and floral aromas. A little waxy, with sharp lemon zest freshness. Interesting, with typically Italian flavours.

Verdicchio Dei Castelli Di Jesi Classico Superiore DOC 2007, Marconi Vini Srl, Marche White
Medium lime-yellow colour, with a slightly cheesy nose. Soft attack, with a nice fruit flavour and tropical character, with reasonable body and length.

Verdicchio Dei Castelli Di Jesi Classico Superiore "villa Talliano" 2007, Azienda Agricola Mancini, Marché White
Clean, bright, and round, with a big nose and almond on the palate. Long lemony harmony.

Verdicchio Di Matelica "Terre Di Valbona" 2008, Cantine Belisario, Marche White
Pale yellow in colour. Clean, broad fruit on the nose. Gentle

attack, with a slight carbon dioxide prickle. Clean, fresh, harmonious palate. Well-balanced, with good depth.
£8.00 LIB

Verdicchio Di Matelica "Vigneti Del Cerro" 2008, Cantine Belisario, Marche White
Very pale lime-yellow colour. Clean fruit, with a ripe, soft attack. Medium to light body, with a clean finish and reasonable length.
£10.00 LIB

Vernaccia Di San Gimignano 2008, Teruzzi&puthod, Tuscany White
Somewhat closed on the nose, with a little dried straw character. The palate is rounder and fruitier, with passable length.

Vesevo Fiano Di Avellino DOCG 2008, Vesevo, Campania White
Delicate fruit on the nose, well-balanced on the palate, good length.
£13.40 HEN, LIB

Villa Lanata Langhe DOC Chardonnay 2008, Az. Agr. Villa Lanata - Distribuito Da Domini Villae Lanata Srl, Piedmont White
Restrained, waxy, mineral aromas. The attack is gentle, but grows on the palate, and shows real Italian typicity. Subtle, but well-made and attractive.
£13.50

Villa Malizia Pinot Grigio 2008, Castellani Spa, Veneto White
Fresh, lightly spiced pear and herb nose. Crisp and medium bodied, with a soft peppery mid-palate and soft, fresh acidity.

Attractive and nicely balanced.
£4.60 ALD

Aglianico Campania 2007, Terredora, Campania Red
Notes of vanilla oak and fragrant cherry on the nose. Sharp tannins.
£7.00 LAY, MON, ODF, WTA

Amarone Della Valpolicella 2006, Cantina Sociale Della Valpantena Sca, Veneto Red
Spicy nose and palate, with notes of caramel and polish. The tannins are well-balanced, with good cherry fruit flavours.

Amarone Della Valpolicella Classico DOC 2005, Terre Di Leone Srl, Veneto Red
Pungent stone fruit on the nose. Rich fruit palate, with notes of spice.

Amarone Della Valpolicella DOC Classico Il Bosco 2004, Gerardo Cesari Spa, Veneto Red
Raisin aromas. Very rich mouthfeel, with some interesting herbal flavours, smooth tannins, and a long, concentrated finish. A delicious and extremely well put-together wine.
£40.00

Amarone Della Valpolicella - Rocca Alata 2006, Cantina Di Soave, Veneto Red
Nice depth of black cherry fruit., with firm grip and a pleasant length.
£14.60 TESC

Amarone Della Valpolicella - Rocca Sveva 2004, Cantina Di Soave, Veneto Red
Deep in colour. Notes of Sweet spice, with Port-like aromas, and notes of raisin, fig and cherry fruit.
£80.00 CTL, VSO

Amarone Pagus Di Bisano 2005, Cantina Sociale Della Valpantena Sca, Veneto Red
Notes of tar and mushroom on the nose. Rich, plummy fruit on a bittersweet on the palate.

Antica Vineria Barbera D'asti 2007, Schenk Italia, Piedmont Red
Creamy, bright focused fruit, with unusual notes of red apple skin. The palate is dry, savoury, and well-balanced.

Avegiano Montepulciano d'Abruzzo 2007, Bove, Abruzzo Red
The nose is dense, but rather subtle, with hints of blueberry, blackberry, and perfumed talcum powder. Palate of damson fruit and blackberries, with tannins leading to a dusty, fine finish.
£8.50 HOH

Barbera D'alba Superiore 2006, Gd Vajra, Piedmont Red
Dark damson fruit, with notes of liquorice. Chewy tannins provide a good structural frame.
£26.00 LIB

Barbera D'Asti 2003, Ca' Del Matt, Piedmont Red
Lots of vanilla and quite fine fruit on the nose, with decent fruit on the palate as well.
£6.70 LIB

Barbera d'Asti Superiore "Le Orme" 2007, Michele Chiarlo, Piedmont Red
Intense yet elegant. Good vanilla aromas. Swathes of tannin blend subtly with crisp cranberry and mouth-watering acidity.
£12.00 HOH

Barolo Arione 2005, Enzo & Gianni Boglietti, Piedmont Red
Herbal and spicy character, with hints of sour cherry on a restrained nose. Mouthwatering acidity and firm tannins.
£44.90 L&W

Bella Modella Nero D'avola 2008, Casa Defra', Sicily Red
Sweet, jammy nose; a vibrant crowd-pleaser. Lots of dark berry and cherry fruits on the palate.
£5.60 HEN, AAW

Benuara 2007, Cusumano, Sicily Red
Deep colour. Richly textured, with a raisin and prune character, and good acidity. Nice integration of oak and fruit.
£14.00 EUW, EVW

Bricco Dei Guazzi - Barbera D'asti 2006, Genagricola Spa, Piedmont Red
Clean fruity nose. Light, but balanced and harmonious, with silky red fruit and soft tannins.

Briccotondo Piemonte Barbera 2007, Fontanafredda, Piedmont Red
Juicy chocolate nose, with chunky smooth ripe fruit. Full, supporting structure, with a slightly dry finish.

Brunello Di Montalcino 2004, Poggio San Polo, Tuscany Red
Bright red cherry on the nose. Black fruit follows on the palate.
£40.00 LIB

Brunello Di Montalcino 2004, Poggio Tempesta, Tuscany Red
Plum on the nose, with notes of spice and cherry. Firm tannins and good balance.
£21.00 LIB

Brunello Di Montalcino DOCG 2004, Loacker Corte Pavone, Tuscany Red
Rich cassis and blueberry nose,

with nice balance and structure. Light and elegant.
£42.00 GWW

Brunello Di Montalcino DOCG 2004, Tenuta Il Poggione, Tuscany Red
Minty and herbal notes, with good ripeness. Red cherry notes, and a dry firm finish.
ENO

Brunello Di Montalcino DOCG Riserva Vigna Paganelli 2003, Tenuta Il Poggione, Tuscany Red
This is a good wine, with true complexity of rounded fruit. Notes of plum and dark cherry, with lovely freshness, lifted acidity, and elegant tannins – will age well.
ENO

Buriano IGT 2004, Rocca Di Castagnoli, Tuscany Red
Lovely oaky blackcurrant and eucalyptus nose, with juicy, meaty, fruity structure. Rich and complex.
EVW

Ca'di Ponti Nero D'avola 2008, Adria, Sicily Red
Intense red pronounced colour, with a nice elegant nose of red fruit. Round and soft, with fruits showing well on the finish.
£5.40 CHH, FLA

Cabernet Sauvignon 2003, Isole E Olena, Tuscany Red
Strong, but balanced fruity aromas. Rich and complex, full of toffee.
£53.00 LIB

Cabernet Sauvignon Garda DOC Val Dei Molini 2008, Cantina Di Custoza, Veneto Red
Touch of greenness on the nose, with notes of oak, but also nice

plummy black fruit and cassis. Well-balanced.
£9.00 EUW

Cagiolo 2006, Cantina Tollo Abruzzo Red
Rustic nose, showing warmth with a soft herby mid-palate. Good balance, with bags of rich fruit.
£13.30 ALI

Cagnulari 2007, Cantina Santa Maria La Palma, Sardinia Red
Deep colour. Herbaceous nose, with some floral and berry notes. Dry, smooth, and elegant, with acidity and tannins on the finish.
£15.00

Caldora Sangiovese Terre Di Chieti IGT 2008, Caldora Vini, Abruzzo Red
Violet hue. Nose shows young, jammy fruit, which follows through onto a sweet ripe palate, with some tannin.
ATM, THI

Campo Della Mura Rosso Piceno Superiore 2005, Terre Cortesi Moncaro Marché Red
Deep, youthful colour. Nicely maturing, with spicy dried fruit on the nose, and some vanilla. Full, dry, spiced berry fruit on the palate. Dry tannins and good balance.

Canaletto Nero D'avola Merlot IGT Sicilia 2008, Casa Girelli Spa, Sicily Red
Garnet red in colour, with blackcurrant fruit and spice. Dry, grippy tannins on the finish.
£6.00 HWL

Canaletto Primitivo IGT Puglia 2006, Casa Girelli Spa, Puglia Red
Fresh and fruity, with red berry flavours and a touch of spice,

culminating in a long finish.
£6.00 WAIT

Capitel Della Crosara Ripasso 2006, Montresor, Veneto Red
Nice depth of colour. Red cherry fruit flavours on a lovely juicy palate, with good tannins.

Casale Vecchio Montepulciano D'abruzzo DOC 2008, Farnese Vini, Abruzzo Red
Floral violet on the nose, palate of dark and red fruits, with rich texture and velvety tannins.
LAI

Castello Di Brolio 2006, Barone Ricasoli, Tuscany Red
Appealing cedarwood nose, with a supple fruity palate. Light tannins and good length.
£25.00

Castero Nobile Di Montepulciano 2006, Schenk Italia, Tuscany Red
Bright colour. Good, quite serious nose, with notes of tobacco. Lush palate, with ripe, stylish fruit, and good backbone. Evolving well.

Cent'Are Nero d'Avola 2007, Duca di castelmonte, Sicily Red
Toasty, ripe black fruits. Rich, succulent cherries, with a long, balanced finish.
£7.50 HOH

Cepparello 2006, Isole E Olena, Tuscany Red
Simple cherry fruit, with herbal notes. Tannins are edgy, but there is elegant, powerful complexity, with decent length.
£46.00 LIB

Chianti 2008, Leonardo, Tuscany Red
Classic Sangiovese nose of oak and blackcurrant. Good fruit

backbone with high acidity. Rich, full-bodied wine with a long finish.
£8.30 HEN, LIB

Chianti Classico Riserva 2005, Carpineto, Tuscany Red
Deep colour, with blackberry and smoke on the nose. Round, smooth, velvety texture. Good fruit and balanced acidity, combined with gentle tannins.
£18.00 HOH

Chianti Colli Fiorentini DOCG "Uggiano" 2007, Uggiano, Tuscany Red
Complex nose of bitter cherry and savoury notes. Attractively chewy on the palate, with layers of red fruit.
£5.70 MRN

Chianti Riserva 2005, Da Vinci, Tuscany Red
Nose of rich dark plum, with some creaminess. Notes of black olive and tobacco. Good complexity, firm tannin, and fresh acidity.
£13.90 HEN, LIB

Chianti Superiore DOCG 2007, Piccini Tuscany Red
Cherry and meat nose, with dark berry concentration and some smoke. Chewy tannins, slightly jammy.
£7.50 SAIN

Colle Secco Montepulciano 2006, Cantina Tollo, Abruzzo Red
Fine aromas. Clean, long, and fresh, with balanced oak and fruit. A drier style, with sweet edges.
£7.60 ALI

Colmello Rosso 2001, Moletto, Veneto Red
Dark cherry and hints of vanilla on the nose. Well-balanced

palate, which develops complexity. Silky smooth tannins.

Colmello Rosso Edizione Speciale 2000, Moletto, Veneto Red

Intense blackcurrant leaf, menthol, and eucalyptus on the nose. The palate is rich and liquorice-like, with succulent blackcurrants and good length.

Cubardi Primitivo Salento Rosso 2004, Schola Sarmenti, Puglia Red

Aromatic raspberry and cherry nose, with juicy black fruit on the palate, and good length.
£16.00 WIN

Edizione 9 Cinque Autoctoni NV, Farnese Vini, Abruzzo & Puglia Red

Bags of sweet fruit on the nose, with powerful legs, rich, sweet flavours, and nice well-balanced tannins.
£13.00 LAI

Familiae Piccini Chianti Riserva DOGC 2006, Piccini, Tuscany Red

Restrained nose, with leafy red berry fruit. Fine, chalky tannins and fresh acidity
£10.00 SAIN

Farnese Sangiovese Terre Di Chieti IGT 2008, Farnese Vini, Abruzzo Red

Youthful, opaque, purple colours., with a floral, cassis nose, following through to the palate. Good length.

Finest Chianti Classico Riserva DOGC 2005, Piccini, Tuscany Red

Modern style. Rich, vanilla oak, with dark cherry fruit and spice on the nose. Soft, smooth palate

with cherry notes. Appealing.
£7.20 TESC

Flaccianello Della Pieve 2006, Fontodi, Tuscany Red

Berry fruit and cherry, with a balsamic note, good acidity, and ripe chewy tannin.
£43.00 LIB

Fojaneghe 2005, Bossi Fedrigotti, Trentino Red

Subtle, herbal, cherry nose. Zippy palate of cherry and blackberry. Good structure, and lovely fruity finish.

Franconia 2007, Moletto Veneto Red

Earthy aromatic nose. Restrained dry fruit on palate. Fresh, supple structure and good length.

Galassi Sangiovese Di Romagna 2008, Gruppo Cevico Soc Coop Agricola, Emilia-Romagna Red

Lots of juicy fruit, with a strong cherry character. Very fragrant, attractive, and youthful. A good red to serve lightly chilled.

Hedone 2007, Valentino Cirulli, Umbria Red

Some sweet fruit, with grippy tannins. Nice oaky cherries on the nose.

Il Principio Aglianico Irpinia 2006, Terredora, Campania Red

Earthy, dense, and spicy. Nice stuff, with firm tannins.
£11.00

Inama Carmenere Più 2006, Michele Wassler, Veneto Red

Clean and well-made, with some spice and dark fruit, and notes of summer fruits. Good individuality.
£14.50 AWW, BDL, BOQ, CVS, FFT, GNW, TAU, WBR

Inferi 2005, Azienda Marramiero, Abruzzo Red
Cherry and raspberry fruit, with a creamy note on the nose. Rich cherry palate, with spicy tannins and a lingering finish.

Itynera Montepulciano D'abruzzo DOC 2007, Mgm Mondo Del Vino, Abruzzo Red
Pleasant, fresh, and simple. Fresh, creamy, red cherry palate. Pure and warm.
CBG

Korem IGT Isola Dei Nuraghi 2006, Argiolas, Sardinia Red
Lovely long, fine tannins, with new oak. Harmonious acidity and good fruit.
£28.00 EUW, EVW

La Segreta Rosso 2008, Planeta, Sicily Red
Attractive sweet ripe nose, showing young cherry fruit. Well-balanced, with good tannins and a fresh finish.
£10.50 ACC, LBS, P&S

Laurana Conero Riserva 2006, Terre Cortesi Moncaro, Marche Red
Sun-baked black fruit nose. Full, ripe palate. Spicy and mineral, with savoury notes.

Laurana Rosso Piceno Superiore 2007, Terre Cortesi Moncaro, Marché Red
Deep youthful purple colour. Fresh clean baked berry fruit, with hints of coffee on the nose. Smooth, dry, spicy palate, with ripe tannins and gentle acidity.

Le Silve Rosso Conero 2007, Terre Cortesi Moncaro, Marché Red
Bright, juicy red fruits. Spicy entry, lively acidity, and soft tannins. Attractive, with good length. A super wine.

Lessona 2005, Proprieta' Sperino, Piedmont Red
Medium brick red in colour. Fruity nose of cherry and red berries. Slightly jammy. Good balance and structure. Drink now.
£43.00 LIB

Lo Zoccolaio Barbera D'alba Sucule' Doc 2005, Cascina Lo Zoccolaio - Distribuito Da Domini Villae Lanata Srl, Piedmont Red
Nice aromas of cinnamon, sweet cherry, raisins, chocolate, and oak. Good length.
£9.50

Marinus Rosso Piceno Superiore 2007, Il Conte Villaprandone, Marche Red
Deep colour, with a vanilla oak nose, and ripe cherry fruit on the palate. Dry and savoury.

Marks & Spencer Baglio Rosso 2007, Cantine Soc. Canicatti, Sicily Red
Deep cherry-red colour. Lifted violet nose, leading to cherry palate. Good balance.
£6.00 M&S

Maso Cervara Teroldego Rotaliano DOC 2006, Cavit, Trentino Red
Purple-red colour, with a brooding dark cherry nose, and notes of violets and truffles. The palate shows rich dark cherry and oaked blackberry fruit. Well -balanced, with acidity and firm tannins, culminating in a dry, long, and rich finish.
£12.00 PBA

Mauro Primitivo 2007, Oenoforos Ab, Puglia Red
Fruity and full-bodied. Very meaty, attractive, and intense. Good quality.
£4.80

Mazzano 2004, Masi Agricola, Veneto Red
Fresh and tangy. Lively acidity, delicious supple style. Aromatic, long, and savoury.

Merlot Primitivo Tarantino Trevini Primo 2007, Mgm Mondo Del Vino S.r.l., Puglia Red
Nose of vanilla, spice, and blackberry fruit. The palate shows zippy green pepper and blackcurrant.

Mhv Chianti Classico DOGC 2007, Piccini, Tuscany Red
A true-to-type Chianti. Clean and simple, with notes of bramble fruit and tea leaf. A good mineral length, with fruit on the finish.
£8.00 MHV

Mhv Chianti Classico Riserva DOCG 2006, Piccini, Tuscany Red
Fruity, with some development. Cherry notes on a rich, complex nose. Good structure and acidity. Pleasant finish.
£9.40 MHV

Mhv Chianti DOCG 2008, Piccini, Tuscany Red
Attractive ripe fruit on the nose. Palate is oaky, with notes of vanilla and blackcurrant. Medium length. Pleasant wine.
£6.00 BNK, MHV

Moi 2005, Vigne And Vini Srl, Puglia Red
Attractive red fruit, with a violet nuance. Bright fruity palate, with lively acidity, and even-textured tannin.

Montefalco Sagrantino DOCG 2005, Cantina Novelli, Umbria Red
Rustic, with lots of brute strength, and some sweet fruit too. Good mouthfeel.

Montepulciano D'abruzzo Materia Prima 2005, Mgm Mondo Del Vino S.r.l., Abruzzo Red
Nose of cocoa and coffee, with some herbal notes and plum fruit. Developed palate, with well-integrated tannins and acidity.
£18.50 WAIT

Montescuro Conero Riserva 2006, Terre Cortesi Moncaro, Marche Red
Dense berry fruit. Smoky and full-bodied, with a heavy tannin structure. Notes of dark fruit and spicy oak.

Morar Amarone Della Valpolicella 2003, Azienda Agricola Valentina Cubi Veneto Red
Palate shows sour cherry fruit and lots of cherry oak. Well-balanced and well-made.
£55.70

Nerio Nardo Riserva Rosso 2003, Schola Sarmenti, Puglia Red
Autumn leaves and notes of chestnuts roasting on a fire. Open, expressive, mature, and unmistakably Italian.
£12.50 WIN

Nero D'avola Aynat 2006, Viticultori Associati Canicatti, Sicily Red
Vibrant ruby colour. Fresh nose of mellow violet and plum. Medium intensity, soft attack. Some cooked damson character on the palate, with fine tannins and good length.
£20.00 VIN

Nero D'avola Villa Seta 2007, Montresor, Sicily Red
Light, fragrant nose. Lovely strawberry fruit, with layers of good, soft tannins and balanced acidity.
£6.00 ASDA

Netrurio 2006, Podere Sperpetua, Tuscany Red
Clean and pleasing on the nose, with good spice on the palate. Puckeringly intense.

Nipozzano Chianti Rufina Riserva 2006, Frescobaldi, Tuscany Red
Complex red fruit and medicinal aromas. Complex fruit core, underpinned by firm, savoury tannins. Has potential to develop further.
£17.00 HOH

Palazzo Comunale Brunello Di Montalcino 2004, Cantina Di Montalcino, Tuscany Red
Deep coffee and leather aromas, with rich fruitiness on the palate, and an attractive, long, sweet finish.
£32.00 LIB

Pasiteo Vino Nobile Di Montepulciano 2005, Fassati, Tuscany Red
Spicy and rich. Well-structured, pleasant, and fruity. Easy-drinking.

Passione 2006, Vigne And Vini Srl, Puglia
Juicy ripe black fruit and grippy tannins. Creamy mid-palate, with a little wood, leading to a spicy finish.

Pinot Nero 2006, Franz Haas, Alto Adige Red
Very pale in colour, with raspberry leaf aromas. Delicate and nicely rounded palate, with refreshing acidity.
£18.00 LIB

Podere Castorani Montepulciano d'Abruzzo 2004, Podere Castorani, Abruzzo Red
Animal notes and tea leaf on the nose, with a palate of ripe

damson. Integrated acidity and oak.
£16.00 HOH

Poggio A' Frati Chianti Classico Riserva Docg 2005, Rocca Di Castagnoli, Tuscany Red
Bright medium red in colour. Clean and elegant on the nose. Full of complex fruit, such as cassis and black cherries. Good acidity and length.
£21.50 EUW, EVW

Poggio Ai Ginepri 2007, Tenuta Argentiera, Tuscany Red
Intense leafy and graphite aromas. Lovely rich, dense fruit, with a streak of bell pepper running through. Perfect balance and poise; complex and long.
£17.30 EUW, EVW

Poggio Alto Chianti Riserva DOCG 2006, Piccini, Tuscany Red
Lovely Sangiovese nose of raisins and wild herbs. Rich fruit, chalky tannins, and fresh acidity.
£9.00 MHV

Poggiotondo Superiore 2007, Tuscany Red
Deep colour, with smooth and rounded fruit, good concentration, chewy tannins, balanced acidity, and full body.
£9.00 LIB

Primitivo Puglia IGT "Feudi Di San Marzano" 2008, Feudi Di San Marzano, Puglia Red
Hints of raisin and toffee on the nose. Smooth tannins and good structure.
ATM, TAN

Primitivo Salento IGT 2007, Cantine Due Palme Soc. Coop. Agricola, Puglia Red
Young, promising cherry fruit on

the nose. Appealing sweet fruit palate.

Raboso 2003, Moletto, Veneto Red
Prominent juicy fruit, balanced by good acidity and ripe tannins. Good length.

Refosco Dal Peduncolo Rosso 2007, Vigna Del Torre, Friuli Venezia-Giulia Red
Leafy, cherry nose which follows into the palate. Plenty of acidic structure, with a long finish.

Remole Toscana Sangiovese 2007, Frescobaldi, Tuscany Red
Fresh, lifted strawberry and raspberry juice, with sour cherry palate, lovely acidity, and soft tannin.
£9.50 HOH

Ricossa Barolo DOCG 2004, Mgm Mondo Del Vino, Piedmont Red
Some development on the nose. Finely structured, with high acidity, and dry tannins. Assertive, but has the finesse to match.
£10.00 TESC

Ripasso Valpolicella DOC Superiore Rocca Sveva 2006, Cantina Di Soave, Veneto Red
Brick red in colour, with an earthy nose. There is some liquorice flavour, with red berry fruit. Clean, with moderate acidity, and good body.
£30.00 AIL, CTL, VSO

Rosso Di Montepulciano 2007, Poliziano, Tuscany Red
Oaky cherries on the nose, with some smokiness, green pepper, and blackberry aromas. Firm, muscular structure.

Rosso Toscano IGT Sarello 2005, Gerardo Cesari Spa, Tuscany Red
Ripe fruit and chocolate aromas. Good tannins, acidity, and fruit intensity.
£13.00

Rosso Veronese IGT "dedicatum" 2006, Terre Di Leone Srl, Veneto Red
Dried rose petals, with some tar on the nose. Intriguing bitterness. Very smooth, with good balance. A good food wine.

San Zio Chianti 2006, Cantine Leonardo, Tuscany Red
Attractive mature nose of complex oak, blackcurrant, and violet. Excellent blackcurrant fruit on the palate. Well-balanced.
£17.00 LIB

Sangiovese Di Romagna DOC Riserva Grifone 2005, Casa Vinicola Botter Carlo & C. S.p.a., Emilia-Romagna Red
Notes of leather and orange on a developed palate, with drying tannins, refreshing acidity, and good concentration.

Sangiovese Merlot Rubicone 2008, Gruppo Cevico Soc Coop Agricola, Emilia-Romagna Red
Ripe cherries on the nose, slightly sweet and smooth on the palate. Well-balanced.

Sediana 2007, Valentino Cirulli, Umbria Red
Deep ruby-purple colour. There is some blackberry fruit and oak on the palate. Fresh ripe fruit and a long finish.

Selciaia Rosso Di Montepulciano 2008, Fassati, Tuscany Red
Lovely brambly character, and

very fruity. Redcurrants on the palate. Splendid example of its type.

Serralunga D'alba Barolo DOCG 2004, Fontanafredda, Piedmont Red
Bright, fruity nose, with notes of leather and tobacco. Moderate tannins.

Sigillo Primo Primitivo 2007, Antica Masseria del Sigillo, Puglia Red
Deep bright red hue. Attractive sour cherry and rhubarb on the nose. Plums and tinned black cherries on the palate.
£7.50 HOH

Somerfield Le Cassiane Montepulciano d'Abruzzo 2007, Umani Ronchi, Abruzzo Red
Some perfumed black fruits on the nose. Nicely cooling sappy fruit on the palate, with a herbal character on the finish, and rather rustic tannins.
£5.00 SMF

Sud Primitivo Di Manduria DOC 2007, Feudi Di San Marzano, Puglia Red
Underlying toffee and pepper, balanced with fresh red berries and plums.
ATM, TAN

Tabano 2006, Montecappone S.a.r.l., Marche Red
Dark berry fruit, with gamey, earthy, chewy tannins, balanced acidity, and a spicy wood finish.

Tanca Farrà 2004, Sella&mosca, Sardinia Red
Clean, floral nose. Fresh black fruit, with crisp acidity, and a long dry finish.
£14.90

Tauleto Sangiovese 2004, Umberto Cesari, Emilia-Romagna Red
Fresh and dried fruit aromas combine on the nose. Full body, with good tannic structure.
£36.00 HOH

Taurasi Campore Riserva 2003, Terredora, Campania Red
Distinctive fresh fruit on the nose, with balanced tannins.

Taurasi Pago Dei Fusi 2003, Terredora, Campania Red
Honey and gentle brown sugar on the nose. Grippy tannins and juicy prunes on the palate.
£16.00 LAY, MON, ODF

Tegole Rosso Toscana Igt 2006, Piccini, Tuscany Red
Prune-like, stewed fruit on the nose and palate. Ripe tannins and good acidity.

Tempore 2006, Giuseppe E Riccardo Olivi, Tuscany Red
Rich flavour. Complex, with ripe fruit, tasty earthiness, and good structure.

Tenute Al Sole Salento 2007, Cantine Due Palme, Puglia Red
Dense, bittersweet nose of dried herbs and oak. Juicy and meaty palate with soft tannins.
£6.00 BTH, CTL

Teroldego Rotaliano DOC Riserva 2005, Lidl, Trentino Red
This wine has a sweet, bitter, dark cherry nose. On the palate it is bright, yet quite elegant, with fresh pure berry and black fruit.
£6.00 LDL

Terragnolo Primitivo Salento IGT Rosso 2003, Apollonio Casa Vinicola Srl, Puglia Red
Engaging blackberry fruit nose.

Appealing, with ripe soft black fruit, and a long, elegant finish.
£9.00

Terrazzano Rosso Piceno Superiore 2006, Terre Cortesi Moncaro, Marché Red
Deepish colour, with a ripe, plummy, spicy nose. Quite a lot of tannin and oak on the palate, but balanced by full plummy fruit. Potential to develop in the short-term.

Terre Di Cariano Amarone Della Valpolicella 2005, Cecilia Beretta, Veneto Red
Deep damson red in colour. Good uplift, with a palate of ripe fruit, and a sweetish edge.
£30.00 ACG, C&B, CTL

Tesco Finest* Barbera D'asti DOC 2005, Fratelli Martini Secondo Luigi, Piedmont Red
Strawberry and new oak fragrance on the nose. Creamy, chewy fruit and soft tannins on the palate.
£7.00 TESC

Tesco Finest* Nero D'avola 2008, Cantine Settesoli, Sicily Red
Bright red in colour, with a light soft nose of sweet and floral notes. Spice and jam are well-mixed on the palate. Very enjoyable and balanced.
£6.00 TESC

Torre A Destra Chianti Classico Riserva 2005, Castello Della Paneretta, Tuscany Red
A moderately intense colour, with a lovely nose, dominated by cassis. Beautiful undertones of vanilla and subtle smokiness. Acidity is gentle but apparent. Moderate length.
VIN

Turriga Vdt 2004, Argiolas, Sardinia Red
Dark ruby colour. Strong pruney, black cherry nose. The palate shows rich fruity notes, with blackberry and bitter chocolate, and firm tannins on the finish.
£50.00 EUW, EVW

Uccelliera Brunello Di Montalcino 2004, Az. Agr. Uccelliera Di Andrea Cortonesi, Tuscany Red
Very rich, complex palate of ripe plummy fruit and pepper.Intense, with firm tannins well-balanced with oak, leading to an elegant finish.
£23.00 AAW

Valle Reale Montepulciano d'Abruzzo Vigne Nuove 2007, Valle Reale, Abruzzo Red
Violet in colour, with fairly subtle aromas. Palate shows a burst of fruit, with firm tannins, and good depth.
£8.60

Valle Reale San Calisto Oak Aged Montepulciano D'Abruzzo 2005, Valle Reale, Abruzzo Red
Smoky cherry nose, with a palate of rich cherries and mocha chocolate, with a sweet creamy edge.
£24.00

Valpolicella 2008, Allegrini, Veneto Red
Beautiful, aromatic cherry nose, which follows onto a fresh, attractive palate.
£9.80 HEN, LIB

Valpolicella Classico Superiore Domini Veneti 2007, Cantina Valpolicella Negrar, Veneto Red
Nice colour, with a garnet core. Oak, cherry, and blackcurrant nose. The palate is fresh and

simple, with a light body.
£6.00

Valpolicella Classico Superiore Ripasso Montecorna 2005, F.lli Farina, Veneto Red
Black fruit, cherry, and wood notes. A fleshy wine, with a soft palate and tannins. Long and fresh.

Valpolicella Ripasso Superiore Torre Del Falasco 2007, Cantina Sociale Della Valpantena Sca, Veneto Red
Good oaky nose, with rich chocolatey berry fruit. Good texture on the palate, with fruity and coffee notes. Nice length.
£12.40 FLA

Vesevo Beneventano Aglianico 2007, Vesevo, Campania Red
Deep in colour, with notes of vanilla and jam on the nose. Black fruit flavours, with jammy sweet tannins, and a long finish.
£9.90 HEN, LIB

Vesevo Taurasi 2005, Vesevo, Campania Red
Very deep plum colour. Oranges and plums on the nose, with a dry finish.
£21.00 HEN, LIB

Via Collina Barbera D'alba 2008, Cantina Terre Del Barolo, Piedmont Red
Some herbal notes. Light to medium depth, with a crunchy, young red fruit nose. There is a good acidic kick on the palate.
GYW

Vigneti Del Parco Conero Riserva 2005, Terre Cortesi Moncaro, Marche Red
Morello cherry fruit, with balsamic tones and creamy oak. Ripe, vibrant, lively acidity, and smooth tannins.
£22.90 EUW, EVW

Vigneto Rancia Chianti Classico Riserva 2006, Felsina, Tuscany Red
Restrained earthy aromas, with savoury meaty notes. Dense sour cherry and butter, with a spicy finish. Needs time to reach its full potential.
£35.00 LIB

Villa Cafaggio San Martino IGT 2004, Basilica Cafaggio, Tuscany Red
Deep raspberry in colour. Intense damson on the nose, with juicy dark cherry and damson on the palate. Lovely tannins, with an excellent finish.
£32.50 WAIT

Villa Magna Montepulciano D'abruzzo DOC 2008, Farnese Vini, Abruzzo Red
Palate of sweet black fruit and spicy oak, with great acidity and tannic structure. Very well-balanced.
LIB

Farnese Montepulciano D'abruzzo Cerasuolo DOC 2008, Farnese Vini, Abruzzo Rosé
Big, quite powerful, and jammy. Hints of strawberries and cream. Lots of fruit and sweet ripeness on the palate. Good length, with cherry acidity to balance.

Pinot Grigio Blush 2007, La Gioiosa, Veneto Rosé
Pale blush colour, with aromas of guava and melon. Nice aromatic subtle palate.
£5.70 TESC

Sangiovese Rosé Rubicone 2008, Gruppo Cevico Soc Coop Agricola, Emilia-Romagna Rosé
Good bright salmon in colour. Subtle redcurrant fruit on the nose. A gentle spritz adds life and zest.

Asda Extra Special Prosecco NV, Adria, Veneto Sparkling
Fine freshness and balance. Clean and bright on the finish.
£7.00 ASDA

Asti Spumanti DOCG NV, Lidl Piedmont Sparkling
Fresh, clear grape and apple nose. The palate is soft but fresh. Lightly spiced.
£4.30 LDL

Berlucchi Cellarius Brut Vendemmia 2005, Guido Berlucchi & C. S.p.a., Lombardia Sparkling
Buttery brioche nose, with a good consistent bead. Savoury notes on a russet apple palate, showing good length.
£25.00

Berlucchi Franciacorta DOCG Cuvée Storica NV, Guido Berlucchi & C. S.p.a., Lombardia Sparkling
Ripe and complex nose. Softly fruity, with some nice aged notes, and a lovely finish.
£25.00

Ca' Morlin Prosecco Spumante 2008, Ca' Morlin, Veneto Sparkling
Light and dry - an austere and refreshing style of Prosecco. Honeysuckle and herbaceous aromas.
£11.50 LIB

Cartizze NV, Garbara, Veneto Sparkling
Clean lively bubbles. Persistent creamy mouthfeel and good acidity, with a citrus finish.

La Gioiosa Prosecco Valdobbiadene DOC (spago) NV, La Gioiosa S.p.a, Veneto Sparkling
A leesy aroma, with hints of lime and melon. Soft texture, with good balance and persistence.

Matiu' Prosecco DOC Di Conegliano Brut 2007, L'antica Quercia, Veneto Sparkling
Very rich and fruity on the nose. Grapey and lively, with lovely bold fruit character.

Prior Brut NV, Bortolomiol, Veneto Sparkling
Light nose. Persistant bubbles, with good viscosity and mouthfeel. Notes of crisp apple and citrus, with balanced acidity.
£9.00

Prosecco Spumante Conegliano Valdobbiadene NV, La Marca, Veneto Sparkling
Drier than a typical Prosecco. Notes of pear. Surprising intensity and length.
£10.50 MWW

Spumante Aromatico Di Qualita' NV, Cantina Produttori Di Valdobbiadene Sac, Veneto Sparkling
Clean, pure, and youthful. Light straw in colour, with balanced dry acidity, and a spicy herbaceous note.

Tesco Finest* Bisol Prosecco Di Valdobbiadene Spumante NV, Bisol Desiderio & Figli, Veneto Sparkling
Creamy aromas with notes of pear. Fresh and well-balanced. Fizzy, relatively dry, and easy-drinking.
£9.10 TESC

Valdobbiadene Prosecco DOC Crede 2007, Bisol Desiderio & Figli, Veneto Sparkling
Clean vigorous mousse. Viscous texture and creamy mouthfeel, with bright, ripe fruit and crisp acidity.

Valdobbiadene Prosecco DOC Spumante Dry "cruner" 2008, Ruggeri Cesare E Renato, Veneto Sparkling
Fruity and firm. Clean and well-balanced, with mouth-filling fruit flavours and a positive finish.
£25.00 C&B

Valdobbiadene Prosecco Extra Dry 2008, Canevel, Veneto Sparkling
Elegant and floral, with fine bubbles and a complex mid-palate. Good length.
£15.00 EVW, HAR, VIN

Valdobbiadene Superiore Di Cartizze Jeio DOC NV, Bisol Desiderio & Figli, Veneto Sparkling
Fruit driven, with a clean, fresh citrus palate. Notes of peach, with a lovely mousse and crisp acidity.

Vino Spumante Prosecco Di Valdobbiadene DOC Millesimato '008 2008, Astoria Vini, Veneto Sparkling
Clean, with some candied notes. Pleasant and refreshing, with a dry finish.

Brachetto D'acqui Cavallino 2008, Araldica Piedmont Sparkling Red
Light red fruit nose, very sweet and rich, with fresh acidity and a clean, light finish.
£9.70 CHH, VGN

Chiarli Grasparossa NV, Chiarli - 1860, Emilia-Romagna Sparkling Red
Deep purple in colour, with an intense, dense nose. Frizzante and very fresh, with nice sweetness.
GYW

Lambrusco Reggiano Concerto 2008, Medici, Emilia-Romagna Sparkling Red
Intense purple in colour, with

a deep nose, clean palate, and fresh flavours.
£11.00 EHB, EVW, HAR, VIN

Prosecco NV, Santero F.lli & C. I.v.a.s.s. S.p.a., Piedmont Sparkling Rose
Clean fresh peach and apricot nose. Off-dry, with a slightly leafy finish.

Marks & Spencer Moscato Freisa Spumante NV, Tosti, Piedmont Sparkling Rosé
Pale red salmon, with lifted rose petals and apple blossom, with fresh upfront strawberries, and a clean finish.
£8.00 M&S

Marks & Spencer Prosecco Raboso NV, Le Contesse Veneto Sparkling Rosé
Pale baby pink. The nose has notes of ripe pear, with hints of apple and apple skin, and a touch of bitterness coming through on the palate. Drier than many Proseccos.
£9.00 M&S

Rose Cuvee Brut 2010, Carpene Malvolti, Veneto, Sparkling Rosé
Quite deep pink. The nose has notes of cherries and hints of marzipan, with the mousse providing a smooth mouthfeel. There is a savoury edge to the tart red fruit, which is gently refreshing.
£11.00 HOH

Rose Royal NV, Montresor, Veneto Sparkling Rosé
Very pale salmon in colour. Attractive nose with subtle creamy fruit. Perfumed and delicate; a bit sherbetty, with some length and hints of bitterness.
£9.80

Shat Mat Rosé- Maschio Dei Cavalieri NV, Cantine Maschio, Veneto Sparkling Rosé
Very pale pink. Stewed red fruits and definite spice, with notes of marzipan and some length.

Brachetto D'Acqui 2008, Contero, Piedmont Sweet
Medium rose-pink in colour. Floral nose with notes of rose petal. Fresh, elegant, and light, with a clean spritz and nice balance. Clean and simple, with a fresh, medium length finish.
£15.00 LIB

Farnito Vin Santo Del Chianti 1992, Carpineto, Tuscany Sweet
Bright orange, apricot colour. Attractive dried apricot and cream, with vanilla aromas. The palate shows lots of spicy, creamy oak. An attractive wine.
£33.00 HOH

Arkezia Muffo Di San Sisto 2005, Fazi Battaglia Marche, Botrytis
Nuts, honey, almonds, apricot and light caramel on the nose. Sweet, with low acidity.
£28.50

Marsala Superiore "Garibaldi" Dolce 2010, Carlo Pellegrino Sicily Fortified
Honeyed nose, with marmalade and hints of cinnamon on the mid-palate. Good acidity and elegant finish.
£6.00 HOH

New Zealand

The land of the long white cloud has steadily increased its average medal tally over the past three years. This may be due to the ongoing investment of time and money spent on improving the vineyards and their vines. Over NZ$1 million (approximately £400,000) has been invested in a Pinot Noir research programme which appears to have paid off already. The country picked up six Golds for this tricky variety from France, four more than Burgundy. While Sauvignon Blanc managed a similar success, it's the aromatic varietals that are developing a greater global interest, with regionality coming through in their expressive styles. Look towards the South Island for a crisp style of Riesling and to Gisborne in the North for Gewürztraminer.

2009 IWC PERFORMANCE

Trophies	13
Gold	20
Silver	91
Bronze	135
Great Value Awards	1

KEY FACTS

Total production
285,000 tonnes of grapes producing around 205 million litres of wine

Total vineyard
27,100ha

Top 10 grapes
1 Sauvignon Blanc
2 Chardonnay
3 Pinot Noir
4 Pinot Gris
5 Merlot
6 Riesling
7 Semillon
8 Cabernet Sauvignon
9 Gewürztraminer
10 Syrah

Top 10 regions
1 Marlborough
2 Hawkes Bay
3 Gisborne
4 Central Otago
5 Nelson
6 Waipara
7 Wairarapa
8 Auckland
9 Canterbury
10 Northland

Producers
584

NEW ZEALAND CHARDONNAY TROPHY

Ata Rangi, Craighall Chardonnay 2007, Wairarapa
White
Intense nose of butter and green beans. Lovely, creamy mouthfeel, with good length and stone fruit. A hint of toffee on the finish. Lots of acidity and good length.
£23.20 NZH, LIB

Century Hill Sauvignon Blanc 2008, Export Union, Marlborough White
Very pale in colour, with a nose of rose petals, with some medium-intensity herbaceous aromas. Long finish on the palate.
£7.00 BRZ

NEW ZEALAND WHITE TROPHY, INTERNATIONAL SAUVIGNON BLANC TROPHY, NEW ZEALAND SAUVIGNON BLANC TROPHY

Clifford Bay Awatere Valley Sauvignon Blanc 2008, Vavasour Wines Limited, Marlborough White
Light pale yellow in colour, with mineral nuances, and notes of green mangos and lemon zest on the nose. Showing incredible finesse on the palate, with perfumed herbal notes, and fresh mango juice. Zesty, with a wonderful freshness, excellent acidity, and real length.
£9.00 B&J

Nautilus Estate Marlborough Sauvignon Blanc 2008, Marlborough White
Green and voluptuous, with hints

of smoke on the nose. Nice balance, crisp, with good length. Quite restrained, almost mineral edge, good and crunchy, with nice length. A classy wine.
£11.00 NZH

Thornbury Sauvignon Blanc 2008, Marlborough White
Grapefruit and asparagus nose. Very interesting, clean palate of nettles and gooseberry, with a long finish, which is mineral and fruity.
£10.30 NZH, ENO

Bridge Pa Louis Syrah 2006, Hawke's Bay Red
Enormous fruit. Wonderful cracked pepper and mulberry, with hints of violet and lavender. Silky richness, and lovely round tannins. Amazingly complex, with an endless spicy finish.
£21.90

Bridge Pa Reserve Syrah 2007, Hawke's Bay Red
Ripe, perfumed nose, with rich, savoury fruit reminiscent of Hermitage. Complex, restrained fruit with perfect balance, great purity and ripeness. Very long and lingering.
£16.50

Cj·Pask Declaration Merlot 2005, Hawke's Bay Red
Rich, silky texture, with good freshness, fruit richness, and tannin. Husk, plum, and spice flavours, with smooth tannins. Will develop well in bottle.
£16.00

Domain Road Pinot Noir 2007, Central Otago Red
A great, meaty, savoury nose, with hints of cherry and berry. Deep cherry fruit on the palate, leading to an intense and powerful finish. A serious wine.
£14.50

 **WAIRARAPA PINOT NOIR TROPHY**

Gladstone Pinot Noir 2007, Wairarapa Red
Strawberries, cream and spice notes on the nose, with complexity that lasts through the finish. Saturated with flavour; spice, cranberry, rhubarb. Lots of red fruit, and a persistent earthiness.
£13.80 CAM, FFT, GWW, NYW

 CENTRAL OTAGO PINOT NOIR TROPHY

Hinton Estate Vineyard Barrel Selection 2007, Central Otago Red
Aromatic red fruit character on the nose, with hints of smoky oak. Ripe and juicy palate, with hints of spice and savoury minerality. Excellent finish and length.

 **NEW ZEALAND RED TROPHY, INTERNATIONAL SYRAH TROPHY, NEW ZEALAND SYRAH TROPHY, AUCKLAND SYRAH TROPHY**

Kennedy Point Waiheke Syrah 2007, Auckland Red
Perfumed floral notes, with some gamey and sweet oaky aromas. Ripe, rich fruit on the palate. Full, with some peppery nuances. Complex and powerful, with great length.

Mission Estate Winery Jewelstone Syrah 2007, Hawke's Bay Red
An elegant and subtle fruit lift, with soft velvety fruit. Pleasant mouthfeel and great finish - an excellent wine for ageing.
£19.00 LAI

 **HAWKE'S BAY SYRAH TROPHY**

Mission Estate Winery Reserve Syrah 2007, Hawke's Bay Red
Lovely sweet perfumed berries on the nose, beautifully balanced with blackberries and oak. Big fruit and spice, with a sweet oak silkiness. Smooth and elegant, with a nice oaky finish.

Peregrine Pinot Noir 2007, Central Otago Red
An evolving nose which is complex and mellow. Mineral fruit on the palate, with ripe tannins and good balance. Good use of oak on a stylish wine, with a balanced, complex finish.
£18.50 NZH, EDC, BB&R, ODD

 **NEW ZEALAND PINOT NOIR TROPHY, MARLBOROUGH PINOT NOIR TROPHY**

Pioneer Block 15 Strip Block Pinot Noir 2007, Saint Clair, Marlborough Red
This wine has a bright cherry-red hue, with a good fruity nose, showing some style, with lovely rich, deep fruit.
£16.10 NZH, HOH

Sandihurst Central Otago Pinot Noir 2007, Central Otago Red
Bramble fruits and berry perfume. Attractive and complex palate, with fresh fruit and minerality. Good balance, and lingering sweet fruit on the finish, with great potential to develop with age.

Harvest Man 2007, The Hay Paddock Limited, Auckland Red
Soft red fruits, with blackberry

and spicy aromas. A great wine, with meaty flavours and ripe fruit on the palate, leading to a lovely, peppery finish.

Waipara West Pinot Noir 2006, Canterbury Red
A high-toned spicy nose, with lots of new oak influence. Fresh and dry, with raisin fruits and creamy, spicy tones. Good length, and a complex, savoury finish.
£15.80 FLA, WAW

Seifried Nelson Winemakers Collection Sweet Agnes Riesling Ice Wine 2008, Nelson Sweet
Deliciously intense notes of sherbet stone fruit and apples. Rich apricot flavours, supported by good acidity, great depth of flavour, and a long finish. Exceptional quality.

SILVER

Astrolabe Voyage Marlborough Sauvignon Blanc 2008, Marlborough White
Green-yellow pale colour. Very intense, creamy, yoghurty nose, and a crisp palate, with a sweet balanced body.
£12.90 NZH

Cape Campbell Sauvignon Blanc 2008, Marlborough White
Grassy, herbaceous green notes. Palate of elderflower, with powerful gooseberry, zingy acidity, and a good, stony-edged body. Lingering fruit finish.

Catalina Sounds Sauvignon Blanc 2008, Marlborough White
Tinned asparagus aromas, which come through on the palate, which also shows green meadow flavours, with a refreshing finish.
£10.40 CHH, NZH

Craggy Range Sauvignon Blanc, Old Renwick Vineyard 2008, Marlborough White
Fresh lime peel aromas, with elements of white fruit. Elegant entrance, with high acidity and a good finish.
£12.00 WAIT

Distant Land Reserve Pinot Gris 2008, Hawke's Bay White
With some minerality, this is fresh, aromatic, dry, and honeyed. Notes of simple spice and pear, in a clean, modern style.

Domain Road Sauvignon Blanc 2008, Central Otago White
Green, herbal pea-pod and asparagus notes, in a European mineral style, with pungent green fruit. This is razor sharp, with good intensity and length.
£10.00

Durvillea Marlborough Sauvignon Blanc 2008, Astrolabe Wines Ltd, Marlborough White
Clean tropical nose, with elegant fresh herbs, gooseberries, and grapefruit. Juicy melon and citrus palate, with a rich, shining style.

Fairleigh Estate Sauvignon Blanc 2008, Marlborough White
Nose of elderflower, with powerful gooseberry aromas, and a touch of leaf. Zingy acidity and good body, with a stony edge. Lingering fruit finish.
£8.00 MWW

Grove Mill Origin Carbon Zero Charonnay 2007, White
Lemon and lime notes, with spice, and creamy , vibrant lime flavours, with bright acidity.

Youthful French and American oak, with citrus aromas and good fruit. Oak is strong, but balanced, and the finish is long.
WRC

Grove Mill Origin Carbon Zero Pinot Gris 2007, Marlborough White
Ripe, creamy, peachy fruit, leading to a soft, smoky finish. Balanced, with good, harmonious length.
WRC

Highfield Sauvignon Blanc 2008, Marlborough White
Aromatic and grapey, with gooseberry and elderflower notes. Fresh, mineral, and fruity. At the green end of the spectrum, with a lovely fresh finish.
£12.50 BBO, WON

Kaituna Hills Forty Knots Sauvignon Blanc 2008 Marlborough White
Clean and ripe, with medium weight and ripe asparagus, with some lovely tropical fruit, intense, vibrant acidity, and good length.
£12.00 M&S

Kaituna Hills Reserve Chardonnay 2007, Marlborough White
A very complete wine, with a wonderful, elegant nose, full body, and a long, creamy finish of sweet fruit.
£9.00 M&S

Kerner Estate Pinot Blanc 2007, Marlborough White
A fresh lemon and lychee nose, with a palate of intense tropical fruit and crisp acidity. Well-balanced.

Montana Reserve Pinot Gris 2008, Hawke's Bay White
Pure, almost pineapple fruit. Quite light and elegant, with

fresh clean flavours. Balanced and well-made.
£9.00

Montana Terroir Series Festival Block Sauvignon Blanc 2008, Marlborough White
Good clear colour. Green tinged notes, with asparagus and passion fruit, showing good intensity, and fresh acidity.
£11.00

Montana Terroir Series Rail Bridge Sauvignon Blanc 2008, Marlborough White
Restrained nose, with balanced fruit and varietal character, with good concentration and acidity. A serious wine, with good depth and length.
£11.00

Mud House Waipara Riesling 2008, Canterbury White
Racy lime flavour, with notes of petrol. Plump mid-palate, and balanced 'cut it with a knife' acidity.
£10.30 NZH

Omaka Reserve Chardonnay 2007, Saint Clair, Marlborough White
Very full oak aspect, with a ripe, fruit-driven character. Good balance of acidity and alcohol.
£13.60 NZH, HOH

Omaka Springs Estates Marlborough Sauvignon Blanc 2008, Marlborough White
Exuberant tropical nose, with notes of passion fruit and mango. Very fresh palate, with good acidity, and medium length.
£8.00

Overstone Marlborough Sauvignon Blanc 2008, Marlborough White
Aromatic, with lovely intense,

grassy, gooseberry fruit. Richly textured and full-flavoured. Very good balance, with fresh acidity.

Oyster Bay Marlborough Sauvignon Blanc 2008, Marlborough White
Tomato leaf and herbs on the nose. Clean and fresh, with some delicateness. The palate is herbaceous, but not green, with passion fruit and lime notes on a flinty finish.
£8.80 NZH, ASDA, SAIN, TESC, WAIT, MWW, THS

Paritua Chardonnay 2008, Hawke's Bay White
Pale gold tone. Pungent butter and burnt toast aromas. A classic, New World Chardonnay, with big, ripe tropical fruit. Great balance of oak and acidity, with a long length and a strong finish.
£16.00 CHH

Pioneer Block 18 Snap Block Sauvignon Blanc 2008, Saint Clair, Marlborough White
Pungent herbs and grassy notes, with a hint of citrus and tropical fruit. Zingy, lemony palate, with hints of tangerine and melon, and a nice finish.
£16.00 NZH, HOH

Pioneer Block 3, 43 Degrees Sauvignon Blanc 2008, Saint Clair, Marlborough White
Mineral and herbaceous; a nice lean style, with a slight peachy element and tropical fruit notes. Atractive weight and good, crisp acidity.
£15.00 NZH, HOH

Pioneer Block 9 Big John Riesling 2008, Saint Clair, Marlborough White
A very well put-together Riesling, with a really fruity, fresh apricot character. Complex wine, with

crisp acidity on the finish.
£18.00 HOH

Saint Clair Riesling 2008, Marlborough White
Concentrated nose, with a hint of sourness. Full fruit flavours dominate up to the intense finish. Good character; a very superior Riesling.
£9.80 NZH, HOH

Saint Clair Wairau Reserve Sauvignon Blanc 2008, Marlborough White
Elegant gooseberry nose, with some mineral, green fig, and white pepper notes. Good structure and balance, with a long, lemony, honeyed finish.
£18.20 NZH, HOH

Seifried Nelson Gewürztraminer 2008, Nelson White
This wine has a delicate rose petal perfume. It is well-balanced and slightly off-dry, with some delicate fruit.
£11.00 LAI, CRI

Sileni Estate Selection Benchmark Block Two Omaka Slopes Sauvignon Blanc 2008, Marlborough White
Soft, restrained fruit. Showing citrus complexity, and vegetal character, with good depth and length.

Spy Valley Wines, Spy Valley Gewürztraminer 2008, Marlborough White
This wine has a very clean, floral, fruity nose, with notes of blossom. Fresh, crisp, lively, clean, and very long.
£11.40 NZH

Stone Paddock Hawkes Bay Chardonnay 2008, Paritua Vineyards, Hawke's Bay White
Very pretty aromatics on the

nose. Soft, silky palate, with hints of citrus and honeysuckle. Clean, subtle, and elegant.
£9.00 CHH

Te Mata Estate, Elston Chardonnay 2007, Hawke's Bay White
Subtle, lime-edged biscuit on the nose. Wood dominates the palate, which is big and buttery on the middle, with an interesting and complex finish.
£18.30 ESL, LEA, NZH

The Crossings Sauvignon Blanc. 2008, Marlborough White
Pale yellow in colour, with notes of citrus, tropical fruit, lemon and lime, with fresh, soft minerality on the palate. The wine is rounded off with tropical fruit, balanced with peppery savouriness, and long persistence.
£9.00 NYW, ODD

Tinpot Hut Marlborough Sauvignon Blanc 2008, Marlborough White
Clean gooseberry and asparagus nose, with a soft, clean palate. Very New Zealand in style.
£9.80 HEN, NZH, LIB

Vavasour Awatere Valley Sauvignon Blanc 2008, Marlborough White
Very clean nose, with zippy lemon zest and hints of aromatics. The palate exhibits vibrant green fruit, lemon zest, and juicy ripeness, with refreshing length.
£10.00 B&J, MWW

Vavasour The Reach Sauvignon Blanc 2008, Marlborough White
Passion fruit and mango aromas. Fresh, really attractive style, with brisk acidity, and ripe, yellow fruit flavours.
£8.20 TESC

Vidal Riesling 2008, Marlborough White
Really nice nose, with a crisp palate of elegant citrus and apples, with elder blossom and notes of petrol. Good balance and length.
£8.70 FLA, NZH, HMA

Villa Maria Cellar Selection Riesling 2008, Marlborough White
This is a really good example of its style and type. Brilliant balance, with nice velvety fruit. Delicate and quite elegant.
£10.00 NZH, HMA

Villa Maria Cellar Selection Sauvignon Blanc 2008, Marlborough White
Floral nose, with green apples, lemons, and gooseberries on the palate. Fine and long, this would be great on a hot summer's day.
£10.00 NZH, TESC, HMA

Villa Maria Single Vineyard Graham Sauvignon Blanc 2008, Marlborough White
Pale green lemon colour, with hints of grassy nettle minerality on the nose. Crisp, refreshing, zippy citrus flavours on the palate, with a lovely long finish.
£13.00 WAIT, HMA

Villa Maria Single Vineyard Maxwell Sauvignon Blanc 2008, Marlborough White
Nuances of asparagus, greengages, and gooseberries, with a fresh, tropical palate, and a long, mineral finish.
£13.00 HMA

Villa Maria Single Vineyard Taylors Pass Sauvignon Blanc 2008, Marlborough White
Pale lemon green, with intense green asparagus on the nose. Lovely mouthfeel, with flavours of lemon, lime, and gooseberry,

with hints of kiwi and pineapple. Excellent acidity, and moderate length.
£13.00 NZH, TESC, HMA

Waimea Estates Spinyback Nelson Pinot Gris 2008, Nelson White

Vegetal character on the nose, with a palate of sweet ripe peachy fruit, and a spicy, peppery finish. Long and balanced.
£9.00 CHN

Waipara West Unoaked Chardonnay 2008, Canterbury White

Light yellow in colour. An earthy style, with pronounced greengage, green apple, and a touch of melon. Lively acidity, and creamy texture.
£9.50 FLA, CBC, WAW

Whitehaven Mansion House Bay 2008, Marlborough White

Bright, inviting nose of light tropical fruit. Good weight on the palate, with well-balanced acidity.
£10.10 NZH, ENO

Wild Rock Elevation Sauvignon Blanc 2008, Wild Rock Wine Company, Hawke's Bay White

Fresh tropical fruit on the nose. Acidity and sugar are nicely balance, and there is good length.
£10.00 WAIT

Wither Hills Chardonnay 2007, Marlborough White

Toasty nose, with hot tropical fruit and honeyed sweetness. The palate leads to a balanced finish, with a nuance of caramel.
£9.90 NZH, WAIT

Wither Hills Rarangi Sauvignon Blanc 2008, Marlborough White

Asparagus and tinned peas on the nose, with fresh, ripe gooseberry and elderflower on the palate, leading to a long, crisp, grapefruit finish.
£13.00 NZH, WSO

Yealands Estate Tawhiri Sauvignon Blanc 2008, Marlborough White

Very herbaceous nose, with a strong gooseberry note. Well-balanced palate, with a lemony finish.
£8.00 LIB

Yealands Sauvignon Blanc 2008, Marlborough White

Intense aromas of cut grass, gooseberries, and asparagus. Soft, sweet, oily palate, with an elegant entry, full body, fresh acidity, and a fresh, fruity finish.
£9.80 NZH, LIB

Averys New Zealand Pinot Noir Marlborough 2007, Marlborough Red

Nose of morello cherry, red berry, and blueberry fruit. The palate is full of lovely juicy cherry fruit, with a pure, dry finish.
£11.00 AVB

CJ Pask Declaration Syrah 2007, CJ Pask Ltd, Hawke's Bay Red

Big meaty nose. Focused, with well-integrated oak. Spicy and Rhône-esque, with hints of chocolate and juicy berries. Good depth and acidity.
£16.00

Craggy Range Merlot, Gimblett Gravels Vineyard 2005, Craggy Range Vineyards Ltd, Hawke's Bay Red

Rich, ripe dark fruit on the nose. The palate shows gravelly minerality, with very silky tannins, and fresh, balanced structure. Lively and stylish.
£17.40 NZH, WAIT

Craggy Range Pinot Noir, Te Muna Road Vineyard 2007, Craggy Range Vineyards Ltd, Wairarapa Red
Rich raspberry and red cherry nose, with juicy fine fruit, good savoury tannins, and a long finish."
£20.40 FLA, NZH, WAIT, AMP, HFB, HFW, WSO

Delegat Reserve Hawke's Bay Cabernet Sauvignon Merlot 2007, Hawke's Bay Red
Elegant bramble fruit, with fresh acidity, and creamy fruit.

Esk Valley Black Label Pinot Noir 2007, Hawke's Bay Red
Fresh, lifted nose, with mild strawberry aromas. Sweet strawberry fruit on the palate. Textbook silky Pinot Noir texture.
£10.00 NZH, HMA

Gardo-Morris Te Mana Syrah 2007, Ben Morris (Gardo-Morris) Red
Delicious brambly and meaty nose, with dark fruit, and peppery notes of vanilla and spicy oak. Very well-balanced and harmonious.

Glazebrook New Zealand Merlot Cabernet 2007, Hawke's Bay Red
Intense ripe cassis on the nose, with chocolatey oak nuances. Concentrated palate of fruit and oak, with good acidity and backbone.

Glazebrook New Zealand Syrah 2007, Hawke's Bay Red
Ripe aromatic berries on the nose, with a palate of rich, ripe berries. Smooth mouthfeel, well-balanced, with good acidity, and a nice fruity finish.

Hinton Estate Vineyard Pinot Noir 2007, Central Otago Red
Aromatic, with a nose of spicy oak and black cherries, with a hint of earthy herbaceousness. Fleshy, juicy palate, with fresh acidity and soft, dry tannins.

Lone Range Gimblett Gravels Red 2007, Hawke's Bay Red
Intense colour, with a rubbery, dark fruit character. Round, with reasonable length. A nice, balanced wine.
£10.00 M&S

Lowburn Ferry 2007, Central Otago Red
Savoury fennel seed character, with notes of candied fruit on the nose. Integrated bramble and wild fruit on the palate, with soft, lingering tannins.
£21.00 HLN

Marks & Spencer Te Kahu 2005, Craggy Range, Hawke's Bay Red
Deep, plummy fruit and vanilla oak on the nose, with a palate of liquorice, plum, and black fruit, underpinned by fine, ripe tannins. A serious wine which will age well.
£17.00 M&S

Marks & Spencer Saddleback Pinot Noir 2007, Peregrine, Central Otago Red
Classic Pinot Noir nose. Lovely complex character, with woody forest floor notes and a gamey character. Rich, ripe palate with a multi-layered finish.
£15.00 M&S

Montana Terroir Series Forgotten Valley Pinot Noir 2007, Marlborough Red
Bright cherry hue, with a good cherry nose, and a similarly appealing fruit-driven palate, finishing with style"
£13.00

Matakana Estate Elingamite Limited Edition Hawke's Bay Merlot Cabernet Franc 2007, Hawke's Bay Red
Attractive smoky damson, cedarwood, and bell pepper on the nose. Very smooth and stylish, with good balance and length.

Mud House Swan Central Otago Pinot Noir 2008, Central Otago Red
Rich, juicy, meaty, clean fruit on the nose. Intense and complex, with a full body, ripe tannins, and a fresh, fruity finish.
£16.00 NZH

Pioneer Block 14 Doctors Creek Pinot Noir 2007, Saint Clair, Marlborough Red
Red and black fruit, with savoury nuances. Medium tannin and acidity, very attractive flavours, and lovely complexity.
£16.20 NZH, HOH, MWW

Pioneer Block 16 Awatere Pinot Noir 2007, Saint Clair, Marlborough Red
Lovely red fruit concentration. Good juicy fruit flavours combine well on the palate, providing a long finish.
£18.00 HOH

Pioneer Block 5 Bull Block Pinot Noir 2007, Saint Clair, Marlborough Red
Good depth of jammy fruit, with lifted acidity, silky texture, and a lovely long, minerally finish.
£16.00 HOH

Schubert Pinot Noir Marion's Vineyard 2007, Wairarapa Red
Well-made, with good firm fruit. A crowd-pleaser, made for rich foods. Good fruitiness on the palate; an elegant style with a long finish.
CVS, EOR, NZH, RWA, SWG, WLY

Southbank Estate Syrah 2006, Hawke's Bay Red
Toasty, spicy, and peppery, with plums and brambles on the nose. Well-structured, with good tannic grip, fruit concentration, and length.
£13.00 HAR, MWW

Te Mata Estate, Awatea, Cabernet Merlot 2007, Hawke's Bay Red
Notes of coffee bean; earthy, dusty, and elegant, with firm, ripe tannins, fresh acidity, and good length.
£16.20 ESL, NZH

Te Mata Estate, Bullnose Syrah 2007, Hawke's Bay Red
Richly spiced bramble fruit. Good weight, with hints of charcuterie, and a touch of pepper. Elegant finish.
£19.60 ESL, NZH

Te Mata Estate, Woodthorpe Gamay Noir 2008, Hawke's Bay Red
Lovely sweet cherry-stone nose, with an attractive fruit palate, good stone fruit character, and a long finish.
£10.80 LEA, NZH, WAIT

The Hay Paddock 2007, Auckland Red
Creamy plum fruit aromas, with a brambly, meaty nose. Rich ripe fruit with a touch of bitterness on the palate. Full-bodied, with a spicy finish.

Villa Maria Cellar Selection Pinot Noir 2007, Marlborough Red
On the nose there are slightly juicy cherry aromas, leading to a concentrated, juicy palate, with baked cherry jam flavour, and a slightly dry, bitter edge, finishing with medium length.
£13.00, NZH, HMA

Villa Maria Reserve Merlot 2006, Marlborough Red
Floral sweet black fruit with toasty oak on the nose. The palate is concentrated, structured, and cedary, with focused ripe fruit.
£16.60 NZH, WAIT, HMA

Villa Maria Single Vineyard Taylors Pass Pinot Noir 2007, Marlborough Red
Mild cherry colour, with a nose that shows good strawberry fruit and apple. Stylish palate, with good fruitiness.
£19.90 NZH, HMA

Waipara Hills Southern Cross Selection Central Otago Pinot Noir 2008, Central Otago Red
Strawberries and raspberries on the nose. Well-balanced, with vanilla oak aromas, very soft tannins, and a spicy structure.
£12.00

Waitiri Creek Pinot Noir 2007, Central Otago Red
Intense strawberry and cherry aromas, nicely blending with wood. Elegant ripe tannins, and a full body, with well-balanced acidity, and a long, coffee finish.

Whitehaven Mansion House Bay 2007, Marlborough Red
A complex nose of red berry and cherry, that leads to a smooth, rounded, fruity palate. It is well balanced with typical Pinot Noir expression.
£14.40 NZH, ENO

Wild Earth Pinot Noir 2007, Central Otago Red
Very light red in colour, with vibrant fruit on the nose. Round and smooth, with some fruit remaining on palate, showing good complexity, and a clean long finish"
£19.30 NZH, LIB

Wild Rock Wine Company Seven Canoes Pinot Noir 2007, Hawke's Bay Red
Lively sweet strawberry and cherry aromas, with a touch of nutmeg. Fine sweet fruit and silky texture, with some savoury spice.
£15.00

Wild Rock Wine Company Seven Canoes Syrah Viognier 2007, Hawke's Bay Red
Toasty, spicy plums and brambles. Soft, creamy palate, well-structured, with good oak integration, and a lingering finish.
£15.00 WRC

Wild Rock Cupid's Arrow Pinot Noir 2007, Hawke's Bay Red
A nose of hedgerow, with ripe, almost strawberry jam fruit. Silky texture, showing some oak.
£12.80 FLA, AMP, BCR, GWI, NZH

GREAT VALUE SPARKLING BETWEEN £5 AND £10

Bluff Hill Brut NV Sparkling
Honey, melon and apricot flavours, with a fine creamy mousse and mature apple fruit on the palate, leading to a long, creamy finish.
£9.00 M&S

Deutz Marlborough Cuvée Blanc De Blancs 2005, Marlborough Sparkling
Good mix of red apple and peach fruit, with a light yeasty note. Attractive, fresh, fruity palate. Clean and appealing.
£13.00

Lindauer Special Reserve NV Sparkling
Pale copper salmon appearance. Very fruity red berry aromas, with good fruit on a crisp

palate, showing touches of strawberry fruit.
£10.00 WAIT

Paritua Dinah Noble Semillon 2008
Hawke's Bay Sweet
Medium gold in colour. Good rich palate of orange peel and over-ripe fruit notes, with layers of honey and citrus peel. Complex, balanced, long, and refreshing.
£17.00 CHH

BRONZE

Asda New Zealand Sauvignon Blanc 2008, Wineco Ltd
White
Tropical fruit aromas, with notes of guava and citrus. Crisp acidity, and a touch of banana, with good length.
£5.50 ASDA

Astrolabe Voyage Marlbrorough Chardonnay 2007, Marlborough White
Pale lemon-green in colour. Lovely sensations of tropical fruit, with underlying hints of herbal, leafy characteristics. Good balance, with persistent fruit on the length.
£13.20 NZH

Babich Black Label Sauvignon Blanc 2008, Marlborough
White
Lemon, lychee, and mineral aromas. Lovely light body, and a good, long finish.
£10.40 NZH

Kim Crawford Marlborough Sauvignon Blanc 2008, Marlborough White
Restrained nose of herbs and juicy fruit. Vegetal character on the palate, with a soft, long finish.
£10.70 HEN, NZH, LIB

Crawford Farm Sauvignon Blanc 2008, Kim Crawford Wines, Marlborough White
Elegant, complex, rounded nose, with soft tropical fruit. Clean palate with good acidity.
£9.00

Delegat Reserve Hawke's Bay Chardonnay 2007, Hawke's Bay White
Oak and vanilla notes on the nose as on the palate, which also shows apple and apricot flavours. Good acidity and medium body.

Delegat Reserve Marlborough Sauvignon Blanc 2008, Marlborough White
Intensely grassy and leafy, with herbal essence, and an impression of minerality.

Delta Vineyard Sauvignon Blanc 2008, Marlborough
White
Quite fragrant and aromatic, with a palate showing minerality and wet pebble flavours. A subtle wine with good length.
£11.10 HEN, NZH, LIB

Esk Valley Black Label Pinot Gris 2008, Hawke's Bay
White
Lush, ripe peachy nose. Full, ripe peach and apricot fruit character. The palate shows pepper and spice, with decent acidity.
£9.40 FLA, NZH, HMA

Esk Valley Black Label Verdelho 2008, Hawke's Bay White
Delicate stone fruit aromas, with a hint of spice and a smoky finish.
£8.80 NZH, HMA

Gladstone Pinot Gris 2008, Wairarapa White
Elegant, perfumed spicy peach. Refreshing acidity.

Persistent minerality, and good concentration of fruit.
£12.60 CAM, GWW

Grove Mill Riesling 2007, NZ Wine Co Ltd, Marlborough
White
Pale straw colour. Floral, mineral nose, with citrus undertones. Fresh, well-balanced mid-palate. German Kabinett style.
£8.50 NZH, THS

Grove Mill Sauvignon Blanc 2008, NZ Wine Co Ltd, Marlborough White
Gooseberry on the nose, with a touch of asparagus. Zesty acidity, concentrated flavours, and rich passion fruit persistence.
£9.10 NZH, ODD, ODF, THS

Marks & Spencer Clocktower Sauvignon Blanc 2008, Wither Hills, Marlborough White
Elegant nose of apples and grass. Zippy acidity, with medium length.
£11.00 M&S

Marks & Spencer Seifried Nelson Sauvignon Blanc 2008, Nelson White
Clean citrus, exotic fruit, gooseberries, and grass, with mineral notes. Pungent and powerful, with fruity sweetness on the palate.
£8.00 M&S

Martinborough Vineyard Sauvignon Blanc 2008, Wairarapa White
Fresh, leafy, spicy green plum on nose. Quite full on the palate, but showing fresh green fruit and acidity.
£12.00 NZH, HAR, HVN

Maven Pinot Gris 2008, Marlborough White
Quite pure and mineral on the nose. Fresh, with some sweetness of fruit, and a rather long, peppery finish.
£13.00

Maven Sauvignon Blanc 2008, Marlborough White
Lemon colour, with a nose of green gooseberry and tropical fruit. Crisp acidity, with notes of pineapple and bananas.
£10.00 TESC

Maven Daisy Rock Sauvignon Blanc 2008, Marlborough
White
Fresh, clean, and lively, with hints of pineapple and honey. Bright acidity, with fresh and grassy fruit on the palate.
£9.00

Montana Ormond Gisborne Chardonnay 2006, Gisborne
White
Deep yellow in colour, with peanut aromas following from nose to palate. Full-bodied and well-balanced, with a long finish.
£12.00

Mud House Marlborough Sauvignon Blanc 2008, Marlborough White
Good fresh aromas, with gentle floral fragrance. Good rich attack, with firm, balanced acidity, and good subtle fruit. Lime and elderflower on the finish.
£11.30 NZH

Mud House Swan Marlborough Sauvignon Blanc 2008, Marlborough White
Attractive, onion character over tropical fruit. Good freshness and balance, with a soft, mineral, limey finish.
£12.00 NZH

Ngatarawa Silks Sauvignon Blanc 2008, Marlborough
White
Pretty, floral aromatics.

Mineral and clean, with a fresh gooseberry character. Good intensity, with firm acidity and balance.

Nobilo Icon Sauvignon Blanc 2008, Marlborough White
Intense grass and passion fruit aromas. Elegant, fresh palate.
£14.00

Oyster Bay Marlborough Chardonnay 2008, Marlborough White
Pure green apples and pears, accented by a touch of vanilla custard. Moderate acidity in support, with touch of spice on the finish. A light style.
£8.70 NZH, SAIN, WAIT, MRN, MWW

Peregrine Chardonnay 2008, Central Otago White
Very clean, vegetal, asparagus-like nose, with a nutty character. Crisp.

Peregrine Riesling 2007, Central Otago White
Surprisingly elegant on the nose, with a palate of lime and flint, and a pleasant finish!
£11.90 NZH, BB&R, ODD

Paua Savignon Blanc 2008, Highfield Estate, White
Lifted passion fruit, with grassy notes and hints of asparagus. Soft, round palate, with zesty acidity.

Pioneer Block 1 Foundation Sauvignon Blanc 2008, Saint Clair, Marlborough White
Restrained nose of apples and pears. Crunchy acidity, and silky structure.
£16.00 HOH

Pioneer Block 11 Cell Block Chardonnay 2007, Saint Clair, Marlborough White
Very fresh, with rich fruit, notes

of butterscotch, caramel, and light lemon. Good acidity, with a long, silky finish.
£16.00 HOH

Pioneer Block 4 Sawcut Chardonnay 2007, Marlborough White
Rich toasty nose, with bold fruit, butter, and spice, leading to lovely green fruit and yeasty notes on a palate, which shows stylish oak, with some lemony freshness.
£16.00 HOH

Pioneer Block 6 Oh Block Sauvignon Blanc 2008, Saint Clair, Marlborough White
Fresh and grassy, with celery aromas. The flavour profile is unusual, yet attractive.
£16.00 HOH

Saint Clair Sauvignon Blanc 2008, Marlborough White
Hint of leafiness, with a lovely mineral intensity, and a delicate finish.
£9.90 NZH, HOH

Sanctuary Pinot Gris 2008, NZ Wine Co Ltd, Marlborough White
Reserved nose, with apple and pear notes. Refreshing acidity and some minerality, with a zesty finish.
£7.00 SAIN

Sanctuary Sauvignon Blanc 2008, NZ Wine Co Ltd, Marlborough White
Very smooth, elegant gooseberry fruit, with pleasant tropical notes, and a good, clean finish.
£7.00 SAIN

Seifried Estate Split Rock Riesling 2007, Nelson White
Deep straw colour. Mineral, honey aroma, with citrus notes on the mid-palate and finish.
£9.00 LAI

Seifried Nelson Winemakers Collection Sauvignon Blanc 2008, Nelson White
Fresh and green-scented, with elderflower and sweet notes of spritz on the palate.

Sileni Cellar Selection Pinot Gris 2008, Hawke's Bay White
Quite fragrant, spicy nose. Tangy palate, with fresh citrus fruit. Well-balanced.
£9.90 NZH

Sileni Cellar Selection Sauvignon Blanc 2008, Marlborough White
Citrus aromas, with complex vanilla and light lemon flavours, leading to an easy, balanced finish.
£8.30 NZH

Sileni Estate Selection Benchmark Block Three Thirteen Rows Sauvignon Blanc 2008, Marlborough White
Intense tropical fruits on the nose, carrying through to a palate of banana and apricot, with sweet fruitiness and good acidity.

Sileni Estate Selection 'The Straits' Sauvignon Blanc 2008, Marlborough White
Elegant mineral nose, with melon and tropical fruit aromas. Nice clean palate, with soft gooseberry note. Well-balanced.
£10.20 TESC

Sileni Satyr Sauvignon Blanc 2008, Marlborough White
Passion fruit and fresh figs, with lemon custard, framed by crisp acidity, and a touch of spicy pepper.
£8.30 TESC

Spy Mountain 2008, Marlborough White
Some minerality and grip, with a tense, tangy, citrus and gooseberry finish.
£8.00

Spy Valley Pinot Gris 2008, Marlborough White
Fresh, tropical fruit nose. Quite concentrated tropical fruit and apricot on the palate. Full and rich, but maintaining freshness and balance.
£11.40 NZH

Spy Valley Riesling 2008, Marlborough White
Mid straw colour. Lime and petrolly notes on the nose, with good lime flavours following through on the palate. Elegant and fine on the finish.
£9.40 NZH, WES

Spy Valley Sauvignon Blanc 2008, Marlborough White
Mineral notes with asparagus, grass, and citrus. Tropical fruits and fresh acidity on the palate.
£9.20 BNK, NZH, WES

Stoneleigh Rapaura Series Pinot Gris 2008, Marlborough White
Aromatic and fresh, with a sweet core of white peach. The palate shows sweet pears, with white peach and ginger spice. Medium-bodied, fresh, soft, and sweetish.
£9.00

Tohu 2008, Marlborough White
Restrained nose of apricot and peach. A warm style, with good length, and balanced acidity. Well-made.
£10.00

Trinity Hill Hawke's Bay Sauvignon Blanc 2008, Hawke's Bay White
Vibrant Sauvignon fruit, showing grass, with and medium acidity

and a savoury finish.
£11.50 NZH, CMR, HOU, RWM

Vavasour The Pass 2008, Marlborough White
Aromas of cut hay, with tropical fruits and gooseberry on the nose. Finishes on a mineral note.
£15.00 THP

Vicarage Lane Marlborough Chardonnay 2007, Marlborough White
Leafy aromas, with green apple fruit, balanced by crisp acidity. A pretty wine, with a floral accent.

Vidal Natural Ferment Chardonnay 2007, Hawke's Bay White
Bright green apple and pear fruit, framed by fresh acidity. Creamy texture, with chalky finish, and notes of spice — an elegant wine.
£8.10 NZH, HMA

Vidal Sauvignon Blanc 2008, Marlborough White
Pineapple on the nose, with lemon on the palate. A fresh, herby wine, with balanced crisp acidity.
£8.10 NZH, HMA

Villa Maria Private Bin Riesling 2008, Marlborough White
Mid-yellow colour, with nice aromatic intensity and purity. Mineral, lime, and floral notes, with nice freshness, and an elegant finish..
£8.10 NZH, WAIT, HMA

Villa Maria Reserve Chardonnay 2007, Marlborough White
Good complexity on the nose, with well-defined stone fruit and custard cream. The palate is ripe, with good acidity, Vibrant and nutty, with lots of energy on the finish.
£10.90 NZH, WAIT, HMA

Villa Maria Reserve Clifford Bay Sauvignon Blanc 2008, Marlborough White
Some layered complexity on the nose, with notes of tropical fruit, green grass, lemon, and lime. The palate shows integrated peppery spice, orange zest, and leafiness, with vibrant acidity.
£13.00 NZH, HMA

Villa Maria Reserve Wairau Valley Sauvignon Blanc 2008, Marlborough White
Attractive herbaceous notes, with some fresh asparagus on a peppery nose. Well-balanced palate, with a good finish.
£12.00 NZH, HMA

Waitrose 'In Partnership' Sauvignon Blanc 2008, Villa Maria Estate, Marlborough White
Light, elegant nose. Nice definition, with touches of orange blossom. Light, but well -defined.
£8.50 WAIT, HMA

Waimea Spinyback Nelson Sauvignon Blanc 2008, Nelson White
Interesting. On the vegetal side, with a touch of minerality. Fresh, clean, fruity palate.
£8.50 CHN

Waimea Nelson Gewürztraminer 2008, Nelson White
Good nose of lychees, toast, and ginger biscuits. Off-dry, with a full body, showing a wide breadth of flavoursome fruit, and a long finish.
£9.50 MWW

Waimea Nelson Sauvignon Blanc 2008, Nelson White
Restrained nose of grass, gooseberries, and broad beans.

Good fruit flavours, with crisp acidity.
£9.00 MWW

Waipara Hills Soul Of The South Marlborough Sauvignon Blanc 2008, Marlborough White
Clean, floral nose of citrus, elderflower, and gooseberry. Palate of citrus fruit, with balanced crisp acidity.
£9.00

Waipara Hills Soul Of The South Waipara Riesling 2008, Canterbury White
Light straw colour. Attractive aromas of melon and lime, with medium-powerful lime notes, and a long finish.
£9.00

Waipara Hills Southern Cross Selection Waipara Pinot Gris 2008, Canterbury White
Pear drop on the nose. Fresh and elegant, with medium weight. Peachy stone fruit palate, with a long, spicy finish.

Waipara Hills Southern Cross Selection Waipara Sauvignon Blanc 2008, Canterbury White
Spicy, green, almost minty note, with intense, vibrant green fruit and spice. Balanced.
£12.00

Waipara West Riesling 2008, Canterbury White
Medium intensity straw colour. Juicy lime, with good development, and strong acidic structure.
£10.00 FLA, CBC, WAW

Waipara West Sauvignon Blanc 2008, Canterbury White
Zesty and grassy, with fresh elderflower notes. Lively green fruit flavours, with a touch of

minerality, and good length and freshness.
£9.70 FLA, DVY, MFS, WAW

Wairau River Riesling 2008, Marlborough White
Pale yellow colour, honey lime notes, good volume, nice balance between the acidity and the sweetness. Persistent.
£11.40 NZH

Wairau River Wines, Wairau River Sauvignon Blanc 2008, Marlborough White
Lime, lemon, and grapefruit on the nose, with restrained grassiness. Elegant and refreshing, with a long finish.
£10.60 NZH

Wither Hills Sauvignon Blanc 2008, Marlborough White
Sweet citrus, tropical, and herbaceous notes on the nose, leading to a long, sweet finish on the palate.
£9.20 BNK, NZH, SAIN, TESC

Yealands Estate Sauvignon Blanc 2008, Marlborough White
Intense asparagus aromas. Juicy acidity, and rich stewed nettle flavours, with nice balance.
£9.80 NZH, LIB

Yealands Riesling 2008, Marlborough White
Profile of clean citrus and ripe fruit. On the palate, there is a sherbet and peachy character, with residual sugar on the finish.
£10.30 NZH, LIB

Astrolabe Voyage Marlbrorough Pinot Noir 2007, Marlborough Red
Cherry fruit and vegetal character on the nose. Supple tannins, and good concentration of sweet cherry fruit.
£16.70 NZH

Astrolabe Durvillea Marlborough Pinot Noir 2008, Marlborough Red
Vibrant attractive cherry and raspberry nose, with a hint of leather and vanilla. Medium-bodied.

Bald Hills Central Otago Single Vineyard Pinot Noir 2006, Central Otago Red
Bright, appealing cherry nose, with good complexity. Palate of fresh black and red berry fruits, with grippy tannins carrying a long, spicy finish.
£24.70 NZH

Bald Hills Central Otago Single Vineyard Pinot Noir 2007, Central Otago Red
Slightly vegetal nose, with hints of spice. Fresh, quite light, elegant, and jammy, with vibrant cherry fruit.
£24.70 NZH

Carrick Winery Unravelled 2008, Central Otago Red
Strawberry fruit, with a cherry and blackberry character. Rich tannins, balanced acidity, and a woody finish.
£12.50 CAM, GWW

CJ Pask Declaration Cabernet Merlot Malbec 2005, Hawke's Bay Red
A little bretty yeastiness. Simple but elegant, with fresh fruit and fine tannins.
£16.00

Craggy Range Pinot Noir, Te Muna Road Vineyard 2006, Wairarapa Red
Ripe fruit, with notes of cherry and raspberry. Lush and sweet, with well-balanced tannin and acidity.
£19.00 FLA, NZHWTSAMP, HFB, HFW

Craggy Range 'Sophia' Gimblett Gravels 2004, Hawke's Bay Red
Nose of creamy damson. Big, powerful, and impressive, with fine tannins and interesting layers of flavour.
£24.80 NZH, WAIT, AMP, HFB, HFW

Craggy Range 'Sophia' Gimblett Gravels 2005, Hawke's Bay Red
Complex, smoky, sweet and savoury aromas. Fine tannins, and lovely, fresh, balancing acidity.
£24.80 NZH, WAIT, AMP, HFB, HFW

Craggy Range Syrah, 'Block 14', Gimblett Gravels Vineyard 2006, Hawke's Bay Red
Cracked black pepper and black cherry notes. Firm and spicy, with lovely balance.
£18.30 FLA, NZH, WAIT, AMP, HFB, HFW

good depth of flavour, and a long finish. An elegant wine.
£12.10 NZH, LIB

Escarpment Pinot Noir 2007, Wairarapa Red
Raspberry, beetroot, and savoury spice, with a dry, intense, spicy finish.
£16.50 DBY, FLA, NZH, THC

Escarpment Kupe Pinot Noir 2005, Wairarapa Red
Lush red cherry, with spicy new oak, and good, dry fruit. Slightly bitter, but with a youthful, savoury character.
£20.30 DBY, NZH, THC

Esk Valley Black Label Merlot / Cabernet Sauvignon / Malbec 2007, Hawke's Bay Red
Nose of soft, ripe black fruit. Soft, earthy palate, which is fragrant, with pleasing length.
£10.30 FLA, NZH, HMA

Esk Valley Reserve Merlot Malbec Cabernet Sauvignon 2006, Hawke's Bay Red
Deep colour. Excellent extraction, with wonderful concentration of dark fruit. An excellent food wine, with good ageing potential.
£17.00 NZH, HMA

Jackson Estate Vintage Widow Pinot Noir 2007, Marlborough Red
Ripe red berries on the nose. Attractive mouthfeel, with balanced oak and soft tannins.
£16.00

Jewelstone Cabernet Merlot Franc Petit Verdot 2007, Mission Estate Winery, Hawke's Bay Red
Balanced, with big coffee notes. Oxidative and complex, with strong, smoky fruit.
£19.00 LAI

Delegat Reserve Hawke's Bay Merlot 2007, Hawke's Bay Red
Bright plum, with plenty of ripeness. Soft core, with some evidence of tannic grip. Fresh and clean.

Delegat Reserve Marlborough Pinot Noir 2007, Marlborough Red
Nose of cherry fruit and smoke. Quite pronounced oak, with a silky texture, and bramble fruit on palate.

Hatter's Hill Pinot Noir 2007, Delta Vineyard, Marlborough Red
Red berry fruit, with a slight beetroot earthiness, and tart acidity. Medium tannins, with subtle rhubarb notes on the finish.
£14.70 HEN, NZH, LIB

Delta Vineyard Pinot Noir 2008, Marlborough Red
Bright red fruit, well supported by acidity. Silky texture, with

Kaituna Hills Reserve Pinot Noir 2007, Marlborough Red
Vibrant fruit, with flavours of tangy cherry and cloves, backed up with smoky oak. There is a bright feel to the finish.
£9.00 M&S

Kennedy Point Waiheke Merlot 2005, Auckland Red
Mint, bitter chocolate, and blackberry fruit on the nose. Fresh acidity, with fine tannins, and a clean finish.

Sp Rise & Shine Pinot Noir 2007, Kim Crawford, Central Otago Red
Well-integrated palate, with lingering cherry and boysenberry flavours, finishing with a touch of fresh minerality.
£19.00 NZH, LIB

Kim Crawford Hawke's Bay Merlot 2007, Hawke's Bay Red
Slightly leafy, fruity, herbal character on the nose. Medium-bodied, fruity palate, with high tannins, and a long finish.
£10.40 NZH, LIB

Marks & Spencer Clocktower Pinot Noir 2007, Wither Hills, Marlborough Red
A leathery, earthy nose, with cherry, and some oak sweetness. Well-structured, with good length.
£11.00 M&S

Martinborough Vineyard Pinot Noir 2007, Wairarapa Red
Warm burnt toast and biscuit nose, with some red fruit. Smooth, round, spicy mid-palate, with a long finish.
£24.70 NZH, HAR, HVN

Montana Terraces Marlborough Pinot Noir 2007, Marlborough Red
Nose of anis and leather, with a bright, fruity, soft, sweet, and well-structured palate.
£14.00

Morton Estate Black Label Marlborough Pinot Noir 2007, Marlborough Red
Clear fragrant nose, with exotic sandalwood spice and rich berry fruit. Nicely juicy and alive.
£14.70 NZH

Mud House Central Otago Pinot Noir 2008, Central Otago Red
Clear ruby violet in colour, with intense red fruit aromas, and fresh notes of cherry and raspberry. Good volume and full body, with fresh acidity, and a long finish"
£16.00 NZH

Nautilus Estate Marlborough Pinot Noir 2007, Marlborough Red
Cherry oak and chestnut, with deep mulberry fruit. The palate is warm, and packed with sweet fruit .
£15.70 NZH

Ngatarawa Silks Syrah 2007, Hawke's Bay Red
Aromatic berries on the nose, with notes of plum fruit and brambles. Well-structured, with grippy tannins, and good fruit concentration.

Nobilo Regional Collection Merlot 2007, Hawke's Bay Red
Nice, dusty character, with some floral notes. Soft, smooth, elegant palate, with spicy vanilla oak.
£9.00 THS

Paritua Syrah 2007, Hawke's Bay Red
Serious wine with lots of fruit. Chunky, savoury, masculine

palate, with big fruit and meatiness. Will age well.
£17.50 CHH

Pond Paddock Te Muna Pinot Noir 2007, Wairarapa Red
Bright, clean, juicy structure, with lots of life and energy, and good, round flavours.

Saint Clair Omaka Reserve Pinot Noir 2007, Marlborough Red
This wine has a bright, cherry red appearance, with a subtle, fruity nose. Well-balanced, with a light finish.
£16.60 NZH, HOH

Saint Clair Pioneer Block 4 Sawcut Pinot Noir 2007, Marlborough Red
Red and black fruit, overlaid with oak. Slightly sappy flavours, and crisp acidity.
£16.10 NZH, HOH

Stockmans Station Pinot Noir 2007, Wild Earth Wines Ltd, Central Otago Red
Attractive cherries on the nose, with a very sweet, fruity structure, and a fairly long, silky chocolate finish.

Stoneleigh Rapaura Series Pinot Noir 2008, Marlborough Red
Meaty, spicy dark cherry nose, with some redcurrants. Silky tannins and medium length.
£11.00

Talisman 2007, The Crossroads Winery, Hawke's Bay Red
Toasty nose, with good fruit, combined with powerful oak.
£22.00 MZC

Tinpot Hut Hawke's Bay Syrah 2007, Hawke's Bay Red
Sweet fruit nose, with cinnamon and spice. Fresh and attractive, with warm fruit.
£13.20 NZH, LIB

Tohu 2007, Marlborough Red
Typical Pinot Noir, with a nice soft palate. A well-structured wine, with medium length.
£14.00

Trinity Hill Hawke's Bay The Trinity 2005, Hawke's Bay Red
Ripe Port-like nose, with a ripe palate of jammy fruit. Full-bodied, with good freshness.
£10.70 NZH

Vavasour Awatere Valley Pinot Noir 2007, Marlborough Red
Light strawberry fruit nose. Soft tannins, and a light body, with pleasant red berry fruit.
£13.00 B&J

Vavasour The Reach Merlot 2007, Hawke's Bay Red
Oaky vanilla aromas, with black cherry on the nose. Full-bodied, with ripe fruit, rounded tannin, and a long finish. Good potential.
£7.10 TESC

Vicarage Lane Marlborough Pinot Noir 2007, Marlborough Red
Fairly light nose, with crisp, bright morello cherries, leading to a similar palate, which is also quite dry and crunchy, bound by spicy tannin.

Vidal Hawke's Bay Pinot Noir 2008, Hawke's Bay Red
Fragrant, sweet, wild strawberry, and violet nose. Full and ripe on the palate. Elegant and fresh.
£10.00 NZH, HMA

Vidal Merlot 2007, Hawke's Bay Red
Plum and cedar nose, with a

palate of sweet black fruit and mint.
£9.10 NZH, HMA

Vidal Syrah 2007, Hawke's Bay Red
Youthful style, with an elegant nose of spiced cherry and tobacco leaves. Balanced and integrated, with dry, gentle acidity, and silky tannins.
£10.00 FLA, NZH, WAIT, HMA

Villa Maria Reserve Pinot Noir 2007, Marlborough Red
Pale raspberry colour, with young raspberry fruit on the nose. Young subtle fruit, and good balance, with fine tannins.
£17.00 NZH, HMA

Vynfields Pinot Noir 2006, Wairarapa Red
Intense red cherry, raspberry, and redcurrant on the nose, with new oak, and rich sweet fruit. Nice palate, with good structure and balance.

Waipara Hills Soul Of The South Waipara Pinot Noir 2008, Canterbury Red
Bright strawberry and mulberry fruit. Fresh medium-weight palate, with cherry fruit and supple tannins.

Wild Rock Gravel Pit Red Merlot Malbec 2007, Hawke's Bay Red
Spicy dark fruit. Lifted and fresh, with good structure. Well-balanced, with lovely length.
£10.50 FLA, NZH, WAIT, AMP, BCR, GWI

Wither Hills Pinot Noir 2007, Marlborough Red
This wine has a typical cherry red appearance, with an intense nose, surrounded by pleasant oak. On the palate, there is elegant cherry and raspberry fruit, with a clean, soft texture, which is in balance with the acidity.
£16.70 BNK, NZH, SAIN, WAIT

Woollaston Estates Ltd Tussock Nelson Pinot Noir 2006, Nelson Red
Delicate cherry nose, with a bit of toast alongside the fruit. Soft, perfumed, plummy palate; warming and delicate.
£14.00

Woollaston Estates Ltd Tussock Nelson Sauvignon Blanc 2008, Nelson Red
A herbal, mineral nose, with some gooseberry, followed by a palate of grassy herbal flavours, and ripe gooseberry and tropical fruit, with some mineral notes, and good intensity.
£10.00 WRC

Woollaston Nelson Pinot Noir 2006, Nelson Red
Lots of very ripe strawberry fruit. Quite jammy, with a little spice. Very smooth attack, with well-judged oak.
£17.00

Mud House Central Otago Rosé 2008, Central Otago Rosé
Bright pink hue. Clean, with lovely fruit, and Pinot character coming through. Excellent levels of acidity.
£11.30 NZH

Tarras Vineyards Florian Reserve Rosé 2008, Central Otago Rosé
Light strawberry nose, with some spiciness. Dry, with good acidity, and flavours of strawberries and cream.
£16.00 BDL, HVN, WIM

Wild Earth Rosé 2008 Central Otago Rosé
Bright pink in colour. Clean Pinot aromas, leading to a pleasant palate, with cutting acidity, giving the wine a zing.

No 1 Family Estate, Cuvée No 1 NV, Marlborough Sparkling
Restrained, lightly honeyed red apple aromas. Ripe fruit, with a little toastiness. Fresh, bright, and attractive.

Deutz Marlborough Cuvée NV Marlborough Sparkling
Attractive floral and lemon herb aromas. Light, citric, and refreshing, with a bready note.
£12.00

Bluff Hill Rose NV Sparkling Rosé
Pronounced berry nose, and a delicate palate, showing good depth of flavour, supported by crisp acidity.
£8.00 M&S

Montana Chardonnay Pinot Noir Rosé NV Sparkling Rosé
Pale pink in colour, with a fresh herby nose, and a soft, fruity palate.
£9.00

KEY FACTS

Total production
7.3m hectolitres

Total vineyard
239,951ha

Top 10 grapes

Whites:
1 Fernão Pires
2 Arinto
3 Alvarinho
4 Loureiro
5 Encruzado

Reds:
1 Touriga Nacional
2 Castelão
3 Trincadeira
4 Aragonês
5 Baga

Top regions
1 Trás-os-Montes
   (includes Douro
   and Porto)
2 Beiras (includes
   Dão, Bairrada,
   Beira Interior)
3 Minho (includes
   Vinho Verde)
4 Estremadura
5 Alentejo
6 Ribatejo
7 T Sado (includes
   Palmela, Setúbal
   and Moscatel)
8 Algarve

Producers
7,000

Portugal

Perhaps the most generous of wine
producing countries, Portugal has
brought so much to the world
in terms of wine styles. In the
white corner we're been treated
to compelling white varieties
such as Arinto and Encruzado,
both gold medal winners, the
multifaceted red and black corner
offering wines of great depth , with
elegance to boot. These wines
are first class passengers on the
Iberian Express, powered in the
engine room by port and Madiera.
Impeccably decorated in awards,
the fortified wines were awarded
sixteen gold, thirty five silver
and twenty three bronze medals.
Portuguese winemakers are worthy
of the recognition and esteem
that is presented to them in the
following pages.

2009 IWC PERFORMANCE	
Trophies	11
Gold	36
Silver	113
Bronze	146
Great Value Awards	1

Marques Dos Vales - White - Primeira Selecção 2008, Quinta Dos Vales , S.A., Algarve White

Really juicy, aromatic, perfumed nose, with notes of lychee, peach, orange, and tangerine. Fabulous oomph follows through onto a balanced and enduring palate.

 **INTERNATIONAL ALVARINHO TROPHY, PORTUGUESE WHITE TROPHY**

Muros Antigos Alvarinho 2008, Anselmo Mendes Vinhos Lda (Wines & Winemakers By Saven), Vinho Verde White

Lemon-green colour. Spicy, waxy dried fruit, with apricot and peach aromas. Sprightly acidity and fleshy yellow fruit on the palate. Aromatic and spicy, with a crisp, zesty finish.

Quinta Dos Carvalhais Encruzado 2007, Sogrape Vinhos S.A., Dão White

Broad, spicy, and oaky, with honey and beeswax complexity. The crisp, balanced palate will hold for some time, with defined flavours of almond, honey, and citrus.

Callabriga Reserva Alentejo 2005, Sogrape Vinhos S.A., Alentejo Red

Ripe liquorice and blackberry nose. Great vigour, and a lovely sensous palate, with soft tannins and medium structure. Very harmonious and understated on the finish.

Esporao Private Selection Red 2005, Alentejo Red

Dried fruit and spice on the nose.

Fine tannins and sleek texture on a palate of plum and blueberry. A lovely graceful finish, and great ageing potential.
£45.00

Esporao Touriga 2007, Alentejo Red

A warm, bright nose of primary berry fruit, with some mint and mocha. Chunky mouthfeel with ripe peppery fruit and soft tannins.

 ALENTEJO TROPHY

Herdade Das Barras 2005, Soc. Agro-pecuaria Do Oeste Alentejano, Lda., Alentejo Red

Rich, Port-like nose. Lovely sweet ripe blueberry and blackcurrant, well-balanced with oak flavours. Vibrant, fresh, and full-bodied, with an attractive, fruity finish.

Herdade Do Peso Reserva 2005, Sogrape Vinhos S.a. Alentejo Red

Sweet cherry and berry fruit, quite moreish, with remarkably good fruit and a mineral finish, which builds tightly with black raspberry flavours.

 **TERRAS DO SADO TROPHY**

Palácio Da Bacalhôa 2005, Bacalhôa Vinhos De Portugal, Terras Do Sado Red

Attractive nose with maturing notes of tar and black fruits, and cooling, refreshing undertones. A dark wine, with ripe tannins. Well-made and charming.
£17.00

Pena De Pato Alentejo Red 2007, Sogrape Vinhos S.A., Alentejo Red

Complex varietal blend, with pleasant lifted dark fruits, and a

**DÃO
TROPHY**

**Quinta Da Garrida 2006,
Alianca, Dão** Red
Black berried fruit, with a touch
of tobacco. Light body, with a
perfumed lift, chewy tannins,
some cigar box oak, and a
warming finish.
£8.70

**Quinta Do Infantado Douro
2007, Douro** Red
Nose of plummy damson
fruit and spice. The palate
is smoky, with silky tannins,
and good refreshing acidity,
making this a solidly
enjoyable drop.
£11.50 LIB

**Quinta Nova Reserva 2006,
Douro** Red
Deep and demure, displaying
stewed fruit with plenty of guts.
Great balance of acidity and
fruit, with a good finish.

**Quinta Vale D. Maria Douro
Red 2006, Lemos & Van Zeller,
Lda, Douro** Red
A spicy nose with notes of berry
fruit and mocha oak. Appealng
forward fruit on the palate, with
delicate, integrated oak, and
good harmony. A great chocolate
finish and decent length.
£18.00 WAIT

 **PORTUGUESE RED
TROPHY, DOURO
TROPHY**

**Xisto 2005, Roquette
E Cazes, Douro** Red
Clean and focused, with a
complex bouquet of floral
aromas, berry notes, and

minerality. Long, rich finish.
A classy wine, with fine
tannins and good ageing
potential.
£33.80 EDC

**10 Year Old Malmsey NV,
Henriques & Henriques,
Madeira,** Madeira
Wonderful complexity, with
molasses and honey flavours
dominating. Golden amber in
colour. Nutty, with lovely acidity.
Well-balanced, with a long,
lingering finish.
£16.50 HAR, HOF, MWW, SEL,
WIM

 **BOAL MADEIRA
TROPHY**

**Blandy's Colheita Bual 1993,
Madeira Wine Company,
Madeira** Madeira
Delicious ripe and concentrated
toffee caramel nose, leading to
a clean palate of smoky mint
and banana, with hints of honey
and almonds. Good acidity and a
long finish.

**Blandy's Colheita Malmsey
1990, Madeira Wine
Company, Madeira** Madeira
Stunning golden amber in colour.
Distinct, complex nose. Rich,
round, and complex, with good
acidity, and great finish. Superb
quality; exceptionally well-made.

**Malvasia 20 Anos, Lote
7199 NV, Vinhos Barbeito
Madeira Lda., Madeira**
Madeira
Gold in colour. Intense nose, with
complex aromas of banana skins.
Palate of sweet upfront flavours;
notes of lemon and orange peel,
with good balance and well-
integrated acidity.
£53.00 REY

**Malvasia Old Reserve 10
Year Old NV, Vinhos Barbeito
Madeira Lda., Madeira** Madeira
Gorgeous golden colour. Intense
and complex nose, with some
cedar and honey aromas. Lovely
palate, with good length. An
extremely good quality Madeira.
£25.00 REY

 **MALMSEY MADEIRA
TROPHY**

**Marks & Spencer Malmsey
Madeira 2001, Henriques &
Henriques, Madeira** Madeira
Extremely attractive, deep amber
brown colour. Lifted raisins and
butterscotch on the nose. Fresh
upfront iced tea and honey on
the palate, with nuts and cloves
on the finish.
£17.00 M&S

 **CHAMPION
FORTIFIED, MADEIRA
TROPHY, VERDELHO
MADEIRA TROPHY**

**Verdelho Old Reserve 10
Year Old NV, Vinhos Barbeito
Madeira Lda, Madeira** Madeira
Lovely rich fruit, with a powerful
and concentrated palate of
walnut and sultana. Clean and
bright, with elegance and a long
finish. A gorgeous Madeira.
£25.00 REY

**Dow's Ribeira 2006,
Symington Family Estates,
Douro** Port
Fresh violet, with and spicy and
exuberant fruit on the nose.
Peppery palate, with an interesting
finish and good length.

**Dow's Vintage 1985,
Symington Family Estates,
Douro** Port
A spicy eucalyptus nose, with

peppery black cherry fruit,
and a long firm finish. Dry and
complex, with a long life ahead.

**Marks & Spencer Vintage
Port 1994, Taylor's, Douro**
Port
Intense, complex nose of red
fruit and liquorice. With good
body and structure, this has
everything in place to develop
into a complex aged Port.
£27.00 M&S

**Mhv Regimental Lbv 2004,
Sandeman, Douro** Port
Ruby red in colour, with a nose
of lifted chocolate and cherry.
Clean, ripe blackberry jam on the
palate, with hints of lavender
and wattle. Very good body with
nice structure.
£10.50 MHV

**Offley 10 Years Old Tawny
NV, Sogrape Vinhos S.A.,
Douro** Port
Nutty and fresh with good
balance. Well-structured, with
fruit all the way through. Very
intense finish, with hints of
sweet spice and dried fruit.

 **TAWNY PORT
TROPHY**

**Porto Ferreira 20 Years Old
Tawny NV, Sogrape Vinhos
S.A., Douro** Port
Intense yet fresh, great body
with good fruit. Elegant golden
amber in colour, with aromatic
orange peel, spice, and nuts,
leading to a complex finish.

 **PORT TROPHY,
VINTAGE PORT
TROPHY**

**Quinta Seara D'ordens
Vintage 2005, Douro** Port
Lively fruity aromas of blackberry,

resin, and fresh flowers, with liquorice undertones. Full sweet palate, with good tannins, and a long and powerful finish.

Sandeman 10 Years Old Tawny NV, Sogrape Vinhos S.A., Douro Port
Clean nose of rich dried fruit, with hints of almond and butterscotch. Very palatable, with full, fresh flavour. Excellent balance and persistent length.

Sandeman 40 Years Old Tawny NV, Sogrape Vinhos S.A., Douro Port
Intense and complex, with freshness and spicy aromas. Dense, round body, with good acidity, and notes of dried fruit, cloves, and Christmas spice, enveloped in exotic wood. A gift to the senses.

Single Quinta Vintage Ervamoira 2007, Adriano Ramos Pinto Vinhos S.A., Douro Port
Dark ruby in colour, with an intense nose of lifted cracked pepper and herbal mint aromas. Fresh fruit, and slightly dry on the palate, with a long finish.

Vesuvio Vintage 2000, Symington Family Estates, Douro Port
Intense concentrated chocolate, black cherry, liquorice, and damson nose. The palate is complex and full, with intense fruit, firm, grippy tannins, good body, and a persistent finish of spice and pepper.

Vista Alegre Late Bottled Vintage - Unfiltered - Port 2003, Douro Port
Deep ruby red in colour, with

a lifted nose of cloves and concentrated black fruit. Full, sweet palate, with a rounded body, grippy tannins, and good length.

 LBV PORT TROPHY

Warre's Lbv 2000, Symington Family Estates, Douro Port
Intense ripe black fruit on an exuberant nose. Rich fruit structure, and a dense, concentrated body, with firm tannins, and an earthy chocolate finish.

Warre's Otima 10 NV, Symington Family Estates, Douro Port
Complex and spicy, with dried figs on the nose. Good body, with nice acidity and a fruity mid-palate, finishing on a rich, complex fruity note.
£13.00 WAIT

Herdade Dos Grous 2008, Alentejo White
Attractive nose with oily, floral hints. Soft, ripe gooseberry flavours, leading to a succulent finish.

Morgadio Da Torre 2007, Sogrape Vinhos S.A., Vinho Verde White
Peachy stone fruit aromas, with a leafy, nettle character. Clean, fresh lime on the palate, alongside peach and apple notes. Crisp acidity.

Morgado Sta. Catherina 2007, Companhia Das Quintas - Vinhos, S.A., Estremadura White
Lemon and oak nose. Zippy acidity, with fresh cream and

honey flavours, and good balance. Long, nutty, and delicious.

Quinta Dos Carvalhais Duque De Viseu White 2008, Sogrape Vinhos S.A., Dão White
Clean, bright, floral and citrus fruit, with liquorice notes. Creamy, delicate palate, with crisp acidity and a long finish.

Quinta Dos Roques Encruzado 2007, Dão White
A vivid nose of orange blossom and grapefruit, leading to a viscous palate, with a touch of vanilla and very good acidity.
£13.00

Vale D'algares White NV, Quatro Âncoras,lda, Ribatejo White
A serious style of Viognier; slightly floral in character, clean and oily, with lightly aromatic, smoky, woody, and lemon flavours, finishing on a creamy note.

Varandas 2008, Adega Cooperativa De Almeirim,c. r.l., Ribatejo White
Deep, rich peachy nose with yeasty, herbal, flower, and oily notes. Well-balanced, with good weight, crisp acidity, and a long finish.
£5.00

Vz Douro White 2008, Lemos & Van Zeller, Lda, Douro White
Aromatic, spicy oak on the nose, leading to a lively mineral and citrus palate with evident integrated oak. Soft, subtle, creamy finish, with fruity acidity.

Adega De Pegoes Selected Harvest Red 2007, Cooperativa Agricola De

Santo Isidro Pegoes Crl, Terras Do Sado Red
Rich blackberry fruit notes, with chocolate, coconut, and vanilla on the nose, and soft strawberry flavours. Good weight, and attractive flavour.

Adega De Pias 2008, Monte Da Capela, Lda, Alentejo Red
Red fruit nose, with a distinctive raspberry character. Bright redcurrant and raspberry aromas follow through on the palate, which also displays subtle vanilla oak.

Alianca Dao Reserva 2006, Dão Red
Aromas of violet and brambly fruit, with spicy vanilla oak. Medium-bodied, with soft chewy tannins, and a lifted, lingering finish.
£6.80

Azul Portugal Palmela 2007, Casa Ermelinda Freitas (wines & Winemakers By Saven), Terras do Sado Red
A soft herbal nose, with wonderful spicy plummy fruit, an intense rounded palate, and excellent length.

Callabriga Reserva Dão 2005, Sogrape Vinhos S.A., Dão Red
Pungent, fruity nose. Palate of berry fruit, with a smooth finish.

Casa Das Mouras Reserva 2005, Quinta Da Veiga Da Casa Da Capela (wines & Winemakers By Saven), Douro Red
Deep in colour, with a complex nose of floral aromas, liquorice, and spice. Palate of concentrated ripe fruit with mineral and meaty notes.

Casa Ermelinda Freitas Reserva 2004, Terras Do Sado Red
Concentrated nose, with good

complexity and depth. Perfumed in the mouth, with dry tannins leading to a long, minty, cassis finish.

Casa Ferreirinha Callabriga 2006, Sogrape Vinhos S.A., Douro Red

A Port-like nose full of bramble fruit. Clean palate of plum and fruitcake, with hints of hedgerow fruits and plenty of vanilla oak.

Cortes De Cima Syrah 2007, Alentejo Red

Deep damson red in colour, with a robust, spicy, and fruity nose. The palate shows rich, stylish good fruit, with great balance. £10.00 WAIT

Cortes De Cima Touriga Nacional 2007, Alentejo Red

Nose of ripe black fruit, with sweet orange notes. On the palate, the wine is big and ripe, with sturdy tannins and oak.

Crataegus 2004, Casal Dos Jordoes, Douro Red

Fresh and lifted savoury fruit on the palate. Firm grippy tannins, showing good concentration, with some elegance and length. £10.00 VER

Different Red 2006, Encosta Do Sobral - Sociedade Agrícola Lda, Ribatejo Red

Rich and smoky, with tightly packed fruit. Full of blueberry and blackberry, with a vanilla finish.

Dona Maria Amantis 2005, Julio Tassara De Bastos, Alentejo Red

Meat, leather, and some fruitiness on the nose. Sweet tannins, black cherry, and oak on the palate. Good complexity and a long finish.

Dona Maria Reserve 2005, Julio Tassara De Bastos, Alentejo Red

Ripe fruit, plum, and juniper. Elegant, enduring fruit, which is balanced and integrated, with a sweet burst on the finish.

Douro Red 2007, Quinta Do Crasto, Douro Red

Nicely textured palate, with balanced savoury and bitter edges. Dark fruit, with good acidity and lingering freshness. £10.00 MWW

Duas Quintas Reserva 2007, Adriano Ramos Pinto, Vinhos S.A., Douro Red

Attractively perfumed fruit, with very dense spice, bitter chocolate, and dark fruit, offering good length and freshness. £22.00

Escapadas, Red Wine 2007, Sociedade Agrícola Quinta Do Conde, Sa, Estremadura Red

Rich nose, full of dark fruit, floral notes, and spice. Good texture, smooth tannins, plummy fruit, and loads of spice on the palate.

Esporão Alicante Bouschet 2007, Alentejo Red

A palate of leather and roasted herbs, with tobacco-scented black fruit. These rich flavours are carried to a dry finish by very firm tannins.

Fiuza Ikon 2007, Ribatejo Red

Damson notes, with a touch of tobacco and spicy fruit on the nose. Good, spicy, supple fruit on the palate, with balanced acidity and good length.

Flor De Crasto 2007, Quinta Do Crasto, Douro Red

Ripe fruit, layers of red fruit and

hints of bitterness, with ripe, grippy tannins.
£9.50

Garrida 2006, Alianca, Dão
Red
Soft, elegant fruit on the nose, with a palate of lively fruit, brambly chewy tannins, and a floral, spicy finish.

Gloria Reynolds 2004, Julian Cuellar Reynolds, Lda., Alentejo Red
Very sweet brambly fruit, with layers of espresso beans and dark chocolate, underlined by super-ripe strawberry compote.
£32.00 HFB

Grou 2005, Sociedade Agrícola Do Vale De Joana (Wines & Winemakers By Saven), Alentejo Red
A complex nose of dried fruit, smoke, and minerality. A big, mouth-filling wine, with firm tannins, ending on a long, peppery note.

Guarda Rios Red NV, Quatro Âncoras,lda, Ribatejo Red
Lovely sweet curranty fruit, with attractive fruitcake character. Full bodied and well-structured. Showing good intensity, and drinking well now.

Herdade Da Maroteira "Cem Reis" 2007, Micheal Brian Mollet, Alentejo Red
Nose of oak and blackcurrant, with spicy chocolate. Rich body of black fruit, violet and bramble, with soft, velvety tannnins carrying a long finish.
£15.00

Herdade Das Servas Vinhas Velhas 2005, Serrano Mira, Sociedade Vinícola S.A., Alentejo Red
Creamy oak, with good balance of alcohol and tannins. Long and well-balanced, with a supple finish.

Herdade Do Peso Colheita 2006, Sogrape Vinhos S.A., Alentejo Red
Sweet fig and damson nose. An extroverted palate. with smooth entry, nice acidity, and notes of Christmas cake and spicy fruit.

Herdade Dos Grous Reserva 2007, Alentejo Red
Bright red in colour. Hints of chocolate on the nose, and dark fruit on the palate, leading to a savoury finish.

João Clara Tinto 2007, Edite Alves, Algarve Red
Powerful spicy oak nose, with a lovely perfumed palate of red and black fruit. Soft tannins, and a rich, ripe, very long finish.

Má Partilha 2006, Bacalhôa Vinhos De Portugal, Terras Do Sado Red
Delicate fresh berries on the nose. Juicy palate with clean, fresh finish, and lively, non-aggressive tannins.

Margalha 2007, Ilex Vinhos, Alentejo Red
Aromatic, herbal blackcurrant nose, with spicy black fruit on a palate which is balanced and dense.

Monte Da Penha Fino 2004, Francisco B. Fino - Sociedade Agrícola, Lda, Alentejo Red
Aromatic nose dominated by dark fruit, and showing development of tertiary aromas, including dried fruit, leather, and earthy oak. There is an attractive hint of spice on the palate.

Monte Medeiros Vino De Mesa Alentejo 2006, Tahora Lda, Alentejo Red
Big sweet coffee and cream nose, with lots of sweet berry fruit. Nice palate, with some raspberry brightness and a long, focused finish.
£7.00 AVB

Montinho São Miguel 2007, Casa Ag. Alexandre Relvas, Alentejo Red
Intense aromas of raisin fruit. Bold, chunky palate, with firm tannins and fresh acidity.
£5.00

Murzelo Reserva 2006, Quinta Da Veiga Da Casa Da Capela (Wines & Winemakers By Saven), Douro Red
Rich and creamy, with dry raspberry and rich blackberry on the palate. Fine tannins and balanced acidity, with a long peppery finish.

Outeiro Do Mouro 2007, Terras De Alter Companhia De Vinhos, Lda, Alentejo Red
Pure and well-defined on the nose, with notes of blackberries and raspberries. Well-balanced, with good integration of oak, and a long finish.

Passadouro Reserva 2006, Douro Red
Deep rich colour. Spicy, peppery nose, with a touch of brett adding complexity. Good long finish.
£25.00 RWD

Patamar 2007, Dfj Vinhos, Douro Red
Fleshy fruit with berries galore and ripe figs. A real food wine.
£7.00 MRN, WRC

Preta 2005, Fita Preta Vinhos, Alentejo Red
Lovely sweet blackberry

and dark cherry fruit on the nose. The palate is sweet and attractive, with spice, and a drying finish.

Quinta Da Fonte Do Ouro Touriga Nacional 2006, Sociedade Agrícola Boas Quintas Lda, Dão Red
Violets, red fruit, and a touch of spice on the nose. Lovely high acidity and sleek tannins. Lots of berry fruit and floral notes on the palate, with well-integrated oak.

Quinta Da Garrida Reserva 2005, Alianca, Dão Red
Aromatic, lifted nose with hints of orange peel. Lovely creamy palate and aromatic character, followed by a long, complex finish.
£13.70

Quinta Do Couquinho Colheita 2006, Quinta Do Couquinho De Maria Adelaide Melo E Trigo, Douro Red
Powerful nose of plum, damson, chocolate, and thyme. Elegant and full-bodied, with good balance and a lingering finish.

Quinta Do Tedo DOC Douro 2007, Douro Red
Vibrant floral nose, with lovely smoky intensity. Notes of berry, brown sugar, and blackcurrant on a palate which is dense, young, and promising.
£8.00 MKV

Quinta Do Tedo Grande Reserva Savedra 2005, Douro Red
Nose of plums, with a hint of vegetal aromas. Silky texture, with red berry fruit, showing good concentration and balance.
£20.00 MKV

Quinta Do Vallado Touriga Nacional 2007, Quinta Do Vallado Sociedade Agrícola, Lda., Douro Red
Nose of cedar and smoke, with sweet plummy fruit. Elegant palate of black fruit, with well-integrated, sweet, cedary oak.
£33.00 BWL

Quinta Dos Carvalhais Colheita 2006, Sogrape Vinhos S.A., Dão Red
Attractive mellow nose, with aromatic notes of ripe plums. Wonderful grainy tannins.

Quinta Dos Carvalhais Duque De Viseu Red 2006, Sogrape Vinhos S.A., Dão Red
A lightly fruity and floral nose, with forward cherry fruits. Fruity and rich on the palate, with lovely length and complexity.

Quinta Dos Roques Reserva 2006, Dão Red
Attractive herbal and floral nose, with hints of red fruit and cassis. Rich style, with depth, good structure, and a well-balanced finish.
£25.00

Quinta Dos Termos Reserva Do Patrão 2006, Beiras Red
Tight and intriguing balsamic nose. Tight tannins, with lots of brambly fruit on a background of American oak and liquorice.

Quinta Nova Grande Reserva 2006, Quinta Nova Nª Srª Do Carmo, Douro Red
Big, fruity wine with hints of raisin and spice. Silky, rounded tannins and good length.

Quinta Nova Touriga Nacional 2006, Quinta Nova Nª Srª Do Carmo, Douro Red
Savoury mineral aromas,

followed by an intense savoury palate of lush fruit, with creamy oak, and a firm grippy finish.

Rayo Premium Red 2007, Sociedade Agrícola D. Diniz, Sa, Alentejo Red
Great colour, and a palate of sweet cherry and red fruit, with hints of meat and green pepper, underpinned by chewy tannins.

Roquevale Reserva 2005, Alentejo Red
Lifted strawberry and red cherry on the nose, with vanilla and oaky spice, and a juicy red berry finish, with smooth and integrated tannins.

S De Soberanas 2005, Terras Do Sado Red
Full-bodied, showing hints of roasted coffee, ripe raspberry and lavender, and a touch of creamy coconut on the finish.

Sexy 2007, Fita Preta Vinhos, Alentejo Red
Deep, rich nose of plummy ripe fruit and coffee, with soft dark fruit, bright tannins and notes of chocolate.

Só Syrah 2006, Bacalhôa Vinhos De Portugal, Terras Do Sado Red
Lush black and red fruit, with balancing acidity and firm ripe tannins. Lovely chocolatey berry finish.
£15.00

Tinto Da Ânfora 2006, Bacalhôa Vinhos De Portugal, Alentejo Red
Brambly black fruit and Christmas cake on the nose. A warmly fruity and juicy wine, with good complexity, and excellent balance.
£6.00 WAIT

**Vale D'algares Red NV,
Quatro Âncoras,lda, Ribatejo
Red**
Intense blackcurrant pastille
nose, with a hint of treacle, and
clean, well-defined perfumed
fruit. Youthful tannins, with a
tingling finish.

**Vallegre DOC Douro Reserva
Especial - Old Vines 2005,
Vallegre, Vinhos Do Porto
S.A., Douro Red**
Deep ruby red, with smoky, dark
fruit on the nose. Balanced,
elegant structure, with good
smoky fruit and length.

**Vista Tr 2006, Alianca, Beiras
Red**
Elegant, concentrated black plum
fruit. Light body and acidity,
with lingering cherry fruit and
spicy vanilla oak flavours coming
through.
£5.80

**Waitrose Douro Valley
Reserva Quinta De La Rosa
2007, Douro Red**
Very leafy, with blackcurrant
and raisin fruit on the nose, and
lovely juicy bramble and some
spice on the palate. Good, lifted,
fresh acidity, with floral tannins,
and great complexity and length.
£10.00 WAIT, JBF

**20 Year Old Malmsey NV,
Henriques & Henriques,
Madeira, Madeira**
Lovely intense baked nose, with
caramel and rich coffee flavours.
Great body, balanced, with a
seductive finish.
£22.00 MZC

**Blandy's Verdelho 1968,
Madeira Wine Company,
Madeira Madeira**
Nose of walnut and spice,
with fruitcake and a hint of
marmalade. The palate is mature,
but still fresh. Bitter chocolate
and toasty walnuts predominate.

**Malvasia 30 Anos, Lote
Especial NV, Vinhos Barbeito
Madeira Lda., Madeira
Madeira**
Lovely amber colour. Very nice,
intense aromas of orange and
marmalade. Very good balance
and harmony.
£85.00 REY

**Sercial Old Reserve 10 Year
Old NV, Vinhos Barbeito
Madeira Lda, Madeira
Madeira**
Golden amber in colour. Fresh
and elegant, with apple and
cinnamon flavours. Extremely
well-balanced.
£25.00 REY

**Single Harvest 1997 Medium
Dry NV, Vinhos Barbeito
Madeira Lda., Madeira
Madeira**
Floral, rose petal character on
the nose, with hints of clean
fresh lemon coming through on
the palate, which ends on a spicy
note Delicious.
£17.50 REY

Dow's 10 Year Old NV, Symington Family Estates, Douro Port

A nose of fresh raisin and subtle chocolate, with nutty aromas and good structure, leading to a fruity finish with notes of juniper berry.

Dow's 20 Year Old NV, Symington Family Estates, Douro Port

Very pale tawny in colour, with a nose of lifted cola and tea leaf. Notes of fresh malt and caramel, with hints of nuts, orange peel, dates, and spice, culminating in an elegant finish.
£27.00 WAIT

Andresen Royal Choice 20 Year Old Tawny NV, Douro Port

Tropical fruit and sweet spices on the nose. Well-balanced, with a complex finish of nuts, caramel, and earthiness.
£25.00 LAI

Andresen Vintage 2005, Douro Port

Ripe, sweet jammy nose. Youthful and fresh, with some chewy tannins. Concentrated and full, with an intense black fruit finish.
£35.00 LAI

Dalva Porto Finest Ruby Reserve NV, C. Da Silva (Vinhos) SA, Douro Port

Dark ruby colour, with a good chocolatey style. Fresh and peppery, with a big fat mouthfeel, and a smooth, velvety finish.

Dalva Porto Vintage 2005, C.da Silva (Vinhos) SA, Douro Port

Complex, elegant nose, which is firm, fresh, and sleek. Dry tannic structure, with clean, pure fruit. Good finesse; a well-made wine.

Dow's Bomfim 1998, Symington Family Estates, Douro Port

Black fruit nose with herbal undertones, an open palate, with good persistence, and a smooth sweet finish with good tannin.

Dow's Crusted 2002, Symington Family Estates, Douro Port

Jammy baked fruit, with a good mouthfeel. Firm but dry, nicely balanced, with smooth tannins.

Ervamoira 10 Years NV, Adrianoa Ramos Pinto Vinhos S.A., Douro Port

A nose of dried fruit and nuts, leading to a palate of fresh fruit, with good body and concentration, with a strong finish.
£29.00 MMD

Fonseca Bin 27 NV, Douro Port

Intense ripe fruit, with a full body and good structure. Lively finish, with floral and peppery hints.
£11.00 F&M, THS

Graham's 20 Year Old NV, Symington Family Estates, Douro Port
Deep amber in colour, with a lifted caramel and cola character. Hints of sweet fruit blossom, with some toffee and butterscotch. A lovely, elegant, well-integrated wine, with harmonious length.
£34.00 WAIT

Graham's Crusted 2002, Symington Family Estates Douro, Port
Clear fruit, with good balance, structure, and age, with some tannins at the end.

Graham's Malvedos 1998, Symington Family Estates, Douro Port
Tight, concentrated berry nose, with mouth-filling compact fruit, chocolate, and blackberry. Full and long.

Graham's Malvedos 1999, Symington Family Estates, Douro Port
Intense fruit on the nose, with plum, cocoa, and resin. Concentrated rich, ripe palate, with a great body that finishes intensely with notes of black fruit and pepper.

Krohn Colheita 1978, Wiese & Krohn, Douro Port
Lovely fragrance, with rich figs and bananas on the nose. Fresh and lively on the palate, with a long hot Douro finish.
£49.10

> **GREAT VALUE FORTIFIED BETWEEN £10 AND £15**

Krohn LBV 2004, Wiese & Krohn, Douro Port
Nose of fresh and dried fruit. Medium-bodied and well-balanced, with great berry fruit

and good length.
£12.60 GGR HFW WWN

Late Bottled Vintage 2004, Adriano Ramos Pinto Vinhos S.A., Douro Port
A rich berry nose, with lovely chocolatey flavours, and a hint of liquorice. Very intense, rich, and complex.

Offley Late Bottled Vintage 2004, Sogrape Vinhos S.A., Douro Port
Concentrated and rich, with ripe fruit and chocolate on the palate. Great structure, with a pleasant blackberry finish.

Poças Vintage Porto 2007, Manoel D. Poças Junior - Vinhos, S.A., Douro Port
Lifted and attractive nose, with intense fruity flavours, and a concentrated finish, with a friendly grip.
HOT

Porto 20 Years Quinta Do Bom Retiro NV, Adriano Ramos Pinto, Vinhos SA, Douro Port
Good balance, good character, and lovely style. Intense cedar and exotic wood aromas, and notes of orange peel, with a structure which is a harmonious, elegant, and ripe.
£49.00 MMD

Porto Ferreira 10 Years Old Tawny NV, Sogrape Vinhos S.A., Douro Port
Amber brown in colour, with notes of lifted cloves and cedar. Fresh upfront sweet spice, nutmeg, and thyme, with a white pepper finish.

Porto Ferreira Dona Antónia NV, Sogrape Vinhos S.A., Douro Port
A nose of lifted cloves and

LOST YOUR BOTTLE?

WHERE CAN I BUY **vini** **portugal**.co.uk PORTUGUESE WINE

nutmeg. Well-made, with fresh cedar and blackberry on the palate, and good balance.

Porto Ferreira Vintage 2003, Sogrape Vinhos S.A., Douro Port
Intense black fruit. Concentrated and complex, with a dense body, firm structure, and good, chewy tannins. Finish of fruit and bitter chocolate.

Quinta Do Tedo Port LBV 2003, Douro Port
Rich, ripe nose, with a concentrated bramble and cherry fruit palate, leading to a rich finish.
£21.00 MKV

Quinta Nova Nª Srª Do Carmo Lbv 2004, Quinta Nova Nª Srª Do Carmo, Douro Port
Ruby red in colour, with a lifted nose of lavender and wattle. Fresh blackberry, strawberry fruit, and cloves on the palate.

Quinta Vale D. Maria Vintage Port 2007, Lemos & Van Zeller, Lda, Douro Port
Dark in colour, with a nose of berry fruit and cassis, leading to a long, dry finish.

Sandeman 20 Years Old Tawny NV, Sogrape Vinhos S.A., Douro Port
White pepper and cedar nose, showing balance and poise on the palate, with good complexity and intensity, and a long, harmonious finish.

Sandeman 30 Years Old Tawny NV, Sogrape Vinhos S.A., Douro Port
Pale tawny in colour, with a nose which is nutty yet citrussy. Caramel and soft spice on the palate, leading to a delicate, soft, lasting finish. Elegant and opulent; a real treat.

Smith Woodhouse LBV 1999, Symington Family Estates, Douro Port
Blackberry nose, with a full, concentrated, firm palate of stone fruit, pepper, and spice. Notes of chocolate, and a long finish.

Taylor's 20 Year Old Tawny NV, Douro Port
Peppery nose and palate, with caramel intensity to finish. A rich palate with good length.
£32.70 WAIT, HAR, SEL

Taylor's Quinta De Terra Feita 1999, Douro Port
Blackcurrant nose and palate, with a concentrated, intense, peppery grip, and a long, warm finish of savoury spice.
£24.00 HOF, MWW, ODD, WIM

Tesco Finest* 10 Year Old Tawny NV, Symington Family Estates, Vinhos, Lda, Douro Port
A delicate tawny, with a soft, spicy, nutty nose, good balance, and a long finish. Lovely, delicate, and elegant.
£11.30 TESC

Vintage 1994, Adriano Ramos Pinto Vinhos S.A., Douro Port
Intense red fruit on a taut nose, wihich spicy, cherry, and resinous notes. Soft lifted tannins, with good structure, and a fruity finish.

Vintage 1995, Adriano Ramos Pinto, Vinhos S.A., Douro Port
Intense aromatic nose, with a chocolate and prune palate. Smooth tannins, and a black fruit overlay, with soft mouthfeel, and an elegant finish.

Vista Alegre Colheita Port 1995, Vallegre, Vinhos Do Porto S.A., Douro Port
Fig, raisin, and caramel nose.

Palate of orange, spice, and toffee, with a very sweet baked flavour, and a long crème brûlée finish.

Warre's Cavadinha 1996, Symington Family Estates, Douro Port

Nose of soft, mature damson fruit, with a hint of almond. Very approachable, with a medium body, and soft tannins.

Warre's Vintage 1980, Symington Family Estates, Douro Port

Rich and figgy on the nose, with soft, luscious fruit on the palate, and chunky tannins.
£47.00 WAIT

Warre's Warrior NV, Symington Family Estates, Douro Port

Deep purple in colour, with a fresh, spicy nose, and notes of blackberry and sherbet on the palate. Grippy tannins and a good finish.
£10.00 WAIT

BRONZE

Adega Cooperativa De Ponte De Lima - Loureiro Selecção 2008, Vinho Verde White

Lemon-yellow in colour, with light, citrus freshness, white flowers, green apple, and classic acidity.

Adega De Pegoes Selected Harvest White 2008, Cooperativa Agricola De Santo Isidro Pegoes Crl, Terras Do Sado White

Very pure, floral, and green, with good acidity, dried lychee, notes of mint, and a light finish.

Adoraz 2008, Sociedade Agricola Casa Pinheiro, Vinho Verde White

Aromatic pear drop aromas on a light spritzy palate. Fresh and simple.

Afros Loureiro 2008, Vasco Croft, Vinho Verde White

Lemon yellolw in colour, with good aromatic intensity, fermentation aromas, and fresh, well-balanced acidity.

Alfaraz Reserva 2007, Henrique Uva/Herdade Da Mingorra, Alentejo White

Dark green-gold in colour, this is a rich and steely wine, which is nutty, with a balanced hint of oak.

Alvarinho Qm 2008, Quintas De Melgaço, S.A., Vinho Verde White

Soft ripe peach and pear aromas. The palate is more intense than the nose would suggest, with pineapple and rich citrus notes, with good underlying acidity.

Defesa White 2008, Esporao S.A., Alentejo White

Star bright, and pale lemon in colour. The nose is light, fruity, clean, and lively. The palate shows dry, clean fruit, with medium length.
£7.00 ATC

Dona Maria Amantis 2007, Julio Tassara De Bastos, Alentejo White

Honeysuckle and roses on the nose, with a heady notes of peach, and rather long, multi-layered finish.

Duas Quintas Branco 2008, Adriano Ramos Pinto, Vinhos S.A., Douro White

Great citrus aromas. Waxy, oily, and powerful, with complex fruity flavours on the palate.

Grainha White 2007, Quinta Nova Nª Srª Do Carmo, Douro White
Floral aromas and sorbet undertones, with notes of melon and apple. The palate has tangy apricot and lime flavours, balanced with good acidity, and bitter lemon on the finish.

Herdade Dos Grous Reserva Branco 2007, Alentejo White
Nose of toasty, which follows through onto a citrussy, creamy palate.

Jp Azeitão White NV, Bacalhôa Vinhos De Portugal, Terras Do Sado White
A sweet flavoursome nose of rose essence. Fresh honey and lemon on the palate, with a soft, gentle, dry finish.
£5.00

Marks & Spencer Vinha De Urze 2008, Rui Maderia, Douro White
Fresh minerally nose, with lovely citrus aromas. Clean, zingy fruit on the palate, with fresh, vibrant acidity.
£8.00 M&S

Mouras De Arraiolos Reserva Branco 2007, Alentejo White
Aromas of stone fruit and almonds, with notes of dried nectarine and apricot. Punchy spice, with leesy notes, good acidic balance, and a substantial, long finish.

Muros Antigos Loureiro 2008, Anselmo Mendes Vinhos Lda (Wines & Winemakers By Saven), Vinho Verde White
Herbaceous and sweet peach aromas. Clean, fresh, and zesty, with some soft melon fruit flavours.

Onda Nova Branco Verdelho 2008, Algarve White
Hint of lees on the nose. Good solid weight, with attractive tropical fruit flavours on the palate.
£10.00

Palpite 2007, Fitapreta Vinhos, Alentejo White
An attractive nose, perfumed with lime, white peach, and honey. Soft, rich, and oaky, with some acidity.

Quinta Da Bacalhôa 2007, Terras Do Sado White
Nose of chocolate powder and notes of lemon curd, with a soft attack and fresh finish.
£11.00

Quinta De Azevedo 2008, Sogrape Vinhos S.A., Vinho Verde White
Melon, apple, and lime flavours, with fresh peach, and a zesty liveliness.
£6.50 WAIT

Sexy Branco 2008, Fita Preta Vinhos, Alentejo White
Pale lemon colour, with citrus notes throughout. Crisp, zingy, and youthful.

Terras D'alter Reserva 2008, Alentejo White
Grass, citrus, and banana aromas on the nose. Soft and rounded, with good structure, and a soft, creamy finish.

Torre De Menagem 2008, Quintas De Melgaço, S.A., Vinho Verde White
Straw yellow in colour, with nice aromatic intensity, and subtle peachy aromas of apple and fresh tropical fruit.

Touquinheiras Alvarinho 2008, Vinho Verde White
Fresh, floral, candied citrus nose,

with nice spicy liveliness, and good fruit on the finish.

Verdelho 2008, Esporao S.A., Alentejo White
Citrus nose, with a zingy lemon palate and good length.
£8.00

Amoras, Red Wine 2008, Casa Santos Lima - Companhia Das Vinhas S.A., Estremadura Red
Opulent plummy aromas, which follow through onto a soft, velvety palate.
LAI

Arco 2008, Esporão, Alentejo Red
A nose of red and black fruit, with hints of spiced plum and baked apple. Balanced structure, with supple tannins.
£10.00 WAIT

Arundel 2007, Joaquim Arnaud, Alentejo Red
Attractive ripe strawberry and plum on the nose. Aromas follow through onto a balanced palate.

Auru 2003, Quinta Do Poral, Douro Red
Attractive, chunky, spicy nose. The palate is light and attractive, with plummy dark cherry fruit, and a lovely meaty character.

Azamor Petit Verdot 2006, Alentejo Red
Dense, brooding nose. Notes of black cherry liqueur, with good weight, and firm tannins.
£15.00 LIB

Azul Portugal Ribatejo Tinto 2007, Companhia Das Lezírias (Wines & Winemakers By Saven), Ribatejo Red
Berry nose, with a touch of smoke, leading into a palate of fresh plum, showing good length.

Barco Negro 2008, François Lurton, Douro Red
Youthful, vibrant wine, with aromas of sweet cherry, with a palate brimming with lively, fresh red fruit and bright acidity.

Barricas, Red Wine 2008, Casa Santos Lima - Companhia Das Vinhas Sa, Estremadura Red
Very ripe, appealing nose, with a medium body, ripe sweet fruit, and a slightly dry, peppery finish.

Cabrita Tinto 2007, Quinta Da Vinha, Algarve Red
Rich ruby red in colour, with notes of green beans, caramel, brown cigar, and tobacco, in an earthy style.

Callabriga Alentejo 2006, Sogrape Vinhos S.A., Alentejo Red
Very ripe raisin, liquorice, and prunes on the nose. Attractive balance on the palate, with good vigour and acidity.

Callabriga Dão 2006, Sogrape Vinhos S.A., Dão Red
Ripe raspberry and cherry nose, with warm spice, grippy tannins, and a fresh finish.

Callabriga Douro 2006, Sogrape Vinhos S.A., Douro Red
Notes of mocha and coffee beans, with jammy fruit and good length. A full, round palate, with good harmony and length.

Callabriga Reserva Douro 2005, Sogrape Vinhos S.A., Douro Red
Deep ruby in colour, with a nose of cherry and menthol. Ripe, fine-grained tannins, balanced with plenty of oak.

**Casa Ermelinda Freitas
- Aragones 2007, Casa
Ermelinda Freitas Vinhos, Lda,
Terras Do Sado** Red
Black fruit and vanilla cream on
the nose. Strong tannins, ripe
fruit, and good structure on
the palate.

**Casa Ferreirinha Quinta Da
Leda 2005, Sogrape Vinhos
S.A., Douro** Red
Pure black fruit, with some
red fruit notes. Rich, pure,
and balanced. Well-made and
seductive.

**Casa Ferreirinha Touriga
Nacional 2005, Sogrape
Vinhos S.A., Douro** Red
Ripe red fruit aromas, with
stewed strawberry fruit, firm
tannins, and a grippy finish.

**Casal Da Coelheira 2008,
Ribatejo** Red
Very youthful colour. Juicy red
berries on the palate, and sweet
spices on the finish.

**Chocapalha Reserva Red
2006, Casa Agrícola Das
Mimosas, Lda., Estremadura**
Red
Some oaky spice notes. Ripe
pruney fruit and vanilla, with
red cherry and berry fruit. Clean
with, good concentration.
C&B

**Collection 2007, Adriano
Ramos Pinto, Vinhos S.A.,
Douro** Red
Blueberry and spice on the
nose, with top quality fruit,
and chunky tannins on the
finish.

**Cortes De Cima 2006,
Alentejo** Red
Heavy tobacco and red berries
on the nose, with lots of fruit,
cocoa, and mint.

**Defesa Red 2007, Esporao
S.A., Alentejo** Red
Rich coffee and chocolate mocha
nose, with plums and violet on
the palate, rounded tannins, and
a long finish.
£9.00

**Douro DOC Altano Biológico
2007, Symington Family
Estates, Douro** Red
Big, primary black fruit aromas.
Concentrated rich fruit on
the palate, with peppery
freshness.

**Esporao Aragones 2007,
Esporao S.A., Alentejo** Red
A big wine, with floral
aromas. Full-flavoured, with
a rich body where dark
fruit, spice, and chocolate
predominate.

**Esporão Red Reserve 2006,
Alentejo** Red
Reserved nose, with dried cherry
fruit and old wood. Warm fruit
on the palate, with attractive
spice on the finish.
£14.00

**Fado 2007, Terras De Alter
Companhia De Vinhos, Lda
Alentejo** Red
Floral primary aromas, with
slick texture and soft tannins.
Blueberries and blackberries
linger.

**Fado Special Selection 2007,
Terras De Alter Companhia
De Vinhos, Lda, Alentejo** Red
Dense nose of dark fruits,
blackcurrant, and strawberry.
Savoury black fruit, with plenty
of tannins.

**Farizoa Reserva 2006,
Companhia Das Quintas -
Vinhos, S.A., Alentejo** Red
Intense nose of black cherry and
sandalwood. Sweet ripe fruit,

with a powerful grainy tannic structure, and fresh acidity.

Foral De Lisboa, Red Wine 2008, Casa Santos Lima - Companhia Das Vinhas S.A., Estremadura Red
Opaque in colour, with coffee and spice on the nose, and a mellow, plummy palate.

Fronteira 2006, Companhia Das Quintas - Vinhos, S.A., Douro Red
Very ripe, almost Porty nose of black fruit. Intense, concentrated palate, with good backbone and potential.

Grand'arte Shiraz 2007, Dfj Vinhos, Estremadura Red
Liquorice and chocolate flavours, with chewy, dense tannins. A good food wine.
£9.00

Grand'arte Tinta Roriz 2005, Dfj Vinhos, Estremadura Red
Fresh, concentrated and peppery. with elegant ripe fruit, and a good finish.
£9.00

Herdade Dos Grous 2007, Alentejo Red
Black and fruit aromas, with soft strawberry fruit character. Medium weight, with fine, tight tannins.

Herdade São Miguel, Colheita Seleccionada 2007, Casa Ag. Alexandre Relvas, Alentejo Red
Peppery damson fruit aromas, with fresh acidity and grippy tannins. A bold rustic style.
£8.00

Jp Azeitão Red NV, Bacalhôa Vinhos De Portugal, Terras Do Sado Red
Fresh red fruit, giving a light

well-balanced wine, which is rustic and food-friendly.
£5.00

Jp Private Selection 2005, Bacalhôa Vinhos De Portugal, Terras do Sado Red
Cherry red appearance, with plenty of young cherry fruit on the nose. A pleasant wine.
£7.00

Julian Reynolds 2004, Alentejo Red
Strawberry jam nose. Cool and rich red flavours on the palate, with black tannins coating the finish.
£12.00 HFB

Marco De Pegoes Red Wine 2007, Cooperativa Agricola De Santo Isidro Pegoes Crl, Terras Do Sado Red
Notes of red and black fruits, cherry, and raspberry on a floral nose. This is pleasant and fruity, with a very green backbone.

Montaria 2006, Goanvi, Lda, Alentejo Red v
Pretty red fruit, with raspberries and black cherries on the nose. Good freshness and velvety tannins, becoming chewy on the finish.

Montefino 2005, Francisco B. Fino - Sociedade Agrícola, Lda, Alentejo Red
Ripe mulberry fruit, with firm tannins. This is very ripe, but balanced by acidity, which flavours the finish.

Mouras De Arraiolos Reserva Tinto 2005, Alentejo Red
Very ripe Porty notes on the nose. Sweet and jammy, with dry tannins.

Olho De Mocho Tinto Reserva 2007, Herdade Do Rocim, Alentejo Red
Inky black fruit, with masses of

vanilla oak on the nose and palate. A baby, with supple tannins, good fruit acidity, and a long finish.

Palha - Canas, Red Wine 2007, Casa Santos Lima - Companhia Das Vinhas S.A., Estremadura Red
Subtle multi-dimensional aromas on the nose, with wonderful balance and elegance.
BWC

Palha - Canas Reserva, Red Wine 2006, Casa Santos Lima - Companhia Das Vinhas S.A., Estremadura Red
Fresh marmalade on the nose, with a palate of aromatic berries and orange zest, backed up by crisp acidity, and firm tannins.

Passadouro 2006, Douro Red
Deep in colour, with elegant spice and strawberry aromas. Multi-faceted flavours on the palate, with a long finish.
£12.00 RWD

Pena De Pato Dão Red 2006, Sogrape Vinhos S.A., Dão Red
Deep damson red, with a light, fruity, floral nose. Fruity and rich on the palate, with a long finish, and plenty of complexity.

Pinalta 2004, António Alves Ferreira, Douro Red
Tobacco and cigar box nose. Red fruit and woody cedar on a well-balanced palate.
£10.00 APW, CBW

Pintas Character Douro Red 2006, Wine&Soul, Lda, Douro Red
Nose of cranberry and dried cherry, with hints of smoke and herbs. Palate of fragant fruit, with firm structure.
£25.00 C&B

Pôpa Tr 2007, Quinta Do Pôpa, Douro Red
Nose of spicy fruit and oak. Good intensity of sweet black fruit and spice on the palate.

Quinta Da Fonte Do Ouro Reserva 2007, Sociedade Agrícola Boas Quintas Lda, Dão Red
Plummy intensity, with floral perfume on the nose, and blueberry fruit on a palate, which shows balanced acidity.

Quinta Da Lagoalva 2007, Ribatejo Red
A smoky nose, with clean ripe cherries, good tannins, and a soft finish, with some length.
£11.00

Quinta Da Terrugem 2006, Alianca, Alentejo Red
Engaging nose, of blackberry, yellow plum, and raisin, with a good mellow finish to the palate.
£14.60

Quinta Das Setencostas, Red Wine 2007, Casa Santos Lima - Companhia Das Vinhas S.A. Estremadura Red
Spicy and juicy fruit aromas, with silky tannins. Well-balanced, with a long, spicy finish.
ODD

Quinta De Chocapalha Red 2006, Casa Agricola Das Mimosas, Lda., Alentejo Red
Red fruit, with some spice and smoke notes. Floral character, with good freshness and structure.
£9.00 C&B

Quinta De Fafide Reserva 2006, Douro Red
Ripe blackcurrant nose, with a fine concentrated palate of cedar and well-defined fruit, gathering

complexity, with fine tannins and integrated oak.
£10.00 M&S

Quinta De Roriz Reserva Douro Red 2004, Douro Red
Spicy fruit, with a firm grip, and drying edge. Good tannins, with a long finish.

Quinta Do Cardo 2006, Companhia Das Quintas - Vinhos, S.a., Beiras Red
Fresh red fruit on the nose. Palate is clean and classic, with good structure, and perfect proportions.

Quinta Do Cardo Reserva 2006, Companhia Das Quintas - Vinhos, S.A., Beiras Red
Clean and linear. Perfect balance of fresh fruit and fine, grippy tannins.

Quinta Do Cardo Selecção Do Enólogo 2005, Companhia Das Quintas - Vinhos, S.A. Red
Simple, fresh, with some fragrant violet notes. Well-balanced and attractive.

Quinta Do Carmo Red 2004, Bacalhôa Vinhos De Portugal, Alentejo Red
Savoury, chewy dried fruit, with a slight bretty character adding complexity. Attractive, with a pleasant tannic structure.
£10.50

Quinta Do Francês Odelouca River Valley 2006, Patrick Agostini,lda, Algarve Red
Ruby colour, with firm tannins, and an interesting finish.

Quinta Do Infantado Reserva Douro 2007, Douro Red
Ripe cherry notes, with a grippy tannic finish. Dense palate, where the tannins remain in control.
£25.00 LIB

Quinta Do Vallado Reserva 2007, Douro Red
Some lifted marzipan notes, with bright strawberry and raspberry on the palate. Sweet oak structure, with great depth.
£37.50 BWL

Quinta Dos Avidagos Reserva 2006, Douro Red
Spicy eucalyptus nose, with cocoa and lots of oak. Intense black fruit, with nice freshness.

Quinta Dos Carvalhais Alfrocheiro 2003, Sogrape Vinhos S.A., Dão Red
Medium damson red in appearance, with an appealing cherry fruit nose. Delicious palate, with a medium-length finish, and decent acidity.

Quinta Dos Carvalhais Reserva 2002, Sogrape Vinhos S.A., Dão Red
Plummy, cherry nose, with a sweet, chocolatey structure, and a light, elegant taste.

Quinta Dos Carvalhais Touriga Nacional 2004, Sogrape Vinhos S.A., Dão Red
Good concentration of dark fruit, with some freshness, and grip. Tannins are a bit drying, but pleasant.

Quinta Dos Carvalhais Único 2005, Sogrape Vinhos S.A., Dão Red
Intense dark baked fruit, with mineral and spice. Firm, meaty palate with complex tobacco notes.

Quinta Dos Quatro Ventos 2006, Alianca, Douro Red
Sweet raspberry fruit on the nose, with slightly dusty vanilla oak, and ripe fruit on the palate.
£14.60

Quinta Dos Roques 2006, Dão Red

Clean, pure nose, with a palate that shows elegance and structure, with dry tannins, good weight, and a long chocolatey finish."

£10.00

Quinta Dos Termos Escolha Virgílio Loureiro 2006, Beiras Red

Clean, peppery, ripe fruit, which is concentrated, savoury, warm, and long. Complex.

Quinta Nova Nª Srª Do Carmo 2007, Quinta Nova Nª Srª Do Carmo, Douro Red

Warm poached fruit flavours, with notes of damson, and soft tannins.

Romeira Reserva 2005, Enoport, Terras do Sado Red

Strong, dark plum nose, with dry tannins leading to a sweet finish.

S. Miguel Das Missoes, Reserva 2007, Casa Ag. Alexandre Relvas Lda, Alentejo Red

Generous, simple, and ripe, with a savoury nose of blackberry. A sweet finish, with medium tannins, and slightly dark wood.

Sainsburys Taste The Difference Douro Red 2007, Quinta Do Crasto, Douro Red

Palate of tannic black fruit, with spice and attractive depth.

£7.90 SAIN

Só Touriga Nacional 2006, Bacalhôa Vinhos De Portugal Terras Do Sado Red

Fresh red fruit and vanilla oak on the nose. Soft, spicy palate of ripe red fruit and chocolatey oak.

£15.00

Solar dos Lobos Regional Tinto 2006, Silveira e Outro, Lda, Alentejo Red

Warm spice and red fruit on the nose, and a stewed fruit palate, with balanced acidity.

Tagus Creek Cabernet Sauvignon/Aragonês NV, Falua - Sociedade De Vinhos S.A., Ribatejo Red

Beaujolais-like nose, with a palate full of savoury, spicy fruit. Soft tannins on a peppery finish.

£6.00 WAIT, NND

Tagus Creek Reserve 2007, Falua - Sociedade De Vinhos Sa, Ribatejo Red

Tannins are in the driving seat here, with gentle fruit, and a firm finish.

£7.00 MRN

Tagus Creek Shiraz/ Trincadeira 2008, Falua - Sociedade De Vinhos Sa, Alentejo Red

Rich, brambly, spicy, and fruit-forward. Lovely balance of fruit, oak, tannins, and acidity, with a long finish.

£5.90 TESC, BTH, MRN, MWW

Tagus Ridge Reserve 2007, Falua - Sociedade De Vinhos S.A., Ribatejo Red

Clean and well-made. Some spice, toast, and dark fruit, with summer fruits apparent on the palate. Showing individuality.

£8.00 THS

Terras D'alter Alicante Bouschet 2007, Alentejo Red

Complex, spicy red fruit aromas, with a bright, solid core of fruit, underpinned by firm tannins.

Tinto Da Ânfora Grande Escolha 2006, Bacalhôa Vinhos De Portugal, Alentejo Red

Good fruit, with excellent berry and cassis aromas. An elegant palate, with lingering soft tannins, and an excellent finish. £16.00

Vale D'algares Syrah/ Viognier Red NV, Quatro Âncoras,lda, Ribatejo Red
Big and bold, with coffee richness and high toast notes. Powerful tannins.

Vale De Nabais Reserva 2007, Quinta Da Alorna, Ribatejo Red
A hint of cough mixture on the nose, with ripe fruit, and Cabernet tannins. Soft and round.

Vale Perdido, Red Wine 2008, Casa Santos Lima - Companhia Das Vinhas Sa Estremadura Red
Soft red fruit on the nose, with hints of cloves and cinnamon. Well-made, with a soft, rounded body.
LAI

Varas, Red Wine 2008, Casa Santos Lima - Companhia Das Vinhas S.A., Estremadura Red
Mellow and rounded, with soft plum and brambly fruit character on the palate.

Versus 2006, Oscar De Almeida Lda, Beiras Red
Red berry nose, with a touch of spice. Refined tannins, refreshing acidity, and good length.

Vinhas Da Ira 2005, Henrique Uva/Herdade Da Mingorra Red
Deep raspberry in colour, with a young, light, fruity nose of attractive cherry fruit. Youthful style.

3 Pomares Rose 2008, Quinta Nova Nª Srª Do Carmo, Douro Rosé
Quite concentrated berry nose, leading to a ripe strawberry and floral palate. Intense, slightly bitter finish.

Adegaborba.pt 2008, Adega Cooperativa De Borba, Alentejo Rosé
Vibrant, with a restrained minerally character. Lovely balance of bright strawberry fruit, and a gentle sweetness.

Amoras, Rosé Wine 2008, Casa Santos Lima - Companhia Das Vinhas S.A., Estremadura Rosé
A big full mouthful of juicy fruit. Well-balanced.
LAI

Bons - Ventos, Rosé Wine 2008, Casa Santos Lima - Companhia Das Vinhas S.A., Estremadura Rosé
Bubblegum and berry notes. Good acidic balance. Citrus notes on a long, refreshing finish.

Dona Helena Rosé 2008, Coop. Santo Isidro De Pegões (wines & Winemakers By Saven), Terras Do Sado Rosé
A light sensation of cherry on the nose. Juicy Genever jam fruits. A user-friendly wine, with soft fruit and a hint of tannins coming through.

Pink Elephant Rose 2008, D F J Vinhos, Estremadura Rosé
Attractive, pale cherry colour, aromas of with bright cherry fruit, and cool ferment characteristics. Nearly dry, with flavours of wild strawberries, this is crisp, with a touch of tannic grip, and a savoury finish.
£5.60 ASDA, SAIN, TESC, MRN, WRC

Stella Rosado Rosé Wine 2008, Cooperativa Agricola De Santo Isidro De Pegoes Crl, Terras Do Sado Rosé
Watery pale pink, with a fading

rim. Light, delicate fruity nose. Medium-sweet, with lovely, clean fruit.

Vida Nova Rosé 2008, Vida Nova Rosé
Very nice nose, with some passion fruit, grapefruit, and bitter cherry notes. Good acidity and length. Quaffable and refreshing.

10 Year Old Sercial NV, Henriques & Henriques, Madeira Madeira
Golden amber in colour. Nutty, dark, tangy nose, with nuts and dried apricots on the palate.
£15.50 WTSF&M, MWW, WIM

15 Year Old Verdelho NV, Henriques & Henriques, Madeira Madeira
Warm, tangy nose of fruitcake, coffee, and walnut. Full, sweet palate with a clean finish.
£19.70 WAIT, SMP

Blandy's 15 YO Malmsey NV, Madeira Wine Company Madeira Madeira
Amber brown in colour, with notes of lifted malt and iced coffee. Hints of fresh caramel, marmalade, nutmeg, and almond. Elegant.
£18.00 WAIT

Blandy's 5 YO Alvada NV, Madeira Wine Company, Madeira Madeira
Medium amber in colour, with a full, rich nose. Excellent balance.
£12.50 WAIT

Blandy's 5 YO Malmsey NV, Madeira Wine Company, Madeira Madeira
Amber brown, with a slightly green hue. Aloe, fresh light tea, and a hint of oil, with caramel malt.

Boal Old Reserve 10 Year Old NV, Vinhos Barbeito Madeira Lda., Madeira Madeira
Nose of figs, sweet dried fruit, honey, and treacle. Sweet palate of spice, with a hint of coffee.
£25.00 REY

30 Years NV, Adriano Ramos Pinto, Vinhos S.A., Douro Port
Amber in colour. Lifted caramel and honey on the nose. Notes of fresh cloves and nutmeg. Complex.
MMD

Colheita Port 2000, Quinta Do Portal, Douro Port
Dried fruit and citrus notes, on this medium bodied wine, with a long apricot finish. Well-balanced and elegant.
CHH, GWW, VLW

Croft Quinta Da Roeda 1997, Douro Port
A nose of cloves, cedar, and blackberry, with a rich texture, and good chocolate acidity.
£19.00 FWL, MWW, NYW, SEL, THS

Croft Triple Crown NV, Douro Port
Deep garnet colour, with fresh damson on the nose, and a long lively finish.
£9.00 MRN, MWW, N&P, NYW

Dow's Crusted 2003, Symington Family Estates, Douro Port
Dried leaves, and a jammy structure with a tannic, earthy finish.

Fonseca Guimaraens 1996, Douro Port
Showing nice evolution, with fresh fruit and spice. Well-balanced, with soft tannins and a pleasant finish.
£24.30 WAIT, F&M, THS

Graham's 10 Year Old NV, Symington Family Estates, Douro Port
Pale strawberry brown colour; clean, ripe, and sweet, with fresh fruit.

Late Bottled Vintage 2003, Quinta Do Portal, Douro Port
Full ruby colour, with a rich herbal and blackcurrant nose, and a ripe, juicy flavour.
£15.90 CSS, ESL, GWW, VLW,

Marks & Spencer 20 Year Old Tawny Port NV, Douro Port
Spicy caramel, and hints of old wood. Full of good tannins on the finish, with a lovely toffee character.
£30.00 M&S

Marks & Spencer LBV Port 2003, Taylor's, Douro Port
Fresh berry and black cherry fruit. Medium weight, with good spice, and a medium-length finish.
£11.00 M&S

Mhv Regimental Ruby Port NV, Sandeman, Douro Port
Bright ruby colour, with fresh red cherry fruit, and a clean, simple structure.
£7.60 MHV

Offley 20 Years Old Tawny NV, Sogrape Vinhos S.a., Douro Port
Intense, complex, and nutty, well-balanced, with a good body. A long finish of dried fruits.

Offley 30 Years Old NV, Sogrape Vinhos S.A., Douro Port
Lovely amber colour. Intense nose of marmalade and orange peel, with some cedar aromas. Elegant and persistent on the palate.

Poças LBV Late Bottled Vintage Porto 2003, Manoel

D Poças Junior - Vinhos S.A., Douro Port
Lifted rhubarb and white pepper, with fresh blackberry and ripe plum, some mint. and a tea-leaf finish.
HOT

Porto Cruz Late Bottled Vintage 2001, Gran-cruz Porto Soc.com.vinhos, Lda, Douro Port
Medium intensity, with bright fruits, good body, and soft structure. The finish is elegant and intensely fruity.

Sandeman Late Bottled Vintage 2004, Sogrape Vinhos S.A., Douro Port
Bright ruby colour, with a nose of lifted blackberry, and hints of cloves and nutmeg.

Taylor's 10 Year Old Tawny NV, Douro Port
Pure nose, leading to a balanced palate of fresh fig, with a hint of red berry on the finish.
£17.40 FLA, ASDA, SAIN, TESC, MWW, SEL, SMF, THS

Taylor's Late Bottle Vintage 2003, Douro Port
Lifted raspberries, with some pepper, and a note of soy on the finish. Medium body and texture.
£12.40 FLA, ASDA, SAIN, TESC, WAIT, MRN, MWW, ODD

Vista Alegre Vintage Port 2006, Vallegre, Vinhos Do Porto S.A., Douro Port
Youthful, with an attractive touch of greenness. Vigorous, and still very young, but destined for a long future.

Secret Spot NV, Gr Consultores, Douro Fortified
Lovely topaz colour. Delicate and sweet, with a fresh, clean nose. Long finish.

Sake

Sake is to the Japanese what wine is to the French or Italians. It is rich in their culture and enjoyed with national cuisine. Dating back as far as the third century, the art of sake making has withstood the test of time and popularity has begun to grow overseas for this fascinating drink. Like grapes, the end product depends on the quality of rice grown and the type of water used for brewing plays a vital role also. The 'Kuramotos' (sake brewers) define the style of sake produced by determining how much of a 'polish' to give the grains of rice and whether to add alcohol or not. Sake enjoyed its most successful year to date with an impressive eighteen Golds. Try these sakes straight from the fridge or gently heat at your leisure and prepare to be astounded.

2009 IWC PERFORMANCE

Trophies	12
Gold	18
Silver	42
Bronze	79
Great Value Awards	1

GINJO-SHU, DAIGINJO-SHU

GOLD

Mifuku Shuzo Co Ltd, Mifuku Daigin Gokujo 2008

Packed full of melon and citrus flavours on the palate and on the nose, with a beautifully focused, integrated acidity. Excellent quality.

 GINJO, DAIGINJO TROPHY

Nemoto Shuzo Co Ltd, Daiginjo Kujinoyama 2008

A sake with a pleasingly fragrant perfumed, tropical nose. It has great length, and a complex, tender, wonderfully satisfying bitterness.

 DAIGINJO MIE REGIONAL TROPHY

Shimizu Jozo Co, Zaku Daiginjo 2008

This is a really superb sake and a great example of daiginjo. Rich and intense, with layers of flavours, including tropical fruits such as lychee and guava.

SILVER

Daishinsyu Breweries Inc, Kozuki Hiden Daiginjo 2007

Very elegant, fruity, and rich, with a youthful, lively fruitiness on the finish.

Inoue Seikichi Co Ltd, Sawahime Daiginjo 2008

A fine sake, with lovely purity, freshness, intensity, and complexity. The palate is rich, with layers of attractive flavour.

Kamotsuru Sake Brewing Co Ltd, Daiginjo Kamotsuru Soukaku 2008

Fragrant, subtle floral notes on the nose, this is fruity, with a hint of mushroom. Very smooth.

Kubota Shuzo Co Ltd, Kinsho Hishimasamune Daiginjo 2007

Fragrant, soft, textured, and mild, with notes of rice powder and banana. Good flavour, with a spicy aftertaste.

Nambu Shuzo Co Ltd, Hanagaki Chotokusen Daiginjo 2008

Focused, with incredible intensity. This is a really complex sake, which is superbly balanced and elegant on the palate.

Sakuramasamune Co Ltd, Daiginjo Ohkaichirin 2008

Fine sake with lovely purity and notes of green spice, and a very special, lovely intensity.

Senjyo Co Ltd, Kuromatsu Senjyo Daiginjo Matsujiro 2008

Lots of expression. This is very focused, intense, and complex, with clean fruit and a nice rice quality.

Toyokuni Shuzo Co Ltd, Ginjo Sinjitu 2008

A youthful but delicate sake, with fine fruitiness on the palate. Quite focused.

Umeda Shuzojo & Co, Honshu-ichi Daiginjo 50% Seihaku 2007

Wonderful freshness! Vibrant and fantastically youthful, with notes of peaches, pears, and lemon zest. Complex and smooth.

BRONZE

Aiyu Shuzo Co Ltd, Aiyu Daiginjo 2008

A fine balance of aromas, with

notes of delicate soft melon. Smooth.

Akita Seishu Co Ltd, Kariho Kohun 2009
Fresh and fruity, with notes of rice, in a clean, commercial style. Very soft.

Dewazakura Shuzo Co Ltd, Dewazakura Daiginjo 2008
Fragrant, with notes of citrus and apple, and intense alcohol power.

Dewazakura Shuzo Co Ltd, Dewazakura Oka Yamadanishiki 2008
Fragrant, focused sake, with delicious apple notes, and an attractive leafy quality.

Hikami Seishu Co Ltd, Hikami Daiginjo Tamahagane Tobingakoi 2008
Notes of soft rice cake, with a nice, subtle fruitiness.

Ichishima Sake Brewery Inc, Ichishima Ginnoyorokobi Daiginjo 2007
Initially sweet impression, with youthful, focused, intense, mineral fruit. Soft and elegant.

Kamotsuru Sake Brewing Co Ltd, Gold Kamotsuru Excellent 2008
A little bit of gentle sweetness, and some nice marshmallow flavours.

Kitagawahonke Co Ltd, Tomio Yamadanishiki 2007
Pronounced umami taste. Modest, subtle aromas. Well-integrated bitterness.

Miyamoto Shuzoten Co Ltd, Mujou Daiginjo Shizuku 2008
An understated style. Wet stone notes, with hints of mineral herb, yet still fruity.

Miyasaka Brewing Company Ltd, Masumi Yumedono 2006
Vibrant and zesty, with some citrus and fruit salad flavours. Clean.

Momokawa Brewing Inc, Momokawa Daiginjo Sake 2008
Smooth, soft, and elegant, with hints of rice powder, and subtle fruity notes.

Murashige Sake Brewing Co Ltd, Kinkan Kuromatsu Daiginjo Nishiki 2009
Fine example of junmai daigonji-shu, with softness and lovely freshness.

Musashino Shuzo Co Ltd, Kasugayama Tentochi 2008
Fantastic intensity, with lovely purity and tropical notes. Floral and balanced.

Nagai Sake Inc, Mizubasho Daiginjo-shu 2007
Mellow and tender, with crisp peach on the palate.

Nagai Sake Inc, Mizubasho Ginjo-shu 2007
Concentrated fruit. Salty, with lovely minerality, and nice purity on the palate.

National Trading Inc. Kimura Brewery, Daiginjo Fukukomachi 2009
Lovely elegance. Round and fruity, with marshmallow character. Smooth.

Ninki Inc, Ninki-ichi Daiginjo-shu 2008
Rich, classic sake, with a nice full body. Complex.

Otani Shuzo Co Ltd, Izumotoji Sakamoto 2007
Shows impressive intensity for 2007. Vibrant, zippy, and zesty; impressive.

Saito Shuzo Co Ltd, Eikun 'iwai 35' Daiginjo-shu 2008
Good quality sake; this is both full and rich.

Saiyashuzoten Co Ltd, Daiginjo Yukinobosha 2008
Fantastic intensity, with nice fruit. Simple, but rich and full-bodied.

Saura Co Ltd, Daiginjo Urakasumi 2007
Note of boiled sweets, with lovely intensity. Vibrant and fresh.

Shindo Sake Brewery Co Ltd, Gasanryu 'kisaragi' 2008
A good, sound example of its type. Very nicely balanced.

Takara Shuzo Co Ltd Shirakabegura, Shoutikubai Daiginjo Muroka Genshu 2008
This has a strong koji (fungus) character. Soft and intense, with a hint of bitterness.

HONJOZO-SHU

 HONJOZO OKAYAMA REGIONAL TROPHY

Kamikokoro Shuzo Co Ltd, Kamikokoro Hihou Honjozo 2008
Beautifully made sake. This is quite well-balanced and elegant, with a sense of umami. Really smooth, with great length.

 HONJOZO TROPHY

Shindo Sake Brewery Co Ltd, Ura Gasanryu 'koka' 2008
Fresh, fruity, and crisp; this is a delicate and fruity honjozo. Full of passion fruit, with a touch of sweetness on palate, and superbly integrated acidity: a lovely expression of honjozo at its best!

Endo Brewery Co, Asashibori Shuppinchozou-shu 2008
Traditional sweet notes on the palate, plus blossom aromas. This can be served at warm temperatures.

Yanagisawa Shuzo Co Ltd, Katsuragawa Honjozo 2008
Exotic and juicy, with a touch of yoghurt, this has real complexity, with super weight. A very nice sake.

Kaetsu Sake Brewery Co Ltd, Kisshozan Senjuhou 2009
Made in a correct, honjozo style: this is fresh, rich, long, and elegant.

Miyasaka Brewing Co Ltd, Tokusen Masumi 2007
Strong, classic, full-bodied honjozo. Well-balanced and youthful.

Musashino Shuzo Co Ltd, Ski-masamune Nyukon 2008
Youthful, with elegant umami, character, and syrup-like cleaned rice aromas.

Nakao Sake Brewery Co Ltd, Seikyo Choukarakuchi 2008
Elegant, with nice, light, smooth texture. Zesty fruit and acidity, with good intensity.

S. Imanishi Co Ltd, Harushika Gokumi 2009
Well-made and correct, with a fresh nose and complex palate.

Sakuramasamune Co Ltd, Honjozo Shumare 2008
Tender, crisp, and spicy, with a strong rice flavour, and salty finish. Elegant.

Umeda Shuzojo & Co, Honshu-ichi Muroka Honjozo 2008
Delicate, with peach and apple fruit, and hints of spice. Showing minerality, ginger, and fresh flowers, with a slight zest. A fine example, with a long finish.

Yamamotohonke Co Ltd, Tokusen Tessai 2008
Full, strong, and smooth-textured. Notes of rice cake, with a touch of salt, and honey purity. Complex.

JUNMAI GINJO-SHU, JUNMAI DAIGINJO-SHU

Bizen Shuzo Honten, Junmai Daiginjo Akita Bizen 2009
Sublime intensity of stone fruit, gooseberry, and a touch of honey, with dried herb. This is a superb sake: smooth, and full of balance and harmony.

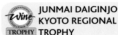
JUNMAI GINJO, JUNMAI DAIGINJO TROPHY

Kodama Brewing Co Ltd, Taiheizan Junmai Daiginjo Tenko 2008
This has really beautiful, intense flavours. Rich, well-balanced, and harmonious, with mineral ity, and real purity of fruit.

Masuda Sake Company, Masuizumi Junmai Daiginjo 2008
Wonderfully tender and elegant, with beautiful texture. This has sublime umami, underpinned by a gentle, subtle fruitiness.

Onuma Shuzoten Co Ltd, Kenkonichi Junmai Daiginjo NV
Very restrained, in an extremely attractive mineral style. Very complex on both nose and palate. A very good, top quality sake.

S. Imanishi Co Ltd, Harushika Kioke Sake 2009
Wonderfully fragrant sake, with plenty of fruitiness, and floral, melon, citrus, and apple notes. Smooth mouthfeel; rich, and fabulously powerful.

JUNMAI DAIGINJO KYOTO REGIONAL TROPHY

Sasaki Shuzo Co Ltd, Jurakudai Junmai Daiginjo-shu 2008
Tremendously soft, this superb sake has a wonderfully appealing creaminess, and a sense of pure, tender peach, and an exotic feel.

JUNMAI DAIGINJO YAMAGATA REGIONAL TROPHY

Takenotsuyu Sake Brewery Co Ltd, Takenotsuyu Junmai Daiginjo Hakurosuishu 2008
Exceptionally well-balanced between fruitiness and minerality. This is extremely pure, but full-flavoured and textured. Beautiful!
£65.00 TZK

JUNMAI DAIGINJO MIYAGI REGIONAL TROPHY

Uchigasaki Shuzouten Ltd, Junmai Daiginjo Hoyo 2008
Superbly well-balanced sake, with a flavours which are

modest and soft, but also focused and rich, with a real feeling of complexity. Superb!

Daishinsyu Breweries Inc, Daishinsyu Teippai 2007
Gently fragrant, with delicious apple and pear, and beautiful steamed rice notes. Initially sweet, it is elegant, fine, pure, and tender.

Dewazakura Shuzo Co Ltd, Dewazakura Aiyama 2007
Intense fruitiness. There is plenty of delicious apple, which is highly refreshing, but there is also a touch of sweetness.

Dewazakura Shuzo Co Ltd, Dewazakura Omachi 2008
A super-styled and elegantly brewed sake, which is brilliant, fragrant, and well-balanced on the palate.

Isojiman Premium Sake Brewery Co Ltd, Isojiman Daiginjo Junmai 50 2008
With very full texture on the palate, this is a very rich, fine sake, with superb purity.

Katoukichibee Shouten, Born: Tokusen Junmai Daiginjo 2007
Strong rice cake flavours, with a bright fruitiness. Mild on the palate, with integrated acidity, juicy freshness, and nice balance.

Komachi Shuzo Co Ltd, Nagaragawa Junmai Ginjo Tenkawa 2008
Wonderful! Tender, with great length, and extremely good balance. Very intense, with tropical notes. Impressive.

Marumoto Sake Brewery Co Ltd, Chikurin Taoyaka (elegance) 2008
A sake of incredible power, with an intense bouquet, and clean, pure rice on the palate. Sublime.
TZK

Onuma Shuzoten Co Ltd, Kenkonichi Chokarakuchi Junmai Ginjo NV
A wonderfully intense sake, with cassis, guava, and some minerality. Smooth, soft, balanced, and textured.

Saito Shuzo Co Ltd, Eikun 'ichigin' Junmai Daiginjo-shu 2008
Showing plenty of fruit and a lasting intensity, but also soft, gentle, and elegant.

Saiyashuzoten Co Ltd, Hidenyamahai Yukinobosha 2008
Sublime umami on the palate, backed up with a modest fruitiness, and a soft, tender texture. Nice balance.

Saura Co Ltd, Yamadanishiki Junmai Daiginjo Urakasumi 2007
Fragrant, with plenty of fruitiness, and melon, citrus, and floral notes

Shimizu Jozo Co, Zaku Miyabi-no-tomo Nakadori 2008
Superbly fragrant, with a smooth fruity palate, and great length. Nice round texture, with a special, complex spiciness.

Takahashi Sukesaku Shuzoten Co Ltd, Matsuwo Junmai Daiginjoby 2006
Super-soft texture, with a lovely smooth mouthfeel, and subtle notes of banana Long, elegant, and balanced.

Watanabe Shuzoten, Nechi Junmai Ginjo-shu 2007
Soft, round, and elegant, with powdery rice notes.

Aiyu Shuzo Co Ltd, Tomoju Junmai Ginjo 2008
Full palate. Powerful and rich, with umami, and wonderful pear flavours.

Akita Seishu Co Ltd, Dewatsuru Hihaku 2009
Crisp and focused, with exotic fruit notes, and a smooth finish.

Akita Seishu Co Ltd, Yamatoshizuku Junmai Ginjo 2009
Strong, ripe notes. Clean and fresh, with some weight and length.

Aramasa Shuzo Co Ltd, Junmai Daiginjo Sato Uhee Sake-komachi 2009
With ripe fruit qualities, this is a commercial style, with impressive freshness.

Asahara Shuzo Co Ltd, Biwano Sazanami Junmai Daiginjo-shu 2008
Elegant, refreshing, super-soft, and tender, with notes of rice powder. Smooth.

Asahi Shuzo Co Ltd, Dassai Junmai Daiginjo-shu Migaki 3 Wari 9 Bu 2008
Nicely smooth and crisp, with herbal hints and banana notes. Round and soft.
TZK

Chiyokotobuki Toraya Co Ltd, Toranoko 2008
Lovely, elegant bouquet, with pears and spice on the palate. Will improve with time.

Daishinsyu Breweries Inc, Daishinsyu Betsukakoi Junmai Daiginjo 2007
Intense but soft, with a touch of sweet mint. Lovely, crisp, and full, with a soft texture.

Hakutsuru Sake Brewing Co Ltd, Hakutsuru Premium Junmai Daiginjo Yamada Ho 2008
Modest, fruity, and fragrant on the palate, with good length. Light style.

Katoukichibee Shouten, Born: Dreams Come True 2004
Nice, fragrant sake, with notes of melon and apples.

Katoukichibee Shouten, Born: Tokishirazu 2003
Pleasant sake, with a nice, round style. Creamy.

Katoukichibee Shouten, Born: Wing Of Japan 2007
Very good. It is fruity, but with a satisfying herbal hint. Wonderfully smooth and long.

Miyamoto Shuzoten Co Ltd, Mujou Junmai Daiginjo Gold 2008
Soft and juicy, with modest, integrated acidity, and wet stone minerality.

Miyasaka Brewing Co Ltd, Masumi Junmai Yumedono 2009
Pure rice aromas. Well-balanced, with good concentration. A smooth, beautifully rich sake.

Morikawa Shuzo Co Ltd, Hakuko Junmai Daiginjo Sarasouju 2007
A lovely example of aged junmai-daiginjo. Still fresh, but with a touch of wood spice and

dried fruit, indicating evolution. A nice sake.

Nagayamahonke Shuzojo Co Ltd, Yamahai Junmai Daiginjo Taka 2007
Focused and still fresh, with zesty citrus notes, and salty complexity. A nice sake, with super length.

Ninki Inc, Ninki-ichi Kuroninki Junmai Ginjo-shu 2008
Full and strong, with a vegetable character, but also nice and soft.

Rihaku Shuzo Co Ltd, Rihaku Junmai Daiginjo 2007
Intense rice note. Focused, but still holding up well. A solid sake.

Sakuramasamune Co Ltd, Kinmare Muroka Junmai Daiginjo Sango 2008
Nicely balanced umami, with rice, fruits, and good acidity.

Shindo Sake Brewery Co Ltd, Ura Gasanryu 'gekka' 2008
This has just a suggestion of bitterness, but it is elegant, with notes of pear and banana.

Sohomare Sake Brewery Co Ltd, Sohomare Kimoto Shikomi Junmai Daiginjo 2006
Prominent herbal notes, but pure and complex, with nice length.

Tamanohikari Sake Brewing Co Ltd, Tamanohikari Junmai Daiginjo Yamahai Yamadanishiki 100% 2007
Understated style, with good junmai spiciness.

Tamanohikari Sake Brewing Co Ltd, Tamanohikari Junmai Ginjo Yamahai 2007
Soft impression, wonderful steamed rice character, with mineral length, and good balance.

Umeda Shuzojo & Co, Honshu-ichi Junmai Ginjo Genshu 2007
Fragrant and focused, with plenty of fruitiness.

Umeda Shuzojo & Co, Honshu-ichi Muroka Junmai Ginjo-shu 2008
Fruity, fragrant style, with bright, pure minerality. Good.

Umeichirin Sake Brewing Co Ltd, Junmai Daiginjo Umeichirin 2008
Spicy, with modest fruitiness, notes of soft marshmallow, and an appley finish.

Yamamotohonke Co Ltd, Tokusen Matsunomidori Junmai Daiginjo 2008
Pure and soft, with notes of baby powder. Smooth on the palate.

JUNMAI-SHU

 JUNMAI TROPHY

Yoshida Sake Brewery Co Ltd, Yamahaishikomi Junmai-shu Tedorigawa 2008
Superb sake, with a beautifully soft, textured palate. Naturally smooth and full of flavour, with a defined, elegant finish. Really top quality.

Gassan Sake Brewery Co Ltd, Ginrei Gassan Junmai Genshu 2008
A really elegant sake. Such finesse and purity, with wonderful complex length. Balanced and spicy.

Kurosawa Sake Brewery Co Ltd, Kurosawa Junmai Kimoto 2007

Very full and intense, in what might be called a "super junmai" style.
TZK

Ono Shuzo Co Ltd, Oigame Koshihikari Junmai 2008

Rich and full-flavoured, with umami to the fore, this shows some signs of development, with a mineral kick, and integrated acidity.

Saiyashuzoten Co Ltd, Yamahai Junmai Yukinobosha 2009

Really quite soft with elegant notes of powdered rice and fragrant fruits. Very smooth.

Shindo Sake Brewery Co Ltd, Ura Gasanryu 'fuka' 2008

Extremely soft and smooth on the palate, this is gorgeously silky and textured. A very luxurious, well-made sake.

Tanakaya Brewing Co Ltd, Mizuo Tokubetsu Junmai-shu Kinmonnishiki Shikomi 2008

Elegant, intense, and full-bodied, the palate is sweet and round, with a pronounced fennel note. Very well-balanced.

Umeda Shuzojo & Co, Honshu-ichi Junmai-shu 2008

A youthful sake, with a slightly bitter hint of freshness. Balanced and well-made, with good concentration. Good.

Yonetsuru Sake Brewery Co Ltd, Yonetsuru Komeno Chikara Kameno O 2007

Extremely elegant, with nice smooth texture on the palate, really great intensity, and some very pale tropical fruit notes.

Akita Seishu Co Ltd, Dewatsuru Matsukura 2009

Fruity, fine, and really flavoursome; a super sake!

Daishinsyu Breweries Inc, Daishinsyu Nagano Appellation Control 2007

A very nice example of the junmai style. Tender, soft, and long.

Ichishima Sake Brewery Inc, Ichishima Junmai Genshu 2008

A pure, fresh, and zesty sake, with a really rich, balanced palate.

Kinshihai Sake Brewery Inc, Yukikage Tokubetsu Junmai 2008

Showing a little development on a mature, balanced, intense palate.

Komachi Shuzo Co Ltd, Nagaragawa Junmai-shu 2008

Herbal hints on the palate. Elegant and balanced, with a rich finish.

Nakao Sake Brewery Co Ltd, Seikyo Junmai Maboroshi 2008

Modest aromas of the junmai style, with notes of steamed rice. Well-balanced.

Nakao Sake Brewery Co Ltd, Seikyo Junmai Takehara 2008

Very intense nose of rain drops, with a fresh, zesty, mineral palate.

Otokoyama Honten Co Ltd, Soutenden Junmai Ginjo-shu 2008

Soft and delicate with a herbal hint. Full-flavoured, with a tender finish.

Sake is brewed with rice, water, and sophisticated and delicate techniques. Sake is born and grows in the changing four seasons of Japan. Surely, it is the fruit of blessing from rich Japanese nature and Japanese wisdom, and is a cultural asset and the pride of Japanese people.

The Sake Samurai Association was established in 2005 as an officially recognized organization of the Japan Sake Brewers Association, and carries out many projects to send messages on sake and sake culture both inside and outside Japan. In particular,

we confer the title of "Sake Samurai" on several people who love sake and sake culture and have a prominent influence in proliferating its splendor, showing our respect for them.

Moreover, since 2007, we have been cooperating with the International Wine Challenge (IWC) as an official coordinator for the sake category at IWC, and dealing with various tasks on preparing for the sake category, for example, to invite participants to enter in the competition and recommend some judges from Japan.

In addition, we do various activities to inform of wonderful and tasty sake to the world through various opportunities at sake seminars, Kuramoto Dinner, and so on.

✉ For further information and inquiry, please contact:
Sake Samurai Secretariat c/o
The Japan Sake Brewers Association Junior Council
1-1-21 West Shimbashi, Minato Ward, Tokyo, JAPAN 105-0003
TEL 03-3501-0101 FAX 03-3501-6018
E-mail info@sakesamurai.jp

Otokoyama Honten Co Ltd, Soutenden Tokubetsu Junmaishu 2008
A modest sake, with notes of herbs and steamed rice. Dry, with integrated acidity underpinning the smooth texture.

Shinozaki Co Ltd, Kunigiku Junmai-shu 2008
An intense nose, with a lovely, sweet palate, and full body. Good.

Takara Shuzo Co Ltd Shirakabegura, Shoutikubai Shirakabekura Kimoto Junmai 2008
A well put-together sake, with a sweet, balanced palate. Good.

Tonoike Shuzoten Co Ltd, Sanran Junmai-shu 2008
Produced in the typical junmai style; a nice, well-made sake.

Uehara Shuzo Co Ltd, Echigotsurukame Junmai 2008
Produced in a typical junmai style; a distinctively fresh, balanced sake.

Umeichirin Sake Brewing Co Ltd, Junmai-shu Umeichirin 2008
Ethereal, light, and delicate; this is textbook light style junmai sake.

Utsunomiya Shuzo Co Ltd, Shikisakura Junmai-shu 2008
Produced in the typical junmai style, this is a modest, humble sake.

Watanabe Shuzo Co Ltd, Tamaka Tokubetsu Junmai-shu 2008
Produced in a very soft and elegant style. Good quality.

Yoshinogawa Co Ltd, Settaya 2007
Fresh, crisp, and balanced, with a good rice character, and a long finish.

KOSHU

 **KOSHU NARA REGIONAL TROPHY**

Choryo Shuzo Co Ltd, Tsukihi Kasanete 1992
Extraordinarily complex sake, with notes of cloves, star anis, steamed rice, and nuts combining on the palate, and leading to a sublime long finish.

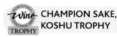 **CHAMPION SAKE, KOSHU TROPHY**

Kinmon Akita Shuzo Co Ltd, Yamabuki 1995
With elegant notes of apricot and dried flowers on the nose and palate, this has a beautiful bright gold colour, and a nice hint of sweetness on the finish.

 **KOSHU MIYAGI REGIONAL TROPHY**

Saura Co Ltd, Yamadanishiki Junmai Daiginjo Koshu Urakasumi 2005
Extremely well-made sake. This has a lovely textured palate, with great softness. The finish is lovely, and very long indeed. Excellent.

Yucho Shuzo Co Ltd, Takacho Bodaimoto Junmai-shu 2003
Extremely well-balanced sake. It is rich, but there is great

harmony too, with sweetness, notes of vanilla, and good acidity and complexity on the palate.

Hanayoi Shuzo Co Ltd, Hanayoi Junmai Koshu 1998
Warm yellow in colour, this has an understated smoky complexity. Intense and very long, with a complex finish.

Ichishima Sake Brewery Inc, Ichishima Ginjo Koshu 2000
A super elegant sake. Very complex, with loads of flavour. Rich, soft, and very fine.

Kaetsu Sake Brewery Co Ltd, Kirin Jijo-shu Vintage 2001
Super sake. Ready to drink now, showing good mature notes, and really lovely complexity.

Morimoto Sake Brewery, Kuromatsu Okina Daiginjo-shu All Japan Competition Gold Prize And More Than 10 Years-old Koshu 1998
This is absolutely textbook koshu-style sake, with a real softness on the palate. Very good quality.

Ono Shuzo Co Ltd, Oigame Chouki Jukusei Honjozo 1995
A very spicy sake, but elegant nonetheless, with a palate of nuts and iodine, and a good finish.

Senjyo Co Ltd, Junmai Ginjo-shu Daimatsu Shuzo-ten 1997
Showing nutty aromas, with sweetness, complexity, and warmth, culminating in a long finish.

Shinozaki Co Ltd, Kunigiku Daiginjo Koshu 1998
A fine, delicate sake, with gentle aromas. The palate is smooth, but full-bodied, with a long finish.

Shiraki Tsunesuke Co Ltd, Darumamasamune 1993
Deep amber in colour, this is textbook mature sake, with a palate full of dried apricot and dates Quite complex and intense.

Tenju Shuzo Co Ltd, Tenjunen Koshu Daiginjo 2001
Very fine, with good length, this is complex, very refined, and elegant. Still very young, it will improve for many years.

Kamotsuru Sake Brewing Co Ltd, Hachinen Hizou Jukusei-shu 2000
This will be a great sake one day, once it has matured, but it is still very young.

Mifuku Shuzo Co Ltd, Mifuku Fueki Ryuko 2006
Very nice texture; smooth and soft, with well-integrated acidity and spice.

Reijin Shuzo Co Ltd, Daiginjo Gonenchozou 2003
Light mature notes on a subtle spicy palate, with notes of roasted nuts. Rich.

Tsuka Shuzo Co Ltd, Otahuku Junmai Ginjo Sannenchozo 2005
Very modest in style, with flavours of nuts. Elegant and soft.

South Africa

KEY FACTS

Total production
The annual harvest in 2006 amounted to 1.3 million tonnes of which 70 per cent was used for wine.

Total vineyard
102,146ha

Top 10 varieties
1 Chenin Blanc
2 Sauvignon Blanc
3 Colombard
4 Chardonnay
5 Shiraz
6 Cabernet Sauvignon
7 Viognier
8 Pinotage
9 Pinot Noir
10 Merlot

Producers
- Worcester
- Paarl
- Stellenbosch
- Malmesbury
- Robertson
- Olifants River
- Orange River
- Little Karoo

Producers
4,185

And so to a nation which has come together as a whole to combat the historic challenges that are synonymous with the African continent. Fair trade, education in the vineyards and ven part ownership for some local communities, are all promising steps for a healthy wine industry. Plantings of Chenin Blanc remain the most dominant grape here, but a broader variety of styles are rapidly gaining global acclaim. Experts have often criticized the 'funky' aromas in the red wines, but winemakers have been determined to eradicate this component. They're on the right track – it's a Cape wine that takes Champion Red in the competition this year.

2009 IWC PERFORMANCE

Trophies	11
Gold	9
Silver	65
Bronze	100

GOLD

Bizoe Henrietta 2008, Western Cape White
Complex, rich, and creamy, with notes of honey, vanilla, and greengage. Brilliantly fresh, with light acidity set against rich, exotic candied flavours. Opulent, but thrillingly refreshing.

SOUTH AFRICAN WHITE TROPHY, SOUTH AFRICAN SAUVIGNON BLANC TROPHY, WESTERN CAPE TROPHY

Groot Constantia Sauvignon Blanc 2008, Western Cape White
Light in colour, with a good fruity nose. The palate has elements of green apple, classic grassy, herbaceous Sauvignon, and great freshness in the mouth.
£10.00 HOH

INTERNATIONAL CHENIN BLANC TROPHY, STELLENBOSCH WHITE TROPHY

Kleine Zalze Vineyard Selection Chenin Blanc 2008, Stellenbosch White
Honeyed colour, with complex butterscotch aromas on a rich, ripe, fruity nose, bolstered by lots of expensive oak. It has a big ripe palate, with lots of apricot fruit and oak - big but balanced.
£8.00

Kwv Mentor Chenin Blanc 2006, Western Cape White
Oaky, vanilla flavours, with creamy coconut notes. Rich and dense on the palate, with a great balance of fruit and oak. Complex, with a long finish.
£5.00

 **CAPE AGULHAS TROPHY**

Lomond Snowbush 2007, Cape Agulhas White
Bright, clean, zesty nose, with honeyed gooseberries, good weight and a long, zesty finish.

Engelbrecht Els Proprietors Blend 2007, Stellenbosch Red
Bright red in colour, with opulent aromas of blackcurrant, blackberry, and cedar oak, with some tight, dry tannins, and a very long, juicy finish.
£20.50 LEA, SAO, THC

THE CHAMPION RED WINE, INTERNATIONAL CABERNET SAUVIGNON TROPHY, SOUTH AFRICAN RED TROPHY, STELLENBOSCH RED TROPHY

Guardian Peak, Lapa Cabernet, Sauvignon 2007, Stellenbosch Red
Flashy black fruit, cassis, and plum. Firm, dense, and extracted, with some dryness too. Elegant, big, powerful, and youthful, with good length.
£16.50 SAO, DBY, L&C

INTERNATIONAL LATE HARVEST TROPHY, SOUTH AFRICAN LATE HARVEST TROPHY

Nederburg Winemasters Reserve Noble Late Harvest 2008, Paarl Sweet
Really attractive aromatic nose of fresh lychees. Good depth of ripe apricot fruit on the palate, balanced with crisp acidity. Long, lingering finish. A very high quality wine.

Tokara Red 2005, Gt Ferreira T/a Tokara, Stellenbosch Red
Cherries and blackcurrants, with leathery pepper tones on the nose. Herbaceous notes and black fruit on a palate which shows elegance and balanced tannins. Very long, pleasant finish.
£20.00 HRR, SBS

SILVER

Asda Extra Special Chenin Blanc 2008, DGB Pty South Africa, Paarl White
Pale colour, with a lovely weighted nose of citrussy apples, with sweet fruit on the palate, and a crisp acidic finish.
£6.00 ASDA

Bellingham Fair Maiden 2008, Coastal Region White
Pale yellow in colour, with smooth delicate fruit, and notes of honey. Good balance of acid, with a lingering, sweet finish.
SAO

Bellingham The Bernard Series Old Vine Chenin Blanc 2007, Coastal Region White
Dark yellow in colour, with a full-on late harvest density. The palate has a floral edge, with a nutty, almost flor-like character. Good oak integration, with a creamy finish.
MWW

Delaire 2008 Stellenbosch White
Displaying strong varietal character, with notes of asparagus and gooseberry, complemented by hints of vanilla and honeyed oak.
£8.00 J&B

Elgin Vintners Chardonnay 2008, Stellenbosch White
Pale golden yellow colour, with an attractively sweet, oaky nose, and touches of tropical fruit. Dry, with medium-rich concentration.

Escapades Sauvignon Blanc 2008, Stellenbosch White
Pale in colour, with a clean, fresh gooseberry and melon nose. Smooth, clean, fresh melon on the palate, which is delicate and light in body, with a long finish.
£11.00

Fairview Oom Pagel Semillon 2007, Paarl White
Pure, youthful Semillon character. Clean and fresh, with notes of cabbage and green fruit on the nose. Off-dry in style, with a fruity taste, complexity, and fine acidic balance.
£12.00

Flagstone Free Run 2008, Elim White
Intense gooseberry aromas, with asparagus and honey notes. The palate is lively, fresh, and fruity, with grassy asparagus, and an intense, creamy texture.
£10.00

Graham Beck Bowed Head Chenin Blanc 2008, Coastal Region White
Spicy oak and toast on the nose, with some creamy apricot notes. Attractive floral character, with good balance between fruit and acidity.

Ken Forrester Chenin Blanc 2008, Stellenbosch White
Elegant, fresh, honeyed tropical fruit and lime, with notes of ripe citrus and peach fruit. Concentrated, with good acidity and length.
£8.00 MWW

Kleine Zalze Cellar Selection Chenin Blanc Select Cuvée

2007, Stellenbosch White
Rich, plump, and juicy, this has
a very heady style, and is full of
rich guava and pineapple fruit. A
very complex wine.

**Kwv Sauvignon Blanc Reserve
2008, Western Cape** White
Aromas of nettles, with
pineapple and lemon notes.
Herbaceous and lemon flavours
on the palate, with high acidity
and good complexity.
£7.00

Mr Dp Burger, Glenwood 2008
White
Nice elegant nose, and a good
smooth palate, with well-
integrated oak and notes of
creamy white peach. Great length.
JKN

**Nederburg Winemasters
Reserve Chenin Blanc 2008,
Western Cape** White
Delicate nose, with rich apple
and nut aromas. Full-bodied,
with some fresh lemony acidity
on the palate, good structure,
and great persistence.

**Paul Cluver Chardonnay
2008, Stellenbosch** White
Clean, complex, rich, integrated,
and chewy. Dry, fresh acidity,
with nice weight of youthful
white Gala melon, which is
balanced with a good finish.
£10.60 BNK, DBY, FLA, THC

**Riebeek Cellars Reserve 2008,
Swartland** White
Fruity on the nose, with honeyed,
buttery aromas. Complex
honey and toasty flavours on
a medium-bodied palate, with
good acidity and structure, and a
long finish.

**Rustenberg Chardonnay
2007, Stellenbosch** White
Classy nose, with fresh ripe fruit

and minerality. Fresh spritzy
palate, with clean grapefruit
flavours, and a long finish. Well-
made.
£10.90 DBY, FLA, LEA, WAIT

**Spier Private Collection
Chenin Blanc 2007,
Stellenbosch** White
Well-defined wine, with an
intense nose of rich tropical fruit.
Very well-balanced and powerful,
with great length.
£13.00 THS

**Stellezicht Semillon
Reserve 2006, Stellenbosch**
White
A pleasant, well-balanced
palate. Lovely waxy notes
combine with hints of grapefruit
and lemon curd. Refreshing
citrus acidity.

**Tokara Chardonnay 2006,
Gt Ferreira T/a Tokara,
Stellenbosch** White
Attractive nose of moderate
complexity, with hints of vanilla
oak and sweet tropical fruit. Fresh
and appealing, with a nice texture
and pineapple acidity.
£15.00 BHL, HGT

**Tokara White 2007,
Gt Ferreira T/a Tokara,
Stellenbosch** White
Banana, coconut, and tropical
fruit on the nose, with good
ripe intensity of melon and
pineapple on the well-balanced
palate.
£16.00 CBW, HGT

**Tokara Zondernaam
Sauvignon Blanc 2008,
Gt Ferreira T/a Tokara,
Stellenbosch** White
Gooseberry ripeness, with a
soft attack on the nose. Good
fruit on the palate, with a long,
herbal finish.
£10.00 MWW

**Zonnebloem Semillon
Limited Edition 2008,
Western Cape** White
Delicate vegetal notes on
the nose, leading to a grassy
palate. A complex blend of dry,
austere, dense notes, along
with a good concentration of
fruit flavours.

**Backsberg Klein
Babylonstoren 2005, Paarl
Red**
Intense nose of cassis, with some
mineral notes. Full-bodied, with
good structure, strong tannins,
and a leathery, peppery finish.
£11.00 CMI, CPV, EOR, IRV,
RWA, SBB

**Bellingham The Bernard
Series Small Barrel S.M.V.
2006, Coastal Region** Red
Dark, ripe, peppery nose. Very
elegant, with a silky structure
and youthful grip, ending on a
long-lasting peppery note.

**Beyerskloof Synergy 2006,
Stellenbosch** Red
Hints of damson and Cape fig
on the nose, with classic San
Francisco wood. The palate
is very clean, with soft Shiraz
tannin and oak, showing a hint
of violet on the long finish.
£9.20 TESC

**Boekenhoutskloof The
Chocolate Block 2007,
Western Cape** Red
Spicy floral, berry fruit nose.
Fresh, clean fruit flavours, with
blackberry and plum fruit, and a
long spicy finish. Well-made.
£19.80

**Bon Courage Inkará Cabernet
Sauvignon 2007, Robertson
Red**
Rounded black fruits and some
liquorice, on a fairly robust
palate. Earthy, intense, and

aromatic. Fine and well-
balanced, with good length.
£16.00 ACG

**Bosman Family Vineyards,
Adama 2007, Paarl** Red
Black fruit, with leafy notes, and
hints of smoky oak. The palate is
nicely balanced, with good depth
of flavour, and an attractive,
spicy finish.
£15.00 CPV, RSV

**Bouchard Finlayson, Hannibal
2006, Walker Bay** Red
Vibrant strawberry on the nose,
with layers of toasty oak and
spice. Refreshing acidity, fine
tannins, and well-integrated oak.
£16.00 LEA

**Brahms Quartet 2006, Paarl
Red**
Deep red colour, with a purple
rim. Elegant, with hints of damson
fruits and juicy blackcurrants
layered over soft ripe tannins.
Ripe fruit, with wide appeal.

**Cape Promise 2008, Western
Cape** Red
Ripe, juicy cherry fruit nose.
Rounded, elegant, and fruity
on the palate, with balanced
acidity, and a long, spicy,
harmonious finish.
£6.00

**Cirrus 2006, Engelbrecht Els
Vineyards, Stellenbosch** Red
Rich smoky black fruit aromas.
Tannins are evident but smooth.
A touch earthy and spicy, with a
good lifted finish.
£25.50 DBY, THC

**Diemersdal Shiraz 2007,
Durbanville** Red
Intense ripe black fruit on the
nose. Multi-dimensional, with
rounded fruit and good weight
on the palate, leading to a long
finish.

Fairview Cyril Back Shiraz 2006, Paarl Red
Cherry menthol on the nose, followed by a clean palate, with hints of prune and a rustic style. Well-balanced and structured, with a good finish.
£26.00

Fairview Primo Pinotage 2007, Paarl Red
Bright red fruit, with chocolate, spice, pepper, blackcurrant, and red fruits. Full and well-balanced in the mouth, with evident silky tannins and well-integrated oak.

Fleur Du Cap Unfiltered Cabernet Sauvignon 2006, Stellenbosch Red
Sweet, ripe fruit and herbs. Tannins are firm but ripe, with good acidity. Good length, with some complexity.

Fleur Du Cap Unfiltered Merlot 2006, Stellenbosch Red
Deep in colour, with spicy oak, raspberry jam, and capsicum on the nose. Chocolatey, ripe fruit on the palate, with quite dry, firm tannins.

Glen Carlou Syrah 2006, Paarl Red
Very ripe fruit and creamy oak on the nose. Palate of fleshy black fruit, with chewy tannins and vibrant acidity.
£15.50 ODD, SAO, SWG

Glen Carlou Zinfandel 2007, Paarl Red
A juicy nose, with ripe fruit and a creamy texture on the palate,. Great weight, and a long, dried fruit finish.
£15.50

Graham Beck The Joshua 2005, Coastal Region Red
Nose of rich ripe dark fruit, with lush, opulent plum and blackcurrant coming through on the palate, supported by firm tannins. A big wine which is built to last.
£19.00 FLA, BWL

Hartenberg Mackenzie 2005, Stellenbosch Red
Notes of green peppers and bay leaves, with a hint of rosemary. The palate has good weight, with developed fruit and roasted coffee, on a background of cocoa.
£33.00 H&H

Hartenberg The Stork 2005, Stellenbosch Red
Very leafy blackcurrant and eucalyptus aromas. Really open and forward on the palate, with a big juicy character, and smooth, chocolatey texture.
£35.00 H&H

Journey's End The Cape Doctor 2005, Stellenbosch Red
Heady, fragrant, peppery, broad and jammy. Big, but refined, with elegent attack and balance, and a long, spicy finish.
£11.00

Kaapzicht Estate, Steytler Pinotage 2006, Stellenbosch Red
Deep in colour, with chocolate and tobacco aromas. Jam and blackcurrant come through on the palate, with dark chocolate. notes. High tannins, and a long finish.
£21.20 SAO

Kwv Cathedral Cellar Shiraz 2006, Western Cape Red
Fresh berry fruit on the palate, creamy and juicy, with fine tannins. Nutty and spicy, with a long, lingering finish.
£9.00

Lourensford Estate Syrah 2007, Stellenbosch Red
Bright briar fruit nose, with lively tangy orange acidity on a juicy fruit palate. Dry finish.
£10.00 HMA

Lord Neethling Laurentius 2004, Stellenbosch Red
Good structure, with elegant fruit aromas, and overtones of oak. Stewed cassis notes, with a sweet blackcurrant finish. Grippy tannins, with quite a long, elegant finish.

Lyngrove Platinum Latitude 2007, Baarsma South Africa (pty Ltd, Stellenbosch Red
Deep colour, with heady cassis, and minty, spicy, orangey notes. Chewy tannins, and plenty of ripe cherry on the palate, with a long finish of leathery, blackcurrant fruit.

Rust en Vrede Estate 2006, Stellenbosch Red
Inky colour, with opulent cassis and tobacco notes on the nose, and plenty of ripe currants and deep jammy fruit on the palate, culminating in a long, rich finish.
£22.50 SAO

Rust en Vrede Shiraz 2006, Stellenbosch Red
Restrained black fruit and savoury aromas. A smoky ashen note on the palate, with some cream and ripe black fruit, and lingering finish.
£16.50 ESL, SAO

Spice Route Flagship Syrah 2006, Swartland Red
Smoky, gamey, and slightly tarry aromas, balanced by sweet blackberry. The palate is full and dry, with sweet fruit, and savoury, peppery notes. With high tannin and acidity, this wine is set to improve further.

Spice Route Pinotage 2007, Paarl Red
With earthy, chunky fruit, deep chocolate, and red berry, this is a lively wine. Solid and tasty, with an elegant, floral finish.
£12.00

Spier Private Collection Shiraz 2005, Stellenbosch Red
Deep red in colour, with a very ripe nose of sweet fruit and vanilla oak. Soft and ripe, with good weight and balance, and a nice finish.
£13.70 ASDA

Spier Vintage Selection Cabernet Sauvignon 2006, Stellenbosch Red
Ruby in colour. Nose of bright attractive fruit and bramble, with good spicy fruit on the palate, and a great cherry finish.
£9.00 MRN

Spier Vintage Selection Shiraz-Mourvèdre-Viognier 2006, Stellenbosch Red
Rich fruit on the nose, with a touch of violet perfume. The palate shows black fruit with a leathery edge, and hint of spice.
£9.80 ASDA

Stellenzicht Golden Triangle Shiraz 2006, Stellenbosch Red
Subtle restrained nose, with a touch of minerality, lovely balance, and fine texture. Complex, restrained, and stylish, with a long, savoury finish.

Stellenzicht Syrah 2002, Stellenbosch Red
Nose of cedar and blackcurrant. The palate shows leathery sweetness, with generous chocolate and coffee layered over gentle mature dark fruit.

 Proud sponsors of International Wine Challenge

T: +44 (0) 1974 272111
F: +44 (0) 1974 272123
www.tynant.com

Vilafonte Series C 2005, Paarl
Red
Nice, intense, elegant aromas of
nuts, cinnamon, fresh black fruit,
and leather. Full-bodied and well-
balanced, with an elegant finish.
£25.00 SAO

Vilafonte Series M 2005,
Paarl Red
Restrained nose of leather and
berries, leading to a well-
balanced palate, with smooth
tannins and good length.
£20.00 SAO

Warwick Estate Three Cape
Ladies 2005, Stellenbosch
Red
Lifted notes of forest fruit and
toasty vanilla. Good structure
and smooth mouthfeel, well-
balanced, with a lingering,
complex finish - a classy wine.
£12.20 FLA, ESL, HAC, WIM,
WWS

Warwick Estate Trilogy 2005,
Stellenbosch Red
Complex sinewy tannins, and
a good core of fruit purity. Dry,
structured finish, showing good
potential.
£18.20 CHH, FLA, LOL

Zonnebloem Laureat
Cabernet Sauvignon Merlot
2006, Western Cape Red
Ruby colour, with a mellow
nose of undergrowth and berry
nose. Soft attack, with a fleshy
mid-palate and fine tannins.
Ripe and slightly dry, with lots of
character and good length.

Fleur Du Cap Noble Late
Harvest 2008, Stellenbosch
Sweet
Orange marmalade and baked
apple on the nose, with notes of
orange peel. Very sweet fruit on
the palate, with lovely balanced
acidity.

Vin De Constance 2004, Klein
Constantia, Western Cape
Sweet
A superb wine, with a citrussy,
honeyed nose with good lift
and barley sugar notes. Spicy,
long, and clean, with great
balance.
£28.00 HAR, HVN, N&P, NYW

Paul Cluver Noble Late
Harvest Riesling 2008,
Stellenbosch Sweet
Powerful honey and spice on the
nose, with floral notes. Sweet,
simple, clean fruit on the palate,
with a long, elegant finish.
£10.30 DBY, FLA, THC

BRONZE

Arniston Bay Reserve
Sauvignon Blanc 2008, The
Company Of Wine People,
Western Cape White
Clean, light colour, with
elderflower and attractive fruit
on the nose. Tropical fruit palate,
with an excellent balance of
fresh, full-bodied fruit acidity.
£7.00

nose. Good mouthfeel, with hints of spice on the palate.
MCT, SAO

Boschendal 1685 Chardonnay 2008, Coastal Region White
Rich, honeyed, and attractive. Soft, clean palate, quite oaky but well-integrated. A nice wine.
£8.00 WAIT, BTH, MWW, SAO, SPR

Bouchard Finlayson, Blanc de Mer 2008, Western Cape White
Elegant perfumed nose, of honey and lemon. Concentrated, with zesty acidity.
£8.50 LEA

Crows Fountain Chenin Blanc 2008, Villiera Wines, Stellenbosch White
Floral, with white blossom with lemon on the nose. Good acidity and minerality, with a lengthy finish.
£6.50 M&S

De Morgenzon Chenin Blanc 2007, Stellenbosch White
A nutty nose of lemon and melon, with creamy oak. A spicy palate of lemon custard, with just the right level of acidity.
£18.00

Diemersdal Wine Estate Single Vineyard Sauvignon Blanc 2008, Durbanville White
Good, fresh, clean palate of apple and gooseberry, with a crisp, clean, medium-weight mouthfeel, and a fresh, acidic finish.

Dornier Wines Donatus White 2008, Stellenbosch White
Gentle grass, pear, and ripe fruit aromas, with balanced acidity and medium weight.
£7.60 MAC

Backsberg Estate Sauvignon Blanc Reserve John Martin 2008, Paarl White
Medium-weight Loire-style Sauvignon, with minerality on the nose, and lots of acidity and lemony zing.
£10.00 CPV, DNL, EOR, RWA, TNG

Bellingham The Bernard Series Hand-picked Viognier 2007, Coastal Region White
Sweet peach nose, followed by a palate of clean fruit and ripe peach, with hints of apple strudel.
MWW

Bergsig Wine Estate White River Chenin Blanc 2008, Breede River Valley White
Delicate, slightly floral nose, with plenty of juicy acidity.
£6.70 LAI

Boschendal Chenin Blanc 2008, Coastal Region White
Light golden colour, with hints of honey and sweet peach on the

Douglas Green Chardonnay 2008, Coastal Region White
Fresh, clean, coastal style, with a very creamy mid-palate, and lots of apples and green melon.
£5.50 WAIT

Douglas Green Chenin Blanc 2008, Coastal Region White
Buttery aromas on the nose. Medium intensity, with good weight in the mouth. Balanced acidity and an elegant finish.
£5.30 MRN, PHM

False Bay Chenin Blanc 2008, Waterkloof, Stellenbosch White
Lively mouthfeel, with cashew nuts and melon. Long and bright, with good balance.
£5.80

Fish Hoek Chenin Blanc 2008, Flagstone, Swartland White
Pale in colour, with notes of wet wool, and a ripe, peachy flavour. Clean and fresh, with notes of soft melon and nice balance.
£6.20 TESC, WAIT

Flagstone Noon Gun 2008, Western Cape White
Pale and green, with good intensity on the nose. Notes of citrus and grassiness, with an attractive finish.
£8.00 TESC

Fleur Du Cap Chardonnay 2008, Stellenbosch White
Clean, fresh, and mineral, with citrus and pear flavours. Dry, pure, and mineral, with a fresh finish.

Fleur Du Cap Unfiltered Semillon 2008, Stellenbosch White
A complex, grassy nose that's almost Sauvignon-like in style. Waxy texture, with hints of walnut and pleasant acidity.

Glen Carlou Quartz Stone 2007, Paarl White
Pale primrose colour, dominated by toasty oak, which overlays lemony fruit. Fine concentrated fruit and acidity.
£15.50 ODD, SAO, SWG

Hartenberg Eleanor 2006, Stellenbosch White
Broad, ripe tropical flavours, with moderate acidity, toasty oak, and pleasant length.
£23.00 H&H

Journey's End Chardonnay 2006, Stellenbosch White
Subtle nose of fruit and spice. Vanilla flavours on the palate, with a pleasing texture and good balance.
£10.70 WAIT, POG, WIM

Journey's End Chardonnay 2007, Stellenbosch White
Bright, pale straw in colour. Interesting woody fruit on the nose, with rich, good fruit on the palate, and an oaky edge.
£13.00 WAIT

Journey's End Destination 2006, Stellenbosch White
Mango, peach, and apricot on a well-defined nose. Clean and light, with a coconut-style palate.
£11.00 EGW, HIG, WIM

Klein Constantia Estate Sauvignon Blanc 2008 Western Cape White
Light lemon, fennel, and grapefruit on the nose, with crisp acidity, but good, fat fruit.
£9.40 WES, B&B, SEL, WIM

Kleine Zalze Cellar Selection Chenin Blanc Bush Vines 2008, Stellenbosch White
Lively, with freshly cut grass on the nose, and a palate of rich

fruit, with fresh acidity, and a long finish.
£6.00

Lanzerac Chardonnay 2008, Stellenbosch White
Rich fruit on the attack, with nice tropical notes and minerality. Good commercial style.
£9.00 ABY, HTF

Le Bonheur Chardonnay 2008, Stellenbosch White
Discreet flower and white peach aromas. Well-balanced, with appley notes, and a lingering aftertaste.

Liberty Chenin Blanc 2008, Western Cape White
Pale in colour, with lots of juicy lime and citrus on the palate.. Rich fruit, creamy character, and gentle acidity.
£7.00 HEN, LIB

Lomond Pincushion Single Vineyard Sauvignon Blanc 2008, Cape Agulhas White
Classic, well-made, and balanced wine, with attractive minerally fruit.

Lomond Sugarbush Single Vineyard Sauvignon Blanc 2007, Cape Agulhas White
Green bean and mangetout notes, with a cool climate character. Crisp and mineral, with good length.

Lyngrove Platinum Chardonnay 2008, Stellenbosch White
Rich, ripe, Meursault-style Cape Chardonnay, with nice use of oak, and a creamy finish.

Marks & Spencer Ses'fikile Pinot Blanc 2008, Western Cape White
Lemony fresh acidity, with some balancing vibrancy, and plenty of varietal character.
£8.50 M&S

Nederburg Ingenuity White Blend 2008, Paarl White
Crisp balance of fruit and acidity, with a pleasurable, clean, fresh palate.

Obikwa Chenin Blanc 2008, Western Cape White
Ripe fruit, with a note of sweet apple, zesty lemon, and citrus.

Olive Brook Chardonnay 2008 Spar Group S.A. Ltd, Robertson White
Clean apple aromas. Well-balanced and fresh on the palate, with a long, lemony finish.

Neil Ellis Sauvignon Blanc 2008, Coastal Region White
Bright minerally nose with herbaceous notes, citrus character, and some weight.
£11.00 MWW

Neil Ellis Stellenbosch Chardonnay 2007, Stellenbosch White
Fresh oak and spice on the nose, with some butter and tropical fruit. Savoury character on the palate. Creamy mouthfeel, with a clean, vibrant finish.
£9.00 TESC

Paul Cluver Sauvignon Blanc 2008, Stellenbosch White
Clean gooseberry and melon nose, with notes of fresh honey, and and a soft attack of clean, fresh melon. Lightweight and delicate, with a long finish.
£9.20 DBY, FLA, THC

Rickety Bridge Chardonnay 2006, Paarl White
Bright, powerful fruit on the nose. Clean and fresh, with pineapple and some herbal notes.

Rustenberg Five Soldiers 2007, Stellenbosch White
Clean, citrus-lemon aromas, with balanced acidity, spicy oak, and a long finish.
£23.50 DBY

Stellenbosch Drive Oaked Chenin Blanc 2008, Origin Wine, Stellenbosch White
A light, delicate straw nose, leading to a delicate, nutty palate, which is slightly coconuty, with good acidity.

Tesco Finest* Ken Forrester Chenin Blanc 2008, Stellenbosch White
Clean, gentle lemon and orange aromas, with oily creamy oak, spicy wood, balanced acidity, and good length.
£7.10 TESC

The Amasimi Kelder Reserve Chardonnay Western Cape 2008, Spier Wines (pty) Ltd, Western Cape White
Intense aromas of flowers, honey, lemon, and minerality. Good mouthfeel, well-balanced, with a lingering finish.
£7.00 LAI

Tokara Walker Bay Sauvignon Blanc 2007, Gt Ferreira T/a Tokara, Stellenbosch White
Elegant, light melon flavours, with some herbal nettle character, a soft sweet attack, and reasonable length.
£15.00 SBS

Tokara Zondernaam Chardonnay 2008, Gt Ferreira T/a Tokara, Stellenbosch White
Fresh, simple style, with an oak-dominated nose. Clean and well-made.
£10.00 EHB, SAO

Tukulu Organic Chardonnay 2007, Swartland White
Apples, limes, and mineral notes on the nose, with a touch of sweet white peach.

Zalze Bush Vine Chenin Blanc 2008, Kleine Zalze, Western Cape White
Clean, fresh, and floral, with minerality and lemon fruit. Fresh, rounded palate.

Zonnebloem Sauvignon Blanc Limited Release 2008 White
Lifted herbaceous notes on the nose. Good citrus palate, with weight and freshness.

African Horizon Pinotage/ Ruby Cabernet 2008, Origin Wine, Western Cape Red
Soft, clean, and juicy. An approachable style, which is appealingly simple and light.

Backsberg Babylons Toren 2003, Paarl Red
Deep plummy nose, with spicy oak complexity. Fresh blackberry and plum fruit, with good, well-integrated, ripe tannins.
£19.00 CPV, EOR, RWA, SBB

Bergsig Pinotage 2005, Breedekloof Red
Spice and black cherry on the nose. Full-bodied, showing black fruit, with notes of oak and chocolate, and a long finish.

Beyers Truter Pinotage 2007, Beyerskloof, Stellenbosch Red
Ruby in colour. Smoky notes, with plenty of spice and black fruit.
£8.20 TESC

Beyerskloof Field Blend 2004, Stellenbosch Red
Dark blackcurrant fruit aromas, with spicy oak and ripe fruit on

the palate. Straightforward, with ripe tannins, and a mild finish.
£20.00

Beyerskloof Pinotage Reserve 2006, Stellenbosch Red
Pleasant wine, with complex cherry fruit, medium body, and good length.
£8.00

Bosman Family Vineyards 2007, Paarl Red
Attractive dark berry fruit and smoky oak. Lively acidity and textured tannins. Exotic spices on the mid-palate and finish.
£15.00 RSV

Bouchard Finlayson, Galpin Peak, Pinot Noir 2008, Walker Bay Red
Complex red fruit and forest floor aromas. An alluring, supple texture, with fine, balanced tannins, and a long, flavoursome finish.
£20.00 BNK, THC

Bouchard Finlayson, Hannibal 2007, Walker Bay Red
Big and juicy, with hints of chocolate and smoke on the nose.
£16.00 LEA

Bouchard Finlayson, Tête de Cuvée, Galpin Peak, Pinot Noir 2007, Walker Bay Red
Attractive raspberry nose, with lifted perfume adding complexity. Good balance of fruit and acidity.
£64.00 LEA, THC

Brahms Shiraz 2005, Paarl Red
Ruby colour, with a soft, fruity palate, and notes of red berry.

Cape Boar 2007, Doolhof Wine Estate, Paarl Red
Youthful, deep red appearance.

Light, elegant, blackcurrant fruit, with dusty tannins providing backbone and aiding length.

Clos Malverne Auret 2007, Stellenbosch Red
Leathery, berry nose, leading to a soft, smooth palate, with integrated tannins, and a long, juicy finish.
£10.50

De Toren Fusion V 2006, Stellenbosch Red
Attractive nose of cassis and damson, with good fruit and oak character. Palate of sweet ripe fruit, with ripe tannins.
£20.00

De Toren Z 2007, Stellenbosch Red
Big, ripe, elegant fruit, with good depth of flavour and vanilla oak. Excellent cassis finish, with appealing purity.
£13.00

Diemersdal Pinotage 2007, Durbanville Red
Leafy, smoky, blackberry fruit. Ripe, creamy, and a bit eccentric, but showing typical dark, smoky flavours.

Dombeya Samara 2005, Stellenbosch Red
Blackberries and a hint of fennel. Excellent intensity, good balance, and ripe tannins.

Fleur Du Cap Pinotage 2007, Stellenbosch Red
Chocolate and tobacco on the nose, as on the palate, which also displays black cherry, jam, and sweet tannins.

Flagstone Dark Horse Shiraz 2007, Western Cape Red
Oaky, spicy, bramble fruit nose. Palate of dark chocolate and

white pepper. Balanced, with firm tannins, and a long finish.
£15.00

Flagstone Music Room Cabernet 2006, Western Cape Red
Deep red in colour. Nose of green peppers, coffee, and a hint of rubber. The palate is a mass of blackcurrant fruit. Balanced and refreshing.
£15.00

Flagstone Writer's Block Pinotage 2007, Worcester Red
Jam, black cherry, and plum on the nose. Sweet tannins and black fruit are evident on the palate.
£15.00

Glen Carlou Grand Classique 2005, Paarl Red
Open nose, showing some mature aromas of black fruit, and leathery spicy notes. Soft tannins and a good finish.
£15.50 SAO, SWG

Glen Carlou Gravel Quarry 2006, Paarl Red
Packed with red fruit, with pronounced tannins, and a smooth mulberry fruit finish.
£25.50 SAO, SWG

Glen Carlou Pinot Noir 2008, Coastal Region Red
The nose shows cherry aromas and hints of smoke, leading to a clean, balanced palate.
£12.00 ODD, SAO, WSO

Golden Kaan Private Collection 2005, Stellenbosch Red
Light, vibrant colour, with notes of chocolate and coffee, a hint of tobacco, and soft marmalade.

Graham Beck The Ridge Syrah 2003, Robertson Red
Smoky bacon and white pepper

on the nose. Nice definition and fine balance. Firm tannins, with white pepper and blackberry. Lovely depth.
£18.00 MWW

Grand Vin Pinotage L'avenir 2006, Laroche Red
Sweet blackcurrant and vanilla flavours, with a nice tang and balance, and an honest, spicy finish.
£26.00

Groot Constantia, Shiraz 2006, Western Cape Red
Tart, spicy palate, balanced with sweet bramble fruit. Bold and tannic, with firm acidity.
£12.00 HOH

Hartenberg Cabernet Sauvignon 2005, Stellenbosch Red
Bright cassis fruit, with herbal overlay. A very smoky palate, with lively, velvet-textured tannins.
£16.00 H&H

Hope's Garden Cabernet Sauvignon 2007, Citrusdal Cellars, Western Cape Red
Elegant combination of spice and black fruit flavours. Fresh mint and eucalyptus, with notes of plum and balanced oak.
£4.50 ASDA

Journey's End Cabernet Sauvignon 2005, Stellenbosch Red
Lovely bouquet of Christmas pudding and spices. Rich, intense palate, elegant and textured, with balanced use of oak use.
£9.50

Journey's End Merlot 2006, Stellenbosch Red
Green pepper, spicy oak, and concentrated, sweet briary black fruit on the nose. Potential to age.

Journey's End Shiraz 2005, Stellenbosch Red
Woody, vegetal nose. Medium-bodied, with nice complexity.
EGW, HIG, POG, WIM

Kaapzicht Estate, Steytler Vision 2006, Stellenbosch Red
Jammy nose. Huge wine, with a delicate black cherry backbone.
£21.00 SAO

Kleine Zalze Family Reserve Cabernet Sauvignon 2006, Stellenbosch Red
Bright stone fruit nose, followed by a multi-layered cherry palate, with a graceful finish.
£20.00

Kleine Zalze Family Reserve Shiraz 2006, Stellenbosch Red
Really nice lifted savoury black fruit aromas. Well-made, balanced, and attractive.
£20.00

Kwv Cathedral Cellar Cabernet Sauvignon 2006, Western Cape Red
Minty chocolate and hints of red fruit. Fine acidity, which balances the tannin.
£9.00

Kwv Cathedral Cellar Pinotage 2006, Western Cape Red
High-toned aromatics, with a full sweet-and-sour palate of juicy, crunchy fruit, showing good intensity.
£9.00

Kwv Mentor Shiraz 2006, Western Cape Red
Spicy baked fruit character, with a jammy dense berry palate, balanced acidity, and a zippy finish.
£5.00

Kwv Shiraz Reserve 2006, Western Cape Red
Restrained raspberry and spice on the nose, followed by a well-defined palate of savoury plummy fruit.
£7.00

Lomond Conebush Single Vineyard Syrah 2007, Cape Agulhas Red
Slightly meaty nose, with a savoury palate, supported by refreshing acidity and good depth of flavour.

Lyngrove Platinum Pinotage 2007, Baarsma South Africa (pty) Ltd, Stellenbosch Red
Good, smoky black fruit aromas. Clean palate, with fresh acidity, and a touch of spice.

Major's Hill Merlot 2007, Robertson Red
Ripe, bright red fruit on the nose, with a well-structured, creamy palate of chewy red fruit and fine tannin.

Marks & Spencer Silver Tree Shiraz 2007, Company Of Wine People, Stellenbosch Red
Silky spice with cassis perfume. Sweet fruit on the palate, dry gentle acidity, and an elegant, warm finish.
£9.00 M&S

Mhv Rouwkes Drift Pinotage 2008 Red
Good, plummy bramble fruit. Simple structure, well-balanced for easy-drinking.
£5.20 BNK, MHV

Nederburg Manor House Cabernet Sauvignon 2007, Paarl Red
Slighty dusty, earthy, and leafy on the nose. An attractive and complex wine.

The Oak Valley Blend 2005, Oak Valley Wines, Stellenbosch Red
Notes of blackcurrant, with cedar and spice, with developed aromas of saddle leather. Supple tannins, with lovely freshness and minerality, and a good length of fruit.

Rust en Vrede Cabernet Sauvignon 2006, Stellenbosch Red
Violet hue. Smoky, leathery nose, with notes of ripe fruit. Nice baked fruit on the palate.
£15.30 DBY

Rustenberg, Brampton Shiraz 2007, Stellenbosch Red
Nose of jammy plum, with ripe strawberry and capsicum. Nicely balanced structure.
£9.10 BNK, DBY, FLA, LEA

6+1 Cabernet Sauvignon/ Shiraz 2005, Seven Oaks, Breedekloof Red
Leafy nose, with green bell pepper, and sweet black fruit. Good concentration, with some length.
£5.00

Spice Route Malabar 2005, Swartland Red
Rich ruby colour, with lovely berry fruit. Rich, peppery palate, with soft tannins and a long finish.
£30.00

Stellenzicht Syrah 2003, Stellenbosch Red
Deep cherry red in colour. Soft and approachable, with good weight and balance.

Table Mountain Merlot 2007, Western Cape Red
Bright, sweet red and black fruit, with balanced acidity, and a little oak influence.

Tokara Zondernaam Cabernet Sauvignon 2006, Gt Ferreira

T/a Tokara, Stellenbosch Red
Spicy earthy aroma, with a smooth attack developing tobacco, earth, and rhubarb notes on the finish. Long, elegant aftertaste.
£11.00 SAO

Tukulu Organic Sangiovese 2007, Swartland Red
Warm, almost fortified nose, with soft layers of black fruit. Deep, structured tannins and good acidity.

Vriesenhof Vineyards, Talana Hill Royale 2003, Stellenbosch Red
A developed wine, with characteristics of leather and cigar box. The palate shows evidence of fine tannins, along with secondary notes of chewy tobacco and dried leaves. A very quaffable wine.
£14.00

Zoetendal Wines Shiraz 2007, Elim Red
Nose of blackberries and spice, with mild hints of oak. Fine tannins and black fruit on the palate
£7.00 WAV

Fish Hoek Rose 2008, Flagstone, Swartland Rosé
Pale, ripe, spicy, sweet fruit. Singularly dry.
£6.40 TESC

Graham Beck Blanc De Blancs 2005, Robertson Sparkling
Toast and lime juice on the nose. Fine mousse, with good balance on the palate.
£13.00 BWL

Graham Beck Brut NV, Robertson Sparkling
Tropical fruit on the nose, with a creamy, peachy, delicate mousse. Persistent double decker finish.
£13.00 WAIT

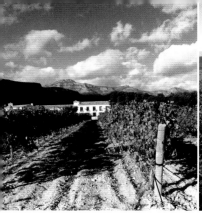

Spain

Accolades were awarded this year to wines from twenty-six regions, a testament to the breadth of styles on offer. What has made Spain such a key player is its diverse native varieties. Even in the new Spain of today, which welcomes international varieties in parts, the originals still deliver. Grapes such as Monastrell and Mencia have been tamed by their masters to create wines of finesse and elegance to weigh against their international counterparts. With vines covering a greater area than any other country in the world it's possible to enjoy styles from all around the country throughout a single meal. Open with a Cava or fino and wrap it up with a lusciously sweet Malaga, with a maze of red and whites along the way.

KEY FACTS

Total production
45m hectolitres

Total vineyard
1.154m hectares

Top 10 regions
1 Castilla-La-Mancha
2 Extramadura
3 Valencia
4 Castilla-Leon
5 Catalonia
6 Murcia
7 Rioja
8 Aragon
9 Andalusia
10 Galicia

Top 10 grapes
1 Airén
2 Tempranillo
3 Bobal
4 Garnacha Tinta
5 Monastrell
6 Pardina
7 Macabeo
8 Palomino
9 Albariño
10 Viura

2009 IWC PERFORMANCE

Trophies	12
Gold	23
Silver	108
Bronze	211
Great Value Awards	2

SPANISH WHITE TROPHY

Maior De Mendoza 2007, Galicia White

Tropical fruit, with fresh, delicate aromas. The palate has a good attack, with a complex, deep, long finish.

Baron De Ley 7 Viñas 2004, Rioja Red

Fine, spicy, creamy oak with sweet cedary fruit and mocha. Youthful concentrated fruit with a lot of oak, but has all the components to age well.
£16.30 TESC

 INTERNATIONAL TEMPRANILLO TROPHY

Campillo Gran Reserva 1995, Rioja Red

Lovely deep colour. Elegant fruit with tannic grip, displaying a complex array of red and black fruit flavours with hints of raisin. Well-balanced and long-lasting.
£23.50 EVW

Campo Dorado Reserva 2005, Bodegas Olarra, S.a., Rioja Red

Rich creamy coconut and raisin aromas; perfumed and elegant. Dark, beautifully textured tannins, with silky layers of red fruit on the palate. Impressive and delicate.
£14.90 MHV

Cillar De Silos 2006, Castilla y León Red

Ripe black raisin and prune combine with basil and chocolate on the nose. Palate of sweet ripe fruit, balanced with crisp acidity, well-structured tannins and a pleasing long finish.
AAW

Coma Vella 2006, Viticultors Mas D'en Gil, S.L., Catalonia Red

Attractive nose of ripe fruit, mint and cedarwood. Absolutely delicious red fruit on the palate with well balanced acidity. Great breadth and long finish.
£22.00 WAIT

 CATALONIA TROPHY

Grupo Codorníu Scala Dei Cartoixa 2006, Catalonia Red

Dark red fruits and high toned spice nose. Immense concentration, big, with well integrated oak. Well balanced, firm tannins and pleasant finish.
£25.00 CPB, HRW, RWW

Imperial Reserva 2004, C.V.N.E, Rioja Red

This is a generous red-fruited Rioja with precise tannins and beautiful fruit on the mid-palate. Clean and grippy with a slight green tinge. Raspberry, cherry, and lovely relaxed jammy fruit. A good, balanced style which is built to last.
£18.30 FLA, WAIT, HMA

 SPANISH RED TROPHY, RIOJA TROPHY

Inspiracion Valdemar Edicion Limitada 2004, Rioja Red

Penetrating, spicy, cedary blackfruit nose with notes of cassis. Intense, deep, dark fruit on the palate. Fine, cedary oak and very elegant tannins. Long, concentrated finish.

> **DID YOU KNOW?**
> The lip of a red wine glass is sloped inward to capture the aromas of the wine and deliver them to your nose.

some cocoa on the palate. Good weight and length. Lovely refreshing, balancing, orangey acidity. Sensational!

 **SHERRY TROPHY, PALO CORTADO SHERRY TROPHY**

Juan Luis Cañas Reserva Selección De La Familia 2001, Rioja Red

A seductive mix of coffee and dark bramble fruit. Attractive, swirling smoke and tobacco on a palate that offers finesse and good length of fruit. Balanced and fine.
£16.50 LAI

Luis Cañas Reserva Selección De La Familia 2003, Rioja Red

Inky and elegant with coffee, chocolate, and spicy strawberry compote aromas. Juicy fruit is balanced by fine tannin, leading to a smoky finish, with lingering spice notes.

Roda I 2004, Rioja Red

Concentrated aromas of sweet black fruit, creamy oak and cocunut. Focused and pure, with savoury spicy notes on the palate. Excellent texture, balance and length.
£33.00 FAW, MWW, NYW, SEL

Viña Zorzal 2007, Vinícola Corellana, Navarra Red

Inky, with blackcurrant, fruit peel, jam and raspberries. Nice rich tannins and juicy structure, with red fruit notes on the finish. Great development potential.
£7.00 IDO, WSO

Príncipe De Viana Vendimia Tardía De Chardonnay 2007, Navarra Sweet

Waxy, rich but firm nose with orange zest. Apricot fruit with

Apostoles Palo Cortado Vors NV, González Byass, Jerez-xérès-sherry Sherry

Medium amber in colour, with a rich toffee muscavado nose. Lifted palate of cashew, toffee, and coffee bean. Great concentration, length, and complexity with a clean smooth finish.
£15.00 WAIT

Lustau Almacenista Palo Cortado 1/50 (vides) NV, Jerez-xérès-sherry Sherry

Lifted barley sugar nose with notes of spice and honey. Delicate, long, and well-balanced. Toffee caramel palate. Elegant, with a savoury finish.
£20.00

 MOSCATEL SHERRY TROPHY

Lustau Solera Reserva Moscatel Emilin NV, Jerez-xérès-sherry Sherry

Amber, caramel colour, like bright coffee. Very dark in character, with Dundee cake and dark chocolate on palate, and long, complex, balanced sweetness, leading to a clean finish.
£14.00

Lustau Solera Reserva Oloroso Don Nuño NV, Jerez-xérès-sherry Sherry

Complex raisin, sultana, and fig nose, with a very dry spicy

palate of cloves and cinnamon. An attractive body with a long Seville marmalade finish.
£12.00

MANZANILLA SHERRY TROPHY

GREAT VALUE CHAMPION FORTIFIED, GREAT VALUE FORTIFIED WINE BETWEEN £5 AND £10

Marks & Spencer Manzanilla Sherry NV, Williams & Humbert, Jerez-xérès-sherry Sherry
Pale gold straw in colour. Nose of lifted salt and bacon rind. Clean and mineral with carnation blossom and hints of lime and a very elegant finish.
£6.00 M&S

PEDRO XIMÉNEZ SHERRY TROPHY

Nectar Pedro Ximénez NV, González Byass Jerez-xérès-sherry Sherry
Toffee butterscotch nose with a citrus lift. Very rich mid-palate, like liquid Christmas pudding. Long, sweet, silky finish with good complexity.

AMONTILLADO SHERRY TROPHY

Sainsburys Taste The Difference Amontillado NV, Emilio Lustau S.a. Jerez-xérès-sherry Sherry
Lifted butterscotch and pine needle nose, showing age and complexity. Fresh, upfront varnish tones and a slight hint of cashew on the finish.
£6.50 SAIN

Sandeman Character, Medium Dry Amontillado Sherry NV, Jerez-xérès-sherry Sherry
Gold in colour, with an intense and complex nose of rancío, yeasty aromas and floral notes. Incredible balance with a complex and elegant finish. A super wine.

FINO SHERRY TROPHY

Waitrose Solera Jerezana Fino Sherry NV, Emilio Lustau Sa, Jerez-xérès-sherry Sherry
Salty and tangy, with lovely weight and concentration. Complex, long and balanced.
£8.00 WAIT

SILVER

Baigorri Blanco Fermentado En Barrica 2006, Rioja White
Nose of creamy peach and apricot, with some sweet vanilla oak. Full of flavour, with real complexity.

Capellania 2004, Marqués De Murrieta, Rioja White
Initial notes of fresh star fruit, pineapple, and apple on the nose, which are then taken over by bright, lemony, and floral elements. This is a bit oaky at the finish, but has rich and lively dry apple and lemon flavours. Good intensity of fruit and full body.
£16.00 FWP, LAI, LLV, TVY

Condesa Eylo 2008, Bodegas Val De Vid, Rueda White
Pale lemon colour with good depth. Elderflower aromas with white peach and citrus notes. A light body with crisp acidity. Long, clean, citrus-infused finish.

Cuatro Rayas Verdejo 2008, Agrícola Castellana, Rueda White

Attractive nose of green pepper, citrus, and white peach. Decent weight on the palate with passionfruit, citrus, and hints of pineapple. Fresh, crisp long finish.
£5.70 M&S, BUC

Fruto Noble 2008, Francisco Gómez, Valencia White

Pale yellow in colour. Clean with a soft attack, and pure, intense guava providing freshness, leading to a good finish.

La Val Crianza Sobre Lias 2004, Galicia White

Wonderfully floral, rounded white fruit on the nose, with more white fruit and marzipan on the palate.
£24.60

Lar De Paula Blanco Fermentado En Barrica 2007, Rioja White

Attractive, nutty, blanched almond aromas. Lovely notes of spice and honey with very fresh acidity and hints of lemon zest.

Los Pecadillos "Envidia" Verdejo Sauvignon 2008, Alliance Wine, Rueda White

Good fresh, creamy, and slightly spicy nose. Creamy peaches on the palate. Balanced fruit and acidity with a fresh fruity finish.
£9.00 AAW

Mas Macia Supreme Garnacha Xarello 2008, Fermi Bohigas, Catalonia White

Fresh, somewhat restrained aromatics. Fine, refreshing, peppery edge to the fruit, with good grip and an appetising off-dry finish.
£11.40

Pazo Señorans 2008, Galicia White

Freshness and mineral complexity that is rich, yet reined in. Tangy with a slight nuttiness, and lovely orange and peach flavours on the palate.

Pazo Señorans Seleccion De Añada 2004, Galicia White

Developed nose. Lots of depth and a good attack. Great concentration, with good acidity and excellent length.

Sol De Señorans 2006, Pazo De Señorans, Galicia White

Pale green in colour, this wine has aromas of meadow and freshly cut grass. A very interesting palate is overlayed with complex grassy, sweet hay flavours. Long, clean, lingering finish.

Txomin Etxaniz 2008, Etxaniz Txacolina, Pais Vasco White

Pale golden hue, with a playful spritz, and floral citrus aromas, fresh crispness and excellent balance. Apple and citrus flavours, with persistent length.
£15.50 MOR, BUT, MKH

Vivanco Viura-Malvasia 2008, Rioja White

Lovely, fresh, green, herbaceous nose, with excellent clean apricot notes and wonderful purity on the palate. Clean citrus character, good balance, with an elegant finish.

150th Anniversary Gran Reserva 2001, Marqués De Riscal, Rioja Red

Warm, spicy nose and palate. Rich juicy fruits on a harmonious palate with a lovely finish and good length.
£42.00 CMR, EDC, HVN, L&W

Agoston- Garnacha & Syrah 2008, Bodegas Virgen Del Águila, Aragón Red
Violet, sweet fragrant nose. Sweet dark cherries and vibrant fruit with some smoky tones. Lovely sweet, round and soft finish.

Altas De Ruesca Garnacha 2007, Jean-Marc Lafage, Aragón Red
Sweet vanilla cream, with spicy plum and redcurrant fruit, slight bitterness on the palate, with some elegant blue fruit, dry tannins, and a smoky finish.
£8.00 BWL

Altos De Luzon 2006, Murcia Red
Clean nose. Intense, complex tones of red cherry, baked fruit, spice and vanilla.
WTR

Altos R Pigeage 2006, Rioja Red
Smoky, chocolatey, and plummy. Soft berry fruit palate with some heat. A nice tannic, serious wine with a rounded finish.

Amaren Reserva 2002, Bodegas Luis Cañas, Rioja Red
Bright and currant y, with plenty of vanilla oak, and creamy, sweet velvety fruit. Quite jammy and sweet, with a long finish.
AAW

Azabache Rioja Reserva 2004, Bodegas Aldeanueva, Rioja Red
Nose of vanilla spice and warm mulberry. Balanced, ripe, and robust fruit palate with a lovely tangy character and a fresh finish.
£12.00 EOR

Baigorri De Garage 2005, Rioja Red
Rich, ripe cherry fruit, and hints of complex spice, beautifully balanced by fresh acidity. Distinctive and concentrated, with a firm, flavourful finish.

Baigorri Reserva 2004, Rioja Red
Sexy wine with good richness. Gently juicy with notes of new oak and hints of coffee and tangy fruit.

Baron De Ley Gran Reserva 1998, Rioja Red
Nose of red berry and truffle, with intriguing hints of spice. Smooth, complex palate of lovely aged fruit. Very elegant wine.
THS

Bodegas Palacio Crianza 2006, Hijos De Antonio Barceló, Rioja Red
Attractive nose of oak and redcurrants. Good fruit, with notes of redcurrant, vanilla, spices and violets.
£7.00 MRN

Borsao Barrica Seleccion 2007, Aragón Red
Sweet, dark, concentrated fruit, with notes of cocoa and balancing acidity. Great complexity, with some dried fruit notes.
£8.00 CHH

Borsao Reserva Campo De Borja Spain 2005, Aragón Red
Sweet blackberries and cherries, with notes of smoke, cream, and raspberries. Firmly structured with great concentration.
£11.00 AVB

Borsao Tres Picos 2007, Aragón Red
Gorgeous violet hue. Rich oaky nose, with some smoky spice

and dark fruit, and rounded mid-weight.
£14.00 FLA

Carchelo 2008, Murcia Red
Attractive new wood aromas, with violet notes. Pleasant mouthfeel, nice acidity, and good chunky length.
£8.20 IDO

Casa De La Ermita Monastrell Ecológico 2008, Murcia Red
Nose of rich juicy fruit. Spicy, with a smooth, velvety entry. Bright raspberry and black cherry on the palate. Good length and complexity.
BWL, ODD

Castaño Monastrell 2008, Murcia Red
Perfumed and spicy nose. Fresh, black cherry fruit with creamy oak, ripe tannins, and a long finish.
£7.00 LIB

Cueva De La Culpa 2006, Bodegas Murviedro, Utiel-Requena Red
Well-ripened black fruit aromas with spicy oak. Full, ripe and fruity palate, well-supported by oak. Ripe tannins and balanced acidity with good length.

Dominio De Valdelacasa 2006, Bodega Del Palacio De Los Frontaura Y Victoria, Castilla y León Red
Brooding with dark fruits, spice and some leather on nose. A lovely balanced palate of sweetly ripe fresh fruit, firm tannins, and well-balanced acidity.
£14.00 P&S

Don Jacobo Crianza Rioja Tinto 2004, Bodegas Corral, Rioja Red
Delicate yet persistent on the nose. Complex, with sweet delicate red fruits, and notes of strawberries and vanilla. Smooth, creamy, and elegant with good balance.
£8.80 MCT

Epulum Gran Reserva 2002, Bodegas La Catedral, Rioja Red
Deep in colour with complex notes of intense dark fruit and well-integrated oak. Very good length and great potential for ageing.

Finca Antigua Petit Verdot 2006, Red
Dense, sweet, blackberry fruit and a smoky flavour. Some spicy and grippy tannin structure and warmth. Good freshness and definition.
£9.00 FLA

Frontaura Reserva 2005, Bodega Del Palacio De Los Frontaura Y Victoria, Castilla y León Red
Bright red colour, with red berry and fig on the nose. Palate of ripe fruit, backed up by chewy tannins.
£29.00 P&S

Fuentespina Crianza 2006, Avelino Vegas S.A., Ribera Del Duero Red
Young farmyard and flinty characteristics, with elegant and subtle black fruit, velvety tannins, and a long balanced finish.
£10.00 MWW

Fuentespina Reserva 2004, Avelino Vegas S.A., Ribera Del Duero Red
Pungent nose with hints of vanilla. Intense, well integrated oak with fresh, soft tannins and a fruity palate. Very long finish.

Glorioso Crianza 2006, Hijos De Antonio Barceló, S.A., Rioja Red
Restrained nose of red fruits,

with a palate of attractive black fruit and savoury notes. Good acidity and integrated tannins.
£8.00 ODD

Grupo Codorníu La Vicalanda Gran Reserva 2001, Bodegas Bilbaínas, Rioja Red

Soft and sleek with lots of new oak to envelop the black fruit. Generous, with a nice complex finish.
£20.00 CPB, FEN, JKN, TAU

Grupo Codorníu Legaris Reserva 2005, Ribera Del Duero Red

Clean, vibrant fruit and well-integrated oak. Rich damson fruit on the nose with a black cherry palate and a lovely finish.
£17.00 L&C, P&R, RWW

Grupo Codorníu Scala Dei Priorat 2005, Catalonia Red

Raspberries and paprika on the nose, with nice, fine, dense flavours. Expressive and plummy, with a long cocoa finish, and a hint of liquorice.
£17.00 AUG, HAC, WUO

Imperial Gran Reserva 1999, C.V.N.E, Rioja Red

Smoky, slightly funky development on an old style. Fairly dry palate.
£24.00 WAIT, HMA

Jaros 2006, Ribera Del Duero Red

Smoky spiciness with dry pepper and firewood on the nose. Smooth palate, soft tannins, and ripe berry fruit, leading to a long rich finish.

Juan Gil Honoro Vera 2008, Murcia Red

Delicate mineral nose. Ripe jammy fruits with a touch of spice. Fresh palate with a good finish.
£5.80

Los Cantos De Torremilanos 2006, Bodegas Peñalba López, S.L., Ribera Del Duero Red

Deep ruby in colour, with an earthy, jammy-scented nose. There are layers of ripe plums, damsons, candied sweets, spice, and scented rose, with dry, soft velvety tannins, and a balanced, spicy finish.

Los Pecadillos "Lujuria" Graciano Garnacha 2007, Alliance Wine, Navarra Red

Full, rich and deep nose of dark fruits and violets. Palate is dense, crisp, and vibrant with a firm finish. Youthful.
£7.00 AAW

Macia Batle Crianza 2006, Mallorca Red

Lovely sweet berry fruit nose. Attractive mouthfeel with ripe blackberries and bramble on the palate. This is very well balanced, with good acidity, and gentle, soft tannins.
£12.80

Macia Batle Reserva Privada 2005, Mallorca Red

Prunes and figs on the nose. Spicy and slightly savoury, with plums, blackberries, and liquorice on the palate. Good concentration of soft fruit, and balanced acidity.
£16.00 FLA

Manuel Quintano Reserva 2004, Bodegas Y Viñedos Labastida, Rioja Red

Tobacco, and earthy, oriental spice aromas, with plenty of ripe strawberry flavours on the palate, and a long, elegant finish.

Marks & Spencer Contino Rioja 2004, C.V.N.E., Rioja Red

Delicate nose of sweet fruit

and creamy oak. Fine intense palate with sweet raspberry and strawberry fruit developing into more savoury notes. Medium body, fine, and quite long.
£22.00 M&S

Marks & Spencer Rioja Campo Aldea Graciano Reserva 2005, Aldanueva, Rioja Red
Old-style nose showing spice and leather tones. Herbaceous with nice red fruit notes on the finish.
£10.00 M&S

Marqués De Arienzo Gran Reserva 1998, Domecq Bodegas, Rioja Red
Rich, complex, juicy and meaty, but still fruity. Well-balanced with a lovely finish.
£13.00

Mas La Plana 2005, Torres, Penedès Red
Ripe, rich, and earthy. Dark cherry and blackcurrant character, is balanced with complex oak and soft tannin.
£25.00 WAIT

Mayor De Castilla Roble 2007, Viña Arnaiz, S.A., Castilla y León
Attractive nose of fruit, coffee, and leather, with notes of vanilla oak. Very juicy, meaty palate with a long sweet finish.

Mogar Roble 2006, Ribera Del Duero Red
Game and chocolate, balanced with sweet fruit on the nose. Good depth and stucture and excellent style.

Mogar Vendimia Seleccionada 2006, Ribera Del Duero Red
Deep garnet colour, with a rich spicy nose of white pepper with floral notes. Quite sweet, ripe fruit mellows out the tannins.

Good, meaty mid-palate with long finish.

O Fournier Spiga 2005, Ribera del Duero Red
Big, rich nose, with a beautiful varietal aroma and deep concentration. Opulent fruit on the palate and velvety tannins.
£18.00 DBY, FLA

Olarra Clasico Reserva 2005, Rioja Red
Attractive leafy dried black fruit aromas with hints of spice. Complex palate with cherry oak, fine tannins, and fresh acidity.

Orben 2005, Rioja Red
Ruby-garnet in colour. Still developing; tight fruit with underlying richness, and a long finish.
£20.00 LIB

Pago De Carraovejas Crianza 2006, Ribera Del Duero Red
Excellent intense red fruit on the nose, with rich fresh fruit on the palate, elegant sutble tannins, and good length.
£33.30 WAIT, MOR, HAR, HDS, HVN, MWW

Pago De Cirsus Cuvee Especial 2004, Navarra Red
Enormous red, jammy, ripe fruit with sweet aromas. Fresh palate and tight tannins. Very expressive, with a good fresh finish.

Pago De Larrainzar 2005, Navarra Red
Ripe red fruits on the nose. Good concentration of flavour. Chocolate and savoury notes on the palate. Nice long finish.
£17.30 GBA

Pago De Larrainzar 2006, Navarra Red
Lovely hue, with red cherry and

a light perfume on the nose.
Tannic, savoury, and salty. A ripe,
gentle wine.
£17.30 GBA

Palacio De Otazu Altar 2004, Navarra Red

Fresh cassis nose with notes of
leather, and showing some oaky
character. Intense cassis and
black fruit on the palate. Chewy,
dry tannins.

Palacio De Otazu Dimension 2005, Navarra Red

Quite rich, plummy nose.
Black fruit on the palate with
some green notes on the finish.
Good acidity, with chewy
tannins.

Peique Viñedos Viejos 2006, Castilla y León Red

Loaded with cherries and plums,
which all consolidate after
fifteen minutes' airing. Excellent
length, wonderful finish,
sumptuous.

Perpetual 2006, Torres, Catalonia Red

Mysterious complex nose. Very
pure and defined. Good quality,
with very elegant tannins. Pure,
classy and complex with a lovely
blackberry finish.

Reserva Martí 2004, Albet I Noya, Catalonia Red

Big fruit on the nose. High
tannins, good oak integration
and fruit intensity, with a long
finish.
VRT

Rivola 2006, Abadía Retuerta, Castilla y León Red

Oaky, spicy fruit on the nose.
Rich and complex palate of
sweet fig and raisin with hints
of roasted chestnut and chewy
tannins.
£12.00 LIB

Secastilla 2005, Viñas Del Vero, Aragón Red

Bright ruby colour, with dried
fruits on the nose. Nicely
rounded warm palate of spice
and dried fruits. Good length and
concentration.

Solar Viejo Crianza 2006, Rioja Red

Clear floral notes combine with
oak and redcurrants on the nose.
Rich, attractive red fruits balance
well with the acidity on the palate.
£8.00

Solluna 2006, Gran Clos, Catalonia Red

Firm nose of ripe fruit with rich
chocolate notes. Forward fruit on
the palate with chewy tannins.
This wine has good ageing
potential.

Taja Reserva 2003, Bodegas Mähler-besse, Murcia Red

Relatively light-bodied, with silky
soft, enduring flavours of figs.
There is a good mineral edge to
the tannic finish. A very sleek wine.

Torresilo 2006, Cillar De Silos S.l, Castilla y León Red

Attractive, lifted black plum
on the nose, with notes of
peppermint and apricot. Very
harmonious, with beautiful svelte
tannins. A very classy wine.
AAW

Ursa Maior Reserva 2005, Bodegas Ondarre, S.a., Rioja Red

Restrained floral, leather,
chocolate, and raisin aromas.
Ripe red and black fruits on the
palate, with chewy tannins and a
long finish.
£9.00 SPR

Valduero Reserva 2005, Ribera Del Duero Red

Pungent violets on the nose and

Spain. As many wineries as landscapes.

In Spain there are almost as many wineries as there are landscapes. The diversity of viticulture in the country is reflected in more than 90 grape varieties from 65 denominations of origin.

Our wines mirror our country's infinite beauty. Soil and climatic conditions ensure variety, personality and richness of style to please all discerning palates.

a rich, ripe, fruit-laden palate.
Subtle oak integration with a
lovely finish.
£19.50

Valtravieso Crianza 2005, Ribera Del Duero Red

A big wine, with lots of intense
berry fruits and dark cherries,
with good concentration of
flavour. Big structure with lots of
ripe tannins, and alcohol which
balances pleasantly with acidity
and length.

Viña Cerrada Reserva 2004, Rioja Vega, Rioja Red

Red fruit and spicy aromas,
with a hint of citrus peel. A
polished palate with good
structure and depth, and an
attractive finish.

Viña Mayor Reserva 2003, Hijos De Antonio Barceló, S.A., Castilla y León Red

Soft and elegant, with strong
varietal character. Ripe and
fruity palate, showing balance,
good depth of fruit, and
concentration.

Viña Mayor Toro 2005, Hijos De Antonio Barceló, S.A., Castilla y León Red

Wonderful colour, lovely dark
chocolate and cherry fruit. Silky,
with decent concentration and
a soft palate. Clear, fine, and
elegant.

Viñasperi 2006, Bodegas Carlos San Pedro Pérez De Viñaspre, Rioja Red

Soft, red fruit nose, with notes
of sour cherry and soft oak.
Attractive jammy palate with
oak providing weight, leading to
a powerful finish.

Vt Tinta Fina 2005, Bodegas Y Viñedos Valtravieso Ribera Del Duero Red

Big, solid, meaty, robust style.
Ripe, bold dark fruit flavours,
with a nice earthy finish.
Quite jammy, with warm oak
influence.

Zabrin Crianza 2005, Viñedos De La Aragona S.l., Murcia Red

Ruby colour. Berries and tobacco
on the nose, following onto
a ripe mid palate with good
length.

De Casta 2008, Torres Catalonia Rosé

Light, elegant wine. Nice
structure and fruitiness, with
light strawberry and cherry
flavours. Good weight. Long,
attractive finish.

Grupo Codorníu Raimat Abadía Rosé 2008, Catalonia Rosé

Dark ruby colour. Fresh fruit, with
a bit of a cream on the nose.
Palate is well-balanced with a
deep fruit character, and notes of
bitter cherry spice. Good acidity
and a sweet finish.
£7.00 MCT

Las Falleras Rosé 2008, Bodegas Murviedro, Utiel-Requena Rosé

Lovely lift on the nose. Good
definition. Fresh and lively with
notes of strawberry, cherry, and
blueberry. Good weight and
length.
£4.00 M&S

Palacio De Sada Rosado 2008, Bodega San Francisco Javier S.C., Navarra Rosé

Dry, fresh, fruity, and
flavoursome with notes of gentle
white pepper. Silky texture and
harmonious finish. An excellent
dry rosé.

Asda Extra Special Mas Miralda Vintage Cava 2005,

Codorníu Sparkling
Lovely pale yellow colour.
Medium intensity nose of dried
apricots, with dried figs and
some toastiness. Nice sweet
palate.
£6 ASDA

**Grupo Codorníu - Reina Maria
Cristina Reserva Vintage Brut
2006, Catalonia** Sparkling
Very rich, floral nose. Well-
balanced creamy taste on the
palate, with elegant lemony
notes and a long citrus finish.
£18.00 P&O

**Grupo Codorníu Raimat Gran
Brut NV, Catalonia** Sparkling
Very subtle bread aromas
and elegant fruit. Creamy
fruity palate, fresh and
balanced, with citrus character
and elegance.

**Mont Marçal Extremarium
Cava Brut NV, Catalonia**
Sparkling
Pale colour and good mousse.
Aromas of fresh, clean green
apples, with a woody edge, waxy
notes, and delicate restraint. A
great fizz.

**Reserva De La Familia 2005,
Juve Y Camps, Penedès**
Sparkling
Lemony and creamy, with
peach, green apple, and pear
aromas. The palate is fruity and
refreshing, with green flavours
and a soft mousse.

**Grupo Codorníu - Codorníu
Pinot Noir Brut NV,
Catalonia** Sparkling Rosé
Lovely, vivid rosé colour.
Dry, fresh, yeasty entry, with
berry fruit and good length.
Crisp and refreshing; excellent
quality.
£11.00 MCT, MWW, ODD, THS,
WUO

**Marqués De Monistrol
Premium Cuvée Vintage Rosé
2006, Catalonia** Sparkling
Rosé
Pale pink hue, with strawberry
and peach fruits, and a touch
of toastiness. Good acidity and
reasonable length.

**Pago De Cirsus Moscatel
Vendimia Tardía 2006,
Navarra** Sweet
Fresh, floral, spicy, and grapey
with notes of sweet orange.
Spicy, gingery, peach and apricot
fruit. Slightly oily, but also fresh,
concentrated, and balanced.

**Silvano García Dulce
Monastrell 2007, Murcia**
Sweet
Pronounced raisined, dried fig
nose. Intensely sweet raisiny
dried figs, with a touch of vanilla.
Very sweet and alcoholic, with
some freshness, and a Port-like
style. Ripe, rich, and spicy
- fantastic!
£9.30

**Classic Manzanilla NV,
Bodegas Fernando De Castilla,
Jerez-xérès-sherry** Sherry
Pale straw colour. Aromas of sea
breeze and fresh pine cone. Clean
and balanced, with a pleasant
finish.
£10.50

**Lustau Almacenista
Manzanilla Pasada (Cuevas
Jurado) NV, Jerez-xérès-
sherry** Sherry
Intense, nutty, slightly yeasty
nose, with hints of light green
apple. Fresh, tangy, and crisp, with
good balance and a long finish.
£20.00

**Lustau Añada Rich Oloroso
1990, Jerez-xérès-sherry**
Sherry
Pale amber colour. Nice complex

nose of dried fruit and caramel. Rich, nutty, powerful palate, with good backbone, balance, and a complex finish.
£17.00 WAIT

Lustau Solera Reserva Manzanilla Papirusa NV, Jerez-xérès-sherry Sherry
Pale straw colour. Lifted vanilla and hints of coconut on the nose. Clear, fresh hints of cinnamon and a dried almond finish.
£11.00

Matusalem Sweet Oloroso Vors NV, Gonzalez Byass, Jerez-xérès-sherry Sherry
Dark amber with green hues. Rich, toasty nose with intense coffee, dried fruit, flowers, and hints of citrus. Great structure and good finish.
£15.00 WAIT

Noé Pedro Ximénez Vors NV, Gonzalez Byass, Jerez-xérès-sherry Sherry
Dark cocoa bean colour, with richness on the nose. Rich chocolate wafer on the palate, with lasting notes fig, syrup and molasses on the finish.

Sandeman Royal Corregidor, Rich Old Oloroso Sherry NV, Jerez-xérès-sherry Sherry
Dark amber colour. Toasty nose with coffee and slightly bitter chocolate notes. Butter and toffee notes on the palate, with a dry and long finish.

Sandeman Royal Esmeralda, Fine Dry Amontillado NV, Jerez-xérès-sherry Sherry
Golden amber colour, with lifted honey and cedar on the nose. The well-balanced palate features notes of vanilla, hazelnut, chocolate, cooked confit, and coffee .

Solera 1847 NV, González Byass, Jerez-xérès-sherry Sherry
Carnation milk, with lifted coffee beans on the nose. Fresh creamy vanilla, ice cream, and slight toffee notes on the palate, with butterscotch on the finish.

Waitrose Solera Jerezana Manzanilla Sherry NV, Emilio Lustau S.A., Jerez-xérès-sherry Sherry
Nose of melon and honey. Sweet, round palate. Savoury tangy flavours, with a crisp, nutty finish.
£8.00 WAIT

BRONZE

Almaraz Rioja Blanco 2007, Bodegas Medievo, Rioja White
Hints of lemon and herbs on the nose, following through to a clean, fresh palate with notes of minerality.
£6.50 AVB

Bodegas Palacio Blanco Viura 2007, Hijos De Antonio Barceló, S.A., Rioja White
Red apple on the nose, with fresh acidity and a hint of honey on the palate.
£7.00 MRN

Burgans 2008, Bodegas Martin Codax, Galicia White
Light fruit and some spice on the nose. Shimmering mineral and salty notes, and apricot on the palate, with an elegant finish.
£9.00

Castel De Bouza 2008, Galicia White
Floral nose, and sweet, ripe fruit on the palate, with good balance and a crisp, flinty finish.
£10.00 AAW

Castillo Monte La Reina Verdejo NV, Castilla y León
White
Scented, bright elderflower and pure fresh fruit. A nicely textured, crisp, refreshing example of the variety.
NOW

Chardonnay Col·lecció 2007, Albert i Noya, Catalonia White
Melon combines with pear and a hint of greengage on the nose. Quite floral, with tropical fruit on finish.
VRT

Colección Cristina Calvache Blanco De Alboloduy 2007, Andalucía White
Reserved in character, with moderate weight and texture, and well-balanced fruit and acidity.

Don Pedro De Soutomaior 2008, Adegas Galegas, Galicia White
Very aromatic, with notes of passion fruit, and a nose reminiscent of Sauvignon Blanc. Good acidic balance.
£11.50

Finca La Colina Verdejo Cien X Cien 2008, Vinos Sanz, S.a., Castilla y León White
Bright, well-balanced tropical fruits, with apricot notes on the nose and palate. Long finish.
£13.00

Fortius Chardonnay 2008, Bodegas Valcarlos, Navarra White
Vibrant apple and mandarin on the nose. Very fruity, balanced by fresh acidity. Spicy mid-palate and finish.
£6.50 BRT

Fulget 2008, Maior De Mendoza Sl, Galicia White
Nicely balanced, with sprightly floral style, and notes of rich peachy fruit.
£9.00 D&M

Grupo Codorníu Raimat Viña 24 Albariño 2008, Catalonia White
Pale, attractive, lemon nose with honey and pleasant acidity on the palate, which ends in an elegant, soft fruity finish.
£8.50 MCT, ODD

Grupo Codorníu The Spanish Quarter Chardonnay/ Albariño 2008, Viñedos De España White
Pale citrussy fruits combine with savoury notes of salty melon and green pepper. Refreshingly crisp finish.
£7.00

Lagar De Bouza 2008, Castel De Bouza, Galicia White
Fruity and stylish nose. With good intensity and acidity, this is very fruity and racy, with a strong finish.
£11.00 AAW

Marks & Spencer Val do Salnes Albariño 2007, Bodegas Castro Martín, Galicia White
A lovely nose which is absolutely typical of the variety. A sweet, open palate, with plenty of intensity on the finish.
£10.00 M&S

Maurel Chardonnay 2007, Bodega Can Bonastre, Penedès White
Rich melon and tropical fruit flavours. Quite fresh, with lively young acidity. At its best now.

Montebuena Blanco 2008, Bodegas y Viñedos Labastida, Rioja White
Delicate spicy fruit on the nose.

Good depth and balance on the palate. Quite complex.

Naia 2008, Bodegas Naia, Rueda White
Vanilla and tropical fruits on the nose and palate. Medium-bodied, in a fruity, commercial style.
IDO

Nora 2008, Galicia White
Ripe exotic fruit nose of papaya and mango. Gentle, with a hint of minerality.
C&D

Pazo De Monterrey 2008, Bodega Pazos Del Rey, Galicia White
Scented, floral, elderflower style. Dry, with a hint of nuttiness, and lovely balance. Understated and appetising.

Príncipe De Viana Chardonnay 2008, Navarra White
Notes of melon, flowers and fresh citrus, with a greengage finish.

Real Compañia De Vinos Blanco 2008, White
Aromatic nose. Fresh and crisp on the palate. Well-balanced.
D&D

Salterio 2008, Bodegas Martín Codax, Galicia White
Floral nose, with sweet, ripe stone fruit on the palate. Nice mouthfeel and crisp finish.
£9.00

Soleira 2008, Bodegas Martín Codax, Galicia White
Inviting aromas of rich peach and honey. Confidently made, with freshness and intensity.
£9.00

Tesco Finest* Palestra Rueda 2008, Bodegas Agrícola

Castellana Scl, Rueda White
Bright nose, and a simple, well-balanced, medium-bodied palate that is juicy, fresh, and ripe.
£7.10 TESC

Tottó 2007, Mata D'abelló, Penedès White
Pale lemon colour. Clean oak and grapefruit on the nose. Light body with crisp acidity.

Val De Vid 2008, Rueda White
A zippy nose which is really fresh, bright, and zesty. Lean, refreshing, zippy palate of pineapple and citrus.

Valdamor 2007, Galicia White
Lovely subtle nose, with a rich, well-balanced palate, showing good acidity with light, attractive fruit.
£15.00 A&A

Viña Mayor Verdejo 2008, Hijos De Antonio Barcelo, S.A., Castilla y León White
Tropical fruit, with gentle acidity, and a fresh and persistent finish. Lovely underlying flavours and complexity.
£7.50

Xarel·lo De Ferré I Catasús 2007, Catalonia White
Light, aromatic blossom notes on the nose. Grapefruit palate with crisp acidity and light body.

1860 Tempranillo 2007, Marqués De Riscal, Castilla y León Red
Sweet raisin, with blackberry and digestive biscuit on the nose. A nutty, tannic palate, showing good ageing potential.
£9.00 ALE, ARM, EOR, EVW

Albret Reserva 2004, Príncipe De Viana, Navarra Red
Minty and herbal, with black fruit

aromas, chewy tannins, and juicy fruit.

Altico 2007, Bodegas Carchelo, S.l, Murcia Red
Dark black fruit aromas leading onto a well-balanced palate of dark fruit, with eucalyptus and herbal flavours.
£9.90 IDO

Altos R Reserva 2004, Rioja Red
Good, balanced style with notes of orange peel and strawberry, and lovely floral edges.
£15.00 LAI

Altozano Tempranillo 2008, Finca Constancia, Tierra De Castilla Red
Youthful, with fresh black fruits on the nose. Juicy, bittersweet fruit palate, with black cherry flavours

Añares Crianza 2007, Bodegas Olarra, S.A., Rioja Red
Oak, and redcurrant spice on the nose. Dry, with well-integrated tannins, and high acidity, and rich, red berry fruit flavours. A pleasant wine.
£7.90 WES, C&D

Artero Crianza 2006, Viñedos Y Bodegas Muñoz, La Mancha Red
Sweet bramble aromas combine with creaminess and berries on the nose. Palate of raspberry and red cherry with spicy oaky character, and good acidity.

Artesa Organic 2007, Rioja Red
Soft, concentrated, ripe fruit nose, with well-balanced fruit, and an attractive, spicy, fruity finish.
£7.40 FLA, WES

Artiga Old Vines Garnacha 2007, Artiga Fustel, Red
Pure Garnacha nose with raspberry, pepper, and mineral flavours. Fruit flavours are ripe but not overpowering, with good retention of freshness and minerality.

Azabache Graciano Reserva 2004, Bodegas Aldeanueva, Rioja Red
Attractive complex nose of vanilla and red berry. Quite lean and dry but with plenty of red fruit.
£15.00 EOR

Baboix 2005, Buil & Giné, Catalonia Red
Good density, with notes of plums, figs, red berries, and perfumed violet. Fresh and elegant, with good minerality.
£14.00 FLA

Badaceli 2005, Bodegas De Cal Grau, Catalonia Red
Dark garnet hue. A very rich nose of black plum and a little prune. A ripe palate with good acidity and flavours of blackberry, damson, and a touch of cigar box on the finish.

Beronia Barrel Fermented Tempranillo 2007, Rioja Red
Nice chocolatey toasty nose, with cooked raspberry on the palate. Mellow, clean and fresh, with good intensity and balance.
£9.00

Beronia Crianza 2006, Rioja Red
Fresh strawberry and cherry notes, with creamy vanilla oak. Good weight and fresh fruit, leading to a gentle, elegant finish.
£9.00

Beronia Rioja Gran Reserva 2001, Rioja Red
Well-developed nose with a pleasingly sweet palate of ripe red fruit with well-balanced tannins.
£16.00

Bodegas Artesa 2006, Rioja Red
Deep black cherry and plum aromas, with a marzipan edge. Good spicy vanilla oak with notes of cherry and mocha.
£7.80

Bodegas Palacio Reserva Especial 2005, Hijos De Antonio Barceló, Rioja Red
Bright, simple blackberry fruit aromas. Light palate with nice peppery notes.
£25.00

Campaneo Old Vines Tempranillo/Merlot 2008, Bodegas Aragonesas, Aragón Red
Deep red in colour, with good concentration of red fruit. Well-structured, with a slight lactic note.

Campo Viejo Gran Reserva 2002, Domecq Wines España S.A., Rioja Red
Rich palate of dark fruit and minerality, with well-integrated oak. Full-bodied, yet fresh and elegant.
£13.00 TESC

Caño Cosecha 2007, Pagos Del Rey Sl, Castilla y León Red
Fresh-scented, plummy, and juicy. Pleasing peppery undertones, with lovely freshness and length.

Cantos De Valpiedra 2006, Finca Valpiedra, S.l., Red
Good colour, with a savoury, spicy nose. Jammy fruit and berry palate, with a good finish.

Canus Verus Viñas Viejas 2005, Covitoro, Castilla y León Red
Pure silky coconut and banana with cherry fruit. Firm and sophisticated, this will age well.
£13.10

Carralero 2007, Vinos Del Bierzo, Castilla y León Red
Nice toasty oak and rich dark cherry fruit aromas leading to a palate of ripe fruit. Good tannins and structure.

Carta Roja 2001, Bodegas Y Viñedos Del Mediterráneo, Murcia Red
Interesting tertiary aromas of dried fruit, fruitcake, and roasted nuts.
£8.00

Casa De La Ermita Crianza Ecológico 2006, Murcia Red
Pure ruby in colour. Dry palate, with notes of fruit jam and black cherry, and high tannins carrying through to the finish.

Casa De La Ermita Idílico 2006, Murcia Red
Plum and cinnamon, with hints of vanilla on the nose. Well-balanced, with a medium body.

Casa De La Ermita Roble 2008, Murcia Red
Red berry fruit nose, with some pencil lead and cedar chip notes.

Castell Del Remei-1780 2005, Catalonia Red
Dried fruits with complex smoke and chocolate character from oak. This complexity carries through to the palate, with very fresh tannins, and notes of coffee on the finish

Castillo Monte La Reina Vendimia Seleccionada NV, Castilla y León Red
Creamy coffee mocha nose, with a palate of spicy, dry, raisiny fruit, and notes of vanilla and coffee on the finish.
NOW

Celeste 2006, Torres, Ribera Del Duero Red
Spicy tobacco on the nose, with ripe berries, stone fruits, and leather on the palate. Dry tannins and moderate length.

Cervoles 2006, Catalonia Red
Deep colour, and leggy muscular style. Palate of ripe fruit and dolly mixtures, with a meaty tannic bite

Cervoles Estrats 2005, Catalonia Red
Aromas of blackberries, leather, roses, and blackcurrants on the nose. Very well-balanced.

Church Mouse Syrah Mazuelo Tempranillo 2008, Bodegas San Marcos, Extremadura Red
Intense black fruit flavours, combine with plums, well-balanced oak, and a generous, seductive palate.
GYW

Clos Reserva 2001, Federico Paternina, Rioja Red
Attractive minty and fruity style. Juicy, meaty structure, with a sweet chocolate finish.
EHL

Colección Jaime Rodríguez 2004, Remelluri, Rioja Red
Rich, jammy, damson nose with good lift. Full-bodied, with good acidity, and an attractive long finish.
£52.00 AAW

Conde De Los Andes 2001, Federico Paternina, Rioja Red
Fresh, balanced palate of spicy dried fruit and hazelnuts, and an elegant cherry finish.
EHL

Contino Reserva 2005, C.V.N.E., Rioja Red
Traditional oaky nose with soft ripe fruit, good balance, and length.
£33.00 WAIT, HMA

Cosme Palacio Reserva 2004, Hijos De Antonio Barceló, S.A., Rioja Red
Nice fruity chocolatey notes, with hints of minty eucalyptus on a very meaty and juicy palate.
£13.00 WAIT

Coto De Imaz Gran Reserva 2000, El Coto De Rioja, S.A., Rioja Red
Aromatic spicy nose of mineral black fruit. Highly structured, quite acidic palate, with a firm, complex, mineral finish.
ACG, CHH, WMA, YOB

Coto De Imaz Reserva 2004, El Coto De Rioja S.A., Rioja Red
Inky and peppery, with damson aromas, and plenty of juicy fruit, with minty, liquorice notes on the palate.
£12.50 CHH, ACG, WMA, YOB

Cruz De Piedra 2007, Co-op Virgen De La Sierra, Aragón Red
Jammy red fruit on the nose, with white pepper, and ripe, mouth-filling tannins, and plenty of fresh spice.
£6.00 CAM, FNW, GWW, WSO

Cuatro Pasos 2007, Bodegas Martín Codax, Castilla y León Red
Warm, rather juicy and fruit nose, with hints of pepper and

rolling tannins on the palate.
£8.90

**Cueva Del Perdón 2006,
Bodegas Murviedro, Valencia
Red**
Dried fruit nose, with smokiness,
spice, and soft, ripe fruit. Good
tannins and notes of toasty
vanilla oak.

**Cuna De Reyes Reserva 2002,
Rioja Red**
Pale garnet in colour. Vegetal
nose, with some fruit and
drying tannins.
£14.80 CNA

**Dinastía Vivanco Crianza
2005, Rioja Red**
Fresh, balanced aromas. Cherry
and raspberry character, with
notes of soft cedar and vanilla
oak, and a gentle bramble fruit
finish.
£11.00 FLA

**El Titan Del Bendito 2005,
Castilla y León Red**
Heavy, chunky, serious style. Big
and bullish with plenty of new
oak, but perhaps needs four or
five years to allow its texture to
settle.

**Epulum Crianza 2007,
Bodegas La Catedral, Rioja
Red**
Oak and redcurrant nose, with
good complexity, and rich red
berry flavours. Very oaky, but
well-made, with integrated
tannins.

**Ferratus 2005, Bodegas
Cuevas Jiménez, Ribera Del
Duero Red**
Damson red in colour, with
youthful mulberry fruit flavours.
Rich, with cinnamon and
powerful fruit.
£25.00 GWW

**Finca L'argata 2006, Joan
D'anguera, Catalonia Red**
Dense, spicy dark fruit nose.
Sweet lush blackberries abound
on the palate.

**Finca Manzanos Joven 2008,
Rioja Red**
Red berry fruit nose, medium
intensity, with fresh berry
flavours, good balance, and
medium length.
£6.00 AAW

**Finca Muñoz Reserva De La
Familia 2006, La Mancha Red**
Sweet dark fruits and spice
combine with oaky vanilla and
cream notes. Firm tannins and
good balance.

**Finca Terrerazo 2006, Bodega
Mustiguillo, Utiel-Requena
Red**
Ripe, spicy baked berries with
a lot of sweet spicy oak on the
nose. Full and ripe, with lots of
oak and extraction, and grainy
tannins.
£25.00 LIB

**Fuenteseca Organic Red 2008,
Ecovitis, Utiel-Requena Red**
Vibrant, young, plummy nose,
with a touch of vanilla oak.
Juicy, medium-bodied, with well
integrated oak and soft tannins.
£6.80

**Garduna 2006, Abadía
Retuerta, Castilla y León Red**
Pleasing aromas of savoury,
rich, and well-managed oak.
Considerable sweetness of fruit,
with smooth tannins, and a fresh
finish.
£62.00 LIB

**Giné Giné 2007, Buil & Giné,
Catalonia Red**
Deep red fruit and caramel spice
on the nose. Ripe, deep palate,

with good weight and grippy tannins.

Gontés 2005, Jesús González Teso, Rioja Red
Rich and dense, with ripe black fruit. Very modern style, with a concentrated black fruit palate, and firm grippy tannins.

Gran Tempranillo 2008, Torrelongares, Cariñena Red
Fresh aromas of cherry and berry, with a ripe, juicy red fruit palate, some vanilla, and a dry finish.
£3.50 HOH

Gran Tesoro Garnacha 2008, Bodegas Borsao S.A., Aragón Red
Light, fresh, fruity nose, and a refreshing, subtle palate, with good fruitiness and fine-grained tannins.
£3.50 TESC

Grans Muralles 2005, Torres, Catalonia Red
Bright, mid-raspberry red. Young raspberry fruit on the nose. Lively rich black fruit palate and moderate length.

Hacienda Shiraz 2007, Bodegas Y Viñedos De La Casa Del Valle, S.A., Castilla-la Mancha Red
Lovely cassis, dark cherry, and damson nose. Rich plummy flavours and sweet vanilla oak, with plenty of tannins.
HOH

Hécula 2006, Bodegas Castaño, Murcia Red
Nose of stone fruit and smokiness, which follows through to the palate. Good length, with green tones on the finish.
£8.50 LIB

Hiru 3 Racimos 2005, Bodegas Luis Cañas, Rioja Red
Lovely concentrated dark black fruit, with creamy overtones, and a hint of mocha and chocolate. Very good length.
AAW

Honoris De Valdubon 2005, Red
Vanilla oak nose with hints of summer berries. Clean, elegant palate.
£35.00

Ijalba Crianza 2005, Rioja Red
Great pungency and elegance. Vibrant fruit, figgy and interesting, with a great modern style.
£9.00 VRT

Ijalba Reserva 2004, Rioja Red
Attractive berry nose. Bright red berry palate, with a simple and pleasing, delicate, floral raspberry flavour and firm tannins.
£11.00 WMA

Inspiración Valdemar 2006, Rioja Red
Hints of green peppercorn combine with primary fruit on the nose. A palate of juicy fruit combined with rich tannins.

Iv Expresión 2006, Bodegas La Purísima, Murcia Red
Bright ruby colour, with an attractive nose of nuts, olives, soft dried fruit, and spice. Quite dry finish, but attractive, with good length.
ASW

Jme 2007, Bodegas Muriel, Rioja Red
Rich gamey fruit on nose. Lots of spice, with rich fruit and savoury flavours on the palate.
D&D

Juan Luis Cañas Reserva 2004
Red
Some smokiness and cherry character. Good structure, with medium weight, nice juicy blackcurrant fruit, and spice.

La Copa Garnacha 2008, Bodegas Aragonesas, Aragón
Red
Bright bramble and mulberry fruit, rich and sweet, with subtle, well-integrated oak tannin.
£8.00 MOR, BUT, MKH

La Copa Tempranillo 2008, Bodegas Aragonesas, Aragón
Red
Fresh red fruit, with elegant, well-balanced and integrated oak. Rounded and structured, with good length.
£8.00 MOR, C&H, TOT

Ladera De La Vega Garnacha 2006, Viñedos Y Bodegas Muñoz, La Mancha Red
Sweet and perfumed, with very seductive oak. Plummy fruit with a crunchy texture, lovely balance and freshness.

Luis Cañas Crianza 2006, Rioja Red
Soft, fleshy red and black fruits on the palate, with great acidity and length.
AAW

Marks & Spencer Bellmunt Priorat 2006, Long Wines, Catalonia Red
Nose of spice, chocolate, and cherry juice. Medium-bodied, with a peppery finish.
£12.00 M&S

Marks & Spencer La Sabrosita Old Vine Garnacha 2007, San Gregorio, Aragón Red
Concentrated and densely flavoured, with well-balanced

red pepper on the nose. Palate of rich red fruits, spice, and balanced acidity, with good intensity and finish.
£6.00 M&S

Marks & Spencer Montsant Old Vine Garnacha 2005, Falset, Catalonia Red
Oak and blackcurrant combine with herbaceous notes. Rich and full-bodied, with firm tannins and long ripe finish.
£9.00 M&S

Marks & Spencer Nos Riqueza Ribera del Duero 2006, Telmo Rodríguez, Ribera del Duero
Red
A gentle nose of ripe, integrated damson, redcurrant, and slightly sour cherry. Medium-bodied, with dry, grippy tannins.
£10.00 M&S

Marks & Spencer Pena del Infierno 2006, Telmo Rodríguez, Ribera del Duero
Red
Light damson red in colour. Showing developed fruit, bubblegum, and cherries. Good length.
£17.00 M&S

Marqués De Arienzo 2003, Domecq Bodegas, Rioja Red
Gentle oak and spice nose with a lot of definition. Oak dominates the palate, with a core of sweet fruit and pleasant finish.
£9.90

Marqués De Cáceres Reserva 2004, Rioja Red
Red fruit aromas, following through to the palate, which shows balanced oak, with good structure and length.
£15.00 EOR, MWW, ODD, WAV

Marqués De Griñon Tempranillo 2007, Rioja Red
Ripe palate of juicy blackberries, reminiscent of leafy hedgerows, balanced by feisty acidity. This would be a good food wine.

Marqués De La Concordía Tempranillo 2007, Rioja Red
Nose of damson fruit, with good quality, dark, spicy fruit on the palate.

Marqués De Terán Edición Especial 2007, Bodegas Regalia De Ollauri S.l, Rioja Red
Nose of dried fruit and spice, with firm tannins and a lingering finish.

Marquesa De La Cruz Tempranillo 2007, Bodegas Santo Cristo, Aragón Red
Sweet, aromatic flavours of cut grass. Good balance, with some bitter tannins but also youthful freshness.
£6.10 WAIT, GYW

Martín Sarmiento 2005, Bodegas Martín Codax, Castilla y León Red
Complex nose, with hints of chocolate. Good tannins and structure.
£9.00 WAIT

Monasterio De Santa Ana Crianza 2005, Bodegas Y Viñedos Casa De La Ermita, S.l., Murcia Red
Ruby red, with blackcurrant, eucalyptus, and mint on the nose. Showing real balance, with notable tannins.
£6.70 TESC

Monasterio De Santa Ana Monastrell 2007, Bodegas Y Viñedos Casa De La Ermita, S.l., Murcia Red
Slightly resinous, traditional bouquet, followed by flavours of dried fruit and herbs. Dryish tannins, but good herby, cedary length.

Montal Garnacha 2007, Vinícola Del País, Tierra De Castilla Red
Blackcurrant and cherry vanilla nose. Ripe dark fruit flavours on the palate. Very drinkable.

Morlanda Crianza 2005, Viticultos Del Priorat S.l, Catalonia Red
Berry fruit aromas, hints of bramble, leading to a rich,

concentrated palate, with fine,
elegant tannins.
£25.00

Museum Real Reserva 2004, Finca Museum S.L., Castilla y León Red

Mushroom and red berry nose,
with full body and good acidity,
underpinned by mouthcoating
tannins.

Navajas Reserva 2004, Rioja Red

Deep plum in colour, with soft
red and black fruit, and hints of
spiciness and cinnamon. Soft,
integrated, grippy tannins, with
good acidic structure, and a long
finish.
£14.60 MOR, CPB

Negralada 2006, Abadia Retuerta, Castilla y León Red

Strawberry and spicy vanilla
aromas, with a big, fairly chunky
mouth-feel of ripe bramble and
strawberry fruit. Firm, tannic
structure provides a backbone,
backed up by toasty oak, and a
big bold, balanced finish.
£60.00 LIB

Pago De Cirsus Opus 11 2006, Navarra Red

Big, bold and chewy with notes
of cassis and black cherry, fruit
jelly, chocolate, violet, and
vanilla. Good complexity.

Pago De Cirsus Seleccion De Familia 2005, Navarra Red

Spicy, intense black fruit
combines with fresh red berries
on the nose. Good structure,
freshness, and length.

Pago De Cirsus Vendimia Seleccionada 2005, Navarra Red

Meaty, spicy, oaky nose with
deep red fruit. Good balance,
with a long, fresh finish.

Peique Selección Familiar 2005, Castilla y León Red

Solid fruit in the mouth,
with grippy tannins on the
finish, and decent length
and structure.

Pleyades Shiraz 2007, Terrai Viñedos Y Crianzas S.L., Cariñena Red

Complex and fruity, with a
spicy black pepper palate, and
concentrated meaty flavours.
£5.00 ASDA

Príncipe De Viana Reserva 1423 2003, Navarra Red

Black fruit and red berries on the
nose. On the palate, the fruit is
integrated, with some secondary
leathery characteristics.

Priorat 2006, Mas La Mola, Catalonia Red

High toned aromatic nose,
perfumed with red fruits. Fresh,
rounded palate, good weight, and
excellent persistence.
£26.00 LIB

Pujanza Norte 2006, Rioja Red

Lovely long chocolate notes on
the palate, and full fruit flavours.
High tannins, and a simple but
pleasant finish.
£38.30 IDO

Quinta De Tarsus 2006, Domecq Wines España S.A., Castilla y León Red

Well-defined nose, with notes
of apricot and orange blossom.
Youthful, assertive palate with
plenty of vigour, and good purity.
PRD

Quinta El Refugio Tinto 2006, Bodegas Torreduero S.A., Castilla y León Red

Meaty and gamey, with a savoury
character, and intense mouthfilling
strawberry fruit. The tannins are

quite firm, and the acidity is balanced, with decent length.
£6.80

Ramón Bilbao Mirto 2006, Rioja Red
Big wine, packed with toastiness, ground coffee, dark, rich berry fruit, and resinous oak. An abundance of fruit stands up to oak and tannins.

Ramón Bilbao Viña Turzaballa 2001, Rioja Red
Complex aromas, with graceful maturity, good rich taste, and a sweet chocolate finish. Will come alive with food.

Real Compañia De Vinos Cabernet Sauvignon 2008, Red
Ripe berry and blackcurrant flavours abound in this young, fresh, vibrant wine.
D&D

Remelluri 2005, Rioja Red
Complex, rich fruit. Elegant, dry fruit on the finish.
£15.00 AAW

Ribereño 2007, Ribera Del Duero Red
Chewy, ripe plum nose, with hints of loganberry. Well-integrated, fruity, silky tannins, floral undertones, and balanced acidity, with medium length.

Rioja Vega Crianza 2006, Rioja Red
Flavours of oak, chocolate, and redcurrants are balanced by dry, chewy tannins. Medium length with attractive oak.

Rioja Vega Reserva 2005, Rioja Red
Notes of leather, coconut, oak, and raisin fruit. Well-balanced blend of traditional and modern styles.

Ruconia Crianza 2004, David Saenz De Santamaria Porres, Rioja Red
Bright, sweet, leafy strawberry notes, with grippy tannins and good acidity.

Sangre De Toro 2007, Torres Catalonia Red
Bright ruby in colour. Bramble nose, with a slight medicinal note, leading to a cherry palate with good length.
£7.00 WAIT

Secreto Reserva 2003, Hijos De Antonio Barceló, S.A., Castilla Y León Red
Showing some development, with farmyard and mushroom character, good acidity, and balanced tannins.
BTH

Selección Especial 2006, Abadía Retuerta, Castilla y León Red
Attractive oaky berries on the nose, with a pleasant mouthfeel, and well-integrated oak.
£17.00 LIB

Senda De Los Olivos Edición Especial 2006, Bodega Pago De Cirsus, Ribera Del Duero Red
Lovely perfumed fruitiness, attractive fresh red berries, soft tannins, delicate acidity, and good integration and balance on the palate.

Señorío De Lampedusa Crianza 2005, Bodega Pago De Cirsus, Navarra Red
Deep rich red, with orange-hued tints. Good, developed red berry notes, with great expression.

Senorio De Sarria Viñedo No 7 2005, Navarra Red
Opaque., with spicy morello cherry aromas. Juicy plums

on the mid-palate, and good, refreshing peppery length.
£8.80

Siglo Reserva 2003, Domecq Wines Espana S.A. (Bodegas Age), Rioja Red
Nose of red fruits, coffee, and vanilla oak. Palate of stewed berry fruit, with lots of woody spice.
£10.00

Syrah Col·lecció 2006, Albert I Noya, Catalonia Red
Rich, ripe, cooked fruit aromas. Sweet cherry flavours with nice finish.
VRT

Taja Excelencia 2005, Bodegas Mähler-besse, Murcia Red
Clean fresh fruit, with some spicy tobacco. Good depth and acidity.

Taja Monastrell 2007, Bodegas Mähler-besse, Murcia Red
Perfumed jammy notes on the nose. Rich, ripe mouthfilling wine with nice length.

Terrai Shiraz 2007, Covinca, Cariñena Red
Slightly vegetal farmyard nose. Juicy fruits on the palate with plum, cherry, and some unripe blackberry. Good length.

The Pilgrimage Mazuelo 2008, Bodegas San Marcos, Extremadura Red
Youthful and brambly, with good soft fruit, and herbaceous and spicy notes on the nose. Smooth tannins and an attractive finish.
£6.60 ASDA, GYW

Torre Beratxa Tinto 2008, Anecoop Bodegas - Bodega Tafalla, Navarra Red
Lovely vibrant fruit on the palate, this is fresh, vigorous and well-made.
£4.00 OHI

Trapio 2006, Bodegas La Purísima, Murcia Red
Youthful, forward fruity nose. Quite an assertive wine with tannic fruit.
£10.00 ASW

Valdubon Reserva 2004, Ribera Del Duero Red
Gamey old fruit on the nose, with some complexity. Good attack and structure, this is rich, fast, and fruity.
£20.00

Valduero Crianza 2006, Ribera Del Duero Red
A dry-edged wine with good tannins, and a palate of violets, blackberry, cherry, and meatiness. This is a wine with potential, good acidity, and moderate length.
£14.50

Valserrano Garnacha 2005, Viñedos Y Bodegas De La Marquesa, Rioja Red
Brambly red fruit. Layers of spice and cigar notes. A serious wine with excellent length.
JAS

Valserrano Reserva 2004, Viñedos Y Bodegas De La Marquesa, Rioja Red
Rich fruit and well-structured, with good oak, firm acid and tannin grip.
AVB, JAS, WIL

Valtravieso Reserva Especial 2004, Ribera Del Duero Red
Good cherry and jammy fruit. Rich and ripe, with evident oak and good length.

Vega Montan Eclipse 2005, Bodegas Adria, Castilla Y León Red
Seductive nose leads seamlessly into a fruit bowl of flavours, with excellent structure and balance.

Will age well and would be a good food wine.

Vega Real Crianza 2006, Ribera Del Duero **Red**
Brambles, damson, and leather on the nose, with lots of sweet black fruit on palate, while excellent extraction enhances the good length.

Vega Tolosa Bobal Old Vines 2007, Castilla-La Mancha **Red**
High-toned, high-baked blackberry notes. The palate is warm and ripe, with black fruit and a peppery, gravy texture.

Viña Al Lado De La Casa 2005, Vila Viniteca, Murcia **Red**
Warm dry fruit notes, some reduction, with an attractive, gentle juicy, jammy fruit palate, and a medium finish.

Viña Albalí Gran Reserva 2002, Félix Solis Avantis S.A. Castilla-La Mancha **Red**
Gorgeous complexity. Milk chocolate and tar notes combine with hints of tobacco. Balanced and smooth, with a great finish.

Viña Cerrada Crianza 2006, Rioja Vega, Rioja **Red**
Plums, damsons, and redcurrants. Youthful, with high acidity and a ripe backbone of red fruits.

Viña Mayor Crianza 2005, Hijos De Antonio Barceló, S.A., Castilla Y León **Red**
Deep red colour with medium intensity. Good fruit, with spice and pepper, very well-balanced and elegant.
£9.90 BTH

Viña Mayor Gran Reserva 2002, Hijos De Antonio Barceló, S.A., Castilla y León **Red**
Black cherry, tar, and blackberry. Full, rich tobacco and leather flavours with dry and astringent tannins, and a long, hot finish.
£20.00

Viña Mayor Roble 2007, Hijos De Antonio Barceló, S.A., Castilla y León **Red**
Scented black fruit, with hints of savoury spice. Flavoursome, with a note of pepper. Good tannins and length.
£7.50

Viña Real Gran Reserva 1999, C.V.N.E., Rioja **Red**
Classic tobacco-tinged Rioja. The nose is generous but elegant, and starting to develop, but with promise of more to come.
£19.00 WAIT, HMA

Vt Vendimia Seleccionada 2005, Bodegas Y Viñedos Valtravieso, Ribera Del Duero **Red**
Well-structured style. Some cassis and blackberry notes. Jammy style, with quite firm tannins.

Yllera Vendimia Seleccionada 2002, Castilla Y León **Red**
Oily, oaky aromas, with dry, sour fruit, notable tannins with grippy nature, and a rather long finish.

Ar, Flor De A10 2008, Anta Bodegas, Castilla y León **Rosé**
Roses and berries on the nose. Confectionary. Good acid balance. Sweet, hot, lingering finish.

Pirineos Merlot Cabernet 2008, Aragón **Rosé**
Soft and fruity, with notes of pear drop. Dry, with good vinosity and length. Pretty serious and persistent.

Príncipe De Viana Rosado Cabernet Sauvignon 2008, Navarra Rosé
Ripe strawberry and raspberry on the nose. Nicely structured, with little spice on the finish. Refreshing.

Stork Tower Tempranillo Shiraz Rosado 2008, Hijos De Antonio Barceló, Castilla y León Rosé
Bubblegum and delicious fruit on the nose. Simple but oh-so drinkable.
£6.10 BTH

Viña Albalí Rosado Tempranillo 2008, Félix Solis Avantis S.A., Castilla-La Mancha Rosé
Lifted floral, strawberry, and bitter notes. Finish is quite long, spicy, and hot.
£6.00 TESC

Cava Brut Nature "Joan Raventos Rosell" NV, Catalonia Sparkling
Lovely herby apple nose, and a toasty herby palate. Mouthfilling mousse and a good finish.

Cava Cristalino Brut Nature Reserva NV, Jaume Serra, Catalonia Sparkling
Herby mineral nose. Rich toasty palate. Lively acidity. Nicely complex.

Clos Monistrol Vintage Brut 2006, Bodegas Marqués De Monistrol, Catalonia Sparkling
Nice, fresh, herbaceous, and slightly mineral nose. Good fine mousse. Clean, refreshing acidity.

Donacella Brut Cava NV, Grupo Codorníu, Catalonia Sparkling
Notes of apples, yeast, and toast. Light in fruit, but elegant, with great balance and length.
SPR

Freixenet Vintage Especial 2007, Catalonia Sparkling
Delicate aromas of flowers, with hints of lemon. Well-made, with well-integrated mousse.
£11.00

Grupo Codorníu Selección Raventós Brut NV, Catalonia Sparkling
Pale gold colour. Very crisp and clean, with fine bubbles leading to a long lasting finish.
£10.00 FEN, MCT, MWW, ODD

Grupo Codorníu Vintage Brut 2006, Catalonia Sparkling
Appealing and atrractive nose with minty, creamy notes, a well-integrated mousse and good length.
£12.00 TESC, P&O

Grupo Codorníu Raimat Brut Nature NV, Catalonia Sparkling
Fresh vibrant nose with round, smooth, mature fruit. Dry citrus finish.

Grupo Codorníu Raimat Chardonnay Brut NV, Catalonia Sparkling
Restrained and delicate nose. Brioche and sweet fruit on the palate, with lemony freshness.

Marqués De La Sardana Brut 2007, Viñedos-Bodegas Covides, Catalonia Sparkling
Fresh, sweet nose. Well-balanced on the palate with good weight. Long citrus finish.
£5.60 MHV

Marqués De Requena Brut Nature NV, Torre Oria, Catalonia Sparkling
Floral nose, with apple fruit and good freshness. This is an elegant Cava in a light style.

Mas Macia Cava Reserva NV, Fermi Bohigas, Catalonia
Sparkling
Pale in colour, with a good mousse, rich oiliness, intense honeyed notes, guava and tropical fruit.
£12.00

Ms 4.7 Cava Brut Nature 2004, Finca Valldosera, S.a. Catalonia Sparkling
Pale yellow colour with intense aromas, and citrus flavours. The palate is round, spicy, and lemony.

Subirat Parent Cava Brut Nature 2006, Finca Valldosera, S.a., Catalonia
Sparkling
Yeasty, toasty nose. The palate shows some finesse, with a good mousse and lots of acidity.

Vilarnau Brut Nature 2005, Vilarnaul Sparkling
Very aromatic, with fresh green apples, grapefruit, and elderflower. Good juicy apple finish.
£10.00

Waitrose Brut Cava NV, Catalonia Sparkling
Green citrus fruit on a delicate, floral palate. Fine bubbles and good length. Clean and fruit-driven.
£6.00 WAIT

Waitrose Cava Castillo Perelada NV, Catalonia
Sparkling
Pale fair mousse, with a yeasty toffee nose which is ripe, clean, and fresh. Soft fizz structure.
£8.00 WAIT

Cava Campoviejo Rosado NV, Domecq Wines Espana S.A., Penedès Sparkling Rosé
Fresh, clean nose. Dry crisp

acidity, and an explosive mousse, with good fruit and reasonable length.

Donacella Rosado Brut Cava NV, Grupo Codorníu, Catalonia Sparkling Rosé
Fresh red berries on the nose, and crisp pink grapefruit and red fruit on the palate. Well-made.
SPR

Flama D'or Cava Brut Rose NV, Castell D'or S.l., Catalonia Sparkling Rosé
Fresh berry fruit on the nose, with mouth-tickling strawberry flavour that is quite enduring.

Lavit Brut Rosado NV, Segura Viudas S.A., Catalonia
Sparkling Rosé
Fresh and clean, with elegant fruit on the nose. Soft creamy mousse, with a strawberry palate, and a noticeably sweet, creamy finish.
£8.00

Sainsbury's Taste The Difference Vintage Cava Rosé Brut 2007, Grupo Codorníu, Catalonia Sparkling Rosé
Sweet red berry nose, and a dry medium-bodied palate, with white fruits and strawberry, leading to a fresh finish.
£10.00 SAIN

Antojo Rubio 2005, Dominio Del Bendito Sweet
Deep golden colour. Apricots and orange marmalade notes. Intensely sweet apricot on the palate, with a very oily texture. Acidity adds freshness to cut through the weight of this wine.

Dulce De Murviedro 2008, Valencia Sweet
Broad, ripe, aromatic flavour,

which has sweetness, balanced acidity, and excellent length. Very attractive, flavoursome wine.

Estrella De Murviedro Rosado 2008, Utiel-Requena Sweet
Deep golden colour. Apricot and orange marmalade notes. Intensely sweet apricot palate. Very oily texture, quite heavy. Some acidity adds freshness.
£5.00 BUC, MRN

La Gitana Manzanilla NV, Jerez-xérès-sherry Sherry
Nutty, appley aromas. Fresh, crisp, and balanced, with a tangy finish.
£8.30 WES, SAIN, TESC, WAIT, MWW, THS

Lustau East India Solera NV, Jerez-xérès-sherry Sherry
Lifted raisin and honey, with some cedar and mint aromas. Very nice palate that is complex and structured.
£9.00 WAIT

Lustau Moscatel De Chipiona NV, Jerez-xérès-sherry Sherry
Lightly nutty with a delicate almond palate, and balanced yeasty sugar cake character, leading to a clean finish.
£5.00 WAIT

Lustau Solera Reserva Puerto Fino NV, Jerez-xérès-sherry Sherry
Pale straw colour. Lifted asparagus and a slightly rubbery nose. Elegant finish.
£11.00

Manzanilla Solear NV, Bodegas Barbadillo, Jerez-xérès-sherry Sherry
Clean, fresh nose. Light style with pleasantly creamy palate and a tangy lift.

Sainsburys Taste The Difference Oloroso Sherry NV, Emilio Lustau S.A., Jerez-xérès-sherry Sherry
Restrained toffee nose, with a simple, spicy toffee palate and moderate length.
£6.50 SAIN

Sandeman Armada, Cream Oloroso NV, Jerez-xérès-sherry Sherry
Golden amber colour. Honey and spiciness on the nose with a good harmonious palate.

Sandeman Royal Ambrosante, Old Solera Pedro Ximenez NV, Jerez-xérès-sherry Sherry
Nice nose, with good intensity, marmalade and cedarwood. Good complexity and elegant finish.

Tio Pepe NV, Gonzalez Byass, Jerez-xérès-sherry Sherry
Intense fruit on a distinguished floral nose, good body, balanced acidity, and a zesty finish.
£9.50 WAIT

Waitrose Manzanilla Fina NV, Emilio Lustau S.A., Jerez-xérès-sherry Sherry
Fresh and fruity. Light with marked acidity and a crisp finish.
£6.00 WAIT

USA

Only a modest fleet of USA wine labels make it to these shores, mostly shadowed by the giant tankers of larger brand names. Their 'Yes We Can' attitude has already bumped them up to second place of UK imports, with varieties such as Petite Sirah and Ruby Cabernet amongst the fruitier styles available. Beyond the 95% dominance of Californian wines lie the more subtle, and pricier, styles found in Washington and Oregon. The latter's Pinot Noir received the only Gold medal for a red wine from the US. The nation has embraced international grapes, and from their multi-temperate climate growers have delivered their own version of these wines in true American fashion.

KEY FACTS

Total production
20m hectolitres

Total vineyard
208,000ha

Top 10 grapes
1. Cabernet Sauvignon
2. Merlot
3. Zinfandel
4. Pinot Noir
5. Syrah
6. Chardonnay
7. Sauvignon Blanc
8. Chenin Blanc
9. Pinot Gris/Grigio
10. Viognier

Top 10 regions
1. San Joaquin Valley
2. Lodi
3. Sonoma
4. Sierra Foothills
5. Napa Valley
6. Monterey
7. Santa Barbara
8. Paso Robles
9. Mendocino
10. Santa Cruz Mountains

Producers
Producers 1,605; Growers 4,500

2009 IWC PERFORMANCE

Trophies	1
Gold	3
Silver	23
Bronze	45

Sonoma-Cutrer Vineyards Sonoma Coast Chardonnay 2006, California White
A superb Chardonnay, with a very rich nose, and loads of good, fat, buttery, and rich flavours. Soft and rounded with good, fresh acidity on the finish.
£15.00 WAIT, BTH, MWW

Domaine Serene Grace Pinot Noir 2006, Oregon Red
Well-balanced, with good complexity, balance, and depth of flavour. A palate of redcurrants, violet, and raspberries, with a mineral underlay, and long lingering finish.

 VERMOUTH TROPHY

Quady Winery Vya Sweet Vermouth 2010, California Vermouth
Cinnamon, clove, and coffee nose, with sweet, intense Seville marmalade on the palate. Intriguingly rich and lingering, with astonishing freshness and length.
£15.00 HOH

SILVER

Beringer Vineyards Napa Valley Chardonnay 2006, California White
Elegant, mineral, quite Burgundian in style. Fine sweetness of fruit, with fresh acidity, lovely overall balance, and a good finish. Top class!
£12.00 THS

Macmurray Ranch Sonoma Coast Pinot Gris 2007, California, E. & J. Gallo Winery White
Pale gold, with an elegant nose

of honey. Intense flavours, with lots of texture and a clean finish.
£12.50

Marks & Spencer Carneros Schug Chardonnay 2007, California White
Apple fruit nose and classy oak, with zippy white fruits on the palate. Good balance with quite a long, fresh finish
£16.00 M&S

Napa Valley Carneros Chardonnay 2006, Robert Mondavi Winery, California White
Clean lemon meringue character. Fruity style, with toast, vanilla, and spice. Fresh ripe fruit and balanced acidity on the palate. Good balance and a clean finish.
£15.00

Beringer Vineyards Bancroft Ranch Merlot 2004, California Red
Dense nose of black fruit, dark chocolate, and oak. Mixed fruit entry, with silky texture and good acidity. Very well-balanced.

Beringer Vineyards Private Reserve Cabernet 2004, California Red
Complex, spicy, jammy, well-balanced and elegant, with a very long, sweet finish. Pleasing cassis fruit, lots of American oak notes.

Gnarly Head Zinfandel 2007, Delicato Family Vineyards, California Red
Lovely fruity nose of cherries and stewed red fruits. Rich, ripe and heavily fruity on the palate. Good length and depth.

Duckhorn Vineyards Merlot 2005, California Red
Clear, medium intensity, with full

flavour on the palate. Medium body, with lots of fruit, aromas of bramble jelly and cherry. Good balance and length.
£35.00 WAIT

E. & J. Gallo Winery Rancho Zabaco Heritage Vines Zinfandel 2007, California Red
Lovely plummy, dark cherry nose. Clean berry fruit, nicely spicy, with integrated alcohol, and a lovely, spicy finish.
£10.00 WAV

Gallo Family Vineyards Estate Cabernet Sauvignon 2003, E. & J. Gallo Winery, California Red
Lovely dark fruit and peppermint spice, with herbal freshness. Good layers of fruit, oak, and tannins. Good balance and lingering mineral length.
WAIT

J. Lohr Carol's Vineyard Cabernet Sauvignon 2005, California Red
Appealing bramble fruit nose. Well-structured, subtle sweet fruit palate, with lovely silky texture and a fine, long finish.

J. Lohr Estates Seven Oaks Cabernet Sauvignon 2007, California Red
Elegant bramble fruit nose, reflected on the rich, stylish palate, with lots of ripe blackcurrants, and a fresh finish.
£15.00

J. Lohr Hilltop Vineyard Cabernet Sauvignon 2006, California Red
Spicy, well-defined nose, showing a pleasing dark fruit character. Plummy, berryish palate, with nice spiciness and complexity. Great length and ageing potential.

Joseph Phelps Le Mistral 2006, California Red
A sweet, spicy nose, with notes of lightly roasted gamey, sweet pepper, and raspberry fruit. Clean, pure, and smooth, with soft oak, good length, and a balanced, fresh finish.
£30.00 WAIT

Ravenswood Lodi Zinfandel 2006, California Red
Lots of pepper, and a ripe mid-palate showing a warm raisiny almond character.
£9.00 MWW

Ravenswood Sonoma County Zinfandel 2006, California Red
An impressive, elegant nose of fermented fruits and spice, with cherry and notable tannins on the palate. This is a big wine with serious oak, powerful fruit, and a long finish.
£12.00

Ravenswood Teldeschi Zinfandel 2006, California Red
Slightly phenolic, with sweet wild cherry on the nose. A soft, round candy-box of ripe fruits, strawberry flumps, raspberry ruffles, and coconut. This is a big mouthful of a wine.
£25.50 MWW

Reynolds Family Winery Reserve Cabernet Sauvignon, Stags Leap District 2006, California Red
Full and rich, with good balance of fruit and oak. Sophisticated length, with nicely integrated oak and juicy berry flavours.
£89.00

Robert Mondavi Winery Napa Valley Cabernet Sauvignon 2006, California Red
Black fruit and cassis aromas,

with notes of spice, cedar, and freshness on the nose. Full, ripe palate of black fruit, dark chocolate, and well-integrated oak., with fine-grained tannins and good balance.
£20.00

Robert Mondavi Winery Napa Valley Carneros Pinot Noir 2007, California Red
Clean, pronounced morello cherry nose. Nice fruity palate, with a lovely balance of fruit and oak.
£20.00 COL

Rosenthal - The Malibu Estate Surfrider Red 2005, California Red
Vibrant cassis fruit and toasty oak. Delicious ripe fruit on the palate, with silky tannins, lively acidity, and textured oak.

Seghesio Sonoma Zinfandel 2007, California Red
Lovely perfumed nose with rich, ripe, complex cedar and spice. Sweet attack of biscuits and liquorice. Good tannins and long length.
£20.00 LIB

Sonoma-Cutrer Vineyards, Sonoma Coast Pinot Noir 2006, California Red
Attractive sweet cherry nose, with a hint of meatiness. Moderate depth and black fruit, with supporting acidity and pleasant, slightly drying length.
£20.00 WAIT, MWW

BRONZE

Badger Mountain Chardonnay 2007, Washington State
White
Pale lemon gold. Soft, juicy apples, pears, and vanilla, with a hint of light spice. Good length and well-balanced.

Beringer Vineyards Private Reserve Chardonnay 2006, California White
Melon and apple notes. Good fat texture, lovely buttery flavours, with quite dominant oak and a soft finish.

Bonterra Chardonnay 2007, California White
Toasty, light topaz coloured wine, with a concentrated cocktail of fruits and a refreshing citrus finish.
£10.00 WAIT, MWW

Dancing Bull Sauvignon Blanc, E. & J. Gallo Winery, 2008, California White
Scent of fennel, aniseed, and green apple. Warm, broad, and juicy, with a ripe finish.
£8.00 THS

Gallo Family Vineyards Estate Chardonnay 2005, E. & J. Gallo Winery, California White
Vanilla oak, very leesy, creamy, and flinty, with a full body and fresh acidity.
£30.00 WAIT

Gallo Family Vineyards Single Vineyard Laguna Ranch Chardonnay 2006, E. & J. Gallo Winery, California White
Intense and quite mineral. Attractive texture, with good acidity and grip. Classy style, very long, with quite strong oak.
£14.00

Estancia Pinnacles Ranches Chardonnay 2006, California White
Restrained tropical fruit and butterscotch aromas. Rich ripe fruit on the palate. Crisp, fresh acidity. Harmonious.
£10.70

Silverado Winery
Napa Valley soul with the heart of a pioneer

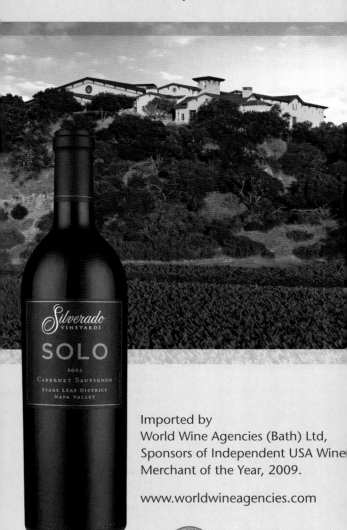

Francis Ford Coppola Presents Director's Cut Russian River Chardonnay 2007, California
White
Clean, ripe stone fruits, with a touch of starburst character. Nicely balanced by fresh acidity.
£17.00 HAX, NYW, ODD

Les Grands Chais De France Burlwood White Wine NV, California White
Lime, lemon, and tropical fruit on the nose. Citrus fruit flavours integrate well with firm acidity to give a youthful, light, pleasant wine.

Concannon Vineyard Single Vineyard Chardonnay 2007, Les Grands Chais De France Group, White
Restrained and complex, with some mineral and lees character, and hints of apricot. Round, soft, and creamy.

Marimar Estate Acero Chardonnay 2007, California
White
Strong, clean appearance. Lots of oak on the nose, along with floral and fruity notes. Creamy palate and a sweet finish.

Robert Mondavi Winery Napa Valley Fumé Blanc 2007, California White
Pale lemon in colour, showing gooseberries and floral hints on the nose. Attractive, with good acidity.
£15.00 HAR

Sonoma-Cutrer Chardonnay "Les Pierres" 2005, California
White
Nose showing finesse with lifted lemon meringue character. The acidity is well-balanced with dryness of oak.
£30.00 MWW

St Supéry 2008, Les Vins Skalli, California White
Rounded herbal and gooseberry flavours, with zingy acidity, good concentration, and length.
£20.00

Beringer Vineyards Founders Estate Old Vine Zinfandel 2006, California Red
Perfumed nose of rich fruit. A rich cake palate, with well-integrated oak.

Beringer Vineyards Stone Cellars Cabernet Sauvignon 2005, California Red
Nice balance of cooked berries and wood on the nose, with full, concentrated blackcurrant and raspberry fruit.

Big House Slammer Shiraz 2006, Les Grands Chais De France Group Red
Cinnamon, clove, liquorice, and tar, with warming spice and concentrated fruit on the palate, and slightly astringent tannins.

cherry compote and cinnamon on the palate, elegant texture, and an enduring finish.
£7.70 FLA, PAT

De Loach Russian River Valley Pinot Noir 2007, California Red

Jammy cherry and some shoe polish notes. Nice, fresh, varietal expression with some spice.
£14.00 LIB

Domaine Carneros Avant Garde Pinot Noir 2006, California Red

Very nice complex aromas of fresh fruit, with some pepper enhancing the structure of the palate.
£17.00 HMA

Eberle Winery Vineyard Selection Cabernet Sauvignon 2006, California Red

Sweet spice, peppermint, and dark fruit. Well-rounded tannins, good structure and length. A big, powerful wine.
£15.50 AAW

Evenstad Pinot Noir 2006, Domaine Serene Winery And Vineyards, Red

Intense bitter cherry nose. Very ripe, sweet fruit on palate with lots of oak. Well-balanced.

Francis Ford Coppola Presents Director's Cut Dry Creek Zinfandel 2006, California Red

Ruby red in colour. Volatile fruit on the nose, with a palate that is fruity, plum-laden, sweet, and dense, with a peppery finish.
£18.50 HAC, POR, RSO

Frei Brothers Reserve Pinot Noir 2006, E. & J. Gallo Winery, California Red

Dark fruit, with notes of cinnamon and spice on the

Brazin Zinfandel 2006, Delicato Family Vineyards, California Red

Perfumed violet nose with soft berry notes. Clean, generous mouthfeel with some spiciness.

Concannon Vineyard Limited Release Petite Sirah 2005, Les Grands Chais De France Group, Red

Black fruit and rhubarb notes, with fine-grained tannins, fresh acidity, and a silky smooth body.

Crossbarn 2005, Paul Hobbs Winery, California Red

Deep red in colour, with huge blackcurrant flavour, and hints of saddle, with very rich currant fruit. Complex, balanced, and very long.
£32.80 AAW

Cycles Gladiator Pinot Noir 2008, Hahn Family Wines, California Red

Bright, clean, juicy fruit, with

nose. Approachable, with dark spicy fruit on the palate, smooth texture, and good length.
£20.00

J. Lohr Estates Los Osos Merlot 2006, California Red
Fragrant black fruit nose, with sweet black fruit on the palate. Silky texture and supple tannins.
£10.00 WAIT

La Crema Sonoma Coast Pinot Noir 2007, Jackson Family Wines, California Red
Rich cherry and berry fruit nose with a spicy edge. Attractive bright cherry fruit palate. A fruit-driven style.
£17.00 WAIT

Marks & Spencer De Loach Pinot Noir 2007, California Red
Attractive, focused sweet cherry fruit. The nose has good definition, and the palate is fresh and full, with attractive fruit, richness and a meaty character.
£19.00 M&S

Marimar Estate "Don Miguel Vineyard" Pinot Noir 2004, California Red
Earthy, spicy, and evolved on the nose. Palate of fresh cherries, with a spicy edge.

Marmesa Cerro Romauldo Syrah 2006, California Red
Spicy, smoky, and earthy, on a developing nose, with a ripe plum palate, showing balanced structure and fruit concentration. Spicy, woody flavour, with notes of elegant spiced plum.
£11.00 FLA

Powers Merlot 2006, Washington State Red
Blackcurrant and raspberry leaf, with hints of soft vanilla. Good berry depth, smoky notes, and soft tannin. Medium weight wine with decent length.

Ravenswood Barricia Zinfandel 2006, California Red
Character of furniture wax, leather, and chocolate, with a tight, dry finish.
£25.50

Robert Mondavi Winery Reserve Cabernet Sauvignon 2005, California Red
Notes of tobacco and chocolate, with soft tannins, powerful fruit. Clean, with a long, fruity finish.
£50.00 HAR

Robert Mondavi Winery Woodbridge Shiraz 2006, California Red
Elegant spicy ripe plum flavours are balanced by refreshing acidity, leading to a good peppery finish.
£8.00 WAIT

Rosenthal - The Malibu Estate Cabernet Sauvignon 2005, California Red
Herbaceous, dusty green tea nose. Soft, elegant, and supple, with a clean finish.

Rosenthal - The Malibu Estate Merlot 2005, California Red
Slightly green cassis and smoky oak, with roasted coffee bean notes on the nose. Savoury and well-structured, with juicy, jammy fruit.

Seghesio Old Vine Zinfandel 2006, Sonoma County, California Red
Stylish, clean, and modern. Slightly varnishy nose with some tight-knit concentrated flavours of black fruit, spice, and oak.
£27.00 WAIT, LIB

Seghesio.Alexander Valley Sangiovese 2006, California Red
Savoury, chunky wine with black fruit flavours, an intriguing white pepper lift, and a long, dry finish.
£83.30 LIB

Smith And Hook Cabernet Sauvignon 2006, Hahn Family Wines, California Red
Well balanced, with a long finish, and good complexity Dark red currant note.
£22.00 FLA, PAT

Zinfandel Steinbeck Vineyard, Wine Bush Vineyard 2006, Eberle Winery, California Red
Perfect plum and cherry nose, with a dark chocolate palate, making a well-balanced wine.
£20.50 AAW

Marmesa Red Harvest Dessert Pinot Noir 2006, California Botrytis
Salmon pink in colour. Rich honey on the nose. Luscious palate.
£9.00

Quady Winery Elysium Black Muscat 2007, California Fortified
Attractive nose of cherry and plums. Clean ginger and cherry fruit on the palate.
£8.80 WES, HOH, MWW

Quady Winery Essensia Orange Muscat 2007, California Fortified
Lifted perfume of mandarin, with fresh pomegranate on the palate, and a violet blossom finish.
£8.80 WES, HOH, MWW

Other Countries

As if learning the wines of Italy and France wasn't enough to keep you busy, the world of wine just keeps getting bigger. This year the IWC welcomed a record 41 countries whose wines competed for international recognition. Amongst them was a Gold medal for an English sparkling wine, an example of the quality of this style on a global stage. Brazil and Mexico are slowly emerging from the Americas where monks and conquistadores brought vines hundreds of years ago; while from two climatic extremes, both Denmark and Thailand are playing their part in vineyard cultivation. India too has invested in vineyards around Mumbai and Bangalore, and with such a population already showing a keen interest in wine we had better hope there's enough left for the rest of us.

2009 IWC PERFORMANCE

Trophies	6
Gold	8
Silver	38
Bronze	75

BRAZIL

SILVER

Casa Valduga, Premium Merlot 2006, Serra Gaucha Red
Almost violet hue, with a good plummy nose of wild fruit, oak and spice, with red fruit flavours.

BRONZE

Casa Valduga, Premium Brut NV, Serra Gaucha Sparkling
Pale yellow gold in colour. Clean nose leading to a dry finish.

Coop. Vinicola Garibaldi, Espumante Garibaldi Moscatel NV Sparkling
Very pale in colour. Fresh and lightly aromatic, with a soft, fruity, easy style, with notes of lychee.

Vinhos Salton S/a Ind. E Com, Salton Volpi Pinot Noir 2007, Serra Gaucha Red
Masses of toast, coffee, and oak on the nose, with rich, velvety fruit beneath. Abundant oak on the palate, but also good fruit flavour.

Irmaos Molon Ltda, Mistela Reggio Di Castela 2004 Fortified
Nose of lifted ice-tea and fresh toffee apple, with a touch of subtle butter. Good acidity and elegant finish.

BULGARIA

BRONZE

Edoardo Miroglio Chardonnay Reserve 2007, Edoardo Miroglio Eood, Thracian Valley White
Peachy nose, notes of gentle oak with vanilla and tropical fruit. Clean and refreshing.

Domaine Boyar Merlot 2008, Domaine Boyar International Ad, Thracian Valley Red
Stewed plum nose with a gravelly edge, and hints of sweet berry and blackcurrants. The palate is slightly herby with beautiful fruit flavour.
£4.50 ASDA, BBZ

Domaine Boyar Solitaire Merlot 2007, Domaine Boyar International Ad, Thracian Valley Red
Creamy, dark fruit on the nose, with notes of herbs and spices. Herby palate with an attractive finish.

Encore 2007, Katarzyna Estate, Thracian Valley Red
Lovely freshness. Rich fruit, with nice creaminess and smooth tannins.

Yatrus Syrah 2007, Terra Tangra, Sakar Red
Sweet, juicy, ripe dark fruit on the nose. Well-balanced, with medium depth.

CANADA

GOLD

Thirty Bench Wine Makers Riesling 2007, Niagara Peninsula White
Begins with steel and petrol, which softens into rich green apple and lime, before stunning acidity slices through it all. A truly wonderful wine.

Inniskillin, Vidal Icewine 2007 Niagara Peninsula Sweet
intense rich aromas of buttery lemon caramel on the nose. Rich palate of luscious marmalade,

pudding, and hints of botrytis.
Long citrus finish with lovely
depth.

 CANADIAN ICEWINE TROPHY

Jackson-Triggs Niagara Estate, Proprietors' Reserve Vidal Icewine 2007, Niagara Peninsula Sweet
Creamy orange nose with beautiful floral, fruity flavours on the palate. Heavy-weight wine, with syrupy orange character, sweet not cloying, very smooth and full-bodied. Balanced, with long marmalade finish.

Southbrook Vineyards, Cabernet Franc Icewine 2006 Niagara Peninsula Sweet
Tawny colour, with a nose of summer pudding, redcurrants, and blackcurrants. Sweet palate, full of fruit, with a liquid honey texture. Delicious length - the astringency of tannins stops it clinging.

SILVER

Hillebrand Winery, Trius Chardonnay Barrel Fermented 2007, Niagara Peninsula White
Tropical peach and oak nose. Quite hot but complex, nutty flavours come through with savoury overtones. Quite classy.

Red Rooster Winery, Red Rooster Reserve Chardonnay 2007, Okanagan Valley White
Nose of guava, mango, butter, and oak. Refreshing acidity and ripe fruit concentration, with citrus, apple and mineral notes coming through on the palate. Finishes well.

Desert Hills, Desert Hills Syrah Select 2005, British Columbia Red
Ripe, with a smoky black fruit character, and spicy herbal notes. Palate of smooth fresh plums, with mouth-watering acidity. Balanced and elegant.

Inniskillin, Cabernet Franc Icewine 2007, Niagara Peninsula Sweet
Rose colour, with golden red tinges, like strawberries and cream in a glass. Good acidity, with medium body and a clean refreshing finish.

Inniskillin, Riesling Icewine 2007, Ontario Sweet
Crystalised lemon nose with a honeyed, almost barley sugar, quality. Good intensity, rich and unctuous, with a good balanced length.
£55.00

Inniskillin, Vidal Gold Icewine 2007, Ontario Sweet
Concentration of tropical fruit aromas, enhanced floral orange, marmalade undertones, and a honeyed persistent finish with excellent acidity.
£45.00

Jackson-Triggs Niagara Estate, Delaine Riesling Icewine 2007, Niagara Peninsula Sweet
Crystalline pineapple and lemon meringue pie, showing some honeyed richness, with hints of lemon and lime underneath. Luscious mouth-feel and very good acidity.

Jackson-Triggs Niagara Estate, Proprietors' Grand Reserve Cabernet Franc Icewine 2007, Niagara Peninsula Sweet
Strawberry, apple, and rhurbarb

on the nose, with good acidity, medium body, and a touch of honeyed sweetness, leading to a cranberry finish.

Peller Estates Winery, Peller Estates Riesling Icewine 2007, Niagara Peninsula Sweet

Quite deep apricot and fig notes, with hints of honey leaf tea. Complex super-sweet palate, lots of richness, sweet concentration, and a long finish.

Peller Estates Winery, Peller Estates Vidal Icewine 2007, Niagara Peninsula Sweet

Lovely floral bouquet, with fresh fruit aromas, and notes of cloves and butter. Honey and marmalade on the palate, with good balanced acidity. Long finish.

Pillitteri Estates Winery, Pillitteri Estates Chardonnay Icewine Vqa 2007, Niagara Peninsula Sweet

Floral and honeyed aromas, intense mouth-feel of dried apricot, sweet marmalade, and ripe melon. A rounded, sweet, luscious wine with good length.

Pillitteri Estates Winery, Pillitteri Estates Vidal Icewine Vqa 2007, Niagara Peninsula Sweet

Orange and lemon pudding on the nose. Rich flavours on the palate with balanced acidity. Fruity orange blossom finish.

BRONZE

Inniskillin, Sparkling Vidal Icewine 2006, Ontario Sparkling

Full, golden-hued fizz with very light mousse. Aromatic, with notes of wet hay and honey, this is characterful, sweet, and fragrant.
£45.00 WAIT

Hillebrand Winery, Showcase Chardonnay Wild Ferment 'oliveira Vineyard' 2007, Niagara Peninsula White

Tropical and full. Rich palate with mild acidity and good restraint. Long finish.

Inniskillin, Winemaker's Series Montague Vineyard Chardonnay 2007, Niagara Peninsula White

Oaky tropical fruit on the nose. Refreshing acidity balanced by concentrated peach and melon flavours. Finishes well.

Mission Hill Family Estate, Perpetua 2006, Okanagan Valley White

Spicy, slightly peppery fruit. Refreshing acidity balanced by citrus apple character. Finishes well.

Mission Hill Family Estate, Reserve Pinot Gris 2007, Okanagan Valley White

A well-made wine with some sweetness, this is smooth and juicy. Pale stone fruits on the palate, with soft fragrance and finish.

Southbrook Vineyards, Triomphe Chardonnay 2006, Niagara Peninsula White

Soft, creamy style, with vanilla and gentle fruit on the palate.

Hillebrand Winery, Trius Red 2007, Niagara Peninsula Red

Blackcurrant, red cherry, cedar, and oak aromas on the nose. Dry black cherry on the palate, with a smooth drying finish.

Mission Hill Family Estate, Reserve Riesling Icewine 2007, Okanagan Valley Sweet
Stewed apple nose, with a palate of baked apple and caramel. Good intensity, with a lovely long fresh finish.

Pillitteri Estates Winery, Pillitteri Estates Cabernet Franc Icewine Vqa 2007, Niagara Peninsula Sweet
Aromas of strawberry and cherry jam. Good acidity, medium body, with bright floral notes and a sweet finish

CYPRUS

SILVER

Domaine Hadjiantonas Cabernet Shiraz 2005, Hadjiantonas Winery Ltd Limassol Red
Dark, ripe fruit with some smoky notes. Big cherry and chocolate flavours, with a long finish.

BRONZE

Domaine Hadjiantonas Chardonnay 2008, Hadjiantonas Winery Ltd, Limassol White
Creamy, opulent nose of citrus fruits. Crisp palate, with a touch of toffee.

CZECH REPUBLIC

SILVER

Hibernal Slámové Víno 2005, Livi Spol. S R.o., Moravia Sweet
Beautiful deep gold colour. Honey and citrus come though on an otherwise fairly neutral nose. Dry on the finish. Well-made.

Osoyoos Larose, Osoyoos Larose 2005, Okanagan Valley Red
Harmonious wine. Chocolate and berry fruit on the nose, with vegetal hints.
£25.00 LIB

Pelee Island Winery, Cabernet Franc 2007, Ontario Red
Ripe berry nose with a touch of coffee. Soft, silky, ripe fruit on the palate, with crisp acidity to balance.

Ganton & Larsen Prospect Winery, Prospect Lost Bars Vidal Icewine 2007, Okanagan Valley Sweet
Clean lemon and lime, with hints of orange and delicate light fruit. Refreshing acidity, and a moderate honeyed finish.

Hillebrand Winery, Trius Vidal Icewine 2007, Niagara Peninsula Sweet
Butter, marmalade, and caramel on the nose. Sweet palate with an orange peel finish.

Chardonnay - Pozdní Sb 2008, Tomá, Moravia White

Star-bright appearance. Clean, inviting, fruity nose. Appealing palate, with balance and volume.

Pálava - Pozdní Sb 2008, Tomá, Moravia White

Bright Muscat-style nose. Palate is full of rich fruit. Finish is smoky, Muscat-like and moreish.

Pálava Pozdni Sber 2008, Winery Mikulica, Moravia White

Nutty peachy aromas are very evident. Quite sweet but the acidity keeps it refreshing.
£6.00

Ryzlink R 2007, Moravské Vina, Moravia White

Lovely, rich peachy flavours. The richness comes through on the palate, with some freshness behind the flesh. A touch simple, but nice fruit.

Ryzlink Vla 2005, Vina, Moravia White

Floral, honeyed nose, with a broad, rich, luscious mouthfeel.

Tramín 2007, Vina, Moravia White

This wine has soft aromas of gingerbread and spice, which are matched on the palate. Medium to full body, with an oily texture.

DENMARK

Don's Orion 2007, Skaersoegaard Vin, Jylland Sparkling

A nose of fresh limes, with a firm, creamy, pristine toastiness. Attractive mousse. What a surprise from Denmark -bravo!

Madeleine Angevine 2008, Skaersoegaard Vin, Jylland White

Pale colour. Very discreet nose of white flowers, apple, and a hint of grass. Citrus fruits and apple on the palate. Good balance.

ENGLAND

 ENGLISH TROPHY

Camel Valley, 2007 Camel Valley Bacchus 2007, South West England White

Bright pale green in colour, with a hint of peach on the nose. Crisp, tangy elderflower and grapefruit flavours. Good intensity, with a fresh clean medium-length finish and a hint of sweetness.
£11.00 WAIT, CVV, WBR

Sharpham Vineyard, Sharpham Bacchus 2007, South-West England White

Grassy nettle notes on the nose, with very distinct citrus and sherbet notes. Spritzy, with a vibrant mouth feel. Good crisp acidity on the finish, balanced by a touch of sweetness.
£11.00 SHR

Sharpham Vineyard, Sharpham Dart Valley Reserve 2007, South-West England White

Gentle floral blossom and apple

on the nose. Refreshing acidity. Quite nicely balanced by citrus and apple fruit. Simple style.
£8.30 CPW, CSS, SAB, SHR

Camel Valley, 2005 Camel Valley White Pinot 2005, South West England Sparkling
Delicate nose of red berries with hints of flowers. Good balance, with medium length and good depth.
£30.00 CVV

Chapel Down Wines, Chapel Down Pinot Reserve 2004, South-East England Sparkling
Fragrant and toasty on the nose, with lifted berry and apple fruit aromas. Crisp finish with a touch of sweetness.
£25.00 ENG, CDO

Nyetimber Limited, Classic Cuvee 2003, South-East England Sparkling
Honeyed, quite complex style, with good acidity and a hint of autolysis. Stylish finish and good length.
£25.90

Ridgeview, Ridgeview Grosvenor (Blanc De Blanc) 2006, South-East England Sparkling
Yellow-green in colour, with a delicate sherbety nose. Fresh, citrussy, and melony. Nice mousse, good acidity and length.
£22.00 BB&R, EWC, F&M, HAR, RVE, SDC

Chapel Down Wines, Chapel Down Rose Brut 2006, South-East England Sparkling Rosé
Very pale rose colour, with a nose of crisp plum. The palate has perfumed red fruits, fragrant length, and fine balance.
£20.70 FLA, ENG, CDO

Astley Vineyards, Astley Severn Vale 2007, West-Central England White
The palate shows spiced apricot and orchard fruits, with a touch of sweetness, which works well. Very English orchard flavours.
£8.00 AST, EOO, HPW, OMB, TCH

Astley Vineyards, Astley Veritas 2007, West-Central England White
Subtle hedgerow, with elderflower blossom and citrus notes on the nose. Appley, with a bit of zestiness and herby character on the finish.
£10.00 AST, TCH

Chapel Down Wines, Chapel Down Bacchus Reserve 2007, South-East England White
Pungent leafy, nettle character. Balanced sweetness and acidity, with a good finish.
£11.80 TESC, ENG, CDO

Warden Abbey Vineyard, Warden Bacchus 2006, East England White
Full, slightly tropical nose, leading to apple on the palate, with a fresh, zesty roundness on the finish.

Warden Abbey Vineyard, Warden Bacchus 2007, East England White
Pale colour, with a supple nose. Crisp, lively, zesty palate of gooseberry and grassiness.

Wickham Vineyard, Wickham Special Release Fumé NV, South-East England White
Lifted, slightly mineral nose, which is light and youthful. Dry, with marked acidity and attractive fruit.
£8.60 WAIT, EOR, EWC, GWW

Camel Valley, 2005 Camel Valley 'Cornwall' Brut 2005, South-West England Sparkling
Biscuits and apples on the nose. Clean body and fresh finish.
£20.00 CVV

Camel Valley, 2006 Camel Valley 'Cornwall' Brut 2006 South-West England
Sparkling
Bright fresh lemony aromas and crisp refreshing flavours. Good acidity, with a touch of honey and nuts.
£20.00 CVV, CWW, GWW, WBR

Chapel Down (English Wines), Chapel Down/ Marks & Spencer English Sparkling Reserve Brut NV, South-East England Sparkling
Attractive yellow-green colour, rounded fermentation aromas, with notes of lemon, a nice mousse, and good acidity.
£17.50 M&S, ENG

Denbies Wine Estate, Greenfields 2002, South-East England Sparkling
Lovely rich yeast and bread nose, with lovely, complex baked apples, giving an elegant and long finish.
£22.00 WAIT, DBS

Denbies Wine Estate, Whitedowns 2004, South-East England Sparkling
Floral, citrus, and red apple notes. Pure fruit character, with refreshing acidity. Zesty and quite concentrated fruit, which retains the balance.
£16.00 WAIT, DBS

Peter Hall, Breaky Bottom Brut - Cuvée John Inglis Hall 2006, South-East England
Sparkling
Joyful yellow-green colour. Nice

fermentation aromas, with a good body, light acidity, and pleasant finish.
£20.00 BBV, BUT, ETV, EWC, HAC, HRY, JAS, SXW

Ridgeview, Ridgeview Knightsbridge (Blanc De Noirs) 2006, South-East England Sparkling
Straw yellow in colour. Lively and fruity, with lots of lemons. Good mouthfeel.
£25.00 RVE

Camel Valley, 2006 Camel Valley Pinot Noir Rosé Brut 2006, South-West England
Sparkling Rosé
Pale salmon colour and a clean nose. Good small bubbles, with some enjoyable crisp fruit and a hint of red berries on the palate.
£25.00 CVV

Ridgeview, Ridgeview Fitzrovia (Rosé) 2006, South-East England
Sparkling Rosé
Nice velvety fruit with yeasty notes. Fresh acidity, light in style, but interesting. Floral and fragrant, with raspberry fruit and good freshness.
£22.00

Astley Vineyards, Astley Late Harvest 2007, West-Central England Sweet
Pale straw in colour. Soft round palate. Balanced.
£10.50 AST, EOO, FLY, OMB, TCH

GEORGIA

SILVER

Saperavi Red Dry 2007, Badagoni Ltd, Kakheti Red
Mid-ruby colour. Floral nose,

leading to a red berry and bubblegum palate. Great intensity of flavour, with tangy acidity. Attractive and refreshing.

BRONZE

Kakhetian Noble White Dry 2005, Badagoni Ltd, Kakheti White
Good acidity, with light citrus, apple and pear. Sensational over-achievement with one of the world's more neutral grapes.

Marani Tvishi 2008, Racha-lechkhumi White
Perfumed nose, notes of sweet bell pepper. Medium-weight juicy body, with a lemon sorbet finish.
£9.40

Marani Kondoli Vineyards Saperavi 2005, Jsc Telavi Wine Cellar, Kakheti Red
Dark ruby in colour, with a palate of mocha, dark fruit, tobacco, and vanilla. Good length.

Marani Kondoli Vineyards Saperavi-Merlot 2007, Jsc Telavi Wine Cellar, Kakheti Red
Inky colour. Mineral aroma, with notes of beetroot on a well-balanced and long-lasting palate.

Orovela 2005, Chandrebi Ltd, Kakheti Red
Ruby in colour. Fresh plum flavours and an aromatic violet character, with attractive round tannins.
£15.70 WAIT, CAV, FAW, SOH

GREECE

GOLD

 **MOSCOPHILERO TROPHY**

Orinos Helios-Mountain Sun White 2008, Semeli Winery, Peloponnese White
Very youthful, lightly aromatic spiced nose. Refined palate, with a fresh lime finish and a good balance of fruit and acidity.
£6.00

 **GREEK WHITE TROPHY**

Ovilos White 2008, Ktima Biblia Chora S.A. White
Lovely nose of passion fruit and pineapple. Round and creamy on the palate, with fresh apple and pear flavours. Fresh, with good body. Great acidity and intense finish.

 RETSINA TROPHY

The Pine 2008, Kechris Winery, Macedonia White
Attractive, clean aromatic nose of flowers and pine cone. Lots of intensity on the palate, with pine wood, light floral notes and a tangy, long finish.

 **GREEK VINSANTO TROPHY**

Sigalas Vinsanto Santorini 2003 Sweet
Very rich aromas of dates and strawberries on the nose, with a fig purée flavour on the palate along with some crème caramel, and a really powerful richness. A

smoky, earthy, volcanic wine.
£17.60 VKB

SILVER

Amethystos Sauvignon Blanc 2008, Domaine Costa Lazaridi Sa, Macedonia White
Light, fresh herbs and fruit on the nose. Clear flavours of lychees on the palate, leading to a delicate and pleasant finish.

Estate Michalakis White Gold Cuvée 2008, Heraklion, Crete White
Aromatic peach fruit with a spicy tone. Fresh, fruity palate with good acidity, depth, and ripeness.

Santorini Assyrtiko 2008, Haridimos Hatzidakis, Santorini White
Concentrated honey-citrus aromas with attractive herbal notes. Refreshing acidity, oily texture, and complex savoury character, leading to hints of kerosene on the finish.
£10.00 FLA, WAIT

Sigalas Barrel VQPRD 2008, Santorini White
Complex, fresh nose with elderflower and mineral notes. Lovely fruity tannins, with a pleasant balance and finish.
£10.80 VKB

Sigalas Santorini VQPRD 2008, Santorini White
Pineapple-citrus aromas. Rich, full palate of sour and savoury notes. Good length, carried by the citrus acidity.
£8.40 VKB

The Pine 2007, Kechris Winery, Macedonia White
Beautifully-made Retsina, exhibiting fine balance, with zesty acidity against a concentrated palate of rosemary and lemon.

Biblinos 2007, Ktima Mouson, Central Greece Red
Lovely characterful wine. Intense currant fruit notes with toasty smoky undertones. Good structure, with a long, intense finish.

Hgemon 2005, George Vassiliou, Peloponnese Red
Fine concentration of grainy tannins. Luscious berry fruit and a long persistent finish with lovely acidity. A well-balanced and pleasant-drinking wine.
£60.00

Nemea / Zacharias Vineyards 2007, Oinotechniki Ltd, Nemea Red
A vigorous nose of attractive raisin, plum, and red fruit. Medium length, with excellent balance, and a fine cocoa finish.

Domaine Gerovassiliou Malagoyzia 2004, Macedonia Sweet
Really nice herbs on the nose, and some attractive coffee sweetness on the palate. Nice and intense; very well-made.
VKB

Melistakto NV, Allagiannis Winery, Attica Sweet
Raisiny, with lovely high acidity and a palate of toffee, sweet coffee, and milk chocolate – almost reminiscent of a Pedro Ximénez.

Samos Anthemis 2002, Union Of Winemaking Cooperatives Of Samos, Samos Sweet
Amber brown in colour, with a nose of lifted honey and butterscotch. Fresh caramel and

malt notes, with some butter and menthol.
£10.00 WAIT

Alpha Estate White 2008, Angelos Latridis, Florina
White
Brilliant colour. Good nose with mineral and floral fruit aromas. Good balance and elegant finish.
£13.50 NOV, VKB

Areti White 2008, Ktima Biblia Chora S.A., White
Citrus nose with hints of German sausage and tropical fruit. Honeyed waxy quality, ending on a fresh spicy note.

Biblia Chora Chardonnay 2008 White
Smoky, mineral, and spice aromas, with a palate of soft apricot and grapefruit, and good, creamy length.

Biblia Chora White 2008, Pangeon White
Attractive lemongrass and grapefruit palate. Fresh mineral finish.

Enotria White 2008, Douloufakis Nikos, Crete White
Crisp vegetal nose. Dolly mixture sweets on the palate, with a very dry finish.

Epathlon Ghis Savatiano 2008, Allagiannis Winery, Attica White
Rich peachy nose. Lovely guava and grapefruit on the palate, with low acidity and a pleasant finish.

Estate Chatzigeorgiou/ 2008, Pageo White
Lifted nose of attractive cut grass and lychees. Crisp palate and good length.

> ## DID YOU KNOW?
> Although over 15,000 bottles were opened at IWC 2008, many more were left untouched. These leftover wines are given away in a charity raffle.

Malaguzia 2008, Simeonidis Polichronis, Pageo White
Nice lemony lime nose. Pleasant acidity and a fresh finish.

Psiles Korfes 2008, Union Of Winemaking Cooperatives Of Samos, Samos White
Lovely, very light elegant nose, with hints of mint and spice on a crisp palate.

Roditis 2008, Simeonidis Polichronis, Pageo White
Slight smoke and slate on the nose, with dried fruit and floral notes, and an elderflower finish.

Sigalas Assyrtico Athiri VQPRD 2008, Santorini White
Soft aromas and good mouthfeel, with a touch of honeyed richness and dry, peppery spice on the finish.
£5.80 VKB

Alpha Estate Red 2006, Angelos Latridis, Macedonia Red
Mineral, black cherry, and spicy aromas. Fruity palate and full body, with a long finish.
£19.00 NOV, VKB

Amethystos Cava 2004, Domaine Costa Lazaridi S.A., Macedonia Red
Coffee beans and minerality,

with a light leafiness, soft
tannins, and a structured, lean
finish.

Black Cubed 2005,
Oinotechniki Ltd. - Zacharias
Vineyards, Peloponnese Red
Rose aromas, with medium
intensity, firm tannins, and a long
finish.

Domaine Gerovassiliou Syrah
2006, Macedonia Red
Lovely dark red fruits. Spicy,
fruity palate. Fresh flavours,
integrated acidity, and a luscious
length.
£15.00 VKB

Pavlidis Tempranillo 2006,
Drama Red
Earthy tobacco aroma, with
juicy strawberries and cream
on palate, and an elegant long
finish.

Semeli Nemea Reserve 2006,
Peloponnese Red
Dusty bramble nose, with a
succulent dusty cherry palate.
Medium length, stylish.
£12.50

Samos Vin Doux 2008, Union
Of Winemaking Cooperatives
Of Samos, Samos Sweet
Delicate citrus nose, soft, very
sweet. Long and silky finish.
£4.90 FLA, ADN, HAX, RDS

HOLLAND

Rossini Bianco NV, Toorank B.
V., Didam Vermouth
Fresh, aromatic, herbal nose with
sweet, fruity, and spicy aromas.
Notes of grapefruit peel on a
palate which is delicate and well-
balanced, with a long menthol
finish.
£3.40 BES

Rossini Rosso NV, Toorank B.
V., Didam Vermouth
Orange zest, grapefruit, and
gentle spice on the nose, with
some herbal notes. Soft, round
attack with a dry length.
£3.40 BES

HUNGARY

 **TOKAJI
TROPHY**

Dobogo' Tokaji Aszu' 6
Puttonyos 2004, Dobogo',
Tokaji Sweet
Layered complexity of fresh
crushed apple with beautiful
crisp acidity and honeyed
lemon. Gentle sense of lime and
honey, with a very long finish.
An extremely well-balanced,
enjoyable wine.
£48.00 LIB

Royal Tokaji Betsek 6
Puttonyos Aszú Wine 2000,
Tokaji Botrytis
Orange-gold in colour. Notes
of intense honey, barley sugar,
baked apple, and cream on
the nose. Complex palate of
burnt sugar, caramel, and some
bramley apple flavour too. Very
long finish.
£25.00 BVD

Csopaki Olaszrizling
Válogatás 2007, Figula
Pincészet Kft., Balatonfüred-
csopak White
Sweet ripe peaches on the
nose. Lovely concentration
of peach and apricot on the
palate, with real depth and a
pleasant finish.

OTHERS

Tokajicum Tokaji "Unfiltered" Furmint 2006, Tokaji White
Creamy white peach and apple aromas with smoky notes. Ripe, crisp stone fruit flavours on the palate, with a mineral, lingering finish.

Béres Tokaji Aszú 5 Puttonyos 2005, Tokaji Botrytis
Straw gold in colour. Clean, fresh style, with a complex nose of lemon and honey. On the palate, there is lemon sharpness to begin with, followed by sweet lemon, with medium acidity and alcohol.
£38.00

Disznók 2000, Tokaji, Botrytis
Rich gold in colour. Sweet apricot and citrus, balanced by zesty acidity on the finish.
£30.00

Patricius Tokaji Aszúeszencia 2002, Patricius Borház Kft. Tokaji Botrytis
Orangey-golden colour. Rich and sweet, with good length and acidity. Walnut and tobacco flavours, with a hint of minerality.

Royal Tokaji 5 Puttonyos Tokaji Aszú Wine 2005, Tokaji Botrytis
Old brassy gold in colour. Oxidative, yeasty nose. Palate of sweet baked lemon acidity, followed by high marmalade and honey notes. Medium acidity.
£12.00 BVD

Tokajicum Tokaji Aszú 6 Puttonyos 2005, Tokaji Botrytis
Deep colour, with marmalade on the nose, and sweet lemon

and barley sugar on the palate. Honeyed finish.

Béres Tokaji Furmint L 2007, Tokaji White
Spicy, almost vegetal style, with lots of fruit depth, and intense aromas of sweet oak with ripe fruits. Some apricot tones on the palate. Well-structured, with very good acidity and a long, pleasant finish.
£14.00

Budai Irsai Olivér 2008, Nyakas Pince Zrt., Etyek-buda White
Fresh and typically fragrant, this has a simple, grapey palate, with good fruit entry. Crisp acidity, rich concentration, and a clean finish.

Budai Riesling 2007, Nyakas Pince Zrt., Etyek-buda White
Toasty, petrol-flavoured balance of fruit and acidity, with a good clean medium-weight body, and a mineral finish.

Campanula Pinot Grigio 2008, Gábor Laczkó, Etyek-Buda White
Ripe, slightly butterscotch aromas, with peppery spice. Excellent fruit concentration and medium-weight palate; a structured and well balanced wine.
£6.00 BTH, LAI

Chapel Hill Grüner Veltliner 2008, János Csernák, Etyek-buda White
Clear colour, with honey and lemony notes on the nose. Fresh, crisp and herbaceous palate. Nice longevity.
£5.00

**Via Canoro Chardonnay 2008,
Hilltop Neszmely, Ászár
Neszmély** White
Floral nose of rose petals. Quite
sweet on the palate with some
lychee character.

**Via Canoro Pinot Grigio 2008,
Hilltop Neszmely, Ászár-
Neszmély** White
Light and floral on the nose, with
ripe pear and apple, medium
weight, and a clean, dry finish.

**Chateau Teleki Villányi
Cabernet Franc 2006, Csányi
Pincészet Zrt., Villány** Red
Opaque, with opulent aromas of
cassis, with notes of violet, silky
tannins. Well-balanced, with a
lingering finish of vibrant raspberry.

**Mereng 2006, St. Andrea Kft.,
Eger** Red
Strawberry and raspberry
aromas. Fresh fruit on the palate,
with nice depth of flavour. Hint
of spice on the finish.

**Selection Egri Kékfrankos
2006, Quality Champions
Kft. / Egri Korona Borház,
Eger** Red
Fresh raspberry nose. Nice, bright
fruit and good length.

Dobogo' Mylitta 2006, Tokaji
Sweet
Beautiful lime blossom and ripe
pear nose. Vivid and pristine on
the palate. Excellent balance.
£17.00 LIB

**Tokaji Aszú 5 Puttonyos 2002,
Patricius Borhaz Kft, Tokaji**
Sweet
Botrytis nose, complex and
intense, with notes of honey and
toast. Rich, sweet, and biscuity,
with a long finish.
£39.00 GWW

ISRAEL

SILVER

**Cabernet Sauvignon Reserve
2006, Teperberg 1870 Winery**
Red
Purple core, with a cherry-coloured
rim. Rich smoky vanilla and
blackcurrant tart on the nose. Ripe,
cedary palate with vanilla oak. Rich
and full, with bright blackberry fruit.
Very smooth and complex.

JAPAN

BRONZE

Koshu Private Reserve Toriibira
Vineyard 2007, Grace Winery,
Yamanashi White
Nose of pure candy floss on a
crisp, pure palate. Delicate and
balanced.

LEBANON

BRONZE

**Château Musar White Gaston
Hochar 1993,** White
Exotic aromas of honey and
lychees. Tangy, waxy palate with
honeyed apple and blossom notes.
£34.60

**Château Musar White Gaston
Hochar 2001** White
Evolved, nutty, exotic palate with
hints of beeswax and honey. Rich
and complex, with firm, nutty
flavours on the finish.
£17.30 WES

**Château Musar Red Gaston
Hochar 2000** Red
Complex, developed, and vibrant
notes of cigar box and clean
pencils. Sweet medium-weight
palate, with structured, dry tannins.
£21.60

Vinicola San Lorenzo, S.A.de C.V., Casa Madero Shiraz 2007, Parras Valley Red
Crushed red fruit character, with minty and herbal overtones, and ripe tannins.

MOLDOVA

BRONZE

Chardonnay Sauvignon Private Reserve 2005, Acorex Wine Holding S.A., Cahul
White
Soft, buttery baked fruits, with herbaceous notes. Rounded and creamy.

ROMANIA

BRONZE

North Ridge Riesling 2008, Rotherfield Properties Romania Srl, Dealu Mare
White
Clean, light, mineral nose. Dry palate with good acidity, quite lean and lemony.

Cuvee "Uberland" 2006, Cramele Recas Red
Green nose with aromas of stewed fruit and spice. Nice berry fruit on the palate, with a spicy finish.

Idle Rock Feteasca Neagra 2008, Rotherfield Properties Romania Srl, Dealu Mare Red
Nose of ripe, fresh fruit and parma violets. Rich jammy fruit on the palate. Appealing and pleasant.

Pinot Noir"Terra Dacica" 2008, Cramele Recas Red
Vibrant ruby colour, with black cherry and almond on the nose. Palate shows fresh acidity and ripe fruit.

SERBIA

BRONZE

Trijumf Barrique 2006, Podrum Aleksandrovic D.O.O., Sumadijsko-velikomoravski
White
Candied aromas of confected fruit. Broad, rich, creamy palate with a mineral finish.

North Ridge Rosé 2008, Rotherfield Properties Romania Srl, Dealu Mare
Rosé
Pretty rose petal character. Fairly dry palate, fruity at first, with a sweet/sour finish. Good.

SWITZERLAND

SILVER

Humagne Blanche De Chamoson 2008, Giroud Vins S.A., Valais White
Some baked apple notes, quite rich and complex, with subtle peach, fine ripeness and length, and tight acidity.

Petite Arvine De Chamoson 2007, Giroud Vins S.A., Valais
White
Delicate tropical fruit on the nose, with peach, melon, and zesty acidity. On the palate, there is green apple, with citrus, peach and apple, and touch of smoky elegance.

BRONZE

Heïda De Chamoson 2008, Giroud Vins S.A., Valais White
Subtle floral notes, combined with peach, melon, and a slightly honeyed texture. Refreshing acidity, with some minerality and spice, balanced by good concentration of fruit. Zingy, spicy notes on the finish.

Muscat De Chamoson 2007, Giroud Vins S.A., Valais White
Clean, fresh, floral notes, with zesty acidity, and citrus, apple, and sophisticated ripe fruit.

Petite Arvine Danse Des Etoiles 2006, Giroud Vins S.A., Valais White
Ripe apple on a developed nose. A pleasant, apple and floral palate. Dry, with softness and mild acidity. A sophisticated wine.

Cornalin De Chamoson 2008, Giroud Vins S.A., Valais Red
A chewy nose, backed up by coffee and mocha oak. There is some very chocolatey oak and very sweet fruit on the palate, with dark bittersweet tannins.

Humagne Rouge De Chamoson 2008, Giroud Vins S.A., Valais Red
Intense redcurrant nose, light, subtle, and peppery. Well-made - a good quaffer!

Syrah De Chamoson 2008, Giroud Vins S.A., Valais Red
Dense, chocolatey, and peppery palate reminiscent of Northern Rhône Syrah, with a very long finish.

Moscato Giroud 2008, Giroud Vins S.A., Valais Sparkling
Grapey nose, which follows through onto a frothy palate. Good balance.

Ballerine 2008, Giroud Vins S.A., Valais Sweet
Peachy nose. Clean and sweet, with a fresh, peachy palate. Good length and balance.

TURKEY

BRONZE

Sarafin Fume Blanc 2007, Doluca Bagcilik Ve Sarapcilik As, Thrace White
Bright, attractive fruity nose with a pure, clean palate. Fresh, charming wine with lovely balance and an interesting mineral finish.

Consensus 3 Me 2006, Idol Organik Gıda, Aegean Red
Oaky coconut nose with notes of berry fruit. Well-made,

Dlc Kalecik Karasi 2007, Doluca Bagcilik Ve Sarapcilik As, Central Anatolia Red
Floral perfume on the nose, with light oak. An attractive style.

URUGUAY

BRONZE

Bouza Merlot B9 2006, Bodega Bouza, Canelones Red
Ripe, sweet cassis fruit and menthol on the nose, with oak aromas and tannin, good grip and clean finish.
£26.00 GWW

The International Wine Challenge

Presents

The Library Collection

The Library Collection

The **Octavian Vaults Library Collection**, in association with the International Wine Challenge, has established an international tasting to promote wines that have withstood the test of time through cellaring.

The purpose of this assessment of wines is to encourage the public to 'trade up', by investing money and time in wine for a greater return.

Focusing on 10 year old and 5 year old wines, the 2008 tasting reviewed the 1998 and 2003 vintages, while the 2009 tasting reviewed the 1999 and 2004 vintages.

Wines are judged blind by an international panel of experts on the 100-point scoring scheme. Tasting notes are provided and also information on how well the wine is expected to develop in future years.

The **Octavian Vaults Library Collection** encourages the knowledgable drinker to invest in current release wines for laying down. A score of 85 or more out of 100 is a significant endorsement of the quality of the wine tasted. Therefore, should the wine consumer be looking for a wine to lay down, such an endorsement helps to build trust in cellaring current vintages of the wine and assures quality for the future.

AUSTRALIA

Brothers in Arms Shiraz 1998 Red

Meaty aromas with some evident liquorice and black fruit, lots of black cherry on the palate with grippy tannins and a long finish. Drink now through 2010.
86

Dr Andrew Pirie Pirie 1998
Sparkling

Deep golden colour, huge intensity of autolytic character. Well structured fruit with creamy, lemony acidity, balanced and lingering on the finish. Drink now through 2010.
88

Howard Park Cabernet Merlot 1998 Red

Good depth of colour, showing some age. The aromas have good clarity revealing black fruit, spice, gentle potpourri. Lively fruit on the palate, youthful, balanced and relaxed. Drink now through 2013.
91

Jim Barry Wine Jim Barry McRae Wood Shiraz 1998 Red

Evolved colour with tobacco and spice on the nose, still quite fresh on the palate and the fruit is still very much alive. Drink now through 2010
88

Peter Lehmann Wines Stonewell Shiraz 1998 Red

Very youthful and oaky on the nose, quite woody on the palate but has plenty of underlying fruit. Ripe, spicy, blackberry fruit that still needs time to develop. Drink now through 2018.
95

AUSTRIA

Erich Machherndl Grüner Veltliner Smaragd Kollmitz 1998 Off-dry White

Bright, full, yet youthful colour. This is a lovely, balanced wine, fresh and lively with notes of white peach and apricot, rounded but vibrant flavours. Delicious now but will keep up to 10 years. Drink now through 2018.
96

FRANCE

Champagne Mailly Grand Cru les Echansons 1998
Sparkling

Pale yellow, showing development on the nose, nutty and buttery on the palate, good acidity with a lingering finish. Drink now through 2013.
91

Champagne Taittinger Taittinger Comtes de Champagne Blanc de Blancs 1998 Sparkling

Biscuit nose, creamy and rich on the palate, quite seductive, lovely fizz with intense bready character. Long finish, toasty and lemony. Drink now through 2020.
95

Champagnes P&C Heidsieck Piper-Heidsieck Rare Millesimé 1998 Sparkling

Lovely fizz, lively mousse, very youthful on the nose with hints of lemon. Very fresh style, balanced with biscuity, brioche character. Has plenty of time and will develop nicely. Drink now through 2018, 2020 if in magnum.
93

NEW ZEALAND

Te Mata Estate Winery Te Mata Estate Coleraine 1998
Red

Very attractive colour, showing a little maturity. Soft, sweet and lively black fruit. Crisp and elegant, well balanced with long length. Drink now to 2012.
95

PORTUGAL

Adriano Ramos Pinto Vinhos SA Late Bottled Vintage 1998
Port

Ripe plum with jammy aromas, rich fruit palate but with a very green edge, big chewy blackberries, figs and raisins. Lush and round. Drink from 2010 - 2016.
89

Hans Kristian Jorgensen Cortes de Cima Reserva 1998
Red

Big, ripe, smoky, showing some development. With ripe, sweet fruit on the palate and generous acidity, fine tannins and a long, sweet finish. Drink now through 2012.
90

Sogevinus Fine Wines Kopke Vintage Port 1998 **Port**

Deep colour, sweet violets and aromatic nose, tight and earthy. Sweet and fleshy with intense flavours and long lingering finish. Drink between 5 and 10 years.
90

SPAIN

Bodegas Primicia Casa Primicia Gran Reserva 1998
Red

Intense, funky, herbaceous and tobacco like notes on the nose, supple and subtle, evolved with dried fruit character, quite restrained but vibrant with fine dry tannins and a long finish. Drink now through 2015.
90

2003

ARGENTINA

Finca la Chamiza Finca la Chamiza Martin Alsina 2003
Red

Deep colour, ripe, bright fruit with spirity warmth on the palate. Firm but good tannins, very pure Malbec character. Drink now through 2010.
88

AUSTRALIA

d'Arenberg The Dead Arm 2003 **Red**

Deep colour, pushing to the rim of the glass. Sweet, sappy and concentrated, crisp acidity with good concentration. Quite lengthy. Drink now through 2011.
88

Howard Park Cabernet Merlot 2003 **Red**

Deep colour, starting to show maturity. Ripe and dense with black fruit aromas, smoky with black cherry character on the palate. Crisp, minty and balanced on the finish. Drink now through 2014.
91

Jim Barry Wine Jim Barry McRae Wood Shiraz 2003 **Red**

Deep core, showing development on the rim. Dense vanilla aromas with creamy black fruit and spice. Rounded and complex with earthy, oaky finish. Drink now through 2016.
93

Orlando Wines Jacob's Creek Centenary Hill 2003 Red
Deep colour, still quite youthful. Ripe but restrained with sweet vanilla notes on the nose. Good acidity, very stylish with excellent balance. Drink now through 2013.
89

Orlando Wines Jacob's Creek Reserve Shiraz 2003 Red
Youthful, sweet and smoky fruit. Cherries and dark berries on the palate with drying tannins and good acidity. Concentrated and well balanced. Drink now through 2011.
86

Peter Lehmann Wines Margaret Semillon 2003 White
Lovely minerality with hints of straw, delicate honey flavours with well balanced fruit. Good, crisp acidity with a long, lively finish. Drink now through 2011.
89

Peter Lehmann Wines Wigan Riesling 2003 White
Bright with vibrant, greenish tint. Petrol and earth aromas on the nose. Crisp citrus peel, petrol and floral notes on the palate. Quite dry with a sweet nutty finish, long and balanced with plenty of character and concentration. Drink now through 2015.
93

Voyager Estate Voyager Estate Chardonnay 2003 White
Pale, finely handled, creamy fruit. Mineral flavours and lively array of tropical fruits, rich and full mouth feel with fine, grippy tannins. Round and

soft on the finish. Drink now through 2011.
93

CHILE

Vina Errazuriz Vina Errazuriz Don Maximiano Founders Reserve 2003 Red
Garnet with a slightly brown edge, eucalyptus nose, youthful with good balance. Lots of ripe fruit and toasted wood, but still needs time. Drink now through 2012.
88

Vina Errazuriz Vinedo Chadwick 2003 Red
Dark ruby, black berries and a touch of wood on the nose. Crisp acidity, well structured with nice tannins, still needs time to open. Drink 2009 through 2014.
90

Viña Seña Cabernet blend 2003 Red
Dark ruby with sweet fruit on the nose. Black cherry and mint, quite fresh. Fleshy and exuberant on the palate, good structure and balance. The acidity will sustain the fruit for a while. Drink now through 2015.
93

FRANCE

Alain Brumont Château Bouscassé Vieilles Vignes 2003 Red
Garnet in colour with a powerful, rich nose. Ripe, black cherries, big mouthful and chewy fruit with tangy acidity. Still full tannins but starting to soften up, will benefit from a bit more time. Drink now through 2015.
90

Alain Brumont Château Montus Prestige 2003 Red
Deep colour, quite pungent on the nose, liquorice and dark fruit

"*Without working for the family a wine like Noble One may never have been created.*"

Darren De Bartoli
De Bartoli Wines since 1928

If you could bottle the passion of generations of winemakers, then Noble One would be the essence. This unique Australian wine has won a host of accolades, making it the most awarded botrytis wine in history. After 25 years of successful vintages, this family legacy is one that will be celebrated throughout time. debortoli.com.au

The Chosen One

palate. Quite a modern style, with ripe, lingering tannins. Drink now through 2014.
89

Alain Brumont Vendemiaire 2003 Sweet
Rich and heavily honeyed, creamy late-harvest style with racy acidity on the palate. Beautiful balance.
96

Arnoux & Fils Seigneur de Lauris 2003 Red
Medium depth with cedar scented aromas, quite floral with red fruit on the palate. Still lively and balanced with good acidity and a lengthy finish. Drinking now.
86

Champagne Mailly Grand Cru Champagne Mailly Grand Cru l'Intemporelle 2003 Sparkling
Quite fat, rounded and rich with biscuit brioche, tangy pineapple and lively acidity. A very fresh and zesty style with a long, lingering finish. Drink now through 2012.
90

Domaine de la Vougeraie Fête de Famille 2003 Sparkling
Very developed nose with complex nutty character, yeasty and bready, good mousse, creamy and very well balanced. Drinking now.
85

Domaine de la Vougeraie Vougeot 1er Cru 'Le Clos Blanc de Vougeot' 2003 White
Golden colour with attractive, lactic notes. Ripe, almost viscous on the palate with a slightly phenolic finish and lingering length. Drink now through 2010.
87

Jaffelin Santenay 1er Cru Beauregard 2003 Red
Clean, cherry fruit, phenolic tannins, well structured with ripe, round character. Angular with good acidity, pungent finish. Drinking now.
88

Jaffelin Vosne Romanée 1er Cru au Dessus Malconsorts 2003 Red
Hint of volatile acidity on the nose with vibrant and fresh fruit underneath, still very ripe but not baked, plum and blackberry on the palate, nicely handled oak with good acidity for the vintage, firm tannins and good length. Drink now through 2011.
91

Jean-Michel Lapalu Château Patache d'Aux 2003 Red
Deep ruby red, quite concentrated nose. Very Bordeaux modern style, spicy fruit with concentrated depth and moderate finish. Drink now through 2011.
89

Louis Jadot Louis Jadot Beaune Boucherottes 2003 Red
Ripe, bretty character, juicy with

plenty of fresh, earthy fruit. Great cherry flavour with rounded raspberries and red fruit. Lingering finish. Drink now through 2011.
88

Maison Albert Bichot Pommard Clos des Ursulines, Monopole, Domaine du Pavillon 2003 Red
Dark, sturdy and structured Pinot, with positive smoky oak notes. Firm tannins, dark raspberry fruit with a cores of sweetness. Well structured length. Drink now through 2014.
91

SCEA M. Marcelis Château Serilhan 2003 Red
Deep colour, rich mocha spice on the nose, ripe red fruit with earthy, tobacco notes on the palate, big tannin with depth and character. Drink now through 2014.
91

Vignobles Lorgeril Les Hauts de la Borie Blanche 2003 Red
Ruby coloured with a nice, fresh nose. Liquorice and spice, still very youthful with good structure and balance. Good acidity and complexity with a savoury finish. Drink now through 2011.
89

Yvon Mau Château Preuillac 2003 Red
Ripe and gorgeous fruit on the nose, good firm tannins, with a hint of mint and chocolate. Ripe red cherry finish. Drink now through 2010.
88

Yvon Mau Château Taillefer 2003 Red
Medium garnet colour, very attractive notes of spice, cloves and red fruit on the nose. Touch of calamine, good acidity and grippy tannins. Drink now through 2010.
89

GERMANY

Weingut St. Urbans-Hof Ockfener Bockstein Riesling Auslese 2003 Sweet
Light gold with abundant fruit on the nose, youthful lemon and honeysuckle on the palate, a delightful wine. Drink from 2010 to 2025.
93

ITALY

Fattoria di Valiano Chianti Classico Riserva DOCG 2003 Red
Appealing red plum, bright and juicy style, structured fruit with grainy tannins, very ripe and warm with a lingering finish. Drink 2009 through 2015.
92

Fattoria di Valiano 'Poggio Teo' Chianti Classico DOCG 2003 Red
Just beginning to show development, vanilla, liquorice and herbal aromas. Full, plumy palate with stewed, jammy fruit. Long, persistent and intense on the finish. Drink 2008 through 2012.
88

Fattoria Varramista Spa Varramista 2003 Red
Deep colour, showing maturity. Dense, concentrated with good balance and lovely acidity. Rounded fruit intensity on the finish. Drink now through 2012.
95

Piccini 'Villa al Cortile' Brunello di Montalcino DOCG 2003 Red
Red fruit, quite young, intense, succulent and juicy on the

palate. Grainy tannins with balanced acidity and round finish. Drink now through 2013.
88

Tenuta Moraia 'Soldi Mela' Monteregio di Massa Marittima DOC 2003 Red
Sweet, slightly oaky with vanilla notes on the nose. Very sweet and ripe on the palate, but persistent acidity balances out the finish. Needs further time to develop. Drink now through 2011.
90

PORTUGAL

Adriano Ramos Pinto Vinhos SA Duas Quintos Reserva Especial 2003 Red
Deep colour, very port like nose without the alcoholic kick. Structured with ripe tannins, long, lush finish. Drink now through 2010.
85

Adriano Ramos Pinto Vinhos SA Duas Quintos Tinto 2003 Red
Rich and youthful with perfumed aroma. Dense, quite closed, but lovely, bright, black fruits. Good structure with lots of aging potential. Drink now through 2015.
90

Adriano Ramos Pinto Vinhos SA Duas Quintos Tinto Reserva 2003 Red
Dark ruby with good, sweet fruit, floral nose and a hint of cedar wood. Rich blackberries and flowers, very ripe tannins with good length. Drink now through 2013.
91

Adriano Ramos Pinto Vinhos SA Late Bottled Vintage 2003 Port
Very dense black fruit, chocolate palate. Fruit forward with a spirity, warm, berry ripeness. Still very young.
89

Adriano Ramos Pinto Vinhos SA Vintage Port 2003 Port
Deep purple in colour, very clean on the nose. Soft on the palate with tea-leaf complexity on the finish. Keep for another 5 years and then enjoy for 10. Elegant, very good.
96

Hans Kristian Jorgensen Cortes de Cima Reserva 2003 Red
Showing some maturity, black cherry and smoky character on the nose. Quite rounded with crisp acidity. Good length and intensity. Drink now through 2012.
88

Sogevinus Fine Wines Barros Vintage Port 2003 Port
Deep ruby, plum nose with rich Christmas cake and toffee. Juicy and round, very pleasant with beautiful fruit finish. Perfectly balanced drink for the next 10 years.
96

SOUTH AFRICA

Hamilton Russell Vineyards Pinot Noir 2003 Red
Pale colour, substantial maturity. Aromas of raspberries with a greenish edge. Palate is quite smoky with attractive complexity and earthy finish. Drinking now.
85

SPAIN

Bodegas Primicia Carravalseca 2003 Red
Rich, red fruit with a peppery spicy aroma, youthful and powerful, modern palate. Well balanced spice with a long and structured finish. Drink now through 2015.
92

Stockists

A

A&A	A & A Wines	01483 274666
AAW	Alliance Wines	01505 506060
ABS	Awin Barratt Siegel Wine Agencies	01780 755810
ABW	Abbey Wines	01902 332122
ABY	Anthony Byrne Wine	01487 814555
ACG	AC Gallie	01534 734596
ACH	Andrew Chapman Fine Wines	01235 821539
ADE	Adel (UK)	020 8994 3960
ADN	Adnams Wine Merchants	01502 727222
AGP	AG Peters	01253 591431
AKT	Arriba Kettle & Co	01386 854700
ALC	Alchemy Wines	01473 290244
ALD	Aldi Stores	01827 711800
ALE	Alexander Wines	0141 882 0039
ALI	Alivini Company	020 8880 2526
ALO	Alouette Wines	0151 608 9900
AMA	Amathus Wines	020 8808 4181
AMP	Amps Fine Wines	01832 273502
AMW	Amey's Wines	01787 377144
ARL	Auriol Wines	01252 843190
ARM	Arthur Rackham Fine Wine Merchants	0870 870 1110
ASDA	Asda Stores	0113 243 5435
ASI	The Aussie Wine Company	07900 301330
AST	Astley Vineyards	01299 822907
ATC	Atlantico UK	020 8649 7444
ATM	Astrum Wine Cellars	020 8870 5252
AUC	The Australian Wine Club	0800 856 2004
AVB	Averys Wine Merchants	01275 811100
AVD	Australian Vineyards Direct	020 7259 8520
AWC	Australian Wine Agencies	01753 544546
AWO	www.australianwinesonline.co.uk	
AWS	Albion Wine Shippers	020 7242 0873
AWW	Andrew Wilson Wines	01782 791 798
AWY	Australasian Wine Company	0117 904 6365

B

BAW	British Airways	0208 513 0422
BBL	Bat & Bottle Wine	08451 084 407
BBO	Barrels and Bottles	01246 453399
BB&R	Berry Bros & Rudd	0870 900 4300
BBS	Barton Brownsdon & Sadler	020 7091 9900
BBV	Breaky Bottom	01273 476427
BCC	Bacchus Wines	01234 711140
BCF	Bon Coeur Fine Wine	020 7622 5244
BCL	Best Cellars of Devon	01364 652546
BDA	Brindisa Foods	020 8772 1600
BDC	Château Bauduc	0800 316 3676
BDG	Las Bodegas	01634 844845
BDL	Bedales	020 7403 8853
BEC	Beaconsfield Wine Cellars	01494 675545
BED	Bellini's Shipley Common	0115 932 0033
BEN	Bennetts Fine Wines	01386 840392
BES	Bestway Cash & Carry	020 8450 9866
BFD	Brian Ford's Discount	
BGL	Bottle Green	0113 205 4521
BHL	Bacchanalia	01223 576 292
BLS	Balls Bros of London	0207 739 1642
BLV	Bacchus Fine Wines	01234 711140
BMK	Benmack International	01435 866 419
BNA	Bona Wines	01666 505911
BNK	Bottleneck (Broadstairs)	01843 861095
BOC	Ballantynes	029 2022 2202
BOF	Bowland Forest Vintners	01200 448688
BOR	De Bortoli Wines UK	01725 516467
BOV	Bookers Vineyard	01444 881 575
BRA	G Bravo & Son	020 7836 4693
BRB	Brown Bros Wines	01628 776446
BRF	Brown-Forman Wines International	020 7478 1300
BRG	Burgundy Wines	01273 870055
BSE	Beer Seller (Folio) Wines	01305 751 300
BST	Bells Stores	020 7695 6000
BTC	Wine Buy The Case	01483 479555
BTH	Booths Supermarkets	01772 251701
BTR	Baton Rouge	07989 516920
BTS	Batleys PLC	0113 387 7000
BTW	Bristol Wine Co	0117 373 0288
BUC	Buckingham Vintners	01753 521336
BUDG	Budgens Stores	020 8422 9511
BUL	CG Bull and Taylor	020 7498 8022

BUT	Butler's Wine Cellar	01273 698724
BWC	Berkmann Wine Cellars	020 7609 4711
BWL	Bibendum Wine	020 7449 4100

C

C&B	Corney & Barrow	020 7265 2400
C&D	C&D Wines	020 8778 1711
C&H	Cairns & Hickey	0113 267 3746
CAF	Colours of Africa	020 8989 0499
CAK	Castel UK	020 8944 4770
CAM	Cambridge Wine Merchants	01223 568991
CAO	C&O Wines	0161 976 3696
CAR	CA Rookes Wine Merchants and Shippers	01789 297777
CAS	Castang Wine Shippers	
CAV	Les Caves de Pyréne	01483 538820
CBC	City Beverage Co	020 7729 2111
CBG	Carlsberg	01604 668866
CBK	Cranbrook Wines	020 8507 8447
CCR	Costcutter	01904 488663
CDO	Chapel Down Wines	01580 763033
CEB	Croque-en-Bouche	01684 565612
CEC	Ceci Paulo	01531 632976
CEL	The Cellar Door	01256 770397
CEN	Centurion Vintners	01453 763223
CER	Cellar 28	01484 710101
CFN	Carringtons Fine Wine	0161 446 2546
CFT	Clifton Cellars	0117 973 0287
CHH	Charles Hennings	01798 872485
CHN	Charles Hawkins	01572 823030
CIB	Ciborio	020 8578 4388
CIT	Cellars of Italy	01435 830902
CLH	Cockburns of Leith	0131 661 8400
CLC	Celtic Wines	01646 681369
CLI	Le Cellier	01670 737825
CMI	Charles Mitchell Wines	0161 775 1626
CMR	Cheers Wines Merchants	01366 382213
CMN	Cadman Fine Wine	0845 121 4011
CNL	Connolly's	0121 236 9269
CNT	Constellation Europe	01483 690000
COC	Corks of Cotham	0117 973 1620
COE	Coe of Ilford (Coe Vintners)	020 8551 4966
COK	Corkscrew Wines	01724 734096
COL	Corks Out	01925 267700
COO	Chandos Deli	0117 974 3275
COOP	The Co-operative Soc	01706 891628
CORD	Codorníu UK	01892 500250
CPC	capewineconnection.co.uk	

CPE	Champagne Par Excellence	0845 838 2860
CPV	Cape Wine and Food	01784 451860
CPW	Christopher Piper Wines	01404 814139
CRU	Crush Wines	01249 811737
CRW	Classic & Rare Wines	01293 525111
CSH	Cheshire Smokehouse	01625 548499
CSS	Charles Steevenson Wines	01822 616272
CTL	Continental Wine & Food	01484 538333
CTY	Cathay Importers	020 8459 3634
CVE	casevalue.com	0845 230 3773
CVS	Caviste	01706 891628
CVV	Camel Valley Vineyard	01208 77959
CWS	The Co-operative Group (CWS)	0161 834 1212
CWW	Wine in Cornwall	01326 379426
CYT	Concha y Toro UK	01865 338013

D

D&D	D&D Wines	01565 650952
DAV	Dartmouth Vintners	01803 832602
DBR	DBR Wines	020 7352 2096
DBS	Denbies Wine Estate	01306 876616
DBY	D Byrne & Co	01200 423152
DDK		www.drinksdirect.co.uk
DEF	Define Food & Wine	01606 882101
DFW	Delibo Fine Wines	01993 886644
DGB	DGB Europe	02088774960
DHA	Dhamecha Foods	020 8903 8181
DHF	Dennhofer Wines	01661 844622
DIO	Dionysus	0208 874 2739
DIW	Direct Wine Importers	01481 726747
DLM	Del Monico's	01726 71412
DMR	Duncan Murray Wines	01858 464935
DMW	Delamere Wines	0161 428 0384
DNL	Dunell's	01534 736418
DOU	Dourthe UK	020 7720 6611
DVY	Davy & Co	020 8858 6011
DWA	Dedicated Wines	01865 343395
DWL	Darlington Wines	01536 446106

E

EDC	Edencroft	01270 629975
EGA	EWGA	01524 701723
EGG	Ernst Gorge	01865 341817
EGW	Eagle's Wines	020 7223 7209
EHB	EH Booth	0800 197 0066
EHL	Ehrmanns	020 7418 1800
ELW	Ell's Fine Wines	028 3833 2306
ENG	English Wines Group	01580 763033
ENO	Enotria Winecellars	020 8961 4411

EOR	Ellis of Richmond	020 8744 5550
EPW	Edward Parker Wines	01328 850588
ESL	Edward Sheldon	01608 661409
ESS	Essentially Wine	01737 557737
ETV	Eton Vintners	01753 790188
ESW	Easy Wine	020 8347 9006
EUW	Eurowines	020 8747 2107
EVE	Everymans	01743 362466
EVI	Evington's Wine	0116 254 2702
EVW	everywine.co.uk	08000 720011
EWC	English Wine Centre	01323 870164
EXL	Excel Wines (Spain)	+34 946 568 325

F

F&F	Food & Fine Wine	0114 266 8747
F&M	Fortnum & Mason	020 7734 8040
FAR	Farr Vintners	020 7821 2000
FAW	Whole Food Market	
FCE	The Fine Cheese Co	01225 483 407
FDB	First Drinks Brands	02380 312000
FEE	Free Run Wines	01672 541006
FEN	Fenwick	0191 232 5100
FFT	Field + Fawcett Winemerchants	01904 489073
FGL	FGL Wine Estates	01932 566703
FHM	Fareham Wine Cellars	01329 822733
FHW	Fairyhill Wines	01792 390139
FLA	Flagship Wines	01727 865309
FLY	Flying Corkscrew	01442 412311
FMV	Fields, Morris & Verdin	020 7921 5300
FNC	Francis Fine Wines	0116 2863521
FNW	The Fine Wine Company	0131 665 0088
FOS	Foster's EMEA	020 8843 8400
FRD	France Domaines	020 7935 1551
FRI	Friarwood	020 7736 2628
FRN	Frenmart	01384 892941
FRV	The Four Vintners	020 7739 7335
FSW	Frank Stainton Wines	01539 731886
FTD	Fortitude Wines	020 8660 8456
FTH	Forth Wines	01577 866001
FUL	Fuller Smith & Turner	020 8996 2000
FWL	Fine & Rare Wines	020 8960 1995
FXT	Freixenet (DWS)	01344 758500

G

G2W	Grape-2-Wine	01531 660599
GBA	George Barbier of London	020 8852 5801
GDM	Giles de Mare	01985 844695
GGR	Great Grog Company	0131 662 4777

GHL	George Hill of Loughborough	01509 212717
GID	Grape Ideas Wholesale	01832 731226
GLL	Gales of Llangollen	01978 860089
GMP	Gordon & MacPhail	01343 545111
GNS	Genesis Wines	020 7963 9062
GNW	Great Northern Wine Co	0113 2304455
GON	Gauntelys of Nottingham	0115 911 0555
GOY	Goyt Wines	01663 734214
GRP	Grapevine	01767 8776100
GSH	The Grape Shop	0207 924 3638
GSL	Gerrard Seel	01925 819695
GWI	The General Wine Company	01428 722201
GWW	Great Western Wine Company	01225 322810
GYW	Guy Anderson Wines	01460 271670
GZB	González Byass UK	01707 274790

H

H&D	Hall & Woodhouse	01258 452141
H&H	H&H Bancroft	020 7232 5450
HAC	Hailsham Cellars	01323 441212
HAM	Hamer Wine	020 8549 9119
HAR	Harrods Wine Shop	020 7225 5662
HAX	Halifax Wine Company	01422 256333
HAY	Hayward Bros (Wines)	0207 237 0576
HBJ	Hayman Barwell Jones	020 7922 1612
HDS	Hedley Wright Wine	01279 465818
HEN	Hengate Wines	01964 532 746
HFB	Handford Wines Old Brompton Road	020 7589 6113
HFW	Handford Wines Holland Park	020 7589 6113
HGT	Harrogate Fine Wine	01423 522 270
HHC	Haynes, Hanson & Clark	020 7259 0102
HIG	Highbury Vintners	020 7226 1347
HJB	HJH Barrel Wines	0118 9722790
HJH	HJH Wines	01909 774990
HKL	Hook and Lambert (South Africa)	+27 11 234 6449
HKN	Hammonds of Knutsford	01565 872872
HLL	Halls of Holywell	01352 711444
HLN	Hellion Wines	07765 472263
HMA	Hatch Mansfield Agencies	01344 871800
HMW	Harvey Miller Wine and Spirit Agencies	0870 241 8459

HND	Hand Picked Wines	07711 414226
HOE	Herbie of Edinburgh	0131 332 9858
HOF	House of Fraser	02079 632000
HOH	Hallgarten Wines	01582 722538
HOT	House of Townend	01482 326891
HPW	Hop Pocket Wine Co.	01531 640592
HRR	Harris Fine Wine	01355 571157
HRW	Hercules Wine Warehouse	01304 617100
HRY	Harvey & Son (Lewes)	01273 480209
HSL	Hanslope Wines	01908 510262
HTG	Hermitage Wine Cellars	
HSW	Henderson Wines	0131 447 8580
HTW	HT White & Co	01323 720161
HVB	John Harvey & Sons	0800 434 6602
HVN	Harvey Nichols	020 7235 5000
HWL	HWCG Wine Growers	01279 873500

I

ICL	Italian Continental Stores	01628 770110
IDO	Indigo Wine	020 7733 8391
IDT	Independent Wines	01481 234440
IRV	Irvine Robertson	0131 553 3521
ITW	The Internet Wine Store	0845 058 0021
ITY	italyabroad.com	0191 565 4884
IVV	Inverarity Vaults	01899 308000

J

J&B	Justerini & Brooks	020 7484 6400
JAK	Aitken Wines	01382 641111
JAR	John Armit Wines	020 7908 0600
JAS	Jascots Wine Merchants	020 8965 2000
JBF	Julian Baker Fine Wines	01206 262358
JCC	Cooden Cellars	01323 649663
JCP	Palmers Brewery	01308 422396
JEF	John E Fells & Sons	01442 870900
JFC	JFC UK	020 8450 4626
JFE	James Fearon Wines	01407 765200
JFR	John Frazier	0121 704 3415
JHE	James Hall & Co	01772 706666
JKN	Jackson Nugent Vintners	020 8947 9722
JKS	Jacksons Stores	020 7695 6000
JNW	James Nicholson Wine Merchant	028 4483 0091
JOB	Jeroboams	020 7259 6716
JSS	John Stephenson & Sons (Nelson)	01282 614618
JWL	J W Lees & Co	

K

KON	John Konig	01794 388000
KOW	Kevin O'Rourke Wines	079415 63433
KSW	Ken Sheather	01242 231231
KWS	Kingsland Wines & Spirits	0161 333 4300

L

L&C	Lewis & Cooper Fine Food & Wine Gifts	01609 772880
L&S	Laymont & Shaw	01872 270545
L&W	Lay & Wheeler	01473 313233
LAI	Laithwaites (Direct Wines)	0870 444 8383
LAY	Laytons Wine Merchants	020 7288 8888
LBS	Luvians Bottle Shop	01334 654820
LBV	Le Bon Vin	0114 256 0090
LCC	Landmark Cash & Carry	01908 255300
LDL	Lidl UK	0870 444 1234
LEA	Lea & Sandeman	020 7244 0522
LEW	John Lewis	01494 462666
LIB	Liberty Wines	020 7720 5350
LID	Lanson International UK	020 7499 0070
LLV	Lakeland Vintners	01539 821999
LNC	Lanchester Wine Cellars	01207 521234
LON	Londis	
LPD	Laurent-Perrier UK	01628 475404
LUS	Emilio Lustau (London)	01932 223398
LVC	latevintage.com	020 8684 9063

M

M&S	Marks & Spencer	0845 603 1603
MAC	Makro UK	0161 786 2256
MAG	Magnums Wine Shop	01793 642569
MAX	Maxxium UK	01786 430500
MBS	Mumbles Fine Wines	01792 367663
MCC	McCabes	028 3833 3102
MCG	McGuigan Simeon Wines UK	see Vinoceros
MCL	McLeod's (USA)	+1 707 822 7307
MCT	Matthew Clark	01275 891400
MFS	Martinez Fine Wine	01943 603241
MFW	Mallards Fine Wines	01328 700071
MGM	Magnum Fine Wines	020 7 839 5732
MHU	Moët Hennessy UK	020 7235 9411
MHV	Booker Cash and Carry	01933 371238
MHW	Mill Hill Wines	020 8959 6754
MKV	McKinley Vintners	020 7928 7300

MLL	Millésima (France)	+33 (0) 557 808 808
MMD	Maisons Marques et Domaines	020 8812 3380
MML	Mason & Mason Wines	01243 536364
MON	Mondial Wine	020 8335 3455
MOR	Moreno Wine	020 7286 0678
MRN	Morrison Supermarkets	01924 875234
MSP	Masterpiece Wines	01634 293141
MTL	Mitchells Wine	0114 274 0311
MTR	Montrachet Fine Wine Merchants	020 7928 1990
MWO	Michael Wooley	020 7262 1114
MWW	Majestic Wine Warehouses	01923 298200
MYL	Myliko International (Wines)	0161 736 9500
MZC	Mentzendorff & Co	020 7840 3600

N

N&P	Nickolls & Perks	01384 394518
NEG	Negociants UK (Yalumba)	01582 462 859
NET	Nethergate Wines	01787 283228
NFW	Nidderdale Fine Wines	01423 711703
NGR	Noble Green Wines	020 8979 1113
NIC	Nicolas UK	020 7436 9338
NND	Nando's	0208 438 4803
NOV	Novum Wines	020 7820 6720
NRW	Noble Rot Wine Warehouse	01527 575606
NTD	Nisa Today's	01724 282028
NWF	Norport Wines and Foods	0131 478 5239
NYW	Noel Young Wines	01223 844744
NZD	New Zealand Wine Distribution Co	0870 240 7460
NZH	The New Zealand House of Wine	01428 648930

O

ODD	Oddbins	020 8944 4400
ODF	Oddbins Fine Wine	0800 917 4093
OFW	Old Forge Wine Cellar	01903 744246
OMB	Ombersley Wines	01905 620580
ONL	O'Neill Fine Wines	0151 924 5767
ORB	Orbital Wines	020 7802 5415
OST	Costco Wholesale	01923 225611
OSW	Old School Wines	01886 821613
OWC	The Oxford Wine Company	01865 301144
OWL	OW Loeb & Co	020 7234 0385
OZW	Oz Wines	0845 450 1261

P

P&R	Peckham's	01414 454555
P&S	Philglass & Swiggot	020 7924 4494
PAN	Palandri Wines	0208 878 1459
PAR	Partridges	020 7730 0651
PAT	Patriarche Wine Agencies	020 7381 4016
PBA	Paul Boutinot	0161 908 1338
PCW	Premier Crew	01985 850 895
PDN	Portal, Dingwall and Norris	01243 377883
PFC	Percy Fox	01279 756200
PFT	Parfrements	02476 503646
PGS	Page & Sons	01843 591214
PGW	Peter Graham Wines	01603 598910
PIM	Pimlico Dozen	020 7630 6254
PLA	Playford Ros	01845 526777
PLB	PLB Wines	01342 318282
PLE	Peter Lehmann	01227 731353
POG	Planet of the Grapes	020 7405 4912
PON	Peter Osborne & Co	01491 612 311
POR	Portland Wine Company	0161 928 0357
POT	Le Pont de la Tour	0207 403 2403
PPW	Portugalia Wines	020 8997 4400
PRD	Pernod Ricard UK	020 8538 4484
PRG	Paragon Vintners	020 7887 1800
PRI	Prime Wines	01737 358057
PRV	Premier Vintners	020 8870 3550
PTD	Promotion Wine	01206 338915
PVC	Private Cellar	01353 721999
PWI	Portland Wine Cellar (Southport)	01704 534299

Q

| QFW | Quaff Fine Wine | 01273 820320 |

R

R&B	Rhythm & Booze	01226 215 195
RAD	Ratcliffe & Brown	0845 603 5485
RAE	Raeburn Fine Wines	0131 3431159
RAR	R&R Fine Wines	0161 763 9363
RBC	Richard Banks & Co	01225 310125
RDS	Reid Wines	01761 452645
REY	Raymond Reynolds	01961 281 5000
RIC	Richard Granger	0191 281 5000
RIH	Richards & Richards	0161 762 0022
RIP	Ripley Wines	01773 570594
RIW	Ri Wine	01344 627411
RKI	Richard Kihl	01728 454455
ROD	Rodney Densem Wines	01270 212200
ROG	Roger Harris Wines	01603 880171
RS2	Richardson & Sons	01946 65334
RSN	Richard Speirs Wines	01548 854473
RSS	Raisin Social	020 8686 8500
RSV	Reserve Wines	0161 438 0101
RVE	Ridgeview Estate Winery	01444 241441

RVL	The Revelstoke Wine Co	020 8545 0077
RWA	Richmond Wine Agencies	01892 668552
RWD	Richards Walford	01780 460451
RWM	Roberson Wine Merchants	020 7371 2121
RWW	Red and White Wines	01548 854473

S

SAB	St Austell Brewery	0845 241 1122
SAD	Sandhams Wine Merchants	01472 852118
SAIN	Sainsbury's Supermarkets	020 7695 6000
SAIO	Sainsbury's Online	0800 917 4092
SAO	SA Wines Online	0845 456 2365
SBB	Susman Best Beef Biltong Co	01273 516160
SBS	Sainsbury Brothers	01392 218186
SCA	GAEC Maulin et Fils (France)	+33 5 5672 9546
SCK	Seckford Wines	01206 23254
SDC	South Downs Cellars	01273 833830
SDW	Smithfield Wine	0161 273 6070
SEL	Selfridges	020 7318 3730
SFW	Strathardle Fine Wines	01389 830643
SGL	Stevens Garnier	01865 263300
SHJ	SH Jones & Company	01295 251179
SMC	Sommerliers Choice	020 8689 9643
SMF	Somerfield Stores	0117 935 9359
SMP	The Sampler	020 7226 9500
SMV	Saint Martin's Vintners	01273 777744
SOH	Soho Wine Supply	020 7636 8490
SOM	Sommelier Wine Co	01481 721677
SPR	Spar (UK)	020 8426 3700
SSU	Stone, Vine & Sun	01962 712351
STC	Sunday Times Wine Club	0870 220 0010
STH	Stephar (UK)	01493650069
STO	Constantine Stores	01326 340226
STT	Stanton Wine Company	01386 852501
SVG	Savage Selection	01451 860896
SVY	Select Vineyards	01206 713 524
SWB	Satchells	01328 738272
SWG	SWiG	08000 272 272
SWS	Stratford's Wine Agencies	01628 810606

T

T&W	T&W Wines	01842 814414
TAN	Tanners Wines	01743 234500
TAU	Taurus Wines	01483 548484
TBO	The Bottle Shop	01925 865 311
TDG	The Drinks Group	0845 260 8870
TEN	10 International	01372 454910
TESC	Tesco Stores	01992 632222
THC	The Haslemere Cellar	01428 645081
THI	Thierry's Wine Services	01794 507100
THM	Thameside Wines	020 8788 4752
THS	Thresher Group	01707 387200
TKW	Talking Wines	01285 650250
TLW	Telford Wines	01952 291129
TMP	Temple Wines	020 8905 9484
TNI	The Nobody Inn	01647 252394
TNR	Trencherman's	01935 432857
TOT	Totnes Wine Company	01803 866357
TOW	Theatre of Wine	020 8858 6363
TPA	The Wine Warehouse	01666 503088
TPE	Terry Platt Wine Merchant	01492 874099
TPM	Topsham Wines	01392874501
TSC	The Secret Cellar	01892 537981
TSS	Tate-Smith	01653 693196
TVY	The Vineyard	01306 876828
TWK	The Wine Keller	01628 620 143
TWR	www.thewineroom.com	
TZK	Tazaki Foods	020 8344 3001

U

UNC	Uncorked	02076385998
UWO	United Wineries UK	020 7393 2829

V

V&C	Valvona & Crolla	0131 556 6066
VDL	V Drinks	0292 048 6130
VDV	Vin du Van Wine Merchants	01223 758727
VER	Vinceremos Wines	0113 244 0002
VGN	Virgin Wines Online	0870 164 9593
VHS	Vintage House	020 7437 2592
VHW	Victor Hugo Wines	01534 508156
VIC	Vica Wines	01273 477132
VIM	Vinimpo	01932 827150
VIN	Vinum	020 8847 4699
VIW	Vintage Wines	0115 947 6565
VKB	Vickbar	020 7490 1000
VKY	Vicki's of Chobham	01276 858374
VLW	Villeneuve Wines	01721 722500
VNO	Vinoceros (UK)	01209 314711
VOA	Vinoteca	020 7253 8786
VPR	Proven PR	0117 924 9303
VRT	Vintage Roots	0118 976 1999
VSE	Vintners Selection	01476 550476
VSO	Vinissimo	01959 563770
VVV	Viader Vintners	029 2039 6665

W

WAD	Wadworth & Co	01380 723361
WAIT	Waitrose	0800 188881

WAV	WaverleyTBS	0131 528 1000
WAW	Waterloo Wine Co	020 7403 7967
WBF	Wine Buffs	01925 659421
WBN	The Winebarn	01256 391 211
WBR	Wadebridge Wines	01208 812692
WBW	William Baber Wines – Tasting Room	01225 463392
WCS	The Wine Cellar (Sanderstead)	0208 657 6936
WES	Wessex Wines	01308 427177
WFF	Woffenden Wines	01204 308081
WHB	Worth Brothers	01543 262051
WHR	Wheeler Cellars	01206 713560
WIB	Wimbledon Wine Cellars (Chiswick)	020 8994 7989
WIE	Wine Importers Edinburgh	0131 556 3601
WIL	Willoughbys	0161 643 2487
WIM	Wimbledon Wine Cellars	020 8540 9979
WIN	The Winery	0207 286 6475
WIS	Wine Importers	01324 482211
WIW	Wine World	08702 414040
WKM	Wickham Vineyard	01329 834042
WMA	Addison Wines UK	01952 686500
WMT	Wine Mart	
WNL	The Wine Cellar	020 8657 6936
WNN	Winning Wine	01382 521159
WOC	Whitesides of Clitheroe	01200 422281
WOE	Worcester Wine Co	01905 425588
WOI	Wines of Interest	0870 224 5640
WON	Weavers of Notts	0115 958 0922
WPL	The Wine Portfolio	020 7843 1600
WPR	Winepress	01684 298002
WRC	Wine Rack – First Quench	01707 387200
WRK	Wine Raks	01224 311460
WRT	Winerite	01132837682
WRW	The Wright Wine Co	01756 700886
WSA	Wineshare	01306 742164
WSO	The Wine Society	01438 741177
WSW	Walkers Wines	01939 290959
WTA	Winetraders (UK)	01865 251851
WTL	Whittalls Wines	01922 636161
WTR	The Wine Treasury	020 7793 9999
WUO	Wine Studio	

WWD	Wineworld	08702 414040
WWT	Whitebridge Wines	01785 817229
WWX	Wooden Wine Box Co	01892 530724

X

XXCLH	Cantrell & Cochrane (Ireland) +353 1 616 1100
XXEPR	Empire Liquor (Australia) +61 88351 7688
XXGGN	Gogan Wine Imports (Germany) +49 6196 902 6939
XXGGP	Great Grapes Wine (Belgium) +31 35 603 8040
XXGOD	Grants of Ireland (Ireland) +353 1 630 4106
XXHGN	Winzerverein Hagnau (Germany) +49 7532 1030
XXKEM	Kemeny's Food & Liquor
XXKGD	Kongernad (Denmark) +45 25 27 69 34
XXLCX	LCBO
XXLSR	Leinster Wines (Ireland) +353 4 586 8425
XXMLL	Millésima (France) + 33 5 5780 8808
XXPLQ	Premium Liquid Assets (France) +33 5 5611 7017
XXRDL	Richmond Hill Wines (Canada) +1 403 686 1980
XXRTG	Rutherglen Wine & Spirits (Australia) +61 3 9646 6666
XXSAA	SAQ (Canada) +1 514 873 2020
XXSPQ	SuperQuinn (Ireland) + 353 1 630 2000
XXVSM	Vine Street Imports (USA) +1 215 533 8463
XXVVT	Vinnovative (USA) +1 704 489 9463
XXWDW	Ward Wines (Sweden) +46 8 678 19 10

Y

YAP	Yapp Brothers	01747 860423
YBW	York Beer & Wine Shop	01904 674136
YOB	Cockburn & Campbell	020 8875 7008
YWD	Youngs Wine Direct	0208 875 7007

Z

| **ZEP** | Zephyr-One | 01625 536172 |

OTHER STOCKISTS

| **3DW** | 3D Wines | 01205 820745 |